Living

Red Dot Design Yearbook 2013/2014
Edited by Peter Zec

reddot design award
product design 2013

Living

Red Dot Design Yearbook 2013/2014
Edited by Peter Zec

Prof. Dr. Peter Zec
Preface of the editor
Vorwort des Herausgebers

Dear Readers,

Do you love to surround yourself with beautiful things? Are you passionate about the world of international design? The volume "Living" is a veritable goldmine of new ideas for maintaining a comfortable and refined lifestyle in the here and now.

This book presents a selection of the best current products created by designers from around the world. Each work has received a distinction from the internationally renowned Red Dot Design Award competition – widely recognised as a hallmark of excellence. The book features spectacular developments and intelligent technologies, including novel ways to significantly improve the functionality of already existing products. We observed a trend towards all things sensual, a design approach that lends itself to capturing and catering to users' more personal predilections. Strong geometric forms stand alongside fascinating organic curves modelled after nature.

"Living" has a clear, intuitive structure and features high-quality illustrations. Readers will easily locate the areas and themes that interest them most. All product categories also put a spotlight on the products awarded with the coveted "Red Dot: Best of the Best" award. Demonstrating excellent design and certain to set new standards, these works captivated and won over the jury in every respect.

The "Living" volume of the Red Dot Design Yearbook is a veritable source of inspiration for designing and furnishing a contemporary home, and for taking part in the lifestyle concepts of tomorrow. In association with the other two volumes ("Doing" and "Working"), "Living" offers an exceptional overview of the best and latest design of our time.

I wish you an engaging and inspiring read.

Sincerely, Peter Zec

Liebe Leserin, lieber Leser,

lieben Sie die schönen Dinge des Lebens und begeistern Sie sich für die Welt des internationalen Designs? Der vor Ihnen liegende Band „Living" bietet Ihnen ein Füllhorn neuer Ideen für ein komfortables und überaus stilvolles Leben im Hier und Jetzt.

Dieses Buch präsentiert eine Auswahl der aktuell besten Produkte, gestaltet von Designern aus aller Welt. Jedes einzelne von ihnen wurde im Rahmen des international renommierten Red Dot Design Award von einer Jury prämiert und ist dabei für sich einzigartig. So finden sich in diesem Band spektakuläre Entwicklungen und intelligente Technologien ebenso wie neue Ansätze, die etwa die Funktionalität eines bereits bekannten Produktes derart verbessern, dass es sich im Alltag hervorragend handhaben lässt. Spürbar wird der Trend zu einem mit allen Sinnen erfahrbaren Design, das die persönlichen Bedürfnisse des Nutzers gekonnt in den Mittelpunkt rückt. Streng geometrische Formen stehen gleichberechtigt neben faszinierend organischen Linien nach Vorbildern aus der Natur.

„Living" ist übersichtlich gegliedert und reich bebildert – es bietet dem Leser eine gute Orientierung. Rasch findet er die Bereiche und Themen, die ihn besonders interessieren. Hervorzuheben sind in jeder Kategorie die Produkte mit der begehrten Auszeichnung „Red Dot: Best of the Best". Diese verfügen über eine herausragende Designqualität, sie setzen neue Maßstäbe und konnten die Jury in jeder Hinsicht begeistern.

In dem Band „Living" des Red Dot Design Yearbook finden Sie zahlreiche Anregungen für die zeitgemäße Planung und Einrichtung Ihres Zuhauses und haben teil an neuen Konzepten für das Leben in der Zukunft. In Verbindung mit den beiden Bänden „Doing" und „Working" bietet „Living" einen einzigartigen Überblick über das beste und neueste Design unserer Zeit.

Ich wünsche Ihnen eine spannungsreiche und inspirierende Lektüre.

Ihr Peter Zec

People who change the world through design

Menschen, die mit Design die Welt verändern

In recognition of its feat, the Red Dot: Design Team of the Year receives the "Radius" trophy. This sculpture was designed and crafted by the Weinstadt-Schnaidt based designer, Simon Peter Eiber. Like all the years before, the Radius changes hands again in 2013. This year Michael Mauer and Style Porsche will pass on the coveted trophy to Yao Yingjia and the Lenovo Design & User Experience Team.

Als Anerkennung erhält das Red Dot: Design Team of the Year den Wanderpokal „Radius". Die Skulptur wurde entworfen und angefertigt von dem Designer Simon Peter Eiber aus Weinstadt-Schnaidt. Auch im Jahr 2013 wechselt der Radius seinen Besitzer: Michael Mauer und Style Porsche geben die begehrte Trophäe an Yao Yingjia und das Lenovo Design & User Experience Team weiter.

For the 26th time in the long history of the competition, one design team will be honoured for its exceptional achievements in the field of design. This year Lenovo Design & User Experience Team led by Yao Yingjia are the recipients of the "Red Dot: Design Team of the Year" award. This is a unique honour and one which is very highly regarded, both within the design scene and beyond, due to the fact that the award is given in recognition of the overall design output of a design team that has generated exceptional products and groundbreaking design over a number of years. Since 1988 the Radius has been presented to a design team as part of the Red Dot Design Award. It has become a tradition that all the prize winners have their names engraved on the trophy before they pass it on to the next year's winner.

Zum 26. Mal wird in der langen Geschichte des Wettbewerbs ein Designteam ausgezeichnet, das durch besondere Leistungen auf sich aufmerksam gemacht hat. In diesem Jahr geht die Ehrenauszeichnung „Red Dot: Design Team of the Year" an das Lenovo Design & User Experience Team unter der Leitung von Yao Yingjia. Diese Würdigung ist einzigartig auf der Welt und genießt über die Designszene hinaus hohes Ansehen, da die gestalterische Gesamtleistung von Designteams honoriert wird, die über mehrere Jahre hinweg mit außergewöhnlichen Produkten und wegbereitenden Gestaltungsleistungen in Erscheinung getreten sind. Seit 1988 wird der Radius im Rahmen des Red Dot Design Award an ein Designteam vergeben. Es ist gute Tradition, dass die Preisträger ihre Namen eingravieren lassen, bevor sie die Trophäe wie einen Wanderpokal weiterreichen.

2013	Lenovo Design & User Experience Team
2012	Michael Mauer & Style Porsche
2011	The Grohe Design Team led by Paul Flowers
2010	Stephan Niehaus & Hilti Design Team
2009	Susan Perkins & Tupperware World Wide Design Team
2008	Michael Laude & Bose Design Team
2007	Chris Bangle & Design Team BMW Group
2006	LG Corporate Design Center
2005	Adidas Design Team
2004	Pininfarina Design Team
2003	Nokia Design Team
2002	Apple Industrial Design Team
2001	Festo Design Team
2000	Sony Design Team
1999	Audi Design Team
1998	Philips Design Team
1997	Michele De Lucchi Design Team
1996	Bill Moggridge & Ideo Design Team
1995	Herbert Schultes & Siemens Design Team
1994	Bruno Sacco & Mercedes-Benz Design Team
1993	Hartmut Esslinger & Frogdesign
1992	Alexander Neumeister & Neumeister Design
1991	Reiner Moll & Partner & Moll Design
1990	Slany Design Team
1989	Braun Design Team
1988	Leybold AG Design Team

»Design today is about being able to predict
and present the look of tomorrow.«
»Im Design geht es heute darum, sich vorstellen
zu können, wie die Produkte von morgen aussehen.«

Yao Yingjia, Vice President
Lenovo Design & User Experience

Red Dot: Design Team of the Year 2013
Lenovo Design & User Experience Team
led by Yao Yingjia
A new legend on the international design map

For the first time in the history of the competition, the honorary title "Red Dot: Design Team of the Year" goes this year to China. The Lenovo Design & User Experience Team, under the leadership of Yao Yingjia, has placed the company and the Lenovo brand firmly in the spotlight. In the last two years alone, the international jury of the Red Dot Award: Product Design has honoured the Chinese manufacturer of PCs, notebooks, tablets, smart TVs and smartphones with the Red Dot a total of 15 times, two of these were the Red Dot: Best of the Best.

A legend out of the garage

The story of the Chinese Company, Lenovo, reads just like the American dream. Reminiscent of the legendary garage-starts of Hewlett-Packard and Apple, Lenovo is following closely behind these legends, not only in terms of the company's history, but also regarding the claim to leadership in computer design. Lenovo founder Liu Chuanzhi made his start in a garage workshop just like William Hewlett and David Packard – with a slight difference: He developed a technology, together with ten colleagues at the Chinese Academy of Sciences in Beijing, which enabled an American computer to be used using Chinese characters. In 1984, with the help of the Chinese Academy of Sciences in Beijing and start-up capital of RMB 200,000 (which at the time was worth around US$ 25,000), Liu Chuanzhi founded New Technology Development Inc., the forerunner of the Legend Group. In 1989, the Beijing Legend Computer Group was born and began with the production of its own computer, which, just one year later appeared on the Chinese market under the name "Legend". The company evolved from a computer dealership into a computer manufacturer and, in 1994, was listed on the Hong Kong stock exchange. Two years later Legend introduced its first laptop under its own brand and became Number 1 on the Chinese market. 1998 also marked the production of the millionth Legend computer and Liu Chuanzhi had become, by this stage, an icon of the Chinese computer industry.

The birth of a new brand

In preparation for its expansion strategy, Legend presented its new brand and company name in April 2003: Lenovo, an artificial word consisting of the initial syllable "Le" from "Legend" and the Latin word "novo" meaning "new". As other companies in many different countries had already registered the "Legend" name as their brand, the new "Lenovo" brand was meant to prepare the ground for and symbolise the move of the Chinese computer and electronics group into the international market.

The overnight emergence of a global player

The strategy was deemed to be successful with the surprise announcement by Lenovo on 8 December 2004 that it wanted to take over IBM's PC division for US$ 1.25 billion. It was a milestone in the history of the company and sent out a signal to the global computer industry. Yang Yuanqing, CEO of Lenovo, was

Erstmals in der Geschichte des Wettbewerbs geht die Ehrenauszeichnung „Red Dot: Design Team of the Year" nach China. Mit dem Lenovo Design & User Experience Team unter der Leitung von Yao Yingjia rücken auch das Unternehmen und die Marke Lenovo in den Blickpunkt. Allein in den letzten beiden Jahren zeichnete die internationale Jury des Red Dot Award: Product Design den chinesischen Hersteller von PCs, Notebooks, Tablets, Smart TVs und Smartphones fünfzehn Mal mit dem Red Dot aus, darunter zwei Mal mit dem Red Dot: Best of the Best.

Die Legende jenseits der Garage

Die Geschichte des chinesischen Unternehmens Lenovo liest sich wie ein amerikanischer Traum. Sie erinnert an die Garagenlegende von Hewlett-Packard und Apple. Lenovo ist diesen Legenden auf der Spur, nicht nur mit Blick auf die eigene Firmengeschichte, auch im Hinblick auf den Führungsanspruch im Computerdesign. Wie William Hewlett und David Packard startet auch Lenovo-Gründer Liu Chuanzhi in einer Garagenwerkstatt – mit einem feinen Unterschied: Gemeinsam mit zehn Kollegen entwickelt er an der chinesischen Akademie der Wissenschaften in Beijing eine Technologie, die es ermöglicht, amerikanische Computer mit chinesischen Schriftzeichen zu betreiben. 1984 gründet Liu Chuanzhi mit Unterstützung der chinesischen Akademie der Wissenschaften in Beijing und einem Startkapital von 200.000 RMB, was zur damaligen Zeit etwa 25.000 US-Dollar entspricht, die New Technology Development Inc., den Vorläufer der Legend Group. 1989 wird die Beijing Legend Computer Group ins Leben gerufen und beginnt mit der Produktion eigener Computer, die nur ein Jahr später unter dem Namen „Legend" auf den chinesischen Markt kommen. Das Unternehmen wandelt sich vom Computerhändler zum Computerhersteller und geht 1994 in Hongkong an die Börse. Zwei Jahre später stellt Legend den ersten Laptop unter eigenem Namen vor und ist erstmals die Nummer eins auf dem chinesischen Markt. 1998 wird der millionste Legend-Computer produziert. Zu diesem Zeitpunkt ist Liu Chuanzhi bereits eine Ikone der chinesischen Computerindustrie.

Die Geburt einer neuen Marke

In Vorbereitung der Expansionsstrategie stellt Legend im April 2003 seinen neuen Marken- und Firmennamen vor: Lenovo, ein Kunstwort aus der englischen Silbe „Le" von „legend" und dem lateinischen Wort „novo" für „neu". Da der Name „Legend" bereits in vielen Ländern von anderen Unternehmen als Marke geschützt ist, soll mit der neuen Marke „Lenovo" auch der internationale Aufbruch des chinesischen Computer- und Elektronikkonzerns vorbereitet und symbolisiert werden.

Über Nacht zum Global Player

Die Strategie geht auf, als Lenovo am 8. Dezember 2004 überraschend bekannt gibt, die IBM PC Division für 1,25 Milliarden US-Dollar übernehmen zu wollen; ein Meilenstein in der Geschichte des Unternehmens und ein Signal für die weltweite Computerindustrie. Lenovos CEO, Yang Yuanqing, ist sich sicher, dass Lenovo zum besten Unternehmen in der Computerindustrie aufsteigen kann. Mit Zustimmung der amerikanischen Behörden ist die Übernahme der IBM PC

certain that Lenovo had the capability of becoming the leader in the computer industry. The takeover of the IBM PC division was officially finalised at the end of April 2005 once the American authorities had given the deal their blessing. Coupled with the goal of entering global markets, this at a stroke turned Lenovo into a global player using the "Think" brand to underline its own product and design quality standards. The acquisition of the IBM computer division and the closely linked Research and Development Centre gave Lenovo the rights to the "Think" brand and to five years usage of the IBM brand.

Outstanding design quality

Over the last few years, Lenovo has based its positioning largely on its product and design quality. In 2005, the company first took part in the Red Dot Award: Design Concept and immediately went on to win the highest award for its Yoga Concept. Further accolades followed. In the last two years alone, the international jury of the Red Dot Design Award has given Yao Yingjia and the Lenovo Design & User Experience Team 15 prizes. On two occasions they have included the highest accolade the competition has to bestow. The Lenovo ThinkCentre Edge 91Z personal computer and the IdeaPad U430s each won the Red Dot: Best of the Best. Both products are proof of Lenovo's Design & User Experience Team's ability to create technological, but also quality-focused products that match today's modern lifestyle and are simple and easy to use. Yao Yingjia and his team have managed to develop a design language that is understood around the globe. This is also repeatedly confirmed by customers. Design is increasingly important to them and has therefore crystallised itself as a clear advantage on the Chinese and global markets.

En route to becoming global market leader

Lenovo is an exception among Chinese brands. In 2012, the company increased its turnover from US$ 21.6 billion to US$ 29.6 billion. It is not only the 37 per cent increase that is surprising, but also the fact that in 2012 Lenovo was already generating 58 per cent of its turnover from overseas markets. With respect to turnover from abroad, Lenovo clearly leads the field among China's most valued brands. The figures back up the company's "Protect & Attack" strategy and the stated aim of its CEO Yang Yuanqing to "become one of the leading technology companies in the world". This goal is just within the company's grasp, as Lenovo is en route to becoming global market leader in its core business, the desktop and laptop segment. This growth is supported by the company's successful design development.

Division Ende April 2005 offiziell abgeschlossen. Verbunden mit dem Ziel, globale Märkte zu erschließen, wird Lenovo mit einem Schlag zum Global Player und unterstreicht mit der Marke „Think" den eigenen Anspruch an Produkt- und Designqualität. Mit der Übernahme der IBM-Computersparte und des damit eng verbundenen Forschungs- und Entwicklungszentrums von IBM erwirbt sich Lenovo auch die Rechte an der Marke „Think" und an der fünfjährigen Nutzung der Marke IBM.

Ausgezeichnete Designqualität

Lenovo positioniert sich insbesondere in den letzten Jahren über seine Produkt- und Designqualität. Erstmals taucht das Unternehmen 2005 im Red Dot Award: Design Concept auf und gewinnt auf Anhieb die höchste Auszeichnung für sein Yoga Concept. Es folgen weitere Auszeichnungen. Allein in den letzten beiden Jahren verleiht die internationale Jury des Red Dot Design Award 15 Auszeichnungen an Yao Yingjia und das Lenovo Design & User Experience Team, darunter zwei Mal die höchste Auszeichnung des Wettbewerbs. Der Personal Computer Lenovo ThinkCentre Edge 91Z und das IdeaPad U430s werden jeweils mit dem Red Dot: Best of the Best prämiert. Lenovos Design & User Experience Team stellt mit beiden Produkten seine Kompetenz unter Beweis, technologische und zugleich qualitätsorientierte Produkte zu gestalten, die dem modernen Lebensstil entsprechen und einfach und angenehm zu benutzen sind. Yao Yingjia und seinem Team ist es gelungen, eine Designsprache zu entwickeln, die überall auf der Welt verstanden wird. Dies wird auch durch die Kunden immer wieder bestätigt, für die gutes Design immer wichtiger wird und somit zum klaren Vorteil im chinesischen und im globalen Markt geworden ist.

Auf dem Weg zum Weltmarktführer

Unter den chinesischen Marken ist Lenovo eine Ausnahmeerscheinung. Im Jahr 2012 konnte das Unternehmen seinen Umsatz von 21,6 Milliarden US-Dollar auf 29,6 Milliarden US-Dollar steigern. Erstaunlich daran ist nicht nur das Wachstum von 37 Prozent, sondern insbesondere die Tatsache, dass Lenovo im Jahr 2012 bereits 58 Prozent seines Umsatzes außerhalb Chinas generiert. Unter Chinas wertvollsten Marken hat Lenovo im Hinblick auf die im Ausland erzielten Umsätze klar die Nase vorn. Die Zahlen unterstreichen die „Protect & Attack"-Strategie des Unternehmens und den Anspruch ihres CEO, Yang Yuanqing, „eines der führenden Technologieunternehmen der Welt zu werden". Das Ziel ist in greifbare Nähe gerückt, denn im Kerngeschäft, dem Segment für Desktop- und Laptop-Computer, ist Lenovo auf dem Weg zum Weltmarktführer. Das Wachstum wird nicht zuletzt von der erfolgreichen Designentwicklung des Unternehmens getragen.

The garage legend has turned into a worldwide success story and today employs more than 30,000 people in over 60 countries. They include 3,000 technicians, researchers and scientists. Lenovo's research and development team have introduced numerous industry firsts as borne out by 2,000 patents and over 100 significant design awards, including 25 Red Dot Design Award prizes.

The new lifestyle era "PC+"

By combining technology and design, Lenovo has managed to emotionalise the brand and not only meet the expectations of Chinese companies and consumers, but also arouse interest and create demand on international markets. Lenovo's Design & User Experience Team is very focused on utilising its technical know-how and experience with computers to create innovative design concepts and solutions. This results in well thought-out and well-made products that meet modern lifestyle needs both in the business-to-business segment and the business-to-consumer sector.

However, Lenovo is much more than just a company that makes PCs. Its CEO Yang Yuanqing and his chief designer Yao Yingjia never tire of emphasising that Lenovo makes a wide range of computer technologies from smartphones to tablets, and smart TVs to PCs. In the smartphone sector, Lenovo is already the second largest supplier in China and is present in countries such as India, Indonesia, Russia, Vietnam and the Philippines. This is all part of what Lenovo calls the "PC+" world, in which people use PCs alongside other intelligent devices whose core technology may make them like PCs, but whose shape and use are very different from those of a traditional computer. The Design & User Experience Team invests a good deal of time into tracking trends. By continuously monitoring and analysing cultural factors and their backgrounds, Yao Yingjia and his team are able to predict future consumer behaviour patterns and so create new design trends. "Lenovo is committed to becoming a global leader in the 'PC+' era, the era of tablets, smartphones, smart TVs and PCs," Yao Yingjia concludes.

The full article on Lenovo and the interview with Yao Yingjia can be found in the "Working" volume of the yearbook.

Die neue Lifestyle-Ära „PC+"

Lenovo gelingt es, durch die Verknüpfung von Technologie und Design, die Marke zu emotionalisieren und nicht nur die Erwartungen der chinesischen Unternehmen und Konsumenten zu erfüllen, sondern auch Wünsche und Begehrlichkeiten auf internationalen Märkten zu wecken. Lenovos Design & User Experience Team arbeitet intensiv daran, das technologische Wissen und die Erfahrung im Umgang mit Computern für innovative Designstudien und Lösungen zu nutzen und sowohl im „Business-to-Business"-Bereich als auch im „Business-to-Consumer"-Bereich gut durchdachte und gut gemachte Produkte anzubieten, die dem modernen Lebensstil entsprechen.

Lenovo ist jedoch weit mehr als nur ein Unternehmen, das PCs herstellt. Lenovos CEO Yang Yuanqing und sein Designchef Yao Yingjia werden nicht müde zu betonen, dass Lenovo eine breite Palette von Computertechnologien entwickelt – von Smartphones über Tablets bis zu Smart TVs und PCs. Mit Blick auf das Marktsegment Smartphones ist Lenovo bereits der zweitgrößte Anbieter in China und in Ländern wie Indien, Indonesien, Russland, Vietnam und auf den Philippinen vertreten. Es ist alles Teil dessen, was Lenovo die „PC+"-Welt nennt, in der die Menschen PCs sowie verschiedene intelligente Geräte nutzen, die von ihrer Kerntechnologie her zwar PCs sind, aber mit Blick auf die Form und Anwendung nicht mehr an die traditionelle Form eines Computers erinnern. Das Design & User Experience Team investiert viel Zeit in das Aufspüren von Trends. Durch laufende Beobachtungen und die Analyse kultureller Faktoren und ihrer Hintergründe ist es Yao Yingjia und seinem Team möglich, künftige Entwicklungen im Verhalten der Verbraucher vorherzusagen und selbst neue Trends im Design zu setzen. „Lenovo hat sich zum Ziel gesetzt, weltweit führend im ‚PC+'-Zeitalter zu werden – der Ära der Tablets, Smartphones, Smart TVs und PCs", sagt Yao Yingjia.

Der ausführliche Artikel über Lenovo und das Interview mit Yao Yingjia sind im Jahrbuchband „Working" nachzulesen.

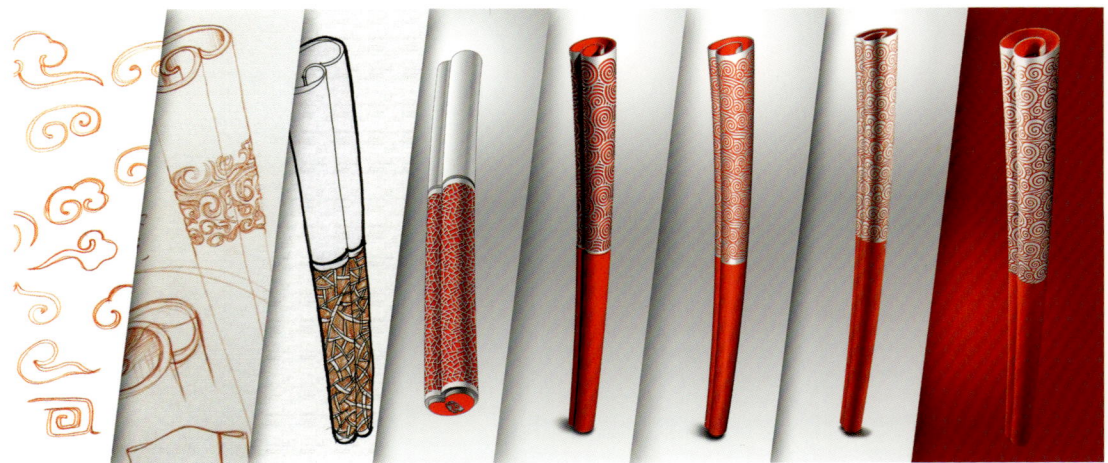

In 2008, Lenovo appeared as sponsor of the Summer Olympics in Beijing and won the design contest for the Olympic torch. The design was reminiscent of a rolled up sheet of paper thereby creating a link to Chinese history and to one of mankind's most important inventions of all time.
Im Jahr 2008 tritt Lenovo als Sponsor der Olympischen Sommerspiele in Beijing in Erscheinung und gewinnt den Wettbewerb für die Gestaltung der olympischen Fackel. Der Entwurf erinnert an ein aufgerolltes Blatt Papier und schlägt eine Brücke zur chinesischen Geschichte und zu einer der wichtigsten Erfindungen der Menschheit überhaupt.

Red Dot: Best of the Best
The best designers of their category
Die besten Designer ihrer Kategorie

The designers of the Red Dot: Best of the Best
Only a few products in the Red Dot Design Award receive the "Red Dot: Best of the Best" accolade. In each category, the jury can assign this award to products of outstanding design quality and innovative achievement. Exploring new paths, these products are all exemplary in their design and oriented towards the future.

The following chapter introduces the people who have received one of these prestigious awards. It features the best designers and design teams of the year 2013 together with their products, revealing in interviews and statements what drives these designers and what design means to them.

Die Designer der Red Dot: Best of the Best
Nur sehr wenige Produkte im Red Dot Design Award erhalten die Auszeichnung „Red Dot: Best of the Best". Die Jury kann mit dieser Auszeichnung in jeder Kategorie Design von außerordentlicher Qualität und Innovationsleistung besonders hervorheben. In jeder Hinsicht vorbildlich gestaltet, beschreiten diese Produkte neue Wege und sind zukunftsweisend.

Das folgende Kapitel stellt die Menschen vor, die diese besondere Auszeichnung erhalten haben. Es zeigt die besten Designer und Designteams des Jahres 2013 zusammen mit ihren Produkten. In Interviews und Statements wird deutlich, was diese Designer bewegt und was ihnen Design bedeutet.

Designer portraits

Lievore Altherr Molina
Saya

»Success for us is to have created, with very simple technology, an object with so much meaning.«
»Erfolg bedeutet für uns, mit einer so schlichten Technik ein Objekt mit so viel Bedeutung geschaffen zu haben.«

Is there a role model or a particular form that inspired your work?
Saya was born of a process rather than an inspiration. A process in which all of the cultural and aesthetic sensibilities we accumulate combine naturally; where even such broad concepts as "Nordic" and "Asian" clearly appear in the synthesis of the multitude of things that Saya represents.

Is there a specific approach that is of significance to your work?
Yes, to embrace the complexity of things in all of their apparent simplicity. To design today means interacting with many other disciplines – tangibly and especially, intangibly.

Gibt es ein Vorbild, das Ihre Arbeit inspiriert hat?
Saya wurde in einem Prozess statt aus einer Inspiration heraus geboren. In einem Prozess, in dem sich alle von uns gebündelten kulturellen und ästhetischen Empfindungen natürlich miteinander verbinden und selbst so weit gefasste Konzepte wie „nordisch" und „asiatisch" in der Synthese der Vielzahl der Dinge, die Saya darstellt, klar erscheinen.

Gibt es einen bestimmten Ansatz, der für Ihre Arbeit von Bedeutung ist?
Ja, die Komplexität der Dinge in all ihrer offenkundigen Schlichtheit zu begrüßen. Gestalten bedeutet heute, mit vielen anderen Disziplinen zu interagieren – materiell und besonders auch immateriell.

Red Dot: Best of the Best
Saya
Chair
Stuhl
See page 60

reddot design award
best of the best 2013

Designer portraits

Alain Gilles
Welded

»When designing, I always try to design something that can age well, both visually and functionally.«
»Meine Gestaltungen versuchen stets, etwas zu erschaffen, das der Zeit funktionell und visuell standhält.«

What do you like in particular about your own award-winning product?
As in all my designs, I want my products to remain highly functional, even if they tend to be sculptural and graphic. In this case, a rather heavy tabletop rests on a visually very light structure. In a way, the table looks more like a small architectural mock-up than a real product.

Is there a role model or a particular form that inspired your work?
Well, I have always been fascinated by the work of the late Oscar Niemeyer. I very much appreciate the readability of his architecture, its unerring simplicity with a nonetheless very personal approach and attention to the shape of his designs.

Was gefällt Ihnen an Ihrem eigenen, ausgezeichneten Produkt besonders gut?
Wie bei all meinen Gestaltungen achte ich darauf, dass sie hochfunktional bleiben, selbst wenn sie zum Skulpturalen oder Grafischen neigen. In diesem Falle ruht eine eher schwere Tischplatte auf einer visuell sehr leichten Struktur. Dadurch mutet der Tisch mehr wie ein kleines Architekturmodell an und weniger wie ein echtes Produkt.

Gibt es ein Vorbild oder eine bestimmte Form, die Ihre Arbeit inspiriert hat?
Nun, ich war schon immer von den Arbeiten des späten Oscar Niemeyer fasziniert. Ich schätze die Lesbarkeit seiner Architektur sehr, ihre unfehlbare Schlichtheit, mit dennoch individuellem Ansatz und Augenmerk für die Form seiner Gestaltungen.

Red Dot: Best of the Best
Welded
Table
Tisch
See page 86

reddot design award
best of the best 2013

Foster + Partners, Industrial Design
Foster 520

»As a practice, we all have a shared belief that the quality of design affects our quality of life.«
»Wir sind der gemeinsamen Überzeugung, dass die Qualität der Gestaltung Einfluss auf die Qualität unseres Lebens hat.«

Is there a role model that inspired your work?
As with all of our projects, the user was our starting point. Rather than resulting from a particular form, the shape derives from ergonomic studies and an extensive period of prototyping – the refined linear profile is designed to visually reduce the chair's volume.

What are the greatest challenges that you currently see in your industry?
Doing more with less – using fewer materials, less energy. The quality of design is therefore vital. If a product or building is well made, then it will endure – longevity is closely linked to sustainability.

Gibt es ein Vorbild, das Ihre Arbeit inspiriert hat?
Ausgangspunkt war der Anwender, wie bei all unseren Projekten. Anstatt einer bestimmten Form zu folgen, ist die Gestalt das Ergebnis von Ergonomiestudien und ausgiebigem Prototyping – das verfeinerte lineare Profil entstand, um die Masse des Stuhls visuell zu reduzieren.

Worin bestehen für Sie aktuell die größten Herausforderungen in Ihrer Branche?
Darin, mehr mit weniger zu erreichen – weniger Materialien, weniger Energieverbrauch. Die Qualität der Gestaltung ist daher von höchster Bedeutung. Wenn ein Produkt oder ein Gebäude gut gestaltet ist, wird es überdauern – Langlebigkeit ist eng verknüpft mit Nachhaltigkeit.

Red Dot: Best of the Best
Foster 520
Armchair
Sessel
See page 74

reddot design award
best of the best 2013

Living rooms and bedrooms

Designer portraits

Moritz Böttcher, Sören Henssler
NEW ORDER

»The simple, distinctive form in combination with eye-catching colours turns these containers into attractive design elements within living spaces.«
»Die schlichte, prägnante Form in Kombination mit markanter Farbgebung macht aus diesen Behältnissen attraktive Gestaltungselemente im Raum.«

Is there a specific approach that is of significance to you and your work?
We believe it is important to get to the heart of things, without becoming trivial. For that reason, our designs may, at first sight, seem restrained. However, upon a second look, users find them surprising as they discover a solution to a detail that they did not expect.

What are the greatest challenges that you currently see in your industry?
The avoidance of obsolescence, consistent recycling of valuable materials, responsible use of increasingly scarce natural resources – in short, the stringent, consistent realisation of the cradle-to-cradle principle.

Gibt es einen bestimmten Ansatz, der für Sie und Ihre Arbeit von Bedeutung ist?
Uns ist es wichtig, die Dinge auf den Punkt zu bringen, ohne dabei banal zu werden. Auf den ersten Blick erscheinen unsere Arbeiten daher als zurückhaltend. Sie überraschen jedoch auf den zweiten Blick, sobald der Nutzer eine Detaillösung entdeckt, die für ihn unerwartet ist.

Worin bestehen für Sie aktuell die größten Herausforderungen in Ihrer Branche?
Unterbindung geplanter Obsoleszenz, konsequentes Wertstoff-Recycling, verantwortungsvoller Umgang mit knapper werdenden Rohstoffen – eben die stringente, konsequente Umsetzung des Cradle-to-Cradle-Prinzips.

Red Dot: Best of the Best
NEW ORDER
Domestic Waste Separation Bags
Taschen zur Mülltrennung im häuslichen Bereich
See page 102

reddot design award
best of the best 2013

Designer portraits

Pia Würtz Mogensen
Pia

»The famous quotation from Ludwig Mies van der Rohe
'less is more' is very characteristic of my design philosophy.«
»Das berühmte Zitat 'weniger ist mehr' von Ludwig Mies van der
Rohe ist sehr charakteristisch für meine Gestaltungsphilosophie.«

What do you like in particular about your own award-winning product?
I like the character of the design – the strong graphical expression, the elegant shape and delicate rounded corners.
I also like the freedom of being able to customise your kitchen with an expression of your personal style.

Is there a designer whom you admire in particular?
Hans Jørgen Wegner. The details, the curves and the elegance of his chairs are very appealing.

Was gefällt Ihnen an Ihrem eigenen, ausgezeichneten Produkt besonders gut?
Ich mag den Charakter der Gestaltung – den starken grafischen Ausdruck, die elegante Formgebung und die leicht gerundeten Ecken. Mir gefällt auch die Freiheit, die eigene Küche mit einem Ausdruck des persönlichen Stils individuell gestalten zu können.

Gibt es einen Designer, den Sie besonders schätzen?
Hans Jørgen Wegner. Die Details, die Kurven und die Eleganz seiner Stühle sind sehr ansprechend.

Red Dot: Best of the Best
Pia
Kitchen Furniture, Kitchen System
Küchenmöbel, Küchensystem
See page 130

reddot design award
best of the best 2013

Brigitte Ziemann
BLANCOSAGA

»We design workplaces. Systemic relationships are therefore a deciding factor in the concept behind our entire product range.«

»Wir gestalten Arbeitsplätze. Deshalb sind systemische Zusammenhänge in unserem gesamten Produktprogramm ein konzeptionell entscheidender Faktor.«

What do you like in particular about your own award-winning product?
The novel operating concept made it possible to reduce the geometry to a cylindrical cross-section. This not only gave it a high formal self-sufficiency, but also resulted in great handling via the sleeve-like slider and made it easy to clean. The product is wonderfully logical.

What are the greatest challenges that you currently see in your industry?
Our markets are very dense due to intense competition. New products are pumped into the various channels at a high frequency; so-called digestion times in trade are not long enough any more.

Was gefällt Ihnen an Ihrem eigenen, ausgezeichneten Produkt besonders gut?
Mit diesem neuartigen Bedienkonzept war es möglich, die Geometrie auf einen zylindrischen Querschnitt zu reduzieren. Neben einer hohen formalen Eigenständigkeit resultieren daraus eine tolle Handhabung über die Manschette und ideale Reinigungseigenschaften. Das Produkt ist wunderbar logisch.

Worin bestehen für Sie aktuell die größten Herausforderungen in Ihrer Branche?
Unsere Märkte sind durch intensiven Wettbewerb stark verdichtet. Neue Produkte werden hochfrequent in die unterschiedlichen Kanäle gepumpt, sogenannte Verdauzeiten im Handel sind nicht mehr ausreichend lang.

Red Dot: Best of the Best
BLANCOSAGA
Mixer Tap
Küchenarmatur
See page 148

reddot design award
best of the best 2013

Designer portraits

2ND WEST
TURMIX

»Demands emerging from the demographic changes to our society will have a substantial influence on the design of the future.«
»Anforderungen, die aus der demografischen Entwicklung unserer Gesellschaft entstehen, werden das Design in Zukunft wesentlich beeinflussen.«

What do you like in particular about your own award-winning product?
The durable technical components and materials, its pleasing tactile surfaces and the simple elegance of these kitchen appliances.

Is there a specific approach that is of significance to you and your work?
The search for simplicity. Approaches focusing on simplicity and the super normal. How can usability be simplified or something be left out without having to compromise.

How would you define the term "design quality"?
Does the product make sense? Does it create added-value? Is it fun?

Was gefällt Ihnen an Ihrem eigenen, ausgezeichneten Produkt besonders gut?
Langlebig in den technischen Komponenten und Materialien, angenehm in den Oberflächen, einfach in der Bedienung und die schlichte Eleganz dieser Maschinen für die Küche.

Gibt es einen bestimmten Ansatz, der für Sie und Ihre Arbeit von Bedeutung ist?
Die Suche nach Einfachheit. Ansätze wie „Simplicity" und „Super-Normal". Wie kann die Bedienung vereinfacht oder etwas ohne Verlust weggelassen werden.

Wie würden Sie den Begriff der Designqualität beschreiben?
Ist das Produkt sinnvoll? Schafft es Mehrwert? Macht es Freude?

Red Dot: Best of the Best
TURMIX
Kitchen Appliances Line
Küchengeräte-Linie
See page 218

reddot design award
best of the best 2013

Designer portraits

Nicholai Wiig Hansen
Geo

»I try not to follow trends, and focus on designing good products that will withstand the test of time.«
»Ich versuche, Trends nicht zu folgen und mich auf das Gestalten guter Produkte zu konzentrieren, die der Zeit standhalten.«

Is there a specific approach that is of significance to you and your work?
All my work starts in my head. I think the product all the way through from the form to production and to the end-user experience before I make a single sketch on paper.

What are the greatest challenges that you currently see in your industry?
One of the biggest challenges is to create economic growth for the companies you work with by using less material and designing products that last longer.

Gibt es einen bestimmten Ansatz, der für Sie und Ihre Arbeit von Bedeutung ist?
All meine Arbeit beginnt in meinem Kopf. Ich durchdenke das Produkt vollständig, von der Form bis zur Produktion und der Erfahrung der Endverbraucher, bevor ich eine einzige Zeichnung auf Papier anfertige.

Worin bestehen für Sie aktuell die größten Herausforderungen in Ihrer Branche?
Eine der größten Herausforderungen ist, ökonomisches Wachstum für die Firmen, mit denen man zusammenarbeitet, zu erzeugen, indem man weniger Material verwendet und Produkte entwirft, die länger halten.

Red Dot: Best of the Best
Geo
Vacuum Flask
Thermoskanne
See page 276

reddot design award
best of the best 2013

Designer portraits

Kazuyuki Kawase, Ken Okuyama
EDA

»The function of EDA is to bring
the essence of nature onto the table.«
»Die Funktion von EDA besteht darin,
das Wesen der Natur auf den Tisch zu bringen.«

Is there a specific approach
that is of significance to your work?
Ken Okuyama: Just as the Arts and
Crafts movement introduced humanity
and culture into industrial products,
we think design is a great tool for
rejuvenating industry and local culture.

How would you define the term
"quality"?
Ken Okuyama: Quality is one of the
most critical values and should be
defined by our customers. Customers
of future products may not have even
been born yet, so designers are required
to have imagination and vision.

Gibt es einen bestimmten Ansatz,
der für Ihre Arbeit von Bedeutung ist?
Ken Okuyama: Ebenso wie die Kunst-
und Handwerksbewegung Menschlichkeit
und Kultur im Industriedesign einführte,
so glauben wir, ist Gestaltung ein groß-
artiges Instrument zur Regenerierung
von Industrie und lokaler Kultur.

Wie würden Sie den Begriff
der Qualität beschreiben?
Ken Okuyama: Qualität ist einer der ent-
scheidendsten Werte und sollte von unseren Kunden definiert werden. Die Kunden
für zukünftige Projekte sind vielleicht
noch gar nicht geboren, deshalb müssen
Gestalter Imagination und Vision besitzen.

Red Dot: Best of the Best
EDA
Cutlery
Besteck
See page 240

Bernhard Elsässer
The Attitude of the Definite – the Square

»Design is much more than just a form-finding process.
It considers societal relationships, reflects them and,
at its best, contributes to solving problems.«
»Design ist weit mehr als ein Formfindungsprozess.
Es nimmt gesellschaftliche Zusammenhänge auf, reflektiert
sie und trägt bestenfalls zu Problemlösungen bei.«

What do you like in particular about your own award-winning product?
What is unusual about this porcelain study is its experimental approach to the material of porcelain and the use of textiles in developing the shape. It is fascinating to see the manufacturing process show through in the end product.

How would you define the term "quality"?
In our affluent society, it is not longer just the sum and quality of all features of a product that are of significance, but the relationship that I can establish with it; that is, the added-value in terms of content and emotion.

Was gefällt Ihnen an Ihrem eigenen, ausgezeichneten Produkt besonders gut?
Das Besondere an der Porzellanstudie ist der experimentelle Umgang mit dem Werkstoff Porzellan und die Verwendung von Textilien im Formfindungsprozess. Es ist sehr reizvoll, am Endprodukt die Herstellungsweise ablesen zu können.

Wie würden Sie den Begriff der Qualität beschreiben?
In unserer Überflussgesellschaft ist nicht mehr nur die Summe und Güte aller Eigenschaften eines Produktes wichtig, sondern die Beziehung, die man mit ihm eingehen kann, mithin sein inhaltlicher und emotionaler Mehrwert.

Red Dot: Best of the Best
The Attitude of the Definite – the Square
Die Attitüde des Bestimmten – das Quadrat
Porcelain Vase
Porzellangefäß
See page 268

Designer portraits

Manabu Tago
OSORO

»Quality is achieved when the concept and role of a product firmly connect with the sensitivity of the customer.«

»Qualität wird erreicht, wenn Idee und Bedeutung eines Produkts mit der Sensibilität des Kunden in einer festen Verbindung stehen.«

Is there a role model that inspired your work?
Similar functionality can be seen in the dinner bowls of Japanese monks. Coupled with traditional Japanese philosophy this functionality has made our product internationally successful.

Which trends have a particularly strong influence on the design of today?
In today's world of super-abundant goods all trends are influential. So there has to be a well-defined reason for introducing yet another product to the world. When designing, it is important to do so with speed so that challenges can be solved in a deliberately ecological way.

Gibt es ein Vorbild, das Ihre Arbeit inspiriert hat?
Eine ähnliche Funktionalität weist die Essensschale eines japanischen Mönchs auf. Sie führte, verbunden mit traditioneller japanischer Philosophie, zum internationalen Erfolg unseres Produkts.

Welche Trends beeinflussen das Design augenblicklich besonders stark?
In der heutigen Welt des Überangebots sind alle Trends einflussreich. Daher muss es einen klaren Grund geben, um noch ein weiteres Produkt in die Welt zu setzen. Bei der Gestaltung ist es wichtig, mit Eile zu agieren, um die Herausforderungen bewusst ökologisch zu lösen.

Red Dot: Best of the Best
OSORO
Open Tableware System
Offenes Geschirrsystem
See page 234

reddot design award
best of the best 2013

Designer portraits

Philippe Starck
Axor Starck Organic

»Quality is about the equilibrium between different parameters. It is very dear to me.«
»Qualität ist das Gleichgewicht zwischen verschiedenen Parametern. Sie liegt mir sehr am Herzen.«

What do you like in particular about your own award-winning product?
This collection was started from scratch with no preconceived ideas, arising purely out of technical requirements, functional parameters and the semantics of symbolism. In an ergonomic way, it allows you to save water easily and harmoniously, which makes the products highly ecological.

Is there a specific approach that is of significance to you and your work?
I always work with the same philosophy: think of the benefit to the final user, and start from the most ambitious vision possible – that should result in a new ethical project.

Was gefällt Ihnen an Ihrem eigenen, ausgezeichneten Produkt besonders gut?
Die Kollektion wurde von Grund auf ohne vorgefasste Vorstellungen entwickelt und entstand lediglich aus technischen Auflagen, funktionalen Parametern und der semantischen Symbolik. Auf ergonomische Weise ermöglicht sie es, einfach und harmonisch Wasser zu sparen, wodurch die Produkte sehr umweltbewusst sind.

Gibt es einen bestimmten Ansatz, der für Sie und Ihre Arbeit von Bedeutung ist?
Ich arbeite immer nach der gleichen Philosophie: Denke an den Vorteil des Endnutzers und gehe von der größtmöglichen Vision aus – das sollte zu einem neuen ethischen Projekt führen.

Red Dot: Best of the Best
Axor Starck Organic
Bathroom Fixtures
Badarmaturen
See page 294

reddot design award
best of the best 2013   39

Designer portraits

Mårten Claesson,
Eero Koivisto, Ola Rune
Blueair Sense

»The specific approach that is of significance to our work is understated elegance with a certain twist – actually a very Scandinavian approach.«

»Der Ansatz, der für unsere Arbeit von besonderer Bedeutung ist, lautet: untertriebene Eleganz mit dem gewissen Extra – ein doch recht skandinavischer Ansatz.«

What do you like in particular about your own award-winning product?
We tried very hard to make something people would like to have in a room – something that looks less electronic. We also like the no-touch user interface, which we designed in place of the number, performance and status diagrams usually present in these kinds of products.

What are the greatest challenges that you currently see in your industry?
To try to maintain the standard of serious design as "design as entertainment" is increasingly filling the media.

Was gefällt Ihnen an Ihrem eigenen, ausgezeichneten Produkt besonders gut?
Wir haben alles daran gesetzt, etwas zu kreieren, das man gerne im Zimmer hat – etwas, das weniger elektronisch aussieht. Uns gefällt auch das berührungslose Interface, das wir anstelle der bei dieser Art von Produkten üblichen Zahlen-, Leistungs- und Statusdiagramme entworfen haben.

Worin bestehen für Sie aktuell die größten Herausforderungen in Ihrer Branche?
Im Versuch, den Grad ernsten Designs hochzuhalten, während immer mehr „Gestaltung als Unterhaltung" die Medien füllt.

Red Dot: Best of the Best
Blueair Sense
Air Purifier
Luftreiniger

See page 332

reddot design award
best of the best 2013

Designer portraits

Jochen Bittermann
Varioline (Special Edition)

»My personal belief is that truly well-conceived design
is timeless.«

»Mein persönlicher Anspruch ist, dass wirklich gelungene
Gestaltung zeitlos ist.«

Red Dot: Best of the Best
Varioline (Special Edition)
Sauna Cabin
Saunakabine
See page 324

Bathrooms, spas and air conditioning

**Is there a role model
that inspired your work?**
Historically, I was inspired by old saunas
in which the heat is generated by an
open fire.

**Is there a specific approach
that is of significance to your work?**
I do not want to create things that are
just "beautiful" or items to be looked
at, but "consumer goods" in the truest
sense of the word; that is objects, which
are easy to use.

**Is there a design object or product,
which you appreciate in particular?**
I admire the "Watercone" by Stephan
Augustin. Its concept reduces the design to the essential – producing one's
own drinking water in the easiest way
possible.

**Gibt es ein Vorbild,
das Ihre Arbeit inspiriert hat?**
Historisch gesehen haben mich alte
Saunen inspiriert, bei denen die Wärme
durch offenes Feuer erzeugt wurde.

**Gibt es einen bestimmten Ansatz, der
für Ihre Arbeit von Bedeutung ist?**
Ich möchte keine reinen „Ansichtssachen"
gestalten, sondern „Gebrauchsgüter" im
Wortsinn, also Objekte, die gut zu gebrauchen sind.

**Gibt es ein Designobjekt oder
Produkt, das Sie besonders schätzen?**
Ich bewundere den „Watercone" von
Stephan Augustin. In dem Entwurf ist das
Design auf das Wesentliche reduziert, auf
einfachstem Weg trinkbares Wasser selbst
herzustellen.

Designer portraits

Issey Miyake
IN-EI

»I think that designers today must be especially conscious of the environment and of our diminishing natural resources.«
»Ich denke, Designer müssen sich heute insbesondere der Umwelt und unserer schwindenden natürlichen Ressourcen bewusst sein.«

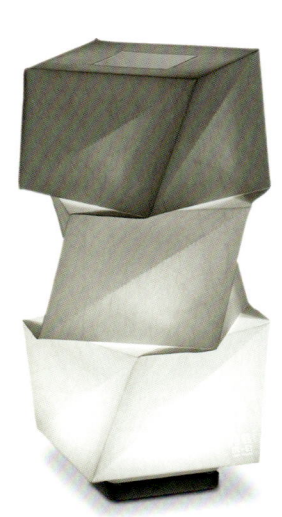

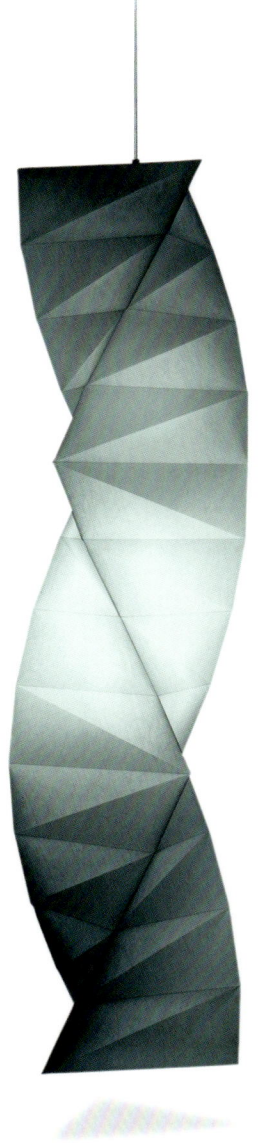

Is there a specific approach that is of significance to you and your work?
No matter how much or how far technology advances, for me the most important element in design will always be the involvement of human hands. To create the folds in the IN-EI lamp shades, each shade must be carefully folded and ironed by hand. I like the precision and the warmth that comes from using our hands.

How would you define the term "design quality"?
I think the most important aspect of design is whether or not it meets people's needs. Design should reflect the fundamental challenges that people face today and look for ways in which to solve them.

Gibt es einen bestimmten Ansatz, der für Sie und Ihre Arbeit von Bedeutung ist?
Ungeachtet dessen, wie sehr oder hoch sich Technologie entwickelt, wird der Einsatz der menschlichen Hand für mich immer das wichtigste Element in der Gestaltung bleiben. Die Falten der Leuchtenschirme IN-EI erfordern es, dass jeder Schirm einzeln von Hand gefaltet und gebügelt werden muss. Ich liebe die Präzision und die Wärme, die durch unsere Hände entsteht.

Wie würden Sie den Begriff der Designqualität beschreiben?
Ich denke, der wichtigste Aspekt einer Gestaltung ist, dass sie den Bedürfnissen der Menschen gerecht wird. Design sollte heute die grundlegenden Probleme der Menschen reflektieren und Wege suchen, um diese zu lösen.

Red Dot: Best of the Best
IN-EI ISSEY MIYAKE
Lighting Collection
Leuchtenkollektion
See page 348

reddot design award
best of the best 2013

Designer portraits

Thomas Cramer,
Hans-Werner Ribjitzki
N8LED

»The better the development, the easier and simpler the handling
– this is what makes a good product!«
»Je einfacher und sicherer das Handling, desto besser war die
Entwicklung – gerade das macht ein gutes Produkt aus!«

What do you like in particular about
the function, use and form of your own
award-winning product?
The merging of functionality and design,
as well as the intuitive handling of the
product – these are its outstanding
characteristics.

What are the greatest challenges that
you currently see in your industry?
The challenge is to develop innovative
products that apply the latest achievements in state-of-the-art technology.

Was gefällt Ihnen an Ihrem
eigenen, ausgezeichneten Produkt
besonders gut?
Die Verschmelzung von Funktionalität
und Design sowie das intuitive Handling
im Umgang mit dem Produkt sind seine
herausragenden Eigenschaften.

Worin bestehen für Sie aktuell die
größten Herausforderungen in Ihrer
Branche?
Die Herausforderung liegt darin, innovative
Produkte zu entwickeln, die sich auf dem
aktuellen Stand der Technik befinden.

Red Dot: Best of the Best
N8LED
360-Degree LED Large Area Lighting
360-Grad-LED-Großflächenbeleuchtung
See page 372

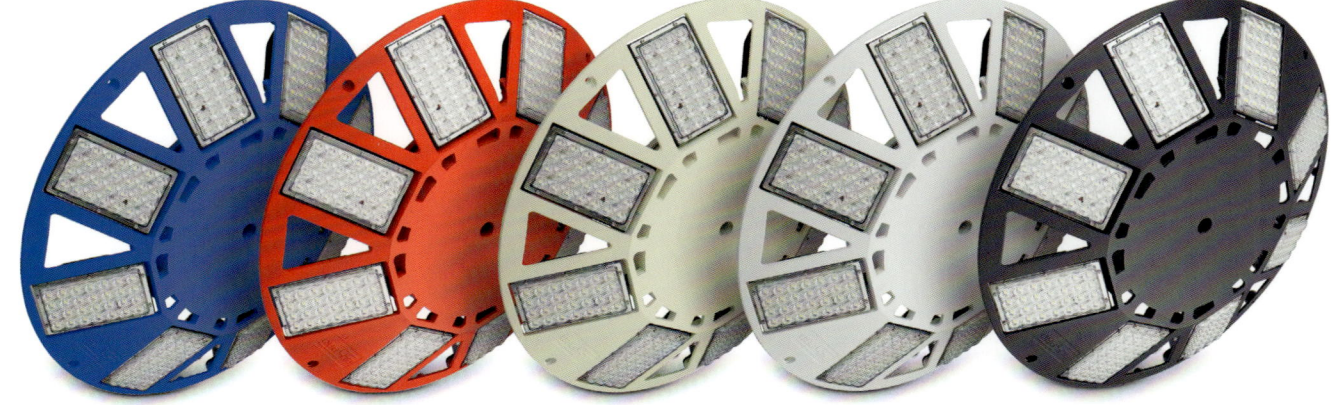

Designer portraits

Philips Design Consumer Lifestyle Team
HF3550

»Throughout the project we made a point of continually challenging ourselves to reduce complexity, to question the value of each additional function.«

»Während des Projekts haben wir uns immer wieder selbst dazu herausgefordert, Komplexität zu reduzieren und den Wert jeglicher Zusatzfunktion zu hinterfragen.«

Were there specific challenges when designing the product which turned out to be really difficult?
The Wake-up Light gives you options for creating the optimum personal wake-up experience via light, sound and visual cues, and it was a big challenge to incorporate all these aspects while at the same time ensuring that the user interface was simple and engaging.

How would you define the term "design quality"?
It's about creating a reaction of surprise or excitement in people. For a product to have real design quality, it must pass this test.

Gab es besondere Herausforderungen bei der Produktgestaltung, die sich als besonders schwierig erwiesen haben?
Die Wake-up Light ermöglicht es Anwendern, sich ein für sie optimales Aufwacherlebnis über Licht, Klang und visuelle Impulse zu schaffen. Es war eine große Herausforderung, all diese Faktoren zu integrieren und gleichzeitig sicherzustellen, dass die Benutzeroberfläche einfach und ansprechend ist.

Wie würden Sie den Begriff der Designqualität beschreiben?
Es geht darum, die Menschen zu begeistern oder zu überraschen. Will ein Produkt wahrhaftige Designqualität aufweisen, muss es diesen Test bestehen.

Red Dot: Best of the Best
HF3550
Wake-up Light
Lichtwecker
See page 368

reddot design award
best of the best 2013

Tokujin Yoshioka
Invisible Table

»I would like to create things that make people happy and touch their emotions.«
»Ich möchte Dinge schaffen, die Menschen glücklich machen und sie emotional berühren.«

Were there specific challenges when designing the product, which turned out to be really difficult?
It was quite challenging to create this minimal form without compromising on strength. The "Invisible Table" seems to camouflage itself in its appearance to escape from our material world. It blends into people's daily lives like air.

Which trends have a particularly strong influence on the design of today?
Rather than picking on a specific area of trends as influences on the design of today, I think that creators naturally find what human beings need based on the mood of the time.

Gab es besondere Herausforderungen bei der Produktgestaltung, die sich als besonders schwierig erwiesen haben?
Es war eine ziemliche Herausforderung, diese reduzierte Form ohne Abstriche bei der Stabilität zu erzeugen. Der „Unsichtbare Tisch" scheint sich in seiner Anmut zu verbergen, um unserer physischen Welt zu entfliehen. Er fügt sich wie Luft in den menschlichen Alltag ein.

Welche Trends beeinflussen das Design augenblicklich besonders stark?
Ohne einen bestimmten Bereich von Trends als Einflussgrößen auf das Design von heute hervorzuheben, denke ich, dass Entwerfer ganz natürlich am Geist der Zeit erkennen, was für die Menschen erforderlich ist.

Red Dot: Best of the Best
Invisible Table
Table
Tisch
See page 394

reddot design award
best of the best 2013

Designer portraits

Tobias Batrla
Origami

»I am fascinated by the way a century-old form of design merges with new technology to create a highly contemporary, luxurious fabric.«

»Mich begeistert, wie eine mehrere Jahrhunderte alte Formensprache durch eine neue Technologie zu topaktuellen, exklusiven Dekorationsstoffen wird.«

Is there a detail of your award-winning product whose solution was really successful?
A jacquard fabric aims to weave all threads into the fabric under the same tension. However, the origami paper-like folding technique we used requires the reconciling of conflicting characteristics, such as stability for the surface areas and the ability to shape the pleats. This allowed for the possibility of creating visual accents at the folds, making this technique substantially different from conventional pleating techniques.

Is there a design object, which you appreciate in particular?
When working, the Variér standing stool impresses me in two ways. It provides sufficient stability for me to carry out delicate work, but gives me full freedom of movement at the same time.

Gibt es ein Detail an Ihrem ausgezeichneten Produkt, dessen Lösung Sie für besonders gut gelungen halten?
Ein Jacquardgewebe ist bestrebt, alle Fäden in einem ähnlichen Spannungszustand einzuarbeiten. Doch die Faltungen der Origamitechnik erfordern die Verbindung gegensätzlicher Eigenschaften wie Stabilität in den Flächen und Formbarkeit an den Kanten. Hieraus entwickelte sich die Möglichkeit der Akzentuierung an den Faltkanten, was diese Technik deutlich von bekannten Plissier-Techniken unterscheidet.

Gibt es ein Designobjekt, das Sie besonders schätzen?
In zweierlei Hinsicht bewegt mich der Stehhocker von Variér bei meiner Arbeit. Darauf finde ich ausreichend Ruhe, um filigrane Arbeiten auszuführen, und bin dabei trotzdem sehr flexibel.

Red Dot: Best of the Best
Origami
Drapery
Dekorationsstoff
See page 400

Designer portraits

BIG Bjarke Ingels Group, Topotek 1, Superflex
Superkilen

»Superkilen is a park reflecting diversity. The project is intended to celebrate the neighbourhood's multi-cultural heritage and unite everybody in one global community.«

»Superkilen ist ein Park der Vielfältigkeit. Das Projekt zielt darauf ab, den multikulturellen Hintergrund der Nachbarschaft zu feiern und alle Bewohner in einer globalen Gemeinschaft zu vereinen.«

Red Dot: Best of the Best
Superkilen
Urban Park
Öffentlicher Park
See page 450

Is there a particular idea that inspired the work for which you received the award?
Taking Superkilen's location in the heart of outer Nørrebro as their point of departure, the team chose to focus on those activities in urban spaces that promote integration across ethnicity, religion, culture and language.

How would you define the term "quality"?
Quality is that special balance between the different elements that the design of a space should advocate. It starts with a strong shape to make identification easy, followed by the essence that in everyday use becomes part of the human experience and which, combined with real physical quality, is able to stand the test of time – in other words, it is sustainable.

Gibt es eine bestimmte Idee, die Ihre prämierte Arbeit inspiriert hat?
Ausgehend von der Lage Superkilens im Herzen des Stadtteils Nørrebro, entschied sich das Team, jene Aktivitäten im urbanen Raum in den Mittelpukt zu stellen, die die ethnische, religiöse, kulturelle und sprachliche Integration fördern.

Wie würden Sie den Begriff der Qualität beschreiben?
Qualität ist jene besondere Ausgewogenheit zwischen unterschiedlichen Elementen, die eine Raumgestaltung verfechten sollte. Ausgangspunkt ist eine konsequente Form, die der Identifikation dient, gefolgt vom Wesentlichen, das in der täglichen Nutzung zur menschlichen Erfahrungswelt wird und in Verbindung mit einer realen physischen Qualität lange überdauern kann, mit anderen Worten zukunftsfähig ist.

Designer portraits

Fernando Seara de Sá, Raul Roque, Alexandre Coelho Lima, Manuel Roque
Platform for Arts and Creativity

»One idea permeates our work: when designing a building, we are eager to see how it turns out, in other words, how our vision will materialise.«

»Eine Idee durchdringt stets unsere Arbeit: Bei der Gestaltung eines Gebäudes sind wir immer gespannt, wie es aussehen wird, das heißt, wie sich unsere Vision materialisieren wird.«

Red Dot: Best of the Best
Platform for Arts and Creativity
See page 440

Is there a particular idea that inspired your award-winning work?
The fundamental idea was to revitalise the space occupied by the marketplace with its historic significance to the city and to turn into a place where people meet and talk, thereby reviving the intense relation it once had with the city. In order to achieve this, we tried to design a building that would act as a reference within the cultural context of the city, by accentuating its eminently contemporary character.

Which developments have a particularly strong influence on the architecture of today?
The quick succession and ease with which new images are currently being created, has completely changed people's way of looking at architecture.

Gibt es eine bestimmte Idee, die Ihre ausgezeichnete Arbeit inspiriert hat?
Die grundlegende Idee bestand darin, den Raum des Marktplatzes mit seiner historischen Bedeutung für die Stadt wiederzubeleben und ihn als Ort der Begegnung wie des Austauschs und damit seine einst enge Beziehung zur Stadt neu zu erschaffen. Wir versuchten daher, ein Gebäude zu entwerfen, das im kulturellen Kontext der Stadt als Referenzpunkt dienen kann, indem wir dessen ausgesprochen zeitgenössischen Charakter hervorhoben.

Welche Entwicklungen beeinflussen die Architektur augenblicklich besonders stark?
Die schnelle Abfolge und Leichtigkeit, mit der neue Bilder derzeit entstehen, hat die Art, wie Menschen Architektur begegnen, vollkommen verändert.

reddot design award
best of the best 2013

Living rooms and bedrooms
Wohnen und Schlafen

Furniture, furniture accessories, stoves, materials, carpets, floorings, wallpaper, mirrors, decorations and accessories
Möbel, Möbelzubehör, Kaminöfen, Stoffe, Teppiche, Bodenbeläge, Tapeten, Spiegel, Dekoration und Accessoires

1

Saya
Chair
Stuhl

Manufacturer
Arper SPA,
Treviso, Italy

Design
Lievore Altherr Molina,
Barcelona, Spain

Web
www.arper.com
www.lievorealtherrmolina.com

reddot design award
best of the best 2013

Graphic sign

In the complex world we live in everything can be seen as a sign. This is how Umberto Eco, one of the most influential proponents of contemporary semiotics, defines the study of signs. The Saya chair is so sharply designed that it resembles a graphic symbol. Saya's lines flow thanks to the warm appearance of wood, with the daring silhouette of the chair set in effective contrast. This incisive shape adds the finishing touch to every room like a signature which makes it clear who the author of a text is. Saya is suitable for use in many ways both in the home and in public spaces. It is available in natural oak or teak, but also in an open-pore varnish. Varnishes in white, black, ochre and three shades of red allow for combinations that add variety, but are nonetheless cohesive. The significant design of Saya goes hand in hand with a high degree of functionality and durability. It has a four-legged frame available either in wood or chromium-plated steel. The latter is stackable, so even the large numbers of chairs needed for conference rooms can be stored without problem. In this way, Saya combines symbolic and concise expression with a high level of suitability for everyday use.

Grafisches Zeichen

Alles kann in unserer komplexen Umwelt zu einem Zeichen werden, so definiert es Umberto Eco, einer der wichtigsten Vertreter der zeitgenössischen Semiotik, der Lehre von den Zeichen. Der Stuhl Saya ist so prägnant gestaltet, dass er einem grafischen Zeichen ähnelt. Die Linien des Saya sind fließend mit der warmen Anmutung des Holzes – in einem gelungenen Kontrast dazu steht die kühne Silhouette dieses Stuhls. Diese Formensprache führt dazu, dass er jeden Raum durch seine Prägnanz vervollständigt: wie eine Unterschrift, die ein Schriftstück eindeutig einem Urheber zuweist. Sowohl im Wohn- wie auch im Objektbereich bietet der Saya vielfältige Möglichkeiten des Einsatzes. Er wird gefertigt in den Holzarten Eiche natur und Teak sowie in der Variante Lasur offenporig. In Verbindung mit den Farben Weiß, Schwarz, Ocker und Rot in drei verschiedenen Tönen ermöglicht dies variable und zugleich geschlossene Kombinationen. Die signifikante Formensprache geht bei dem Stuhl Saya zudem einher mit einem hohen Maß an Funktionalität und Langlebigkeit. Er ist gestaltet mit einem vierbeinigen Gestell in den Ausführungen Holz oder verchromter Stahl. Die vierbeinige Version in Stahl verchromt ist zudem stapelbar, sodass sich auch große Stückzahlen zur Bestuhlung von Versammlungsräumen problemlos verstauen lassen. Der Stuhl Saya verbindet auf diese Weise seine zeichenhafte und prägnante Aussage mit einem hohen Maß an Alltagstauglichkeit.

Statement by the jury

The iconic shape of this wooden chair is surprisingly new. It possesses a quality of form that is unique and will stand the test of time. Saya's ergonomics are thought through offering the user good back support. The chair is functional, durable and versatile in use even for public spaces.

Begründung der Jury

Dieser Holzstuhl ist überraschend neu in seiner ikonografischen Formensprache. Er verfügt über eine formale Qualität, die einzigartig ist und deshalb die Zeit überdauern wird. Er ist ergonomisch durchdacht und bietet dem Rücken einen guten Halt. Der Stuhl Saya ist dabei funktional, langlebig und vielseitig auch im Objektbereich einsetzbar.

Masters
Chair
Stuhl

Manufacturer
Kartell,
Milan, Italy
Design
Starck Network (Philippe Starck),
Paris, France
Eugeni Quitllet,
Paris, France
Web
www.kartell.it
www.starcknetwork.com
www.eugenidesign.com

Masters is a tribute to three classic chairs – Series 7 by Arne Jacobsen, the Tulip Armchair by Eero Saarinen and the Eiffel Chair by Charles Eames. Their unmistakable silhouettes combine into a sleek entity, with a particularly noticeable back, created through three curvaceous, intersecting poles. Masters is stackable and available in many different colours. It can be used both indoors and out.

Der Stuhl Masters ist eine Hommage an drei Stuhl-Klassiker – die Serie 7 von Arne Jacobsen, den Tulip Armchair von Eero Saarinen sowie den Eiffel Chair von Charles Eames. Deren unverwechselbare Silhouetten vereinen sich in einem geschmeidigen Gebilde. Dabei fällt besonders die Rückenlehne auf, die durch drei kurvenreiche, sich überkreuzende Lehnenstangen gebildet wird. Stapelbar und erhältlich in vielen Farben, kann Masters auch im Freien verwendet werden.

Statement by the jury
Masters displays an original mix of styles based on classic, iconic chairs. The interplay of lines and the special finish give it a sensuous appeal.

Begründung der Jury
Masters präsentiert sich als originelle Stil-Mischung klassischer Stuhl-Ikonen. Das Spiel der Linien und die besondere Verarbeitung verleihen ihm Sinnlichkeit.

Audrey
Chair
Stuhl

Manufacturer
Kartell,
Milan, Italy
Design
Lissoni Associati
(Piero Lissoni),
Milan, Italy
Web
www.kartell.it
www.lissoniassociati.it

The versatility and modernity of Audrey is the result of the simple and uncluttered lines of its frame, manufactured from only two components in a die-casting process. The innovative use of aluminium in combination with plastic, whose surface is polished in an automatic process make the chair light and robust. It is multifunctional and can be used in almost any environment both indoors and outdoors, at home or in a public space.

Audrey ist dank des einfachen und schlichten, aus nur zwei Teilen gefertigten Druckgussgestells ein vielseitiger und moderner Stuhl. Der innovative Einsatz von Aluminium und dessen Verbindung mit Kunststoff sowie die durch ein automatisiertes Verfahren ermöglichte Politur machen ihn leicht und widerstandsfähig. Der Stuhl ist multifunktional und für nahezu alle Anwendungsmöglichkeiten geeignet: für innen wie für außen, für den Wohn- wie den Objektbereich.

Statement by the jury
Simple, clean lines characterise this chair, which is manufactured using an innovative process, which avoids any visible welding seams or screws.

Begründung der Jury
Einfache, klare Linien bestimmen die Gestaltung dieses Stuhls, der durch ein innovatives Herstellungsverfahren ohne sichtbare Schweißnähte oder Schrauben auskommt.

Juno
Chair
Stuhl

Manufacturer
Arper SpA,
Treviso, Italy
Design
James Irvine Srl,
Milan, Italy
Web
www.arper.com
www.james-irvine.com

This plastic chair is manufactured in a single operation and is characterised by its flowing lines and light weight. It combines the advantages of a simple, uncomplicated form with efficiency and versatility, thus meeting customers' individual needs. The chair comes in six colours, with an open or closed back, with or without armrests and with an optional, elegantly upholstered seat and back. Juno is at home in domestic and office environments and can be used both indoors and out. What is more, all variations are stackable, so that the large numbers required for conference rooms, for example, can be stored without problem.

Dieser in nur einem Arbeitsgang hergestellte Kunststoffstuhl zeichnet sich durch fließende Linien und ein geringes Gewicht aus. Er kombiniert die Vorteile einer einfachen, schlichten Form mit Effizienz und Vielseitigkeit. Dadurch kommt er auch individuellen Kundenwünschen entgegen. Den Stuhl gibt es in sechs Farben, mit offener oder geschlossener Rückenlehne, mit und ohne Armlehnen und auch mit eleganter, gepolsterter Sitzfläche und Rückenlehne. Er eignet sich für den Wohn- wie für den Bürobereich, für innen wie für außen. Sämtliche Varianten sind außerdem stapelbar, sodass sich auch große Stückzahlen zur Bestuhlung von beispielsweise Versammlungsräumen problemlos verstauen lassen.

Statement by the jury
A lightness of form and weight is the predominant characteristic of this versatile and robust chair.

Begründung der Jury
Leichtigkeit in Form und Materialität ist das hervorstechende Merkmal dieses vielseitigen, robusten Stuhls.

The Andersen Chair
Chair
Stuhl

Manufacturer
Brødrene Andersen Møbelsnedkeri A/S,
Hinnerup, Denmark
Design
byKATO
(Karl Rüdiger Rossell, Tonny Glismand),
Aarhus, Denmark
Web
www.brdr-andersen.dk
www.bykato.com

The legs of the Andersen Chair are
made of solid wood. At the top of each
of the legs, a brass ring creates a lovely
transition to the seat while at the same
time protecting the wood from splitting.
The sturdy, slightly curved fibre-glass
seat is only around 6 mm thick and
provides an extremely comfortable
sitting experience by supporting the
body in all the right places. The chair
legs are identical in size and shape and
are attached to the chair using four
tapered fixtures.

Der Andersen Chair hat Stuhlbeine aus
massivem Holz. Einen schönen Übergang
zur Sitzfläche bildet jeweils ein Messing-
ring, der das Holz davor schützt zu reißen.
Der feste, leicht gewölbte Glasfasersitz ist
nur ca. 6 mm dick und sorgt für ausgezeichneten Sitzkomfort, da der Körper an
den richtigen Stellen gestützt wird. Die
Stuhlbeine sind in Größe und Form iden-
tisch und werden mit vier kegelförmigen
Befestigungen am Stuhl fixiert.

Statement by the jury
This chair is remarkable for its mix of
materials from solid wood to brass
and fibre-glass. Its carefully planned
construction is at once aesthetically
pleasing and practical.

Begründung der Jury
Dieser Stuhl fällt auf durch den Materialmix aus Vollholz, Messing und Glasfaser.
Durch seine durchdachte Konstruktion
ist er ästhetisch reizvoll und praktisch
zugleich.

Panama
Chair
Stuhl

Manufacturer
GABER S.r.l.,
Caselle di Altivole (Treviso),
Italy
Design
Stefano Sandonà,
Selvazzano Dentro (Padova), Italy
Web
www.gaber.it
www.sandonadesign.it

Panama is a symbiosis of the past and present, of innovative materials such as plastic and traditional ones like solid wood. Its light and airy design creates an even, harmonious appearance. The comfortable chair comes with and without armrests, with wooden or technopolymer legs and in various colours, making it suitable for the home and for public spaces. It can be used both indoors and outdoors.

Statement by the jury
The large number of available versions make this elegant chair an up-to-date and highly practical piece of seating furniture.

Panama ist eine Symbiose zwischen Vergangenheit und Gegenwart, zwischen innovativen Materialien wie Kunststoff und traditionellen wie Massivholz. Das leichte, luftig wirkende Design schafft eine gleichmäßige, harmonische Form. Den bequemen Stuhl gibt es mit oder ohne Armlehnen, mit Stuhlbeinen aus Holz oder Technopolymer und in verschiedenen Farbtönen. Er eignet sich daher für zu Hause und für den Objektbereich, für den Innen- und Außeneinsatz.

Begründung der Jury
Dank vieler verfügbarer Varianten ist dieser formschöne Stuhl ein zeitgemäßes und äußerst praktikables Sitzmöbel.

Malmö
Chair
Stuhl

Manufacturer
Pedrali Spa,
Mornico al Serio, Italy
Design
Michele Cazzaniga,
Simone Mandelli,
Antonio Pagliarulo,
Lentate sul Seveso, Italy
Web
www.pedrali.it

The Malmö collection was inspired by an imaginary journey to a Scandinavian lake. The snugness of the wood gives the chair a warm atmosphere, which evokes a feeling of homecoming. The ash frame supports a multilayered, wooden seat shell. The gentle, figure-hugging lines, which characterise this chair, make it elegant and comfortable. Upholstered versions provide even more relaxation.

Statement by the jury
The aura evoked by the quality of the wood makes this chair come alive. The properties of the wood have been cleverly incorporated into its design.

Die Kollektion Malmö beruht auf einer imaginären Reise an einen skandinavischen See. Sie erweckt das Gefühl von Heimkehr – dank der Behaglichkeit des Holzes, das eine warme Atmosphäre verbreitet. Das Gestell aus Eschenholz trägt eine Sitzschale aus mehrschichtigem Holz. Das durch seine sanften, anschmiegsamen Linien charakterisierte Sitzmöbel ist formschön und komfortabel. Die Bequemlichkeit lässt sich durch gepolsterte Varianten zusätzlich erhöhen.

Begründung der Jury
Dieser Stuhl lebt ganz von der auratischen Qualität des Holzes, dessen Materialität bei der Gestaltung geschickt genutzt wurde.

Pit
Chair
Stuhl

Manufacturer
Tonon & C. spa,
Manzano, Italy
Design
MHK Peter Maly Birgit Hoffmann Christoph Kahleyss, Aumühle, Germany
Web
www.tononitalia.com
www.mhk-design.com

The Pit collection of chairs is a perfect combination of design and craftsmanship that is sensitive to the environment. The minimalist form of the seat shell, available fully upholstered, with elegant stitching or with a wooden back, offers very comfortable seating. The workmanship using precious woods such as American walnut and oak underlines the high quality of the products.

Statement by the jury
The contemporary, reduced design of this collection of chairs is also expressed in the perfectly executed workmanship.

Die Stuhlkollektion Pit stellt eine perfekte Kombination zwischen Design und Handwerk dar, mit Sensibilität für die Umwelt. Die minimalistische Form der Sitzschale, die sowohl vollgepolstert, mit eleganter Absteppung oder mit Rückenansicht in Holz gewählt werden kann, bietet höchsten Sitzkomfort. Die Verarbeitung von edlen Hölzern wie Amerikanischer Nussbaum und Eiche unterstreicht die Wertigkeit der Produkte.

Begründung der Jury
Die zeitgemäße, reduzierte Gestaltung dieser Stuhlkollektion kommt auch in der handwerklichen Perfektion der Ausführung zum Ausdruck.

Mirah
Armchair
Sessel

Manufacturer
Sollosbrasil, Princesa,
Santa Catarina, Brazil
In-house design
Jader Almeida
Web
www.sollos.ind.br

This armchair reveals new details from every perspective. Its wealth of details and a particularly sophisticated design give this timeless product its individuality. Different colour tones are achieved through the use of hardwood, making Mirah adaptable to a variety of settings. The lightness and simplicity of the construction in combination with the precise execution make for a welcoming, contemporary piece of furniture.

Aus jedem Blickwinkel offenbart dieser Sessel andere Details. Diese Detailfülle und eine auch sonst anspruchsvolle Gestaltung verleihen diesem zeitlosen Produkt Identität. Der Einsatz von Hartholz erlaubt zudem verschiedene Farbtöne, sodass sich Mirah unterschiedlichen Umgebungen anpasst. Die Leichtigkeit und Einfachheit der Konstruktion in Kombination mit der präzisen Ausführung bilden die Grundlage für dieses freundlich anmutende und zeitgemäße Sitzmöbel.

Statement by the jury
The high-quality design of materials and form turn Mirah into an object of timeless appeal for every room of the home.

Begründung der Jury
Die qualitativ hochwertige Gestaltung in Material und Form macht Mirah zu einem Objekt von zeitlosem Charakter für jeden Wohnraum.

Flexa
Chair
Stuhl

Manufacturer
Andreu World,
Valencia, Spain
Design
Piergiorgio Cazzaniga,
Lentate sul Seveso, Italy
Web
www.andreuworld.com

Flexa is a new collection of light, functional multi-purpose chairs with a seat shell made of fibre-glass reinforced thermopolymer. The chairs are therefore particularly suitable for long-term use in public spaces, wherever there is need for a simple, practical, hardwearing and functional chair. A wide selection of different variations is available, with steel and aluminium feet with skids or swivel function, with or without wheels, upholstered and also stackable.

Flexa ist eine neue Kollektion von leichten, funktionalen Mehrzweck-Stühlen mit einer Sitzschale aus glasfaserverstärktem Thermopolymer. Die Stühle sind deshalb besonders geeignet für den Dauereinsatz im öffentlichen Raum, überall dort, wo ein einfacher, praktischer, widerstandsfähiger und funktionaler Stuhl benötigt wird. Zur Auswahl stehen viele verschiedene Varianten, mit Stahl- und Aluminiumfüßen, mit Kufen oder Drehgestell, mit und ohne Rollen, gepolstert und auch stapelbar.

Statement by the jury
Flexa captivates not only due to its functional and aesthetic appeal, but also because of its ergonomic design.

Begründung der Jury
Die Gestaltung von Flexa besticht nicht nur durch Funktionalität und Ästhetik, sondern auch durch Ergonomie.

Liz
Chair
Stuhl

Manufacturer
Walter Knoll AG & Co. KG,
Herrenberg, Germany
Design
Claudio Bellini,
Milan, Italy
Web
www.walterknoll.de
www.claudiobellini.com

Swaying lines define this chair's silhouette – cleverly emphasised by the coloured piping. Liz gently spans its expanses of fabric or leather for seat and back. The delicate framework gives the elastic inner textile stability. Developed for aviation, the high-tech material provides extra comfort. Innovative like the Antimott armchair of the 1930s with its horizontal coil springs, the chair comes either with or without armrests. The cover can be removed.

Statement by the jury
Purism combined with a nonetheless distinctive language of form are not mutually exclusive. In addition, Liz is comfortable and very versatile in use.

Schwingende Linien gestalten die Silhouette dieses Stuhls – trefflich betont durch die farblich akzentuierte Biese. Leicht spannt Liz seine Flächen aus Stoff oder Leder für Sitz und Rücken auf. Das filigrane Gestell gibt dem elastischen Gewebe im Innern Halt. Für die Luftfahrt entwickelt, leistet das Hightech-Material den besonderen Komfort. Innovativ wie der Antimott-Sessel mit seiner horizontalen Spiralfeder in den 30er Jahren. Den Stuhl gibt es mit und ohne Armlehnen. Der Bezug ist abnehmbar.

Begründung der Jury
Purismus und eine dennoch aparte Formensprache schließen sich nicht aus. Liz ist zudem bequem und vielseitig verwendbar.

Lova
Chair
Stuhl

Manufacturer
A. Venjakob GmbH & Co. KG,
Gütersloh, Germany
Design
Design Ballendat
(Martin Ballendat),
Simbach am Inn, Germany
Web
www.venjakob-moebel.de
www.ballendat.com

Lova is a cantilever chair with an expressive form whose special feature is an independent, elliptic steel tube. The unbroken line of the curved frame combines with the slanting profile on the floor to create an elegant form and stylishly incorporate the seat shell. The harmonious flow of the tubing together with the seat shell complement each other to form a comfortable chair. The frame has a chrome or matt chrome finish and the hide-covered seat shell shows leather stitching.

Statement by the jury
The sleek contours and ergonomic upholstery of this chair redefine the classic cantilever chair.

Lova ist ein sinnlich gestalteter Freischwinger mit der Besonderheit eines eigenständigen, elliptischen Stahlrohres. Das in einer durchgängigen Linie gebogene Gestell bildet mit der Profilschrägstellung am Boden eine elegante Gestalt und beim Sitzschalenanschluss eine stilvolle Einbettung. Der harmonische Rohrverlauf ergänzt sich mit der Schale zu einem bequemen Sitzobjekt. Das Gestell ist verchromt oder matt verchromt; der Schalenkörper in Kernleder mit Ledernähten ausgeführt.

Begründung der Jury
Die schlanke Kontur, verbunden mit einer ergonomischen Polsterung, macht diesen Stuhl zu einer aufregenden Neudefinition des klassischen Freischwingers.

Melk-i
Ergonomic Stool
Gesundheitsschemel

Manufacturer
georgmuehlmann,
Jenesien, Italy
In-house design
Web
www.georgmuehlmann.it

Simplicity and sustainability are the mark of the Melk-i ergonomic stool, modelled on a traditional object of daily use, the milking stool. By sitting on Melk-i, the spinal column is therapeutically relaxed and the muscles in the back, stomach and legs are strengthened. In addition, the resins and essential oils contained in the wood used, the Swiss pine (Pinus cembra), have a calming effect on the cardiovascular system and contribute to a general sense of well-being. The Swiss pine is the typical wood of the alpine region, from where the milking stool originates.

Schlichte Einfachheit und Nachhaltigkeit prägen den Gesundheitsschemel Melk-i, der einem traditionellen Gebrauchsgegenstand, dem Melkschemel, nachempfunden ist. Wohltuend lockert sich durch das Sitzen auf Melk-i die Wirbelsäule und die Rücken-, Bauch- und Beinmuskulatur wird gestärkt. Die Harze und ätherischen Öle der verwendeten Zirbelkiefer (Arven-Holz), dem typischen Holz des Alpenraums, der Ursprungsregion des Melkschemels, wirken zudem beruhigend auf das Herz-Kreislauf-System und tragen zum allgemeinen Wohlbefinden bei.

Dutch Design Chair
Stool
Hocker

Manufacturer
Timon Enterprise BV,
Haarlem, Netherlands
In-house design
Marcel Hellemons,
Tim Várdy
Web
www.dutchdesignchair.com

The innovative construction of the Dutch Design Chair is sturdy and practical. An unusual design concept has resulted in a modern, feather-light piece of furniture, an environmentally friendly chair with many different areas of use. In seconds, seven movements turn the convenient box made of high-quality, FSC-certified, 100 per cent recyclable, corrugated cardboard into an extremely sturdy stool that can support up to 200 kg in weight.

Statement by the jury
Chair, stool or occasional table – the Dutch Design Chair impresses with its imaginative design and exceptional versatility.

Die innovative Konstruktion des Dutch Design Chair ist praktisch und stabil. Dank einer ungewöhnlichen Gestaltungsidee entsteht ein modernes, federleichtes Möbelstück, ein umweltfreundlicher Stuhl mit vielfältigen Einsatzmöglichkeiten. In Sekunden wird der handliche Karton aus hochwertiger, FSC-zertifizierter, zu 100 Prozent recyelbarer Wellpappe mit sieben Handgriffen zum äußerst stabilen, bis 200 kg belastbaren Hocker gefaltet.

Begründung der Jury
Stuhl, Hocker oder Beistelltisch – der Dutch Design Chair beeindruckt durch seine einfallsreiche Gestaltung und außerordentliche Vielseitigkeit.

Angus, Almas, Agnes
Stool Series
Hockerserie

Manufacturer
Pozsgai Möbelschreinerei,
Heitersheim, Germany
In-house design
Raphael Pozsgai
Web
www.brettgeschichten.net

The stools from this range are contemporary interpretations of the classic milking stool. The chamfered legs, as well as the glue-free assembly of the components are all reminiscent of the stool's origin. The seat is available either in Valchromat, an FSC-certified MDF panel with solid through-colouring using organic dyes (Angus, Almas) or in white HPL coated birch plywood (Agnes). The legs are made of oiled oak (Angus, Almas) or untreated ash (Agnes).

Statement by the jury
This carefully executed range of stools is an innovative, contemporary re-interpretation of a traditional stool.

Die Hocker dieser Serie sind zeitgenössische Interpretationen des klassischen Melkschemels. Daran erinnern die gefasten Hockerbeine sowie die leimlose Verbindung der Komponenten. Die Sitzfläche besteht aus Valchromat, einer FSC-zertifizierten, mit organischen Farbstoffen durchgefärbten Holzfaserplatte (Angus, Almas), oder aus mit weißem HPL beschichtetem Birkensperrholz (Agnes). Für die Beine wurde geölte Eiche (Angus, Almas) und naturbelassenes Eschenholz (Agnes) verwendet.

Begründung der Jury
Diese sorgfältig ausgeführte Hockerserie ist eine innovative, zeitgemäße Neuinterpretation eines traditionellen Sitzmöbels.

Flexa
High Chair
Hochstuhl

Manufacturer
Flexa4Dreams,
Hornsyld, Denmark
In-house design
Kristine Schmidt,
Mikael Nissen
Design
Hans Sandgren Jakobsen,
Grenaa, Denmark
Web
www.flexa.dk
www.hans-sandgren-jakobsen.dk

The Flexa high chair is designed for babies and their continually changing needs, because eating is part of children's development of motor skills. The chair is made of a modern combination of solid beech and plastic, and offers a child excellent ergonomics and comfort. The seat, legs and the attachable tray table all have rounded edges and a smooth surface. The footrest can be adjusted to seven different positions, the height of the seat to three.

Der Flexa-Hochstuhl wurde für Babys und deren sich ständig verändernde Ansprüche entworfen, denn für Kinder geht das Essen auch mit der Entwicklung ihrer motorischen Fähigkeiten einher. Der aus einer zeitgemäßen Kombination von massivem Buchenholz und Kunststoff bestehende Hochstuhl bietet dem Kind ausgezeichnete Ergonomie und Komfort. Sitz, Füße und die zusätzliche Tischablage sind alle abgerundet und von glatter Struktur. Die Fußstütze kann auf sieben verschiedene, die Sitzhöhe auf drei verschiedene Positionen eingestellt werden.

Statement by the jury
Top-quality design down to the last detail characterises this high chair. Its gentle and natural look and feel give it timeless appeal and make it suitable for any environment.

Begründung der Jury
Dieser Hochstuhl zeichnet sich durch eine bis ins Detail hochwertige und funktionale Gestaltung aus. Seine sanfte und natürliche Anmutung macht ihn zeitlos und passend für jedes Ambiente.

Foster 520
Armchair
Sessel

Manufacturer
Walter Knoll AG & Co. KG,
Herrenberg, Germany

Design
Foster + Partners,
London, GB

Web
www.walterknoll.de
www.fosterandpartners.com

reddot design award
best of the best 2013

A charming oasis of tranquility

The salon culture that was prevalent in the 1920s combines a sense of style with a highly developed approach to life. The club chairs in these salons were the site of intense debates or just bantering chit-chat. The concept of Foster 520 reinterprets the tradition of the club chair, making it extremely comfortable, but also timelessly elegant. Its design harmoniously unites sweeping lines with perfectly balanced proportions, underlined by a choice of materials that give Foster 520 added panache. The smooth leather used for the seatback has a distinctive pattern, which is combined with aplomb with the natural look of the textiles on the seat. The complex decorative stitching brings to the fore the bold lines of the chair that extend from the seatback over the armrests to the luxurious seat. The armchair is available with a high or low seatback. A suitably designed footstool completes its role as an oasis of tranquil comfort. The design of Foster 520 unites powerful elegance with a touch of "laisser-faire". Thus it is perfectly suited for long evenings of charming conviviality. As a contemporary representative of the salon culture, it fulfils its function just as well in a hotel lobby as in the home.

Charmanter Ruhepol

Die Salonkultur, wie sie besonders in den 1920er Jahren gelebt wurde, verbindet Stilempfinden mit einem hoch entwickelten Lebensgefühl. In den Clubsesseln dieser Salons wurde intensiv diskutiert oder bei einem Drink charmant geplaudert. Die Gestaltung des Sessels Foster 520 interpretiert die Tradition der Clubsessel neu hin zu einem überaus bequemen Sitzmöbel von zeitloser Eleganz. Harmonisch verbindet seine Gestaltung schwungvolle Linien mit perfekt austarierten Proportionen. Seine Ausdruckskraft erlangt der Sessel Foster 520 auch durch seine Materialgebung. Auf souveräne Weise wird ein, mit einer markanten Zeichnung versehenes, Glattleder für den Rücken mit natürlich anmutenden Stoffen für den Sitz kombiniert. Eine aufwendig gearbeitete Ziernaht betont dabei die schwungvollen Linien des Sitzkörpers vom Rücken über die Armlehnen bis in den opulent anmutenden Sitz. Erhältlich ist dieser Sessel mit einem hohen oder niedrigen Rücken, ein dazu passender Hocker vervollständigt seine Funktion als ein komfortabler Ruhepol. Die Gestaltung des Sessels Foster 520 vereint kraftvolle Eleganz mit der Anmutung eines Lebensgefühls des Laisser-faire. Damit ist er perfekt geeignet für lange Abende charmanter Gastlichkeit. Als ein neuer Vertreter der Salonkultur erfüllt er diese Funktion in der Hotellobby ebenso wie zu Hause.

Statement by the jury

The more one looks at it, the more one becomes aware of the unusual shape of this chair. By sitting in it, one experiences its lightness. One feels safe and wants to linger as it is so comfortable. Foster 520 is a real beauty whose form unites power with elegance.

Begründung der Jury

Je intensiver man hinschaut, umso mehr erschließt sich die besondere Formensprache dieses Sessels. Sitzt man in ihm, offenbart sich sogleich seine Leichtigkeit. Man fühlt sich geborgen und will lange in ihm verweilen, da er zudem sehr komfortabel ist. Der Sessel Foster 520 ist eine wahre Schönheit, dessen Gestaltung Kraft mit Eleganz vereint.

Furniture

CP.1
Lounge Chair
Lounge-Stuhl

Manufacturer
Bernhardt Design,
Lenoir, USA
Design
Charles Pollock,
Lenoir, USA
Web
www.bernhardtdesign.com

Charles Pollock's iconic office chair from 1965 came to symbolise the modern office. A successor seems to have been found in this lounge chair. Decorative seams along with individual, hand-quilted seat and back covers in leather, suede or felt are the hallmark of the CP.1. The comfortable seat shell rests on a polished stainless steel frame.

Charles Pollocks ikonischer Bürostuhl aus dem Jahr 1965 wurde zu einem Symbol des modernen Büros. Einen Nachfolger scheint er in diesem Lounge-Stuhl gefunden zu haben. Den CP.1 kennzeichnen Ziernähte sowie individuelle hand-gesteppte Bezüge aus Leder, Wildleder oder Filz für die Polsterung von Sitz und Rückenlehne. Der bequeme Sitzkörper ruht auf einem Rahmen aus poliertem Edelstahl.

Statement by the jury
The CP.1 appears to float thanks to its delicate construction. Its timeless design and clean lines make for simple, chic elegance.

Begründung der Jury
Durch seine filigrane Konstruktion scheint der CP.1 förmlich zu schweben. Sein zeitloses Design mit klaren Linien ist von schlichter, stilvoller Eleganz.

Butterfly Twin Chair
Two-Seater Sofa
Zweisitzer-Sofa

Manufacturer
Weinbaum,
Frankfurt/Main, Germany
In-house design
Barbara Gimenez Weinbaum
Web
www.weinbaum.com.de

A re-interpretation of the Hardoy Butterfly Chair design classic from 1938, this sofa extends the original's sculptural use of form. Based on the original design, the two-seater updates the harmonious geometry of the original chair. It is very comfortable to sit in and versatile – from hotel bars to reception areas and from offices to patios. The Butterfly Twin Chair is timeless eye-catcher and aesthetic sofa rolled into one.

Dieses Sofa ist eine Neuinterpretation des stilprägenden Hardoy Butterfly Chair von 1938, dessen skulpturale Formensprache es erweitert. Basierend auf dem ursprünglichen Entwurf schreibt der Zweisitzer die harmonische Geometrie des Sessels fort, überzeugt mit hohem Sitzkomfort und vielfältigen Einsatzmöglichkeiten: von der Hotelbar bis zur Rezeption, vom Büro bis zur Terrasse. Der Butterfly Twin Chair ist zeitloser Blickfang und ästhetisches Sitzmöbel in einem.

Asienta
Upholstered Furniture Range
Polstermöbelprogramm

Manufacturer
Wilkhahn,
Bad Münder, Germany
Design
Jehs+Laub GbR
(Markus Jehs, Jürgen Laub),
Stuttgart, Germany
Web
www.wilkhahn.de
www.jehs-laub.com

Asienta combines distinctive appeal with ergonomic comfort and superb craftsmanship. The seating cubes and delicate aluminium frame with four legs form a stable unit. The precisely contoured upholstery of the chair lends it a soft look, while nonetheless providing firm ergonomic support. The sophisticated textile or leather covers are folded around the upholstery, so that the seating boxes appear perfectly wrapped in one piece.

Asienta verbindet markante Eigenständigkeit, ergonomischen Komfort und handwerkliche Perfektion: Ein filigranes, vierbeiniges Aluminiumtraggerüst bildet mit den Sitzkuben eine stabile Einheit. Die innenseitigen, präzisen Überwölbungen vermitteln visuelle Weichheit und bieten straffe, ergonomische Abstützung. Die edlen Textil-/Lederbezüge sind um die Polster herumgefaltet, wodurch die Kuben wie aus einem Stück perfekt eingepackt erscheinen.

Statement by the jury
Asienta is eye-catching due to the successful interplay of contrasts. At the same time angular and rounded, voluminous and delicate, it communicates elegance and cosiness.

Begründung der Jury
Asienta fällt ins Auge durch das gelungene Spiel mit Kontrasten. Kantig und rund, voluminös und filigran zugleich vermittelt es Eleganz und Wohnlichkeit.

Structure
Armchair
Sessel

Manufacturer
Tonon & C. spa,
Manzano, Italy
Design
Massive Design Sp. z o.o.
(Przemyslaw Mac Stopa),
Warsaw, Poland
Web
www.tononitalia.com
www.massivedesign.pl

Structure combines elements of classic design with organic shapes and gains its almost artistic verve through a three-dimensional geometric pattern on the exterior of its round shell. The shape of the pleasantly soft inner shell has been adapted to fit the human body and is very comfortable to sit in. The seat shell is available in ten fresh colours while the attractive four-legged base comes either in steel or in wood.

Statement by the jury
Due to the use of modern technology and innovative foam, Structure is a visually appealing and comfortable armchair.

Structure kombiniert klassische Elemente mit organischen Formen und gewinnt durch eine dreidimensionale geometrische Struktur auf der Außenseite der runden Schale eine geradezu künstlerische Ausdruckskraft. Die angenehm weiche Innenschale ist in ihrer Form dem menschlichen Körper angepasst und bietet besten Sitzkomfort. Die Sitzschale ist erhältlich in zehn frischen Farben, das attraktive Vierfußuntergestell ist sowohl in einer Variante aus Stahl als auch in Holz lieferbar.

Begründung der Jury
Dank des Einsatzes moderner Technologie und eines innovativen Schaumstoffes ist Structure ein visuell ansprechendes und bequemes Sitzmöbel.

Kyo
Bucket Chair
Schalensessel

Manufacturer
Walter Knoll AG & Co. KG,
Herrenberg, Germany
Design
PearsonLloyd
(Luke Pearson, Tom Lloyd),
London, GB
Web
www.walterknoll.de
www.pearsonlloyd.com

Appreciated and desired for generations, bucket seats are the ultimate in good taste. Elegant lines, soft curves – Kyo safely envelops its owner. Striking seams structure the upholstery – sweeping and elegant like the seats of a sports car. Its shell – on the outside, like the original, in plastic or completely covered with leather – ensures exceptional seating comfort. With a slight swivel action on the four-star or tubular steel base, Kyo offers new perspectives whichever way you look at it.

Statement by the jury
Kyo is a majestically imposing piece of furniture without however being over-powering – a classic bucket seat of the highest quality.

Über Generationen hinweg geschätzt und begehrt: Schalensessel stehen für guten Geschmack. Elegante Linien, sanfte Rundungen – sicher umhüllt Kyo seinen Besitzer. Markante Nahtbilder modulieren die Polster – schwungvoll-elegant wie bei den Sitzen eines Sportwagens. Die Schale – außen originär in Kunststoff oder komplett mit Leder bezogen – sorgt für ausgezeichneten Sitzkomfort. Leicht drehbar auf dem Vierfuß- oder dem Stahlrohrfußkreuz bietet Kyo von jeder Seite ein anderes Bild.

Begründung der Jury
Kyo ist ein majestätisch anmutendes Sitzmöbel, ohne aufdringlich zu wirken. Ein klassischer Schalensessel höchster Qualität.

Seating Stones
Armchair
Sessel

Manufacturer
Walter Knoll AG & Co. KG,
Herrenberg, Germany
Design
UNStudio/Ben van Berkel,
Amsterdam, Netherlands
Web
www.walterknoll.de
www.unstudio.com

Seating Stones bring natural fundamentals back into the home. The new seating landscapes fulfil the longing for naturalness and original forms of seating – cheerful, free and variable. Users intuitively follow the possibilities on offer: sitting or lounging around, relaxing or concentrating, on your own or in company. As a single piece or side by side, arranged as desired. For creative spaces: in lobbies, in the spaces between desks, in a welcoming entrance hall.

Statement by the jury
The organic styling inspired by nature is an irresistible invitation to get comfortable and snuggle up.

Die Seating Stones holen die Archaik ins Haus. Die neuen Sitzlandschaften erfüllen die Sehnsucht nach Natürlichkeit und der Urform des Sitzens – fröhlich, frei und variabel. Intuitiv folgen die Besitzer den Möglichkeiten: sitzen oder lümmeln, entspannen oder konzentrieren, allein oder im Gespräch. Als Solitär oder Seite an Seite in freier Komposition. Für kreative Räume – in der Lobby, im Freiraum zwischen den Arbeitsplätzen, im einladenden Entree.

Begründung der Jury
Die von der Natur inspirierte, organische Formgebung ist eine unwiderstehliche Einladung, es sich bequem zu machen und anzuschmiegen.

1303 Nano
Functional Armchair
Funktionssessel

Manufacturer
Intertime AG,
Endingen, Switzerland
Design
Martin Birrer,
Benny Mosimann
Web
www.intertime.ch

Nano is the most compact of the Intertime armchairs. Its simple, clear contours and soft lines make it the ideal partner for the Frame sofa. Despite its compact size, Nano is extremely comfortable due to its separately adjustable foot rests, back and head rests, which can be stored in the chair back. The chair is mounted on a 360-degree swivel base and is available with a foot made of polished chrome, smoked chrome, brushed chrome or powder-coated in RAL colours.

Statement by the jury
In this chair, elegance, comfort and functionality are combined to create a virtually unbeatable symbiosis.

Der Nano ist der kompakteste unter den Intertime-Relaxsesseln und passt mit seiner einfachen, klaren Form und weichen Linienführung ideal zum Sofa Frame. Trotz seiner Kompaktheit bietet Nano besten Komfort mit getrennt verstellbarer Fußstütze und Rückenlehne sowie dem Nackenkissen, das sich im Rückenkissen verstauen lässt. Der Sessel verfügt über ein 360-Grad-Drehgestell und ist mit Fuß in Glanz-Chrom, Rauch-Chrom, Chrom gebürstet oder pulverbeschichtet in RAL-Farben erhältlich.

Begründung der Jury
Eleganz, Bequemlichkeit und Funktionalität gehen bei diesem Sessel eine kaum zu schlagende Symbiose ein.

Work Lounge Furniture
Arbeits-Lounge-Möbel

Manufacturer
Coalesse,
San Francisco, USA
Design
Patricia Urquiola,
Milan, Italy
Web
www.coalesse.eu
www.patriciaurquiola.com

As work and life become more integrated, people appreciate a relaxed environment for working whether at home, in the office or on the go. Hosu, a comfortable lounge chair, encourages relaxed postures to think, work, read and relax with your feet up. In one simple motion, the lounge converts into a chaise. Convenient side and rear pockets offer storage space. A grommet at the base of the lounge allows for power cords to reach to the user.

Arbeit und Privatleben verschmelzen zunehmend miteinander. Daher wird eine entspannte Arbeitsumgebung immer wichtiger – ob zu Hause, im Büro oder unterwegs. Die bequeme Arbeitslounge Hosu ermöglicht entspanntes Denken, Arbeiten, Lesen und Ausruhen in bequemen Positionen. Mit einem einzigen Handgriff kann die Lounge in ein Liegesofa verwandelt werden. Praktische Seiten- und Rückentaschen bieten großzügigen Stauraum, während die Kabeldurchführung am Fuß der Lounge für eine elegante Stromversorgung sorgt.

Statement by the jury
Hosu is a very comfortable, functional and well thought-through chair that creates an intimate oasis of peace in the midst of everyday life's stress and makes it possible to combine work and relaxation in an intelligent way.

Begründung der Jury
Hosu ist ein sehr bequemer, funktional durchdachter Sessel, der eine erholsame, geradezu intime Oase inmitten des alltäglichen Stresses bildet, um Arbeit und Entspannung intelligent zu verbinden.

Yuuto
Sofa

Manufacturer
Walter Knoll AG & Co. KG,
Herrenberg, Germany
Design
EOOS Design GmbH
(Martin Bergmann, Gernot Bohmann,
Harald Gründl), Vienna, Austria
Web
www.walterknoll.de
www.eoos.com

This range of upholstery offers very comfortable spacious seating. All-encompassing and modular, the interaction of volumes with deep seat elements and opulent upholstery creates a sofa landscape for the entire family, friends and guests. Whether as a single sofa, recamiere or large corner configuration – there are a range of shapes for individual lifestyles from cosy apartment to spacious loft. But Yuuto is much more than a landscape of cushions. The "coussins indépendants" were developed in the search for added comfort: a framework, stretched straps, with soft upholstery on top. Every seat cushion is effectively a sofa in itself. Top-quality surfaces draw attention to the detail: upholstered areas made of natural fabrics, armrests and boards in sturdy saddle leather.

Dieses Polsterprogramm bietet großzügiges Sitzen mit hohem Komfort. Raumgreifend und modular – im Spiel der Volumina mit tiefen Sitzflächen und opulenten Polstern entsteht eine Sofalandschaft für die ganze Familie, für Freunde und Gäste. Ob als Einzelsofa, Récamiere oder große Ecke – vielfältige Formen für individuelle Lebensweisen vom kleinen Wohnraum bis zum geräumigen Loft. Doch Yuuto ist mehr als eine Landschaft aus Kissen. Auf der Suche nach der besonderen Bequemlichkeit wurden die „coussins indépendants" entwickelt: Rahmen, gespannte Gurte, darauf das weiche Polster. Jedes Sitzkissen für sich ist wie ein Sofa. Wertige Oberflächen öffnen den Blick fürs Detail: Polsterflächen aus natürlichen Stoffen, dazu Armlehnen und Ablageflächen in griffigem Blankleder.

Statement by the jury
Yuuto is an eye catcher for any room, but it is also versatile enough to adapt to any space. Its very high degree of comfort and premium quality materials meet all expectations.

Begründung der Jury
Yuuto ist ein Blickfang in jedem Raum, fügt sich aber ebenso variabel und anpassungsfähig ein. Höchster Sitzkomfort und hochwertige Materialien lassen keine Wünsche offen.

Modular Sofa System
Modulares Sofasystem

Manufacturer
Sitzfeldt,
Berlin, Germany
Design
Atelier Steffen Kehrle,
Munich, Germany
Web
www.sitzfeldt.com
www.steffenkehrle.com

The harmonious basic form of this sofa is defined by four elements. Everything else can be assembled freely: arm and back rests, seats, cushions and covers, as well as colours. The balanced proportions lend themselves to classic combinations just as much as to individual room concepts. Assembly is simple and self-explanatory: the back and arm rests are attached with screws and the seats are connected with Velcro.

Die harmonischen Grundformen dieses Sofas sind durch vier Bauteile vorgegeben, alles andere lässt sich frei zusammenstellen: Arm- und Rückenlehnen, Sitzflächen, Kissen und Bezüge sowie Farben. Dabei eignen sich die ausgewogenen Proportionen für klassische Kombinationen ebenso wie für individuelle Raumkonzepte. Das Befestigungssystem ist einfach und selbsterklärend: Die Rücken- und Armlehnen werden verschraubt, die Sitze durch einen Klett-Strap miteinander verbunden.

Statement by the jury
This sofa system almost turns the user into a designer. The ingenious modular concept allows for the highest degree of variability and adaptability.

Begründung der Jury
Durch dieses Sofasystem wird der Nutzer beinahe selbst zum Designer. Das ausgeklügelte modulare Konzept erlaubt höchste Variabilität und Anpassbarkeit.

Open Space
Folding Bed
Klappbett

Manufacturer
CLEI Srl,
Carugo, Italy
In-house design
Pierluigi Colombo,
Oscar Grimoldi
Web
www.clei.it
Honourable Mention

This unusual bed has the appearance, size and technical characteristics of a normal high-end bed. The real innovation is in the living philosophy underlying the project. Before Open Space, the bedroom and especially all the square metres occupied by the bed were just used for sleeping. This system makes it possible to use bedroom space in a very flexible way. All of this without compromising on sleep comfort or the attractiveness of product.

Dieses außergewöhnliche Bett hat das Aussehen, die Größe und die technischen Charakteristiken eines normalen High-End-Bettes. Die eigentliche Innovation besteht in der dem Projekt zugrunde liegenden Wohnphilosophie. Vor Open Space waren Schlafzimmer und vor allem die vom Bett beanspruchten Quadratmeter allein zum Schlafen da. Dieses System hingegen bietet die Möglichkeit, den Schlafraum absolut flexibel zu nutzen – ohne dabei den Schlafkomfort und die Attraktivität des Produkts zu mindern.

Statement by the jury
By simply folding up this high-quality, elegant bed, it is possible to make a practical lifestyle a reality.

Begründung der Jury
Durch einfaches Hochklappen lässt sich mit diesem hochwertigen und eleganten Bett ein praktikabler Lebensstil verwirklichen.

Welded
Table
Tisch

Manufacturer
Bonaldo Spa,
Villanova di Camposampiero
(Padova), Italy

Design
Alain Gilles / The Studio
(Alain Gilles),
Brussels, Belgium

Web
www.bonaldo.it
www.alaingilles.com

reddot design award
best of the best 2013

Powerful minimalism
The cultural history of the table not only concerns simple wooden constructions, but also massive ones which are nothing more than two slabs of stone laid on top of one another. The design of Welded is fascinating due to the combination of materials that seem heavy with the simple, clean lines of the support. The inspiration for this table came from the manufacture of heavy machinery. The legs are made of laser-cut sheet steel, which are subsequently welded together. This process gives the table its name – Welded – as if it were formed from one piece of metal. Its clean form gives it a high degree of visual lightness. The colours of the legs, available in white, anthracite grey, bright red, orange, green and matt brown, are also very harmonious as they help to stress the legs' innovative construction. This table is very versatile and easily suits all types of interior and areas of life. Welded is available in four rectangular table-top sizes, in various types of wood and crystal, as well as in the original format in matt-white Carrara marble. Its form combines minimalism with an impressive presence – thus imposing a strong personality on its environment.

Kraftvoller Minimalismus
In der Kulturgeschichte des Tisches finden sich neben einfachen Holzkonstruktionen ebenso sehr schwergewichtige Varianten, die im Grunde nur aus zwei übereinandergestellten Steinplatten bestehen. Die Gestaltung des Tisches Welded fasziniert durch eine Kombination solch schwer erscheinender Materialien mit einer klar und schlicht anmutenden Linienführung des Untergestells. Inspiriert wurde die Gestaltung dieses Tisches von Verfahren aus dem Schwermaschinenbau. Seine Beine aus Stahl werden mit dem Laser geschnitten und anschließend miteinander verschweißt. Die Fertigung im Schweißverfahren führt dazu, dass der Tisch Welded aus einem Stück zu bestehen scheint. Seine klare Linienführung verleiht ihm zugleich ein hohes Maß an visueller Leichtigkeit. Sehr stimmig ist auch die Farbgebung der Tischbeine in den Farben Weiß, Anthrazitgrau, leuchtend Rot, Orange, Grün und matt Braun, da diese seine innovative Konstruktion noch einmal betont. Dieser Tisch ist variabel und kann sich leicht in alle Interieurs und Lebensbereiche einfügen. Die rechteckige Tischfläche des Welded in vier Größen ist in unterschiedlichen Holz- und Kristallglasvarianten und in der originellen Ausführung aus mattem weißen Carrara-Marmor erhältlich. Seine Gestaltung verbindet Minimalismus mit einer beeindruckenden Präsenz – im Raum verkörpert der Welded damit eine starke Persönlichkeit.

Statement by the jury
The minimalist lines of this table are unique and make a lasting impression on anyone who sees them. The design successfully achieves a powerful contrast between the metal structure and the stone top. It is a truly striking solution that thoroughly redefines the table.

Begründung der Jury
Die minimalistische Linienführung dieses Tisches ist einzigartig und prägt sich dem Betrachter ein. Gestalterisch gelungen ist bei dem Welded auch der starke Kontrast zwischen der Metallstruktur und der darauf liegenden Steinplatte. Eine wirklich bemerkenswerte Lösung, die einen Tisch auf völlig neue Weise definiert.

Furniture

Lucy
Folding Table
Klapptisch

Manufacturer
Johanson Design,
Markaryd, Sweden
Design
Alexander Lervik,
Stockholm, Sweden
Web
www.johansondesign.se
www.lervik.se
Honourable Mention

What sets Lucy, a folding table, apart is an S-shaped clip that locks the movement of the fold-out table leg whether it is folded out or back. One part of the leg is fixed, while the other part can manually be moved along the clip. In this way, the table legs are securely held in place when extended. Lucy is very versatile in use, from conference to function rooms, but also suitable for flexible modern workplaces.

Das Besondere am Klapptisch Lucy ist eine S-förmige Halteschiene, durch die sich das faltbare Tischbein in der ein- wie auch ausgefalteten Position arretieren lässt. Dies ist möglich, weil der eine Teil des Beins fixiert ist, während der andere Teil manuell in der Führungsschiene bewegt wird. Die Beine werden in der ausgestreckten Position sicher gehalten. Lucy kann vielfältig eingesetzt werden, in Konferenz- und Funktionsräumen oder auch an flexiblen modernen Arbeitsplätzen.

Statement by the jury
Lucy is the intelligent next step of the practical, multi-purpose folding table – innovative in function, clean in shape.

Begründung der Jury
Lucy ist eine intelligente Weiterentwicklung des praktischen, vielseitigen Klapptisches – innovativ in der Funktion, klar in der Form.

Faltwerk
Dining Table
Esstisch

Manufacturer
Melz Design,
Röttingen, Germany
Design
Melz Design Ltd. (Christian Melz),
Beijing, China
Web
www.line-eins.com
www.melz-design.com

This dining table, which has a solid cherry wood top and a fine steel base, is mainly intended for large, open-plan living and dining areas. Faltwerk can be extended by a metre to a total length of 3.4 metres, thereby offering enough space for ten people. The table's key feature is its mechanism, which makes it possible to unlock and extend the table from both ends without having to clear it. The mechanism is smooth to operate. Wire cables effect the synchronised extension and render all interior movement visible.

Dieser Esstisch aus massivem Kirschbaum und Stahl ist hauptsächlich für offene und große Wohn- und Essbereiche gedacht. Faltwerk kann um einen Meter auf eine Länge von 3,40 Meter ausgezogen werden. So können bis zu zehn Personen bewirtet werden. Das Hauptaugenmerk liegt dabei auf der Mechanik. Diese macht ein Entriegeln und Ausziehen von beiden Seiten möglich, der Tisch muss dazu nicht einmal abgeräumt werden. Die Mechanik lässt sich sanft bedienen, die Drahtseile erlauben das synchrone Ausziehen und machen alle Bewegungen im Inneren sichtbar.

Still
Table
Tisch

Manufacturer
Bonaldo Spa,
Villanova di Camposampiero (Padova),
Italy
Design
Bartoli Design,
Monza, Italy
Web
www.bonaldo.it
www.bartolidesign.it

Still is characterised by the combination of cement and wood. The conical cement table legs create a unique decorative feature in the centre of the table-top which comes in solid walnut or white lacquered wood and is available in square, rectangular and round versions.

Statement by the jury
The striking and deftly executed combination of wood and cement turns this table into an experience that can be both seen and felt.

Still ist durch die Kombination von Zement und Holz gekennzeichnet. Die konischen Tischbeine aus Zement bilden ein originelles Dekor in der Mitte der Tischplatte, die in massivem Nussbaumholz oder in weiß lackiertem Holz und in quadratischer, rechteckiger oder runder Ausführung verfügbar ist.

Begründung der Jury
Die auffällige und geschickt ausgeführte Kombination von Holz und Zement sorgt bei diesem Tisch sowohl für ein visuelles wie auch haptisches Erlebnis.

flaye
Table
Tisch

Manufacturer
TEAM 7 Natürlich Wohnen GmbH,
Ried im Innkreis, Austria
In-house design
Jacob Strobel
Web
www.team7.at

flaye is a new generation of pull-out tables. The revolutionary non-stop synchronised pull-out mechanism makes it possible to move the insert panel in and out automatically and smoothly in a matter of seconds. A single tug is all it takes – intuitive just like using a touch screen. A leather frame in a contrasting colour underlines the table's almost weightless appearance.

Statement by the jury
The use of natural wood and a sculptural design language are the key characteristics of this sensual table.

flaye führt den Auszugstisch in eine neue Ära: Die bahnbrechende „Nonstop"-Synchron-Auszugstechnik ermöglicht ein automatisches, gedämpftes Ein- und Ausschwenken der Einlegeplatte in Sekundenschnelle: mit nur einem Handgriff und in einem Zug. Ein einfaches Ziehen, intuitiv wie bei einem Touchscreen. Zur Anmutung der Leichtigkeit trägt die farblich kontrastierende Lederzarge bei.

Begründung der Jury
Der Gebrauch von Naturholz und eine skulpturale Formensprache sind die Hauptkennzeichen dieses die Sinne ansprechenden Tisches.

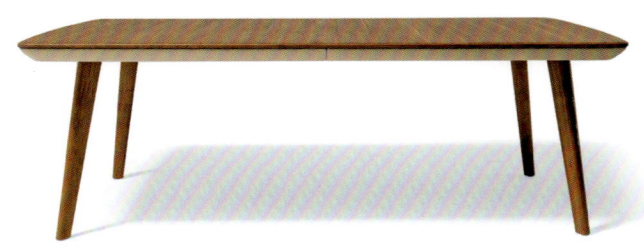

Paustian ASAP Table
Table
Tisch

Manufacturer
Paustian A/S,
Copenhagen, Denmark
Design
Foersom & Hiort-Lorenzen
(Johannes Foersom, Peter Hiort-Lorenzen),
Copenhagen, Denmark
Web
www.paustian.com
www.f-h-l.dk

The Paustian ASAP Table is elegant and understated. The interplay of wood and colourful details is friendly and inviting, with slightly angled legs giving the table a dynamic appearance. This makes it fit into both modern and classic interiors. By way of example, it can be used as a dining table, in a café or canteen, as a small table in the kitchen or as a desk or conference table.

Statement by the jury
The Paustian ASAP Table sets itself apart through its skilful combination of materials and forms, which epitomise dynamism and solidity at the same time.

Der ASAP Table von Paustian ist elegant und zurückhaltend. Das Wechselspiel zwischen Holz und farbigen Details wirkt freundlich und einladend. Die leicht abgewinkelten Beine geben dem Tisch ein dynamisches Erscheinungsbild. Der Tisch passt sowohl zu modernen als auch klassischen Einrichtungen. Er kann beispielsweise als Esstisch, Café- oder Kantinentisch, als kleiner Tisch in der Küche und als Arbeits- oder Konferenztisch genutzt werden.

Begründung der Jury
Der ASAP Table von Paustian besticht durch die geschickte Kombination der Materialien und Formen. So verkörpert er gleichermaßen Dynamik und Gediegenheit.

Basket
Side Tables
Beistelltische

Manufacturer
Makomim Ltd.,
Izmir, Turkey
Design
Koz Susani Design (Defne Koz),
Chicago, USA
Web
www.megaron.org
www.kozsusanidesign.com

These side tables are reminiscent of baskets. Their curved handles make it easy to move them from the sofa to the armchair or to any place desired. They can also be used as trays when there are visitors. The tables are made of a light composite material and are available with a high-gloss or a matt surface in a variety of different colours.

Statement by the jury
The coffee or dining table can often be too small or you simply need a place to put something down. This is where these practical, winsome side tables provide an elegant solution.

Diese Beistelltische erinnern in ihrer Form an einen Korb. Sie können durch ihren gebogenen Griff vom Sofa zu einem Stuhl bewegt oder an jedem beliebigen Ort platziert werden. Wenn man beispielsweise Gäste hat, können sie fast wie Tabletts verwendet werden. Die Tische werden aus leichtem Verbundwerkstoff mit entweder hochglänzender oder matter Oberfläche und in verschiedenen Farben hergestellt.

Begründung der Jury
Oft ist der Couch- oder Esstisch zu klein oder es fehlt einfach eine Möglichkeit, irgendwo etwas abzustellen. Hier schaffen diese praktischen, gefälligen Beistelltische elegant Abhilfe.

Fino
Furniture Collection
Möbelkollektion

Manufacturer
ANREI,
Pabneukirchen, Austria
Design
Thomas Feichtner,
Vienna, Austria
Web
www.anrei.at
www.thomasfeichtner.com

Fino is a furniture range made of solid wood. All the pieces of furniture in the collection use a type of chassis as a sub-construction. The interplay of fibres and joints, as well as the conically shaped table top edges and the tapered legs make the solid wood pieces appear light and overcome their typical weight and massive quality. Individual pieces of furniture can be used together, but also work well on their own.

Statement by the jury
Perfect craftsmanship and ecological sustainability are the hallmark of this collection of furniture, whose design is both intelligent and contemporary.

Fino ist eine Möbelkollektion in Massivholz. Alle Möbel der Kollektion haben durchgängig eine Art Chassis als Unterkonstruktion. Das Zusammenspiel von Fasen und Fugen sowie die konisch zulaufende Tischkante oder die sich nach unten verjüngenden Beine verleihen den Massivholz-Möbeln Leichtigkeit und nehmen ihnen ihre typische Schwere und Wuchtigkeit. Die einzelnen Möbel können nicht nur untereinander kombiniert werden, sondern wirken auch als Einzelstücke.

Begründung der Jury
Perfekte Verarbeitung und ökologische Nachhaltigkeit zeichnen diese Möbelkollektion aus, die intelligent und zeitgemäß gestaltet ist.

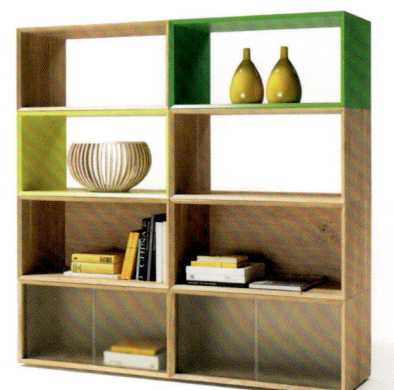

Ottawa
Furniture Collection
Möbelkollektion

Manufacturer
BoConcept A/S,
Herning, Denmark
Design
Karim Rashid,
New York, USA
Web
www.boconcept.com
www.karimrashid.com
Honourable Mention

The Ottawa collection is a complete dining room set consisting of a table, chairs and sideboard whose colours and materials can all be customised. The leaf shape of the comfortable dining chairs was inspired by nature. The extendable dining table is functional with a soft, sensual appearance while the sideboard is eye-catching due to the colourful, interchangeable inserts on the sides and behind the handles on the front.

Statement by the jury
This highly individual, but nonetheless pleasantly reticent furniture collection is the embodiment of modern, urban living.

Die Ottawa-Kollektion umfasst ein komplettes Esszimmer-Set mit Tisch, Stühlen und Sideboard. Alle Stücke können in der Wahl der Farben und Materialien angepasst werden. Die bequemen Ess-Stühle sind mit ihrer Blattform von der Natur inspiriert. Der ausziehbare Esstisch ist funktionell und hat eine weiche, sinnliche Anmutung. Das Sideboard fällt besonders durch die farbigen, veränderbaren Einsätze an den Seiten und hinter den Griffen der Fronten auf.

Begründung der Jury
Diese charaktervolle und dennoch angenehm unaufdringlich wirkende Möbelkollektion verkörpert ein modernes, urbanes Wohngefühl.

cubus pure
Living Programme
Wohnprogramm

Manufacturer
TEAM 7 Natürlich Wohnen GmbH,
Ried im Innkreis, Austria
In-house design
Sebastian Desch
Web
www.team7.at

Clean cubic shapes and a sensuous mix of wood and coloured glass are what make the cubus pure system programme so fascinating. The delicate, coloured glass frames the front like a picture mount, highlighting the natural wood and giving this piece of furniture its clear, contemporary modernity. Whether it is used as a sideboard, high board or home entertainment system, cubus pure always appears graceful and ethereal.

Das Systemprogramm cubus pure fasziniert durch kubisch klare Formen und einen sinnlichen Materialmix aus Holz und Farbglas. Das zarte Farbglas fasst die Fronten wie ein Passepartout ein, hebt das Naturholz auf eine Bühne und verleiht dem Möbel eine zeitgemäß klare Modernität. Ob Anrichte, Highboard oder Home-Entertainment – cubus pure mutet stets filigran und schwerelos an.

Statement by the jury
cubus pure lives up to its name. The system's clean, reduced lines and its precise surfaces and edges are beguiling.

Begründung der Jury
Der Name ist hier Programm. cubus pure beeindruckt durch seine klare, reduzierte Formensprache mit ihren präzisen Flächen und Kanten.

WALL
Side-/Lowboard

Manufacturer
die COLLECTION,
Buchen, Germany
MAB Betschart,
Muotathal, Switzerland
Design
Althaus Design (Thomas Althaus),
Düsseldorf, Germany
Web
www.die-collection.de

WALL is a side- and lowboard range of minimalist design and delicate proportions. The front and the cover panels consist of high-quality, rear-lacquered crystal in clear or matt Optiwhite quality. All side- or lowboards are available for wall-hanging, mountable in variable widths, or on feet with an innovative extension technique. Both the side- and lowboard are therefore eminently suited to every type of room. Vertical container elements can be added to create modern, constantly changing combinations for all living areas.

Statement by the jury
The variability – WALL on feet can even be used as a room divider – and the high-quality craftsmanship are particularly striking.

WALL ist ein Side- und Lowboardprogramm in reduzierter Formensprache und filigranen Proportionen. Die Fassade und Abdeckplatte bestehen aus hochwertigem, hinterlackiertem Kristallglas in Optiwhite-Qualität klar oder matt. Alle Side- oder Lowboards können entweder wandhängend, breitenvariabel montierbar, oder auf Füßen mit einer innovativen Auszugstechnik geliefert werden. Beide Varianten können sich dadurch Raumsituationen optimal anpassen und durch vertikale Container-Elemente zudem zu modernen, immer wieder veränderbaren Wohnkombinationen ergänzt werden.

Begründung der Jury
Die Variabilität – WALL auf Füßen kann sogar als Raumteiler verwendet werden – und hochwertige Ausführung überzeugen hier besonders.

Cut-Y
Sideboard System

Manufacturer
Sudbrock GmbH Möbelwerk,
Rietberg-Bokel, Germany
Design
Haverkamp Interior Design
(Manfred F. Haverkamp),
Herford, Germany
Web
www.sudbrock.de
www.h-id.com

The surprise of Cut-Y is the interplay between "depth" and "surface". The result is a sideboard that plays on contrasts. Closed and open components, generous surfaces and small niches, light and shade all alternate. In order to make the play with depth succeed, oblique body modules come into play. If these slanted components are combined, open recesses full of nooks and crannies appear. All components of a row can furthermore be combined at will.

Statement by the jury
An adept contouring and numerous configuration possibilities turn this sideboard into a very individual piece of furniture.

Cut-Y überrascht durch das Wechselspiel von „Tiefe" und „Fläche". Das Ergebnis ist ein Sideboard, das mit Gegensätzen spielt. Geschlossene und offene Elemente, großzügige Flächen und kleine Nischen, Licht und Schatten wechseln sich ab. Damit das Spiel mit der Tiefe gelingt, kommen abgeschrägte Korpus-Module zum Einsatz. Kombiniert man diese abgeschrägten Elemente miteinander, entstehen offene, verwinkelte Vertiefungen. Alle Zeilenelemente lassen sich zudem beliebig miteinander kombinieren.

Begründung der Jury
Eine geschickte Formgebung und viele Konfigurationsmöglichkeiten machen dieses Sideboard zu einem sehr individuellen Möbelstück.

X System
Shelf System
Regalsystem

Manufacturer
Kdomázidlibydlí s.r.o.,
Prague, Czech Republic
In-house design
Jan Vacek
Web
www.kdomazidlibydli.cz

The length and height of this flexible shelf system depend on the number of modules. The system consists of only three components: one vertical panel, the shelf floor and the connecting metal element, which allows for assembly of the shelf units. The system can be built to lean up against a wall or as a unit standing free in the room.

Statement by the jury
This shelf is simple and original just like the idea behind it. Produced in plain black and white it gives the impression of movement and dynamism.

Bei diesem flexiblen Regalsystem werden Länge und Höhe des Regals abhängig von der Anzahl der Module bestimmt. Das System besteht aus nur drei Komponenten: einer vertikalen Platte, dem Regalboden und dem verbindenden Metallelement. Die Regaleinheiten werden mithilfe des Verbindungselements zusammengefügt. Das System kann an der Wand lehnend oder frei im Raum stehend aufgebaut werden.

Begründung der Jury
Einfach und originell wie die zugrunde liegende Gestaltungsidee zeigt sich dieses Regal insgesamt. In schlichtem Schwarz und Weiß vermittelt es den Eindruck von Bewegung und Dynamik.

Manufacturer
Globe Zero 4 A/S,
Aarhus, Denmark
Design
busk+hertzog
(Flemming Busk, Stephan Hertzog),
London, GB
Web
www.globezero4.dk
www.busk-hertzog.com

Penny is a coat stand of unconventional and unforgettable style. The asymmetric design endows the product with another dimension, making it look different from every angle so that the viewer has repeatedly fresh perceptual experiences. Penny simultaneously fulfils its primary purpose as a receptacle for coats, hats and umbrellas, but in a new and beautiful way.

Penny ist ein Garderobenständer mit einer unkonventionellen und eindrücklichen Gestaltung. Das asymmetrische Design fügt dem Produkt eine weitere Dimension hinzu, sodass es aus jedem Blickwinkel anders aussieht und damit dem Betrachter immer wieder neue Wahrnehmungser-lebnisse beschert. Zugleich erfüllt Penny aber auch seine primäre Aufgabe – er nimmt Mäntel, Hüte und Schirme auf, aber in einer neuen und schönen Weise.

Statement by the jury
Thanks to its sculptural styling, Penny is an eye-catcher in any room, though it can also simply be used for its intended purpose.

Begründung der Jury
Penny ist dank seiner skulpturalen Anmu-tung ein sehenswertes Objekt in jedem Raum, kann aber auch ganz schnöde für seine eigentliche Aufgabe genutzt werden.

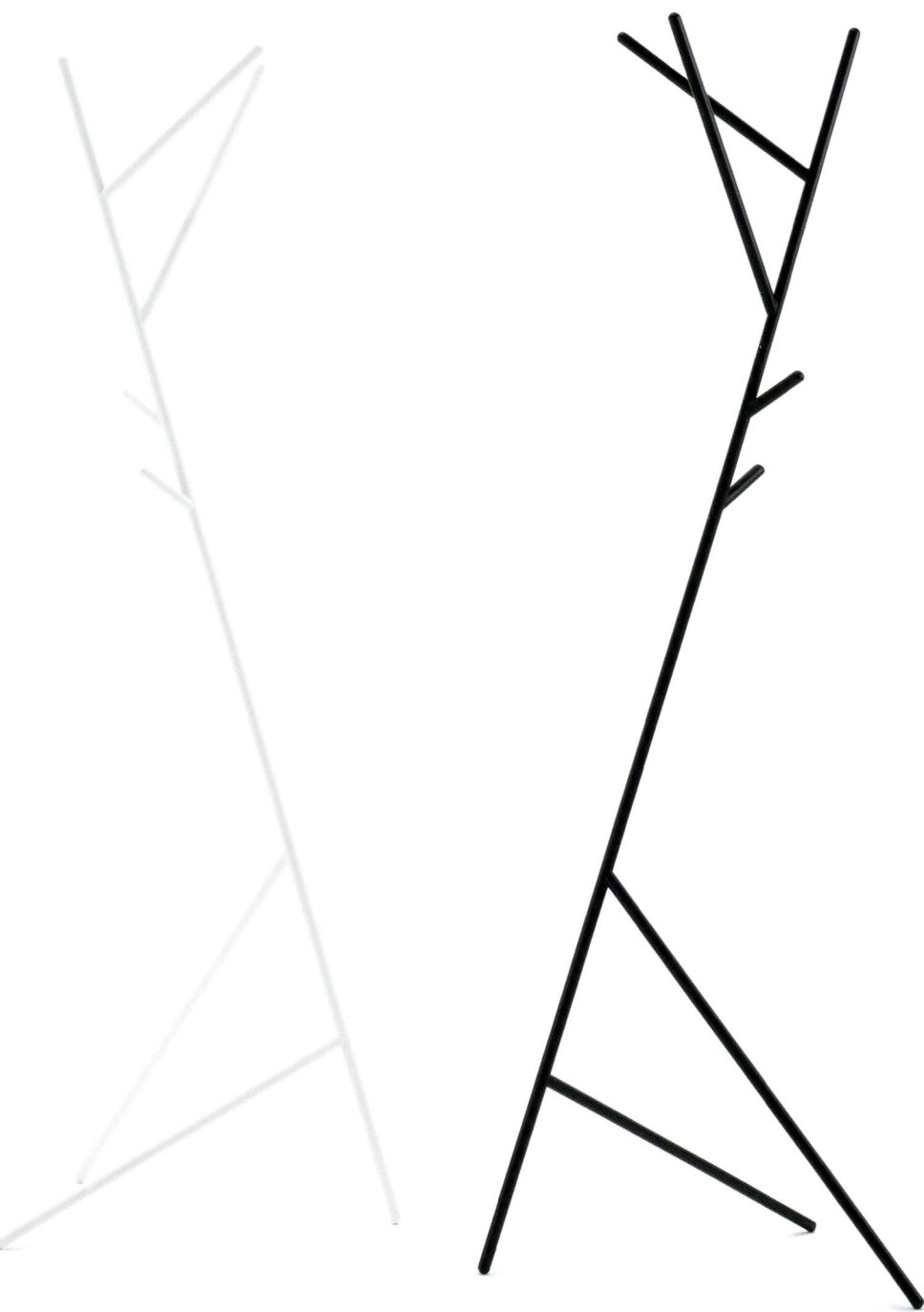

Madra
Log Basket
Holztrage

Manufacturer
Blomus GmbH,
Sundern, Germany
Design
Flöz Industriedesign (Oliver Wahl),
Essen, Germany
Web
www.blomus.com
www.floez.de

Madra not only has an attractive appearance but is also practical to use. Simply pick up the textile basket, go to the log pile or down into the cellar, carry the wood easily to the fireplace and place the textile basket in the elegant stainless steel stand. It is simple to attach the log basket using the clip fixings. Plastic gliders protect the floor and the easy-care synthetic-textile cover is hardwearing.

Madra hat nicht nur ein attraktives Äußeres, sondern ist auch praktisch im Gebrauch. Einfach die Tragetasche abheben, zum Holzstapel oder in den Keller gehen, das Holz bequem transportieren und mit dem Textil im eleganten Edelstahlgestell vor dem Kamin ablegen. Die Holztrage wird mit Clip-Verbindungen ganz leicht montiert. Kunststoffgleiter schonen den Fußboden. Der Kunstfaser-Bezug ist pflegeleicht und strapazierfähig.

Statement by the jury
Madra proves that intelligent design, which pays attention to detail, can even make a log basket functionally utilitarian and aesthetically appealing at the same time.

Begründung der Jury
Madra zeigt, dass dank einer bis ins Detail intelligenten Gestaltung auch eine Holztrage zweckmäßig funktional und ästhetisch ansprechend sein kann.

Elements
Stove System
Kaminofensystem

Manufacturer
Skantherm Wagner GmbH & Co. KG,
Oelde, Germany
Design
Prof. Wulf Schneider und Partner,
Stuttgart, Germany
Web
www.skantherm.de
www.profwulfschneider.de
Honourable Mention

Although this stove system has only three different elements, they can be combined to produce an endless number of designs to suit every taste and available space. All the elements are held together by a special magnetic technology. The two elements of different width can be positioned above, below or at the sides of the combustion chamber, either upright or flat.

Mit nur drei unterschiedlichen Elementen, aber unendlich vielen Gestaltungsmöglichkeiten kann das Kaminofensystem Elements ganz nach den individuellen Vorstellungen und dem Platzangebot kombiniert werden. Alle Elemente werden mit einer speziellen Magnettechnik einfach miteinander verbunden. Die zwei Elemente unterschiedlicher Breite lassen sich oberhalb, unterhalb, seitlich und auch hochkant der Brennkammer anordnen.

Statement by the jury
This stove is astonishing for its versatility and variability, turning it into an integral part of any living space.

Begründung der Jury
Dieser Kaminofen erstaunt durch seine Vielseitigkeit und Variabilität, die ihn zu einem integralen Bestandteil eines jeden Wohnraums machen.

Delhi
Stove
Kaminofen

Manufacturer
Hase Kaminofenbau GmbH,
Trier, Germany
In-house design
Walter Blasius,
Fernando Najera
Web
www.hase.de

Delhi's combustion chamber, with its panoramic window, can be rotated through almost 90 degrees to perfectly showcase the spectacle of flickering flames. Carefully designed details make the stove easy to use; for example, the combustion chamber door can be opened without bending down and its handle is designed to remain pleasantly cool at all times. The cast iron floor of the combustion chamber has a rotatable grate, so that ash can be removed effortlessly. A slide with a double function makes it easy to regulate the air supply and the rotating mechanism.

Statement by the jury
The slim, cylindrical form and effective display of the fire, which is visible from many angles, enhance the appeal of Delhi.

Der um fast 90 Grad drehbare Feuerraum mit seiner Panoramascheibe setzt beim Kaminofen Delhi das Flammenspiel perfekt in Szene. Ausgereifte Details sorgen für eine komfortable Bedienung: Die Feuerraumtür lässt sich im Stehen öffnen, der Türgriff bleibt dabei angenehm kühl. Dank des gusseisernen Feuerraumbodens mit drehbarem Feuerrost kann die Asche bequem entfernt werden. Für Luftsteuerung und Drehmechanismus gibt es einen einfach zu bedienenden Doppelfunktionsschieber.

Begründung der Jury
Delhi gefällt durch seine schlanke zylindrische Form und die gelungene Inszenierung des Feuers, das man aus vielen Blickwinkeln genießen kann.

wodtke Holiday
Wood-Burning Stove
Kaminofen

Manufacturer
wodtke GmbH,
Tübingen, Germany
In-house design
Web
www.wodtke.com

The wodtke Holiday stove is rotatable left and right through 48 degrees. Its special firebox geometry and post combustion features facilitate reduced emission combustion. Thanks to the wodtke HiClean-Filter, an innovative, ceramic-foam depth filter, the combustion of soot particles leaves virtually no residue. Optional room-air independent operation makes it possible to install the stove in low-energy or passive houses with controlled room ventilation.

Statement by the jury
In this wood-burning stove, an aesthetic, rectilinear use of form is combined with a high degree of technically advanced practical value.

wodtke Holiday ist ein um 48 Grad nach rechts und links drehbarer Kaminofen. Seine spezielle Feuerraum-Geometrie und Nachverbrennung unterstützen eine emissionsarme Verbrennung. Dank des wodtke HiClean-Filters, eines neuartigen Tiefenfilters aus Schaumkeramik, werden Rußpartikel fast rückstandslos verbrannt. Die Möglichkeit der raumluftunabhängigen Betriebsweise erlaubt den Einsatz in Niedrigenergie- oder Passivhäusern mit kontrollierter Wohnraumlüftung.

Begründung der Jury
Eine ästhetische, geradlinige Formensprache verbindet sich bei diesem Kaminofen mit einem hohen, technisch avancierten Gebrauchswert.

Vision
Wood-Burning Stove
Kaminofen

Manufacturer
Skantherm Wagner GmbH & Co. KG,
Oelde, Germany
Design
Sebastian David Büscher,
Gütersloh, Germany
Web
www.skantherm.de
www.sebastian-buescher.de

Inspired by the modern television, the unusual and timeless design of the Vision wood-burning stove brings the fire into the observer's direct line of vision. In doing so, Vision opts for a puristic and at the same time exciting shape by cleverly shifting the centre of gravity to the back of the base due to the use of a counter weight, thus accentuating the fire.

Statement by the jury
A well thought-out design with a distinctive style turns this stove into an eye-catching, central focus in every living room.

Der Kaminofen Vision bringt das Feuer in das direkte Blickfeld des Betrachters durch ein außergewöhnliches und zeitloses Design, welches an einen modernen Fernseher angelehnt ist. Vision setzt dabei auf eine puristische und zugleich spannende Formgebung, indem der Fuß geschickt durch ein Kontergewicht nach hinten versetzt wird und dadurch dem Feuer Dominanz verleiht.

Begründung der Jury
Eine durchdachte Gestaltung mit markanter Form macht diesen Kaminofen zu einem auffälligen, zentralen Blickfang in jedem Wohnraum.

Households
Haushalt

Washing machines, driers, vacuum cleaners, cleaning devices, iron systems, ventilators, domestic appliances
Waschmaschinen, Trockner, Staubsauger, Reinigungsgeräte, Bügelsysteme, Ventilatoren, Haushaltsgeräte

2

NEW ORDER
Domestic Waste Separation Bags
Taschen zur Mülltrennung im häuslichen Bereich

Manufacturer
Berliner Stadtreinigungsbetriebe
(BSR), Berlin, Germany

Design
böttcher+henssler
(Moritz Böttcher, Sören Henssler,
Clémentine Caurier),
Berlin, Germany

Web
www.trenntmoebel.de
www.boettcher-henssler.de

New intrinsic value

Separating domestic waste, necessary in order to sustain the environment, is a task that is often performed hidden from the eye. Different types of waste are either stored in a kitchen cabinet or collected in the subbasement for later dumping. The design of the New Order reinterprets waste separation by taking an entirely novel approach: the waste is collected in a series of coloured bags hanging on the wall in full view. Boldly placing waste centre stage, this concept won first prize in a competition organised by public cleansing service Berlin Stadtreinigung in collaboration with the design network "Create Berlin" as part of the "Trenntstadt Berlin" (waste separation city) campaign. The New Order bags are made of a robust, easily washable and recyclable textile. Thanks to integrated magnets, the bags open intuitively with only one hand, turning daily waste separation into an easy task. On their inside, these aesthetically looking bags feature a functional and removable holder that keeps the actual inner waste bag in place. When a bag becomes full, the user can carry it safely with the solid handle to dispose of the contents in the outside waste container. The systematic concept of the New Order implies that this very bag can be used for shopping immediately afterwards. The dedicated reinterpretation of the topic led to the emergence of an innovative system – bags used for separating waste turn into multifunctional and cherished design objects.

Neue Wertigkeit

Die für die Erhaltung der Recyclingkreisläufe nötige Trennung des Hausmülls geschieht meist im Verborgenen. Entweder werden die unterschiedlichen Müllsorten in einem Schrank zwischendeponiert oder im Keller gesammelt. Die Gestaltung von New Order interpretiert das Thema Müllsortierung auf völlig neue Art und Weise: Für jeden sichtbar wird der Müll in bunten, an der Wand hängenden Taschen sortiert. Dieses Konzept, welches als Gewinner aus einem Wettbewerb hervorging, den die Berliner Stadtreinigung mit dem Design-Netzwerk „Create Berlin" im Rahmen der Kampagne „Trenntstadt Berlin" veranstaltete, rückt den Müll visuell in den Mittelpunkt. Die Taschen von New Order bestehen aus einem robusten, gut waschbaren und recycelfähigen Textilgewebe. Für die tägliche Mülltrennung lassen sie sich durch eingearbeitete Magnete intuitiv und mit nur einer Hand öffnen. In ihrem Inneren sind diese ästhetischen Taschen mit einem funktionalen, herausnehmbaren Einsatz gestaltet, der als Halterung für den Müllbeutel dient. Ist eine der Taschen mit Müll gefüllt, kann sie der Nutzer mittels eines stabilen Henkels bis zur Mülltonne tragen. Das systemische Konzept von New Order impliziert, dass sie dabei anschließend gleich wieder zum Einkaufen genutzt werden. Die engagierte Neuinterpretation des Themas brachte hier ein innovatives System hervor – Behälter für die Mülltrennung wandeln sich in multifunktionale, begehrte Designobjekte.

Statement by the jury

The design of the New Order reinterprets the importance of waste separation using a novel approach. They are washable, recyclable and facilitate an almost effortless separation of waste. These multifunctional and aesthetically pleasing bags communicate a sense of freshness in the kitchen. They create an entirely new style.

Begründung der Jury

Die Gestaltung von New Order interpretiert das wichtige Thema Mülltrennung auf innovative Art und Weise. Sie sind wasch- und recycelbar und erlauben eine mühelose Sortierung des Mülls. Diese multifunktionalen und ästhetischen Taschen kommunizieren in der Küche die Anmutung von Frische. Sie kreieren einen neuen Style.

Mobile waste system

BLANCOSELECT
Waste System
Abfallsystem

Manufacturer
BLANCO GmbH + Co KG,
Oberderdingen, Germany
In-house design
Brigitte Ziemann
Design
formteam Produktdesign,
Schorndorf, Germany
Web
www.blanco-germany.com/de
www.formteam.de

Blancoselect is a waste system that can be installed inside the sink cabinet. It follows a consistently function-oriented design principle and equally focuses on utilising the available space, providing optimum stability and cleanliness.
The bins are hung neatly side by side in the all round, unsupported frame construction, guaranteeing maximum availability of the full capacity. The geometry tilts to the inside so that it serves as a funnel for the waste.

Statement by the jury
The practical waste system in subtle shades of anthracite fits into contemporary kitchen cabinets, being functionally and visually appealing.

Blancoselect ist ein Abfallsystem zum Einbau in den Spülenunterschrank. Es folgt einem konsequent funktionsorientierten Gestaltungsansatz und fokussiert gleichermaßen eine gute Raumausnutzung, überzeugende Stabilität und Sauberkeit.
In der umlaufenden, frei tragenden Rahmenkonstruktion werden die Eimer bündig nebeneinander eingehängt und bieten eine maximale Volumenausnutzung. Die nach innen geneigte Geometrie wirkt wie ein Trichter für den Abfall.

Begründung der Jury
Das praktische Abfallsystem in dezenten Anthrazittönen fügt sich funktional und visuell ansprechend in zeitgemäße Küchenschränke ein.

Waste system

MR6500
Robot Vacuum Cleaner
Roboter-Staubsauger

Manufacturer
Moneual,
Seoul, South Korea
In-house design
Park Hongseuk,
Jeong Yeonwook
Web
www.moneual.co.kr
Honourable Mention

Composed of eco-friendly materials while providing a variety of functions, excellent functionality and sophisticated design, the robot vacuum cleaner MR6500 is composed for families with young children, dual-income families, pet owners and senior citizens. The innovative Shadow Cleaning Mode detects and performs concentrated cleaning in areas that do not receive direct light, for example underneath large furniture such as couches and beds.

Gefertigt aus umweltfreundlichen Materialien, bietet der Roboter-Staubsauger MR6500 eine variable Funktionalität und eine anspruchsvolle Gestaltung. Der Staubsauger wurde für Familien mit kleinen Kindern, berufstätige Eheleute, Haustier-Besitzer und Senioren entworfen. Der innovative Shadow Cleaning Modus entdeckt die unzureichend beleuchteten Bereiche unter großen Möbeln wie Sofas und Betten und reinigt diese intensiv.

BSGL50S
Vacuum Cleaner
Staubsauger

Manufacturer
Robert Bosch Hausgeräte GmbH,
Munich, Germany
In-house design
Daniel Dockner, Jörg Schröter, Helmut Kaiser
Design
Brandis Industrial Design,
Nuremberg, Germany
Web
www.bosch-hausgeraete.de
www.brandis-design.de

The innovative design concept of the vacuum cleaner Free'e ProSilence combines high suction power with a low-noise level. The focus is on the sophisticated SilenceSound system. The contrasting baffle in the exhaust area provides additional sound absorption. Integrated bumper guards are easy on furniture and walls. Swivel castors, a patented 360-degree ball joint and an operating range of 15 metres grant high mobility.

Das innovative Gestaltungskonzept des Staubsaugers Free'e ProSilence verbindet eine hohe Saugleistung mit einem niedrigen Geräuschpegel. Im Fokus steht das ausgefeilte SilenceSound System, wobei ein farblich abgesetzter Schalldämpfer im Ausblasbereich für zusätzliche Schallabsorption sorgt. Integrierte Stoßleisten schonen Möbel und Wände. Für viel Mobilität sorgen Lenkrollen, ein patentiertes 360-Grad-Kugelgelenk und ein Aktionsradius von 15 Metern.

Statement by the jury
Stringent lines characterise the overall appearance of a vacuum cleaner that impresses by ease of operation and functionality.

Begründung der Jury
Eine stringente Linienführung prägt das Gesamtbild eines Staubsaugers, der durch Bedienkomfort und Funktionalität überzeugt.

BGS40
Bagless Vacuum Cleaner
Beutelloser Staubsauger

Manufacturer
Robert Bosch Hausgeräte GmbH,
Munich, Germany
In-house design
Daniel Dockner,
Helmut Kaiser
Web
www.bosch-hausgeraete.de

With its powerful design, this bagless vacuum cleaner represents a high performance level. Its compact form with a rounded front and XXL wheels, homogeneously integrated in the corpus, support its manoeuvrability. The dust container has a handle and is very easy to clean. The device-specific „bagless disk" is an additional feature.

Dieser beutellose Staubsauger kommuniziert durch sein kraftvolles Design Leistungsstärke. Die kompakte Form mit abgerundetem Bugbereich und die homogen in den Korpus integrierten XXL-Räder unterstützen die Wendigkeit. Ein Tragegriff erleichtert den Transport des Gerätes. Ebenfalls mit einem Tragegriff ausgestattet, lässt sich der Staubauffangbehälter mühelos reinigen. Zusätzliches Gestaltungsmerkmal ist die gerätetypische, kreisförmige „bagless disk".

Statement by the jury
A compact case in a striking shade of black emphasises a high technical standard and innovative functionality.

Begründung der Jury
Ein kompaktes Gehäuse in markantem Schwarz unterstreicht einen hohen technischen Anspruch und eine innovative Funktionalität.

Aura CleanmaxSPLUS
RobocleanSPLUS
Cleaning Robot
Reinigungsroboter

Manufacturer
Ihlas Ev Aletleri Iml. San. Tic. A.S.,
Istanbul, Turkey
In-house design
Omer Kamber,
Zafer Yucesoy,
Umit Altun
Web
www.iea.com.tr

The Aura CleanmaxSplus cleaning robot
is a water filter vacuum cleaner. It is
intuitively activated via a touch screen
control panel. The appliance was designed
as a vacuum cleaner with washing
and cleaning function: it features the
additional function of an air freshener
with a capacity of 200 m³/hour. The
ambient air can be optionally perfumed
with aromas. The form of the corpus
was designed with respect to function,
ergonomics and user-friendliness.

Bei dem Aura CleanmaxSplus Reinigungsroboter handelt es sich um einen Staubsauger mit Wasserfilter. Er lässt sich intuitiv über ein Touchscreen-Panel ansteuern.
Das als Staubsauger mit Wasch- und
Reinigungsfunktion konzipierte Gerät
bietet zusätzlich die Funktion eines Luft-
erfrischers für ein Volumen von 200 m³/
Stunde. Optional kann die Raumluft mit
Aromen beduftet werden. Der Korpus ist
funktional, ergonomisch und benutzer-
freundlich konstruiert.

Ultra One Mini
Vacuum Cleaner
Staubsauger

Manufacturer
AB Electrolux,
Stockholm, Sweden
In-house design
Electrolux Group Design
Small Appliances
Web
www.electrolux.se

Ultra One Mini is a compact, high-capacity vacuum cleaner for demanding, urban consumers. The Ultra One Mini is small in size and easy to store away. Its large, soft wheels enable particularly quiet rolling and ease of manoeuvrability. The remote control is integrated in the handle and the hidden display visualises advanced technology. The graphic patterns on the housing suggest the picture of airflow.

Ultra One Mini ist ein kompakter, leistungsstarker Staubsauger für den anspruchsvollen Verbraucher in der Stadt. Der Ultra One Mini ist klein und platzsparend zu verstauen. Seine großen, weichen Räder laufen ungewöhnlich leise und lassen sich leicht lenken. Im Griff befindet sich eine Fernbedienung, zudem visualisiert das versteckte Display eine hoch entwickelte Technologie. Die grafischen Muster auf dem Gehäuse deuten einen Luftstrom an.

Statement by the jury
With its emotionally appealing colours and rounded contours, the vacuum cleaner offers modern aesthetics.

Begründung der Jury
Mittels einer emotional ansprechenden Farbgebung und abgerundeter Konturen zeigt der Staubsauger eine zeitgemäße Ästhetik.

b2c Carpet Cleaner
b2c Teppichreiniger

Manufacturer
sarasa.com Inc.,
Tokyo, Japan
Design
Sketch collective noun Co., Ltd
(Masashi Okawa),
Tokyo, Japan
Web
www.sarasa-design.com
www.sketchcollective.net

With the aim of making the handy carpet cleaner as attractive as possible, a cleaning device was designed that can be arranged in homes like an art object, visible to everybody. Thanks to its pleasant casing, the carpet cleaner does not have to be hidden in a cabinet. The unit is ready to hand if required and provides ease of simple cleaning.

Mit der Zielsetzung, den handlichen Teppichreiniger möglichst attraktiv zu gestalten, entstand ein Reinigungsgerät, das gleich einem Kunstobjekt für alle sichtbar an einem passenden Ort in der Wohnung aufgestellt werden kann. Aufgrund seines gefälligen Gehäuses muss der Teppichreiniger nicht im Schrank versteckt werden. Das Gerät ist im Bedarfsfall schnell zur Hand und bietet die Nutzerfreundlichkeit einer unkomplizierten Reinigung.

Statement by the jury
This carpet cleaner is a successful example of how to unite two components to become a perfectly fitting, compact product solution.

Begründung der Jury
Der Teppichreiniger ist ein gelungenes Beispiel dafür, wie sich zwei Bestandteile passgenau zu einer kompakten Produktlösung verbinden können.

Floor Wiper Holder
Wischerständer

Manufacturer
Marna Inc.,
Tokyo, Japan
In-house design
Web
www.marna-inc.co.jp/en

This decorative floor wiper holder easily hides any wiper or mop and doesn't need much space. By its discreet design, it flexibly adapts to different rooms and is particularly suitable for being placed in a cabinet or the corner of a room. The cleaning tool is thus immediately at hand.

Der dekorative Wischerständer verbirgt jeden Wischer unkompliziert und platzsparend. Durch seine dezente Formensprache passt er sich unterschiedlichen Räumlichkeiten flexibel an und eignet sich besonders gut für die Platzierung in einer Schrank- oder Zimmerecke. Das Reinigungsutensil ist dadurch sofort griffbereit.

Statement by the jury
The refined appearance of the smoothly curved wiper holder is reminiscent of a vase, but a vase which features surprising benefits when being used.

Begründung der Jury
Mit seiner edlen Anmutung erinnert der sanft geschwungene Wischerständer an eine Vase, die überraschende Gebrauchsvorteile bietet.

Laurastar Lift
Ironing System
Bügelsystem

Manufacturer
LauraStar SA,
Châtel-St-Denis, Switzerland
Design
Les Ateliers du Nord
(Antoine Cahen),
Lausanne, Switzerland
Web
www.laurastar.com
www.adn-design.ch

When the Laurastar Lift ironing system was created, the idea was to develop an ironing station with the best possible comfort. The ironing system is available in four different colours. It effectively protects users from burns. The design concept allows lower weight and easy handling. The iron can be safely placed on the station immediately after use, even if it is still hot.

Bei der Gestaltung des Bügelsystems Laurastar Lift ging es darum, eine Bügelstation mit größtmöglichem Komfort zu entwickeln. Das Bügelsystem ist in vier verschiedenen Farben erhältlich und schützt den Benutzer effektiv vor Verbrennungen. Das Gestaltungskonzept ermöglicht ein geringes Gewicht und eine einfache Handhabung. Das noch heiße Bügeleisen kann direkt nach dem Gebrauch in der Station sicher verstaut werden.

Statement by the jury
A minimalist design concept succeeds in meeting the standards of a functionally sophisticated ironing system.

Begründung der Jury
Ein minimalistisch anmutendes Gestaltungskonzept begegnet hier erfolgreich den Anforderungen eines funktional hochwertigen Bügelsystems.

  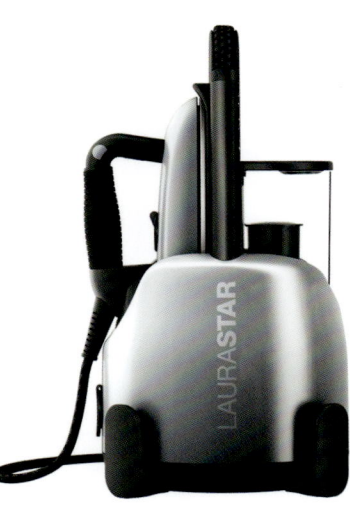 

Compact Clothes Dryer
Kompakt-Wäschetrockner

Manufacturer
Foshan Shunde LionHeart Electric Co., Ltd.,
Shunde, China
Design
Nova Design (Shanghai) Ltd
(Peng Jia, Kai Wang),
Shanghai, China
Web
www.lionheartelec.com
www.e-novadesign.com
Honourable Mention

The compact clothes dryer is a product solution that has a small footprint and is easy to transport. Accordingly, the dryer can be taken on travel. This technically simple method of hot air drying is easy to use. Thus, wet clothes are dried in no time and wrinkles smoothed out, too. The compact appliance features an extractable hanging rail on which the clothing is hung.

Statement by the jury
The innovative design concept for this portable clothes dryer offers a high practical value.

Der Kompakt-Wäschetrockner ist eine Produktlösung, die nur eine kleine Standfläche benötigt und leicht zu transportieren ist. Entsprechend lässt sich der Trockner auch auf Reisen mitnehmen. Diese technisch einfache Heißlufttrocknung lässt sich unkompliziert nutzen, um nasse Kleidung in kürzester Zeit zu trocknen und zudem faltenfrei zu glätten. Das kompakte Gerät verfügt über eine ausziehbare Kleiderstange, auf der die Kleidung aufgehängt wird.

Begründung der Jury
Die innovative Gestaltungsidee dieses portablen Wäschetrockners bietet den Nutzern einen hohen Gebrauchswert.

PowerLegato
Energy Storage System
Energie-Speichersystem

Manufacturer
AU Optronics Corporation,
Hsinchu, Taiwan
Design
Qisda Creative Design Center,
Taipei, Taiwan
Web
www.auo.com
www.qisda.com
Honourable Mention

PowerLegato is a solar energy storage system with a capacity of six kilowatt-hours. The desired amount of solar energy to be stored can be programmed via touch screen. In case of a natural disaster or a power outage, the stored energy can be used independently. The device is made of metal and plastics and has a robust structure. Bottom wheels and handles on both sides make it easily manoeuvrable.

Statement by the jury
This expediently designed storage system for solar energy allows consumers to be independent from electricity providers.

PowerLegato ist eine Solar-Akkubank mit einer Kapazität von sechs Kilowattstunden. Über einen Touchscreen lässt sich der gewünschte Umfang der zu speichernden Solarenergie programmieren. Während einer Naturkatastrophe oder eines Stromausfalls kann die gespeicherte Energie autark genutzt werden. Das Gerät aus Metall und Plastik besitzt eine robuste Struktur. Räder und Griffe an den Seiten machen das Gerät leicht bewegbar.

Begründung der Jury
Dieses zweckmäßig gestaltete Speichersystem für Solarenergie bietet dem Verbraucher eine Unabhängigkeit von Stromanbietern.

WING
Hanger
Kleiderbügel

Manufacturer
cw-concept (Horst Weihrauch),
Reichelsheim, Germany
Design
Designbüro Wenisch und Partner
(Heinrich Wenisch),
Lauenförde, Germany
Web
www.cw-concept.de
www.dbwetp.de

The Wing hanger comes in many colours. It is slightly bent forward to adapt to the shape of a human body. In an interesting way, the design concept refines previous hanger forms. Broad shoulder parts provide for protective storage so that the slender ends of the hanger do not leave any traces on the garment. The hanger is made of unbreakable plastic. It has a rough surface, giving it a sophisticated look.

Statement by the jury
Aesthetically pleasing, the hanger combines an expressive style with persuasive functionality.

Der in vielen Farben erhältliche Kleiderbügel Wing ist, leicht nach vorne geschwungen, der Körperform nachempfunden. Sein Gestaltungskonzept entwickelt bisherige Kleiderbügelformen auf interessante Weise weiter. Die breiten Schulterauflagen sorgen für eine schonende Aufbewahrung, sodass sich keine schmalen Bügelenden auf dem Kleidungsstück abbilden können. Der Bügel aus bruchfestem Kunststoff hat eine raue Oberfläche, die ihm ein edles Aussehen verleiht.

Begründung der Jury
Ästhetisch ansprechend verbindet der Kleiderbügel Wing eine ausdrucksstarke Formensprache mit einer überzeugenden Funktionalität.

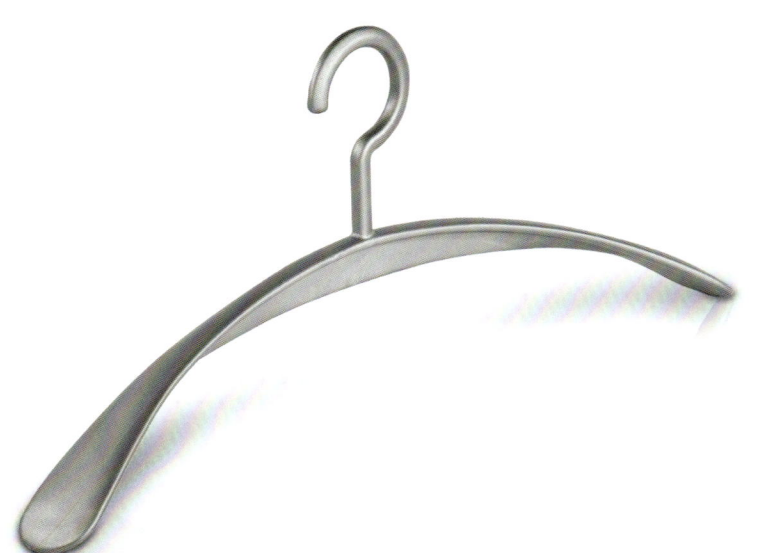

PFAFF Passport 2.0
Sewing Machine
Nähmaschine

Manufacturer
VSM Group,
Huskvarna, Sweden
Design
Zenit Design
(Caroline Formby, Oskar Ponnert,
Marten Rittfeldt), Malmö, Sweden
Web
www.pfaff.com
www.zenitdesign.se

The Passport 2.0 sewing machine is so compact and lightweight it can easily be taken to sewing classes and travels. The white rounded back, in contrast to the edge shaped black front, emphasises the clear separation between sewing area and operating panel. Its sleek lines and eye-catching details are carefully balanced to meet the demands for sewing ergonomics and convenience. The minimalistic design allows an intuitive operation.

Statement by the jury
This portable sewing machine in black and white has an appealing design. Its panel structure is easy to understand.

Die kompakte und leichte Passport 2.0 Nähmaschine eignet sich zum Mitnehmen zu Kursen und auf Reisen. Die weiße abgerundete Rückseite, im Kontrast zu der kantig gehaltenen schwarzen Vorderseite, betont eine klare Trennung des Nähbereichs zum Bedienfeld. Ihre elegante, ausgewogene Linienführung sowie auffällige Details entsprechen Ergonomie- und Komfortansprüchen. Das minimalistische Gestaltungskonzept ermöglicht eine intuitive Bedienung.

Begründung der Jury
Formal ansprechend wirkt diese portable Nähmaschine in Schwarz-Weiß, deren Bedienfeld leicht verständlich strukturiert ist.

Gorenje SensoCare
Washing Machine
Waschmaschine

Manufacturer
Gorenje d.d.,
Velenje, Slovenia
In-house design
Gorenje Design Studio d.o.o.
(Borut Kerzic)
Web
www.gorenje.com
www.gorenjedesignstudio.com

The distinct aesthetics of the Gorenje SensoCare washing machine underlines its most important features such as user interface and door handle. Its robust impression illustrates a high technical standard and promises long lasting performance. The user interface on the slant front panel is clearly visible. In fast mode, programmes are selected via two steps according to the user's needs.

Die klare Ästhetik der Gorenje SensoCare Waschmaschine betont ihre wichtigsten Elemente wie die Benutzeroberfläche und den Türgriff. Der robuste Eindruck vermittelt einen hohen technischen Anspruch und verspricht eine dauerhafte Leistungsfähigkeit. Die geneigte Frontplatte macht die Benutzeroberfläche übersichtlich. Im Schnell-Modus erfolgt die Programmauswahl über zwei Stufen, wodurch das Waschprogramm bedarfsgerecht eingestellt werden kann.

Statement by the jury
The pronounced stylistic elements of the door emphasise the functional overall appearance of this washing machine. The control panel features a two-step programme selection.

Begründung der Jury
Die prägnante Türgestaltung prägt bei dieser Waschmaschine ein funktionales Gesamtbild. Das Bedienfeld bietet eine zweistufige Programmwahl.

Adora SLQ WP
Washing Machine
Waschmaschine

Manufacturer
V-Zug AG,
Zug, Switzerland
In-house design
Peter Pfenniger
Design
Albatros Design GmbH
(Zacharias Baur),
Zürich, Switzerland
Web
www.vzug.ch
www.albatrosdesign.ch

This washing machine successfully incorporates an energy-saving heat pump technology. The Adora SLQ WP offers a choice of three different EcoHybrid levels. Power consumption beats the values of energy efficiency class A+++ by 40 per cent. The steam anti-crease function allows smoothing out creases in the washing so in most cases ironing is no longer necessary. The anti-mite programme completely removes mites and their allergens.

Bei dieser Waschmaschine ist es gelungen, eine energiesparsame Wärmepumpentechnologie einzusetzen. Die Adora SLQ WP bietet die Wahl zwischen drei verschiedenen EcoHybrid-Stufen. Der Stromverbrauch unterschreitet die Energieeffizienzklasse A+++ um 40 Prozent. Beim Programm Dampfglätten wird die Wäsche so gründlich geglättet, dass Bügeln meist überflüssig wird. Mit dem Milbenstopp-Programm werden Milben und deren Allergene restlos entfernt.

WF-F500E (WF80/WF81, WF70/WF71, WF7A/WF8A)
Washing Machine Series
Waschmaschinen-Serie

Manufacturer
Samsung Electronics Co., Ltd.,
Seoul, South Korea
In-house design
Jin Nam Kim,
Seung Bin Im
Web
www.samsung.com
Honourable Mention

The WF-F500E washing machine series demonstrates the intentional use of the double injection moulding method, which produces metallic effects, thus making further chrome plating unnecessary. Therefore, it is possible to reduce material costs and make the manufacturing process more eco-friendly. In addition, a clear crystal appearance with a transparent effect is created. It visually symbolises the cleanliness of the laundry desired by the consumer.

Bei der Waschmaschinen-Serie WF-F500E erzielt der bewusste Einsatz des dualen Spritzgussverfahrens metallische Effekte, welche eine weitere Verchromung überflüssig machen. Somit gelingt es, Materialkosten zu reduzieren und das Herstellungsverfahren umweltfreundlicher zu gestalten. Zudem entsteht eine klare, transparent wirkende Kristall-Anmutung, welche dem Benutzer die angestrebte Sauberkeit der Wäsche visuell vermittelt.

Statement by the jury
The aesthetically pleasing surface design emphasises the independent look of this washing machine series.

Begründung der Jury
Die ästhetisch ansprechende Oberflächengestaltung unterstreicht bei dieser Waschmaschinen-Serie einen eigenständigen Charakter.

Profilo CM1001LTR
Washing Machine
Waschmaschine

Manufacturer
BSH Bosch und Siemens Hausgeräte GmbH,
Munich, Germany
In-house design
Ralph Pietruska
Web
www.bsh-group.com

The Profilo CM1001LTR washing machine combines elegant design with impressive functionality. The central component is the user interface area, featuring a large programme selector and option buttons which are operated from left to right. They are formally limited by a circumferential frame to ensure intuitive operation. Furthermore, the most important interactive elements are colour-coded for quick use when in a hurry.

Statement by the jury
As an outstanding quality feature, the user-friendly interface design of the Profilo washing machine makes a positive impression.

Die Profilo Waschmaschine CM1001LTR verbindet eine elegante Gestaltung mit überzeugender Funktionalität. Zentrales Element ist der Interfacebereich mit dem großen Programmwähler und den in Leserichtung zu bedienenden Optionstasten, der durch einen umlaufenden Rahmen formal abgegrenzt wird und eine intuitive Handhabung ermöglicht. Für die schnelle Bedienung unter Zeitdruck sind die wichtigsten Interaktionselemente zudem farblich gekennzeichnet.

Begründung der Jury
Als herausragendes Qualitätsmerkmal fällt bei der Profilo Waschmaschine die bedienungsfreundliche Interface-Gestaltung positiv auf.

Profilo CM1021LTR
Washing Machine
Waschmaschine

Manufacturer
BSH Bosch und Siemens Hausgeräte GmbH,
Munich, Germany
In-house design
Ralph Pietruska
Web
www.bsh-group.com

The matt silver surface adds a sophisticated edge to the Profilo CM1021LTR washing machine and the control elements are of high quality. The well-thought out design of the front panel visually divides the surface into harmonious areas. The central component is the user interface area, featuring a large rotary selector and option buttons which are operated from left to right. Thus, it ensures intuitive operation; it is formally defined by a circumferential frame.

Statement by the jury
The high-quality design of the corpus underlines the superior functionality of the user-friendly Profilo washing machine.

Die matt silberfarbene Oberfläche der Profilo Waschmaschine CM1021LTR wirkt edel, die Materialität der Bedienelemente hochwertig. Durch den durchdachten Aufbau der Blende ist die vordere Oberfläche visuell stimmig gegliedert. Als zentrales Element ermöglicht der Interfacebereich mit seinem großen Programmwähler und den in Leserichtung zu bedienenden Optionstasten eine intuitive Handhabung. Er ist formal durch einen umlaufenden Rahmen abgegrenzt.

Begründung der Jury
Die hochwertige Korpusgestaltung der Profilo Waschmaschine unterstreicht die gehobene Funktionalität des nutzerfreundlichen Gerätes.

Electrolux SteamSystem
Washing Machine
Waschmaschine

Manufacturer
Electrolux Major Appliances EMEA,
Stockholm, Sweden
In-house design
Electrolux Group Design EMEA
Web
www.electrolux.com
www.electrolux.it

Professional laundries freshen and
steam iron clothes. The household
washing machine of the Inspiration
Range is to offer consumers the same
functions. Optionally, the versatile
programmes can be selected directly
by pressing a button or turning a
chromed transparent knob. The design
concept confers an exclusive look and
emphasises the silver-coloured control
panel with its white LED icons and
touch buttons.

Professionelle Wäschereien frischen
Wäsche auf und glätten sie mit Dampf –
die Waschmaschine der Inspiration
Range soll dem Nutzer die gleichen
Funktionen bieten. Optional können die
vielseitigen Programme direkt per Tastendruck oder mittels eines verchromten
Drehknopfs ausgewählt werden. Ein
exklusiv anmutendes Gestaltungskonzept
betont die silberfarbene Bedienblende
mit ihren weißen Symbolen und Sensortasten.

Statement by the jury
Clear lines visually enhance the
innovative functionality of a washing
machine that is convenient to use.

Begründung der Jury
Eine klare Linienführung unterstreicht
visuell die innovative Funktionalität einer
Waschmaschine, die komfortabel zu
bedienen ist.

Electrolux EcoCare
Tumble Dryer
Wäschetrockner

Manufacturer
Electrolux Major Appliances EMEA,
Stockholm, Sweden
In-house design
Electrolux Group Design EMEA
Web
www.electrolux.com
www.electrolux.it

This tumble dryer works with low temperatures thus treating the clothes gently and saving energy. Smooth lines emphasise exclusivity and a transparent inlay in silver highlights the edges of the operating panel. White LED icons and touch buttons form a homogenous image. The programmes can be selected by pressing a button or turning a knob so that the user can choose between different control options.

Dieser Wäschetrockner arbeitet mit niedrigen Temperaturen, was die Kleidung schont und Energie spart. Glatte Linien unterstreichen Exklusivität, während eine transparent silberne Einlage den Abschluss der Bedienblende betont. Weiße Symbole und Sensortasten prägen ein homogenes Bild. Die Programme können per Tastendruck oder Knopf gewählt werden, sodass verschiedene Bedienelemente dem Nutzer zur Wahl stehen.

Statement by the jury
A clearly structured and easy-to-use control panel visualises the high functionality of this tumble dryer.

Begründung der Jury
Ein klar strukturiertes und nutzerfreundlich angeordnetes Bedienfeld visualisiert die hohe Funktionalität des Wäschetrockners.

Beko WKY 61031 C
Washing Machine
Waschmaschine

Manufacturer
Arçelik A.S.,
Istanbul, Turkey
In-house design
Soner Ilgin,
Ozgur Mutlu Oz
Web
www.arcelik.com.tr

The overall appearance of the Beko washing machine is characterised by a minimalist style. Due to its small depth, it fits easily in small rooms while offering a loading capacity of 6 kg. The large-sized door allows convenient loading and unloading. A simple and clearly arranged interface ensures efficiency and precise operation. The slant front panel ensures comfortable reading.

Statement by the jury
This washing machine offers a space-saving solution and high ease of operation. It features a surprisingly large washing drum.

Das Gesamtbild der Beko-Waschmaschine ist durch eine minimalistische Formensprache charakterisiert. Mit ihrer geringen Tiefe fügt sie sich problemlos in kleine Räume ein und bietet dennoch eine Beladungskapazität von 6 kg. Dank ihrer großen Tür gestaltet sich das Be- und Entladen komfortabel. Ein einfaches und klar angeordnetes Interface bietet Effizienz und präzise Bedienung, wobei die schräge Frontblende gut lesbar ist.

Begründung der Jury
Als platzsparende Produktlösung bietet diese Waschmaschine einen guten Bedienkomfort und eine überraschend große Waschtrommel.

Grundig GWN 58472 C
Washing Machine
Waschmaschine

Manufacturer
Arçelik A.S.,
Istanbul, Turkey
In-house design
Arçelik Industrial Design Team
Design
Designaffairs GmbH,
Munich, Germany
Web
www.arcelik.com.tr
www.designaffairs.com
Honourable Mention

This energy-saving washing machine realises a minimalist design concept demonstrated by the linear black or stainless steel surface of the operation panels. The innovative technology comprises special sensors for detecting load and fabric type. The sensor data, which are indicated on the display, regulate water temperature and duration of washing programmes depending on the degree of soiling.

Statement by the jury
The precision crafted operation panel visualises the high functionality of this washing machine, which features a compelling sensor technology.

Bei der energiesparsamen Waschmaschine äußert sich ein minimalistisches Gestaltungskonzept durch die linear schwarze bzw. Edelstahloberfläche der Bedienpanele. Die innovative Technologie umfasst spezielle Sensoren zur Erkennung von Beladungsmenge und Textiltyp. Dementsprechend werden Wassertemperatur und Dauer des Waschprogramms dem jeweiligen Verschmutzungsgrad angepasst und im Display angezeigt.

Begründung der Jury
Das präzise ausgearbeitete Bedienfeld visualisiert die hohe Funktionalität dieser Waschmaschine, welche mit Sensorentechnologie überzeugt.

Grundig GTN 48271 GC
Condenser Dryer
Kondenswäschetrockner

Manufacturer
Arçelik A.S.,
Istanbul, Turkey
In-house design
Arçelik Industrial Design Team
Design
Designaffairs GmbH,
Munich, Germany
Web
www.arcelik.com.tr
www.designaffairs.com
Honourable Mention

The design of this condenser dryer is typical of the brand and features an energy saving heat pump technology. Energy consumption falls below the levels of class A by 65 per cent. Thanks to the brushless motor and a variable speed control, the laundry can be dried faster. The dryer is distinguished by high condensation efficiency. Sound-absorbing sidewalls, cabinet insulation and brushless motor technology ensure low-noise operation.

Statement by the jury
Distinct lines and contrasting materials in the control panel emphasise the convenient handling of the condenser dryer.

Der markentypisch gestaltete Kondenswäschetrockner verfügt über eine energiesparsame Wärmepumpentechnologie und unterschreitet den Energieverbrauch der Klasse A um 65 Prozent. Dank eines bürstenlosen Motors und einer variablen Geschwindigkeitsregelung wird die Wäsche schneller trocken. Den Trockner zeichnet eine hohe Kondensationseffizienz aus. Dämmende Seitenwände, Gehäuseisolierung sowie bürstenlose Motortechnologie sorgen für einen geräuscharmen Betrieb.

Begründung der Jury
Eine klare Linienführung und kontrastreiche Materialien im Bedienfeld betonen die komfortable Handhabung des Kondenswäschetrockners.

PWT 6089
Commercial Stackable Washer and Dryer Unit
Gewerbliche Wasch-Trocken-Säule

Manufacturer
Miele & Cie. KG,
Gütersloh, Germany
In-house design
Web
www.miele.de

This commercial stackable washer and dryer unit is a space-saving solution adjusted to the needs of laundry operators. Changing staff can easily and accurately operate the ergonomically arranged, intuitive controls. Without having to carry the laundry, it can be dried right after washing, thus saving resources. The appliance combination achieves high operating efficiency; it is long-lasting and visually appealing.

Diese gewerblich nutzbare Wasch-Trocken-Säule ist als platzsparende Lösung auf die Bedürfnisse von Wäschereibetreibern abgestimmt. Die ergonomisch angeordnete, intuitiv bedienbare Steuerung lässt sich leicht und fehlerfrei von einer wechselnden Belegschaft bedienen. Ressourcensparend und ohne lange Wege kann die Wäsche nach dem Waschen getrocknet werden. Das Geräteduo erreicht eine hohe Wirtschaftlichkeit, ist langlebig und visuell ansprechend.

Statement by the jury
This stackable washer and dryer unit has a professional look that represents high quality; its multifunctionality aims at using space efficiently.

Begründung der Jury
Gleichsam professionell und hochwertig wirkt diese Wasch-Trocken-Säule, deren Multifunktionalität auf eine effektive Raumnutzung abzielt.

Vieser One
Floor Drain
Bodenablauf

Manufacturer
Serres Oy, Kauhajoki,
Finland
In-house design
Serres R&D team
Design
Buorre Design Agency,
Vaasa, Finland
Web
www.vieser.fi
www.buorre.fi

Vieser One is a special floor drain designed for challenging installations even under harsh winter conditions. It has an innovative adjustable support structure and a water trap that automatically fits into place. These combined with intuitive assembly instructions make it quick and easy to install. The upper flange serves as an attachment platform for the mounting feet. The Vieser One floor drain system range is optimized for all installations, without the need for special tools.

Vieser One ist ein besonderer Boden-ablauf, der für anspruchsvolle Installa-tionen, selbst unter harten Winterbedin-gungen, konzipiert wurde. Er verfügt über eine innovative, einstellbare Tragstruktur sowie einen Wasserabscheider, der auto-matisch und passgenau einrastet und kombiniert mit einer intuitiven Montage-anleitung die Installation beschleunigt. Der obere Flansch dient als Plattform für die Befestigung der Montagefüße. Das Vieser One Bodenablaufsystem ist für alle Installationen optimiert, ohne spezielle Werkzeuge notwendig zu machen.

Statement by the jury
The design of Vieser One focuses entirely on its function and simple use and this is what makes it such a high-quality product, suited to even the most difficult conditions.

Begründung der Jury
Die ganz auf seine Funktion und einen problemlosen Gebrauch ausgerichtete Gestaltung macht Vieser One zu einem hochwertigen Produkt, das auch für schwierige Bedingungen geeignet ist.

Braun BNC013
Weather Station
Wetterstation

Manufacturer
Zeon Ltd,
London, GB
Design
Braun Design Team,
Kronberg im Taunus, Germany
Web
www.braun-clocks.com
Honourable Mention

The design of this weather station focuses on easy readability and operation. Weather symbols, temperature and time are indicated simultaneously to get all information at a glance. On its right side, the station's display can be intuitively set and personalised to indicate the individually desired information. The battery compartment serves as the base of the display, which is tilted backwards for better reading.

Die Gestaltung der Wetterstation fokussiert eine gute Ablesbarkeit und Bedienbarkeit. Wettersymbole, Temperatur und Uhrzeit werden gleichzeitig angezeigt, um alle Informationen auf einen Blick zu haben. Die Station ist an der rechten Seite intuitiv einstellbar und kann personalisiert werden, um individuell gewünschte Informationen anzuzeigen. Das Batteriefach wird als Fuß für das Display genutzt, welches sich zur besseren Lesbarkeit nach hinten neigt.

Statement by the jury
The compact weather station features a full-screen display that communicates high quality, which is typical for this brand.

Begründung der Jury
Die kompakte Wetterstation vermittelt mithilfe eines vollflächigen Displays die markentypisch hohe Wertigkeit.

Kitchens
Küche

Kitchen furniture, kitchen equipment, cooking implements, heaters and hobs, microwaves, extractor hoods, dishwashers, sink units, refrigerators and freezers, kitchen utensils and accessories, coffee machines, toasters, mixers, professional kitchens

Kücheneinrichtung, -möbel und -technik, Öfen und Kochfelder, Mikrowellen, Abzugshauben, Spülmaschinen, Spülbecken, Kühl- und Gefriergeräte, Küchengeräte und -zubehör, Kaffeemaschinen, Toaster, Mixer, Gastronomie

3

Pia
Kitchen Furniture, Kitchen System
Küchenmöbel, Küchensystem

Manufacturer
allmilmö-Zeiler Möbelwerk
GmbH & Co. KG,
Zeil am Main, Germany

Design
Pia Würtz Mogensen,
Aalborg, Denmark

Web
www.allmilmoe.com
www.piawuertz.dk

reddot design award
best of the best 2013

In tune with the times

Kitchen design has always been a reflection of the times. Take for example the Frankfurt kitchen of 1926, which set out to create a multifunctional environment where one could work efficiently. The concept behind the Pia kitchen system defines the kitchen as a functional oasis of calm, which aesthetically enhances the home. Designed with gently rounded corners, this kitchen system looks as if it has been framed by an all-encompassing delicate passepartout. This frame is painted and covered at the edges with a decorative durable stainless steel border. The Pia kitchen system design idea allows for numerous versatile configurations that will combine to form an impressively coherent unified concept. But this kitchen system is also functional and makes access and storage easy. The front panels are available in all RAL colours in matt, diamond lacquered and high-gloss finish to adapt to changing and specific user requirements. With its clear lines and finely rounded corners, the Pia kitchen system harmoniously suits contemporary architecture. Its design awakens a feeling of harmony in those using and working in it.

Im Rahmen des Zeitgeistes

Die Gestaltung von Küchen ist stets ein Ausdruck des Zeitgeistes. So war es etwa das Anliegen der 1926 konzipierten Frankfurter Küche, einen multifunktionalen Ort zu schaffen, an dem effektiv gearbeitet werden konnte. Die Gestaltung des Küchensystems Pia definiert die Küche als einen funktionellen Ruhepol, der das Zuhause auf ästhetische Weise bereichert. Dieses Küchensystem ist mit weich gerundeten Ecken gestaltet. Es wirkt wie gerahmt von einem rundum verlaufenden, filigranen Passepartout. Dieses Passepartout ist lackiert und an der Kante mit einer langlebigen Edelstahldekorkante beschichtet. Das Gestaltungskonzept des Küchensystems Pia erlaubt vielfältige Konfigurationen, die sich zu einem beeindruckend schlüssigen Gesamtkonzept vereinen. Dieses Küchensystem ist zudem funktional und ermöglicht einen einfachen Zugriff und eine einfache Vorratshaltung. Um sich den wechselnden und individuellen Wünschen des Nutzers anpassen zu können, sind die Fronten in Mattlack, Diamantlack und Hochglanzlack jeweils in allen RAL-Farbtönen erhältlich. Mit ihrer klaren Linienführung und ihren fein abgerundeten Ecken fügt sich das Küchensystem Pia stimmig in die zeitgemäße Architektur ein – seine gestalterische Harmonie überträgt sich auch auf die Bewohner und Küchenbenutzer.

Icon
Kitchen
Küche

Manufacturer
Ernestomeda S.p.A.,
Montelabbate, Italy
Design
GB Studio
(Giuseppe Bavuso),
Seregno, Italy
Web
www.ernestomeda.com

The Icon furniture programme shows a distinctive, powerful elegance. It includes versatile, innovative and practical kitchen furniture, which are constantly advanced in terms of material and design. Each individual kitchen element offers high-tech solutions such as opening and closing systems or extendable table systems. In addition to environmental sustainability, hygiene and well-being were further key notes in the development.

Eine charakteristische, kraftvolle Eleganz strahlt das Einrichtungsprogramm Icon aus. Es umfasst vielseitige, innovative und praktische Küchenmöbel, die ständig hinsichtlich Material und Ausführung weiterentwickelt werden. Jedes einzelne Küchenelement bietet High-Tech-Lösungen, beispielsweise bei den Öffnungs- und Schließsystemen oder den auszieh- baren Tischsystemen. Weitere Leitmotive bei der Entwicklung waren neben der Umweltverträglichkeit auch Hygiene und Wohlbefinden.

Statement by the jury
In this kitchen programme, high quality materials provide for a homely touch. With distinct lines and stylish colours, Icon is captivating.

Begründung der Jury
Hochwertige Materialien sorgen bei diesem Küchenprogramm für eine wohnliche Anmutung. Icon besticht durch klare Linien und stilvolle Farben.

Concept Kitchen
Mobile Kitchen
Mobilküche

Manufacturer
Naber GmbH,
Nordhorn, Germany
Design
Kilian Schindler Produktdesign
(Kilian Schindler),
Karlsruhe, Germany
Web
www.naber.de
www.kilianschindler.com

This mobile kitchen flexibly adapts to users' lifestyles. Whether as a standalone solution or in combination with a traditional kitchen unit, the modules can be arranged as desired. The system is based on five modules: worktop with integrated hob, sink centre, butcher block, storage rack and technology tower. The stainless steel base elements can be disassembled. They feature grid holes for the flexible positioning of structural and plain shelves. A simple plug-in principle allows easy assembly and disassembly without tools.

Die Mobilküche lässt sich flexibel an das Leben des Benutzers anpassen. Ob als Insellösung oder in Kombination mit einer klassischen Küchenzeile, die Module können nach Belieben angeordnet werden. Das System basiert auf fünf Modulen: einer Arbeitsfläche mit integrierter Kochfläche, einem Spülzentrum, einem Butcher-Block, einem Lagerregal sowie einem Technik-Tower. Die aus Stahl gefertigten Grundelemente sind zerlegbar und verfügen über Rasterbohrungen für die flexible Anordnung von Konstruktions- und Regalböden. Ein einfaches Steckprinzip ermöglicht den unkomplizierten Auf- und Abbau ohne Werkzeugeinsatz.

Statement by the jury
An original overall appearance characterises this mobile kitchen, which allows users a high degree of flexibility and mobility.

Begründung der Jury
Ein originelles Gesamtbild charakterisiert diese Mobilküche, die den Nutzern ein hohes Maß an Flexibilität und Mobilität ermöglicht.

Convoy Premio
Larder Unit
Hochschrank

Manufacturer
Kesseböhmer GmbH,
Bad Essen, Germany
In-house design
Web
www.kesseböhmer.com
Honourable Mention

The door and the integrated shelves of the Convoy Premio larder unit move smoothly. Wide-angle hinges allow a door opening up to 135 degrees. Thus, Convoy Premio provides convenient access from three sides when pulled out. The shelves are locked in a single-tube support frame. Inch-perfect, they can be infinitely height adjusted and thus adapted to the size of the stored items.

Statement by the jury
This functionally mature larder unit and the pull-out shelves allow convenient access to the items inside of it.

Beim Hochschrank Convoy Premio lassen sich die Tür sowie die im Schrankinneren eingebauten Tablare mühelos bewegen. Weitwinkelscharniere ermöglichen eine Türöffnung von bis zu 135 Grad, damit bietet der ausgefahrene Convoy Premio einen komfortablen Zugriff von drei Seiten. Die Tablare sind an einem Einrohr-Tragrahmen arretiert und lassen sich stufenlos und zentimetergenau in der Höhe variieren und damit an die Größe des Staugutes anpassen.

Begründung der Jury
Der funktional durchdachte Hochschrank mit seinen ausziehbaren Tablaren erlaubt einen bequemen Zugriff auf den Schrankinhalt.

LeMans II
Swivel Fitting
for Corner Cabinets
Eckschrank-Schwenkbeschlag

Manufacturer
Kesseböhmer GmbH,
Bad Essen, Germany
In-house design
Web
www.kesseböhmer.com
Honourable Mention

The LeMans II swivel fitting for corner cabinets allows direct access to everything that is stored: each of the elegant trays with their chrome-plated railings can be completely pulled out of the corner cabinet separately. They are height-adjustable without tools and can thus be adapted flexibly to individual needs. The cushioned self-closing mechanism can be attached to the right place without the use of tools. It ensures smooth and silent closing and offers special ease of use.

Statement by the jury
This flexibly placeable swivel fitting for corner cabinets offers a high utility value.

Der Schwenkbeschlag LeMans II ermöglicht den direkten Zugriff auf das Staugut: Die eleganten Tablare mit ihrer verchromten Reling lassen sich einzeln, jeweils komplett aus dem Eckschrank herausfahren. Sie sind werkzeuglos höhenverstellbar und können so flexibel den individuellen Bedürfnissen angepasst werden. Für besonderen Bedienkomfort und einen sanften und leisen Einzug sorgt der gedämpfte, werkzeuglos aufsteckbare Selbsteinzug.

Begründung der Jury
Einen hohen Gebrauchswert bietet dieser flexibel platzierbare Schwenkbeschlag für Eckschränke.

SPACE TOWER
with LEGRABOX free and LEGRABOX pure
Larder Unit and Box System
Vorratsschrank und Boxsystem

Manufacturer
Julius Blum GmbH,
Höchst, Austria
In-house design
Web
www.blum.com

The larder unit Space Tower offers much storage space. Its flexibly designed inner pull-outs can be used individually and accessed from three sides. The inner pull-outs feature the innovative Legrabox system. This box system is available in two programme lines that differ in materiality: "free" is made of different metals, while the "pure" version combines glass and wood or stone.

Statement by the jury
The precise and cross-material implementation of a distinct style succeeds with this larder unit including a box system.

Der Vorratsschrank Space Tower bietet viel Stauraum, seine flexibel gestalteten Innenauszüge sind einzeln herausziehbar und von drei Seiten zugänglich. Die Innenauszüge sind mit einem innovativen Boxsystem namens Legrabox ausgestattet. Dieses Boxsystem ist in zwei Programmlinien erhältlich, die sich hinsichtlich ihrer Materialität unterscheiden: Während „free" aus unterschiedlichen Metallen besteht, werden bei „pure" Glas, Holz oder auch Stein kombiniert.

Begründung der Jury
Bei diesem Vorratsschrank inklusive Boxsystem gelingt die stringente und materialübergreifende Umsetzung einer klaren Formensprache.

a-Box
Drawer and Pull-out System
Schubkasten- und Auszugssystem

Manufacturer
allmilmö–Zeiler Möbelwerk GmbH & Co. KG,
Zeil am Main, Germany
In-house design
Web
www.allmilmoe.com

a-Box is an elegant and at the same time functional drawer and pull-out system. The drawers and pull-outs are made of four mitred side parts, which are 10 mm thick. Three different heights allow full use of the cabinet interior. The system runs on undermount glides and features a soft closing system, offering much comfort. Customers can choose between four different surface finishes: white, metal black, real wood veneer and stainless steel decor.

Statement by the jury
This functionally well-devised drawer and pull-out system meets many requirements and offers high ease of use.

a-Box ist ein elegantes und zugleich funktionelles Schubkasten- und Auszugssystem. Die Schubkästen und Auszüge sind aus 10 mm starken Seitenteilen gefertigt, die vierseitig auf Gehrung gearbeitet wurden. Drei verschiedene Höhen ermöglichen die vollständige Nutzung des Schrankinnenraums. Auf Unterflurschienen laufend und mit gedämpftem Einzug ausgestattet, bietet das System viel Komfort. Je nach Kundenwunsch stehen vier verschiedene Oberflächen zur Option: Weiß, Metallschwarz, Echtholzfurnier oder Edelstahllook.

Begründung der Jury
Das funktional durchdachte Schubkasten- und Auszugssystem erfüllt viele Anforderungen und bietet einen hohen Bedienkomfort.

MATA
Cutlery Insert
Organisationssystem für Schubkästen

Manufacturer
Dirks GmbH & Co.KG,
Vlotho, Germany
Design
byform design
(Thorsten Rosenstengel),
Bielefeld, Germany
Web
www.dirks-kunststoff.de
www.byform.de

The Mata organisation system is a cutlery insert which can be locked in any position. All compartments are individually adjustable in size. They can be set by simply moving metal brackets on a high quality magnetic mat. With regard to the use of materials and design, the system is reduced to its basic functions. The efficient use of space and the simple assembly of the dividing elements provide high practical value.

Statement by the jury
In line with an impressive functionality, this organisation system for drawers features a puristic overall appearance.

Das Organisationssystem Mata ist ein stufenlos zu arretierender Besteckeinsatz für Schubladen. Alle Fächer sind in der Größe individuell anpassbar und durch einfaches Verschieben der Metallwinkel auf einer hochwertigen Magnetunterlage einzustellen. Hinsichtlich Materialeinsatz und Linienführung ist das System auf das Wesentliche reduziert. Die effiziente Nutzung des Raums und eine einfache Montage der Streben gewährleisten einen hohen Gebrauchswert.

Begründung der Jury
Im Einklang mit einer überzeugenden Funktionalität zeigt dieses Organisationssystem für Schubkästen ein puristisches Gesamtbild.

Meisterstück profession +
Cooking Centre
Kochcenter

Manufacturer
Küppersbusch Hausgeräte GmbH,
Gelsenkirchen, Germany
Design
Keicheldesign
(Klaus Keichel),
Düsseldorf, Germany
Web
www.kueppersbusch-hausgeraete.de

This gourmet cooking centre was
inspired by the fine restaurant cuisine
and offers an innovative concept of
integrated kitchen islands. Demanding
customers, such as top chefs, can
arrange their kitchen according to their
wishes: a 90 cm wide maxi oven, an
induction hob, a Tepan Yaki or lava stone
grill as well as a wok hob and warming
drawers are some of the features that
are available.

Statement by the jury
Due to its monolithic presence, the
cooking centre attracts everyone's
attention and becomes a compact
centre of the kitchen.

Inspiriert von der gehobenen Restaurant-
küche bietet das Gourmet-Kochcenter ein
innovatives Konzept integrierter Kochin-
seln. Anspruchsvolle Kunden können sich,
wie es auch Spitzenköche machen, ihre
Küche nach eigenen Wünschen zusammenstellen lassen: Ein 90 cm breiter
Maxibackofen, ein Induktionskochfeld, ein
Teppan Yaki- oder Lavastein-Grill sowie
Wok-Mulden und Wärmeschubladen sind
einige der Ausstattungsmöglichkeiten, die
zur Auswahl stehen.

Begründung der Jury
Aufgrund seiner monolithischen Präsenz
zieht das Kochcenter alle Blicke auf sich
und wird zum kompakten Mittelpunkt der
Küche.

Kitchen furniture

Kochwagen®

Manufacturer
Kreativzentrum Peter Gregor,
Berlin, Germany
In-house design
Peter Gregor
Web
www.kochwagen.de

This cooking trolley offers increased mobility. Each cooking trolley is made in single-item production and can be adapted to individual needs. The hand-made chassis is made of high-strength aluminium and is complemented with a worktop made of selected types of solid wood. The flexibly placeable cooking furniture features high quality gas hobs, which are connected to a customary gas cylinder.

Mehr Mobilität in der Küche bietet der Kochwagen. Jeder Kochwagen ist eine Einzelanfertigung und kann auf individuelle Wünsche abgestimmt werden. Das von Hand gefertigte Chassis besteht aus einer hochfesten Aluminium-Legierung und wird von einer Arbeitsplatte aus ausgesuchtem Massivholz vervollständigt. Das flexibel platzierbare Kochmöbel ist mit hochwertigen Gas-Kochmulden, die mit einer handelsüblichen Gasflasche verbunden sind, ausgestattet.

Statement by the jury
This custom-made cooking trolley offers high practical use. Thanks to the use of different materials, it can be adapted to particular kitchen interiors.

Begründung der Jury
Der individuell gefertigte Kochwagen bietet einen hohen Gebrauchswert und lässt sich in seiner Materialgebung dem jeweiligen Kücheninterieur anpassen.

Flex
Kitchen Unit
Küchenblock

Manufacturer
Xiamen Solux Industries Co., Ltd.,
Xiamen, China
In-house design
Tang Qinfeng, Wang Quanlao,
Yin Yanmei, Wang Min, Chen Yiying
Web
www.solux.com.cn
Honourable Mention

With its complex design, Flex enables multi-functional use in the smallest space. For cooking, the table cover is pushed aside and the kitchen tap is taken out so that the cooking area is ready for use. When there is no cooking to be done, the table cover is on top and the kitchen cabinet turns into a decorative table. The design of the unit base is not only convenient and functional but also plain and space-saving.

Statement by the jury
This functionally designed kitchen unit offers a space-saving solution for limited living space.

Mit seiner komplexen Gestaltung ermöglicht Flex eine multifunktionale Nutzung auf kleinstem Raum. Zum Kochen wird die Tischplatte beiseite geschoben, die Küchenarmatur hervorgeholt und somit ist der Kochbereich einsatzbereit. Wenn nicht gekocht wird, liegt die Abdeckplatte obenauf und der Küchenblock verwandelt sich in einen dekorativen Tisch. Der Unterschrank ist nicht nur komfortabel und praktisch, sondern zudem schlicht und platzsparend konzipiert.

Begründung der Jury
Dieser funktional durchdachte Küchenblock bietet eine platzsparende Lösung für einen begrenzten Wohnraum.

A1
Multifunctional Sink
Multifunktionale Spüle

Manufacturer
Zhejiang Marssenger
Kitchenware Co., Ltd.,
Jiaxing, China
In-house design
Xiangcheng Zhang
Web
www.marssenger.com

A1 is a sink which is integrated into a kitchen unit and can be closed with a cover when not in use. Thus, an additional worktop is created and kitchen space can be used flexibly. The handmade stainless steel sink was designed for the Asian market and is equipped with useful accessories. Innovative features such as a small electric kettle, a water filter and a waste processor complement the operating concept.

Statement by the jury
This multifunctional sink impresses as a practical product solution for kitchens with limited space.

A1 ist eine in die Küchenzeile integrierte Spüle, die bei Nichtgebrauch mit einem Deckel verschlossen werden kann. Somit entsteht eine zusätzliche Arbeitsfläche und der Küchenraum wird flexibel genutzt. Die für den asiatischen Markt konzipierte Edelstahlspüle ist handgefertigt und mit praktischem Zubehör ausgestattet: Innovative Funktionen wie ein kleiner elektrischer Wasserkocher, ein Wasserfilter sowie ein Müllprozessor ergänzen das Bedienkonzept.

Begründung der Jury
Die multifunktional nutzbare Spüle überzeugt als praktische Produktlösung für Küchen mit wenig Platz.

X7
Cooking Unit
Kocheinheit

Manufacturer
Zhejiang Marssenger
Kitchenware Co., Ltd.,
Jiaxing, China
In-house design
Xiangcheng Zhang
Web
www.marssenger.com

This cooking unit integrates the functions of a hood, a gas stove and a disinfection cabinet to meet the needs of Chinese consumers. The modular design allows easy removal of individual elements such as oil screen, cooktop, turbine or control panel for regular maintenance. A Teflon coating and the surface finishing of the stainless steel prevent soiling and fingerprints.

Statement by the jury
This multi-functional cooking unit offers high ease of use. In addition, high quality materials provide for a high-contrast overall look.

Diese Kocheinheit vereint die Funktionen einer Dunstabzugshaube, eines Gasherds und eines Desinfektions-Schranks in einem Gerät und erfüllt so die Bedürfnisse der chinesischen Verbraucher. Das modulare Design ermöglicht den leichten Ausbau einzelner Elemente wie Ölsieb, Platte, Turbine oder Bedienpanel zur regelmäßigen Wartung. Eine Teflon-Beschichtung sowie eine Oberflächenveredelung des Edelstahls verhindern Verschmutzungen und Fingerabdrücke.

Begründung der Jury
Diese multifunktionale Kocheinheit bietet einen hohen Bedienkomfort. Zudem sorgen hochwertige Materialien für ein kontrastreiches Gesamtbild.

CRISTADUR® Mono D-100

Kitchen Sink
Küchenspüle

Manufacturer
Schock GmbH,
Regen, Germany
Design
Mukomelov Studio
(Aleksandr Mukomelov),
Simferopol, Ukraine
Web
www.schock.de
www.mukomelov.com

The Mono D-100 kitchen sink was designed for kitchens where space is limited. Thanks to its flat sides, this kitchen sink is suitable for installation both on and under the worktop. The patented Cristadur material is pleasing to the touch and features high performance capabilities and dirt resistance. The concept is complemented by practical accessories such as a wooden chopping board and a pull-out colander.

Die Küchenspüle Mono D-100 wurde für Küchen mit wenig Platz konzipiert. Sie kann aufgrund ihrer flachen Seiten sowohl als Aufsatz als auch als Unterbauspüle in die Arbeitsplatte integriert werden. Das patentierte Material Christadur zeichnet sich durch seine angenehme Haptik, eine hohe Funktionsfähigkeit sowie einen Abperleffekt aus. Praktische Zubehörartikel wie ein Holzschneidbrett oder eine Resteschale runden das Konzept ab.

Statement by the jury
This compact kitchen sink is characterised by clear lines and corners, a prominently positioned overflow and surfaces that are pleasing to the touch.

Begründung der Jury
Eine klare Linienführung, ein auffälliger Überlauf sowie eine haptisch angenehme Oberfläche charakterisieren diese kompakte Küchenspüle.

RODI ART
Sink
Spüle

Manufacturer
RODI, Sinks and Ideas,
Eixo (Aveiro), Portugal
In-house design
Ana Silva, Claudia Felgar,
Fábio Duarte
Web
www.rodi.pt

The Rodi Art sink made of brushed stainless steel is characterised by a minimalist style. At a height of 50 mm, its plain yet robust shape shows to particular advantage. The bowl with a small volume of 500 x 400 x 200 mm is completed by a rectangular outlet and a rectangular overflow. For ecological reasons, recycled stainless steel is largely used in the production.

Die Spüle Rodi Art aus gebürstetem Edelstahl zeichnet sich durch eine minimalistische Formensprache aus. Ihre schlichte und dennoch robuste Form wird durch eine Höhe von 50 mm verstärkt zur Geltung gebracht. Das Becken mit einem kleinen Volumen von 500 x 400 x 200 mm wird mit einem rechteckigen Ventil und einem rechteckigen Überlauf vervollständigt. Aus ökologischen Überlegungen wird bei der Herstellung zum größten Teil recycelter Edelstahl verwendet.

Statement by the jury
The overall timeless and elegant appearance of this sink, which features a centrally positioned bowl, emphasises its high quality.

Begründung der Jury
Das zeitlos elegante Gesamtbild dieser Spüle, die mit einem mittig platzierten Becken ausgestattet ist, betont deren Hochwertigkeit.

BLANCOATTIKA
Kitchen Sink
Küchenspüle

Manufacturer
BLANCO GmbH + Co KG,
Oberderdingen, Germany
In-house design
Brigitte Ziemann
Web
www.blanco-germany.com/de

Authentic material aesthetics and striking manufacture features characterise the Blancoattika kitchen sink. The outstanding rim design with its solid appeal and delicately shaped corner radii serves as a formal leitmotif. It functionally defines the active zone of the wet working area. Thanks to the interplay of a lowerable tap and a movable chopping board, made of a high quality ash compound, the sit-on bowl can be covered.

Authentische Materialästhetik und ausgeprägte Manufaktur-Merkmale kennzeichnen die Küchenspüle Blancoattika. Die außergewöhnliche Randgestaltung mit ihrer massiven Anmutung und den filigran gebogenen Eckradien dient als formales Leitmotiv und grenzt funktional die Aktivzone des Nassarbeitsbereichs ab. Durch das Zusammenspiel von absenkbarer Armatur und verschiebbarem Arbeitsbrett aus hochwertigem Esche-Compound lässt sich das Aufsatzbecken abdecken.

Statement by the jury
A minimalist formal style unifies the flexible components of this kitchen sink, creating a striking overall impression.

Begründung der Jury
Eine minimalistische Formensprache vereint die flexiblen Bestandteile dieser Küchenspüle zu einem charakteristischen Gesamtbild.

Bossan SCM–BSA–C608S
Food Purification Sink
Spüle zum Säubern
von Lebensmitteln

Manufacturer
China National Food (Beijing) Purification
Technology Development Co., Ltd.,
Beijing, China
In-house design
Xinsheng Shi
Web
www.cfcjh.com
Honourable Mention

With its satin finish and the asymmetric bowl, this handcrafted stainless steel sink shows an original stylistic language. A hydroxy purification technology is used for the hygienically impeccable cleaning of food. It removes chemical residues from agriculture, germs and other harmful residues when rinsing. Like a cascade, the filtered water pours out into the left sink.

Das handgefertigte Spülbecken aus Edelstahl zeigt mit seiner satinierten Oberfläche und den asymmetrischen Becken eine originelle Formensprache. Zum hygienisch einwandfreien Säubern von Nahrungsmitteln kommt eine Hydroxy-Reinigungstechnologie zum Einsatz. Diese entfernt beim Abspülen die chemischen Rückstände aus der Landwirtschaft, Keime und andere schädliche Rückstände. Wie ein Wasserfall ergießt sich das gefilterte Wasser in das linke Spülbecken.

Statement by the jury
This sink is characterised by a high practical use. Its innovative technology ensures hygienic food preparation.

Begründung der Jury
Ein hoher Gebrauchswert zeichnet diese Spüle aus, ihre innovative Technologie gewährleistet eine hygienische Zubereitung von Speisen.

Franke Sinos SNX
Sink
Spüle

Manufacturer
Franke Küchentechnik AG,
Aarburg, Switzerland
In-house design
Christian Bomatter
Web
www.franke.ch

The Sinos stainless steel sink is suitable for flush mounting or to mount from above. The design concept picks up the trend toward organic shapes, curved contours create a contemporary interpretation of the retro style. The chopping board made of antibacterial material is another eye-catcher, embellished with a twine pattern. A matching tap completes the overall appearance.

Statement by the jury
Sink, chopping board and tap join together to form an aesthetic overall picture. The rounded edges underscore the elegant appearance.

Die Edelstahlspüle Sinos eignet sich für den flächenbündigen Einbau sowie den Einbau von oben. Das Gestaltungskonzept greift den Trend zu organischen Formen auf, mit geschwungenen Konturen entsteht eine zeitgemäße Interpretation des Retro-Stils. Ein weiterer Blickfang ist das Rüstbrett aus antibakteriellem Material, verziert mit einem Ranken-Muster. Das Gesamtbild wird durch eine passende Armatur abgerundet.

Begründung der Jury
Spüle, Schneidbrett und Armatur fügen sich zu einem ästhetischen Gesamtbild zusammen. Die abgerundeten Ecken unterstreichen die elegante Anmutung.

Eisinger Design-Line EDX
Sink
Spüle

Manufacturer
Franke Küchentechnik AG,
Aarburg, Switzerland
In-house design
Christian Bomatter
Web
www.franke.ch

Style and perfection are the principal elements of the Design-Line sink which is suitable for inset-, under-, as well as flush mounting. Its 12 mm flanges set off the sink edge. It takes one click to open and to close the patented push-button waste. The hygienic overflow outlet harmonises with the square waste outlet, and the chopping board with integrated hygiene function provides permanent protection against bacteria.

Statement by the jury
The visually harmonious interplay of sink, fittings and accessories has a high aesthetic appeal.

Stil und Perfektion prägen die Spüle der Design-Line, die sich sowohl von unten, von oben und flächenbündig einbauen lässt. Radien von 12 mm schmeicheln dem Spülbeckenrand. Das patentierte Druckknopfventil lässt sich mit einem Klick bequem öffnen und schließen. Harmonisch passt sich das hygienische Überlaufventil dem rechteckigen Bodenablauf an. Das Rüstbrett mit integrierter Hygienefunktion schützt dauerhaft vor Bakterien.

Begründung der Jury
Ein hohes Maß an Ästhetik vermittelt das visuell ausgewogene Zusammenspiel von Spülbecken, Armatur und Zubehör.

Nevada 18-30
Sink Series
Spülen-Serie

Manufacturer
Reginox B.V.,
Rijssen, Netherlands
In-house design
Wim Ter Steege
Web
www.reginox.com

The Nevada sink series comes with an aesthetic draining board and a 10 mm corner radius. Its tight, weld-free corner processing allows easy cleaning of the sink unit. The square basket strainer and the overflow provide for a homogenous overall effect. Nevada is available as a single bowl or double bowl unit both with draining board and as left- or right-sided version.

Statement by the jury
The lines of this sink series achieve a formal lightness that is consistent with its elaborate functionality.

Mit einer ästhetischen Abtropffläche und einem 10-mm-Eckradius präsentiert sich die Spülen-Serie Nevada. Dank ihrer straffen, schweißnahtfreien Eckenverarbeitung lässt sich die Spüleinheit problemlos reinigen. Das viereckige Korbventil sorgt gemeinsam mit dem Überlauf für eine homogene Gesamtwirkung. Nevada ist als Einzelspüle mit Abtropffläche und als Doppelspüle mit Abtropffläche erhältlich, beide Ausführungen sind links- und rechtsseitig lieferbar.

Begründung der Jury
Die Linienführung dieser Spülen-Serie erreicht eine formale Leichtigkeit, die im Einklang mit der ausgereiften Funktionalität steht.

Texas Tapwing
Texas Hahnlochbank
Sink
Spüle

Manufacturer
Reginox B.V.,
Rijssen, Netherlands
In-house design
Wim Ter Steege
Web
www.reginox.com

The Texas sink is made of brushed stainless steel. Formally, the characteristic tapwing was kept extra small. The slim silhouette of the tap harmonises particularly well with the 10 mm radius of the sink corners. They are pressed into the sink in one piece so that no welds were needed. The combination of kitchen tap and brushed stainless steel sink gives the kitchen a radiant look.

Statement by the jury
As an aesthetic product solution with little space requirement, the Texas sink achieves a purist, stringent style.

Die Spüle Texas ist aus gebürstetem Edelstahl gefertigt. Formal charakteristisch wurde die Hahnlochbank extra klein gehalten. Die schlanke Silhouette der Armatur harmoniert ausgewogen mit dem 10-mm-Radius der Spülbeckenecken. Diese sind in die Spüle am Stück eingepresst, sodass auf Schweißnähte verzichtet werden konnte. Die Kombination von Küchenarmatur und Spüle aus gebürstetem Edelstahl verleiht der Küche eine strahlende Anmutung.

Begründung der Jury
Als ästhetische Produktlösung mit wenig Flächenbedarf zeigt die Spüle Texas eine puristische, stringent durchdachte Formensprache.

Pebel
**Kitchen Sink
Product Range**
Küchenspülen-
Produktreihe

Manufacturer
Franke,
Falkirk, GB
In-house design
Tommy Paton
Design
Cramasie Ltd
(Simon Salter),
Edinburgh, GB
Web
www.franke.com
www.cramasie.com

The Pebel range of granite kitchen sinks captures the trend toward curvy retro lines. Elegant, minimalist details are incorporated into the sink edges and combined with flowing contours. The detailed design of the draining board takes advantage of the properties of the moulded material to enhance the overall appearance. The sink is available in a variety of different colours.

Statement by the jury
The haptically appealing materials and curvy contours of this kitchen sink product range form an impressive unit.

Die Granitspülenserie Pebel greift den Trend einer kurvenreichen Retro-Linienführung auf. Elegante, minimalistische Details zeigen sich an den Beckenkanten und werden mit fließenden Konturen kombiniert. Die detailliert ausgearbeitete Abtropffläche nutzt die Eigenschaften eines gegossenen Materials und unterstreicht das Gesamtbild. Die Spüle ist in verschiedenen Farben verfügbar.

Begründung der Jury
Haptisch reizvolle Materialien und schwungvolle Konturen fügen sich bei dieser Küchenspülen-Produktreihe zu einem überzeugenden Ganzen.

SE-211
Sink
Spüle

Manufacturer
Ningbo Oulin Kitchen Utensils Co., Ltd,
Ningbo, China
In-house design
Lei Gong, Zhaoqian Huang
Web
www.oulin-global.com

This stainless steel sink was designed for the Asian market and features an iconic cleaning technology which works like a water catalyst. Thus, pesticides and bacteria can be reliably removed. Fruit, vegetables, meat and rice are cleaned and sterilised. The sink is easy to use without producing any noise. This allows consumers to cook in a hygienic, healthy and easy manner.

Statement by the jury
In line with a well thought out functionality, the elegant lines of this sink are impressing.

Diese Spüle aus Edelstahl wurde für den asiatischen Markt konzipiert und bietet eine ionische Reinigungstechnologie, die wie ein Wasserkatalysator funktioniert. Somit können Pestizide und Bakterien zuverlässig beseitigt werden – Obst, Gemüse, Fleisch und Reis werden gereinigt und gleichzeitig sterilisiert. Die Spüle ist leise und leicht zu bedienen. Sie ermöglicht Verbrauchern ein hygienisches, gesundes und bequemes Zubereiten.

Begründung der Jury
Im Einklang mit einer gut durchdachten Funktionalität überzeugt bei dieser Spüle die Eleganz der Linienführung.

Genea 100
Kitchen Sink
Küchenspüle

Manufacturer
systemceram GmbH & Co. KG,
Siershahn, Germany
In-house design
Christoph Erll
Design
Pechmann Design
(Dieter Pechmann),
Essen, Germany
Web
www.systemceram.de

The harmonious design of this kitchen sink places high demands on ceramic shaping technology. The drain board runs off nearly horizontally at the sides, allowing a continuous plane to be formed when installed flush with the work surface. The two basins feature perfectly fitted standard stainless steel gastronomy containers. The basin in the middle allows vegetables and other cooked foods to be safely set down for drainage.

Die harmonische Gestaltung dieser Küchenspüle setzt hohe Ansprüche an die keramische Formgebung. So läuft die Abtropffläche seitlich gegen Null aus, sodass sie beim flächenbündigen Einbau mit der Arbeitsplatte eine durchgehende Ebene bildet. In beide Becken werden passgenau Standard-Gastronomiebehälter aus Edelstahl eingesetzt. Das mittig platzierte Becken eignet sich zum Abtropfen von Gemüse und anderem Gargut.

Statement by the jury
In combination with the drainage containers, this generously proportioned kitchen sink offers multi-functional usability.

Begründung der Jury
Diese großzügig proportionierte Küchenspüle ermöglicht im Zusammenspiel mit den Abtropfbehältern eine multifunktionale Nutzung.

BLANCOSAGA
Mixer Tap
Küchenarmatur

Manufacturer
BLANCO GmbH + Co KG,
Oberderdingen, Germany

In-house design
Brigitte Ziemann

Web
www.blanco-germany.com/de

reddot design award
best of the best 2013

Elegant control

Food preparation and cooking require a constant supply of water in the kitchen, which is why kitchen taps are undoubtedly at the heart of these tasks. Blancosaga mixers will surprise the user with an innovative mode of operation that create many exciting new experiences. To regulate the water manually, a cartridge has been concealed coaxially in the body of the spout. Water flow and temperature are regulated using a sleeve-like slide control, picked out in distinctive black, that allows for fine tuning. By moving the slide control backwards and forwards, users can regulate water flow. To achieve exactly the right temperature, the control is turned to the right or left. The design of the Blancosaga mixer has kept the technical appearance minimalist by manufacturing the body and spout from a single arched stainless-steel tube. The matt surface finish of gently brushed stainless steel combined with the matt black sleeve lends the mixer's technical appearance a simple elegance. The new, comfortable user concept of the Blancosaga kitchen tap is harmoniously combined with a design approach that visually highlights its versatility.

Elegante Steuerung

Für das Vorbereiten und Kochen wird in der Küche stetig Wasser benötigt, weshalb die Küchenarmatur unzweifelhaft den Mittelpunkt all dieser Arbeiten definiert. Die Küchenarmatur Blancosaga überrascht mit einer innovativen Bedientechnik, die dem Nutzer spannungsreiche neue Erfahrungen bietet. Eine Kartusche zur manuellen Wassersteuerung ist koaxial, im Auslaufkörper dieser Küchenarmatur liegend, versteckt. Die Wassermenge wie auch die Temperatur werden über einen markant schwarz abgesetzten Schieberegler gesteuert, der die Feinabstufung erlaubt. Mit einer Vorwärts- und Rückwärtsbewegung des Schiebereglers steuert der Nutzer die Wassermenge. Für eine punktgenaue Temperatureinstellung dreht er den Regler nach rechts oder links. Die technisch anmutende Form der Küchenarmatur Blancosaga ist gestalterisch auf ein Minimum reduziert. So werden ihr Standkörper und der Auslauf aus einem einzigen gebogenen Edelstahlrohr hergestellt. Die matte Oberflächengestaltung von sanft gebürstetem Edelstahl in Kombination mit der mattschwarzen Manschette verleiht ihrer technischen Anmutung zusätzlich eine schlichte Eleganz. Das neue und komfortable Bedienkonzept der Küchenarmatur Blancosaga verbindet sich so mit einer Formensprache, die ihre vielseitigen Möglichkeiten auf stimmige Weise visualisiert.

Statement by the jury

The innovative concept behind the operation of the Blancosaga kitchen tap is its most striking feature. Water flow and temperature can be regulated very precisely. The user will be impressed by the ease with which it is controlled. With its clear and minimalist form, as well as contrasting black sleeve this kitchen tap provides a highlight in any kitchen.

Begründung der Jury

Bei der Küchenarmatur Blancosaga beeindruckt das innovative Konzept ihrer Bedienung. Die Wassermenge wie auch die Temperatureinstellung lassen sich damit gezielt steuern; der Nutzer erlebt intensiv den Komfort dieser Art der Steuerung. Mit ihrer klaren und minimalistischen Formensprache sowie der kontrastreich schwarz abgesetzten Manschette setzt diese Küchenarmatur Akzente in der Küche.

Mixer taps

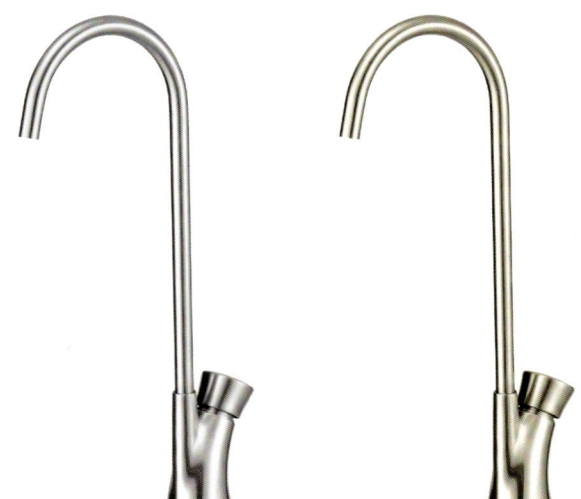

Tai Chi
Drinking Water Faucet
Trinkwasserhahn

Manufacturer
Shengtai Brassware Co., Ltd.,
Chang Hua, Taiwan
In-house design
JUSTIME Design Team
Web
www.justime.com

The designers of this faucet took their inspiration from the harmonious exercises of the Chinese martial art of Tai Chi. The faucet is available in two material versions and allows economical water consumption. On top of that, it is also suitable for public buildings. The faucet, which is made of recyclable stainless steel or copper, is durable and easy to clean, and its antimicrobial copper material kills bacteria and prevents contamination.

Statement by the jury
The curved Tai Chi faucet features a particularly elegant look and its purist lines stylishly emphasise the material.

Die Gestalter dieses Wasserhahns haben sich von den harmonischen Bewegungen der chinesischen Kampfkunst Tai Chi inspirieren lassen. Die in zwei Materialien erhältliche Armatur ermöglicht einen sparsamen Wasserverbrauch und eignet sich auch für den Einsatz in öffentlichen Gebäuden. Der Wasserhahn aus recycelbarem Edelstahl oder Kupfer ist langlebig und leicht zu reinigen. Die antimikrobielle Kupferbeschichtung tötet Bakterien ab und verhindert Verschmutzungen.

Begründung der Jury
Der geschwungene Wasserhahn Tai Chi wirkt ausgesprochen elegant. Seine puristisch anmutende Linienführung bringt das Material stilvoll zur Geltung.

BLANCOSEDA
Mixer Tap
Küchenarmatur

Manufacturer
BLANCO GmbH + Co KG,
Oberderdingen, Germany
In-house design
Brigitte Ziemann
Design
Uwe Spannagel™,
Cologne, Germany
Web
www.blanco-germany.com/de
www.uwespannagel.com

The Blancoseda mixer tap has filigree design features that go very well with small or single-bowl sinks. The clever swivel principle of the spout in vertical direction offers the possibility to fill even tall containers and ensures that there is no splashing in normal position. The combination of chrome and matt black in the surface creates an elegant tension in the minimalist mixer tap, which is composed of two cylindrical bodies.

Statement by the jury
In the Blancoseda mixer tap, a design concept is implemented that impresses by both form and function.

Blancoseda ist eine filigran gestaltete Küchenarmatur, die gut mit kleinen Spülen oder Einzelbecken kombiniert werden kann. Das raffinierte Schwenkprinzip des Auslaufs in vertikaler Richtung bietet die Möglichkeit, auch hohe Gefäße zu befüllen und sorgt in Normallage für spritzarmes Arbeiten. In der Oberflächenkombination von Chrom mit Mattschwarz erhält die minimalisierte Armatur, bestehend aus zwei zylindrischen Körpern, eine elegante Spannung.

Begründung der Jury
Bei der Küchenarmatur Blancoseda gelingt die Umsetzung einer Gestaltungsidee, die formal und funktional überzeugt.

GROHE Blue Mono
Water Filtration System
Wasserfiltersystem

Manufacturer
Grohe AG,
Düsseldorf, Germany
In-house design
Web
www.grohe.com

The Blue Mono water filtration system offers a smart alternative to buying bottled mineral water. The system provides freshly filtered and chilled table water, carbonated, medium or still, according to needs. The reduced stylistic idiom is based on carefully proportioned cylinders and an unadorned lever, which is arranged at right angles to the tap body. Clear icons indicate the carbonation levels. The ProGrip enhancement of the lever tip intuitively guides the hand of the user to the ergonomically best possible grip position.

Das Wasserfiltersystem Blue Mono bietet eine intelligente Alternative zum Kauf von in Flaschen abgefülltem Mineralwasser. Das System liefert frisch gefiltertes und gekühltes Tafelwasser, nach Wunsch sprudelnd, medium oder still. Die reduzierte Formensprache basiert auf sorgfältig proportionierten Zylindern und einem schnörkellosen Hebel, der rechtwinklig am Armaturenkörper ansetzt. Eindeutige Symbole kennzeichnen die Kohlensäurestufen. Die ProGrip-Veredelung der Hebelspitze führt die Hand des Bedieners intuitiv zur ergonomisch vorteilhaftesten Griffposition.

Statement by the jury
As an eco-friendly product concept, the Blue Mono water filtration system particularly scores with functionality and elegant lines.

Begründung der Jury
Als umweltfreundliche Produktidee punktet das Wasserfiltersystem Blue Mono vor allem durch seine Funktionalität und die elegante Linienführung.

Bauknecht BlackLine
Kitchen Appliance Product Range
Küchengeräte-Produktreihe

Manufacturer
Bauknecht Hausgeräte GmbH,
Stuttgart, Germany
In-house design
Vincenzo Gadaleta, Sander Brouwer
Web
www.bauknecht.de

The timeless aesthetics of the BlackLine kitchen appliance product range is based on the use of high quality materials. An especially designed black mirror glass highlights its superior character; in addition it is both especially high quality and durable. The BlackLine range comprises a built-in oven, a combined steamer, a microwave compact oven, a freezer, a cabinet refrigerator and two design hoods. All appliances are highly functional and harmoniously blend in with modern kitchen furniture.

Die zeitlose Ästhetik der BlackLine Küchengeräte-Produktreihe beruht auf der Verwendung hochwertiger Materialien. Ein eigens entwickeltes, schwarzes Spiegelglas betont den edlen Charakter und ist zudem besonders hochwertig und belastbar. Die BlackLine-Serie umfasst einen Einbau-Backofen, einen Kombi-Dampfgarer, einen Mikrowellen-Kompakt-Backofen, einen Gefrierschrank, einen Vollraumkühlschrank sowie zwei Design-hauben. Sämtliche Geräte bieten eine hohe Funktionalität und lassen sich harmonisch in eine zeitgemäße Kücheneinrichtung integrieren.

Statement by the jury
The stringent implementation of a striking design line characterises the homogenous overall picture of this kitchen appliance range.

Begründung der Jury
Die stringente Umsetzung einer markanten Gestaltungslinie prägt das homogene Gesamtbild dieser Küchengeräte-Serie.

Black Diamond
Built-in Appliance
Product Range
Einbau-Geräte-
Produktreihe

Manufacturer
Guangdong Midea
Microwave and Electrical
Appliances Manufacturing Co., Ltd.,
Guangdong, China
In-house design
Kim Jaehoon, Kim Woonhyong,
Zhu Zhi
Web
www.midea.com

Black Diamond is an innovative
combination of microwave and oven
with a built-in side-by-side refrigerator.
The aim is to create a simple but
luxurious overall picture. Atmospheric
lines frame the front panel, while the
diamond cut of the no fingerprint black
glass surface creates a strong contrast
of light and shadow. The dynamic LED
screen is easy to use.

Statement by the jury
The glossy glass front of this built-
in appliance product range creates a
luxurious impression. A purist design
with emotional appeal.

Black Diamond ist eine innovative Kombination aus Einbau-Mikrowelle und Backofen mit einem eingebauten Side-by-Side
Kühlschrank. Ziel ist es, einen schlichten
und gleichzeitig luxuriösen Gesamteindruck zu vermitteln. Stimmungsvolle Linien
umrahmen die Gerätefront, während der
Diamantenschliff des schwarzen Glases mit
seiner vor Fingerabdrücken geschützten
Oberfläche einen starken Kontrast aus
Licht und Schatten erzeugt. Bedienungs-
komfort bietet der dynamische LED-
Bildschirm.

Begründung der Jury
Die glänzende Glasfront vermittelt bei
dieser Einbau-Geräte-Produktreihe eine
luxuriöse Anmutung. Ein puristischer
Entwurf, der Emotionen weckt.

Scandinavia
Built-in Appliance
Product Range
Einbau-Geräte-
Produktreihe

Manufacturer
Guangdong Midea
Microwave and Electrical
Appliances Manufacturing Co., Ltd.,
Guangdong, China
In-house design
Kim Jaehoon, Cao Pei,
Kim Soyoung
Web
www.midea.com

The Scandinavia range of built-in
appliances includes a combination of
microwave and oven as well as a
side-by-side refrigerator. The unique
design is based on large surfaces made
of black glass. The handles, which are
made of aluminium and wood, support
a cosy facet. The intuitive-to-use
control panels create a calm, premium
impression that fits in well with
modern kitchen settings.

Statement by the jury
This product range is distinguished by
an independent formal vocabulary.
The white or black glass surface is an
appealing contrast.

Die Einbau-Geräte-Produktreihe Scandinavia umfasst eine Mikrowellen-Backofen-
Kombination und einen Side-by-Side
Kühlschrank. Die unverwechselbare Gestaltungslinie nutzt großflächiges schwarzes
Glas. Die Griffe aus Aluminium und Holz
tragen zu einem wohnlichen Eindruck bei.
Die Bedienfelder sind dank des Punkt-
Matrix-LED-Displays intuitiv nutzbar und
vermitteln eine ruhige und edle Anmutung,
die gut zu zeitgemäßen Küchenausstattun-
gen passt.

Begründung der Jury
Diese Produktreihe fällt aufgrund ihrer
eigenständigen Formensprache auf.
Stilistisch reizvoll hebt sich die weiße
oder schwarze Glasfläche hervor.

Bonbon
Built-in Appliance Product Range
Einbau-Geräte-Produktreihe

Manufacturer
Guangdong Midea
Microwave and Electrical
Appliances Manufacturing Co., Ltd.,
Guangdong, China
In-house design
Kim Soyoung, Kim Woonhyong,
Chen Hongmei
Web
www.midea.com

The Bonbon built-in appliance product range comprises a combination of microwave and oven as well as a side-by-side refrigerator. White tempered glass creates a pure but luxurious impression and handles, made of aluminium and wood, generate a homely atmosphere. The use of wood is the expression of a trendy design concept. The control panels have an invisible dot matrix LED display.

Statement by the jury
Details such as a handle bar in contrasting colours account for the visual appeal of this purist combination of appliances.

Die Einbau-Geräte-Produktreihe Bonbon umfasst eine Mikrowellen-Backofen-Kombination sowie einen Side-by-Side Kühlschrank. Das weiße Standard-Hartglas vermittelt einen schlichten und gleichzeitig luxuriösen Eindruck. Die Griffe aus einer Aluminium-Holz-Kombination erwecken eine wohnliche Anmutung. Der Einsatz von Holz dient dabei als Ausdruck eines trendbewussten Gestaltungskonzepts. Die Bedienfelder haben ein nicht sichtbares Dot-Matrix-LED-Display.

Begründung der Jury
Ansprechende Details wie eine farbig abgesetzte Griffleiste machen den visuellen Reiz dieser puristisch wirkenden Geräte-kombination aus.

DG 6800
Built-in Steam Oven
Einbau-Dampfgarer

Manufacturer
Miele & Cie. KG,
Gütersloh, Germany
In-house design
Web
www.miele.de

The DG 6800 is the premium model of the steam oven generation 6000. The device features the innovative MTouch control. Thanks to its MultiSteam technology, it achieves reliable cooking results. MultiSteam combines powerful steam output with a system that distributes steam through eight ports. The backlit module is integrated into the rear panel of the cooking chamber. A transparent plastic water container facilitates filling.

Statement by the jury
High functionality and technical precision are the characteristic features of this built-in steam oven. In addition, the front of the device has an appealingly elegant look.

Der DG 6800 ist die Premium-Ausführung der Dampfgarer-Generation 6000. Das Gerät umfasst eine innovative MTouch-Steuerung und liefert dank seiner MultiSteam-Technologie zuverlässige Gar-Ergebnisse. MultiSteam kombiniert eine leistungsstarke Dampferzeugung mit einer Dampfverteilung durch acht Dampfeinlässe. Das hinterleuchtete Modul ist an der Garraumrückwand platziert. Ein durchsichtiger Kunststoff-Wassertank vereinfacht die Befüllung.

Begründung der Jury
Eine hohe Funktionalität und technische Präzision zeichnen diesen Einbau-Dampfgarer aus, darüber hinaus wirkt die Gerätefront ansprechend elegant.

M 6260 TC
Built-in Microwave Oven
Einbau-Mikrowelle

Manufacturer
Miele & Cie. KG,
Gütersloh, Germany
In-house design
Web
www.miele.de

This built-in microwave oven features numerous automatic programmes for the preparation of various dishes. The innovative EasyControl system in the upper operating area offers a variety of useful advantages. The stainless steel cooking chamber in XL format has a 46-litre capacity and is equipped with LED lighting. With a diameter of 40 cm, the turntable allows the simultaneous use of containers of different size.

Statement by the jury
Coherently, the design of this built-in microwave device follows the independent style of the device series.

Diese Einbau-Mikrowelle verfügt über zahlreiche Automatikprogramme für die Zubereitung diverser Speisen. Eine Innovation ist die Easy-Control-Steuerung im oberen Bedienbereich, welche zahlreiche Vorteile bietet. Der Edelstahlgarraum im XL-Format verfügt über 46 Liter Volumen und ist mit einer LED-Beleuchtung ausgestattet. Mit einem Durchmesser von 40 cm erlaubt der Drehteller den gleichzeitigen Einsatz unterschiedlich großer Gefäße.

Begründung der Jury
Stringent führt die Gestaltung der Einbau-Mikrowelle die eigenständige Formensprache der Geräteserie fort.

Gen6000 PureLine
Built-in Appliance Product Range
Einbau-Geräte-Produktreihe

Manufacturer
Miele & Cie. KG,
Gütersloh, Germany
In-house design
Web
www.miele.de

The PureLine design concept for the generation 6000 built-in appliances realises a high proportion of glass in the fronts of the devices, creating timeless elegance. The CleanSteel stripes emphasise the horizontal alignment and support a harmonious combination of different devices of the product line. The handle is a striking element and seems to hover in front of the devices. The 6.2" TFT touch colour display, which is consistently used in this product range, simplifies operation.

Statement by the jury
The built-in appliances of this product range use an independent formal vocabulary which is consistent with their impressive functionality.

Das Gestaltungskonzept PureLine für die Einbau-Geräte-Generation 6000 setzt einen hohen Glasanteil in den Fronten um, was zeitlos elegant wirkt. Durch die CleanSteel-Streifen wird die horizontale Ausrichtung betont und die Geräte der Produktserie können harmonisch miteinander kombiniert werden. Als markantes Element scheint der Griff vor den Geräten zu schweben. Das übergreifend eingesetzte 6,2" TFT-Touch-Farbdisplay vereinfacht die Handhabung.

Begründung der Jury
Die Einbau-Geräte dieser Produktreihe zeigen eine eigenständige Formensprache, die mit der überzeugenden Funktionalität im Einklang steht.

Gen6000 ContourLine
Built-in Appliance Product Range
Einbau-Geräte-Produktreihe

Manufacturer
Miele & Cie. KG,
Gütersloh, Germany
In-house design
Web
www.miele.de

The ContourLine of the generation 6000 built-in appliances shows a precise interplay of glass and stainless steel. The stainless steel frame of the door has a traditional and yet timelessly elegant look. Thanks to the CleanSteel stripes in the panel, the appliances can be combined both horizontally as well as vertically. The door frame encloses and integrates the straight-lined handle. The touch controls and TFT displays simplify operation.

Statement by the jury
An appealing composition of materials determines the overall impression of this high-quality generation of built-in appliances.

Die Gestaltungslinie ContourLine der Einbau-Geräte-Generation 6000 zeigt ein präzises Zusammenspiel von Glas und Edelstahl, wobei der Edelstahlrahmen der Tür traditionell und dennoch zeitlos elegant wirkt. Die CleanSteel-Streifen in der Blende ermöglichen eine horizontale wie auch vertikale Gerätekombination. Der gradlinige Griff wird vom Türrahmen umschlossen und integriert. Die Touch-Bedienung und die TFT-Displays vereinfachen die Nutzung.

Begründung der Jury
Eine attraktive Materialzusammenstellung prägt das Gesamtbild dieser hochwertigen Einbau-Geräte-Generation.

Gen6000 Obsidian Black
Gen6000 Obsidianschwarz
Built-in Appliance Product Range
Einbau-Geräte-Produktreihe

Manufacturer
Miele & Cie. KG,
Gütersloh, Germany
In-house design
Web
www.miele.de

The Obsidian Black version for the generation 6000 built-in appliances achieves a homogenous overall appearance. Thanks to the black glass fronts, the appliances have a puristic and timelessly elegant look. A high proportion of glass allows a harmonious combination of various appliances. Rich in contrast, the eye-catching aluminium handle seems to hover in front of the appliances. The 6.2" TFT touch colour display, which is consistently used in all appliances, can be operated intuitively.

Statement by the jury
Boasting high quality, the black version of this product range introduces visual aspects and stands out sharply from the kitchen interior.

Mit der Farbvariante Obsidianschwarz vermittelt die Einbau-Geräte-Generation 6000 ein homogenes Gesamtbild, das aufgrund der schwarzen Vollglasfronten puristisch und zeitlos elegant wirkt. Durch einen hohen Glasanteil wird eine harmonische Kombination der Geräte ermöglicht. Kontrastreich scheint der markante Aluminiumgriff vor den Geräten zu schweben. Das übergreifend eingesetzte 6,2" TFT-Touch-Farbdisplay kann intuitiv bedient werden.

Begründung der Jury
Qualitätsbewusst setzt die schwarze Variante dieser Einbau-Geräte einen visuellen Akzent und hebt sich aus dem Kücheninterieur markant hervor.

Electrolux 3D Oven
Oven Product Range
Backofen-Produktreihe

Manufacturer
Electrolux Major Appliances EMEA,
Stockholm, Sweden
In-house design
Electrolux Group Design EMEA
Web
www.electrolux.com
www.electrolux.it

The exceptional design concept of this oven product range is characterised by a stainless steel control panel behind glass. There, white LED icons as well as several operating elements such as touch keys, knobs and buttons are accommodated. Using graphic patterns, the diversity of functions is displayed on the door. Other aspects such as the especially large baking trays, flexible telescopic runners and a soft-closing door system round off the concept.

Das exklusive Gestaltungskonzept dieser Backofen-Produktreihe wird durch eine Edelstahl-Bedienblende unter Glas geprägt. Hier befinden sich weiße LED-Symbole und verschiedene Bedienelemente wie Sensortasten, Drehknöpfe und Tasten. Die Vielfalt der Funktionen wird mittels Grafiken auf der Tür abgebildet. Weitere Aspekte wie besonders große Backbleche, flexible Teleskopschienen und der gedämpfte Türschließmechanismus runden das Konzept ab.

Electrolux Compact
Compact Product Range
Kompakt-Produktreihe

Manufacturer
Electrolux Major Appliances EMEA,
Stockholm, Sweden
In-house design
Electrolux Group Design EMEA
Web
www.electrolux.com
www.electrolux.it

This product range consists of compact ovens, coffee makers and warming drawers. The combination of the required appliances can be aligned in horizontal as well as in vertical direction to other built-in kitchen appliances of the Inspiration Range. The control panel behind glass creates a distinctive image that is complemented by white LED icons as well as touch keys, knobs and buttons in a coherent way.

Diese Produktreihe besteht unter anderem aus Kompaktbacköfen, Kaffeemaschinen und Warmhalteschubladen. Die Kombination der benötigten Geräte kann sowohl in horizontaler als auch in vertikaler Ausrichtung zu anderen Kücheneinbaugeräten der Inspiration Range erfolgen. Die Bedienblende unter Glas erzeugt ein charakteristisches Bild, welches durch weiße LED-Symbole sowie Sensortasten, Drehknöpfe und Tasten sinnvoll ergänzt wird.

Statement by the jury
Formally expressive and functionally mature, this compact product range allows various combinations of appliances.

Begründung der Jury
Formal ausdrucksstark und funktional ausgereift präsentiert sich diese Kompakt-Produktreihe, welche unterschiedliche Gerätekombinationen ermöglicht.

Grundig GEZM 47000 B
Built-in Multifunction Oven
Einbau-Multifunktionsbackofen

Manufacturer
Arçelik A.S.,
Istanbul, Turkey
In-house design
Arçelik Industrial Design Team
Design
Designaffairs GmbH,
Munich, Germany
Web
www.arcelik.com.tr
www.designaffairs.com

This built-in multifunction oven features a linear stainless steel look in all its control panels, representative of the product-family design language. It consumes ten per cent less energy than products in the A energy efficiency class and is astonishingly quiet. The operational noise level has been reduced to 46 dB(A). With its 75 litres of net oven capacity, this oven offers generous space, while its "nano" coating prevents residues accumulating on the inner door.

Statement by the jury
The distinctive and elegant look of the front panel visualises the convincing functionality of this built-in oven.

Der Einbau-Multifunktionsbackofen zeigt mit seinen linear angeordneten Edelstahl-applikationen eine markentypische Formensprache. Er verbraucht zehn Prozent weniger Energie als Produkte der Energieeffizienzklasse A und ist bemerkenswert leise. Die Betriebsgeräusche konnten auf 46 dB(A) verringert werden. Mit einer Netto-Ofenkapazität von 75 Litern bietet der Backofen viel Platz, zudem verhindert die „Nano"-Beschichtung Schmutzablagerungen an der Innentür.

Begründung der Jury
Eine markante und zugleich elegante Gerätefront visualisiert die überzeugende Funktionalität dieses Einbau-Backofens.

Grundig GEBM 46000 B
Built-in Multifunction Oven
Einbau-Multifunktionsbackofen

Manufacturer
Arçelik A.S.,
Istanbul, Turkey
In-house design
Arçelik Industrial Design Team
Design
Designaffairs GmbH,
Munich, Germany
Web
www.arcelik.com.tr
www.designaffairs.com

This electronic multifunction oven follows a minimalist design concept. The built-in device consumes 20 per cent less energy than products of the A energy efficiency class and is two times quieter than previous models, reaching a maximum noise level of 46 dB(A). This oven has a net oven capacity of 65 litres and features a Cooking Guide with various dishes from international cuisine. Its "nano" coating surface prevents the accumulation of residues.

Statement by the jury
The consistent implementation of the brand's distinctive design principle lends this electronic multifunction oven a high degree of recognition.

Der Multifunktionsbackofen folgt einem minimalistischen Gestaltungskonzept. Das Einbaugerät verbraucht 20 Prozent weniger Strom als Produkte der Energieeffizienzklasse A und arbeitet zweimal leiser als Vorgängermodelle, es wird ein Maximalwert von 46 dB(A) erreicht. Der Backofen hat eine Netto-Ofenkapazität von 65 Litern und bietet zudem Garanleitungen für internationale Gerichte. Eine „Nano"-Beschichtung verhindert die Ablagerung von Speiseresten.

Begründung der Jury
Die stringente Umsetzung eines markentypischen Gestaltungsprinzips sorgt bei diesem Multifunktionsbackofen für einen hohen Wiedererkennungswert.

KQD84-R08K
Electric Oven
Elektro-Backofen

Manufacturer
Ningbo Oulin Kitchen Utensils Co., Ltd,
Ningbo, China
In-house design
Hao Chen, Lingli Guo
Web
www.oulin-global.com

This electric oven offers eight intelligent modes of temperature control to meet different cooking requirements. As a further feature, a rotary motor allows uniform barbecuing on all sides. The black tempered glass and the handle, which is made of aluminium alloy, add a discreet, at the same time elegant look. By contrast, the red LED display indicates the programme functions. The oven door is equipped with a child-proof lock.

Statement by the jury
High functionality characterises this electric oven. In addition, an independent stylistic vocabulary emphasises its high quality.

Der Elektro-Backofen bietet acht intelligente Modi der Temperaturkontrolle, um unterschiedlichen Kochanforderungen gerecht zu werden. Als weitere Funktion ermöglicht ein Drehmotor das gleichmäßige Grillen von allen Seiten. Das schwarze Hartglas sowie der Griff aus einer Aluminiumlegierung wirken dezent und gleichzeitig elegant. Im Kontrast dazu zeigen rote LEDs die Programmfunktionen. Die Backofentür ist mit einer Kindersicherung ausgestattet.

Begründung der Jury
Eine hohe Funktionalität zeichnet diesen Elektro-Backofen aus, zudem unterstreicht eine eigenständige Formensprache dessen Hochwertigkeit.

Siemens HB76GB560
Built-in Oven
Einbau-Backofen

Manufacturer
Siemens-Electrogeräte GmbH,
Munich, Germany
In-house design
Frank Rieser
Web
www.siemens-home.de

This built-in oven provides a simple, directly controllable operating concept featuring a 3-fold display. The brand-specific impression is characterised by the specific design of stainless steel trims in the shape of a portal. The control panel is split into two parts and supports brand recognition. The innovative design concept includes the integration of the door into the frame of the appliance and improves the lateral connection of the oven to the other kitchen furniture.

Statement by the jury
High ease of use and a consistently distinctive formal vocabulary characterise this built-in oven.

Dieser Einbau-Backofen bietet ein einfaches, direkt steuerbares Bedienkonzept mit einem 3-fachen Display. Das markenspezifische Gesamtbild wird durch die besondere Gestaltung der Edelstahlapplikationen in Form eines Portals geprägt. Auch die zweigeteilte Bedienblende dient als Wiedererkennbarkeits-Parameter. Das neuartige Aufbaukonzept umfasst die Einbindung der Tür in den Geräterahmen und verbessert die seitliche Anbindung des Backofens zu anderen Küchenmöbeln.

Begründung der Jury
Ein gehobener Bedienkomfort und eine konsequent markante Formensprache zeichnen diesen Einbau-Backofen aus.

OB60SL11DEPX1
Built-in Oven 60 cm
Einbau-Backofen 60 cm

Manufacturer
Fisher & Paykel Appliances Ltd,
Auckland, New Zealand
In-house design
Fisher & Paykel Design Team
Web
www.fisherpaykel.co.nz

Black, reflective glass and stainless steel finishes give this 60 cm wide built-in oven a distinctive appearance. It offers a usable capacity of 77 litres with maximised height to enable multi-shelf cooking. Smooth and balanced controls enable precise temperature adjustment. The active venting system ensures an optimised balance between reliable cooking performance, condensation management and energy consumption.

Statement by the jury
This built-in oven, devised for the Australian market, gives proof of an impressive design concept with regard to form and function.

Schwarzes, verspiegeltes Glas und Edelstahlapplikationen verleihen diesem 60 cm breiten Einbau-Backofen eine auffällige Anmutung. Er bietet eine Nutzkapazität von 77 Litern sowie eine maximierte Höhe zum Backen auf mehreren Ebenen. Glatte und ausgewogene Regler ermöglichen eine präzise Einstellung der Temperatur. Das aktive Entlüftungssystem sorgt für ein gutes Gleichgewicht aus zuverlässiger Kochleistung, Kondensationsmanagement und Energieverbrauch.

Begründung der Jury
Der für den australischen Markt konzipierte Einbau-Backofen stellt ein formal wie funktional überzeugendes Gestaltungskonzept unter Beweis.

Zanussi New Quadro Oven
Oven Product Range
Backofen-Produktreihe

Manufacturer
Electrolux Major Appliances EMEA,
Stockholm, Sweden
In-house design
Electrolux Group Design EMEA
Web
www.electrolux.com
www.electrolux.it

These easy-to-use ovens take their cues from the manufacturer's own Quadro product range. Beside the typical arc-shaped handle, the amber LEDs as well as the black tinted glass of the dot patterned doors are distinctive design elements. Intuitive control panels, large knobs and touch controls allow for easy programme selection with distinctive symbols in a clear architectural framework.

Statement by the jury
In this oven product range, functionality, modern configuration details and a striking overall impression stand out.

Diese einfach zu bedienenden Backöfen sind an die herstellereigene Quadro-Produktreihe angelehnt. Charakteristische Gestaltungselemente sind, neben dem typischen Griff in Bogenform, die bernstein-farbene LED-Anzeige sowie das schwarz getönte Türglas mit Punktmuster. Intuitive Bedienblenden, große Knöpfe und Touch Controls ermöglichen eine Programmaus-wahl mittels unverwechselbaren Symbolen in einem klaren architektonischen Rahmen.

Begründung der Jury
Funktionalität, zeitgemäße Ausstattungs-details sowie ein markantes Gesamtbild zeichnen diese Backofen-Produktreihe aus.

Zanussi New Quadro
Compact Product Range
Kompakt-Produktreihe

Manufacturer
Electrolux Major Appliances EMEA,
Stockholm, Sweden
In-house design
Electrolux Group Design EMEA
Web
www.electrolux.com
www.electrolux.it

The objective of a trouble-free and effort-less life at home characterises the design concept of the New Quadro compact product range. The ovens are distinguished by an easy-to-use control panel, large knobs and touch controls. The vertical alignment of the short handle sets itself apart from contrasting surfaces, which creates an architectural impression. In addition, the amber LEDs and black glass with dot pattern round off the concept.

Statement by the jury
In limited space, the characteristic overall appearance and the high practical value of this compact product range are impressive.

Die Zielvorstellung eines mühelosen Lebens zu Hause prägt das Gestaltungskonzept der New Quadro-Kompakt-Produktreihe. Die Backöfen zeichnen sich durch einfach zu handhabende Bedienblenden, große Knöpfe und Touch Controls aus. Eine architektoni-sche Anmutung erzielen die kontrastreichen Oberflächen, von denen sich der vertikale Kurzgriff abhebt. Zudem vervollständigen bernsteinfarbene LEDs sowie schwarzes Glas mit Punktmuster das Konzept.

Begründung der Jury
Auf begrenztem Raum überzeugen das charakteristische Gesamtbild und der hohe Gebrauchswert dieser Kompakt-Produkt-reihe.

Siemens HB73GB550
Built-in Oven
Einbau-Backofen

Manufacturer
Siemens-Electrogeräte GmbH,
Munich, Germany
In-house design
Frank Rieser
Web
www.siemens-home.de

This built-in oven is distinguished by a new design concept, which is particularly evident through the integration of the door into the frame. In addition, the lateral connection to adjacent kitchen furniture was improved. Brand-specific design aspects are expressed by the arrangement of stainless steel trims in the shape of a portal as well as a two-part control panel. The reduced use of stainless steel is intended to emphasise the metaphoric style of the oven.

Statement by the jury
Like a picture frame, the slim stainless steel surfaces draw the attention to the control panel of this built-in oven.

Ein neuartiges Aufbaukonzept, das sich vor allem in der Türeinbindung zeigt, prägt diesen Einbau-Backofen. Dadurch wurde die seitliche Anbindung zu den angrenzenden Küchenmöbeln verbessert. Markenspezifische Gestaltungsaspekte äußern sich mittels der Anordnung der Edelstahlapplikationen in Form eines Portals sowie durch eine zweigeteilte Bedienblende. Der reduzierte Einsatz von Edelstahl soll die Bildhaftigkeit des Backofens steigern.

Begründung der Jury
Gleich einem Bilderrahmen lenken die schmalen Edelstahlflächen den Blick auf das Bedienfeld des Einbau-Backofens.

Siemens HB24D552
Steam Oven
Dampfgarer

Manufacturer
Siemens-Electrogeräte GmbH,
Munich, Germany
In-house design
Frank Rieser
Web
www.siemens-home.de

The conservation of nutrients and flavour of fresh food is one of the benefits of healthy steam cooking. This steam oven also offers the possibility of combining a versatile installation programme and thus harmoniously integrates into the respective kitchen environment. The control panel, split into two parts, as well as the portal-shaped arrangement of the stainless steel trims provide high recognition value.

Statement by the jury
This advanced steamer shows the consistent implementation of a brand-specific design concept.

Zu den Vorteilen des gesunden Dampfgarens gehört die Erhaltung der Nährstoffe und des Geschmacks frischer Lebensmittel. Dieser Dampfgarer bietet darüber hinaus die Kombinationsmöglichkeit eines vielfältigen Einbauprogramms und ordnet sich dadurch harmonisch in die jeweilige Küchenlandschaft ein. Die zweigeteilte Bedienblende sowie die portalähnliche Anordnung der Edelstahlapplikationen sorgen für einen hohen Wiedererkennungswert.

Begründung der Jury
Bei dem technisch ausgereiften Dampfgarer zeigt sich die konsequente Umsetzung eines markenspezifischen Gestaltungskonzeptes.

Built-in ovens, steam ovens

HGV74X456T
Free-Standing Cooker
Standherd

Manufacturer
Robert Bosch Hausgeräte GmbH,
Munich, Germany
In-house design
Alexander Marsch, Robert Sachon
Web
www.bosch-hausgeraete.de

This reinterpretation of a free-standing gas cooker features high quality materials and is characterised by its specific use of glass and stainless steel. The glass front underlines the excellent view of the extra-large oven interior. On the cooktop, the glass enables easy cleaning. Dishwasher-proof cast iron pan supports and a solid metal handle underscore not only the powerful burners but also the high standard of the precisely designed appliance.

Statement by the jury
In this free-standing gas cooker, clear lines and the use of large glass surfaces create a distinctive overall picture.

Diese Neuinterpretation eines Gas-Standherds mit hochwertigen Materialien ist durch den prägnanten Einsatz von Glas und Edelstahl geprägt. Auf der Frontseite betont das Glas den Einblick in den großen XXL-Backraum, auf dem Kochfeld ermöglicht es eine leichte Reinigung. Spülmaschinengeeignete Gusstopfträger und ein Vollmetallgriff unterstreichen neben den leistungsstarken Brennern die Wertigkeit des präzise gestalteten Gerätes.

Begründung der Jury
Mittels einer klaren Linienführung und der Verwendung von großen Glasflächen entsteht bei diesem Standherd ein charakteristisches Gesamtbild.

Siemens HC858543
Free-Standing Cooker
Standherd

Manufacturer
Siemens-Electrogeräte GmbH,
Munich, Germany
In-house design
Heiko Thielen
Web
www.siemens-home.de

The free-standing stainless steel cooker enables comfortable operation. Its four powerBoost induction zones are controlled via touch sensors which are particularly easy to clean. The oven controls follow an innovative operating concept that comprises ten heating modes and 40 programmes. The large 67-litre oven features a self-cleaning system, which, at the push of a button, turns even persistent dirt into dust.

Statement by the jury
Corresponding to brand-specific design features of this appliance series, this free-standing cooker conveys appealing quality.

Der Edelstahl-Standherd ermöglicht eine komfortable Bedienung. Seine vier powerBoost-Induktionsfelder werden über Touchfelder gesteuert, die besonders reinigungsfreundlich sind. Die Backofensteuerung folgt einem innovativen Bedienkonzept, das 10 Heizarten und 40 Programme umfasst. Der Großraum-Backofen mit einem Volumen von 67 Litern besitzt eine Selbstreinigungs-Automatik, wodurch auf Tastendruck selbst hartnäckiger Schmutz zu Staub zerfällt.

Begründung der Jury
In Anlehnung an die herstellertypischen Gestaltungsmerkmale dieser Geräteserie vermittelt der Standherd eine ansprechende Hochwertigkeit.

Luna
Free-Standing Cooker
Standherd

Manufacturer
Guangdong Midea
Microwave and Electrical
Appliances Manufacturing Co., Ltd.,
Guangdong, China
In-house design
Wu Ziming, Hou Bangbin, Lu Wei
Web
www.midea.com

A striking mix of materials characterises the Luna free-standing cooker. The black tempered glass of the body surfaces is framed by a decorative, eight mm wide aluminium alloy bar. The easy-to-operate cooker features a rear control panel and full touch control. The glass surfaces are easy to clean and the slim handle bar unobtrusively blends in with the overall picture.

Ein markanter Materialmix prägt den Standherd Luna. Das schwarze Hartglas der Korpusflächen wird mit einer dekorativen, 8 mm breiten Leiste aus einer Aluminiumlegierung kombiniert. Der Herd ist mit einem im hinteren Bereich platzierten Bedienfeld und einer Full-Touch-Steuerung ausgestattet und lässt sich leicht handhaben. Die Glasflächen sind komfortabel zu reinigen. Dezent fügt sich die schmale Griffleiste in das Gesamtbild ein.

Statement by the jury
This free-standing cooker is striking for its independent design vocabulary. The choice of material conveys high quality.

Begründung der Jury
Mit einer eigenständigen Formensprache überzeugt dieser Standherd, wobei die Materialwahl Hochwertigkeit zum Ausdruck bringt.

EWMK 6550.0J-BV
**Built-in Compact Oven
with Integrated Microwave**
Einbau-Kompakt-Backofen
mit integrierter Mikrowelle

Manufacturer
Küppersbusch Hausgeräte GmbH,
Gelsenkirchen, Germany
Design
Keicheldesign
(Klaus Keichel),
Düsseldorf, Germany
Web
www.kueppersbusch-hausgeraete.de

The combination of black glass with
a matt black handle underscores
the superior usability of this built-in
combined solution. The compact oven
with integrated microwave features
horizontally aligned lines displaying
an aesthetic elegance. Six oven and
microwave functions as well as an
integrated grill function are operated by
a fully electronic sensor touch control.

Statement by the jury
The refined appearance of this built-
in appliance is based on homogenous
colours and the use of high quality
materials.

Die Kombination aus schwarzem Glas mit
einer mattschwarzen Griffleiste unterstreicht den gehobenen Gebrauchswert
dieser Einbau-Kombilösung. Der Kompakt-
Backofen mit integrierter Mikrowelle zeigt
eine elegante Ästhetik mit einer horizontal
ausgerichteten Linienführung. Seine sechs
Backofen- und Mikrowellenfunktionen
sowie eine integrierte Grillfunktion werden
durch eine vollelektronische Sensor-Touch-
Bedienung gesteuert.

Begründung der Jury
Die edle Anmutung dieses Einbau-Geräts
beruht auf einer homogenen Farbgebung
und dem Einsatz hochwertiger Materialien.

Artemis (MW233RW)
Microwave Oven
Mikrowelle

Manufacturer
LG Electronics Inc.,
Seoul, South Korea
In-house design
Song-Yi Han, Hong-Sik Kwon,
Soo-Yun Kim
Web
www.lg.com

The design concept of this microwave
oven discreetly hides the handle for
easy opening in the door. The minimalist
appearance completes the modern
concept. The extra large window allows
easy inspection of the cooked food.
Its ergonomically elaborate structure
is continued in the control elements,
running top-down, while the small
number of components enables effective
device management.

Statement by the jury
A striking black and white contrast
characterises the overall impression of
this functionally well-devised microwave
oven.

Diese Mikrowelle verfolgt ein Gestaltungskonzept, welches den leicht zu öffnenden
Griff dezent in der Türklappe verbirgt. Die
minimalistische Anmutung ergänzt ein
zeitgemäßes Konzept. Das verbreiterte
Sichtfenster ermöglicht ein müheloses
Prüfen des Garguts. Die ergonomisch
durchdachte Struktur setzt sich an den von
oben nach unten verlaufenden Bedienelementen fort, während die geringe Anzahl
von Bauteilen ein effektives Gerätema-
nagement erzielt.

Begründung der Jury
Ein prägnanter Schwarz-Weiß-Kontrast
prägt das Gesamtbild dieses funktional
durchdachten Mikrowellenofens.

Siemens HF25G5L2
Built-in Microwave Oven
Einbau-Mikrowelle

Manufacturer
Siemens-Electrogeräte GmbH,
Munich, Germany
In-house design
Frank Rieser
Web
www.siemens-home.de

This built-in microwave oven features a combination of shiny, black glass surfaces with stainless steel trims and control elements. A newly developed control concept includes a direct-selection mode, a white/black display and a blue button confirmation, which altogether support technical, innovative design standards. The interplay of the materials focuses on a reduced use of stainless steel.

Statement by the jury
This built-in microwave oven is part of an appliance series, which is distinguished by circumferential stainless steel trims. It visualises high formal quality.

Diese Einbau-Mikrowelle zeigt eine Kombination von glänzenden, schwarzen Glasflächen mit Edelstahlapplikationen und Bedienelementen aus Edelstahl. Ein neu entwickeltes Bedienkonzept umfasst einen Direktwahlmodus, eine weiß-schwarze Displayanzeige sowie eine blaue Tasten-quittierung, die den technisch-innovativen Gestaltungsanspruch unterstützen. Das Zusammenspiel der Materialien setzt auf einen reduzierten Einsatz von Edelstahl.

Begründung der Jury
Eine hohe formale Qualität visualisiert diese Einbau-Mikrowelle einer Gerätereihe, welche sich durch umlaufende Edelstahl-applikationen auszeichnet.

Siemens HS363500W
Steriliser
Sterilisator

Manufacturer
Siemens-Electrogeräte GmbH,
Munich, Germany
In-house design
Julia Ehrensberger
Web
www.siemens-home.de

Laterally positioned stainless steel strips and handles which are integrated into the glass surfaces characterise this steriliser. A brand-specific 2-zone panel ensures the combination with other household appliances of the manufacturer. Functional controls in connection with an information zone as well as centrally positioned cursor buttons guarantee ease of use. The 100-litre capacity of the appliance round off the concept in a coherent way.

Statement by the jury
The overall impression of the steriliser is distinguished by slim stainless steel panels and the division into two zones.

Seitlich aufgesetzte Edelstahl-Streifen sowie in die Glasflächen integrierte Griffe charakterisieren diesen Sterilisator. Eine markentypische Zwei-Zonen-Blende stellt die Kombinierbarkeit mit anderen Haus-haltsgeräten des Herstellers sicher. In Ver-bindung mit einer Infozone gewährleisten Funktionstasten und mittig positionierte Cursor-Tasten eine anwenderfreundliche Bedienbarkeit. Die Geräteraum-Größe von 100 Litern rundet das Konzept stimmig ab.

Begründung der Jury
Das Gesamtbild des Sterilisators wird durch schmale Edelstahlblenden und die Auftei-lung in zwei Zonen geprägt.

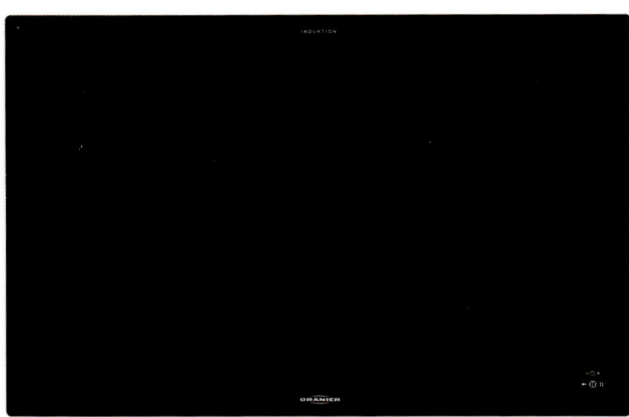

FLI 2088 SL+
Induction Hob
Induktionskochfeld

Manufacturer
Oranier Küchentechnik GmbH,
Gladenbach, Germany
In-house design
Thomas Tete
Web
www.oranier.com

This free-zone induction hob with six cooking zones is distinguished by a pot position detection system. As soon as a pot is put down, the corresponding slider lights up and indicates which zone is to be regulated. The hob surface features a carbon-like, criss-cross braided structure, emphasising its high quality and protecting the surface. The appliance can be mounted flush or with stainless steel side strips.

Statement by the jury
The free-zone induction hob is both formally and functionally well conceived.

Dieses Flächen-Induktionskochfeld mit sechs Kochzonen zeichnet sich durch eine Topf-Positions-Erkennung aus. Sobald ein Topf abgestellt wird, leuchtet der entsprechende Slider auf und zeigt an, welche Zone zu regeln ist. Die Oberfläche des Kochfeldes hat eine karbonartige, über Kreuz geflochtene Struktur, wodurch die Hochwertigkeit betont und die Oberfläche geschützt wird. Das Gerät kann flächenbündig oder mit Edelstahl-Seitenleisten montiert werden.

Begründung der Jury
Das Flächen-Induktionskochfeld ist sowohl formal als auch funktional schlüssig durchdacht.

PIV375N17E, PIV675N17E, PIV975N17E
Induction Hob
Product Range
Induktionskochstellen-Produktreihe

Manufacturer
Robert Bosch Hausgeräte GmbH,
Munich, Germany
In-house design
Ulrich Goss, Robert Sachon,
Fabian Puls, Christoph Ortmann
Web
www.bosch-hausgeraete.de
Honourable Mention

Thanks to generous cooking zones, the FlexInduction hob product range is flexible with regard to the positioning as well as the shape and size of the cookware. According to their needs, users can choose between three differently sized induction hobs, from the slim Domino to the generous 90 cm hob. The selected power level is indicated in form of an intuitively comprehensible light line. The clear graphical structure provides orientation.

Statement by the jury
Reduced to the essential, the surface structure characterises the FlexInduction hob range.

Die Kochstellen-Produktreihe FlexInduction erlaubt durch ihre großzügigen Induktionskochzonen Flexibilität bezüglich der Platzierung, Form und Größe des Kochgeschirrs. Bedarfsorientiert besteht die Auswahl zwischen drei unterschiedlichen Kochfeldgrößen, vom schmalen Domino bis hin zum großzügigen 90 cm Kochfeld. Die gewählte Leistungsstufe wird in Form einer intuitiv verständlichen Lichtlinie angezeigt, wobei die klare grafische Gliederung Orientierung gibt.

Begründung der Jury
Eine auf das Wesentliche reduzierte Oberflächengestaltung kennzeichnet die FlexInduction Kochstellen.

HI9272SV
Built-in Induction Hob
Einbau-Induktionskochstelle

Manufacturer
ATAG Nederland BV,
Duiven, Netherlands
In-house design
Björn Flinterhoff, Iris Hogervorst,
Wouter Ditters, Wilbert van Emous,
Vincent Hofstee
Web
www.atag.nl

The ceramic glass of this elegant built-in induction hob with Iris Slide Control was provided with an innovative enamel matt black finish, making it not only scratch resistant but also easier to clean. Each of the five induction zones is equipped with a separate control. The four individual square zones on the left and the right can be combined to form large rectangular zones. Each induction zone features an independent timer.

Statement by the jury
With its reduced design, this induction hob fits in well with kitchen interiors. Especially the look of the ceramic glass is appealing.

Bei dieser eleganten Einbau-Induktionskochstelle mit Iris Slide Control hat die Glaskeramik ein innovatives mattschwarzes Emaille-Dekor erhalten, wodurch sie nicht nur kratzunempfindlich, sondern darüber hinaus auch einfacher zu reinigen ist. Alle fünf Induktionszonen sind mit einer eigenen Bedienung konfiguriert. Die vier einzelnen quadratischen Zonen links und rechts können zu großen rechteckigen Zonen verbunden werden. Jede Induktionszone ist mit einem unabhängigen Timer ausgestattet.

Begründung der Jury
Durch ihre minimalistische Gestaltung fügt sich die Induktionskochstelle gut in das Kücheninterieur ein, wobei insbesondere die Glaskeramik visuell reizvoll erscheint.

TF 7487 N
FreeInduction Hob
FreeInduction-Kochfeld

Manufacturer
Constructa-Neff Vertriebs GmbH,
Munich, Germany
In-house design
Thomas Knöller, Elena Leinmüller
Web
www.neff.de

The design of the discreetly chequered FreeInduction ceramic glass visualises plain elegance. 48 inductors are integrated underneath the hob and enable a continuously usable cooking zone. As soon as pots and pans are placed on the hob, the appliance automatically recognises the combined area of inductors that is occupied. This is graphically indicated on the touch TFT display where the temperature is set by the press of a finger.

Die Gestaltung der dezent gerasterten FreeInduction-Glaskeramik visualisiert schlichte Eleganz. Unter dem Kochfeld wurden 48 Induktoren eingebaut, die eine durchgängig nutzbare Oberfläche ermöglichen. Sobald Töpfe oder Pfannen aufgestellt werden, erkennt das Gerät automatisch den durch das Kochgeschirr belegten Verbund an Induktoren und stellt dies auf dem Touch-TFT-Display grafisch dar. Durch einfaches Berühren mit dem Finger wird dort die Temperatur eingestellt.

Electrolux InfinitePure™
Hob
Kochmulde

Manufacturer
Electrolux Major Appliances EMEA,
Stockholm, Sweden
In-house design
Electrolux Group Design EMEA
Web
www.electrolux.com
www.electrolux.it

The elegant InfinitePure hob features rimless flush glass surfaces. It is fully backlit in an innovative way. When not in use, the hob is entirely black. The cooking zones and the controls are only illuminated when in use. The induction zones are flexible and adapt to the size of the respective cookware. Direct access rotary electronics offer instant heat control.

Statement by the jury
The minimalist clearness of this hob characterises a modern piece of kitchen equipment which fully dispenses with visible operating controls.

Die elegante Kochmulde InfinitePure weist randlose und flächenbündige Glasflächen auf. Auf innovative Weise ist sie vollständig von hinten beleuchtet. Bei Nichtbenutzung bleibt die Kochmulde komplett schwarz, erst beim Gebrauch werden die Kochzonen sowie die Bedienelemente illuminiert. Die Induktionsfelder passen sich flexibel der Größe des Kochgeschirrs an. Eine Drehelektronik mit Direktzugriff bietet eine sofortige Wärmeregelung.

Begründung der Jury
Mit ihrer minimalistischen Klarheit prägt diese Kochmulde eine zeitgemäße Küchenausstattung, die auf sichtbare Bedienelemente verzichtet.

Zanussi Induction Range
Induction Hob
Product Range
Induktionskochmulden-Produktreihe

Manufacturer
Electrolux Major Appliances EMEA,
Stockholm, Sweden
In-house design
Electrolux Group Design EMEA
Web
www.electrolux.com
www.electrolux.it

Taking inspiration from the Quadro ovens, an induction hob product range was created the design of which conveys the brand value of an easy-to-use appliance. The iconic design of the glass ceramic control panel guides users and thus allows for an intuitive, self-explanatory cooking experience. Enhancing the brand message, the hob is to be perceived as an expedient kitchen partner with a distinctive personality.

Statement by the jury
An independent style is characteristic of the overall impression of the induction hob product range. It provides compelling functionality.

In Anlehnung an die Quadro-Backöfen wurde eine Induktionskochmulden-Produktreihe geschaffen, deren Gestaltung den Markenwert eines einfach zu benutzenden Geräts vermittelt. Informative Symbole im Bedienfeld der Glaskeramik leiten den Benutzer und ermöglichen somit ein intuitiv selbsterklärendes Kocherlebnis. Imageprägend soll das Kochfeld als praktischer Küchenpartner mit einer unverwechselbaren Persönlichkeit wahrgenommen werden.

Begründung der Jury
Eine eigenständige Formensprache prägt das Gesamtbild der Induktionskochmulden-Produktreihe. Sie vermittelt eine überzeugende Funktionalität.

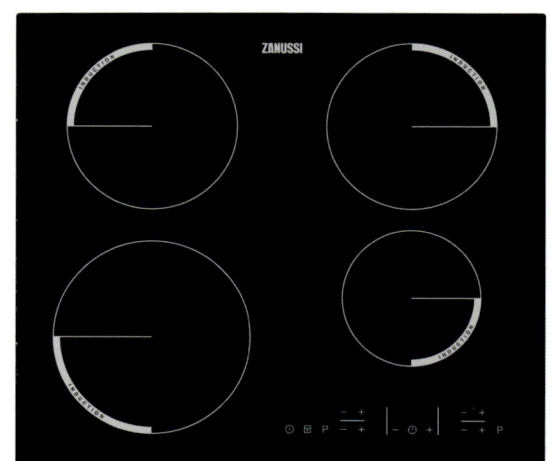

Gas and Induction Hob
Gas- und Induktionskochstelle

Manufacturer
Ningbo Fotile Kitchen Ware Co., Ltd.,
Cixi, Ningbo, China
In-house design
Dengguan He, Xiaogang Liu, Yun Zhang
Web
www.fotile.com

This hob, with its microcrystalline glass surface, unites the advantages of a gas cooker with those of an induction cooker. The designers were inspired by the display of a dashboard and created a minimalist-looking panel with two rotary knobs. Users can adjust the cooking heat in twelve levels and the respective heating level is displayed by means of orange LED symbols.

Diese Kochstelle mit ihrer mikrokristallinen Glasscheibenoberfläche vereint die Vorteile eines Gas- mit denen eines Induktionsherds. Die Gestalter wurden von der Anzeige eines Armaturenbretts inspiriert und schufen ein minimalistisch wirkendes Bedienfeld mit zwei Drehknöpfen. Der Benutzer kann damit die Kochhitze in zwölf Stufen regulieren, wobei die jeweilige Heizstufe mittels orangefarbener LED-Symbole angezeigt wird.

Statement by the jury
The many-sided practical value of this combined gas and induction hob visualises a subtle, synchronously aligned style.

Begründung der Jury
Den vielseitigen Gebrauchswert dieser kombinierten Gas- und Induktionskochstelle visualisiert eine dezente, synchron ausgerichtete Formensprache.

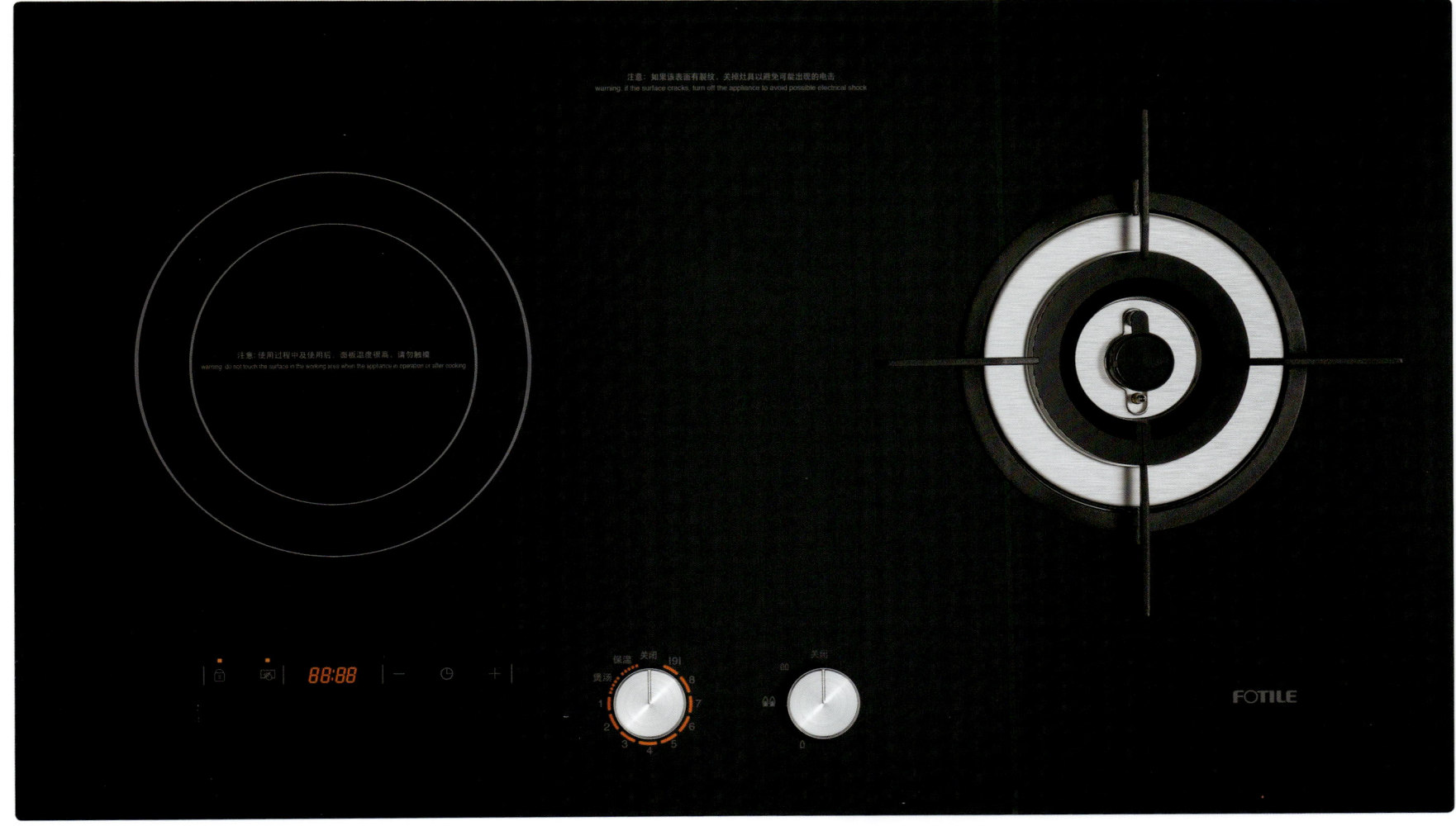

HG3171MB
Built-in Gas Hob
Einbau-Gaskochstelle

Manufacturer
ATAG Nederland BV,
Duiven, Netherlands
In-house design
Design
Waacs, Rotterdam, Netherlands
Van Berlo, Eindhoven, Netherlands
Buro Brand, Den Haag, Netherlands
Web
www.atag.nl
www.waacs.nl
www.vanberlo.nl
www.burobrand.nl

This modular built-in gas hob features the innovative Fusion Volcano wok burner. The "volcano" renders concentrated heat into the middle of a wok pan, saving up to 50 per cent on gas consumption compared with other wok burners. The desired burning power can be controlled accurately with the solid metal control knob. The base of the hob consists of a ceramic glass plate with a sophisticated screening.

Statement by the jury
Boasting a professional appearance, this robust gas hob features a burner technology that saves on gas yet has high performance.

Die modular einbaubare Gaskochstelle ist mit dem innovativen „Fusion Volcano"-Wokbrenner ausgestattet. Dieser „Vulkan" leitet konzentrierte Hitze durch ein rotierendes Flammenbild an die Mitte der Wok-Pfanne, wodurch bis zu 50 Prozent weniger Gas verbraucht wird. Die gewünschte Leistung kann punktgenau mit dem massiven metallenen Drehknebel eingestellt werden. Die Basis des Kochfeldes bildet ein keramisches Glas mit einem eleganten Dekor.

Begründung der Jury
Einen professionellen Eindruck macht diese robuste Gaskochstelle, deren Brenner-Technologie energiesparsam und effektiv arbeitet.

HG8411MBA
Built-in Gas Hob
Einbau-Gaskochstelle

Manufacturer
ATAG Nederland BV,
Duiven, Netherlands
In-house design
Design
Waacs, Rotterdam, Netherlands
Van Berlo, Eindhoven, Netherlands
Buro Brand, Den Haag, Netherlands
Web
www.atag.nl
www.waacs.nl
www.vanberlo.nl
www.burobrand.nl

This 80 cm wide built-in gas hob combines the innovative Fusion Volcano wok burner with three other gas burners. The arrangement of those four burners, and the fact that the wok burner is positioned on the left, creates generous space for different kinds of pots and pans. The wok burner can switch from an inner flame to an outer flame. With up to 6 kW, it provides a very strong flame and is well suited for large pans with flat bottoms or wok pans. The simmer function reduces the performance to only 0.2 kW, which is even suitable for melting chocolate.

Statement by the jury
A function-oriented design principle distinguishes this gas hob, of which the energy-efficient burner technology is impressive.

Die 80 cm breite Gaskochstelle kombiniert den innovativen „Fusion Volcano"-Wokbrenner mit drei weiteren Gasbrennern. Die Anordnung der vier Gaskochstellen, mit dem links positionierten Wokbrenner, ergibt einen großzügigen Raum für verschiedenste Töpfe und Pfannen. Der Wokbrenner kann von einer inneren Flamme auf eine äußere Flamme umgeschaltet werden. Diese mit bis zu 6 kW sehr kräftige Flamme eignet sich gut für große Pfannen mit flachem Boden oder für Wokpfannen. Die Schmorfunktion reduziert die Leistung auf nur 0,2 kW und eignet sich sogar zum Schmelzen von Schokolade.

Begründung der Jury
Ein funktional ausgerichtetes Gestaltungsprinzip prägt diese Gaskochstelle, deren energieeffiziente Brenner-Technologie überzeugt.

Siemens ER76K230MP
Gas Hob
Gaskochstelle

Manufacturer
Siemens-Electrogeräte GmbH,
Munich, Germany
In-house design
Karsten Willmann, Tim Richter
Design
südkamp designstudio GbR
(Judith Südkamp, Rouven Südkamp),
Wildeshausen, Germany
Web
www.siemens-home.de
www.suedkamp-design.de

With an innovative pot support design and a digital timer, these wok burners become an efficient gas hob of the best energy class. The appliance was developed for Asian cooking habits and is distinguished by a reduced design. It is functional and easy to clean. Its quality and its intrinsic value are underlined by elegant, ergonomically impressing control knobs and the lateral stainless steel kickboards on black glass.

Statement by the jury
The independent formal vocabulary of this gas hob achieves a distinctive aesthetics. In addition, it scores with its material arrangement.

Ein innovatives Topfträgerdesign sowie ein digitaler Timer machen diese Wokbrenner zu einer effizienten Gaskochstelle der besten Energieklasse. Das für asiatische Kochgewohnheiten entwickelte Gerät zeichnet sich durch eine reduzierte Gestaltung aus, ist funktional und leicht zu reinigen. Qualität und Wertigkeit werden durch elegante, ergonomisch überzeugende Schwertknebel sowie die seitlichen Stoßleisten aus Edelstahl auf schwarzem Glas unterstrichen.

Begründung der Jury
Die eigenständige Formensprache dieser Gaskochstelle erreicht eine charakteristische Ästhetik, zudem punktet die Materialanordnung.

Siemens ER76K251MP
Gas Hob
Gaskochstelle

Manufacturer
Siemens-Electrogeräte GmbH,
Munich, Germany
In-house design
Karsten Willmann, Tim Richter
Design
südkamp designstudio GbR
(Judith Südkamp, Rouven Südkamp),
Wildeshausen, Germany
Web
www.siemens-home.de
www.suedkamp-design.de

The integrative connection between pan supports and top sheet emphasises the flat design of this gas hob. Typical of this brand, the control panel is set off against the stainless steel cooking zone by contrasting black glass. The indentations for collecting liquids are elegantly covered by the pan supports thus complying with the planar character of the hob. High quality control knobs ensure safe operability.

Statement by the jury
The design concept employs the effect of highly contrasting materials. Thus, the structure of the gas hob conveys a sophisticated impression.

Eine formschlüssige Anbindung der Topfträger an das Stahlmuldenblatt unterstützt bei dieser Gaskochstelle die flächenbündige Gestaltung. Markentypisch wird das Bedienpanel durch kontrastierendes, schwarzes Glas von der Edelstahlkochfläche abgesetzt. Die Prägungen zum Auffangen von Flüssigkeiten sind elegant durch die Topfträger abgedeckt, was dem flächigen Charakter gerecht wird. Hochwertige Schwertknebel sorgen für eine sichere Bedienbarkeit.

Begründung der Jury
Visuell ansprechend nutzt das Gestaltungskonzept die Wirkung kontraststarker Materialien, die Gaskochstelle wirkt dadurch raffiniert strukturiert.

Zanussi Ultra Flat
Gas Hob
Gaskochmulde

Manufacturer
Electrolux Major Appliances EMEA,
Stockholm, Sweden
In-house design
Electrolux Group Design EMEA
Web
www.electrolux.com
www.electrolux.it

This 75 cm stainless steel gas hob offers generous cooking space for various pots and pans. The design vocabulary of the pan supports is striking. The wok burner is conveniently placed on the left to take up even large cookware. The hob is easy to clean thanks to its ultra flat design and the auto-ignition is ideal for one-hand operation.

Diese 75 cm breite Gaskochmulde aus Edelstahl bietet eine großzügige Kochfläche für unterschiedliche Töpfe und Pfannen. Prägnant wirkt die Formensprache der Topfträger. Der Wok-Brenner ist bequem auf der linken Seite platziert, um auch größeres Kochgeschirr verwenden zu können. Die ultraflach gestaltete Mulde ist einfach zu reinigen und die Selbstentzündung eignet sich hervorragend für die Bedienung mit einer Hand.

Statement by the jury
Due to its outstanding pan supports, this flush mountable stainless steel hob provides a formally independent and functional impression.

Begründung der Jury
Aufgrund ihrer auffallenden Topfträger wirkt die flächenbündig einbaubare Edelstahlmulde formal eigenständig und funktional durchdacht.

CG903D Series
Gas on Glass
Gas Hob 90 cm
Gas auf Glas
Gaskochfeld 90 cm

Manufacturer
Fisher & Paykel Appliances Ltd,
Auckland, New Zealand
In-house design
Fisher & Paykel Design Team
Web
www.fisherpaykel.co.nz

Minimal in design, this 90 cm wide Gas on Glass 903 hob combines the cleanability of glass surfaces with the performance of a gas hob. Its sophisticated aesthetic is enhanced by the polished metal trim, which marks the transition from the black reflective glass control panel to the black ceramic glass cooking zone. The three-in-a-row format is ergonomically sound and ensures a high degree of safety.

Minimalistisch gestaltet, verbindet dieses 90 cm breite Kochfeld „Gas auf Glas 903" die Reinigungsfähigkeit eines Glaskochfeldes mit der Leistung eines Gasherdes. Seine elegante Ästhetik betont der polierte Metallstreifen, der als Übergang vom schwarzen Bedienfeld aus verspiegeltem Glas zum schwarzen Glaskeramik-Kochfeld dient. Die drei, aus ergonomischen Überlegungen nebeneinander angeordneten, Brenner sorgen für ein hohes Maß an Sicherheit.

Statement by the jury
Balanced elegance and high practical value define this three-burner gas hob.

Begründung der Jury
Eine ausgewogene Eleganz sowie ein hoher Gebrauchswert definieren dieses Gaskochfeld mit drei Brennern.

JZ-S09
Gas Hob
Gaskochmulde

Manufacturer
Ningbo Oulin Kitchen Utensils Co., Ltd,
Ningbo, China
In-house design
Ning Ma, Huibin Xu
Web
www.oulin-global.com

This two-flame gas hob features a timer which can be used to set a cooking time of up to 199 minutes. In addition, the appliance has a protective function that prevents burning to no avail. The special burner design ensures unimpaired cooking even in side winds. Ignition and size of the flame can be controlled by easy-to-handle knobs.

Statement by the jury
Harmonious proportions characterise this gas hob. Both the arrangement of the burners and the control panel allow comfortable use.

Diese zweiflammige Gaskochmulde verfügt über eine Zeitschaltuhr, optional kann eine Kochzeit von bis zu 199 Minuten eingestellt werden. Zudem ist das Gerät mit einer Schutzfunktion gegen Leerbrennen ausgestattet. Aufgrund der Brennergestaltung ist selbst bei Seitenwind ein unbeeinträchtigtes Kochen möglich. Die stromlinienförmige Mulde ist leicht zu reinigen. Mittels einfach zu handhabender Drehknöpfe können die Zündung sowie die Größe der Flamme gesteuert werden.

Begründung der Jury
Ausgewogene Proportionen prägen diese Gaskochmulde. Sowohl die Anordnung der Brenner als auch das Bedienfeld erlauben eine komfortable Nutzung.

Android
Gas Hob and Exhaust Hood
Gaskochfeld und
Dunstabzugshaube

Manufacturer
Guangdong Midea
Microwave and Electrical
Appliances Manufacturing Co., Ltd.,
Guangdong, China
In-house design
He Yanhuan, Yang Jie, Liang Wengan
Web
www.midea.com
Honourable Mention

In this product combination, the choice of materials is the connecting link. Both the exhaust hood and the matching gas hob are made of black glass and aluminium alloy. The glass structure provides the slim products with their characteristic aesthetic quality. The rectangular hob features a touch control as well as a timer function. The white light of the knobs takes up the design of the hood.

Bei dieser Produktkombination wird die Materialwahl zum verbindenden Element: Sowohl die Dunstabzugshaube als auch das dazu passende Gaskochfeld werden aus schwarzem Glas und einer Aluminiumlegierung gefertigt. Die Glasstruktur verleiht den schmal konstruierten Produkten eine charakteristische Ästhetik. Das rechteckige Kochfeld ist mit einer Touch-Bedienung inklusive einer Zeituhr-Funktion ausgestattet. Das weiße Licht der Drehknöpfe nimmt die Gestaltung der Abzugshaube auf.

Statement by the jury
This ensemble, consisting of a gas hob and an exhaust hood, displays striking lines.

Begründung der Jury
Das Ensemble, bestehend aus einem Gaskochfeld und einer Dunstabzugshaube, zeigt eine prägnante Linienführung.

Galaxy Slim
Gas Hob and Exhaust Hood
Gaskochfeld und
Dunstabzugshaube

Manufacturer
Guangdong Midea
Microwave and Electrical Appliances
Manufacturing Co., Ltd.,
Guangdong, China
In-house design
Le Jinliang, Zhou Zongxu,
Zhang Zhe
Web
www.midea.com
Honourable Mention

The exhaust hood and the gas hob follow the same design principle and display a distinctly divided structure. The exhaust hood hides a condenser made of aluminium alloy, which ensures reliable fume extraction. The condenser plate, made of oxidised and brushed aluminium, can be recycled. The touch control panel is equipped with white LEDs and offers a choice of three speeds. The installable hob has two gas burners, which are operated via a photoelectric switch and rotary buttons.

Sowohl die Dunstabzugshaube als auch das Gaskochfeld folgen dem gleichen Gestaltungsprinzip und zeigen eine deutlich unterteilte Struktur. In der kompakten Abzugshaube verbirgt sich ein Kondensator aus einer Aluminiumlegierung, der für einen zuverlässigen Rauchabzug sorgt. Die Kondensatorplatte aus oxidiertem und gebürstetem Aluminium ist recycelbar. Das Touch-Bedienfeld ist mit weißen LEDs ausgestattet und bietet die Wahl zwischen drei Gebläsestufen. Das einbaubare Kochfeld bietet zwei Gasbrenner, deren Bedienung über einen photoelektrischen Schalter und Drehknöpfe erfolgt.

Statement by the jury
In this combination of a gas hob with an exhaust hood, contrasting materials create a classic-elegant look.

Begründung der Jury
Kontrastreiche Materialien lassen bei dieser Kombination eines Gaskochfelds mit einer Dunstabzugshaube eine klassisch elegante Anmutung entstehen.

Art Gallery
Cooker Hood
Dunstabzugshaube

Manufacturer
Whirlpool Europe S.r.l.,
Comerio (Varese), Italy
In-house design
Global Consumer Design
Web
www.whirlpool.com
Honourable Mention

The Art Gallery is a cooker hood hidden behind a panel of contemporary art. It consists of a body and exchangeable glass panels that can be installed without technical support. With a range of six select works of art, the product offers a wide range of motifs, from subtle to strikingly colourful. The digital printing technology on the panels opens up the opportunity for customization. Thus, the household appliance disappears behind a selected favourite picture.

Die Art Gallery ist eine hinter einer Blende zeitgenössischer Kunst versteckte Dunstabzugshaube. Sie besteht aus einem Edelstahlkörper und austauschbaren Glasscheiben, die ohne Werkzeug installiert werden können. Mit einer Reihe von sechs ausgewählten Kunstwerken bietet das Produkt eine breite Auswahl an Motiven, von dezent bis auffallend bunt. Der Digitaldruck auf Glasscheiben bietet die Möglichkeit für eine komplett individuelle Gestaltung. So verbirgt sich das Haushaltsgerät hinter einem ausgewählten Lieblingsbild.

Statement by the jury
The implementation of an innovative design concept turns Art Gallery into a visually multi-faceted cooker hood.

Begründung der Jury
Die Umsetzung einer innovativen Gestaltungsidee führt bei Art Gallery zu einer visuell vielseitigen Dunstabzugshaube.

Siemens LS26753TI
Wall-Mounted Chimney Hood
Wandesse

Manufacturer
Siemens-Electrogeräte GmbH,
Munich, Germany
In-house design
Tim Richter, Minghao Shi,
Julia Ehrensberger
Web
www.siemens-home.de

This wall-mounted chimney hood for the Chinese market offers a specific technology as well as aesthetics. The inclined angle provides for much headroom. The reduced width of 75 cm enables space-saving installation of the hood. The front-positioned lamps provide glare-free illumination. At the bottom of the unit, there is a long oil-collecting container, the capacity of which is adjusted to cooking with a lot of oil.

Statement by the jury
Rich in contrast, the glass panel of this wall-mounted chimney hood sets itself apart from the stainless steel frame. The blue light bar increases brand recognition.

Diese Wandesse für den chinesischen Markt bietet eine spezifische Technologie und Ästhetik. Durch die Neigung entsteht viel Kopffreiheit und mittels einer reduzierten Breite von nur 75 cm lässt sich die Esse platzsparend integrieren. Die vorne positionierten Lampen sorgen für eine blendfreie Beleuchtung. Auf der Unterseite des Geräts befindet sich ein langer Öl-Auffangbehälter, dessen Kapazität auf das Kochen mit viel Öl abgestimmt ist.

Begründung der Jury
Kontrastreich setzt sich bei der Wandesse die schwarze Glasplatte vom Edelstahlrahmen ab. Die blaue Lichtlinie erhöht den Wiedererkennungswert.

Tiffany
Cooker Hood
Dunstabzugshaube

Manufacturer
Elica,
Fabriano (Ancona), Italy
Design
Fabrizio Crisà
Web
www.elica.com

Tiffany is a vertical cooker hood that is optionally available with black or white glass. The plain composition features a front panel with rounded corners that conceal a powerful technology. The extraction system extends over a length of three metres and captures cooking fumes and vapours at any point. All extraction and lighting features can be managed via an infrared control system.

Statement by the jury
The elegant character of this cooker hood emphasises advanced features allowing high ease of use.

Tiffany ist eine vertikale Abzugshaube, die optional mit schwarzem oder weißem Glas erhältlich ist. Die schlichte Komposition besteht aus einem Front-Panel mit abgerundeten Ecken, hinter dem sich eine leistungsstarke Technologie verbirgt. Das Absaugsystem erstreckt sich über eine Länge von drei Metern und fängt an allen Punkten Rauch und Kochdünste ein. Über ein Infrarot-Steuersystem lassen sich alle Absaug- und Beleuchtungsfunktionen regeln.

Begründung der Jury
Der elegante Charakter dieser Dunstabzugshaube betont eine innovative Ausstattung, die einen gehobenen Bedienkomfort ermöglicht.

Ergoline BKH 90 EG
Exhaust Hood
Kopffreihaube

Manufacturer
berbel Ablufttechnik GmbH,
Rheine, Germany
Design
Studio Ambrozus
(Stefan Ambrozus),
Cologne, Germany
Web
www.berbel.de
www.studioambrozus.de

The design of this slanted exhaust hood grants users plenty of headroom. Its elegant sensor-touch control panel harmoniously complements the clear, straight-lined style. The Back-Flow technology offers additional functional benefit. It ventilates the decorative surface from below so that no condensed water can accumulate. For easy cleaning, the glass surface can be folded down and the drip tray can be removed.

Statement by the jury
Balanced proportions characterise the overall appearance of an exhaust hood that impresses with different colour and material variations.

Die Gestaltung dieser abgeschrägten Dunstabzugshaube lässt dem Nutzer viel Kopffreiheit. Die klare, geradlinige Formensprache wird durch die elegante Sensor-Touch-Steuerung stimmig ergänzt. Einen funktionalen Mehrwert bietet die Back-Flow-Technologie. Diese belüftet die Dekorfläche von unten, sodass sich dort kein Kondenswasser absetzen kann. Zur komfortablen Reinigung kann die Glasfläche heruntergeklappt und die Auffangschale herausgenommen werden.

Begründung der Jury
Ausgewogene Proportionen prägen das Gesamtbild einer Kopffreihaube, die in unterschiedlichen Farb- und Materialausführungen überzeugt.

CXW-200-JQ01T

Range Hood
Dunstabzugshaube

Manufacturer
Ningbo Fotile Kitchen Ware Co., Ltd.,
Cixi, Ningbo, China
In-house design
Bo Ma, Xing Zheng, Yi Jin
Web
www.fotile.com
Honourable Mention

The design concept for this slanted range hood was inspired by the natural phenomenon of a total solar eclipse. In the operating mode, the three-part glass front opens allowing a particularly effective extraction. Dark brown glass surfaces blend well with a touch screen control panel which shows bright orange-coloured circles and icons. A light finger touch starts the visually appealing interplay of light and shadow.

Inspiriert von dem Naturphänomen einer totalen Sonnenfinsternis entstand das Gestaltungskonzept für eine abgeschrägt konstruierte Dunstabzugshaube. Die dreigeteilte Glasfront öffnet sich im Betriebsmodus und ermöglicht eine besonders effektive Absaugung. Dunkelbraune Glasflächen harmonieren mit einem Touch-Screen-Bedienfeld, welches orangefarbig leuchtende Kreise und Symbole zeigt. Eine leichte Berührung startet das visuell ansprechende Zusammenspiel von Licht und Schatten.

Statement by the jury
The design of this dynamic looking hood visualises high functionality and high ease of use.

Begründung der Jury
Die Gestaltung dieser dynamisch wirkenden Dunstabzugshaube visualisiert eine hohe Funktionalität und viel Bedienkomfort.

CXW-200-IF8
Range Hood
Dunstabzugshaube

Manufacturer
Ningbo Oulin Kitchen Utensils Co., Ltd,
Ningbo, China
In-house design
Sheng Sun, Tongjin Chen
Web
www.oulin-global.com

This powerful range hood absorbs 99 per cent of the cooking smells and soot particles thanks to its innovative technology. Due to a 45-degree inclination angle, the distance to the cooking area can be minimised, which improves suction performance. In addition, the appliance offers correspondingly large headroom. The touch control panel can be activated by a body-inductive technology and provides an intelligent protective function.

Statement by the jury
Distinct lines characterise the elegant overall picture of this range hood; furthermore, the elegant black-white contrast is captivating.

Die leistungsstarke Dunstabzugshaube nimmt aufgrund ihrer innovativen Technologie 99 Prozent der Kochgerüche und Russpartikel auf. Durch die Neigung in einem 45-Grad-Winkel kann der Abstand zum Kochplatz möglichst gering gehalten werden, was die Absaugeffektivität erhöht. Zudem bietet das Gerät eine entsprechend große Kopffreiheit. Das Touch-Bedienfeld wird über Körperinduktion aktiviert und bietet eine intelligente Schutzfunktion.

Begründung der Jury
Eine klare Linienführung prägt das elegante Gesamtbild dieser Dunstabzugshaube, zudem besticht der elegante Schwarz-Weiß-Kontrast.

Illumia
Range Hood
Dunstabzugshaube

Manufacturer
Ciarko Sp. z o.o. S.K.A.,
Sanok, Poland
Design
Lukasz Paszkowski,
Zabrze, Poland
Web
www.ciarkodesign.pl
www.lukaszpaszkowski.pl
Honourable Mention

Illumia is an innovative range hood, which can be operated via touch panel control and also via Android smartphones. A tasteful combination of black glass surfaces and metal trims visualises a high quality standard. The energy-saving device features a brushless motor, which enables high efficiency and a low noise level. The LED lighting is omnidirectional.

Statement by the jury
This range hood stands out due to its unique formal vocabulary. In addition, it provides innovative ease of use.

Illumia ist eine innovative Dunstabzugshaube, die neben der Touch-Panel-Steuerung auch über Android-Smartphones zu kontrollieren ist. Eine geschmackvolle Kombination von schwarzen Glasflächen mit Metallapplikationen visualisiert einen hohen Qualitätsanspruch. Das energiesparsame Gerät verfügt über einen bürstenlosen Motor, der eine hohe Effizienz und einen niedrigen Geräuschpegel ermöglicht. Die LED-Beleuchtung ist flexibel und kann in alle Richtungen geschwenkt werden.

Begründung der Jury
Diese Dunstabzugshaube fällt durch ihre eigenständige Formensprache auf. Sie bietet zudem einen innovativen Bedienkomfort.

Zanussi Casual Hood
Cooker Hood
Dunstabzugshaube

Manufacturer
Electrolux Major Appliances EMEA,
Stockholm, Sweden
In-house design
Electrolux Group Design EMEA
Web
www.electrolux.com
www.electrolux.it

The cooker hood of the Casual Hood product range features a smoothly polished, decorative front. The hood allows flexible adaptation to different cooking habits. Users can choose between three speed levels and use an additional power programme for maximum extraction. The control panel on front side of the hood is equipped with push buttons, facilitating the setting of the required level.

Statement by the jury
An independent style enhances this powerful hood in an appealing way. The lighting concept is impressive as well.

Die Dunstabzugshaube der Produktreihe Casual Hood zeigt eine glatt polierte, dekorative Gerätefront. Die Haube ermöglicht eine flexible Abstimmung auf unterschiedliche Kochgewohnheiten. Der Benutzer kann zwischen drei Leistungsstufen und einem zusätzlichen Intensiv-Programm für maximalen Dunstabzug wählen. Die mit Drucktasten ausgestattete Bedienleiste auf der Haubenvorderseite erleichtert die Einstellung der bedarfsgerechten Stufe.

Begründung der Jury
Eine eigenständige Formensprache wertet diese leistungsstarke Dunstabzugshaube ansprechend auf. Auch das Beleuchtungskonzept überzeugt.

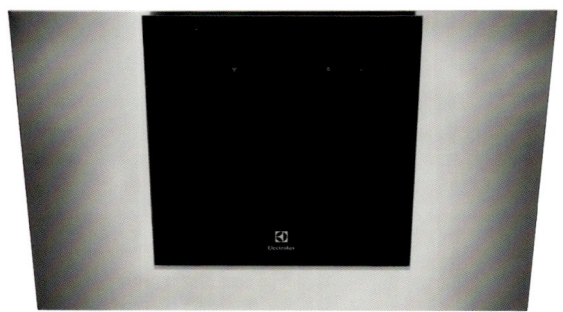

Electrolux Window Hood
**Cooker Hood
Product Range**
Dunstabzugshauben-
Produktreihe

Manufacturer
Electrolux Major Appliances EMEA,
Stockholm, Sweden
In-house design
Electrolux Group Design EMEA
Web
www.electrolux.com
www.electrolux.it

The energy saving cooker hoods of the Window Hood product range show architectural lines that match the products of the Inspiration Range. Actually, its technology was developed for professional kitchens. Direct access controls enable infinitely adjustable setting of the desired absorption and illumination intensity. In addition, these cooker hoods feature comprehensive perimeter aspiration.

Statement by the jury
The contrast between the stainless steel frame and the centrally positioned functional unit with a black glass front is visually appealing.

Die energiesparsamen Dunstabzugshauben der Produktreihe Window Hood zeigen eine architektonische Linienführung, abgestimmt auf Produkte der Inspiration Range. Ihre Technologie wurde ursprünglich für professionelle Küchen entwickelt. Bedienelemente mit Direktzugriff erlauben eine stufenlose Einstellung der gewünschten Absaug- und Beleuchtungsintensität. Diese Abzugshauben sind zusätzlich mit einer umfassenden Perimete-Absaugung ausgestattet.

Begründung der Jury
Visuell reizvoll wirkt hier der Kontrast zwischen dem Edelstahlrahmen und der mittig platzierten Funktionseinheit mit einer schwarzen Glasfront.

AEG Madison Hood
**Cooker Hood
Product Range**
Dunstabzugshauben-
Produktreihe

Manufacturer
Electrolux Major Appliances EMEA,
Stockholm, Sweden
In-house design
Electrolux Group Design EMEA
Web
www.electrolux.com
www.electrolux.it

The cooker hoods of the Madison Hood product range are completely made of stainless steel and give kitchens a professional look. The high-speed motor powerfully and efficiently extracts any cooking fumes. The 90 cm wide hood is ideal for large cooking areas. With regard to ergonomics and suction performance, its tilted design ensures optimal positioning just above the hob.

Statement by the jury
This cooker hood product range embodies a striking, sculptural aesthetics. The material and the purposive design vocabulary go well together.

Die Dunstabzugshauben der Produktreihe Madison Hood sind komplett aus Edelstahl gefertigt und verleihen der Küche ein professionelles Aussehen. Der Hochgeschwindigkeitsmotor saugt leistungsstark und effizient alle Kochdünste ab. Die 90 cm breite Haube eignet sich insbesondere für große Kochflächen. Ihre schräge Anordnung garantiert eine ergonomisch und absaugtechnisch günstige Positionierung der Abzugshaube direkt über dem Kochfeld.

Begründung der Jury
Eine prägnant skulpturale Ästhetik verkörpert diese Dunstabzugshauben-Produktreihe. Das Material harmoniert mit der zweckgerichteten Formensprache.

AEG Movida Hood
**Cooker Hood
Product Range**
Dunstabzugshauben-
Produktreihe

Manufacturer
Electrolux Major Appliances EMEA,
Stockholm, Sweden
In-house design
Electrolux Group Design EMEA
Web
www.electrolux.com
www.electrolux.it

The designers of the Movida Hood product range combined black glass with stainless steel, emphasising the modern look of the 80 cm wide hoods. Its elaborate concept includes advanced features to meet high performance standards: the high-speed motor powerfully and efficiently extracts any cooking fumes, while the front cover can be opened for easy access to the grease filter.

Statement by the jury
The strikingly slim silhouette of this cooker hood product range attracts the attention of the viewer. An elegant design.

Die Gestalter der Produktreihe Movida Hood kombinieren schwarzes Glas mit Edelstahl, was die zeitgemäße Anmutung der 80 cm breiten Abzugshaube betont. Ihr anspruchsvolles Konzept enthä t erweiterte Funktionen zur Erfüllung hoher Leistungsstandards: Der Hochgeschwindigkeitsmotor saugt leistungsstark und effizient alle Kochdünste ab, während die vordere Abdeckung für ein einfaches Zugreifen auf den Fettfilter geöffnet werden kann.

Begründung der Jury
Eine auffallend schmale Silhouette zieht bei dieser Dunstabzugshauben-Produktreihe die Aufmerksamkeit des Betrachters auf sich. Ein eleganter Entwurf.

Electrolux Pearl Hood
**Cooker Hood
Product Range**
Dunstabzugshauben-
Produktreihe

Manufacturer
Electrolux Major Appliances EMEA,
Stockholm, Sweden
In-house design
Electrolux Group Design EMEA
Web
www.electrolux.com
www.electrolux.it

The design concept of this cooker hood product range strives for a characteristic appearance. The control panel made of black glass is embedded in a stainless steel corpus. The simple touch of the control panel enables stepless adjustment of the desired absorption and illumination intensity. Sensor technology combined with perimeter aspiration reliably removes odours and smoke.

Statement by the jury
Elegant looking lines emphasise the compelling functionality of the Pearl Hood product range.

Das Gestaltungskonzept dieser Dunst-abzugshauben-Produktreihe strebt ein charakteristisches Erscheinungsbild an. Die Bedienblende aus schwarzem Glas ist in einen Korpus aus Edelstahl eingebettet. Einfaches Berühren der Bedienelemente erlaubt eine stufenlose Einstellung der gewünschten Absaug- und Beleuchtungs-intensität. Die Sensortechnologie entfernt im Zusammenspiel mit der Perimeter-Absaugung zuverlässig Kochgerüche und Rauch.

Begründung der Jury
Eine elegant wirkende Linienführung unterstreicht die überzeugende Funktiona-lität der Pearl Hood Dunstabzugshauben-Produktreihe.

Electrolux Wing Hood
**Cooker Hood
Product Range**
Dunstabzugshauben-
Produktreihe

Manufacturer
Electrolux Major Appliances EMEA,
Stockholm, Sweden
In-house design
Electrolux Group Design EMEA
Web
www.electrolux.com
www.electrolux.it

The Wing Hood product range comes with a distinctive material combination of glass and stainless steel. Digital slider controls with a pure white LED display enable stepless adjustment of the desired absorption and illumination intensity. Features such as inverter technology, dimmable LED lighting and comprehensive perimeter aspiration enhance the premium quality of the hoods.

Statement by the jury
Due to the lateral glass surfaces, the cooker hood product range appears to be remarkably compact. Thus, the hoods discreetly blend in with kitchen interiors.

Die Dunstabzugshauben der Produktreihe Wing Hood verfügen über eine charak-teristische Materialkombination aus Glas und Edelstahl. Die digitalen Schieberele-mente mit einer reinweißen LED-Anzeige ermöglichen eine stufenlose Einstellung der gewünschten Absaug- und Beleuch-tungsintensität. Funktionen wie eine Inverter-Technologie, eine dimmbare LED-Beleuchtung sowie eine umfassende Perimeter-Absaugung steigern die Hoch-wertigkeit der Hauben.

Begründung der Jury
Aufgrund der seitlichen Glasflächen wirkt die Dunstabzugshauben-Produktreihe auffallend kompakt. Die Hauben fügen sich daher dezent ins Kücheninterieur ein.

Zanussi Curva Hood
**Cooker Hood
Product Range**
Dunstabzugshauben-
Produktreihe

Manufacturer
Electrolux Major Appliances EMEA,
Stockholm, Sweden
In-house design
Electrolux Group Design EMEA
Web
www.electrolux.com
www.electrolux.it

The Curva product range comprises cooker hoods with curved glass surfaces that are visually striking and harmoniously blend in with homely kitchen environments. Simplicity is one of their assets. Special care has been taken to design the lighting concept – from comfortable ambient lighting to the bright halogen lighting of the cooking area. Maximum absorption performance is activated by a single touch of the control panel.

Statement by the jury
With elegantly curved lines, the cooker hood product range emotionally appeals to viewers. Altogether a high-quality impression.

Die Produktreihe Curva besteht aus Dunstabzugshauben mit geschwungenen Glasflächen, die visuell auffallen und sich in wohnliche Küchensituationen harmo-nisch einfügen. Schlichtheit ist eine ihrer Stärken. Besondere Sorgfalt wurde auf das Beleuchtungskonzept verwendet – von ei-ner angenehmen Raumbeleuchtung bis hin zur hellen Halogenbeleuchtung des Koch-bereichs. Die maximale Absaugleistung wird bereits durch einmaliges Berühren des Bedienfeldes aktiviert.

Begründung der Jury
Mittels einer elegant geschwungenen Li-nienführung spricht die Dunstabzugshau-ben-Produktreihe die Betrachter emotional an. Ein hochwertiges Gesamtbild.

Bosch Glass Cover
DWK09M850
Wall-Mounted
Chimney Hood
Wandesse

Manufacturer
Robert Bosch Hausgeräte GmbH,
Munich, Germany
In-house design
Robert Sachon,
Christoph Ortmann,
Oliver Kraemer
Web
www.bosch-hausgeraete.de

Due to its harmonious proportions and innovative structure, the Glass Cover chimney hood harmoniously blends in with any kitchen scenario. The folding cover makes this hood visually and functionally unique. When closed, the filters are covered and the chimney hood looks like a piece of furniture. When the glass panel is open, it serves as a functional and easy-to-clean splash guard which protects the wall behind the cooking area. The panel blends in well with glass surfaces, which are often used in kitchens.

Aufgrund der ausgewogenen Proportionen und des innovativen Aufbaus fügt sich die Wandesse Glass Cover harmonisch in die Küchenlandschaft ein. Ihre klappbare Blende macht die Abzugshaube visuell und funktional unverwechselbar. Im geschlossenen Zustand werden die Filter abgedeckt, was der Esse eine möbelartige Anmutung verleiht. Ist die Glasblende geöffnet, dient diese als funktionaler und leicht zu reinigender Spritzschutz, der die Wand hinter der Kochstelle schützt. Die Glasblende harmoniert mit Glasoberflächen, wie sie in Küchen häufig zu sehen sind.

Statement by the jury
A high degree of functionality is characteristic of this wall-mounted chimney hood. Its fold-out glass panel satisfies many needs.

Begründung der Jury
Ein hohes Maß an Funktionalität zeichnet diese Dunstabzugshaube aus, deren aufklappbare Glasblende multifunktional nutzbar ist.

Siemens LC98KA570
Extractor Hood
Dunstabzugshaube

Manufacturer
Siemens-Electrogeräte GmbH,
Munich, Germany
In-house design
Julia Ehrensberger
Design
Digitalform,
Munich, Germany
Web
www.siemens-home.de

The slanted extractor hood consists of a solid piece of glass that is 6 mm thick in which movable filter panels are inserted. They can be pulled out to operate the extraction vents. The thin, dimmable LED light band at the lower edge of the glass panel illuminates the hob across the whole width. The feature-rich touch screen is equipped with the brand-specific blue lightLine.

Statement by the jury
The appeal of this extractor hood lies in its functionality and the delicate nature of its material – an impressive design.

Diese Schrägesse besteht aus einer 6 mm dünnen, aus einem Stück gefertigten Glasscheibe, in welche bewegliche Filterpaneele eingelassen sind. Diese lassen sich aus der Fläche herausbewegen und geben somit die Absaugöffnungen frei. Das dünne, dimmbare LED-Lichtband an der unteren Kante der Glasscheibe beleuchtet das Kochfeld in voller Breite. Die funktionsreiche Touch-Bedienung ist mit einer herstellertypischen blauen lightLine ausgestattet.

Begründung der Jury
Ein beeindruckender Entwurf, bei welchem die filigrane Beschaffenheit des Materials und die Funktionalität der Dunstabzugshaube überzeugen.

Siemens LD97AA670
Downdraft
Tischlüfter

Manufacturer
Siemens-Electrogeräte GmbH,
Munich, Germany
In-house design
Julia Ehrensberger
Web
www.siemens-home.de

This downdraft is installed in the worktop in the immediate vicinity of the hob. It can be silently extended to a height of 406 mm. The activation of a light strip, spanning the entire width, is coupled to it. Thus, optimum illumination of the hob is achieved. A touch control on the upper part of the glass cover rounds off the design of future-oriented rim ventilation.

Statement by the jury
Harmoniously matching stainless steel and glass surfaces underline the elegance of this rim ventilation for cooking fumes.

Dieser Tischlüfter, der in unmittelbarer Nähe des Kochfeldes in die Arbeitsfläche eingebaut wird, lässt sich lautlos auf eine Höhe von 406 mm herausfahren. Daran gekoppelt ist das Einschalten eines über die gesamte Breite laufenden LED-Lichtbandes. Somit wird eine optimale Beleuchtung des Kochfeldes erreicht. Eine Touch-Control auf der Oberseite der Glasabdeckung rundet das Konzept einer zukunftsweisenden Randabsaugung ab.

Begründung der Jury
Harmonisch aufeinander abgestimmte Edelstahl- und Glasflächen unterstreichen die Eleganz dieses Tischlüfters.

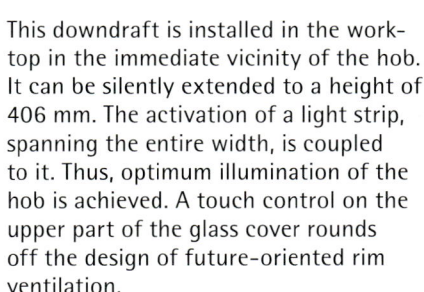

Electrolux Compact
Compact Dishwasher Product Range
Kompakt-Geschirrspüler-Produktreihe

Manufacturer
Electrolux Major Appliances EMEA,
Stockholm, Sweden
In-house design
Electrolux Group Design EMEA
Web
www.electrolux.com
www.electrolux.it

The small-format dishwashers of the Inspiration Range Compact require only little space. Their distinctive corpus is characterised by clear lines and colours (glossy white, black or red), material properties and a specific handle. The intuitive LED user interface is discreetly hidden on the upper edge of the door. Users can choose between six automatic programmes that are activated at the push of a button.

Statement by the jury
These compact dishwashers are both visually and haptically appealing. A practical product solution which can be installed easily.

Mit ihrem Kleinformat haben die Geschirr-spüler der Inspiration Range Compact einen nur geringen Platzbedarf. Ihr cha-rakteristischer Korpus ist von klaren Linien und Farben (glänzend Weiß, Schwarz oder Rot), der Materialbeschaffenheit und dem typischen Griff geprägt. Eine intuitiv hand-habbare LED-Bedienoberfläche ist dezent auf der oberen Türkante versteckt. Der Verbraucher hat die Wahl zwischen sechs Automatikprogrammen, die per Tasten-druck aktiviert werden.

Begründung der Jury
Sowohl visuell als auch haptisch anspre-chend wirken diese Kompakt-Geschirrspü-ler. Eine praktische Produktlösung ohne Einbauaufwand.

Aline
Dishwasher
Geschirrspüler

Manufacturer
Vestel Beyaz Esya San. ve Tic. A.S.,
Manisa, Turkey
In-house design
Vestel White Industrial Design Group
(Serpil Sedef Yağcı)
Web
www.vestel.com.tr

The design of the Aline dishwasher reflects high-grade brand quality. The glass front is available in different colours and it can be integrated in kitchen units in various ways. The chrome coated, slim profile underlines an elegant appearance. While the most frequently used controls are arranged on the tilted panel, the other elements hide on top of the door.

Statement by the jury
The shining glass front of this dishwasher provides clarity and purity, an appealing product solution with a bold colour scheme.

Aline ist ein Geschirrspüler, dessen Ge-staltung eine hochwertige Markenqualität reflektiert. Die in verschiedenen Farben er-hältliche Glasfront lässt sich variantenreich in Küchenzeilen integrieren. Das mit Chrom beschichtete, schlanke Profil betont ein elegantes Erscheinungsbild. Während sich die am häufigsten verwendeten Bedienele-mente auf dem geneigten Panel befinden, verbergen sich die übrigen Elemente auf der Oberseite der Tür.

Begründung der Jury
Die glänzende Glasfront dieses Geschirr-spülers vermittelt Klarheit und Reinheit, eine ansprechende Produktlösung mit Mut zur Farbe.

Electrolux RealLife
Free-Standing Dishwasher
Stand-Geschirrspüler

Manufacturer
Electrolux Major Appliances EMEA,
Stockholm, Sweden
In-house design
Electrolux Group Design EMEA
Web
www.electrolux.com
www.electrolux.it

The free-standing dishwasher of the RealLife Inspiration Range has an exclusive look. A transparent control panel and a well-arranged user interface with white LED displays are easy to understand and meet the most common user needs. The XXL tub and the innovative spray arm are combined with an intelligent Auto-Flex programme, which provides reliable cleaning results at the push of a button.

Statement by the jury
The independent style of this dishwasher is a striking feature and emphasises the compelling functionality of the appliance.

Der Stand-Geschirrspüler der Inspiration Range RealLife erzielt eine exklusive Anmutung. Eine transparente Bedienblende und eine gut strukturierte Bedienoberfläche mit weißen LED-Anzeigen decken die gängigsten Nutzerbedürfnisse leicht verständlich ab. Der XXL-Bottich und der innovative Sprüharm sind mit einem intelligenten AutoFlex-Programm kombiniert, das auf Tastendruck zuverlässige Spülergebnisse erreicht.

Begründung der Jury
Bei diesem Geschirrspüler fällt die eigenständige Formensprache auf, welche seine überzeugende Funktionalität betont.

Electrolux RealLife
Semi-Integrated Dishwasher Product Range
Halbintegrierte Geschirrspüler-Produktreihe

Manufacturer
Electrolux Major Appliances EMEA,
Stockholm, Sweden
In-house design
Electrolux Group Design EMEA
Web
www.electrolux.com
www.electrolux.it

The semi-integrated dishwashers of the RealLife Inspiration Range are equipped with integrated control panels and convey an overall impression of high quality. The brand-typical inverted handle fits in harmoniously with modern kitchen units. An intuitive user interface with white and amber LEDs provides for a convenient programme selection. The intelligent AutoFlex programme can be activated at the push of a button.

Statement by the jury
With its classy design, the front panels of these dishwashers blend in with their surroundings in a visually appealing way.

Ein hochwertiges Gesamtbild zeigen die halbintegrierten Geschirrspüler der Inspiration Range RealLife mit integrierter Bedienblende. Der markentypisch invertierte Griff fügt sich harmonisch in zeitgemäße Küchenzeilen ein. Eine intuitiv nutzbare Bedienoberfläche mit weißen oder bernsteinfarbenen LED-Anzeigen bietet eine komfortable Programmauswahl. Per Tastendruck lassen sich die intelligenten AutoFlex-Programme ansteuern.

Begründung der Jury
Visuell ansprechend fügt sich die exklusiv gestaltete Gerätefront der Geschirrspüler in ihre Umgebung ein.

Siemens SN56V594EU
Built-in Dishwasher
Einbau-Geschirrspüler

Manufacturer
Siemens-Electrogeräte GmbH,
Munich, Germany
In-house design
Wolfgang Kaczmarek,
Klaus Foersterling
Web
www.siemens-home.de

This built-in dishwasher with metal-Touch operation indicates the selected cycle, special functions, preset time and cycle status. In addition, the eco forecast visualises the water and energy consumption. The appliance features an automatic cleaning cycle, three automatic programmes for different temperature ranges as well as a blue interior light. The time-saving varioSpeedPlus programme shortens the process of cleaning by 66 per cent.

Statement by the jury
This dishwasher features a unit front that suits the kitchen furniture. In addition, its innovative technology is impressive.

Dieser Einbau-Geschirrspüler mit metalTouch-Bedienung zeigt das gewählte Programm, Sonderfunktionen, Zeitvorwahl sowie den Programmablauf an. Zudem visualisiert die Eco-Prognose den Wasser- und Energieverbrauch. Das Gerät verfügt über eine Reinigungsautomatik, drei Auto-Programme für unterschiedliche Temperaturbereiche sowie eine blaue Innenbeleuchtung. Für eine Zeitersparnis von 66 Prozent sorgt die Programmoption varioSpeedPlus.

Begründung der Jury
Eine Gerätefront passend zur Kücheneinrichtung bietet dieser Geschirrspüler, zudem überzeugt die innovative Technik.

Siemens SN26V893EU
Free-Standing Dishwasher
Stand-Geschirrspüler

Manufacturer
Siemens-Electrogeräte GmbH,
Munich, Germany
In-house design
Klaus Foersterling,
Wolfgang Kaczmarek
Web
www.siemens-home.de

The metalTouch control panel of this free-standing dishwasher enables not only programme selection but also the activation of special functions and the preselection of time. Water and energy consumption is indicated by eco forecast. Limited to 44 decibels, the dishwasher is comfortably quiet. A zone for heavily soiled dishes is integrated in the lower basket. The 3-level height adjustment of the upper basket allows varying the loading capacity.

Statement by the jury
As to functionality and handling, this dishwasher with stainless steel body provides convincing proof of meeting high requirements.

Das metalTouch-Bedienfeld des Stand-Geschirrspülers ermöglicht neben der Programmauswahl die Aktivierung von Sonderfunktionen sowie einer Zeitvorwahl. Der Wasser- und Energieverbrauch wird mittels Eco-Prognose angezeigt. Mit 44 Dezibel arbeitet der Geschirrspüler angenehm leise. Im Unterkorb steht eine Zone für stark verschmutztes Geschirr zur Verfügung. Die 3-stufige Höhenverstellbarkeit des Oberkorbes variiert die Beladungskapazität.

Begründung der Jury
Einen gehobenen Anspruch an Funktionalität und Bedienbarkeit stellt dieser Geschirrspüler mit Edelstahlkorpus glaubhaft unter Beweis.

SMI69U65EU
Integrated Dishwasher
Integrierter Geschirrspüler

Manufacturer
Robert Bosch Hausgeräte GmbH,
Munich, Germany
In-house design
Thomas Ott, Robert Sachon
Web
www.bosch-hausgeraete.de

In addition to a well-structured, minimalist panel, this integrated dishwasher is characterised by an intuitive touch control. The high-definition colour TFT display provides information on programmes as well as usage and dosage recommendations. The programme status can be read from a distance. Inside, the resource-saving appliance features flexible baskets and a cutlery drawer.

Statement by the jury
The design concept of this dishwasher conveys high quality and functionality. It discreetly integrates into kitchen units.

Neben einer klar gegliederten, minimalistischen Blende zeichnet sich der integrierte Geschirrspüler durch eine intuitive Touch-Bedienung aus. Das hoch auflösende Farb-TFT-Display bietet Informationen zu Programmen sowie Hinweise zur Nutzung und Verbrauchsmittelzugabe. Dabei kann der Programmstatus auch aus größeren Entfernungen abgelesen werden. Im Inneren bietet das ressourcensparame Gerät flexible Körbe und eine Besteckschublade.

Begründung der Jury
Hochwertigkeit und Funktionalität vermittelt das Gestaltungskonzept eines Geschirrspülers, der sich dezent in die Küchenzeile einfügt.

SMV69U60EU
Fully Integrated Dishwasher
Vollintegrierter Geschirrspüler

Manufacturer
Robert Bosch Hausgeräte GmbH,
Munich, Germany
In-house design
Thomas Ott, Robert Sachon
Web
www.bosch-hausgeraete.de

The design concept of this fully integrated dishwasher dispenses with a control panel which is visible from the outside. Instead, the appliance projects the remaining cycle time and other information on the floor. Inside, the dishwasher impresses with elaborate equipment such as the atmospheric light, flexible baskets, an intuitive touch control and a resource-saving technology.

Statement by the jury
In an innovative way, users are informed about the current programme status of the dishwasher, an inventive design concept.

Das Gestaltungskonzept des vollintegrierten Geschirrspülers verzichtet auf eine von außen sichtbare Bedienblende. Stattdessen projiziert das Gerät während des Spülbetriebs die Programmrestzeit und weitere Informationen auf den Boden. Im Inneren überzeugt der Geschirrspüler durch gut durchdachte Ausstattungsdetails wie das atmosphärische Licht, flexible Körbe, eine intuitive Touch-Bedienung sowie eine ressourcensparame Technik.

Begründung der Jury
Auf innovative Weise wird der Nutzer über den aktuellen Programmstatus des Geschirrspülers informiert, eine originelle Gestaltungsidee.

Profilo BM5380MA
Free-Standing Dishwasher
Stand-Geschirrspüler

Manufacturer
BSH Bosch und Siemens Hausgeräte GmbH,
Munich, Germany
In-house design
Ralph Pietruska, Ulrich Goss
Web
www.bsh-group.com

The harmonious interplay of matt silver coated surfaces and brushed stainless steel distinguishes this free-standing dishwasher. Clear lines and an intuitive user interface with direct selection buttons and backlit symbols characterise the control panel. The key element is the ergonomically shaped, recessed grip. Convenience is provided by six programmes, a start timer and the special functions VarioSpeed and "half load".

Das harmonische Zusammenspiel von matt silberfarbenen Lackoberflächen und gebürstetem Edelstahl prägt diesen Stand-Geschirrspüler. Eine klare Linienführung und eine intuitive Bedienoberfläche mit Direktanwahl-Tasten und hinterleuchteter Symbolik charakterisieren die Bedienblende. Zentrales Element ist die ergonomisch geformte Griffmulde. Für Komfort sorgen sechs Programme, eine Zeitvorwahl sowie die Sonderfunktionen VarioSpeed und „Halbe Beladung".

Statement by the jury
In this free-standing dishwasher with stainless steel body, the stringent implementation of a distinct design concept is impressive.

Begründung der Jury
Die stringente Umsetzung eines markanten Gestaltungskonzepts überzeugt bei diesem Stand-Geschirrspüler mit Edelstahl-Korpus.

Profilo BM6480MG
Free-Standing Dishwasher
Stand-Geschirrspüler

Manufacturer
BSH Bosch und Siemens Hausgeräte GmbH,
Munich, Germany
In-house design
Ralph Pietruska, Ulrich Goss
Web
www.bsh-group.com

This free-standing dishwasher features high quality materials; the matt silver plastic elements and brushed stainless steel surfaces match in a harmonious way. The focus of its design is on the front panel with an ergonomically shaped handle positioned in its centre. The horizontally aligned display shows the respective settings. The economical "half load" function saves energy, water and time.

Der Stand-Geschirrspüler zeigt eine hochwertige Materialität, wobei matt silberfarbene Kunststoffelemente und gebürstete Edelstahlflächen harmonisch aufeinander abgestimmt sind. Im Fokus der Gestaltung steht die Frontblende, in deren Zentrum der ergonomisch geformte Griff positioniert ist. Eine horizontal gestaltete Anzeige kommuniziert die aktuellen Einstellungen. Ökonomisch sinnvoll spart die „Halbe Beladung"-Funktion Energie, Wasser und Zeit.

Statement by the jury
The distinct overall picture of this dishwasher is due to a metal body from which control panel and recessed grip stand out, producing a strong contrast.

Begründung der Jury
Sein prägnantes Gesamtbild verdankt dieser Geschirrspüler einem Metall-Korpus, von welchem sich Bedienblende und Griffmulde kontrastreich absetzen.

Electrolux FreshPlus
Refrigerator
Product Range
Kühlschrank-Produktreihe

Manufacturer
Electrolux Major Appliances EMEA,
Stockholm, Sweden
In-house design
Electrolux Group Design EMEA
Web
www.electrolux.com
www.electrolux.it

The refrigerators of the Inspiration Range feature an electronic touch display with white LEDs. The high quality interior is distinct and offers plenty of space for food storage. The cooling system is based on the technology of refrigerators in restaurants; two separate cooling circuits ensure fresh climate in the refrigerator and prevent icing in the freezer.

Statement by the jury
The refrigerators of this product range rises like monoliths, while the distinctive display emphasises functionality.

Die Kühlschrank-Produktreihe der Inspiration Range zeichnet sich durch ein elektronisches Sensordisplay mit weißen LEDs aus. Die hochwertige Innengestaltung ist klar und bietet viel Platz für die Lebensmittellagerung. Die von Restaurant-Kühlschränken abgeleitete Kühltechnik mit zwei getrennten Kühlkreisläufen sorgt für ein Frischeklima im Kühlschrank und verhindert die Vereisung im Gefrierbereich.

Begründung der Jury
Monolithisch ragen die Geräte der Kühlschrank-Produktreihe auf, während das charakteristische Display die Funktionalität unterstreicht.

Electrolux Kitchen Line
Refrigerator
Product Range
Kühlschrank-Produktreihe

Manufacturer
Electrolux Major Appliances EMEA,
Stockholm, Sweden
In-house design
Electrolux Group Design EMEA
Web
www.electrolux.com
www.electrolux.it

The appearance of the exterior of this professionally designed refrigerator product range is distinguished by a polished stainless steel front and an architectural handle. The interior design is transparent and there is plenty of storage space in different shelves and compartments. The applied TwinTech cooling technology, which is commonly used in restaurant kitchens, constantly provides for a fresh climate in the cooling zone and prevents icing.

Statement by the jury
Behind puristic and refined stainless steel fronts hide functionally elaborate refrigerators with expedient equipment features.

Die Außenansicht der professionell gestalteten Kühlschrank-Produktreihe zeichnet sich durch eine polierte Edelstahlfront und einen architektonisch anmutenden Griff aus. Die Gestaltung im Inneren ist transparent und bietet viel Stauraum in verschiedenen Fächern und Ablagen. Die von Kühlschränken in Restaurantküchen abgeleitete TwinTech-Kühltechnik liefert ein konstantes Frischeklima im Kühlbereich und verhindert die Vereisung.

Begründung der Jury
Hinter puristisch und edel wirkenden Edelstahlfronten verbergen sich funktional durchdachte Kühlschränke mit praktischen Ausstattungsdetails.

3D-GEN2
Refrigerator
Kühlschrank

Manufacturer
Haier Group,
Qingdao, China
Design
Haier Innovation Design Center
(Li Xiang, Huang Zeping,
Chi Shasha, Chang Yonghun),
Qingdao, China
Web
www.haier.com

This refrigerator follows the My Zone design concept, which advances look, interior and system features of the first generation of three-door refrigerators. Employing an air-cooling technology and the variable frequency DC compressor, the product achieves the energy efficiency rating A+++. This allows individual setting of temperature zones. The upper, precisely stamped stainless steel door can be opened both to the left and right. The two lower drawers are distinguished by a subtle handle design.

Dieser Kühlschrank folgt dem My-Zone-Gestaltungskonzept, welches die erste Generation der dreitürigen Kühlschränke hinsichtlich ihrer äußeren Gestaltung, der Innenausstattung und Systemfunktion weiterentwickelt. Die Nutzung einer Luftkühlung sowie eines variablen Kompressors erreicht den Energieverbrauchsstandard A+++ und ermöglicht individuell temperierbare Zonen. Die obere, präzise gestanzte Edelstahltür kann sowohl nach links als auch nach rechts geöffnet werden. Die beiden unteren Schubladen zeichnen sich durch eine dezente Griffgestaltung aus.

Statement by the jury
A distinct, puristic style dominates the elegant-looking refrigerator. Its ease of use meets high standards.

Begründung der Jury
Eine klare, puristische Formensprache prägt den elegant wirkenden Kühlschrank. Der Bedienkomfort entspricht gehobenen Anforderungen.

REF-M4CS
Refrigerator
Kühlschrank

Manufacturer
Haier Group,
Qingdao, China
Design
Haier Innovation Design Center
(Li Xiang, Chang Yonghun, Li Qiang),
Qingdao, China
Web
www.haier.com

This refrigerator is an eco-friendly appliance that uses a CFC-free cooling agent. In addition, it is most effectively insulated. Thanks to its flexible technology, the cooling system features individually selectable temperature ranges, which can be precisely controlled and set by the user. Innovative technologies prevent the formation of odours. The design concept combines two doors and three drawers to form a homogenous overall picture.

Dieser Kühlschrank ist ein umweltfreundliches Gerät mit einem FCKW-freien Kühlmittel. Darüber hinaus ist er besonders effektiv isoliert. Das Kühlsystem bietet aufgrund seiner variablen Technik individuell wählbare Temperaturbereiche, die vom Benutzer exakt kontrolliert und eingestellt werden können. Innovative Technologien verhindern das Entstehen von Gerüchen. Das Gestaltungskonzept integriert die beiden Türen sowie die drei Schubfächer zu einem homogenen Gesamtbild.

Statement by the jury
The design of the handles characterises the distinctive look of this refrigerator. Its freely selectable temperature ranges are innovative.

Begründung der Jury
Die Gestaltung der Griffleisten charakterisiert die prägnante Anmutung dieses Kühlschranks. Innovativ sind seine frei wählbaren Temperaturbereiche.

REF-S6CG
Refrigerator
Kühlschrank

Manufacturer
Haier Group,
Qingdao, China
Design
Haier Innovation Design Center
(Chang Yonghun, Li Xiang,
Zhou Shu, Li Qiang),
Qingdao, China
Web
www.haier.com

This CFC-free refrigerator features several insulation layers and a variably adjustable cooling system. According to individual needs, users can select up to seven different temperature zones in order to freeze or store fish, meat, vegetables and fruit gently. The body and the interior of the appliance are easy to clean. With regard to the habits of Chinese consumers, there is no water dispenser. The energy-saving appliance consumes less than one kilowatt per day.

Der FCKW-freie Kühlschrank wurde mit mehreren Isolationsschichten und einem variabel ausgerichteten Kühlsystem ausgestattet. Je nach Bedarf kann der Benutzer bis zu sieben unterschiedliche Temperaturzonen einstellen, um Fisch, Fleisch, Gemüse und Obst schonend zu lagern oder einzufrieren. Der Gerätekorpus sowie der Innenbereich sind unkompliziert zu reinigen. Unter Berücksichtigung der Gewohnheiten chinesischer Verbraucher wurde auf einen Wasserspender verzichtet. Das energiesparsame Gerät verbraucht pro Tag weniger als ein Kilowatt.

Statement by the jury
In this refrigerator, the combination of shining surfaces and gently curved handles forms a harmonious overall impression.

Begründung der Jury
Glänzende Oberflächen und sanft geschwungene Griffleisten verbinden sich bei diesem Kühlschrank zu einem harmonischen Gesamtbild.

Changhong BCD-537WIPB
Refrigerator
Kühlschrank

Manufacturer
Sichuan Changhong Electric Co. Ltd.
Chengdu (Sichuan), China
In-house design
Homwee Technology Co. Ltd.,
Innovative Design Center
Web
www.changhong.com

The frameless glass front gives this refrigerator an elegant high-grade appearance. The design uses a new space management: the Magic Box System is a modular system comprising a set of transparent containers that can be flexibly arranged. An innovative air purification technology provides for freshness. The use of environment-friendly materials, frequency conversion technology as well as fluoride-free refrigeration make this BCD-537WIPB an eco-friendly appliance.

Die rahmenlose Glasfront verleiht diesem Kühlschrank eine elegante, hochwertige Anmutung. Die Innenraumgestaltung nutzt ein neues Raum-Management: Das Magic Box System besteht aus einem Satz transparenter Behälter, die flexibel nach dem Baukastenprinzip untergebracht werden können. Für Frische sorgt eine innovative Luftreinigungstechnologie. Die Verwendung von umweltfreundlichen Materialien, der Frequenzumwandlungstechnologie sowie die fluoridfreie Kältetechnik machen den BCD-537WIPB zu einem umweltfreundlichen Gerät.

Statement by the jury
An independent style and high ease of use characterise this refrigerator. Its material is particularly striking.

Begründung der Jury
Eine eigenständige Formensprache und ein hoher Bedienkomfort zeichnen diesen Kühlschrank aus. Vor allem die Materialität fällt auf.

Changhong Cabinet
Refrigerator
Kühlschrank

Manufacturer
Sichuan Changhong Electric Co. Ltd.,
Chengdu (Sichuan), China
In-house design
Homwee Technology Co. Ltd.,
Innovative Design Center
Web
www.changhong.com

The Changhong Cabinet refrigerator shows an elegant, minimalist appearance. Its double door design allows for easy access to frequently needed food. In addition, less energy is consumed when the door is opened. The temperature of the cold fresh drawer, located at the bottom of the main compartment, can be independently controlled using its own touch operation panel. The appliance features a microprocessor with a tracking system that helps consumers, e.g. to draw up a shopping list. Users can interact with the refrigerator using the touchscreen on the door or remotely from a smartphone or computer.

Der Kühlschrank Changhong Cabinet zeigt eine elegante, minimalistische Formensprache. Seine zweitürige Bauweise ermöglicht den leichten Zugang zu häufig benötigten Lebensmitteln, zudem wird beim Öffnen der Tür weniger Energie verbraucht. Die Temperatur der Kühlschublade, die sich im unteren Gerätebereich befindet, kann separat über das Touch-Bedienfeld gesteuert werden. Das Gerät verfügt über einen Mikroprozessor mit einem Tracking-System, das den Nutzern z.B. die Erstellung einer Einkaufsliste ermöglicht. Die Verbraucher können den Kühlschrank über den Tür-Touchscreen sowie aus der Ferne über Smartphone oder Computer steuern.

Statement by the jury
Innovative features enhance the practical value of this refrigerator. Furthermore, the striking overall appearance is impressive.

Begründung der Jury
Innovative Ausstattungsmerkmale steigern bei diesem Kühlschrank den Gebrauchswert. Darüber hinaus überzeugt das markante Gesamtbild.

G-Zone 2
(GS9366NSSZ/GS9366NECZ)
Refrigerator
Kühlschrank

Manufacturer
LG Electronics Inc.,
Seoul, South Korea
In-house design
Kyu-Kwan Choi, Sun-Il Cho,
Jae-Young Kim
Web
www.lg.com

In this refrigerator, the centrally positioned display was designed not as an independent element but as a dividing line matching the minimalist form. The metal surfaces of the body harmoniously fit in with different kitchen settings, while the incremental LED lighting introduces attractive accents. A special door-in-door system allows easy access at the push of a button without the need to open the refrigerator.

Bei diesem Kühlschrank wurde das zentral positionierte Display als Teilungslinie und nicht als unabhängiges Element entworfen, was die minimalistische Gestaltung unterstützt. Die Metallflächen des Korpus passen sich harmonisch in unterschiedliche Küchen ein, während die Stufen-LED-Beleuchtung attraktive Akzente setzt. Ein spezielles Tür-in-Tür-System erlaubt einen einfachen Zugang per Tastendruck, ohne dass der Kühlschrank geöffnet werden muss.

Statement by the jury
Clear lines and an unobtrusive display arrangement create a purist overall impression of the refrigerator.

Begründung der Jury
Mittels einer klaren Linienführung und dank einer dezenten Display-Anordnung entsteht bei diesem Kühlschrank ein puristisches Gesamtbild.

Siemens KG23D1110W
Fridge-Freezer
Kühl-Gefrier-Kombination

Manufacturer
Siemens-Electrogeräte GmbH,
Munich, Germany
In-house design
Tim Richter, Christoph Becke,
Yao Xingen, Wang Kai
Web
www.siemens-home.de

Designed specifically for the Chinese market, this fridge-freezer offers two freezer compartments with different temperature zones. Behind the centre door is a 1-star freezer compartment, ideal for keeping fresh fish, meat and vegetables; the 3-star freezer is arranged below. Due to the integrated handles, the design of the door looks functional and timeless. It underscores the freezingFresh quality label.

Statement by the jury
A tripartite division of the body shapes the purist overall impression of the fridge-freezer and provides users with a compelling functionality.

Speziell für den chinesischen Markt entwickelt, bietet diese Kühl-Gefrier-Kombination zwei Gefriereinheiten mit unterschiedlichen Temperaturzonen. Hinter der Mitteltür befindet sich ein 1-Stern-Gefrierbereich, der sich zum Frischhalten von Fisch, Fleisch und Gemüse eignet, darunter ist das 3-Sterne-Gefrierfach. Die Gestaltung der Türen wirkt aufgrund der integrierten Griffleisten funktional und zeitlos, sie hebt das Qualitätsmerkmal freezingFresh hervor.

Begründung der Jury
Eine Dreiteilung des Korpus prägt das puristische Gesamtbild der Kühl-Gefrier-Kombination und bietet den Nutzern eine überzeugende Funktionalität.

KKF287S5TI
Refrigerator
Kühlschrank

Manufacturer
Robert Bosch Hausgeräte GmbH,
Munich, Germany
In-house design
Tim Richter, Ralph Staud,
Yao Xingen, Wang Yueru
Web
www.bosch-hausgeraete.de

Frameless white glass panels with a "nature-line" print pattern characterise this emotionally appealing refrigerator. Integrated handles on both sides define the front and underline the clarity of the appliance. The fully transparent bowls and shelves are practical and are optimally matched. The 3-circuit cooling system precisely regulates the temperatures in the three compartments, which also contributes to energy savings.

Statement by the jury
The surface design of this refrigerator achieves a charming effect by fine lines that visually freshens the glass front.

Weiße Glasflächen ohne Rahmen, bedruckt mit einem „Nature-line"-Muster, prägen den emotional ansprechenden Kühlschrank. Die integrierten Griffe auf beiden Seiten definieren die Front und unterstreichen die Klarheit des Geräts. Die volltransparenten Schalen und Regalböden sind optimal aufeinander abgestimmt und praktisch. Das 3-Kreis-Kühlsystem regelt die Temperaturen in den drei Fächern sehr präzise, was auch zur Energieeinsparung beiträgt.

Begründung der Jury
Einen reizvollen Effekt erreicht die Oberflächengestaltung dieses Kühlschranks, indem feine Linien die Glasfront visuell beleben.

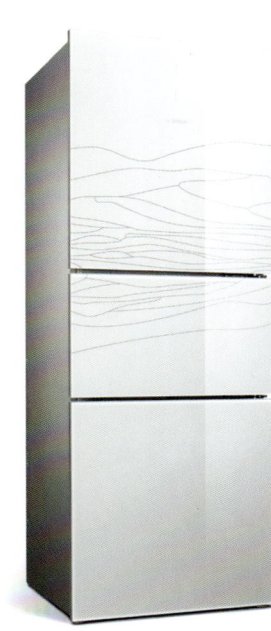

KMF40S20TI
Refrigerator
Kühlschrank

Manufacturer
Robert Bosch Hausgeräte GmbH,
Munich, Germany
In-house design
Ralph Staud, Thomas Tischer,
Tim Richter, Yao Xingen
Design
Eisele Kuberg Design,
Neu-Ulm, Germany
Web
www.bosch-hausgeraete.de

The design of the body of this multi-door refrigerator is characterised by the use of real materials. The doors and drawers are made of ColorGlass, and the handles are completely made of brushed metal. Thanks to the double door, chilled goods are ergonomically easy to reach and are clearly arranged at eye level. The touch control display behind glass enables easy operation, while the flexxibleStorage-system optimises the use of the interior space.

Statement by the jury
The combination of high quality materials highlights the homely look and feel of a refrigerator which fits in with contemporary open plan kitchens.

Die Korpusgestaltung des Multidoor-Kühlschranks zeichnet sich durch den Einsatz von Echtmaterialien aus. So sind die Türen und Schubladen aus ColorGlass und die Griffe komplett aus gebürstetem Metall. Durch die Doppeltür ist das Kühlgut ergonomisch günstig und übersichtlich auf Augenhöhe erreichbar. Das Touch-Control-Display hinter Glas ermöglicht eine leichte Bedienung, während das flexxibleStorage-System das Platzangebot im Innenraum optimiert.

Begründung der Jury
Die Kombination hochwertiger Materialien unterstreicht die wohnliche Anmutung eines Kühlschranks, der sich zeitgemäß in offene Küchen einfügt.

China Verve
Refrigerator
Kühlschrank

Manufacturer
Haier Group,
Qingdao, China
Design
Haier Innovation Design Center
(Wu Jian, Zhao Shilei,
Wang Tianjian, Liu Haibo),
Qingdao, China
Web
www.haier.com

For this refrigerator, ceramic materials have been used in an innovative way. Based on the Chinese porcelain artistry of the Song Dynasty, a traditional manufacturing method is employed to meet today's needs and to give each surface a unique look. The robust material is acid- and alkali-resistant and durable. The manufacturing process is environment-friendly since no ink is used when the ornamentation is created.

Auf innovative Weise werden bei diesem Kühlschrank keramische Werkstoffe eingesetzt. In Anlehnung an die chinesische Porzellankunst der Song-Dynastie wird ein traditionelles Herstellungsverfahren zeitgemäß genutzt, sodass jede Korpusoberfläche eine einzigartige Anmutung erhält. Das robuste Material ist säure- und alkalibeständig sowie langlebig. Der Herstellungsprozess ist umweltfreundlich, da bei der Gestaltung der Ornamentik keinerlei Tinte eingesetzt wird.

Statement by the jury
The two-door refrigerator presents a particularly exquisite look. The front of the appliance is made of innovative material.

Begründung der Jury
Ein besonders edles Gesamtbild zeigt dieser zweitürige Kühlschrank, dessen Gerätefront aus einem innovativen Material besteht.

Nature Mark
Refrigerator
Kühlschrank

Manufacturer
Haier Group,
Qingdao, China
Design
Haier Innovation Design Center
(Zhao Shilei, Wu Jian, Shao Yanan,
Luo Yanping, Yang Maosheng),
Qingdao, China
Web
www.haier.com

Due to its innovative surface design, the Nature Mark refrigerator has a distinct and high quality look. The three dimensional surface structure of the appliance creates an emotional impression. By using a metallic stove-enamelled finish, the coating undergoes a special process causing an aesthetically appealing crack formation. The surface is durable, stable and eco-friendly.

Eine innovative Oberflächengestaltung lässt den Kühlschrank „Nature Mark" unverwechselbar und hochwertig erscheinen. Die dreidimensionale Oberflächenstruktur verleiht dem Gerät eine emotionale Anmutung. Unter Verwendung eines Metallic-Einbrennlacks durchläuft die Beschichtung einen Prozess, durch den es zu einer ästhetischen Rissbildung kommt. Die Oberfläche ist langlebig, stabil und umweltfreundlich.

Statement by the jury
An unusual finish, which resembles a stone surface, characterises the independent overall picture of this refrigerator.

Begründung der Jury
Eine ungewöhnliche Lackierung, die an eine Steinfläche erinnert, prägt das eigenständige Gesamtbild dieses Kühlschranks.

Siemens KG39NXW30, KG39NXL30, KG39NXI40
Fridge-Freezer
Kühl-Gefrier-Kombination

Manufacturer
Siemens-Electrogeräte GmbH,
Munich, Germany
In-house design
Christoph Becke, Max Eicher
Web
www.siemens-home.de

The energy-saving noFrost appliance is characterised by its formal reduction and its surface materials. In addition, the stainless steel handles and the ergonomically positioned control of the appliance bring in appealing aspects. The functional interior ensures high practical value: large drawers in the cooling and freezing compartments combine simplicity and easy access. In the cooling compartment, different temperature zones can be used according to requirements.

Statement by the jury
A timeless and high quality appearance distinguishes this fridge-freezer. The functional interior equipment provides operating advantages.

Dieses energiesparsame noFrost-Gerät ist durch eine formale Reduktion und die verwendeten Oberflächenmaterialien geprägt. Zudem setzen Edelstahlgriffe und eine ergonomisch positionierte Gerätebedienung ansprechende Akzente. Die funktionale Ausstattung bietet einen hohen Gebrauchswert: Große Schubladen in Kühl- und Gefrierfach verbinden Übersichtlichkeit mit einem leichten Zugriff. Im Kühlfach sind je nach Bedarf unterschiedliche Klimazonen nutzbar.

Begründung der Jury
Ein zeitlos und hochwertig wirkendes Gesamtbild charakterisiert diese Kühl-Gefrier-Kombination. Die funktionale Innenraumgestaltung bietet Bedienvorteile.

Siemens GS36DPI20, KS36WPI30
Twincenter Refrigerator and Freezer
Twincenter Kühl- und Gefrierschrank

Manufacturer
Siemens-Electrogeräte GmbH,
Munich, Germany
In-house design
Max Eicher, Christoph Becke
Web
www.siemens-home.de

Refrigerator and freezer are positioned side-by-side to form a large-volume food storage centre. Automated water and ice dispensers add visual accents. In addition to its large volume, Twincenter impresses with high-energy efficiency, glare-free LED illumination and robust trims in areas that are subject to heavy wear such as the handles. The cooling area also features a special climate zone for fruits and vegetables.

Statement by the jury
The shiny stainless steel body of this fridge-freezer achieves a visual conciseness which expresses quality and significance.

Kühl- und Gefrierschrank bilden durch ihr Side-by-Side-Konzept ein großvolumiges Vorratszentrum. Visuelle Akzente setzen die automatisierten Spender für Wasser und Eis. Neben seinem großen Volumen besticht das Twincenter durch eine hohe Energieeffizienz, eine blendfreie LED-Beleuchtung und robuste Applikationen an stark beanspruchten Bereichen wie etwa den Griffen. Zudem bietet der Kühlbereich eine spezielle Klimazone für Obst und Gemüse.

Begründung der Jury
Der glänzende Edelstahlkorpus des Kühl- und Gefrierschranks erreicht eine visuelle Prägnanz, die Qualität und Wertigkeit zum Ausdruck bringt.

Siemens KG36WVL30
Fridge-Freezer
Kühl-Gefrier-Kombination

Manufacturer
Siemens-Electrogeräte GmbH,
Munich, Germany
In-house design
Christoph Becke, Max Eicher
Web
www.siemens-home.de

This fridge-freezer features a water tank with integrated filter. Cooled water can easily be filled into a glass or carafe through the ergonomically positioned outlet. In addition, the energy-efficient appliance has electronic device control. The style is reduced both inside and outside and thus timeless. Along with the water, the bottle rack adds attractive visual accents.

Statement by the jury
Particularly due to its integrated water dispenser, this fridge-freezer features a puristic design and has a high practical value.

Die Kühl-Gefrier-Kombination verfügt über einen Wassertank mit integriertem Filter. Das gekühlte Wasser kann bequem über die ergonomisch günstig positionierte Ausgabe direkt in ein Glas oder eine Karaffe gefüllt werden. Darüber hinaus bietet das energieeffiziente Gerät eine elektronische Gerätesteuerung. Die Formensprache ist außen wie innen reduziert und somit zeitlos. Neben der Wasserausgabe setzt die Flaschenablage im Innenraum visuelle Akzente.

Begründung der Jury
Einen hohen Gebrauchswert besitzt diese puristisch gestaltete Kühl-Gefrier-Kombination insbesondere dank ihres integrierten Wasserspenders.

KDN56SM40N
Fridge-Freezer
Kühl-Gefrier-Kombination

Manufacturer
Robert Bosch Hausgeräte GmbH,
Munich, Germany
In-house design
Robert Sachon, Ralph Staud,
Thomas Tischer
Web
www.bosch-hausgeraete.de

This extra-wide top freezer realises the concept "stainless steel behind glass" and aims at underscoring its claim to be a trendsetter. The conspicuous composition of the materials and the colouring differ from other products in the household appliance sector. An innovative bonding method allows the frameless coating of materials with differing degrees of lustre and creates a unique depth effect.

Statement by the jury
The finish of this fridge-freezer attracts attention and is produced in an innovative manufacturing process.

Diese überbreite Top Freezer-Variante in einer edlen Edelstahl-hinter-Glas-Ausführung verfolgt die Zielsetzung, einen Trendsetter-Anspruch zu unterstreichen. Die prägnante Materialkomposition und Farbgebung unterscheidet sich von anderen Produkten im Hausgerätebereich. Ein innovatives Klebeverfahren ermöglicht die rahmenlose Schichtung der unterschiedlich glänzenden Materialien und generiert eine unverwechselbare Tiefenwirkung.

Begründung der Jury
Die Oberflächengestaltung dieser Kühl-Gefrier-Kombination zieht die Aufmerksamkeit auf sich und wird durch ein innovatives Herstellungsverfahren ermöglicht.

KDD74AL20N
Fridge-Freezer
Kühl-Gefrier-Kombination

Manufacturer
Robert Bosch Hausgeräte GmbH,
Munich, Germany
In-house design
Ralph Staud, Thomas Tischer
Web
www.bosch-hausgeraete.de

This innovative XXL fridge-freezer provides generous space for the storage of food. Its exterior design is characterised by the consistent use of authentic materials. Thus, the control panel is inserted flush with the door. It can easily be read and is easy to use by specially developed, high quality metal touch sensors. The beverage dispenser is also integrated flush into the door.

Statement by the jury
A striking overall appearance emphasises individual features and underlines the practical value of this XXL fridge-freezer.

Die innovative XXL-Kühl-Gefrier-Kombination bietet einen großzügigen Stauraum für die Lagerung von Lebensmitteln. Ihre Außengestaltung zeichnet sich durch den konsequenten Einsatz von Echtmaterialien aus. So ist das Bedienpanel flächenbündig in die Türe eingesetzt. Es lässt sich bequem ablesen und per speziell entwickelten, hochwertigen Metal-Touch-Sensoren einfach bedienen. Auch der Getränke-Spender wurde flächenbündig in die Tür eingefügt.

Begründung der Jury
Ein prägnantes Gesamtbild betont einzelne Ausstattungsdetails und unterstreicht den Gebrauchswert dieser XXL-Kühl-Gefrier-Kombination.

KGV36VD30S, KGV36VE30S, KGV36VH30S
Fridge-Freezer Product Range
Kühl-Gefrier-Geräte-Produktreihe

Manufacturer
Robert Bosch Hausgeräte GmbH,
Munich, Germany
In-house design
Ralph Staud, Thomas Tischer
Web
www.bosch-hausgeraete.de

In this coloured fridge-freezer product range, a minimalist design language is combined with an innovative, velvet-like finish and discreetly integrated handles. The matt surface comes in three different colours which are both aesthetically appealing and, above all, particularly easy to clean. Each of these versions harmoniously blends in with modern, homely kitchen environments.

Statement by the jury
A trendy colour concept characterises this fridge-freezer range, the elegant front of which is emotionally appealing.

Eine reduzierte Formensprache wird bei dieser farbigen Kühl-Gefrier-Geräte-Produktreihe mit einer innovativen, samtartigen Oberflächenbeschichtung und dezent integrierten Griffen kombiniert. Dabei ist die in verschiedenen Farben erhältliche, matte Oberflächenstruktur nicht nur ästhetisch ansprechend, sondern vor allem auch besonders pflegeleicht. Die drei Farbvarianten lassen sich harmonisch in zeitgemäß wohnliche Küchenumfelder integrieren.

Begründung der Jury
Ein trendbewusstes Farbkonzept prägt diese Serie von Kühl-Gefrier-Geräten, deren elegante Front emotional ansprechend wirkt.

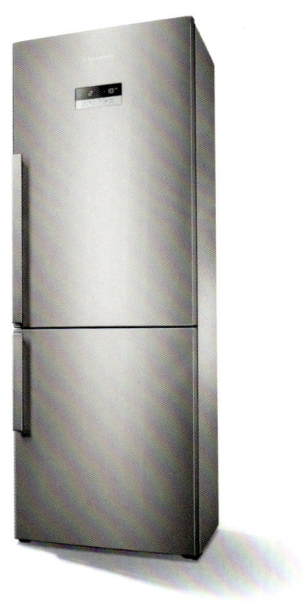

Grundig GKN 16830 X
Free-Standing Fridge-Freezer
Stand-Kühl-Gefrier-Kombination

Manufacturer
Arçelik A.S.,
Istanbul, Turkey
In-house design
Arçelik Industrial Design Team
Design
Designaffairs GmbH,
Munich, Germany
Web
www.arcelik.com.tr
www.designaffairs.com

This fridge-freezer of minimalist design is a full no-frost device of A+++ energy efficiency class. The free-standing refrigerator features a Super Fresh Zone (0 to 3 degrees Celsius) to keep food fresher for a longer time. An antibacterial carbon filter in combination with Hygair ioniser technology prevents the formation of bacteria, mould and fridge odours. The unit is equipped with an eco mode and a vacation function.

Statement by the jury
This free-standing fridge-freezer is characterised by an overall brand-typical design and is also functionally convincing.

Die minimalistisch gestaltete Kühl-Gefrier-Kombination ist ein frostfreies Gerät der Energieeffizienzklasse A+++. Der freistehende Kühlschrank bietet einen Superfrisch-Bereich (0 bis 3 Grad Celsius), in dem Lebensmittel länger frisch gehalten werden. Ein antibakterieller Kohlefilter in Kombination mit der Hygair-Ionisator-technologie verhindert die Entstehung von Bakterien, Schimmel und Kühlschrankge-rüchen. Das Gerät ist mit Öko-Modus und Urlaubsfunktion ausgestattet.

Begründung der Jury
Ein markentypisch schlichtes Gestaltungs-prinzip prägt das Gesamtbild einer frei-stehenden Kühl-Gefrier-Kombination, die auch funktional punktet.

IKBP 3554
Integrable Refrigerator
Integrierbarer Kühlschrank

Manufacturer
Liebherr-Hausgeräte GmbH,
Ochsenhausen, Germany
In-house design
Design
PRODESIGN Brüssing GmbH & Co. KG
(Bernd Brüssing),
Neu-Ulm, Germany
Web
www.liebherr.com
www.prodesign-ulm.de

This integrable refrigerator meets high standards with its elegant overall appearance, quality and innovative ideas such as dual-sided LED light column. In the development phase, special attention was paid to achieving the energy efficiency rating A+++ as well as making the fridge easy to use. Characteristic features include safety glass storage shelves with stainless steel profile, a GlassLine inner door with plastic containers as well as integrated stainless steel profiles.

Statement by the jury
High quality materials, plenty of storage space and high functionality distinguish this refrigerator with BioFresh function.

Der integrierbare Kühlschrank erfüllt hohe Ansprüche mit seinem eleganten Gesamt-bild, seiner Qualität und seinen innova-tiven Ideen wie der beidseitigen LED-Lichtsäule. Bei der Entwicklung wurde auf die Energieeffizienz A+++ und den Bedienkomfort besonderen Wert gelegt. Charakteristisch für die Geräte sind die Ablageflächen aus Sicherheitsglas mit Edelstahlprofil, die GlassLine-Innentür mit Kunststoff-Halteteilen sowie die integrier-ten Edelstahlprofile.

Begründung der Jury
Qualitativ hochwertige Materialien, viel Stauraum und eine hohe Funktionalität zeichnen den mit BioFresh ausgestatteten Kühlschrank aus.

ICBP 3256
Integrable Fridge-Freezer
Integrierbare Kühl-Gefrier-Kombination

Manufacturer
Liebherr-Hausgeräte GmbH,
Ochsenhausen, Germany
In-house design
Design
PRODESIGN Brüssing GmbH & Co. KG
(Bernd Brüssing),
Neu-Ulm, Germany
Web
www.liebherr.com
www.prodesign-ulm.de

With innovative ideas, elegant design and quality, this integrable BioFresh fridge-freezer combination meets the highest requirements. In the development process, particular importance was attached to combining the energy efficiency level A+++ and ease of use. Characteristic are the storage shelves made of safety glass with stainless steel profile, the elegant GlassLine door interior with plastic storage elements as well as the harmoniously integrated stainless steel profiles.

Statement by the jury
The LED lit interior of this fridge-freezer provides an all-embracing overview. The division is variably customisable.

Die integrierbare BioFresh Kühl-Gefrier-Kombination erfüllt mit innovativen Ideen, eleganter Gestaltung und Qualität höchste Ansprüche. Bei der Konzeption wurde auf die Kombination von Energieeffizienz A+++ und Bedienkomfort besonderen Wert gelegt. Charakteristisch sind die Abla-geflächen aus Sicherheitsglas mit Edel-stahlprofil, die elegante GlassLine-Innentür mit Kunststoff-Halteteilen sowie die harmonisch integrierten Edelstahl-Profile.

Begründung der Jury
Der LED-beleuchtete Innenraum dieser Kühl-Gefrier-Kombination lässt sich gut überblicken, die Aufteilung ist variabel individualisierbar.

Siemens KI87SAD30, KI86NAD30, KI82LAD30
Built-in Refrigerator Product Range
Einbau-Kühlschrank-Produktreihe

Manufacturer
Siemens-Electrogeräte GmbH,
Munich, Germany
In-house design
Max Eicher, Christoph Becke
Web
www.siemens-home.de

This built-in refrigerator product range offers technical innovations in terms of space utilisation and ergonomics: pull-out shelves and bins allow for neatly arranged storage and facilitate access. The design of the interior containers combines highly insulating materials and maximum useable volume. Laterally arranged, glare-free LEDs ensure perfect illumination. Metal trims protect areas that are subject to heavy wear.

Statement by the jury
An impressive functionality characterises this product range. Inside, the spacious built-in refrigerators are neatly arranged.

Die Einbau-Kältegeräte bieten Neuerungen hinsichtlich Raumnutzung, Energieeffizienz und Ergonomie: Ausziehbare Fachböden und Schalen ermöglichen eine übersichtliche Lagerung und erleichtern den Zugriff. Die Innenbehälter-Gestaltung kombiniert isolationsstarke Materialien mit einem großen Nutzvolumen, wobei blendfreie LED-Seitenlichter für eine gute Ausleuchtung sorgen. Metall-Applikationen schützen stark belastete Bereiche.

Begründung der Jury
Eine überzeugende Funktionalität zeichnet diese Produktreihe aus, die geräumigen Einbau-Kühlschränke sind innen übersichtlich unterteilt.

K 37472 iD
Built-in Refrigerator
Einbau-Kühlschrank

Manufacturer
Miele & Cie. KG,
Gütersloh, Germany
In-house design
Web
www.miele.de

This built-in refrigerator provides an innovative lighting concept. Illumination inside is glare-free, the light sources being invisible to the customer. Nevertheless, they can be flexibly positioned. The touch controls feature all the design attributes of the corresponding Miele appliance series. In the PerfectFresh drawers in the lower part of the refrigerator, food can be carefully stored for a longer time than in conventional refrigerators.

Statement by the jury
This built-in refrigerator, the brand-specific design of which aims at homogeneity, embodies a puristic aesthetic style.

Dieser Einbau-Kühlschrank bietet ein innovatives Lichtkonzept: Der Innenraum wird blendfrei ausgeleuchtet, wobei die Lichtquellen für die Kunden unsichtbar sind und sich dennoch flexibel positionieren lassen. Die Touch-Bedienung weist alle Gestaltungsmerkmale der Miele-Kücheneinbaugeräte auf. In den PerfectFresh-Schubladen im unteren Kühlbereich lassen sich Lebensmittel schonend und länger lagern als in einem herkömmlichen Kühlschrank.

Begründung der Jury
Eine puristische Ästhetik verkörpert der Einbau-Kühlschrank, dessen markenspezifische Gestaltung Homogenität anstrebt.

KFN 37452 iDE
Built-in Fridge-Freezer
Einbau-Kühl-Gefrier-Kombination

Manufacturer
Miele & Cie. KG,
Gütersloh, Germany
In-house design
Web
www.miele.de

This energy-saving fridge-freezer is characterised by an illumination concept that gently lights up and can be individually positioned. Through the intuitive touch control, which shows all the brand-specific features, the cooling device fits harmoniously into the family of built-in appliances as well. The easy-to-use water tank can be filled according to customers' preferences. In addition, the appliance is equipped with a soft-close door mechanism.

Statement by the jury
The lighting concept and other features enhance the practical value of this fridge-freezer.

Die energiesparende Kühl-Gefrier-Kombination zeichnet sich durch eine sanft aufleuchtende Beleuchtung aus, die individuell platziert werden kann. Durch die intuitive Touch-Bedienung, die alle markenspezifischen Merkmale zeigt, reiht sich auch das Kältegerät harmonisch in die Familie der Einbaugeräte ein. Der einfach zu handhabende Wassertank lässt sich je nach Kundenwunsch befüllen. Zudem ist das Gerät mit einem Türschließdämpfer ausgestattet.

Begründung der Jury
Das Beleuchtungskonzept und weitere Ausstattungsdetails steigern den Gebrauchswert dieser Kühl-Gefrier-Kombination.

EKV 6500.1–BV
Fully Automatic Built-in Coffee Maker
Einbau-Kaffeevollautomat

Manufacturer
Küppersbusch Hausgeräte GmbH,
Gelsenkirchen, Germany
Design
Keicheldesign
(Klaus Keichel),
Düsseldorf, Germany
Web
www.kueppersbusch-hausgeraete.de

This automatic built-in coffee maker is distinguished by the option to programme the water amount for three different cup sizes as well as a special milk heating feature to prepare cappuccino, latte macchiato and white coffee. In addition, the milk container is removable and provides for comfortable operation. Thanks to its innovative sensor touch electronics, the device is self-explanatory and easy to operate. Plain text display guides the user through all the functions of the device.

Der Einbau-Kaffeevollautomat zeichnet sich durch eine Mengenprogrammierung für drei verschiedene Tassengrößen und eine echte Milchfunktion für Cappuccino, Latte Macciato oder Milchkaffee aus. Für besonderen Bedienkomfort sorgt zudem die herausnehmbare Milcheinheit. Dank einer innovativen Touch-Control-Elektronik wird die Bedienung des Gerätes selbsterklärend einfach. Per Klarschriftdisplay wird der Benutzer durch sämtliche Funktionen des Gerätes geführt.

Statement by the jury
High functionality and an elegant, brand-specific design vocabulary are combined in this fully automatic built-in coffee maker.

Begründung der Jury
Eine hohe Funktionalität verbindet sich bei diesem Einbau-Kaffeevo lautomaten mit einer eleganten, marken:ypischen Formensprache.

CVA 6805
**Built-in Fully Automatic
Coffee Maker**
Einbau-Kaffeevollautomat

Manufacturer
Miele & Cie. KG,
Gütersloh, Germany
In-house design
Web
www.miele.de

This built-in fully automatic coffee maker with whole coffee bean system is available in stainless steel, Obsidian Black, Brilliant White and Havana Brown. Its fully automatic CupSensor adjusts the coffee spout at an ideal distance to the height of the cup placed below. The One Touch for Two function allows the simultaneous preparation of two coffee specialities. With one movement, the milk jar can be inserted from the front or removed thanks to the EasyClick system.

Der Einbau-Kaffeevollautomat mit Bohnensystem wird in Edelstahl, Obsidianschwarz, Brillantweiß und Havannabraun angeboten. Sein CupSensor bewegt den Kaffeeauslauf vollautomatisch in einen idealen Abstand zur Tassenhöhe. Die „One Touch for Two"-Zubereitung ermöglicht es, mit einer Taste zwei Kaffeespezialitäten zeitgleich zuzubereiten. Mittels EasyClick-System kann das Milchgefäß in einer Bewegung von vorne eingesetzt oder entfernt werden.

Statement by the jury
This built-in fully automatic coffee maker elegantly fits in different kitchen units. Its high ease of use is also impressive.

Begründung der Jury
Elegant fügt sich dieser Einbau-Kaffeevollautomat in die jeweilige Küchenzeile ein, auch der hohe Bedienkomfort überzeugt.

QUARZA
**Fully Automatic
Coffee Maker**
Kaffeevollautomat

Manufacturer
Suzhou Industry Park
Kalerm Electric Appliances Co., Ltd,
Suzhou, China
Design
Segnoinverso Design Studio
(Nicola Zanetti, Bettina Di Virgilio,
Giordano Redaelli),
Flero (Brescia), Italy
Web
www.kalerm.com
www.segnoinverso.com

This fully automatic coffee maker
prepares a wide range of specialities
from whole or ground beans via touch
screen control. The user-friendly
OLED display visualises five different
programmes, which can be selected by
double-click. The coffee spout can be
flexibly adjusted to the height of the
cup. Due to the "one button mode",
the cup need not be moved for the
preparation of a cappuccino.

Ein breites Spezialitäten-Repertoire
aus ganzen oder gemahlenen Bohnen
bereitet dieser Kaffeevollautomat per
Touchscreen-Steuerung zu. Das benut-
zerfreundliche LED-Display visualisiert
fünf verschiedene Programme, die mittels
Doppelklick ausgewählt werden. Je nach
Tassengröße ist der Kaffeeauslauf flexibel höhenverstellbar. Aufgrund des
„One-Button-Modus" muss auch bei der
Cappuccino-Zubereitung die Tasse nicht
verschoben werden.

Statement by the jury
This fully automatic coffee maker
is characterised by clear lines and
impresses by its functionality.

Begründung der Jury
Dieser Kaffeevollautomat zeichnet sich
durch eine überzeugende Funktionalität
und eine klare Linienführung aus.

Nespresso U
Coffee Maker
Kaffeemaschine

Manufacturer
Nestle Nespresso SA,
Lausanne, Switzerland
Design
Les Ateliers du Nord (Antoine Cahen),
Lausanne, Switzerland
Web
www.nespresso.com
www.adn-design.ch

Based on the principle of motor-driven extraction, the design goal was to create a coffee maker of minimalist appearance. Thus, manual user elements such as handles and buttons have vanished. Instead, coffee is made by operating the Nespresso U's "slider" in one finger movement, without having to push any buttons. Following a modular approach, the water tank is held in place by magnets and can move and swivel around. Peripheral elements are also flexibly fixed by magnets. The machine is available in two versions and four colours.

Ausgehend vom Prinzip der motorisierten Extraktion bestand das Gestaltungsziel darin, eine minimalistische Kaffeemaschine zu entwickeln. Entsprechend sind manuelle Bedienelemente wie Griffe und Tasten verschwunden. Die Nespresso U ermöglicht es, durch eine einfache Bewegung des Sliders einen Kaffee ganz ohne Knopfdruck zuzubereiten. Einem modularen Aufbau folgend, kann der Wassertank flexibel platziert und mit Magneten befestigt werden. Auf die gleiche Weise wird das Zubehör flexibel genutzt. Das Gerät ist in zwei Versionen und vier Farben erhältlich.

Statement by the jury
The Nespresso U coffee maker embodies the consistent realisation of a purist design principle, convincing in both form and function.

Begründung der Jury
Bei der Kaffeemaschine Nespresso U gelingt die konsequente Umsetzung eines puristischen Gestaltungsprinzips, formal wie funktional überzeugend.

Svart Presisjon
Coffee Maker
Kaffeemaschine

Manufacturer
AS Wilfa,
Hagan, Norway
In-house design
Arild Jorgensen,
Ann-Katrin Lislevand
Design
Designit A/S,
Copenhagen, Denmark
Web
www.wilfa.com
www.designit.com

The design of the Svart Presisjon automatic coffee maker was inspired by Nordic coffee culture. Its basic elements consist of a removable fresh water tank, a precise heating system and an innovative pump, delivering the last drop of water so that the coffee maker stays free from stagnant water. By means of a flow control, users can regulate amount and strength of coffee to their preferences. The sleek finishes match contemporary kitchens.

Statement by the jury
The Svart Presisjon coffee maker shows an independent style. The unusual structure of the two-part coffee maker produces a creative look.

Das Gestaltungskonzept der Svart Presisjon Automatik-Kaffeemaschine wurde durch die nordische Kaffee-Kultur inspiriert. Ihre Grundbestandteile sind ein abnehmbarer Frischwassertank, ein präzises Heizungssystem und eine innovative Pumpe, welche dafür sorgt, dass in der Maschine kein stehendes Wasser zurückbleibt. Mittels Ablaufsteuerung kann der Benutzer, je nach Vorlieben, die Menge und die Stärke des Kaffees regulieren. Das elegante Finish passt sich zeitgemäßen Küchen an.

Begründung der Jury
Die Svart Presisjon zeigt eine eigenständige Formensprache. Kreativ wirkt die ungewohnte Struktur der zweigeteilten Kaffeemaschine.

KISS (Keep It Simply Swiss)
Espresso Machine
Espessomaschine

Manufacturer
Gotec S.A.,
Sion, Switzerland
In-house design
Web
www.gotec.ch

The KISS (Keep It Simply Swiss) espresso machine features a remarkably compact housing. With a height of only 210 mm and a diameter of 160 mm, it is easy to transport. The energy-saving appliance contains the manufacturer's own all-in-one technology and uses only little water. Its matt polished aluminium housing is available in different colours.

Statement by the jury
This handy little espresso machine shows an independent style. The materials used are rich in contrast creating an appealing look.

Das auffallend kompakte Gehäuse der Espressomaschine KISS (Keep It Simply Swiss) misst eine Höhe von nur 210 mm und einen Durchmesser von 160 mm. Entsprechend lässt sich diese Maschine unkompliziert transportieren. Das energiesparsame Gerät mit der herstellereigenen All-In-One-Technologie verbraucht nur wenig Wasser. Sein matt poliertes Aluminium-Gehäuse kann in unterschiedlichen Farben gewählt werden.

Begründung der Jury
Eine eigenständige Formensprache zeigt diese handlich kleine Espressomaschine. Die verwendeten Materialien wirken reizvoll kontrastreich.

Pump Vacuum Jug
Pump-Isolierkanne

Manufacturer
Eva Solo A/S,
Måløv, Denmark
Design
Tools Design
(Henrik Holbæk, Claus Jensen),
Copenhagen, Denmark
Web
www.evasolo.com
www.toolsdesign.com

The design of this pump vacuum jug is inspired by models from the 1970s, adorned with flower stickers. As a modern refinement, it differs from its predecessors by a sophisticated vacuum mechanism. The purist jug has a metal handle and features high quality plastics inside and outside. It is available in black and white and has a capacity of 1.8 litres.

Statement by the jury
In this pump vacuum jug, an elegant style is combined with proven functionality. Its spout is formally striking.

Die Gestaltung dieser Pump-Isolierkanne lehnt sich an mit Blumenaufklebern dekorierte Modelle aus den 1970er Jahren an. Als eine zeitgemäße Weiterentwicklung unterscheidet sie sich von ihren Vorgängern durch die Ausstattung mit einem ausgeklügelten Vakuum-Mechanismus. Die puristisch gestaltete Kanne hat einen Metallhenkel und ist außen und innen aus hochwertigem Kunststoff gefertigt. Sie ist in Schwarz und Weiß erhältlich und bietet ein Fassungsvermögen von 1,8 Litern.

Begründung der Jury
Eine elegante Formensprache verbindet sich bei dieser Pump-Isolierkanne mit einer ausgereiften Funktionalität – formal auffällig ist ihr Ausguss.

Electric Moka Pot
Electric Coffee Maker
Elektrische Kaffeekanne

Manufacturer
Foshan Shunde LionHeart Electric Co., Ltd,
Shunde, China
Design
Nova Design (Shanghai) Ltd
(Kai Wang, Tsu Hao Liu),
Shanghai, China
Web
www.lionheartelec.com
www.e-novadesign.com
Honourable Mention

The design concept of this electric coffee maker takes up the classic style of the traditional Moka pot. Equipped with an electronic heating element, the compact device provides additional flexibility. The convenient pot is a convenient device at home, in hotel rooms or at the workplace. Its large, heat-resistant handle and its simple key operation offer a high level of user comfort.

Statement by the jury
The distinctly designed electric coffee maker offers users a comfortable and flexible handling.

Das Gestaltungskonzept dieser elektrischen Kaffeekanne greift die klassische Formgebung der traditionellen Moka-Kanne auf. Ausgestattet mit einem elektrischen Heizelement, bietet das kompakte Gerät einen Mehrwert an Flexibilität. Die komfortable Kanne ist daheim, im Hotelzimmer oder am Arbeitsplatz unkompliziert einsatzbereit. Ihr großer, hitzebeständiger Griff und ihre einfache Tastenbedienung bieten einen hohen Bedienkomfort.

Begründung der Jury
Die prägnant gestaltete elektrische Kaffeekanne bietet dem Nutzer eine komfortable und flexible Handhabung.

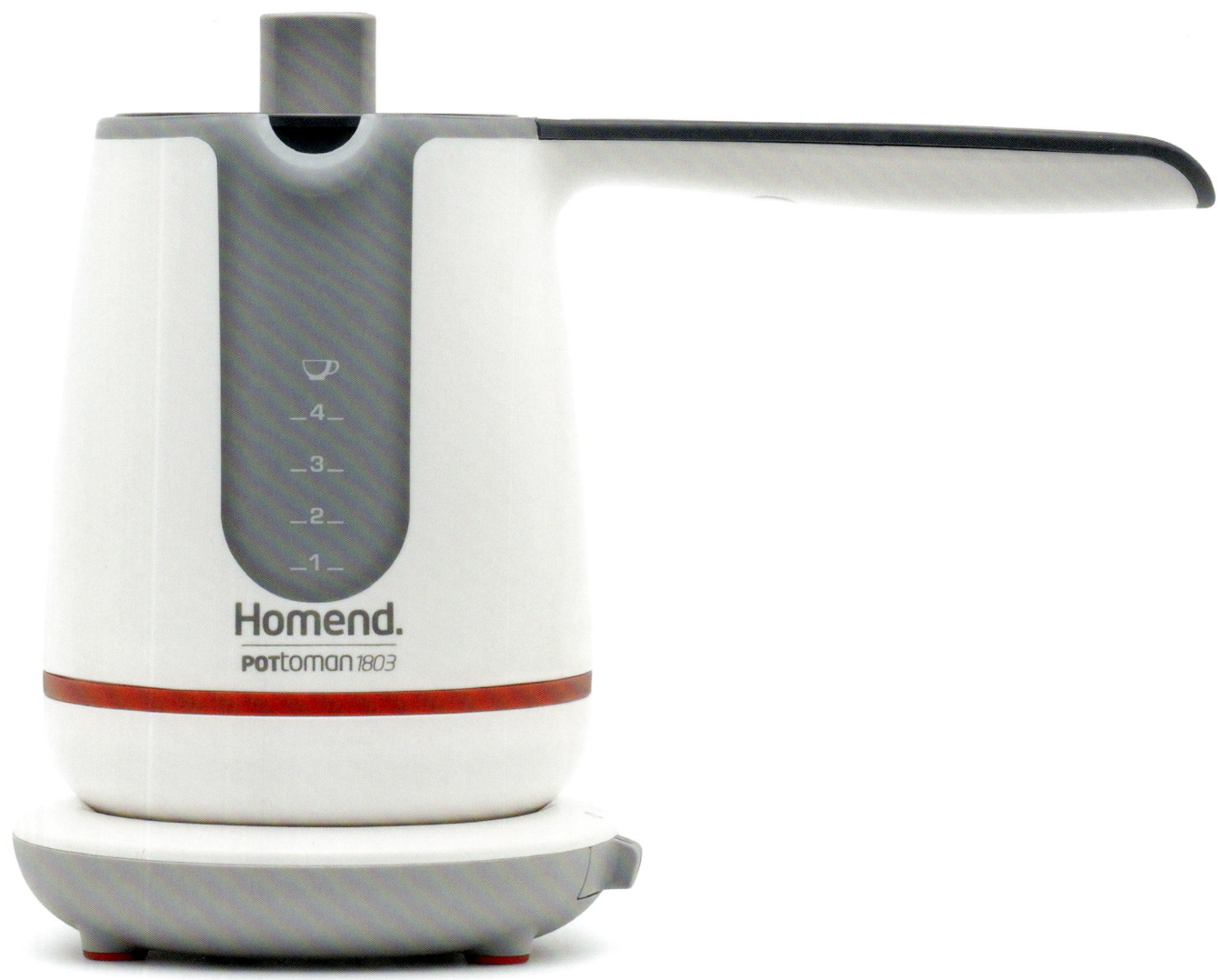

Homend Pottoman
Turkish Coffee Maker
Türkische Mokkakanne

Manufacturer
Homend Elektrikli Cihazlar San. ve Tic. A.S.
Istanbul, Turkey
Design
DesignUM
(Ümit Altun, Rinaldo Filinesi),
Istanbul, Turkey
Web
www.homend.com.tr
www.design-um.com
Honourable Mention

Traditionally, Turkish coffee is brewed in a copper pot on an open fire. This ritual is an integral part of Turkish culture. Pottoman is an electric Turkish coffee maker, which significantly simplifies the process of brewing coffee. The water level is visible from outside making cumbersome measuring unnecessary. The heater coil technology accelerates the brewing process and supports the emergence of an aromatic head of froth. The contour represents a synthesis of modern trends and the shape of a traditional copper pot.

Traditioneller Weise wird türkischer Mokka in einem Kupferkännchen auf dem offenen Feuer gebrüht, dieses Ritual ist fester Bestandteil der türkischen Kultur. Pottoman ist eine elektrische Mokkakanne, die den Prozess des Kaffeebrühens wesentlich vereinfacht. Der Wasserstand ist von außen ablesbar, was das mühevolle Dosieren überflüssig macht. Eine Heizspiralentechnik beschleunigt das Aufbrühen und unterstützt das Entstehen einer aromatischen Schaumkrone. Die Kontur stellt dabei eine Synthese aus zeitgemäßen Trends und der Form eines traditionellen Kupferkännchens dar.

Statement by the jury
As a reinterpretation of a traditional copper pot, this electric Turkish coffee maker allows easy handling.

Begründung der Jury
Als Neuinterpretation eines traditionellen Kupferkännchens erlaubt diese elektrische Mokkakanne eine komfortable Handhabung.

Homend RoyalTea
Electric Tea Maker
Elektrischer Teekocher

Manufacturer
Homend Elektrikli Cihazlar San. ve Tic. A.S.,
Istanbul, Turkey
Design
DesignUM
(Ümit Altun, Rinaldo Filinesi),
Istanbul, Turkey
Web
www.homend.com.tr
www.design-um.com

The RoyalTea tea maker was developed
with regard to the needs of Turkish
consumers. Following the concept
of traditional tea makers, the device
includes two separate pots. In the lower
larger one, water is boiled, while in the
upper small pot, tea is brewed. RoyalTea
sterilises the water by boiling it to
100 degrees centigrade and then cools
it down to the desired temperature for
different drinks.

Der Teekocher RoyalTea wurde unter
Berücksichtigung der Bedürfnisse und
Wünsche türkischer Verbraucher entworfen. In Anlehnung an traditionelle Tee-
kannen umfasst das Gerät zwei separate
Kannen. In der großen unteren wird das
Wasser gekocht, während in der kleineren
oberen der Tee aufgebrüht wird. RoyalTea
sterilisiert das Wasser durch Abkochen
auf 100 Grad und kühlt es danach auf die
gewünschte Temperatur für unterschiedliche Getränke ab.

Statement by the jury
This functional electric tea maker offers
users a high practical value and relaxed
comfort during preparation.

Begründung der Jury
Dieser funktional gestaltete elektrische
Teekocher bietet dem Nutzer einen hohen
Gebrauchswert und angenehmen Komfort
bei der Zubereitung.

Electric Kettle
Wasserkocher

Manufacturer
Supor,
Hangzhou, China
In-house design
Chen Jian, Ma Han
Web
www.supor.com
Honourable Mention

This electric kettle unites the positive characteristics of stainless steel and plastics in its double-layered covering. The reliably insulating double layer not only enhances ease of use but also ensures excellent durability. The elegantly curved kettle is available in two emotionally appealing colours. At the top end, a small stainless steel rim underscores the contrast to the black lid.

Dieser elektrische Wasserkocher vereint in seiner doppelschichtigen Ummantelung die positiven Eigenschaften von Edelstahl und Kunststoff. Die zuverlässig isolierende Doppelschicht steigert nicht nur den Bedienkomfort, sondern sorgt zudem für eine langlebige Qualität. Der elegant geschwungene Wasserkocher ist in zwei emotional ansprechenden Farbvarianten erhältlich. Am oberen Rand betont ein schmaler Edelstahlrand den Kontrast zum schwarzen Deckel.

Statement by the jury
Gently flowing contours harmoniously accentuate the elegance of this electric kettle.

Begründung der Jury
Sanft fließende Konturen bringen die Eleganz dieses elektrischen Wasserkochers harmonisch zur Geltung.

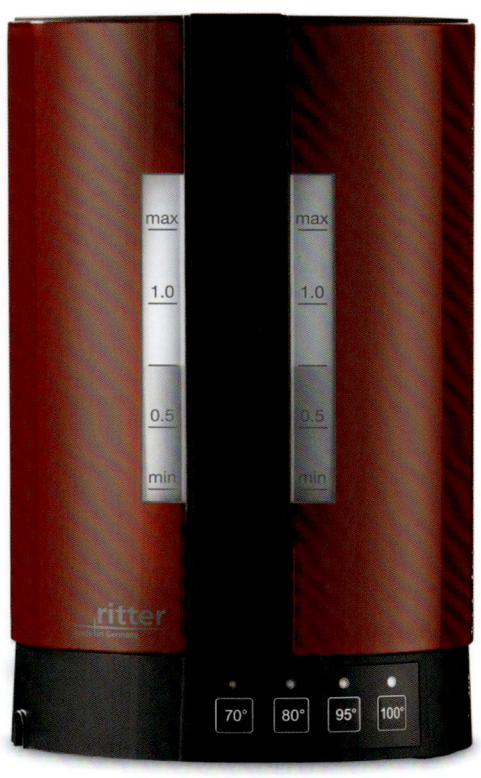

fontana 5
Kettle
Wasserkocher

Manufacturer
Ritterwerk GmbH,
Gröbenzell, Germany
Design
Martin Dettinger Industriedesign
(Martin Dettinger),
Planegg, Germany
Web
www.ritterwerk.de
www.martindettinger.de

The fontana 5 kettle aims at a symbiosis of zeitgeist and elements of the Bauhaus style. The cordless kettle with a 360-degree rotating base station has a heat insulated external housing made of high-grade acrylic glass and comes in black, white or red. A water level viewing window on both sides indicates the filling quantity. The water temperature can be set precisely and is shown on a LED display.

Mit dem Wasserkocher fontana 5 wird eine Symbiose von Zeitgeist und Elementen des Bauhaus-Stils angestrebt. Der kabellose Wasserkocher mit einer 360-Grad-Basis-station hat ein wärmeisoliertes Außen-gehäuse aus hochwertigem Acrylglas in Schwarz, Weiß oder Rot. Durch ein beidsei-tiges Wasserstands-Sichtfenster lässt sich die Füllmenge ablesen. Die Wassertempe-ratur kann gradgenau eingestellt werden und wird mittels LED-Anzeige visualisiert.

Statement by the jury
The functional design concept of fontana 5 impresses with distinct lines and high quality materials.

Begründung der Jury
Ein funktional ausgerichtetes Gestaltungs-konzept überzeugt bei fontana 5 mit klaren Linien und der Verwendung hochwertiger Materialien.

SodaStream Source
Home Water Carbonator
Trinkwassersprudler

Manufacturer
SodaStream Israel Ltd.,
Airport City, Israel
Design
fuseproject (Yves Behar),
San Francisco, USA
Web
www.sodastream.com
www.fuseproject.com

With SodaStream Source, consumers can make carbonated beverages from tap water, a sustainable alternative to buying beverages in plastic bottles. The sleek, monolithic style provides for visual clarity. The clearly arranged user interface simplifies handling. The surface of the concave portion which houses the bottle is adorned with a myriad of water droplets.

Mit SodaStream Source lassen sich kohlensäurehaltige Getränke aus Leitungswasser herstellen, eine nachhaltige Alternative zum Kauf von Getränken in Plastikflaschen. Die glatte, monolithische Formensprache verschafft visuelle Klarheit, während die übersichtlich gestaltete Benutzeroberfläche die Handhabung vereinfacht. Die Oberfläche des gewölbten, für die Flasche vorgesehenen Geräteteils ist mit unzähligen Wassertropfen verziert.

Statement by the jury
The SodaStream Source home water carbonator owes its aesthetic appeal to a design principle that uses visual and haptic stimuli.

Begründung der Jury
Seine ansprechende Ästhetik verdankt der Trinkwassersprudler SodaStream Source einem Gestaltungsprinzip, das visuelle und haptische Reize nutzt.

Home water carbonator

Changhong CH-A90
Water Dispenser
Wasserspender

Manufacturer
Sichuan Changhong Electric Co. Ltd.,
Chengdu (Sichuan), China
In-house design
Homwee Technology Co. Ltd.,
Innovative Design Center
Web
www.changhong.com

The Changhong CH-A90 is a wall-mounted water dispenser that can be installed in kitchens, living rooms or offices. It provides cold or warm water at any time since it is connected to the water supply of the building. The touch screen panel has the shape of a large toggle switch and can be used to switch the water dispenser on and off. This facilitates filling different kinds of containers, especially bottles. Different LEDs at the edge of the nozzle indicate different water temperatures: blue for cold water, orange for warm water and red for hot water.

Der Changhong CH-A90 ist ein wandmontierter Wasserspender, der in der Küche, im Wohnzimmer oder im Büro angebracht werden kann. Er stellt jederzeit kaltes oder warmes Wasser zur Verfügung, da er an die Wasserversorgung des Gebäudes angeschlossen wird. Das Touchscreen-Bedienfeld hat die Form eines großen Kippschalters und kann zum An- und Ausschalten des Wasserspenders genutzt werden. So wird das Befüllen unterschiedlicher Behälter, wie z.B. Flaschen, vereinfacht. Rund um die Düsenkante leuchten mittels LEDs verschiedene Farben auf: Blau für kaltes, Orange für warmes und Rot für heißes Wasser.

Statement by the jury
This appealing water dispenser is connected to the water supply system. It stands out as an eco-friendly product solution.

Begründung der Jury
Dieser ansprechend gestaltete Wasserspender, der an das Leitungssystem angeschlossen wird, überzeugt als umweltfreundliche Produktlösung.

BAUER quantum
Water Purifier
Wasseraufbereitungsanlage

Manufacturer
BaUer Beteiligungs GmbH,
Bielefeld, Germany
In-house design
Harry Brakowski, Hans Epp
Design
Andre Baran, Tarkan Yetiskin
Web
www.bauer-international.com
Honourable Mention

This drinking water purifier was designed for the use in private households as well as in office or factory canteens. Thanks to its refined design, the Bauer quantum can be used as a visible desktop unit. By employing innovative filter technologies and the reverse osmosis principle, the four-phase filter system allows reducing harmful and toxic substances by more than 99 per cent. Thus, drinking water qualities are achieved.

Statement by the jury
The hydraulically operated drinking water purifier shows an impressive functionality.

Diese Trinkwasserreinigungsanlage wurde für den Gebrauch im privaten Haushalt sowie in Büro- oder Betriebsküchen entwickelt. Dank seiner edel anmutenden Gestaltung lässt sich der Bauer quantum als sichtbares Auftischgerät einsetzen. Durch die Verwendung innovativer Filtrationstechnologien sowie des Umkehrosmose-Prinzips ermöglicht das vierstufige Filtersystem eine Reduzierung von Schad- und Giftstoffen von über 99 Prozent und erreicht Trinkwasserqualität.

Begründung der Jury
Eine überzeugende Funktionalität weist die hydraulisch betriebene Trinkwasserreinigungsanlage auf.

Siemens DG60155BW
Water Heater
Wasserboiler

Manufacturer
Siemens-Electrogeräte GmbH,
Munich, Germany
In-house design
Tim Richter
Web
www.siemens-home.de

This water heater adopts a new style within its product category. Its geometrical body is combined with the control unit arranged on the bottom side, creating a strong contrast. Thanks to its fast heating function, weekly tracking, timer and anode monitoring, the appliance meets future requirements. The logical design of the interface with touch functionality ensures easy operation.

Statement by the jury
The horizontal alignment of the water heater is surprising and embodies the successful implementation of an innovative design concept.

Dieser Wasserboiler wählt eine neue Formensprache innerhalb seiner Produktkategorie. Seine geometrische Grundform wird mit der auf der Unterseite angeordneten Bedieneinheit kontrastreich kombiniert. Mit seiner Schnell-Heiz-Funktion, der Wochenkontrolle, dem Timer und dem Anoden-Monitor erfüllt das Gerät zukunftsorientierte Anforderungen. Das logisch gestaltete Interface mit Touch-Funktionalität garantiert eine einfache Bedienbarkeit.

Begründung der Jury
Die horizontale Ausrichtung des Wasserboilers überrascht und verkörpert die gelungene Umsetzung einer innovativen Gestaltungsidee.

TURMIX
Kitchen Appliances Line
Küchengeräte-Linie

Manufacturer
DKB Household Ltd.,
Zürich, Switzerland

Design
2ND WEST
(Michael Thurnherr),
Rapperswil, Switzerland

Web
www.turmix.com
www.2ndwest.ch

reddot design award
best of the best 2013

Stylish kitchen aids

Kitchen appliances are indispensable aids in the modern kitchen. The Turmix kitchen appliances line consists of a standard food processor, a stick blender, a hand-held blender and a juicer and exhibits a design with clean lines and noteworthy styling. Cleverly pared down to the essentials, the design and the sophisticated innovative functionality of each item are impressive. Take for example the stick blender: Its innovate three-bladed Turmix knife and powerful motor make for efficient and clean puréeing while the food processor is equipped with a six-bladed Turmix knife. The beautiful shape of its mixing jug is a visual delight. The hand mixer combines kitchen aids such as a hand-held whisk, stick blender and dough-kneading machine in a well thought-out, multi-functional design. The Turmix Platinum juicer offers a very tough grater surface made of steel as well as offset teeth. It is very efficient, but nonetheless looks like a stylish design object in any kitchen. Thanks to their ergonomic design all these kitchen aids are comfortable and pleasant to use. They are equipped with powerful motors that function quietly and almost without vibration. The Turmix kitchen appliances line unites elegance with a high degree of user-friendly functionality. Chopping, puréeing, mixing and juicing turn into an experience for the senses that will inspire ever new culinary creations.

Stilvolle Küchenhilfen

Küchengeräte sind unerlässliche Helfer für die moderne Küche. Die Gestaltung der Turmix Küchengeräte-Linie vereint einen Stand-, Stab- und Handmixer sowie einen Entsafter in einer klaren und wertig anmutenden Formensprache. Beeindruckend ist ihre gekonnt auf das Wesentliche reduzierte Gestaltung und eine jeweils ausgefeilte innovative Funktionalität. Der Stabmixer etwa ermöglicht durch seine Ausstattung mit einem innovativen Turmix-Messer mit drei Flügeln sowie einem leistungsstarken Motor ein effizientes und sauberes Pürieren. Der Standmixer arbeitet mit einem Turmix-Messer mit sechs Flügeln und begeistert visuell durch eine formschöne Mixkaraffe. Der Handmixer dieser Küchengeräte-Linie vereint die Küchenhelfer Handrühr-gerät, Stabmixer und Teigknetmaschine in einer durch-dachten, multifunktionalen Gestaltung. Der Entsafter Turmix Platinum verfügt über eine sehr harte Raffel-scheibe aus Stahl sowie versetzte Zähne. Er arbeitet effektiv und mutet in der Küche wie ein stilvolles Design-objekt an. Aufgrund ihrer ergonomischen Gestaltung bieten diese Geräte eine komfortable und angenehme Handhabung. Sie sind mit leistungsstarken Motoren ausgestattet und arbeiten leise und vibrationsarm. Die Turmix Küchengeräte-Linie verbindet Eleganz mit einem hohen Maß an nutzerfreundlicher Funktionalität. Das Zerkleinern, Pürieren, Mixen und Entsaften wird zu einem sinnlich erfahrbaren Erlebnis, welches zu immer neuen Kreationen anregt.

Statement by the jury
The clean, purist lines of the Turmix kitchen appliances line are captivating. The use of high quality metal surfaces and top of the range plastics endow these appliances with an appearance of classical elegance. Every single detail has been precisely executed. The innovative functionality of all tools in this kitchen appliances line is an inspiration. Notwithstanding, each one is still comfortable and easy to use.

Begründung der Jury
Die Turmix Küchengeräte-Linie fasziniert durch ihre puristische und klare Formensprache. Der Einsatz edler Metalloberflächen und hochwertiger Kunststoffe ver-leiht diesen Geräten die Anmutung klassischer Eleganz. Jedes ihrer Details ist präzise ausgeführt. Die einzelnen Geräte dieser Küchengeräte-Linie begeistern mit einer innovativen Funktionalität. Sie sind dabei komfortabel und liegen gut in der Hand.

Kitchen utensils

Multipro Sense FPM800
Compact Food Processor
Kompakt-Küchenmaschine

Manufacturer
Kenwood Limited,
Havant, GB
In-house design
Robin Ferraby, David Faram,
Nick Jays, Aaron Wilcock
Web
www.kenwoodworld.com

A robust corpus, high quality materials and a solid base characterise the Multipro Sense food processor. A range of accessories deliver broad functionality. Variable speeds and an intelligent auto function offer flexible control. The solid metal die cast body together with the BPA-free, shatterproof Tritan plastic bowl convey significance and durability.

Ein robuster Korpus, hochwertige Materialien und eine stabile Basis kennzeichnen die Kompakt-Küchenmaschine Multipro Sense. Eine Reihe von Zubehörteilen ermöglicht vielseitige Funktionen. Variable Geschwindigkeiten und eine intelligente Auto-Funktion gestalten die Steuerung flexibel. Der solide Metall-Druckguss-Korpus vermittelt in Verbindung mit der BPA-freien, bruchsicheren Tritan-Schüssel Wertigkeit und Langlebigkeit.

Statement by the jury
This compact food processor impresses by the consistent use of robust materials and its wide range of applications.

Begründung der Jury
Durch den konsequenten Einsatz robuster Materialien und dank ihres breiten Anwendungsspektrums überzeugt diese Kompakt-Küchenmaschine.

Homend FunctionAll
Hand Blender Set
Stabmixer-Set

Manufacturer
Homend Elektrikli Cihazlar San. ve Tic. A.S.,
Istanbul, Turkey
Design
DesignUM
(Ümit Altun, Rinaldo Filinesi),
Istanbul, Turkey
Web
www.homend.com.tr
www.design-um.com
Honourable Mention

FunctionAll is an advanced, space saving and at the same time versatile hand blender. Depending on the field of application, the all-in-one solution can be used as hand blender, mixer, chopper and grater. In the development process, special attention was paid to hygienic considerations, simple cleaning and handling as well as to user safety. All functional components, especially the bowl, the cutting blades and the feed tube are designed for high user comfort.

FunctionAll ist ein fortschrittliches, platzsparendes und zugleich vielseitiges Stabmixer-Set. Die Multifunktionslösung kann je nach Anwendungsbereich als Handrührstab, Mixer, Häcksler oder Reibe verwendet werden. Bei der Entwicklung wurde vor allem auf hygienische Gesichtspunkte, eine einfache Reinigung und Handhabung sowie auf Anwendersicherheit Wert gelegt. Alle Funktionsbauteile, speziell die Schüssel, die Schneidmesser und der Einschub, sind auf einen hohen Bedienkomfort ausgelegt.

Statement by the jury
The functionally mature hand blender is a compact product solution that offers users a variety of applications.

Begründung der Jury
Das funktional durchdachte Stabmixer-Set ist eine kompakte Produktlösung, welche dem Nutzer vielseitige Einsatzmöglichkeiten bietet.

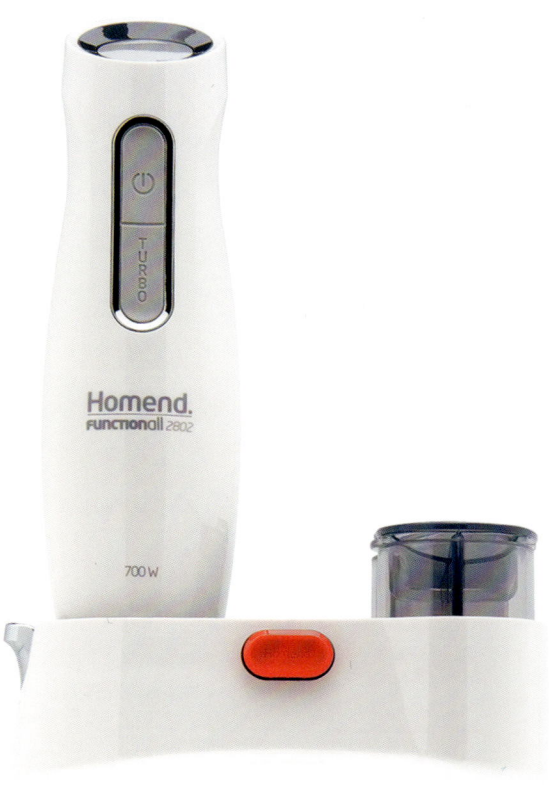

Kitchen utensils

HAUS 2.0
Hand Blender
Stabmixer

Manufacturer
Buwon Electronics Co., Ltd,
Daegu, South Korea
In-house design
Moon Eun Gi, Kim Min Seok,
Kim Hyun Tae
Web
www.tokebi.com

In comparison to other hand blenders with separate accessory, the Haus 2.0 blender accommodates its tools in the handle. Thus, it is easy to find and store the accessory. In addition, when a detector registers that the blender tilts over and reaches an angle of 45 degrees, it automatically stops the motor. According to their needs, users can set the rotation speed of the mixer to five different stages.

Im Vergleich zu anderen Stabmixern mit separaten Extras verstaut der Haus 2.0 sein Zubehör im Handgriff. Es ist so entsprechend leicht zu finden und aufzubewahren. Zudem registriert ein Detektor, sobald der Mixer umkippt und einen Winkel von über 45 Grad erreicht, und stoppt den Motor automatisch. Die Drehgeschwindigkeit des Mixers kann von den Benutzern je nach Bedarf in fünf unterschiedlichen Stufen eingestellt werden.

Statement by the jury
Inspired by a traditional formal vocabulary, this hand blender has a compact appearance and is easy to store.

Begründung der Jury
In Anlehnung an eine traditionelle Formensprache zeigt dieser Stabmixer ein kompaktes Gesamtbild und lässt sich unkompliziert verstauen.

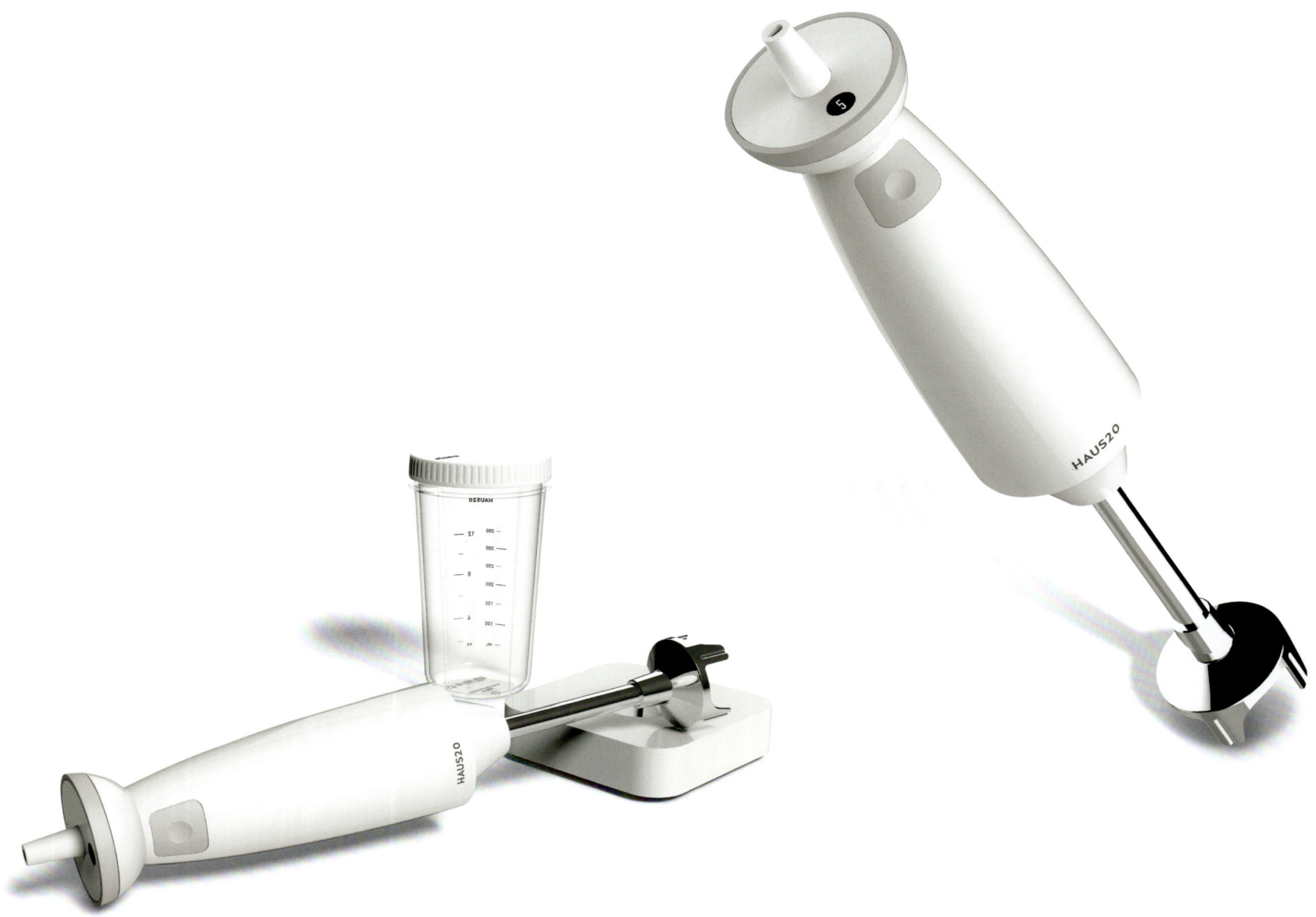

Daily Collection
Kitchen Appliance Product Range
Küchengeräte-Produktreihe

Manufacturer
Royal Philips Electronics,
Eindhoven, Netherlands
In-house design
Philips Design Consumer Lifestyle Team
Web
www.philips.com
Honourable Mention

Familiar forms, generous details and subtle splashes of colour help create the archetypical appeal of the Daily Collection range. The range of products, designed for daily use, includes a kettle, a hand blender, a blender, a food processor and a toaster. The simple, functional and friendly design offers good value for money and dependable brand quality.

Statement by the jury
Aesthetic and balanced proportions characterise the subtle overall picture of this kitchen appliance product range.

Bekannte Formen, großzügige Details und dezente Farbtupfer tragen zum archetypischen Aussehen der Geräteserie Daily Collection bei. Das für den täglichen Gebrauch konzipierte Sortiment umfasst einen Wasserkocher, einen Handmixer, einen Stabmixer, eine Küchenmaschine und einen Toaster. Die einfache, funktionelle und ansprechende Gestaltung bietet ein gutes Preis-Leistungs-Verhältnis bei einer verlässlichen Markenqualität.

Begründung der Jury
Ästhetische und ausgewogene Proportionen prägen das dezente Gesamtbild dieser Küchengeräte-Produktreihe.

BBL 605 Kinetix™ Control
Blender
Standmixer

Manufacturer
Breville Group,
Sydney, Australia
In-house design
Richard Hoare, Greg Upston
Web
www.breville.com.au
Honourable Mention

The Kinetix Control 1200W blender incorporates a patented technology. Extra wide stainless steel blades are offset to a hemispherical surface eliminating all dead zones. To reduce components, the co-polyester jug features integrated blades and is impact-resistant, BPA free and dishwasher safe. The control panel has five speeds, pre-programmed settings and pulse feature, giving the control to create exceptionally uniform blends.

Statement by the jury
This blender, the clear control panel of which allows intuitive handling, makes a robust impression.

Der Standmixer Kinetix Control 1200W beinhaltet eine patentierte Technologie. Extra breite Klingen aus rostfreiem Stahl reichen bis zum halbkugelförmigen Schüsselboden. Um die Komponenten zu reduzieren, verfügt der schlagfeste Polyester-Krug über integrierte Klingen, er ist BPA-frei und spülmaschinenfest. Das Bedienfeld bietet fünf Geschwindigkeiten, Programme sowie eine Puls-Funktion, welche die Kreation außergewöhnlich cremiger Mischungen ermöglicht.

Begründung der Jury
Einen robusten Eindruck macht dieser Standmixer, dessen übersichtliches Bedienfeld eine intuitive Handhabung ermöglicht.

JuicePresso CJP-03
Juicer
Entsafter

Manufacturer
Coway,
Seoul, South Korea
In-house design
Hun-Jung Choi, Dae-Hoo Kim,
Mi-Youn Kyung
Web
www.coway.com

The JuicePresso juices fruits and vegetables and also prepares jam, cocktails and mash. A comparatively low speed preserves the quality of the food. The juicer drum is in one piece and easy to clean. 20 per cent smaller than its predecessor model, this standalone unit requires only little space. The hopper inlet is available in two different shapes and colours.

Statement by the jury
This compact juicer combines an aesthetic style with ease of use and functionality.

Mit dem JuicePresso können Früchte und Gemüse entsaftet sowie Marmeladen, Cocktails oder Brei zubereitet werden. Eine vergleichsweise niedrige Drehzahl bewahrt die Qualität der Lebensmittel. Die Trommel des Entsafters besteht aus einem Stück und lässt sich mühelos reinigen. 20 Prozent kleiner als sein Vorgängermodell, nimmt dieses Standgerät nur wenig Platz ein. Der Trichtereinlauf wird in zwei verschiedenen Formen und Farben angeboten.

Begründung der Jury
Eine ästhetische Formensprache verbindet sich bei diesem kompakten Entsafter mit Bedienkomfort und Funktionalität.

HH-SBF06

Juicer
Entsafter

Manufacturer
Hurom L.S. Co., Ltd.,
Gimhae City, South Korea
In-house design
Yong Cheol Kim, Byoung Ho An
Web
www.hurom.com

This juicer features an innovative construction that optimises handling. Its technology enables users to make juices, ice smoothies and even baby food. Gradation markings on the drum surface allow accurate measuring of the desired amount of juice. The juicer can be cleaned easily and quickly. Marks on the drum and strainer facilitate effortless assembly and disassembly of each part of the machine. Its overall appearance is defined by curved smooth surfaces and an easy-to-reach handle that harmonises with the body shape. The operation switch is easy to handle because of its form and size.

Der innovative Aufbau des Entsafters optimiert dessen Handhabung. Mit seiner Technologie lassen sich diverse Säfte, Eis-Smoothies oder auch Babynahrung herstellen. Durch die Skala an der Trommeloberfläche kann die gewünschte Saftmenge genau abgemessen werden. Der Entsafter lässt sich schnell und einfach reinigen. Markierungen an Trommel und Sieb vereinfachen das Abnehmen und Einfügen einzelner Geräteteile. Sanft abgerundete Oberflächen charakterisieren das Gesamtbild, wobei der gut erreichbare Griff mit der Geräteform harmoniert. Der komfortable Bedienschalter ist handlich in Größe und Form.

Statement by the jury
The juicer is characterised by a high degree of functionality. Both the materials used and the feature details lend it a robust appearance.

Begründung der Jury
Ein hohes Maß an Funktionalität zeichnet den Entsafter aus. Die verwendeten Materialien und Ausstattungsdetails machen einen robusten Eindruck.

Kitchen utensils

Manufacturer
Royal Philips Electronics,
Eindhoven, Netherlands
In-house design
Philips Design Consumer Lifestyle Team
Web
www.philips.com
Honourable Mention

The HomeCooker is the first of a series of kitchen appliances co-created with British chef Jamie Oliver. The kitchen appliance can chop and grate ingredients as well as stir, steam and sauté, then be left cooking unattended. Thanks to the specially developed AutoStir technology, the food will not burn while cooking. The system is flexible and modular, easy to disassemble and dishwasher safe.

Der HomeCooker ist das erste einer Reihe von Küchengeräten, die gemeinsam mit dem englischen Koch Jamie Oliver entwickelt wurden. Das Küchengerät kann Zutaten hacken und raspeln sowie rühren, dämpfen und sautieren und anschließend unbeaufsichtigt weiterkochen. Aufgrund einer speziell entwickelten AutoStir-Technologie brennt während des Kochens nichts an. Das System ist flexibel und modular aufgebaut, leicht zu demontieren und spülmaschinenfest.

Statement by the jury
With the HomeCooker, users benefit from high functionality and save time in the preparation of food.

Begründung der Jury
Beim HomeCooker profitiert der Nutzer von einer hohen Funktionalität und einer Zeitersparnis bei der Zubereitung von Speisen.

TURBOLINE
Salad Spinner
Salatschleuder

Manufacturer
EMSA GmbH,
Emsdetten, Germany
In-house design
Markus Helb
Web
www.emsa.de

Turboline is a salad spinner with an innovative turbo function, allowing a rotational speed that is 50 per cent faster than usual. For a pleasant feel, its cord has a Soft-Touch handle. When drying lettuce, a functional colander ensures complete water drain. A stop button, the integrated drain in the lid and the non-slip bottom of the bowl offer further advantages. The salad spinner is available in three versions.

Turboline ist eine Salatschleuder mit einem innovativen Turbo-Gang, der eine um 50 Prozent höhere Drehgeschwindigkeit ermöglicht. Für eine angenehme Haptik ist das Seil mit einem Soft-Touch-Griff ausgestattet. Beim Salattrocknen sorgt der funktionale Seiher für einen vollständigen Wasserabfluss. Weitere Vorteile bieten der Stopp-Knopf, der integrierte Ausguss im Deckel sowie der rutschfeste Schalenboden. Die Salatschleuder gibt es in drei Varianten.

Statement by the jury
This salad spinner presents itself as a sophisticated product development achieving high practical use.

Begründung der Jury
Eine funktional durchdachte Produktweiterentwicklung erzielt bei dieser Salatschleuder einen hohen Gebrauchswert.

Grundig Toaster

Manufacturer
Arçelik A.S.,
Istanbul, Turkey
In-house design
Mehmet Oney
Web
www.arcelik.com.tr

The design concept of this toaster follows a geometric language of form to lend it a minimalist, clean and function-oriented appearance. Showcasing simple, classic and aesthetic lines, the toaster allows users to choose between seven heat levels. The toaster includes a stop-function, among other features, as well as a defrost function to unfreeze frozen foodstuffs. The toaster is easy-to-clean thanks to its removable crumb tray.

Statement by the jury
The timeless aesthetics of this toaster addresses users emotionally. The technically sophisticated device offers convincing ease of use.

Das Gestaltungskonzept dieses Toasters zeigt eine geometrische Formensprache, die Minimalismus, Funktionalität und Sauberkeit zum Ausdruck bringt. Der mit schlichten, klassischen Linien gestaltete Toaster bietet die Wahl zwischen sieben Röst-Stufen. Das unter anderem mit einer Stopp-Funktion ausgestattete Gerät eignet sich auch zum Auftauen von Tiefkühlprodukten. Eine herausnehmbare Krümel-schublade erleichtert die Reinigung.

Begründung der Jury
Die zeitlose Ästhetik dieses Toasters spricht den Nutzer emotional an. Das technisch ausgereifte Gerät bietet einen überzeugenden Bedienkomfort.

NC-DF1, NT-DP1
Breakfast Range
Frühstücksserie

Manufacturer
Panasonic Deutschland,
Hamburg, Germany
In-house design
Suzuki Tomohisa, Tsuruha Toshiaki
Web
www.panasonic.de

Clear lines, stainless steel and high-quality, translucent materials were used for this breakfast range in trendy black. The products offer high quality standards, easy-to-use functionality and top-quality processing. The NC-DF1 filter coffee maker with its puristic jug protects the flavour of the coffee while brewing it. The clear lines are also consistently used in the design of the NT-DP1 Toaster.

Statement by the jury
This black breakfast range looks striking. Angular contours emphasise its characteristic lines.

Klare Formen, Edelstahl und hochwertige, transluzente Materialien wurden bei dieser Frühstücksserie trendbewusst in Schwarz umgesetzt. Die Produkte bieten eine hohe und bequem nutzbare Funktionalität und eine hochwertige Verarbeitung. Die Filterkaffeemaschine NC-DF1 brüht den Kaffee geschmacksschonend in die puristische Glaskanne. Stringent wird die klare Linienführung auch beim Toaster NT-DP1 fortgeführt.

Begründung der Jury
Prägnant wirkt diese Frühstücksserie in Schwarz, wobei eckige Konturen die charakteristische Linienführung hervorheben.

WMF LINEO
Breakfast Set
Frühstücksset

Manufacturer
WMF Consumer Electric GmbH,
Jettingen-Scheppach, Germany
Design
TEAGUE GmbH
(Alf Hackenberg, Tim Zurmöhle,
Björn Frank, Lisa Töpfer),
Munich, Germany
Web
www.wmf-ce.de
www.teague.com

The Lineo breakfast set, including filter coffee machine, kettle and toaster, brings innovation and classic design to the kitchen, combining advanced technologies with superior craftsmanship. With an intuitive user interface and uniform ergonomic handle, the set is precisely manufactured and one-of-a-kind with cylindrical shapes, clean lines and high-end materials including stainless steel and Cromargan.

Das Lineo Frühstücksset, einschließlich Kaffeemaschine, Wasserkocher und Toaster, bringt Innovation und klassisches Design in die Küche. Fortschrittliche Technologie wird mit hoher Fertigungsqualität kombiniert. Das Set ist mit seiner intuitiven Benutzer-Schnittstelle und einem einheitlichen, ergonomischen Griff präzise gefertigt und dank zylindrischer Formen, klarer Linien und hochwertiger Materialien wie Edelstahl und Cromargan unverwechselbar.

Statement by the jury
Highly polished materials effectively underline the timeless elegance of the Lineo breakfast set.

Begründung der Jury
Glänzend polierte Materialien unterstreichen wirkungsvoll die zeitlos elegante Ästhetik des Lineo Frühstückssets.

Kitchen utensils

Butterfly Sensor Can
Trashcan
Abfalleimer

Manufacturer
simplehuman,
Torrance, USA
In-house design
Frank Yang
Design
Dashdot Studios
(Daniel Ballou),
Long Beach, USA
Web
www.simplehuman.com
www.dashdotstudios.com

The sensor trashcan was developed with multi-sense technology that reacts and adapts to consumer behaviour. The touch-free lid technology offers three different modes: a ready mode, a task mode, and a 30-second mode that makes the lid stay open for tasks that take longer. The slim shape of the trashcan is space-saving, yet offers enough capacity. The full top surface lid opens from the centre like a butterfly.

Dieser Sensor-Abfalleimer ist mit einer „multi-sense"-Technologie ausgestattet, die sich dem Nutzerverhalten anpasst. Diese berührungsfreie Schließtechnik nutzt drei verschiedene Modi: einen Bereitschaftsmodus, einen Arbeitsmodus und einen 30-Sekunden-Modus, bei dem der Deckel länger geöffnet bleibt. Die schmale Form des Abfalleimers spart Platz und bietet dennoch genügend Volumen. Der großzügige Schmetterlingsdeckel öffnet sich in der Mitte.

Statement by the jury
This trashcan is characterised by a design of high functional orientation and equipped with innovative sensor technology in the lid.

Begründung der Jury
Eine funktional orientierte Gestaltung zeichnet diesen Abfalleimer, der über eine innovative Sensortechnologie verfügt, aus.

Fire Detector
Brandmelder

Manufacturer
Cavius Aps,
Silkeborg, Denmark
In-house design
Glenn Hojmose
Web
www.cavius.com

With a diameter of only 40 mm, this fire detector is comparatively small and discreetly blends in with any kitchen decor. The device has been designed for quality and efficiency. The risk of false alarm set off by non-hazardous emission of smoke caused by cooking could be minimised. An innovative feature is the battery service life of ten years, making frequent battery replacements unnecessary.

Statement by the jury
Elaborate functionality distinguishes this fire detector, the design of which is remarkably compact.

Mit einem Durchmesser von nur 40 mm ist dieser Brandmelder vergleichsweise klein und fügt sich unauffällig in die Küchensituation ein. Das Gerät ist auf Qualität und Effizienz ausgelegt. Es konnte das Risiko eines Fehlalarms aufgrund einer gefahrlosen Rauchentwicklung, die etwa durch Kochen verursacht wird, minimiert werden. Als innovative Neuerung hat die Batterie eine Lebensdauer von zehn Jahren, wodurch häufiges Batteriewechseln entfällt.

Begründung der Jury
Eine durchdachte Funktionalität zeichnet diesen Brandmelder aus, der zudem bemerkenswert kompakt konstruiert ist.

RAUVISIO crystal
Polymer Glass Laminate
Polymeres Glaslaminat

Manufacturer
REHAU AG + Co,
Rehau, Germany
In-house design
Web
www.rehau.de
Honourable Mention

The Rauvisio crystal surface product range opens up new possibilities for creating glass finishes. This glass laminate combines the visual characteristics of glass with the advantages of a polymeric material. Furniture manufacturers can thus produce furniture fronts with a high quality glass finish in mass production. Products previously had to be laboriously manufactured outside the serial production. Now it is possible to produce almost any form in mass production accurate to dimension.

Statement by the jury
The development of this innovative glass laminate allows the simplified production of furniture fronts with a high quality glass finish.

Das Möbel-Oberflächenprogramm Rauvisio crystal eröffnet neue Möglichkeiten bei der Gestaltung von Glasfronten. Dieses Glaslaminat kombiniert die visuellen Eigenschaften von Glas mit den Vorteilen eines polymeren Werkstoffes. Möbelhersteller können damit auf Serienanlagen hochwertige Möbelfronten mit Glasanmutung herstellen. Wo bislang aufwendig außerhalb des Serienprozesses gefertigt werden musste, kann nun maßgenau nahezu jede Form auf Serienanlagen hergestellt werden.

Begründung der Jury
Die Entwicklung dieses innovativen Glaslaminats ermöglicht eine vereinfachte Herstellung von vollflächigen Möbelfronten mit Glasanmutung.

RAUKANTEX visions
Duo-Design
Edgeband
Kantenwerkstoff

Manufacturer
REHAU AG + Co,
Rehau, Germany
In-house design
Web
www.rehau.de
Honourable Mention

The newly developed Duo-Design version of the Raukantex visions edgeband product range uses the material PMMA. It facilitates the design of furniture glass fronts. In combination with glass laminate, Duo-Design creates the visual effect of a flush-mounted glass panel. It can be used both continuously and with a V groove. It offers the processing advantages of polymeric materials. Thus, kitchen fronts can be produced more cost effective.

Statement by the jury
The advanced Raukantex visions Duo-Design edgeband material impresses in combination with the manufacturer-specific glass laminate.

Das Kantenprogramm Raukantex visions mit seiner neu entwickelten Variante Duo-Design nutzt den Werkstoff PMMA und erleichtert die Gestaltung von Möbel-Glasfronten. Duo-Design ermöglicht in Kombination mit Glaslaminat den visuellen Effekt einer bündig aufliegenden Glasplatte und findet sowohl stufenlos als auch mit V-Nut Verwendung. Es bietet die Verarbeitungsvorteile eines polymeren Werkstoffs, sodass eine Küchenfront kostengünstiger gestaltet werden kann.

Begründung der Jury
Der fortschrittliche Kantenwerkstoff Raukantex visions Duo-Design überzeugt im Zusammenspiel mit dem herstellereigenen Glaslaminat.

Tableware
and decoration
Tableware
und Dekoration

Dining, porcelain, cookware and dinnerware, table decoration, table textiles, glass, ceramics, cutlery, accessories
Dining, Porzellan, Koch- und Küchengeschirr, Tischdekoration und -textilien, Glas, Keramik, Besteck, Accessoires

4

OSORO
Open Tableware System
Offenes Geschirrsystem

Manufacturer
Narumi Corporation,
Nagoya, Aichi, Japan

Design
MTDO Inc. (Manabu Tago),
Tokyo, Japan
Wellness Arena Corporation
(Takako Kajikawa),
Tokyo, Japan (Supervisor)

Web
www.osoro.jp
www.narumi.co.jp
www.mtdo-ch.com
www.warena.net

reddot design award
best of the best 2013

Modular lightness

Tableware has always been an expression of the
contemporary zeitgeist. In the 1920s, Bauhaus
designer Walter Gropius for instance created simple
and distinctive plates and bowls that merged the
areas of table and kitchen through their functionality.
The design of the Osoro defines contemporary
tableware according to the maxim of a highly
functional and formal openness. This tableware
system aims at presenting a straightforward solution
for everyday life as it adapts easily to people's
changing demands and lifestyles. Coming in different
sizes, the various Osoro tableware items are compact
in design, easy to stack and offer users a multitude
of individual variations and combinations. For storing
dinner leftovers in the fridge or keeping them fresh
for a short period, Osoro offers the possibility of
sealing the bowls and plates with differently coloured
lids – a perfectly matched silicon ring keeps the
foodstuffs inside well protected. Due to this new
interpretation of modularity and functionality, the
gaps between the areas of cooking, refrigerating,
freezing and storing are bridged easily. The Osoro
tableware offers a multitude of aesthetically pleasing
form and colour variations – it conveys a new
sense of lightness that connects all areas of life.

Modulare Leichtigkeit

Ein Essgeschirr ist immer Ausdruck des aktuellen Zeitgeistes. So gestaltete etwa in den 1920er Jahren der
Bauhaus-Designer Walter Gropius schlichte und markante Teller und Schalen, die durch ihre Funktionalität
die Bereiche Tafel und Küche miteinander vereinten. Die
Gestaltung von Osoro definiert ein zeitgemäßes Geschirr
durch die Maxime einer sehr weitreichenden funktionalen und formalen Offenheit. Dieses Geschirrsystem
will unkomplizierte Lösungen für den Alltag bieten,
indem sich die Anforderungen und Lebensumstände
rasch verändern können. Die unterschiedlich großen
Geschirrteile von Osoro sind kompakt gestaltet und gut
ineinander stapelbar – alle einzelnen Geschirrelemente
lassen sich frei untereinander kombinieren und variieren.
Um Reste im Kühlschrank aufzubewahren oder kurz
einmal frischzuhalten, bietet das Osoro die Möglichkeit,
Schüsseln und Platten mit verschiedenfarbigen Deckeln
zu verschließen: Ein exakt abdichtender Silikonring hält
die Speisen dabei gut verschlossen. Durch diese neu
interpretierte Modularität und Funktionalität können die
Bereiche des Kochens, Kühlens, Einfrierens und Lagerns
gut überbrückt werden. Das Geschirrsystem Osoro
ermöglicht mit seiner Formen- und Farbenvielfalt ein
ästhetisches Miteinander – es kommuniziert eine neue
Art von Leichtigkeit, die alle Lebensbereiche verbindet.

Statement by the jury

The Osoro tableware system brings joy to everyday
life. It follows the concept of merging different things
into a fresh and clear language of form. The modular
design facilitates a myriad of uses – the function
constantly adapts to the need. The combination
of traditional materials with new ones creates an
appealing contrast.

Begründung der Jury

Das Geschirrsystem Osoro bringt Freude in den Alltag.
Es ist ein neues Konzept, unterschiedliche Dinge in
einer frischen und klaren Formensprache miteinander
zu verbinden. Durch seine modulare Gestaltung
entstehen viele Einsatzmöglichkeiten – die Funktion
verändert sich stetig. Die Kombination traditioneller
Materialien mit modernen schafft einen reizvollen
Kontrast.

Dinnerware

Light
Tableware
Geschirrserie

Manufacturer
Asa Selection GmbH,
Höhr-Grenzhausen, Germany
In-house design
Aleks Samek
Web
www.asa-selection.de

All items of the Light tableware are of snow-white porcelain. The porcelain is so thin that it appears almost transparent and is particularly light. The lines are organic, whereby the elegant forms are slightly asymmetric. The collection consists of four round and two oval pieces, salt and pepper set as well as beaker and water carafe.

Alle Elemente der Geschirrserie Light bestehen aus schneeweißem Porzellan. Das Porzellan ist so dünn verarbeitet, dass es fast durchscheinend wirkt und besonders leicht ist. Die Linienführung ist organisch, dabei sind die eleganten Formen leicht asymmetrisch. Zur Serie gehören vier runde und zwei ovale Teile, Salz- und Pfefferstreuer sowie Becher und Wasserkaraffe.

Statement by the jury
The Light collection lives up to its name: it impresses with a charming lightness of design and workmanship.

Begründung der Jury
Die Serie Light hält, was ihr Name verspricht: Sie besticht mit einer anmutigen Leichtigkeit in Gestaltung und Ausführung.

MOOD
Dinnerware
Geschirrserie

Manufacturer
Asa Selection GmbH,
Höhr-Grenzhausen, Germany
In-house design
Romi Bohnenberg
Web
www.asa-selection.com

Nature is the godfather of this dinnerware collection. Mood is inspired by the age rings of a tree. The age ring décor is finely embossed on the delicate porcelain surface of the service, interplaying with light and shadow. The contrast between the shine of the glazed plate and unglazed edge provides an additional visual and haptic charm. The dinnerware is dishwasher proof and microwave safe.

Die Natur stand Pate für diese Geschirr-serie. Mood ist inspiriert von den Jahres-ringen eines Baumes. Aus den zarten, rein weißen Porzellanoberflächen des Services ist das Jahresringdekor als fein erhabenes Relief herausgearbeitet, das mit Licht und Schatten spielt. Der Kontrast zwischen glasiertem Spiegel und unglasiertem Rand übt einen zusätzlichen optischen und haptischen Reiz aus. Das Geschirr ist spül-maschinenfest und mikrowellengeeignet.

Statement by the jury
Mood dinnerware transmits a natural phenomenon cleverly into a contemporary decor. This results in simple elegance and strong sensuality.

Begründung der Jury
Die Geschirrserie Mood übersetzt ein Naturphänomen gekonnt in ein zeitgemä-ßes Dekor. Das Ergebnis ist von schlichter Eleganz und starker Sinnlichkeit.

Artesano Original
Tableware
Geschirrserie

Manufacturer
Villeroy & Boch AG,
Mettlach, Germany
In-house design
Henrike Stein,
Helmut Frank
Design
Studio Christian Haas,
Munich, Germany
Web
www.villeroy-boch.com
www.christian-haas.com
Honourable Mention

Artesano Original reflects the philosophy of modern life in harmony with nature. The form language is correspondingly characterised as minimalist and handcrafted. The concept is further emphasised by the material mix: premium Fine China porcelain encounters grained acacia wood, cork and slate. The collection consists of 32 items which are distinguished by a pleasant haptic and various tableware elements. Thus the multifunctional collection provides products for every culinary occasion.

Artesano Original spiegelt die Philosophie eines modernen Lebens im Einklang mit der Natur wider. Entsprechend minimalistisch und handwerklich geprägt ist die Formensprache. Das Konzept wird durch die Materialwahl noch betont: edles Fine China Porzellan trifft auf stark gemasertes Akazienholz, Kork und Schiefer. Das Sortiment besteht aus 32 Artikeln, die sich durch eine angenehme Haptik und Multifunktionalität auszeichnen. So bietet die vielfältige Kollektion die richtigen Produkte für jeden kulinarischen Anlass.

Lina
Tableware
Geschirrserie

Manufacturer
Villeroy & Boch AG,
Mettlach, Germany
In-house design
Dorothea Ollinger
Design
Werner Bohr, Agentur für Gestaltung,
Trier, Germany
Web
www.villeroy-boch.com
www.wernerbohr.de
Honourable Mention

Lina is an uncomplicated everyday concept proposing a plethora of individual combinations. The decors gleam in typical vintage colours with three designs: one graphic raster design in potato print optic, one continuous decor and one floral decor. The basic forms of all tableware components derive from two established collections of the manufacturer, both of which have a very reduced design. This way the vibrant colours are highlighted particularly vividly.

Lina ist ein unkompliziertes Every-Day-Konzept, das mit seiner individuellen Kombinierbarkeit begeistert. Die Dekore leuchten in Vintage-typischen Farben und drei Mustern: ein grafisches Rasterdekor in Kartoffeldruck-Optik, ein Verlaufsdekor und ein florales Dekor. Die Grundformen aller Geschirrelemente sind zwei etablierten Serien des Herstellers entlehnt, die beide ein sehr reduziertes Design haben. So kommen die kräftigen Farben und einzigartigen Dekore besonders gut zur Geltung.

Statement by the jury
This service with its cheerful vintage decors brings joie de vivre to the table with simple forms and many possibilities for combination.

Begründung der Jury
Dieses Service bringt mit seinen verspielten Vintage-Dekoren, schlichten Formen und vielen Kombinationsmöglichkeiten Lebensfreude auf den Tisch.

EDA
Cutlery
Besteck

Manufacturer
Ken Okuyama Design Co., Ltd.,
Tokyo, Japan

In-house design
Ken Okuyama

Web
www.kenokuyamadesign.com

Organic elegance

Classical cutlery, consisting of knives, forks and spoons, comes in many different shapes and looks. Filigree, almost delicate-looking cutlery designs can be found right next to minimalist creations of formal austerity. The design of the EDA cutlery is inspired by the natural shape of a tree with branches and twigs lending it a highly organic appearance. The prongs of the fork seem to extend like branches from the trunk of a tree and all pieces of the cutlery set share the same twig-like patterns. The aim behind this branch motif form was to bring a high degree of the feeling of naturalism to the daily table. The EDA cutlery is made of premium-grade stainless steel. However, featuring a tree-like brown colour and when laid out on the table, the cutlery at first sight creates the impression of an artistic arrangement of organic elements collected from nature. Another outstanding feature of this cutlery is how its organic appearance consistently embodies the guiding design principle of asymmetry. All elements are harmoniously proportioned and feature lines that are equally well balanced. The design concept of the EDA cutlery centres around the idea of universal usability. The aim was to create cutlery that matches well and adds to the ambience of almost any environment, including cafes and restaurants. Therefore, the cutlery is highly durable and perfectly honed to the last detail. Inspired by the shape and look of branches, this design concept manages to lend cutlery an entirely novel aesthetics – playful in appearance paired with high functional usability.

Organische Eleganz

Die Form des klassischen Bestecks, bestehend aus Messer, Gabeln und Löffeln, ist sehr variabel. Es existieren zierliche und filigran gestaltete Bestecke ebenso gleichberechtigt neben strengen und minimalistischen Formen. Das Besteck EDA ist in seiner Gestaltung den natürlichen Verästelungen eines Baumes angelehnt und mutet damit sehr organisch an. Wie Äste scheinen die Zinken der Gabel aus einem Stamm herauszuwachsen; alle Besteckteile haben ähnlich zweigartige Verästelungen. Das Ziel dieser Gestaltung mit Zweigmotiven war es, ein hohes Maß an Natürlichkeit auf den Tisch zu bringen. Das Besteck EDA ist aus einem hochwertigen Edelstahl gefertigt. Da dieser jedoch eine baumähnliche Farbe hat, wirkt es auf den ersten Blick, als lägen kunstvoll arrangierte Pflanzenteile auf dem Tisch. Auffällig ist bei diesem Besteck zudem, wie sich seine organische Anmutung gekonnt mit der gestaltungsleitenden Maxime der Asymmetrie verbindet. Alle Elemente sind gut proportioniert und in ihren Radien ebenso gut aufeinander abgestimmt. Bei der Gestaltung des Besteckes EDA stand eine offene Art der Nutzung im Mittelpunkt. Es sollte ein vielseitig verwendbares Besteck entstehen, welches zum Beispiel in Cafés auf ungezwungene Art eingesetzt werden kann. Für diesen Einsatz ist es sehr langlebig und in all seinen Details perfekt ausgearbeitet. Die gestalterischen Anleihen an die Form von Ästen führte hier zu einem Besteck mit einer völlig neuen Ästhetik – es wirkt spielerisch und ist dennoch hochfunktional.

Statement by the jury

The design of the EDA cutlery manages in a highly impressive way to translate natural forms found in nature into cutlery. It convinces with an appearance that is both sensual and organic. Its ergonomic shaped rests well in the hand and perfectly satisfies all requirements for use in the catering industry.

Begründung der Jury

Der Gestaltung des EDA gelingt es auf beeindruckende Art und Weise, in der Natur vorkommende Formen in ein Besteck zu überführen. Es besticht durch seine sinnliche wie organische Anmutung. Es liegt ergonomisch gut in der Hand und erfüllt auf perfekte Weise alle Anforderungen für einen Einsatz im Gastronomiebereich.

Cutlery

Molton
Cutlery
Besteck

Manufacturer
Robert Welch Designs Ltd,
Chipping Campden, GB
In-house design
Kit De Bretton Gordon
Web
www.robertwelch.com

Molton Cutlery, with its finely sweeping contours and smooth edges in the lower handle area, reflects the basic form of a plate. The cutlery handle is well balanced; thanks to its weight and the flowing form it lies in the hand quite naturally and is effortless to use. The cutlery set is made of high quality stainless steel. The knives are forged out of especially hardened stainless steel for a particularly fine cutting edge.

Molton Cutlery reflektiert mit seinen fein geschwungenen Konturen und weichen Kanten im unteren Griffbereich die Grundform eines Tellers. Der Griff des Bestecks ist gut ausbalanciert, dank seines Gewichts und der fließenden Formen liegt es ganz selbstverständlich in der Hand und lässt sich mühelos nutzen. Das Besteck besteht aus hochwertigem Edelstahl; die Messer sind für eine besonders feine Schneide aus speziell gehärtetem Edelstahl geschmiedet.

Statement by the jury
The sweeping lines of the cutlery provide high form quality which further enhances the tableware accompanying it.

Begründung der Jury
Die geschwungene Linienführung des Bestecks ist von hoher formaler Qualität, die zusätzlich das Geschirr, neben dem es eingedeckt wird, aufwertet.

Cutlery

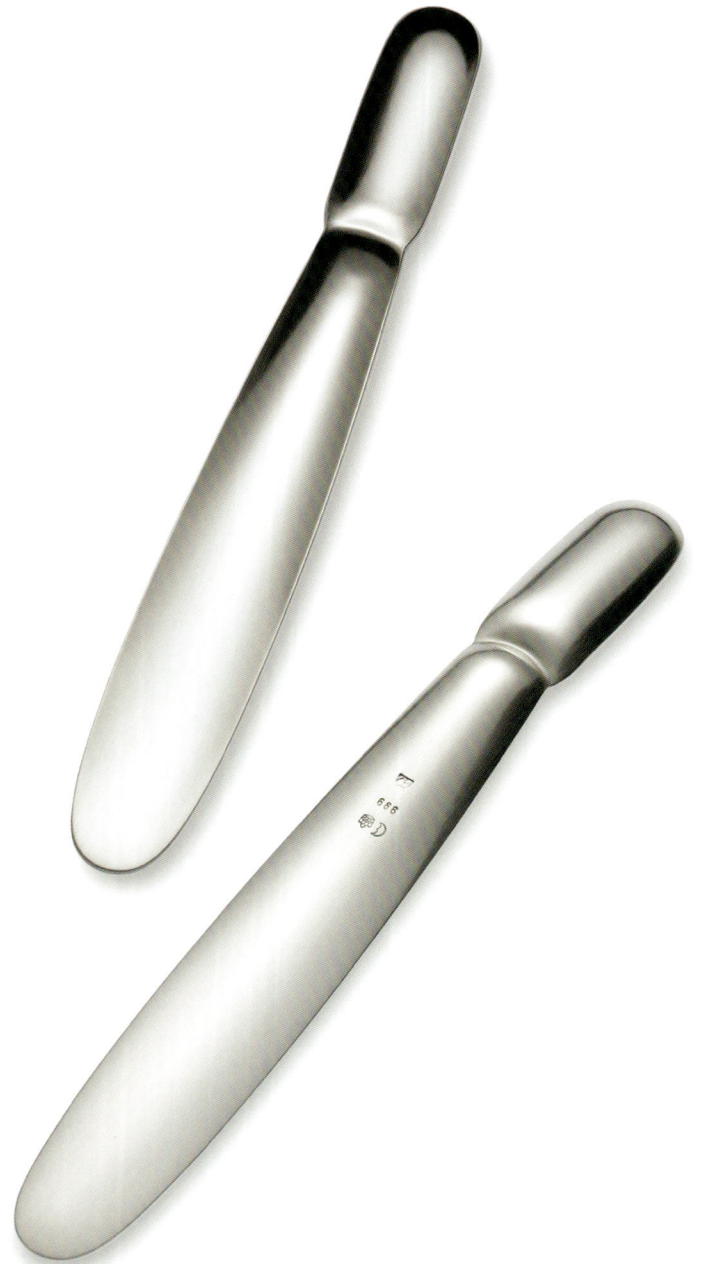

Dragonfly
Libelle
Espresso Spoon
Espressolöffel

Manufacturer
Atelier Bindernagel,
Hildesheim, Germany
In-house design
Marit Bindernagel
Web
www.atelierbindernagel.de

Designed and manufactured by a lady silversmith, these espresso spoons combine precise artisan handwork with an artistic approach. Their wide, lightly arched handle, which becomes flatter as it tapers upwards, provides a pleasant haptic experience. Due to the reduced, narrow form of the front part of the spoon, the function of stirring is emphasised. The spoon is made of shiny, fine silver.

Statement by the jury
Its delicate, balanced design and the high quality of manufacturing craftsmanship make Dragonfly a timeless design object.

Von einer Gold- und Silberschmiedin gestaltet und hergestellt, verbinden diese Espressolöffel eine präzise handwerkliche Verarbeitung mit einer künstlerischen Herangehensweise. Ihr breiter, leicht gewölbter und nach oben immer flacher auslaufender Griff verspricht eine angenehme haptische Erfahrung. Durch die reduzierte, schmale Form des vorderen Löffelteils wird die Funktion des Rührens betont. Der Löffel besteht aus glänzendem Feinsilber.

Begründung der Jury
Ihre grazile, ausgewogene Gestaltung und die hohe handwerkliche Qualität der Herstellung machen Libelle zu einem zeitlosen Designobjekt.

Cutlery Wave
Besteck Elan

Manufacturer
Ornamin-Kunststoffwerke,
Minden, Germany
In-house design
Ornamin Design Team
(Thorsten Erdelt, Janine Sparmann)
Web
www.ornamin.com
Honourable Mention

This cutlery set for handicapped people can be used fully intuitively and individually, as there are no fixed holding positions. Spoon and fork are S-shaped and also have pads which can be slid on to support use when hand and finger movement is impaired. One possible position of the knife blade is for example between the middle and the forefinger and allows for safe cutting also in case of motoric hindrance.

Statement by the jury
With this cutlery the requirements of Universal Design, particularly in the field of ergonomics and haptic have been convincingly implemented.

Dieses Besteck für Menschen mit Handicap kann völlig intuitiv und individuell benutzt werden, denn es gibt keine festgelegten Griffpositionen. Löffel und Gabel haben eine S-Form und zusätzlich aufschiebbare Kissen, die auch bei eingeschränkter Hand- und Fingerbeweglichkeit den Gebrauch unterstützen. Eine mögliche Position der Klinge beim Messer liegt beispielsweise zwischen Mittel- und Zeigefinger und erleichtert auch bei motorischen Einschränkungen ein sicheres Schneiden.

Begründung der Jury
Bei diesem Besteck wurden die Anforderungen des Universal Design insbesondere in den Bereichen Ergonomie und Haptik bemerkenswert umgesetzt.

Hoverware
Cutlery
Besteck

Manufacturer
Manifesto Design Lab
Seoul, South Korea
In-house design
Jeeyong An
Sang Hwa Lee
Design
Manifesto Architecture P.C.
New York, USA
Web
www.mfarch.com

Hoverware is a simply designed set of wooden cutlery with one special feature at the underside: in the upper part of the handle it has a small stand, inspired by bamboo node, which prevents the mouthpiece of the cutlery from contact with the table. The stand is so positioned that it does not interfere when the cutlery is held in the hand. If, on the other hand, pressure is needed when cutting or forking, this can be applied by means of the support. The cutlery is handmade of Sawo, Japanese wood.

Hoverware ist ein schlicht gestaltetes Holzbesteck mit einer Besonderheit an der Unterseite: Es hat im oberen Bereich des Griffs einen kleinen Steg, der verhindert, dass das Mundstück des Bestecks auf dem Tisch aufliegt. Der Steg ist so positioniert, dass er beim Greifen nicht stört. Muss hingegen beim Schneiden Druck ausgeübt werden, kann dieser über den Steg noch verstärkt werden. Das Besteck wird in Handarbeit aus japanischem Sawo-Holz gefertigt.

Xline
Knife Series
Messerserie

Manufacturer
Ed. Wüsthof Dreizackwerk KG,
Solingen, Germany
In-house design
Viola Wüsthof,
Harald Wüsthof
Design
Nicolas Thomkins,
Lüneburg, Germany
Web
www.wuesthof.com

By means of an innovative forging technology, in this knife series handle and blade are attached in a special X-form. The lines extend to the blade and are accentuated by the bolster and handle. The X-shaped transition between handle and blade leads intuitively to the right handling of the knife and optimal blade guiding. A newly developed transparent ceramic coating gives the blade even more robustness.

Statement by the jury
In this knife series traditional brand characteristics combine with innovative production and design approaches to realise one harmonious unit.

Durch die innovative Schmiedetechnik verbinden sich Griff und Klinge bei dieser Messerserie in einer speziellen X-Form. Die Linien werden von der Klinge aufgenommen und über Kropf und Griff noch hervorgehoben. Der X-förmige Übergang zwischen Griff und Klinge führt intuitiv zur richtigen Handhabung der Messer und einer optimalen Klingenführung. Eine neu entwickelte transparente Keramikbeschichtung macht die Klinge noch widerstandsfähiger.

Begründung der Jury
Bei dieser Messerserie verbinden sich traditionelle Markenmerkmale und innovative Produktions- und Gestaltungsansätze zu einem stimmigen Ganzen.

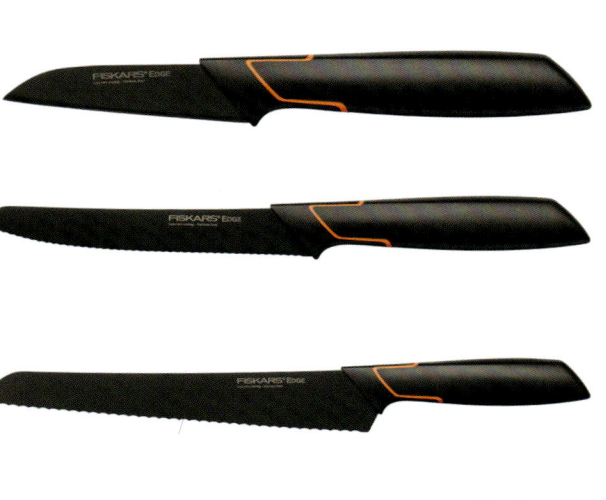

Fiskars Edge™
Knife Series
Messerserie

Manufacturer
Fiskars,
Helsinki, Finland
Design
Tobias Wandrup,
Copenhagen, Denmark
Web
www.fiskars.com

The kitchen knives of the Edge series are versatile: Elements of the greatest variations in knife styles are reflected here. High-grade steel and the knife blade grinding assure long-term sharpness. The flowing transition between ergonomically formed handle and blade facilitate various cutting techniques and optimal handling. Due to their special black, non-stick coating the knives are easy to clean and durable.

Statement by the jury
The knives of the Edge series fascinate at first glance due to their distinctive design and are additionally convincing when in use.

Die Küchenmesser der Edge Serie sind vielseitig: Elemente der unterschiedlichsten Messer-Stile finden sich in ihnen wieder. Hochwertiger Stahl und der Schliff der Klinge gewährleisten lang anhaltende Schärfe. Der fließende Übergang zwischen ergonomisch geformtem Griff und Klinge ermöglicht verschiedene Schnitttechniken und eine optimale Handhabung. Durch ihre spezielle schwarze Antihaft-Beschichtung sind die Messer leicht zu reinigen und haltbar.

Begründung der Jury
Die Messer der Edge-Serie faszinieren bereits auf den ersten Blick durch ihre markante Gestaltung und überzeugen darüber hinaus in der Anwendung.

Seki Magoroku Composite
Chef's Knife Series
Messerserie

Manufacturer
Kai Industries Co., Ltd.,
Gifu, Japan
In-house design
Kai R&D Center Co., Ltd.
(Katsumi Hasegawa)
Web
www.kai-group.com

The blades of this eight-piece knife series are composed of two different types of steel: one is the high-gloss polished cutting edge made of extremely sharp VG-Max steel and a satinised back of SUS420J2 steel. The types of steel are developed from aircraft construction technology and are bonded using a special copper brazing technique. The fine bonding line thus created remains as a decorative design feature.

Die Klingen dieser achtteiligen Messerserie setzen sich aus zwei verschiedenen Stahlsorten zusammen: einer hochglanz-polierten Schneide aus extrem scharfem VG-Max Stahl und einem satinierten Rücken aus SUS420J2 Stahl. Die Stahlsorten werden nach einer dem Flugzeugbau entlehnten Technologie mit einer speziellen Kupferlötung verbunden. Die dabei entstehende feine Kupferlinie zwischen den Sorten bleibt als Gestaltungselement sichtbar.

Knife Series
Messerserie

Manufacturer
Neoflam Inc.,
Seoul, South Korea
In-house design
Joon-Hee Noh
Web
www.neoflam.com

The knives of the Aveco series are made of hardened stainless steel and coated with an environmentally friendly ceramic finish, which makes the blades particularly solid and durable. The centre of gravity of the knives is with regard to optimal handling accurately balanced. The coloured knife handles stand out from the knife block and facilitate the ease of use, since each colour denotes a particular type of blade.

Statement by the jury
The Aveco series with its distinctive, colourful design stands out immediately and convinces in the long term due to its high quality and degree of utility.

Die Messer der Aveco Serie sind aus gehärtetem Edelstahl gefertigt und mit einer umweltfreundlichen, keramischen Beschichtung überzogen, welche die Klingen besonders solide und langlebig macht. Der Schwerpunkt der Messer ist im Hinblick auf eine optimale Handhabung exakt ausbalanciert. Die farbigen Messergriffe heben sich vom Messerblock ab und erleichtern die Benutzung, da jede Farbe einer bestimmten Klingenform zugeordnet ist.

Begründung der Jury
Die Aveco Serie fällt mit ihrer markanten, farbenfrohen Gestaltung sofort auf und überzeugt langfristig durch hohe Qualität und Gebrauchstauglichkeit.

Aveco
Knife Block
Messerblock

Manufacturer
Neoflam Inc.,
Seoul, South Korea
In-house design
Joon-Hee Noh
Web
www.neoflam.com

Plain and simplistic in design, the Aveco knife block can hold Aveco knives of various sizes and forms. The anti-bacterial brushes of the knife block facilitate insertion of the knives in any direction. Due to its double-wall construction, the knife block is particularly robust. Thanks to its slim form, it takes up only little room on the work surface.

Statement by the jury
The slim knife block convinces with its flexible interior and reduced form allowing it to fit into every kitchen environment.

Schlicht und minimalistisch im Design, lassen sich im Messerblock Aveco Messer unterschiedlicher Größe und Form aufbewahren. Die antibakteriell ausgestatteten Bürsten des Messerblocks ermöglichen das Einsetzen der Messer in beliebiger Richtung. Durch seine doppelwandige Struktur ist der Messerblock besonders robust. Dank seiner schmalen Form benötigt er nur wenig Platz auf der Arbeitsfläche.

Begründung der Jury
Der schlanke Messerblock überzeugt mit seinem flexiblen Innenleben und einer reduzierten Formensprache, durch die er sich in jede Küchenumgebung einfügt.

MicroCook
Containers for Microwave Use
Behälter für die Mikrowelle

Manufacturer
Tupperware France S.A.,
Joué-lès-Tours, France
In-house design
Tupperware Worldwide
Product Development Team
Design
Heiberg Industrial Design,
Gentofte, Denmark
Web
www.tupperwarebrands.com

The collection consists of two stackable casseroles and a jug for microwave cooking. The casseroles have vent openings at the edge of the lid so that the steam can escape and no vacuum is created when cooling. Separate, fresh-keeping lids make it possible for the food afterwards to be cooled down or frozen in the same container. The interiors of all containers are made better for use by rounding off the corners. The ergonomic handles provide safe handling.

Die Serie umfasst zwei stapelbare Kasserollen und eine Kanne für das Garen in der Mikrowelle. Die Kasserollen haben Entlüftungsöffnungen im Deckelrand, damit Dampf entweichen und beim Abkühlen kein Vakuum entstehen kann. Separate Frischhaltedeckel ermöglichen, die Speisen anschließend im selben Behälter zu kühlen oder einzufrieren. Das Innere aller Gefäße ist zum besseren Gebrauch abgerundet. Die ergonomischen Griffe erlauben eine sichere Handhabung.

Statement by the jury
This innovative microwave cooking set is flexible in use, well considered in detail and has a high utility factor.

Begründung der Jury
Dieses innovative Mikrowellen-Kochset ist flexibel einsetzbar, bis ins Detail durchdacht und hat einen hohen Gebrauchswert.

Tableware and decoration

Collapsible Cooking Pot
Cookware
Kochgeschirr

Manufacturer
Ricco Engineering International Inc.,
Nantou City, Taiwan
In-house design
Ronald Tuan
Web
www.riccoeng.com
Honourable Mention

This cooking pot can be folded from its cooking height of 15.8 cm to a space-saving 7.6 cm. It consists of a stainless steel base plate and a silicone body and can be used on almost every kind of cooker. Thanks to its small size when folded and its weight of only 690 grams, this pot is suitable not only for the home cooker but it is also the ideal companion for a camping holiday, trekking tours etc.

Statement by the jury
High user value and a well thought-out functionality characterise this versatile cooking pot.

Dieser Kochtopf lässt sich von seinen 15,8 cm Kochhöhe auf platzsparende 7,6 cm zusammenfalten. Er besteht aus einer Edelstahl-Bodenplatte und einem Silikonkörper und ist auf nahezu jedem Herd einsetzbar. Dank der geringen Größe in zusammengefaltetem Zustand und einem Gewicht von nur 690 Gramm eignet sich der Topf nicht nur für den heimischen Herd, sondern ist auch der ideale Begleiter für Campingurlaube, Trekkingtouren etc.

Begründung der Jury
Ein hoher Nutzwert und eine gut durchdachte Funktionalität kennzeichnen diesen vielseitigen Kochtopf.

ELO Multilayer
Cookware
Kochgeschirr

Manufacturer
ELO Stahlwaren GmbH & Co. KG,
Spabrücken, Germany
In-house design
Marcus Grünewald
Web
www.elo.de
Honourable Mention

The distinctiveness of this cookware collection lies in its special material construction: The pans are composed of precisely matched laminates of stainless steel, pure aluminium and aluminium alloy, bonded into an akkutherm storage system. This assures for all cooker types a constant heat distribution up to the edge of the side walls. In this way, the content of the pan is heated to the same degree overall.

Statement by the jury
In the case of this cookware, a clear design and intelligent use of materials are combined, with the aim of saving energy and time when cooking.

Die Besonderheit dieser Kochtopfserie liegt in ihrem speziellen Materialaufbau: Die Töpfe bestehen aus präzise aufeinander abgestimmten Schichten aus Edelstahl, reinem Aluminium und Aluminium-Legierungen, die sich zu einem Akkutherm-Speichersystem verbinden. Dieses sorgt auf allen Herdarten für eine konstante Wärmeverteilung bis hinauf zum Rand der Seitenwände. So wird der Inhalt des Topfes immer gleichmäßig erhitzt.

Begründung der Jury
Bei diesem Kochgeschirr trifft eine klare Gestaltung auf einen intelligenten Materialeinsatz mit dem Ziel, beim Kochen Energie und Zeit einzusparen.

BK Flow
Cookware
Kochgeschirr

Manufacturer
BK Cookware BV,
Zoetermeer, Netherlands
In-house design
Nadia Wijstma
Web
www.bk.nl

The cookware collection Flow has an intelligent pouring system by which the lids can be locked for pouring by a simple twist. The items are of high quality stainless steel and have a sandwich base which conducts the heat quicker and distributes it optimally. Flow is suitable for all heat sources including induction. The handles are positioned far up, which means the pots can be stacked to save space.

Statement by the jury
Flow convinces with its linearity of form and its particularly functional pouring system.

Die Topfserie Flow hat ein intelligentes Abgießsystem, bei dem die Deckel zum Abgießen mit einer einfachen Drehung verriegelt werden können. Die Töpfe sind aus hochwertigem Edelstahl hergestellt und haben einen Sandwichboden, der die Hitze schneller aufnimmt und die Wärme optimal verteilt. Flow eignet sich für alle Wärmequellen, einschließlich Induktion. Die Griffe sind weit oben angebracht, dadurch sind die Töpfe platzsparend stapelbar.

Begründung der Jury
Flow überzeugt mit Geradlinigkeit in der Formgebung und seinem besonders funktionellen Abgießsystem.

12'o'Clock
Cookware
Kochgeschirr

Manufacturer
Sambonet Paderno Industrie S.p.A.,
Casalino (Novara), Italy
In-house design
Paola Longoni
Web
www.corporate.sambonet.it

12'o'Clock – this cookware takes its name from that moment when the midday meal is prepared. The pans are of stainless steel and have a sandwich base which assures optimal heat distribution. The eye-catching handles made of terracotta coloured silicone allow safe handling. The large handle of the lid is so designed that the glass lid, when turned upside down, stands firmly and provides the novel coaster.

Statement by the jury
With the double function of the lid and the particularly ergonomic handle, this collection provides real added value to cooking.

12'o'Clock – der Zeitpunkt, zu dem das Mittagessen vorbereitet wird, ist namensgebend für dieses Kochgeschirr. Die Töpfe bestehen aus Edelstahl und haben einen Sandwichboden, der eine optimale Wärmeverteilung gewährleistet. Die auffälligen Griffe aus weichem terrakottafarbenem Silikon erlauben eine sichere Handhabung. Der große Griff des Deckels ist so gestaltet, dass der Glasdeckel umgedreht sicher steht und zum originellen Topfuntersetzer wird.

Begründung der Jury
Mit der Doppelfunktion des Deckels und den besonders ergonomischen Griffen bietet diese Kollektion einen echten Mehrwert beim Kochen.

The Multi Chef
Rice Cooker
Reiskocher

Manufacturer
Breville Group,
Sydney, Australia
In-house design
Richard Harrod,
Vyvyan Rose
Web
www.breville.com.au

The Multi Chef is an advanced cooker with temperature controlled programs that can make tender slow cooked meals, risotto without the need to stir, fluffy rice and quinoa. Fresh ingredients can be sautéed with the sear setting, and one can also steam food using the integrated steam tray. An intuitive interface, elegant stainless steel housing with cool touch handles and a removable cooking bowl makes this product easy to use, clean and store.

Statement by the jury
This technically advanced rice cooker has a high practical value. A stringent, independent implementation of the formal vocabulary is impressive as well.

Multi Chef ist ein Kocher mit temperaturkontrollierten Kochprogrammen, mit dem sich geschmorte Mahlzeiten, Risotto, lockerer Reis oder Quinoa zubereiten lassen. Darüber hinaus können Zutaten scharf angebraten oder in einem integrierten Einsatz gedämpft werden. Dank seiner übersichtlichen Bedieneinheit, dem eleganten Edelstahl-Gehäuse mit Cool Touch-Handgriffen und einer abnehmbaren Kochschale ist das Produkt leicht zu bedienen, zu reinigen und zu verstauen.

Begründung der Jury
Technisch ausgereift bietet der Reiskocher einen hohen Gebrauchswert, auch formal überzeugt eine stringente, eigenständige Umsetzung.

The Thermal Pro Grill
Fry Pan
Grillpfanne

Manufacturer
Breville Group,
Sydney, Australia
In-house design
Mario Rosian,
Greg Upston
Web
www.breville.com.au

The Thermal Pro Grill features a variable temperature controlled thermostat that allows searing at high heat without overheating the pan, thus protecting the PFOA free non-stick coating. An optimally engineered powerful heating element and vessel geometry ensures even heat distribution and fast temperature recovery across the entire cooking surface. This pan also features an elegant design with ergonomic handles that can all go in the dishwasher.

Statement by the jury
As a compact product solution, this combination of heating element and fry pan is impressive. It is flexible as it can be used at any place.

Der Thermal Pro Grill bietet einen variablen, temperaturgesteuerten Thermostat, der scharfes Anbraten ohne Überhitzung der Pfanne und ihrer PFOA-freien Antihaftbeschichtung ermöglicht. Das optimal konstruierte Heizelement und die Pfannengeometrie sorgen für eine gleichmäßige Wärmeverteilung über die gesamte Grilloberfläche. Die Pfanne ist elegant gestaltet, verfügt über ergonomische Griffe und ist spülmaschinenfest.

Begründung der Jury
Als kompakte Produktlösung überzeugt diese Kombination aus Heizelement und Grillpfanne. Sie ist flexibel ortsunabhängig einsetzbar.

Detachable Series
Cookware
Kochgeschirr

Manufacturer
Zhejiang Citic Kitchen Utensils Co., Ltd,
Yongkang, China
In-house design
Wei Sun,
Bing Liu
Web
www.zhongxincookware.com

Detachable Series is a cookware series with detachable handles. The cookware is made of coated aluminium for rapid and even heat distribution. For the entire series only four handles are necessary: one long handle, one handle for the lids and two compact cooking pot handles. The cookware can thus be easily stacked and takes up only little room. The handles are designed from an ergonomic viewpoint and easily and variably fitted. A special locking device assures safe handling.

Detachable Series ist eine Kochtopfserie mit abnehmbaren Griffen. Das Kochgeschirr ist für eine schnelle und gleichmäßige Wärmeverteilung aus beschichtetem Aluminium gefertigt. Für die gesamte Serie werden nur vier Griffe benötigt: Ein Stiel, ein Griff für die Deckel und zwei kompakte Topfgriffe. Dadurch ist das Kochgeschirr gut stapelbar und nimmt wenig Platz ein. Die Griffe sind unter ergonomischen Gesichtspunkten gestaltet und einfach und variabel anzubringen. Eine spezielle Verschlusstechnik sorgt für eine sichere Handhabung.

Statement by the jury
Detachable Series has a variable handle solution which is logical, also from economic aspects.

Begründung der Jury
Detachable Series hat eine variable Grifflösung, die nicht nur funktionell, sondern auch unter ökonomischen Aspekten sinnvoll ist.

Premio
Processing Bowl
Arbeitsschüssel

Manufacturer
Betty Bossi,
Zürich, Switzerland
In-house design
Valentin Engler
Design
Nose Design AG
(Lennart Behrmann),
Zürich, Switzerland
Web
www.bettybossi.ch
www.nose.ch

This stainless steel processing bowl is designed with double walls and thus keeps hot food longer hot and cold food longer cool. The bowl has a wide base with non-slip silicone coating which provides stability. A lightly declining, angular edge makes it easy, for instance, to beat eggs. The interior of the bowl, on the other hand, is completely round – and thus the optimal basis for mixing, kneading etc.

Diese Arbeitsschüssel aus Edelstahl ist doppelwandig gestaltet und hält dadurch heiße Speisen länger heiß und kalte länger kalt. Die Schüssel hat einen breiten Boden mit Anti-Rutsch-Silikonbeschichtung, der für Standfestigkeit sorgt. Ein leicht nach innen abfallender, kantiger Rand erleichtert etwa das Eieraufschlagen. Das Innere der Schüssel hingegen ist vollkommen rund – und damit die optimale Grundlage fürs Rühren, Kneten etc.

Statement by the jury
Premio is eminently suitable as processing bowl and thanks to its elegant simplicity, it furthermore acts decoratively as a bowl with any table setting.

Begründung der Jury
Premio eignet sich hervorragend als Arbeitsschüssel, dank ihrer edlen Schlichtheit ziert sie darüber hinaus als Schale auch jeden gedeckten Tisch.

Shake & Bake
Bakeware
Backformen

Manufacturer
Betty Bossi AG,
Zürich, Switzerland
In-house design
Valentin Engler
Design
Formfabrik AG
(Christoph Jaun, Dominic Spiess),
Zwillikon, Switzerland
Web
www.bettybossi.ch
www.formfabrik.ch
Honourable Mention

Shake & Bake consists of two baking forms for ring cakes which can be connected by a plastic ring with a twist closure. By means of a novel, non-stick coating, greasing the bakeware is not necessary. To make the cake dough, all ingredients are filled into one of the two forms, the other is screwed on and the content well shaken. Finally the lower form can be simply placed in the oven for baking.

Shake & Bake besteht aus zwei Backformen (Napfkuchen und Gugelhupf), die durch einen Kunststoffring mit Drehverschluss verbunden werden können. Durch eine neuartige Antihaftbeschichtung erübrigt sich das Einfetten der Backformen. Zum Zubereiten des Teigs werden alle Zutaten in eine der beiden Formen gefüllt, die andere aufgeschraubt, und der Inhalt gut geschüttelt. Anschließend kann die untere Form einfach zum Backen in den Ofen geschoben werden.

Statement by the jury
Shake & Bake is bowl, mixer and baking form in one. This makes preparation easy, saves time and meets the spirit of the times.

Begründung der Jury
Shake & Bake ist Schüssel, Mixer und Backform in einem. So erleichtert es die Zubereitung, ist zeitsparend und trifft damit den Zeitgeist.

BISTRO Mixing Bowl 1.4 l
BISTRO Rührschüssel 1,4 l

Manufacturer
Bodum AG,
Triengen, Switzerland
In-house design
Bodum Design Group
Web
www.bodum.com

The Bistro mixing bowl is optimally suitable for preparing foods. While most new mixing bowls on the market are made of melamine, these bowls are manufactured from recyclable, BPA-free plastic. The bowls have a non-slip, rubber coated handle and base. Rubber nubs, strategically located on the bowl's outer surface provide additional stability when mixing.

Statement by the jury
With their high quality of form and optimal functionality, these bowls more than fulfil the demands of a modern kitchen utensil.

Die Bistro-Rührschüsseln eignen sich optimal für die Zubereitung von Speisen. Während die meisten neuen Rührschüsseln auf dem Markt aus Melamin bestehen, werden diese Schüsseln aus recyclingfähigem BPA-freien Kunststoff hergestellt. Die Schüsseln haben eine rutschfeste Gummierung an Griff und Unterseite. Strategisch auf der Oberfläche der Schüssel angebrachte Gummipunkte sorgen für zusätzliche Stabilität beim Rühren.

Begründung der Jury
Mit ihrer hohen formalen Qualität und optimalen Funktionalität werden diese Schüsseln den Anforderungen an ein modernes Küchenutensil mehr als gerecht.

BISTRO Mixing Bowl 2.8 l
BISTRO Rührschüssel 2,8 l

Manufacturer
Bodum AG,
Triengen, Switzerland
In-house design
Bodum Design Group
Web
www.bodum.com

An eye-catching feature of this mixing bowl series are the small rubber nubs on the outside of the bowls. These spots, together with the rubberised base provide additional stability when mixing. This bowl, with 2.8 l capacity, can thus be tilted for beating eggs without danger of it slipping. The bowls are made of recyclable BPA-free plastic with added rubber coatings.

Statement by the jury
The small rubber spots improve the handling and contrast as design element with the otherwise greatly reduced form language of the bowls.

Hervorstechendes Gestaltungsmerkmal dieser Rührschüssel-Serie sind die kleinen Gummipunkte an der Außenseite der Schüsseln. Sie sorgen neben der Gummierung am Boden während des Rührens für zusätzliche Stabilität. So kann diese Schüssel mit 2,8 Litern Fassungsvermögen etwa zum Eischaumschlagen schräg gestellt werden, ohne wegrutschen zu können. Die Schüsseln sind aus recyclingfähigem BPA-freiem Kunststoff mit zusätzlicher Gummierung hergestellt.

Begründung der Jury
Die kleinen Gummipunkte verbessern die Handhabung und kontrastieren als Gestaltungselement die sonst sehr reduzierte Formensprache der Schüsseln.

BISTRO Mixing Bowl 4.7 l
BISTRO Rührschüssel 4,7 l

Manufacturer
Bodum AG,
Triengen, Switzerland
In-house design
Bodum Design Group
Web
www.bodum.com

This biggest bowl of the Bistro series holds 4.7 litres and can therefore even marinate a large roast or be used for preparing great amounts of salad or dough. It stands thereby securely on the work surface at all times due to its slip-free, rubber coated base and the rubber nubs typical for the series. The other bowls of the set can be stacked to save space. The mixing bowls are available in various colours.

Statement by the jury
The semi-spherical design of the lower half of the bowl is characterising for the harmonious overall impression of these functional bowls.

Diese größte Schüssel der Bistro-Serie fasst 4,7 Liter und kann damit sogar zum Marinieren großer Braten oder der Vorbereitung großer Salat- oder Teigmengen genutzt werden. Dabei steht sie mit ihrer rutschfesten Boden-Gummierung und den serientypischen Gummipunkten jederzeit sicher auf der Arbeitsfläche. Die anderen Schüsseln des Sets können in dieser platzsparend gestapelt werden. Die Rührschüsseln sind in verschiedenen Farben erhältlich.

Begründung der Jury
Die halbkugelförmige Gestaltung der unteren Schüsselhälfte ist prägend für den harmonischen Gesamteindruck dieser funktionalen Schüsseln.

BISTRO Mixing Bowl 0.3 l
BISTRO Rührschüssel 0,3 l

Manufacturer
Bodum AG,
Triengen, Switzerland
In-house design
Bodum Design Group
Web
www.bodum.com

This Bistro mixing bowl with a capacity of 0.3 litres is ideally suitable for mixing small amounts of sauce, dips or the like. By means of the pourer, which naturally is integrated in the lines of the bowl, its content can easily be distributed over the prepared foods. The slip-free rubber coating on the handle and the rubber elements in the bottom third of the bowl ensure safe handling.

Statement by the jury
The smallest bowl of the Bistro series is in no way inferior to its siblings: it has a well-considered design and is convincing when used.

Diese Bistro-Rührschüssel mit einem Fassungsvermögen von 0,3 Litern eignet sich hervorragend für das Anrühren kleinerer Mengen an Sauce, Dips oder Ähnlichem. Mithilfe des Ausgusses, der sich ganz selbstverständlich in die Linienführung der Schüssel integriert, lässt sich ihr Inhalt gut über die fertigen Speisen verteilen. Die rutschfeste Gummierung am Griff und Gummielemente im unteren Drittel der Schüssel machen die Handhabung sicher.

Begründung der Jury
Die kleinste Schüssel der Bistro-Serie steht ihren großen Geschwistern in nichts nach: Sie ist durchdacht gestaltet und überzeugt im Gebrauch.

BISTRO Mixing Bowl 0.7 l
BISTRO Rührschüssel 0,7 l

Manufacturer
Bodum AG,
Triengen, Switzerland
In-house design
Bodum Design Group
Web
www.bodum.com

The 0.7 litre capacity of this bowl of the Bistro series has the right size for mixing, for instance, desserts in it. As with the other models in the collection, the bowl is made of BPA-free plastic. The bowl is therefore suitable even for heating the ingredients in the microwave (without oil). After use it can be cleaned in the dishwasher without problem.

Statement by the jury
The choice of recyclable, BPA-free plastic as material for the Bistro series further extends the bowls' radius of functionality.

Mit 0,7 Litern Fassungsvolumen hat diese Schüssel der Bistro-Serie die richtige Größe, um darin beispielsweise Desserts anzurühren. Wie die anderen Modelle der Kollektion ist die Schüssel aus BPA-freiem Kunststoff gefertigt. Dadurch eignet sich die Schüssel sogar zum Erhitzen von Zutaten in der Mikrowelle (ohne Öl). Nach dem Gebrauch kann sie problemlos in der Spülmaschine gereinigt werden.

Begründung der Jury
Die Wahl eines recyclingfähigen BPA-freien Kunststoffs als Material für die Bistro-Serie erweitert den Funktionsradius der Schüsseln zusätzlich.

BISTRO Mixing Jug 1 l
BISTRO Rührbecher 1 l

Manufacturer
Bodum AG,
Triengen, Switzerland
In-house design
Bodum Design Group
Web
www.bodum.com

This jug with its high sides is ideally suited for kitchen work which is not performed quite without splashing – for instance when whipping cream or as vessel for pureeing foods. The mixing jug has a capacity of one litre. As with the other models of the series, the jug, thanks to the rubber coating, is slip-free, good to handle and easily cleaned after use.

Statement by the jury
The mixing jug differs from the other bowls of the series by the change in proportions; it keeps, however, the high formal quality.

Dieser Rührbecher mit seinen hochgezogenen Seitenwänden eignet sich ideal für Küchenarbeiten, die nicht ganz spritzfrei vonstattengehen – etwa zum Sahneschlagen oder als Gefäß zum Pürieren von Lebensmitteln. Der Becher hat ein Fassungsvolumen von einem Liter. Wie die übrigen Modelle der Serie ist der Becher dank der Gummierungen rutschfest, gut zu handhaben und kann nach Gebrauch leicht gereinigt werden.

Begründung der Jury
Der Rührbecher unterscheidet sich von den anderen Schüsseln der Serie durch veränderte Proportionen, die hohe formale Qualität bleibt jedoch erhalten.

YOOCOOK Chocolate Tablet
Silicone Mould
Silikonform

Manufacturer
YOOCOOK a brand of Tellier SAS,
Argenteuil, France
Design
Cappandco
(Alexandre Chinon, Philippe Portheault),
Paris, France
Web
www.yoocook.fr
www.cappandco.com
Honourable Mention

This silicone mould makes it possible to produce totally individual tablets of chocolate. The mould contains point-shaped recesses in a grid form. This allows the avant-garde form to "pixelate" a chocolate tablet using two different kinds of chocolate and thus to mould letters, words, messages or complete images in chocolate. The mould is made of high-grade, food-safe silicone and assures easy removal of the chocolate.

Diese Silikonform ermöglicht die Herstellung ganz individueller Schokoladentafeln. Die Form ist durch punktförmige Vertiefungen gerastert. Diese avantgardistische Form erlaubt es, eine Tafel Schokolade mithilfe von zwei verschiedenen Schokoladensorten zu „verpixeln" und so Buchstaben, Wörter, Nachrichten oder ganze Grafiken in Schokolade zu gießen. Die Form besteht aus hochwertigem Nahrungssilikon und garantiert ein leichtes Herauslösen der Schokolade.

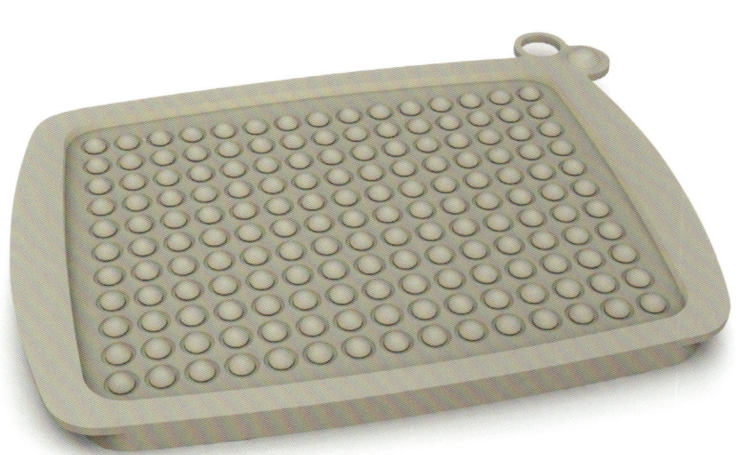

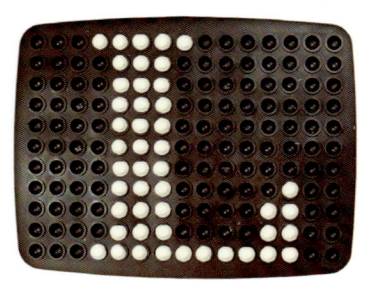
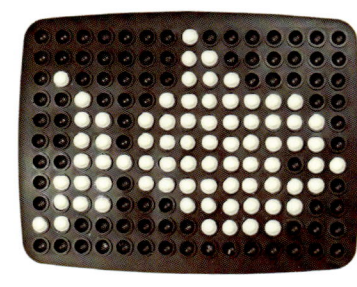
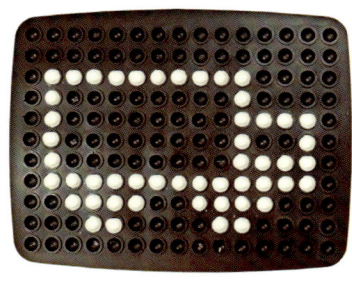
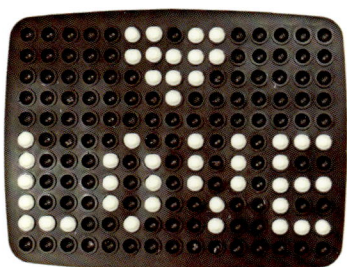

258

PopPan
Bakeware
Backformen

Manufacturer
LICO (HK) Manufacturing Ltd,
Hong Kong
In-house design
Mario John Chaves Barker
Web
www.licohk.com
www.pop-pan.com

The PopPan collection comprises a range of baking tins, making use of both silicone as well as metal: The non-stick coated metal provides an even heat distribution, so that the cake becomes crispy and brown on the outside. The silicone pop-out ring in the bottom of the form makes it easy to simply push out the finished cake. For this the cake form is pressed lightly down – the silicone ring acts as a spring which gently pushes the cake out.

Die PopPan-Serie umfasst eine Reihe von Backformen, bei der sowohl Silikon als auch Metall zum Einsatz kommen: Das antihaftbeschichtete Metall sorgt für eine gleichmäßige Wärmeverteilung und lässt den Kuchen knusprig werden. Der Pop-out-Ring aus Silikon im Boden ermöglicht ein einfaches Herausdrücken des fertigen Kuchens. Dazu wird die Form leicht nach unten gedrückt – der Silikonring wirkt wie eine Feder, die den Kuchen sanft herausschiebt.

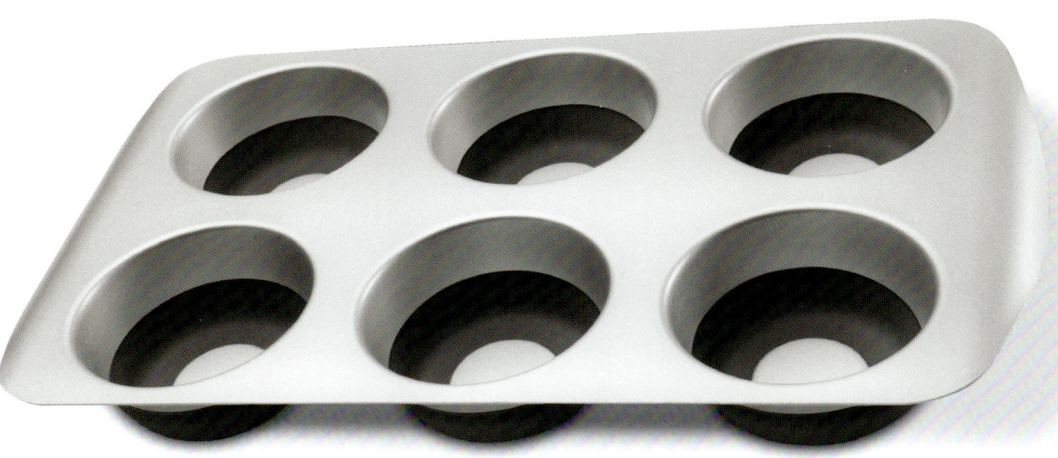

Williams-Sonoma Cooks' Tools Collection

Kitchen Tools
Küchenutensilien

Manufacturer
Williams-Sonoma,
San Francisco, USA
Design
Ammunition LLC
(Victoria Slaker, Kenneth Sweet,
Jonas Lagerstedt, Xuan Shu,
Rhys Bonahoom),
San Francisco, USA
Web
www.williams-sonoma.com
www.ammunitiongroup.com

The items in this collection all have small design details which make them particularly functional. For example, the fish spatula has a thin, flexible tip which is designed so that it effortlessly glides under every fillet. Each kitchen tool is made of heavy gauge stainless steel and ergonomically contoured and balanced as to allow precise control. The design of the handles assures secure and comfortable handling.

Die Geräte dieser Serie haben alle kleine Designdetails, die sie besonders funktionell machen. So hat etwa der Fisch-Pfannenwender eine dünne, flexible Spitze, die so gestaltet ist, dass er mühelos unter jedes Filet gleitet. Alle Küchenhelfer sind aus dickwandigem Edelstahl gefertigt und ergonomisch so konturiert und ausbalanciert, dass sie präzise Kontrolle erlauben. Die Gestaltung der Griffe unterstützt eine sichere und komfortable Handhabung.

Statement by the jury
The high degree of functionality of these kitchen utensils is the result of their development and design with love of detail.

Begründung der Jury
Die hohe Funktionalität dieser Küchen-utensilien resultiert daraus, dass sie mit Liebe zum Detail entwickelt und gestaltet wurden.

Kitchen utensils

GarlicCard
Garlic Grater
Knoblauchreibe

Manufacturer
Rasmusons Matbyrå Ab,
Lidingö, Sweden
AD-Plast AB,
Anderstorp, Sweden
In-house design
Nils Herman Rasmuson
Web
www.garliccard.com
Honourable Mention

GarlicCard is the invention of the Swedish chef Herman Rasmuson and is a genuine alternative to regular, often difficult to clean garlic presses or razor-sharp kitchen graters. The plastic card has a specially embossed grating surface which allows for shredding garlic cloves quickly and without effort. GarlicCard is easy to handle, being only about the size of a credit card, and has a holding surface which is bent slightly upwards.

GarlicCard ist die Erfindung des schwedischen Kochs Herman Rasmuson und eine echte Alternative zu normalen, meist schwer zu reinigenden Knoblauchpressen oder rasiermesserscharfen Küchenreiben. Die Kunststoffkarte hat eine speziell geprägte Reibefläche, auf der man Knoblauchzehen schnell und mühelos zerkleinern kann. Nur etwa so groß wie eine Kreditkarte und mit einer leicht nach oben gebogenen Grifffläche, ist die GarlicCard sehr handlich.

Statement by the jury
This little, colourful kitchen aid meets the challenge of shredding garlic in a new way – conveniently, usefully and innovatively.

Begründung der Jury
Dieser farbige kleine Küchenhelfer löst die Herausforderung des Knoblauchreibens auf neue Weise – handlich, nützlich und innovativ.

Milli
Mortar and Pestle
Mörser und Stößel

Manufacturer
Silver Ball GmbH,
Berlin, Germany
Design
Emamidesign
(Arman Emami),
Berlin, Germany
Web
www.emamidesign.de

For this mortar the ceramic pestle head is so designed that roughness, which provides the necessary friction, consists of concave indents. The edges of the extensive indents are ground sharp. This particular form facilitates the grinding process and ensures that nothing remains sticking to it. The sensitive ceramic is only used for the pestle head and the interior of the mortar; the rest is made of silicone.

Bei diesem Mörser ist der Keramikkopf des Stößels so gestaltet, dass die Unebenheiten, die für die notwendige Reibung sorgen, konkav nach innen geformt sind. Die Ränder der großflächigen Vertiefungen sind scharf geschliffen. Diese besondere Formgebung erleichtert den Reibeprozess und sorgt dafür, dass nichts haften bleibt. Die zerbrechliche Keramik kommt nur am Kopf des Stößels und im Schüsselinneren zum Einsatz, der Rest besteht aus Silikon.

Statement by the jury
This kitchen aid is impressive due to an innovative design which provides a high degree of usefulness.

Begründung der Jury
Dieser Küchenhelfer überzeugt durch eine innovative Gestaltung, die zu einer hohen Gebrauchstauglichkeit führt.

Squeezable Tools
Kitchen Utensil Set
Küchenhelfer-Set

Manufacturer
Magisso Ltd.,
Helsinki, Finland
In-house design
Juhani Siren
Web
www.magisso.com

The Squeezable Tools set consists of three innovative spatulas with dual functions: spatula-spoon, spatula-spaghetti lifter and spatula-skimmer. For the additional functions the flexible handle is lightly pressed together and the tools fold along the length at the colour-highlighted fold lines. Under the surface, hinges of heat-resistant nylon and silicone assure stability.

Statement by the jury
The Squeezable Tools impress by their intriguingly simple dual functionality which is communicated formally by their coloured, prominent fold lines.

Die Squeezable Tools-Serie setzt sich aus drei innovativen Pfannenwendern mit Doppelfunktion zusammen: Pfannenwender/Löffel, Pfannenwender/Spaghettiheber und Pfannenwender/Schaumlöffel. Für die Zusatzfunktion wird der flexible Griff leicht zusammengedrückt, und die Geräte knicken der Länge nach an den farbig hervorgehobenen Faltlinien ein. Unter der Oberfläche aus hitzebeständigem Nylon und Silikon sorgen Scharniere für Stabilität.

Begründung der Jury
Die Squeezable Tools bestechen mit ihrer verblüffend einfachen Doppelfunktion, die formal durch die farblich abgesetzten Faltlinien kommuniziert wird.

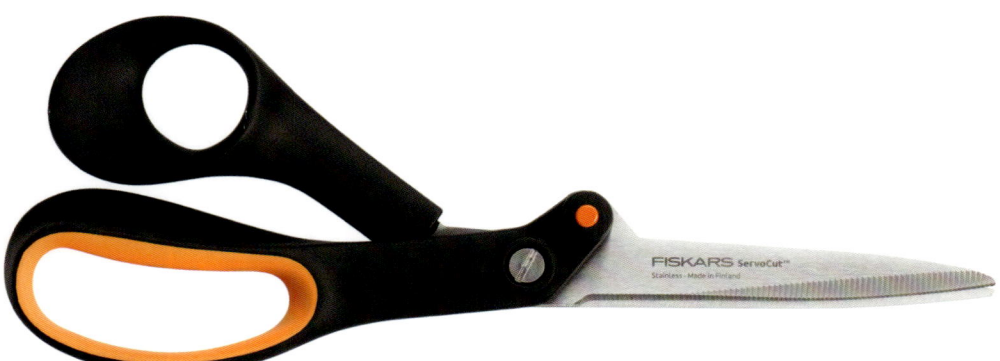

Fiskars Amplify™ and ServoCut™
Scissors
Scheren

Manufacturer
Fiskars,
Helsinki, Finland
In-house design
Heikki Savolainen,
Jens Housley
Web
www.fiskars.com

These premium scissors were developed for cutting very thick materials. Amplify and ServoCut technology senses blade separation when cutting thick materials and forces the blades back together for crisp, clean cuts every time. The scissors with their ergonomic finger grips are made of stainless premium steel. They are available in various sizes both as professional model for craftsmen as well as for domestic use.

Statement by the jury
Innovative technologies and an ergonomic design using corporate colour merge here in optimised functionality.

Diese Premium-Scheren sind zum Schneiden von sehr dicken Materialien entwickelt worden. Sie haben eine bewegliche Klinge, die dank Amplify- und ServoCut-Technologie die Energie an eine Übersetzung weiterleitet und einen sauberen Schnitt gewährleistet. Die Scheren mit ihren ergonomischen Griffen sind aus rostfreiem Premium-Stahl. Sie sind in verschiedenen Größen sowohl als Profimodelle für Handwerker als auch für den Hausgebrauch erhältlich.

Begründung der Jury
Innovative Technologien und eine ergonomische Gestaltung unter Verwendung der markanten Unternehmensfarbe münden hier in einer optimierten Funktionalität.

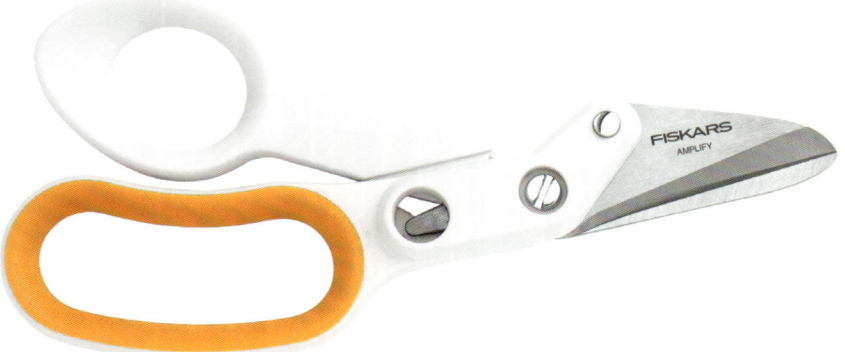

Multi-Masher
Stampfer

Manufacturer
Kool Limited,
Hong Kong
In-house design
Ho, Yip Shing Jason
Web
www.kool.com.hk
Honourable Mention

The Multi-Masher is a masher with three different work surfaces, in order to produce various puree textures: a ribbed side for coarse mashing, a side with medium-sized round holes as well as a side with fine, hexagonal recesses. The removable handle of non-slip rubber is simply pushed onto the edge which is opposite the required surface. The Multi-Masher is made of sturdy plastic.

Statement by the jury
The innovative functionality of the Multi-Masher is a result of the design solution of the flexible handle which stands out from the rest in colour and material.

Der Multi-Masher ist ein Stampfer mit drei unterschiedlichen Arbeitsflächen, um verschiedene Püree-Texturen herzustellen: eine gerippte Seite zum groben Stampfen, eine Seite mit mittelgroßen kreisförmigen Löchern sowie eine Seite mit feinen sechseckigen Aussparungen. Der abnehmbare Griff aus rutschfestem Gummi wird einfach an der Kante, die der benötigten Fläche gegenüberliegt, aufgeschoben. Der Multi-Masher ist aus robustem Kunststoff gefertigt.

Begründung der Jury
Die innovative Funktionalität des Multi-Masher beruht auf der Designlösung des flexiblen Griffs, der sich durch Farbe und Material vom Rest abhebt.

Elite Series
Kitchen Graters
Küchenreiben

Manufacturer
Microplane,
Russellville, Arkansas, USA /
Hamburg, Germany
In-house design
Jon Schmidt
Design
Carter McGuyer Design Group, Inc.
(Carter McGuyer),
Muscle Shoals, USA
Web
www.microplane.com
www.cartermcguyer.com
Honourable Mention

The graters of the Elite series are of durable stainless steel and have elegant, flowing lines. Thanks to the special form of the grater, the non-slip coated edges and the ergonomic handle, the grater can be used in an upright as well as a flat position. The transparent protection cover surprises with an additional function: it can be pushed onto the back of the grater and serves then as collecting vessel and measuring container.

Statement by the jury
The Elite series makes kitchen work easier with optimal functionality.

Die Reiben der Elite-Serie aus langlebigem Edelstahl haben eine elegante, fließende Linienführung. Dank der speziellen Reibenform, der rutschfest beschichteten Kanten und des ergonomischen Griffs, lässt sich die Reibe sowohl aufrecht als auch liegend nutzen. Die transparente Schutzhülle überrascht mit einer Zusatzfunktion: Sie kann auf die Rückseite der Reibe geschoben werden und dient dann als Auffangbehälter und Messbecher.

Begründung der Jury
Die Elite-Serie erleichtert die Küchenarbeit mit optimierter Funktionalität.

LOFT
Premium Storage Container
Premium-Vorratsbehälter

Manufacturer
Rotho Kunststoff AG,
Würenlingen, Switzerland
In-house design
Nicola Nowak
Web
www.rotho.ch

Loft is a modular system consisting of eight storage containers which can be individually combined and thereby always result in the same width, length and height. The containers are of high quality, transparent plastic. The red seals on the lids close the boxes not only aroma-tight but, due to the dual component seal, especially hygienically – they are at the same time a concise design characteristic of the reduced design containers.

Loft ist ein modulares System aus acht Vorratsbehältern, die sich individuell kombinieren lassen und dabei immer wieder gleiche Breiten, Tiefen und Höhen ergeben. Die Behälter sind aus hochwertigem, hochtransparentem Kunststoff. Die roten Dichtungen an den Deckeln verschließen die Boxen nicht nur aromadicht und durch eine Zwei-Komponenten-Dichtung besonders hygienisch. Sie sind zugleich prägnantes Gestaltungsmerkmal der reduziert gestalteten Behälter.

Statement by the jury
Of high quality overall, Loft impresses with the manner in which it draws attention to its fresh-keeping function by emphasising the seals.

Begründung der Jury
Insgesamt von hoher Qualität, überzeugt Loft damit, wie es seine Frischhaltefunktion durch die Akzentuierung der Dichtung in Szene setzt.

VentSmart™ Range
KlimaOasen
Containers for Vegetables and Fruits
Aufbewahrungsbehälter für Obst und Gemüse

Manufacturer
Tupperware Belgium N.V.,
Aalst, Belgium
In-house design
Tupperware Worldwide
Product Development Team
Web
www.tupperwarebrands.com
Honourable Mention

The VentSmart Range comprises storage containers for fruit and vegetables, developed specially for the refrigerator. A three-stage ventilation system means that the climate in the containers can be controlled so that fruit in the refrigerator is kept fresh for a long period of time. A freshness chart on the containers shows the right setting for the most common types. The various fruits lie in containers, dry and airy, on a freshness grid.

Statement by the jury
The well considered functionality of the VentSmart Range is additionally enhanced by the self-explanatory quality of the containers.

Die KlimaOasen sind Aufbewahrungsbehälter für Obst und Gemüse, die speziell für den Kühlschrank entwickelt wurden. Mit einem dreistufigen Belüftungssystem lässt sich das Klima in den Behältern so steuern, dass Früchte im Kühlschrank lange frisch bleiben. Eine Frischetabelle auf den Behältern zeigt die richtige Einstellung für die gängigsten Sorten. Die Früchte lagern in den Behältern trocken und luftig auf einem Frischegitter.

Begründung der Jury
Die durchdachte Funktionalität der Klima-Oasen wird durch die Selbsterklärungs-qualität der Behälter zusätzlich verstärkt.

Daykips
Storage Container
Vorratsbehälter

Manufacturer
Komax Industrial Co., Ltd.,
Seoul, South Korea
In-house design
Ja-il Koo,
Hyeong-yeol Park,
Na-young Jee,
Beom-suk Chae
Web
www.ikomax.com
Honourable Mention

Daykips are storage containers which facilitate storage using a simple system. By means of two rotating rings at the top edge of the containers, the day and month of expiry or of the initial storage can be set. This shows at first glance how long the food can still be used. The storage jars can be sealed airtight and leak-proof with a lid that matches the colour of the date rings.

Statement by the jury
The charmingly simple storage containers of the Daykips series surprise with a simple extension of the function in the form of slim-line date rings.

Die Vorratsbehälter Daykips erleichtern die Vorratshaltung durch ein einfaches System. Mithilfe von zwei drehbaren Ringen am oberen Rand der Gefäße lassen sich Tag und Monat des Ablaufens oder der Einlagerung einstellen. So zeigen sie auf den ersten Blick, wie lange die Lebensmittel noch verwendet werden können. Die Vorratsgläser lassen sich mit einem farblich auf die Datumsringe abgestimmten Deckel luft- und wasserdicht verschließen.

Begründung der Jury
Die anmutig-schlichten Vorratsgefäße der Daykips Serie überraschen mit einer einfachen Erweiterung der Funktion in Form von schlanken Datumsringen.

TriScale – Compact folding digital scale
Kitchen Scale
Küchenwaage

Manufacturer
Joseph Joseph Ltd.,
London, GB
In-house design
Antony Joseph
Design
Morph UK Ltd.
(Bill Holding, Ben Cox),
London, GB
Web
www.josephjoseph.com
www.morphuk.com
Honourable Mention

The TriScale kitchen scale can be folded up to an extremely compact size; therefore making it perfect for storing in a kitchen drawer. When unfolded, the three arms provide a stable platform for jugs and bowls. The scale has a tare weighing function and an easy to read LCD display with optional readings in grams, pounds, ounces, fluid ounces or millilitres. When folded up, the arms lie protectively around the display and operating elements.

Statement by the jury
This small, compact, foldable scale is the ultimate space-saving kitchen accessory.

Die Küchenwaage TriScale lässt sich extrem kompakt und platzsparend zusammenfalten und passt in jede Schublade. Auseinandergeklappt bilden ihre drei Arme eine stabile Stellfläche für Becher oder Schüsseln. Die Waage hat eine Zuwiegefunktion und ein leicht abzulesendes LCD-Display, welches das Gewicht wahlweise in Gramm, Pfund, Unzen, Flüssigunzen oder Millilitern anzeigt. Beim Zusammenfalten legen sich die Arme schützend um Display und Bedienelemente.

Begründung der Jury
Diese kleine, kompakt zusammenfaltbare Waage ist der Inbegriff eines platzsparenden Küchenaccessoires.

The Attitude of the Definite – the Square
Die Attitüde des Bestimmten – das Quadrat
Porcelain Vase
Porzellangefäß

Design
Bernhard Elsässer,
Halle (Saale), Germany

Web
www.bernhard-elsaesser.com

reddot design award
best of the best 2013

The attitude of the definite – the square

The manufacture of china has maintained an air of mystery until this very day, as a process of applying high heat to a mix of many different ingredients turns it into softly shimmering porcelain. The research during the porcelain study "The Attitude of the Definite – the Square" led to an innovative technical process that lends porcelain vessels a new appearance. The initial shape of the china is formed by flexible textile wraps sewed from sponge cloth. Consisting of renewable celluloses and cotton fibre, this sponge cloth is extremely absorbent and takes over the function of plaster mould in the design process. The result of this innovative process is astounding: the cloth extracts the liquid from the china mass moulded into the wrap to form a shard with squared structures. The textile origin remains visible on the outside, lending this porcelain vase a strong visual character. This impression is enhanced further by the highly biscuit surface. In order to allow for reproduction, the form is fixated by a cast procedure. In order to offer variations, different versions of pedestals can be combined with the base body. Focusing on the aspect of randomness in the working process, the design study "The Attitude of the Definite – the Square" defines this procedure as its starting point and thus led to the creation of a highly attractive porcelain vase – an approach that also opens up new paths for the future of china manufacture.

Die Attitüde des Bestimmten - das Quadrat

Die Herstellung von Porzellan ist ein auch heute noch geheimnisumwitterter Prozess, in dem viele Zutaten schließlich in großer Hitze das weich schimmernde Porzellan ausbilden. Bei der Entstehung der Porzellanstudie „Die Attitüde des Bestimmten – das Quadrat" führte ein innovatives technisches Verfahren zu einer neuen Anmutung eines Porzellangefäßes. Seine Ausgangsform bilden zunächst flexible, aus Schwammtuch genähte Textilhüllen. Dieses nachwachsende Material aus Cellulose und Baumwollfasern ist extrem saugfähig, weshalb es im Gestaltungsprozess die Funktion einer Gipsform übernehmen kann. Die Wirkung dieses innovativen Verfahrens ist verblüffend: Wird Porzellanmasse in die Textilhülle eingegossen, entzieht diese der Masse die Flüssigkeit und es entsteht ein Scherben mit quadratischen Strukturen. Der textile Ursprung wird äußerlich sichtbar und verleiht diesem Porzellangefäß eine starke Ausdruckskraft. Die Wirkung auf den Betrachter wird zusätzlich durch seine bisquite Oberfläche verstärkt. Für die Vervielfältigung wird die Form über ein Abgussverfahren fixiert. Um Varianten zu ermöglichen, können zudem unterschiedliche Sockel mit dem Grundkörper variiert werden. Aus einer Designstudie, die den Aspekt des Zufalls im Arbeitsprozess bewusst an ihren Anfangspunkt stellte, ging mit „Die Attitüte des Bestimmten - das Quadrat" ein überaus reizvolles Porzellangefäß hervor. Sein Gestaltungsprozess eröffnet zudem neue Perspektiven für die Zukunft der Porzellanherstellung.

Statement by the jury

The porcelain vase "The Attitude of the Definite – the Square" is the result of a highly creative design process. The language of form of this vase impresses with its plasticity. The way the textile origin remains visible, creating distinctive structures, is also fascinating. The vase gives proof of how an extended, evolutionary design understanding can lead to the emergence of something truly novel.

Begründung der Jury

Das Porzellangefäß „Die Attitüde des Bestimmten – das Quadrat" ist Ausdruck eines überaus kreativen Schaffensprozesses. Die Formensprache dieses Gefäßes beeindruckt durch ihre Plastizität. Faszinierend ist zudem, wie der textile Ursprung sichtbar wird und immer wieder neue Strukturen bildet. Hier wird deutlich, wie durch ein erweitertes, evolutionäres Designverständnis etwas völlig Neues entstehen kann.

Table decoration

farmer
Magnetic Bowl Set
Magnetisches Schalen-Set

Manufacturer
JJJM Design,
Aachen, Germany
In-house design
Marco Preussener,
Patrick Bergs
Web
www.farmer-block.eu

farmer is a modular set consisting of bowls which vary in colour, material and size. The magnetic bowls can be arranged individually next to each other or one on top of the other – for snacks, collecting or organising. With its flexibility, farmer symbolises growth and interaction and puts these on the table in reduced aesthetics.

Statement by the jury
The concept of farmer with its range of variations has not only a high quality of form, it involves the user and makes him an architect.

farmer ist ein modularer Baukasten aus Schalen, die in Farbe, Material und Größe variieren. Die magnetischen Schalen können ganz individuell neben- oder übereinander arrangiert werden – zum Snacken, Sammeln oder Ordnen. Mit seiner Flexibilität symbolisiert farmer Wachstum und Interaktion und bringt sie in reduzierter Ästhetik auf den Tisch.

Begründung der Jury
Das Konzept von farmer mit seiner Variantenvielfalt hat nicht nur eine hohe formale Qualität, es bindet den Nutzer auch mit ein und lässt ihn zum Architekten werden.

Aireado
Fruit Bowl
Obstschale

Manufacturer
BV Koninklijke Van Kempen & Begeer,
Zoetermeer, Netherlands
In-house design
Joffrey Walonker
Design
Flip Ziedses Des Plantes,
Amsterdam, Netherlands
Web
www.royalvkb.com
www.fzdp.com

Aireado is Spanish for airy and thus says it all for this fruit bowl: the fruit in the bowl lies on a soft, knitted mat of synthetic material which allows the air to circulate and prevents bruising. The outer metal cover provides a striking contrast to the soft interior. The bowl can be placed in ever different positions on a rubber ring which acts as base.

Statement by the jury
The innovative combination of materials allows Aireado to perform optimally its two tasks: the storage and the presentation of fruit.

Aireado ist das spanische Wort für luftig und damit Programm für diese Obstschale: Die Früchte liegen in der Schale auf einer weichen, gestrickten Matte aus Synthetik, die die Luft zirkulieren lässt und Druckstellen verhindert. Einen spannungsreichen Kontrast zum weichen Inneren bildet die äußere Metallhülle. Die Schale kann auf einem Gummiring, der als Basis dient, in immer wieder unterschiedlichen Positionen platziert werden.

Begründung der Jury
Die innovative Materialkombination führt dazu, dass Aireado ihre beiden Aufgaben, die Aufbewahrung und die Präsentation von Früchten, optimal erfüllt.

Gio Ponti Centerpiece
Centerpiece
Tafelaufsatz

Manufacturer
Sambonet Paderno Industrie S.p.A.,
Casalino (Novara), Italy
In-house design
Paola Longoni
Web
www.corporate.sambonet.it

The Gio Ponti Centerpiece consists of two bowls with a foot. They are made of stainless steel and are also available in a silver plated version. Each bowl alone is an elegant lifestyle accessory which can be used to hold flowers or fruit, but they develop their greatest effect when put together. When placed one on top of the other they present an imposing, spherical object, a sculpture in the room.

Statement by the jury
Gio Ponti Centerpiece is a charming object of great quality of form – a luxurious item within one's own four walls.

Der Gio Ponti Tafelaufsatz setzt sich aus zwei Schalen mit Fuß zusammen. Sie sind aus Edelstahl gefertigt und auch in einer versilberten Version erhältlich. Jede Schale für sich allein ist ein elegantes Wohnaccessoire, das mit Blumen oder Früchten gefüllt werden kann. – Erst gemeinsam entfalten sie jedoch ihre größte Wirkung: Aufeinandergestellt bilden sie ein auffälliges sphärisches Objekt, eine Skulptur im Raum.

Begründung der Jury
Gio Ponti Centerpiece ist ein charmantes Objekt von hoher formaler Qualität - ein Stück Luxus für die eigenen vier Wände.

La Vague
Fruit Bowl
Obstschale

Manufacturer
Manor AG,
Basel, Switzerland
Design
Mizko Design GmbH
(Sarah Hügin, Benedikt Löwenstein,
Maurice Calanca), Buchs, Switzerland
Web
www.manor.ch
www.mizkodesign.ch

The La Vague fruit bowl for the Swiss department store Manor is based on the simple principle of expanded metal, in which metal is given parallel cuts and then expanded. It is a simple and cost-effective method which, in the case of La Vague, produces an exciting result: The bowl appears just as filigree and light as simple and timeless. From a holistic viewpoint it is produced totally in Switzerland.

Statement by the jury
The attraction of this bowl lies in its intensely aesthetic appeal, which is achieved by means of a conceivably simple production method.

Die Obstschale La Vague für das Schweizer Kaufhaus Manor basiert auf dem simplen Prinzip des Streckblechs, bei dem Metall mit parallelen Einschnitten versehen und dann auseinandergezogen wird. Eine einfache und günstige Produktionsmethode, die im Falle von La Vague zu einem spannenden Ergebnis führt: Die Schale wirkt ebenso filigran und leicht wie schlicht und zeitlos. Sie wird unter ganzheitlichen Gesichtspunkten komplett in der Schweiz gefertigt.

Begründung der Jury
Der Reiz dieser Schale liegt in ihrer starken ästhetischen Wirkung, die mit einer denkbar einfachen Produktionsmethode erzielt wird.

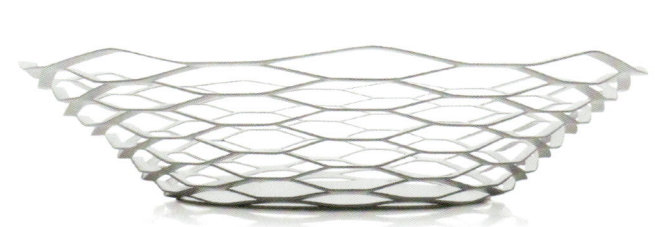

"Fruit and vegetable peels"
Ceramic Cups
Keramikbecher

Manufacturer
HXH Group.,
Zhubei City, Hsinchu County, Taiwan
Design
ViiCHEN DESIGN
(Ju Wei Chen),
Zhubei City, Hsinchu County, Taiwan
Web
www.hesxhers.blogspot.tw
www.viichendesign.blogspot.tw

With these ceramic cups the focus is on the haptic experience. The collection consists of six cups with geometric relief patterns on the outside which remind one of various kinds of fruit and vegetables. Holding the cups that way arouses associations which lead to a haptic experience by the feel of the cups, releasing an emotional component. The cups are produced in white ceramic using plaster casting.

Statement by the jury
The organic relief patterns result not only in an interesting haptic experience; they also convey them a special aesthetic.

Bei diesen Keramikbechern steht die haptische Erfahrung im Mittelpunkt. Die Serie umfasst sechs Becher mit geometrischen Reliefmustern, die an die Schalen verschiedener Obst- und Gemüsesorten erinnern. Beim Berühren der Becher sollen so Assoziationen geweckt werden, die dazu führen, dass die Nutzung der Becher durch die haptische Erfahrung eine emotionale Komponente bekommt. Die Gefäße aus weißer Keramik werden mithilfe von Gipsformen hergestellt.

Begründung der Jury
Die organischen Reliefmuster machen die Becher nicht nur zu einer interessanten haptischen Erfahrung; sie verleihen ihnen auch eine besondere Ästhetik.

an&angel DECO
Glass Bowls
Glasschalen

Manufacturer
Angel Glass Design, Ltd.,
Riga, Latvia
In-house design
Artis Nimanis
Web
www.angel.lv

The an&angel DECO collection consists of various mouth-blown glass bowls which radiate cultural elegance due to their simple geometric form, their colouring and their subtle mirror effects. The mirror coating of the bowls is the result of painstaking experiments to coat glass with stainless steel. This technology achieves the effect that the bowls reflect their environment and thus match all possible variations of furnishing styles.

Statement by the jury
This collection impresses due to its elegant design which has been achieved by the use of new technologies for glass coating.

Die an&angel DECO-Serie umfasst verschiedene mundgeblasene Glasschalen, die mit ihrer schlicht-geometrischen Formensprache, ihrer Farbgebung und ihren raffinierten Spiegeleffekten kultivierte Eleganz ausstrahlen. Die Spiegelbeschichtung der Schalen ist das Ergebnis langwieriger Experimente, Glas mit Edelstahl zu beschichten. Diese Technologie bewirkt, dass die Schalen ihre Umgebung widerspiegeln und sich so den verschiedensten Einrichtungsstilen anpassen.

Begründung der Jury
Diese Kollektion überzeugt durch eine elegante Gestaltung, die unter Einsatz neuer Technologien für die Glasbeschichtung erreicht wird.

Lucky Punch
Nutcracker
Nussknacker

Manufacturer
Take2 Designagentur GmbH & Co. KG,
Rosenheim, Germany
In-house design
Markus Roling
Design
Hermann Staudinger,
Rosenheim, Germany
Web
www.take2-design.de

The function of this nutcracker is actuated by the piston which is spring-loaded. The piston can move freely inside the housing, and cracks the nutshell upon impact. The nut is simply placed in the opening and the shutter closed. A single sweeping downwards motion is sufficient to cause the mobile piston inside to crack the shell. Lucky Punch is operated with one hand and little effort.

Statement by the jury
The functionality of Lucky Punch is just as straightforward and simple as the outer appearance – with sweeping success.

Die Funktion dieses Nussknackers basiert auf einem an einer Feder aufgehängten Kolben, der sich im Inneren des Gehäuses frei bewegt und beim Aufschlag die Nussschale aufbricht. Die Nuss wird einfach in die Öffnung gelegt und der Schieber geschlossen. Eine einzige schwungvolle, nach unten gerichtete Bewegung genügt, damit der bewegliche Kolben im Inneren die Schale knackt. Lucky Punch funktioniert einhändig und mit geringem Kraftaufwand.

Begründung der Jury
Ebenso geradlinig und schnörkellos wie die äußere Formgebung ist die Funktionsweise von Lucky Punch – mit durchschlagendem Erfolg.

Naomi
Nutcracker
Nussknacker

Manufacturer
Take2 Designagentur GmbH & Co. KG,
Rosenheim, Germany
In-house design
Markus Roling
Web
www.take2-design.de

Naomi cracks nuts by means of a helical spring with a striker attached inside: The nut is placed in the stainless steel bowl of the nutcracker, and the spring body placed over it. The spring is fixed at the table top with two fingers aside, and the ball on the end of the spring is pulled upwards. When it is released, the striker shoots down and cracks the nut. At the same time the spiral spring closes to prevent shell pieces from flying around.

Statement by the jury
The nut cracker Naomi combines aesthetics, functionality and the adventurous character of usage in one successful item.

Naomi knackt Nüsse mit Hilfe einer Kegelfeder, in deren Inneren ein Schlagbolzen befestigt ist: Die Nuss wird in die Edelstahlschale des Nussknackers gelegt und der Federkörper darüber platziert. Wird die Feder seitlich mit zwei Fingern fixiert und die Kugel an der Spitze der Feder nach oben gezogen, spannt sich die Feder. Wird sie losgelassen, schnellt der Schlagbolzen nach unten und knackt die Nuss. Im gleichen Moment schließt sich die Spiralfeder um die Nuss und verhindert so, dass Schalenstücke umherfliegen.

Begründung der Jury
Beim Nussknacker Naomi verbinden sich Ästhetik, Funktionalität und der Erlebnischarakter der Anwendung zu einem gelungenen Ganzen.

Squeeze
Salt and Pepper Shaker
Salz- und Pfefferstreuer

Manufacturer
Auerhahn Bestecke GmbH,
Altensteig, Germany
Design
TEAGUE GmbH
(Alf Hackenberg),
Munich, Germany
Web
www.auerhahn-bestecke.de
www.teague.com

The Squeeze salt and pepper shaker radiates a playful elegance. The body consists of a specially bent stainless steel tube segment. The kink in the tube clearly separates the salt and the pepper sides and forms a stable stand – at the same time it really invites you to spin Squeeze on the table. The removable salt and pepper containers are made of ABS plastic and can be supplied in white or black.

Der Salz- und Pfefferstreuer Squeeze strahlt eine verspielte Eleganz aus. Sein Körper besteht aus einem speziell gebogenen Edelstahlrohrsegment. Der Tuben-Knick separiert Salz- und Pfefferseite deutlich und bildet eine solide Standfläche – gleichzeitig lädt er geradezu dazu ein, Squeeze auf dem Tisch kreiseln zu lassen. Die herausnehmbaren Salz- und Pfefferbehälter sind aus mattem ABS-Kunststoff gefertigt und in weiß oder schwarz erhältlich.

Statement by the jury
Squeeze combines elegant lines and high quality materials to produce a surprising aspect: the challenge to play.

Begründung der Jury
Eine elegante Linienführung und hochwertige Materialien vereinen sich bei Squeeze mit einem überraschenden Aspekt: der Aufforderung zum Spielen.

ZWILLING Sommelier Waiter's Knife Classic
ZWILLING Sommelier Kellnermesser Classic

Manufacturer
ZWILLING J. A. Henckels AG,
Solingen, Germany
Design
Kurz Kurz Design
(Dorian Kurz),
Solingen, Germany
Web
www.zwilling.com
www.kurz-kurz-design.de

The compact foldable waiter's knife is made of stainless steel and combines three functions in one tool: Foil cutter, corkscrew and bottle opener for crown caps. The Micarta coated handle has a slim and ergonomic form. The hardened, forged and ribbed spindle has a non-stick coating. The two-stage lifter has a flexible joint which makes drawing the cork an easy matter.

Statement by the jury
The compact and classically styled waiter's knife impresses with its pleasant haptic and easy and functional operation.

Das kompakt zusammenklappbare Kellnermesser aus Edelstahl vereint drei Funktionen in einem Werkzeug: Folien-schneider, Korkenzieher sowie einen Flaschenöffner für Kronkorkenver-schlüsse. Der Micarta-veredelte Griff ist schlank und ergonomisch geformt. Die gehärtete, geschmiedete und geriffelte Spindel ist mit einer Antihaftbeschich-tung versehen. Der zweistufige Heber hat ein flexibles Gelenk, wodurch das Herausziehen des Korkens leicht von der Hand geht.

Begründung der Jury
Kompakt und klassisch gestaltet be-eindruckt das Kellnermesser mit seiner angenehmen Haptik und einer leichten und funktionellen Handhabung.

Adjustable Manual Knife Sharpener
Justierbarer manueller Messerschärfer

Manufacturer
Smiths Consumer Products, Inc,
Hot Springs, USA
In-house design
Louis Chalfant
Design
Carter McGuyer Design Group, Inc.
(Carter McGuyer),
Muscle Shoals, USA
Web
www.edgewareproducts.com
www.cartermdesign.com

With this manually adjustable knife sharpener it is possible to adjust the grinding surface quite simply so that every knife can be sharpened in the grinding angle originally set by the manufacturer. This way there is less metal abrasion. The knife sharpener has three grinding slots: one with ceramic rods for light re-sharpening, one with diamond for sharpening blunt or damaged knives as well as one with serrations for a serrated blade.

Statement by the jury
Thanks to its innovative technology and the ergonomic design, the knife sharpener is easy to handle yet functions, however, very accurately.

Dieser manuelle Messerschärfer ermög-licht es, die Schleifflächfe ganz einfach so zu justieren, dass jedes Messer im Originalwinkel, in dem es ursprünglich zugeschliffen wurde, geschärft werden kann. So verringert sich der Metallabrieb. Der Messerschärfer hat drei Schleif-schlitze: einen mit Keramikstäben für leichtes Nachschleifen, einen mit Diamanten zum Schärfen von stumpfen oder beschädigten Messern sowie einen mit Wellenschliff für Sägemesser.

Begründung der Jury
Dank seiner innovativen Technik und der ergonomischen Gestaltung ist der Messerschärfer einfach zu handhaben, arbeitet dabei jedoch sehr präzise.

Geo
Vacuum Flask
Thermoskanne

Manufacturer
Normann Copenhagen,
Copenhagen, Denmark

Design
Nicholai Wiig Hansen,
Copenhagen, Denmark

Web
www.normann-copenhagen.com

reddot design award
best of the best 2013

Geometric harmony

Vacuum flasks keep beverages fresh on a daily basis and, as they are often placed within easy reach on a table, pass through many hands. Dedicating himself to redesign this vessel of daily use with the creative idea of "making a vacuum flask that has character," Danish designer Nicholai Wiig Hansen has transformed it into a fascinating object of strictly geometric appearance. The search for a new shape for the vacuum flask led him to in-depth research and sketching of "various possible lines, circles and forms" in order to "create a geometric harmony and give the flask weight and stability," the designer explained. This process of creative reinterpretation resulted in the concept of a vacuum flask defined by a surprisingly masculine appearance with sharp edges. In addition, the "geometric harmony" of the Geo vacuum flask is complemented by a well thought-out colour concept – the flask is available in six different, lively colour combinations that each possesses a distinct personality. Geo holds one litre of warm or cold drinks and is easy and self-explanatory to use. Based on a subtle design investigation, the creative design process led to a vacuum flask with a strong impression.

Geometrische Harmonie

Die Thermoskanne ist ein viel genutztes Gefäß, welches tagtäglich auf dem Tisch steht und dort von Hand zu Hand geht. Der dänische Designer Nicholai Wiig Hansen widmete sich diesem Alltagsgefäß und wandelte es mit der gestaltungsleitenden Idee „eine Thermoskanne mit Charakter zu gestalten" in ein faszinierendes, streng geometrisch anmutendes Objekt. Die Suche nach einer neuen Form für die Thermoskanne führte ihn zu intensiver Arbeit mit „verschiedenen möglichen Linienführungen, Kreisen und Formen", um auf diese Weise „eine geometrische Harmonie zu schaffen und der Kanne Schwere und Stabilität zu verleihen", so ihr Designer. Das Ergebnis dieses gestalterischen Neuordnens ist das Konzept einer Thermoskanne mit überraschend maskulin und klar anmutenden Kanten. Die „geometrische Harmonie" der Thermoskanne Geo verbindet sich zudem stimmig mit einem gut durchdachten Farbkonzept – in sechs verschiedenen, lebendigen Farbkombinationen zeigt sie jeweils eine eigene Persönlichkeit. Die Geo fasst 1 Liter heiße oder kalte Getränke und lässt sich leicht und selbsterklärend bedienen. Durch eine feinsinnige gestalterische Auseinandersetzung entstand hier eine Thermoskanne mit einer starken Ausdruckskraft. Sie gesellt sich überaus harmonisch zu den übrigen Dingen auf dem Tisch.

Statement by the jury

The graphic and geometric form language of the Geo vacuum flask fascinates at first sight. It has a well-balanced minimalist shape stripped of all unnecessary details. Complemented by a visually appealing colour concept, the flask offers users an individual choice of contrasting colours. The flasks are functional and rest well in the hand.

Begründung der Jury

Die grafische und geometrische Formensprache der Thermoskanne Geo begeistert auf den ersten Blick. Ihre gelungen minimalistische Gestaltung verzichtet auf überflüssige Details. Einen reizvollen Kontrast bietet ihr Farbkonzept, welches es dem Nutzer erlaubt, diese Thermoskanne individuell auszuwählen. Sie ist funktional für den täglichen Gebrauch und liegt gut in der Hand.

Vacuum flasks

Tea Maker TEO, with Infusers
Kanne TEO, mit Teesieben

Manufacturer
Tescoma s.r.o.,
Zlin, Czech Republic
In-house design
Ladislav Skoda
Web
www.tescoma.com
Honourable Mention

Teo is different from other tea jugs, above all due to its two sieves: the bigger filter has vertical slits for brewing fresh mint or similar herbs. The smaller filter with horizontal meshes can be placed in the bigger filter and thus provides a very fine sieve for loose tea sorts. The jug is made of borosilicate glass and plastic and is a continuation of the traditional craftsmanship of Bohemian glass workers.

Teo unterscheidet sich von anderen Kannen vor allem durch ihre beiden Siebe: Der größere Filter hat vertikale Schlitze zum Aufbrühen frischer Minze oder Ähnlichem. Der kleinere Filter mit horizontalen Maschen kann in den größeren Filter eingelegt werden und wird so zu einem sehr feinen Sieb für lose Teesorten. Die Kanne ist aus Borosilikatglas und Kunststoff gefertigt und knüpft an die traditionsreiche Handwerkskunst der böhmischen Glasmacher an.

Statement by the jury
Teo convinces by the symbiosis of simple forms and harmonious proportions with intelligent functionality and traditional manufacturing craft.

Begründung der Jury
Teo überzeugt durch die Symbiose einfacher Formen und harmonischer Proportionen mit einer intelligenten Funktionalität und traditionellen Fertigungsart.

My Big Tea
Teapot
Teekanne

Manufacturer
Eva Solo A/S,
Måløv, Denmark
Design
Tools Design
(Henrik Holbæk, Claus Jensen),
Copenhagen, Denmark
Web
www.evasolo.com
www.toolsdesign.com

This teapot with knitted tea cosy not only keeps the tea hot for longer – it radiates warmth and cosiness. The elastic wool sleeve is offered in a variety of colours and patterns and is machine-washable. The teapot itself has a simplistic form, is made of white porcelain and has a large handle of stainless steel. The teapot holds 1.5 litres which can be poured cleanly thanks to a drip-free spout.

Statement by the jury
The contrasting interplay between a plain porcelain teapot and the soft woollen sleeve with its emotional content is convincing.

Diese Teekanne mit Stricküberzug hält Tee nicht nur lange heiß – sie strahlt auch Wärme und Gemütlichkeit aus. Die elastische Wollmanschette wird in verschiedenen Farben und Strickmustern angeboten und kann in der Maschine gewaschen werden. Die Teekanne selbst hat eine reduzierte Formensprache, besteht aus weißem Porzellan und hat einen großen Edelstahlhenkel. Die Kanne fasst 1,5 Liter, die sich dank einer tropffreien Tülle sauber ausgießen lassen.

Begründung der Jury
Das kontrastierende Zusammenspiel zwischen schlichter Porzellankanne und der weichen Wollmanschette mit ihrer emotionalen Komponente ist überzeugend.

Infusion
Teapot
Teekanne

Manufacturer
Viva Scandinavia,
Aabyhoej, Denmark
In-house design
Peng Lin,
Nina Bruun Faerch-Jensen
Web
www.vivascandinavia.com

Infusion is a teapot which possesses everything needed for fresh tea making. It has a fine tea strainer which reaches deeply into the pot. By this means the tealeaves can whirl around, thus releasing its full taste potential. Thanks to a special spout, the tea can be poured drip-free and silently. The reduced form lines of the teapot are an expression of contemporary Scandinavian design.

Statement by the jury
The Infusion teapot captivates with its harmonious, clear design and sophisticated functionality.

Infusion ist eine Teekanne, die alles, was für einen frischen Teeaufguss nötig ist, mit sich bringt. Sie hat ein feines Teesieb, das tief in die Kanne reicht. Dadurch können die Teeblätter beim Aufgießen umherwirbeln und so ihr volles Geschmackspotenzial entfalten. Dank einer speziellen Tülle kann der Tee tropffrei und geräuschlos eingeschenkt werden. Die reduzierte Formensprache der Kanne ist Ausdruck zeitgenössischen skandinavischen Designs.

Begründung der Jury
Die Teekanne Infusion besticht mit ihrer harmonischen, klaren Gestaltung und ausgereiften Funktionalität.

Madam Solo
Coffee Maker
Kaffeebereiter

Manufacturer
Eva Solo A/S,
Måløv, Denmark
Design
Tools Design
(Henrik Holbæk, Claus Jensen),
Copenhagen, Denmark
Web
www.evasolo.com
www.toolsdesign.com

Madam Solo was created to mark the 100th anniversary of Eva Solo and is an homage to the iconic Danish coffee pot "Madam Blue". The white porcelain body of Madam Solo is of puristic design. The spout, on the other hand, with its lightly curved form is along the lines of the role model. Thanks to a flexible filter, Madam Solo facilitates the preparation of two kinds of coffee – direct immersion and filter coffee – directly in the porcelain coffee jug.

Statement by the jury
Madam Solo is a contemporary new interpretation of the earlier coffee maker and epitomises a harmonious combination of tradition and innovation.

Madam Solo wurde anlässlich des 100-jährigen Jubiläums von Eva Solo kreiert und ist eine Hommage an die dänische Kaffeekannen-Ikone „Madam Blue". Der weiße Porzellankörper von Madam Solo ist puristisch gestaltet. Der Ausguss hingegen mit seiner leicht geschwungenen Form zitiert das Vorbild. Madam Solo ermöglicht dank eines flexiblen Filters die Zubereitung von zwei Arten von Kaffee – Direktaufguss und Filterkaffee – direkt in der Porzellankanne.

Begründung der Jury
Madam Solo ist eine zeitgemäße Neuinterpretation der früheren Kaffeebereiter und verkörpert eine harmonische Verbindung von Tradition und Innovation.

Teapot for Travelling
Reiseteekanne

Manufacturer
Lupao Fine China Co. Ltd,
Taipei, Taiwan
In-house design
Jacky Tseng
Web
www.lohaspottery.com

This teapot is very suitable for travelling. The upper part is double-walled, insulated particularly well and protects against burning the fingers when handling. The bottom half, in contrast, is made in one piece, in order to reduce the weight of the teapot and to give it an elegant appearance. The ring pattern on the outside wall provides a good haptic. The inner wall in front of the pouring spout is perforated like a tea strainer and filters the tealeaves out.

Diese Teekanne eignet sich gut für die Reise: Der obere Teil ist doppelwandig, isoliert besonders gut und schützt beim Anfassen vor Verbrennungen. Die untere Hälfte ist dagegen aus einem Stück gefertigt, um das Gewicht der Kanne zu reduzieren und ihr eine elegante Anmutung zu verleihen. Das Spiralmuster auf der Außenwand sorgt für eine gute Haptik. Die innere Wand vor der Ausgussöffnung ist wie ein Teesieb perforiert und filtert Teeblätter aus.

Zenique „Double Drink" Mug
Tea Mug
Teebecher

Manufacturer
Intermezzo International Co., Ltd.,
Taipei, Taiwan
In-house design
Shih-Chieh Huang
Web
www.zenique.net
Honourable Mention

Tea making in Taiwan has a long and almost artistic tradition. In the everyday hectic, however, occasional pragmatic solutions are needed, such as the Zenique "Double Drink" mug. This simple tea mug has a filter insert, facilitating quick tea making with loose tea. The loose tea is simply put in the mug, the filter placed on top and the tea brewed by pouring on boiling water.

Teezubereitung hat in Taiwan eine lange und beinahe künstlerische Tradition. Im hektischen Alltag jedoch braucht es bisweilen pragmatische Lösungen wie den Zenique „Double Drink" Mug. Dieser schlichte Teebecher hat einen Filtereinsatz, der eine schnelle Teezubereitung mit losem Tee ermöglicht. Die Teeblätter werden einfach in die Tasse gegeben, der Filter darüber gesetzt und der Tee mit heißem Wasser aufgebrüht.

Statement by the jury
This mug for making tea shows that from a design as well as functional viewpoint, a good solution can sometimes be very simple.

Begründung der Jury
Dieser Becher für die Teezubereitung zeigt in gestalterischer wie funktionaler Hinsicht, dass eine gute Lösung manchmal sehr einfach sein kann.

Tea Egg
Tea Infuser
Tee-Ei

Manufacturer
Normann Copenhagen,
Copenhagen, Denmark
Design
Made By Makers,
Copenhagen, Denmark
Web
www.normann-copenhagen.com
www.madebymakers.dk
Honourable Mention

Tea Egg is a charming and simultaneously functional tea infuser with which
a cup of tea can be brewed in a quick
and uncomplicated way. The tea infuser
consists of silicone and can be dis-
mantled easily into two parts for filling
and later cleaning. The tea infuser is
available in six different colours, so
that different colours can be chosen
according to personal preference and
better differentiation of every type
of tea or each tea drinker.

Statement by the jury
The tea infuser combines a clear, elegant form with fresh colours and a high
degree of functionality.

Tea Egg ist ein anmutiges und gleichzeitig funktionelles Tee-Ei, mit dem sich
rasch und unkompliziert eine Tasse Tee
aufbrühen lässt. Das Tea Egg besteht
aus Silikon und lässt sich zum Füllen und
zur späteren Reinigung einfach in zwei
Teile zerlegen. Das Tee-Ei ist in sechs
verschiedenen Farben erhältlich, so dass
man je nach persönlicher Vorliebe und zur
besseren Unterscheidung für jede Teesorte
oder jeden Teetrinker eine andere Farbe
verwenden kann.

Begründung der Jury
Das Tea Egg verbindet eine klare, elegante
Formensprache mit frischen Farben und
hoher Funktionalität.

Tea Egg

Press
Juicer
Fruchtpresse

Manufacturer
Xindao B.V.,
Rijswijk, Netherlands
In-house design
Antoine Persyn
Web
www.xindao.nl
Honourable Mention

This fruit press is a juicer and carafe in one: The top is a distinctive, functional press attachment made of black plastic, below is a simple glass receptacle with soft lines. Two different sized attachments can be chosen, according to the size of the fruit to be pressed. The juice produced is collected in the glass carafe and can be served immediately by means of the attached spout.

Statement by the jury
Press is impressively simple in form and functionality, yet at the same time very effective.

Diese Fruchtpresse ist Entsafter und Karaffe in einem: Oben der markante, funktionale Pressaufsatz aus schwarzem Kunststoff, unten ein schlichtes Glasgefäß mit sanfter Linienführung. Je nach Größe der auszupressenden Früchte kann zwischen zwei unterschiedlich großen Aufsätzen gewählt werden. Der austretende Saft wird in der Glaskaraffe aufgefangen und kann mithilfe des dazugehörigen Ausgießers sofort serviert werden.

Begründung der Jury
Press ist in formaler wie funktionaler Hinsicht bestechend einfach, gleichzeitig jedoch sehr effektiv.

Tea-Jay on the rocks
Ice Tea Maker
Eistee-Zubereiter

Manufacturer
Blomus GmbH,
Sundern, Germany
Design
Flöz Industriedesign
(Oliver Wahl),
Essen, Germany
Web
www.blomus.com
www.floez.de
Honourable Mention

This ice tea maker with its simple, modern carafe form combines the work stages of making tea and cooling it down in a process similar to shock: The ice cubes are put in the glass receptacle; the tea brews in the stainless steel container. As soon as the tea is ready, the passage between the upper container and the glass receptacle is opened by turning, and the hot tea flows over the ice. The cold tea can be served immediately.

Statement by the jury
The puristic designed Tea-Jay enacts tea making as an interactive experience and is therefore an innovative contribution to table culture.

Dieser Eistee-Zubereiter mit seiner schlichten, modernen Karaffen-Form verbindet die Arbeitsgänge von Teezubereitung und schockähnlichem Abkühlvorgang: Die Eiswürfel werden ins Glasgefäß gegeben, der Tee zieht im Edelstahlbehälter. Sobald er fertig ist, wird der Durchfluss zwischen oberem Behälter und Glasgefäß mit einer Drehbewegung geöffnet, und der heiße Tee fließt über das Eis. Der kalte Tee kann sofort serviert werden.

Begründung der Jury
Der puristisch gestaltete Tea-Jay inszeniert die Zubereitung des Tees als interaktives Erlebnis und ist damit ein innovativer Beitrag zur Tischkultur.

Sukori
Water Filter Bottle
Wasserfilter-Flasche

Manufacturer
Fan Bao Co., Ltd.,
New Taipei City, Taiwan
In-house design
William Wen-Der Yang,
Yin Chun Wang
Web
www.fbao95.com
Honourable Mention

Sukori is a water bottle with integrated filter function. The filter is activated as required by means of a simple hand grip. In order to produce drinking water, the inner vessel with the filter at the bottom is pulled out and the water to be purified is filled into the main vessel. Thereafter, the element with the carbon filter is pushed through the water and thereby removes the chlorine, heavy metals, chemical substances and odours.

Statement by the jury
The Sukori water bottle convinces due to its simple handling and its high degree of practical usefulness.

Sukori ist eine Wasserflasche mit integrierter Filterfunktion. Der Filter lässt sich je nach Bedarf durch einen einfachen Handgriff aktivieren. Um Trinkwasser herzustellen, wird das innere Gefäß mit dem Filter im Boden herausgezogen und das zu reinigende Wasser in das Grundgefäß gefüllt. Anschließend wird das Element mit dem Karbonfilter durch das Wasser gedrückt und befreit es so von Chlor, Schwermetallen, chemischen Stoffen und Gerüchen.

Begründung der Jury
Die Wasserfilter-Flasche Sukori überzeugt durch ihre einfache Handhabung und ihren hohen praktischen Nutzwert.

Contigo Morgan
Travel Mug
Thermobecher

Manufacturer
Kambukka BVBA,
Hasselt, Belgium
In-house design
Stijn Lowette
Web
www.mycontigo.com
Honourable Mention

Contigo surprises with the new Morgan coffee mug. It has a classical look for users on the move by means of one particular feature: thanks to its patented Autoseal closing system in the lid, the mug is absolutely spill- and leak-proof. The drinking aperture opens only by pressing the Autoseal button and closes automatically when the button is released. The mug is made of plastic with a soft-feel and the double wall construction acts as thermal insulation that keeps drinks warm or cold.

Statement by the jury
This innovative coffee mug for travellers convinces due to its functionality combined with a puristic design.

Der Formensprache nach ein klassischer Kaffeebecher für unterwegs überrascht Contigo Morgan durch eine Besonderheit: Dank seines patentierten Autoseal-Verschluss-Systems im Deckel ist der Becher absolut auslaufsicher. Die Trinköffnung öffnet sich nur durch Knopfdruck und schließt sich automatisch, wenn der Finger vom Knopf genommen wird. Der Becher ist aus Kunststoff gefertigt und isoliert durch einen doppelwandigen Aufbau.

Begründung der Jury
Dieser innovative Kaffeebecher für unterwegs überzeugt durch seine Funktionalität in Verbindung mit einer puristischen Gestaltung.

Hallasu
Glass-Bottled Drinking Water
Trinkwasser in Glasflaschen

Manufacturer
Jeju Special Self-Governing Province Development
Corp., Jeju City, Jeju Province, South Korea
In-house design
Seung Sin Yang,
Ji Yeon Kim
Design
Hye Won Sohn,
Soo Chung
Web
www.jpdc.co.kr

Hallasu is a premium water brand from
Korea whose water has its source
on Mount Halla on the volcanic island
of Jeju. The mountain's silhouette is
reflected prominently in the form of the
base of the bottle. The design lines of
the vessel with its rounded square basic
form are gentle and clear. The black
stopper serves as a drinking vessel. The
calligraphy of the Chinese character for
water dominates graphically the design.

Hallasu ist eine Premium Wassermarke
aus Korea, deren Wasser am Mount
Halla auf der Vulkaninsel Jeju entspringt.
Die Silhouette des Berges findet sich als
auffälliges Gestaltungselement in der Form
des Flaschenbodens wieder. Die Linienführung des Gefäßes mit seiner abgerundeten
quadratischen Grundform ist sanft und
klar. Der schwarze Deckel dient als Trinkgefäß. Grafisch dominiert die Kalligrafie
des chinesischen Schriftzeichens für
Wasser die Gestaltung.

Statement by the jury
The aesthetic balance of the water
bottle communicates the premium claim
of the brand emphatically and without
straining after effect.

Begründung der Jury
Die ästhetische Ausgewogenheit der
Wasserflasche kommuniziert den Premi-
um-Anspruch der Marke eindringlich
und ohne Effekthascherei.

Dopper –
The perfect bottle for tap water!
Drinking Bottle
Trinkflasche

Manufacturer
Dopper BV,
Haarlem, Netherlands
Design
Rinke van Remortel,
Goes, Netherlands
Web
www.dopper.com
www.vanremortel.nl
Honourable Mention

Dopper was developed in the course of an initiative to promote the drinking of tap water. The form is puristic; the functionality of the bottle is enhanced by the fact that the white upper part of the bottle can be screwed off and used as a drinking vessel. The plastic bottle has no climatic impact and no plasticiser. It is produced in the Netherlands. A Dopper app gives information on where water can be obtained free of charge.

Dopper wurde im Rahmen einer Initiative zur Förderung des Trinkens von Leitungs-wasser entwickelt. Die Formgebung ist puristisch, die Funktionalität der Flasche dadurch erweitert, dass der obere weiße Teil der Flasche abgeschraubt und als Trinkgefäß genutzt werden kann. Die Kunststoff-Flasche wird klimaneutral und ohne Weichmacher in den Niederlanden produziert. Eine Dopper-App gibt Auskunft darüber, wo kostenlos Wasser gezapft werden kann.

Statement by the jury
With its clear, contemporary design, Dopper is a convincing ambassador for sustainability.

Begründung der Jury
Mit seiner klaren, zeitgemäßen Gestaltung ist Dopper ein überzeugender Botschafter für Nachhaltigkeit.

Unda
Collection of Glass Objects
Glas-Kollektion

Manufacturer
Berendsohn AG,
Hamburg, Germany
Design
Alfredo Häberli Design Development
(Alfredo Häberli),
Zürich, Switzerland
Web
www.berendsohn.com
www.alfredo-haeberli.com
Honourable Mention

This glass collection consists of one carafe and two glasses and was designed specially with the enjoyment of tap water in mind. The organic form of the body is orientated by the water flow. The hand-blown glass, coloured throughout, makes each item distinctive and unique. The wavy contour of the products is ergonomic and provides a secure grip. Unda is supplied in the colour variations smoky and aquamarine.

Die Glas-Kollektion besteht aus einer Karaffe und zwei Gläsern und wurde speziell im Hinblick auf den Genuss von Leitungswasser gestaltet. Die organische Form der Körper orientiert sich am Fluss des Wassers. Das durchgefärbte, mundgeblasene Glas macht jedes Objekt zu einem Unikat. Die wellenförmige Kontur der Produkte ist ergonomisch und ermöglicht ein sicheres Halten. Unda ist in den Farbvarianten Rauch und Aquamarin erhältlich.

Statement by the jury
With their soft lines and traditional manufacturing method the glass vessels present water in an elegant and respectful manner.

Begründung der Jury
Mit ihren weichen Linien und der traditionellen Art der Fertigung präsentieren die Glasgefäße Wasser auf elegante und respektvolle Weise.

Glass objects

Wine Classics
Series of Gourmet Glasses
Gourmetglasserie

Manufacturer
Zwiesel Kristallglas,
Zwiesel, Germany
In-house design
Irmgard Braun-Ditzen
Web
www.zwiesel-kristallglas.com

Wine Classics consists of 13 different
goblet-shaped glasses and three
decanters and was developed in
cooperation with the International
Wine Institute. The linear, concise form
of the hand-made crystal glass series
with its wide, reflecting surface and
high, curved body (so called "chimney")
supports ideally the development of
aromas in the glass. The filigreed walls
of the glasses provide them with a
special haptic and lightness.

Statement by the jury
Wine Classics combines lightness and
charm of lines with artistic craftsmanship to a mature functionality: the
special, pleasurable experience.

Wine Classics besteht aus 13 verschiedenen Kelchgläsern und drei Dekantern
und wurde in Zusammenarbeit mit dem
International Wine Institute entwickelt.
Die geradlinige, prägnante Formensprache
der handgefertigten Kristallglasserie unterstützt mit breitem Oberflächenspiegel
und hohem, geschwungenem Kamin
ideal die Entfaltung von Aromen im Glas.
Die filigranen Wände der Kelche bewirken
eine besondere Haptik und Leichtigkeit
der Gläser.

Begründung der Jury
Wine Classics verbindet Leichtigkeit und
Anmut in der Linienführung mit Handwerkskunst zu einer ausgereiften Funktionalität: dem besonderen Genusserlebnis.

Tasting Goblet
Sensorik-Pokal
Tasting Glass
Degustationsglas

Manufacturer
Sahm GmbH & Co. KG,
Höhr-Grenzhausen, Germany
In-house design
Annette Neunzig
Web
www.sahm.de

This goblet is a development in glass form for beer tasting which provides neutral, constant and comparative results for the sensory evaluation of beers. Its volume allows for optimal assessment of the colour density of each beer; the aroma development is furthered due to the upward tapering shape of the glass. The slightly flaring glass rim allows an optimal assessment of the various flavor components. The beer can be ideally tasted.

Statement by the jury
With this beer tasting glass the plain yet elegant form is optimally suited for the sensory assessment of various beer types.

Mit diesem Pokal wurde eine Glasform für die Bierverkostung entwickelt, die neutrale, konstante und vergleichbare Ergebnisse für die sensorische Bewertung von Bieren liefert. Sein Volumen erlaubt eine optimale Einschätzung der Farbdichte des jeweiligen Bieres. Durch die sich nach oben verjüngende Glasform wird die Aroma-Entwicklung gefördert. Der leicht ausgestellte Glasrand ermöglicht es, alle Geschmackskomponenten optimal zu beurteilen. Das Bier lässt sich ideal verkosten.

Begründung der Jury
Bei diesem Bier-Degustationsglas ist die schlicht-elegante Form optimal auf die sensorische Beurteilung verschiedener Biersorten abgestimmt.

Arc
Goblet
Kelch

Manufacturer
Ken Okuyama Design Co., Ltd.,
Tokyo, Japan
In-house design
Ken Okuyama
Web
www.kenokuyamadesign.com

Arc is a charming goblet of stainless steel. It is composed of six individual parts which are merged together in a special manufacturing process to one smooth form. The double wall structure acts as insulation; its interior is enhanced additionally by lavish polishing which has the effect that the beer in the tankard produces a particularly fine froth. The tankard has a stable centre of gravity which makes it pleasant to hold.

Statement by the jury
Arc impresses not only by its sculptural form, but also due to the unusual choice of materials and its high quality.

Arc ist ein anmutiger Kelch aus Edelstahl. Er setzt sich aus sechs Einzelteilen zusammen, die in einem besonderen Herstellungsprozess zu einer einzigen glatten Form zusammengefügt werden. Die doppelwandige Struktur des Kelchs isoliert; seine Innenseite ist zusätzlich durch eine aufwändige Politur veredelt, die bewirkt, dass Bier in dem Gefäß einen besonders feinen Schaum bildet. Der Kelch hat einen stabilen Schwerpunkt und ist dadurch angenehm zu halten.

Begründung der Jury
Arc besticht nicht nur durch seine skulpturale Form, sondern auch durch die ungewöhnliche Materialwahl und die qualitativ hochwertige Ausführung.

Bathrooms, spas and air conditioning
Bad, Wellness und Klima

Bathroom furnishings, bathroom accessories, sanitary installations, heating and air-conditioning technology, saunas, solaria, massage equipment
Badausstattungen, Badaccessoires, Sanitäreinrichtungen, Heiz- und Klimatechnik, Saunen, Solarien, Massageausrüstungen

5

Axor Starck Organic
Bathroom Fixtures
Badarmaturen

Manufacturer
Hansgrohe SE,
Schiltach, Germany

Design
Starck Network
(Philippe Starck),
Paris, France

Web
www.hansgrohe.com
www.starcknetwork.com

Natural presence

The philosophers of Greek antiquity had already written about the fundamental significance of water. The pre-Socratic philosopher and astronomer Thales of Miletus for instance defined water as the element and principle of all things that are. The design of the Axor Starck Organic collection is inspired by and draws upon this idea of water as the first principle. The clear and harmonious lines of the bathroom fixtures are reminiscent of shapes found in nature. An organic and flowing form lends them an appearance of exciting and powerful immediacy. The handles of the bathroom fixtures blend in visually with the body of the faucets to adopt the appearance of a self-sufficient unity – like natural sculptures they blend harmoniously with almost any environment. In addition, they feature an ergonomic design and are intuitive to use. Equipped with innovative technology, these bathroom fixtures use water and energy economically, since water volume and temperature are controlled separately. A newly developed spray with a low flow rate of only 3.5 litres per minute means that much less water is used, without compromising functionality. The design of the Axor Starck Organic bathroom fixtures thus merges a surprisingly natural and organic appearance with a user concept that sets new standards for the future.

Natürliche Präsenz

Schon die frühen Philosophen thematisierten die Bedeutung des Elements Wasser. Der antike griechische Philosoph und Astronom Thales von Milet etwa sah im Wasser den Urstoff allen Seins. Die Axor Starck Organic Kollektion knüpft in ihrer Gestaltung an diese ursprüngliche Bedeutung des Elements Wasser an. Die klaren und harmonischen Linien der Badarmaturen sind an Silhouetten angelehnt, wie man sie aus der Natur kennt. Eine organisch fließende Formensprache verleiht ihnen dabei die Anmutung von Spannung und Kraft. Die Griffe dieser Badarmaturen verschmelzen visuell mit den Armaturenkörpern und wirken auf den Betrachter geschlossen – wie naturähnliche Skulpturen bereichern sie jedes Ambiente. Die Axor Starck Organic Badarmaturen sind zudem ergonomisch dem Nutzer zugewandt und können intuitiv bedient werden. Durch eine Ausstattung mit innovativen Technologien ermöglichen diese Badarmaturen einen ökonomischen Umgang mit Wasser und Energie, denn die Wassermenge und die Wassertemperatur werden separat gesteuert. Eine neu entwickelte Strahlart trägt mit einem geringen Durchfluss von nur 3,5 Litern pro Minute zudem dazu bei, dass erheblich weniger Wasser verwendet wird. Die überraschend natürliche, organisch anmutende Formensprache verbindet die Gestaltung der Axor Starck Organic Badarmaturen so mit einem Nutzerkonzept, welches neue Wege in die Zukunft aufzeigt.

Statement by the jury

The Axor Starck Organic bathroom fixtures possess an outstanding design quality and formal distinction. They are highly visible sculptures with an appearance of organically flowing naturalness. Their feel and ergonomics are also astounding. The individual elements merge symbiotically into an overly well-thought-out unity.

Begründung der Jury

Die Axor Starck Organic Badarmaturen sind von außerordentlicher gestalterischer Qualität und Prägnanz. Es sind unübersehbare Skulpturen mit der Anmutung organisch fließender Natürlichkeit. Auch ihre Ergonomie und Haptik ist verblüffend. Die einzelnen Elemente schaffen in ihrer Gesamtheit eine gelungene Symbiose.

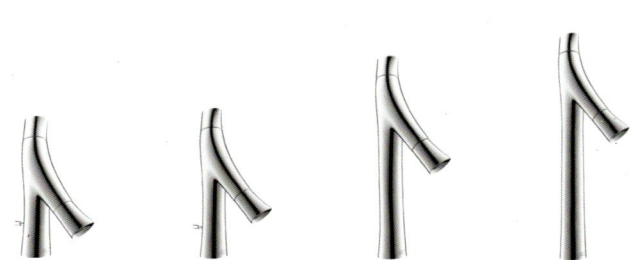

Sanitary installations

Spirit Collection
Single-Lever Mixer
Einhebel-Waschtischmischer

Manufacturer
AM.PM,
Berlin, Germany
Design
Design 3
(Bjoern Vibrans),
Hamburg, Germany
Web
www.ampm-world.com
www.design3.de

AM.PM Spirit combines organic flow and geometric precision. The compact, pure and timeless shape leans towards the user and allows comfortable and easy handling. The soft handle offers a very good surface feel for precise water regulation. In addition, economic consumption is assured by built-in water and energy saving functions.

AM.PM Spirit verbindet organische Weichheit und geometrische Strenge. Die kompakte, klare und zeitlose Form neigt sich zum Nutzer und ermöglicht eine komfortable Handhabung. Die Gestaltung des Hebels sorgt für eine besonders gute Haptik zur präzisen Wasserregulierung. Zusätzlich gewährleistet die integrierte Wasser- und Energiesparfunktion einen ökonomischen Verbrauch.

Statement by the jury
The striking, modern look of the single-lever mixer from the AM.PM Spirit collection is at the cutting edge, as is its functionality and ergonomic design.

Begründung der Jury
Neben der markanten, modernen Gestaltung ist der Einhebel-Waschtischmischer der AM.PM Spirit-Kollektion auch hinsichtlich Funktionalität und Ergonomie auf der Höhe der Zeit.

Spirit Collection
Single-Lever Bathtub Mixer
Einhebel-Wannenmischer

Manufacturer
AM.PM,
Berlin, Germany
Design
Design 3
(Bjoern Vibrans),
Hamburg, Germany
Web
www.ampm-world.com
www.design3.de

The bathtub mixer of AM.PM's Spirit collection combines organic flow and geometric precision. The overall shape is very compact, precisely defined and allows comfortable handling. The soft sculptured surfaces of the handle offer a very good surface feel for precise water regulation. In addition, economic consumption is assured by built-in water and energy saving functions.

Auch die Wannenarmatur der AM.PM Spirit-Kollektion verbindet organische Weichheit mit geometrischer Strenge. Die Form ist kompakt, klar definiert und ermöglicht eine komfortable Handhabung. Die überwölbten Flächen des Hebels sorgen für eine besonders gute Haptik. Die integrierte Wasser- und Energiesparfunktion sorgt für einen ökonomischen Verbrauch.

Statement by the jury
The single-lever bathtub mixer from AM.PM's Spirit collection is pleasing due to its memorable shape, as well as the pleasant handling that it assures in daily use.

Begründung der Jury
Der Einhebel-Wannenmischer der AM.PM Spirit-Kollektion gefällt durch seine eindrucksvolle Formgebung, die zudem eine angenehme Handhabung im alltäglichen Gebrauch gewährleistet.

Laufen Cityplus
Wash Basin Fitting
Waschtischarmatur

Manufacturer
Laufen Bathrooms AG,
Laufen, Switzerland
Design
platinumdesign
(Andreas Dimitriadis),
Stuttgart, Germany
Web
www.laufen.com
www.platinumdesign.com

Laufen Cityplus represents the link between purist planar design and horizontal proportions. In addition to the elegant surface grip, it features a compact zero handle, which can be fitted with a square coloured inlay. Particular attention was paid to making the appliance easy to clean by avoiding unnecessary edges, integrating a flush-mounted aerator and by minimising clearance gaps in the manufacturing process.

Laufen Cityplus steht für die Verbindung von puristisch flächigem Design und horizontalen Proportionen. Zusätzlich zum eleganten Flächengriff wird ein kompakter Zerogriff angeboten. Dieser kann mit einem quadratischen Farbeinleger bestückt werden. Besonderes Augenmerk wurde auf die Reinigungsfreundlichkeit durch das Vermeiden von unnötigen Kanten, einen flächenbündig eingearbeiteten Strahlregler und durch Einhaltung von minimalen Spaltmaßen in der Fertigung gelegt.

Statement by the jury
Clean lines make this series of fittings modern and contemporary in appearance. Its colour inlays also give it a very individual character.

Begründung der Jury
Diese Armaturenserie wirkt durch ihre klaren Linien nicht nur modern und zeitgemäß, sondern gewinnt durch einen farbigen Akzenteinleger auch eine individuelle Note.

Natura
Bath Collection
Badkollektion

Manufacturer
Bisk S.A.,
Łubna, Poland
Design
Colorofon
(Magda Kiełkiewicz, Kuba Gurnik),
Warsaw, Poland
Web
www.bisk.eu
www.colorofon.pl

The design of the Natura collection follows classic minimalist patterns without, however, losing its own identity. The ergonomic shape gives it a modern look. Environmental awareness has led to the use of aerators to reduce water consumption, and of durable, corrosion-resistant PEX tubes. The entire collection is 100 per cent recyclable.

Statement by the jury
The soft, natural looking lines are characteristic of the Natura collection. It also appeals thanks to the use of mature technology.

Das Design der Kollektion Natura orientiert sich durchgehend an klassischen minimalistischen Mustern, ohne seinen eigenen Charakter aufzugeben. Die ergonomische Form verleiht ihr ein modernes Aussehen. Aus ökologischen Gründen werden zudem wassersparende Luftsprudler und haltbare korrosionsbeständige PEX-Schläuche eingesetzt. Die gesamte Kollektion ist zu 100 Prozent recycelbar.

Begründung der Jury
Eine weiche, natürlich wirkende Linienführung kennzeichnet die Kollektion Natura, die zudem durch ihre ausgereiften technischen Aspekte zu gefallen weiß.

Ophir
Tap
Armatur

Manufacturer
AWA Faucet Ltd,
Taipei, Taiwan
In-house design
Christian Laudet,
Warran Hoy
Web
www.awafaucet.com

Purist lines, top quality and balanced proportions are the hallmark of this tap which also eschews any sharp edges to ensure optimal handling. This European designed masterpiece benefits from the outstanding skills of Taiwan's manufacturing. Within this context, this strength enables the creation of an incredibly thin handle for Ophir. Together with a tap body of high-quality brass this makes for a product of superior workmanship and maximum durability.

Statement by the jury
Elegant minimalism paired with perfect craftsmanship are the key features of this stylish tap.

Eine puristische Linienführung, höchste Qualität und ausgewogene Proportionen kennzeichnen diese Armatur. Zusätzlich wurden für ein besseres Handling alle scharfen Kanten vermieden. Dieses meisterhaft ausgeführte Produkt mit europäischem Design profitiert von den ausgezeichneten Fähigkeiten taiwanesischer Fertigung. Diese Qualität ermöglicht die Kreation eines extrem dünnen Einstellhebels für Ophir. Zusammen mit dem Armaturenkörper aus hochwertigem Messing führt dies zu einem Produkt von höchster Verarbeitungsqualität und maximaler Haltbarkeit.

Begründung der Jury
Ein eleganter Minimalismus gepaart mit handwerklicher Perfektion sind die Hauptmerkmale dieser stilvollen Armatur.

Sanitary installations

Hand Dryer
Händetrockner

Manufacturer
Dyson Ltd.,
Malmesbury, Wiltshire, GB
In-house design
James Dyson
Web
www.dyson.co.uk
Honourable Mention

The Dyson Airblade Tap hand dryer washes and dries hands without needing to leave the wash basin. Infrared sensors register the position of the hands and activate the jet of water. To dry the hands, an integrated electronic system subsequently activates two high-velocity streams of air, which come out of the tap's branches. The major components of the system are housed separately under the wash basin.

Der Dyson Airblade Tap Händetrockner wäscht und trocknet die Hände, ohne dass man das Waschbecken verlassen muss. Infrarot-Sensoren registrieren die Handposition und aktivieren den Wasserstahl. Um die Hände zu trocknen, werden anschließend über die integrierte Elektronik zwei Hochgeschwindigkeits-Luftströme aktiviert, die aus den Armen des Wasserhahns abgegeben werden. Die Hauptbestandteile befinden sich dabei in einem separaten Gehäuse unter dem Waschbecken.

Statement by the jury
The Dyson Airblade Tap is a good example of how successful design based on an inventive idea and high-quality implementation can make everyday life that bit easier.

Begründung der Jury
Der Dyson Airblade Tap ist ein gutes Beispiel dafür, wie gelungenes Design dank einer originellen Idee und einer hochwertigen Ausführung den Alltag vereinfacht.

Multiplex Trio Ergo
Bath Handle and Water Inlet
Wannengriff und Wasserzulauf

Manufacturer
Viega GmbH & Co. KG,
Attendorn, Germany
Design
ARTEFAKT industriekultur,
Darmstadt, Germany
Web
www.viega.de
www.artefakt.de

Multiplex Trio Ergo is a novel bath handle with an integrated water inlet. This combination is suitable for many different bathtubs and guarantees that the bathroom interior will be up to date for years to come. A wide water inlet fills the bath up in virtually no time and the heat-insulated handle is always safe to touch. Installation could not be easier. Multiplex Trio Ergo just needs to be attached to a tap.

Multiplex Trio Ergo ist ein neuartiger Wannengriff mit integriertem Wassereinlauf. Diese Kombination ist für zahlreiche Badewannentypen geeignet und gewährleistet eine zukunftssichere Ausstattung im Bad. Mittels eines breiten Schwallauslaufs ist die Badewanne in kurzer Zeit gefüllt, wobei der wärmeisolierte Griff in seiner Handhabung stets sicher bleibt. Um die Multiplex Trio Ergo in Betrieb nehmen zu können, muss sie lediglich an eine Armatur angeschlossen werden.

Statement by the jury
Multiplex Trio Ergo stands out as a functional unit with an appearance of high quality that combines bath handle and water inlet.

Begründung der Jury
Multiplex Trio Ergo brilliert als funktionale Einheit von hoher formaler Qualität, die Wannengriff und Wasserzulauf in sich vereint.

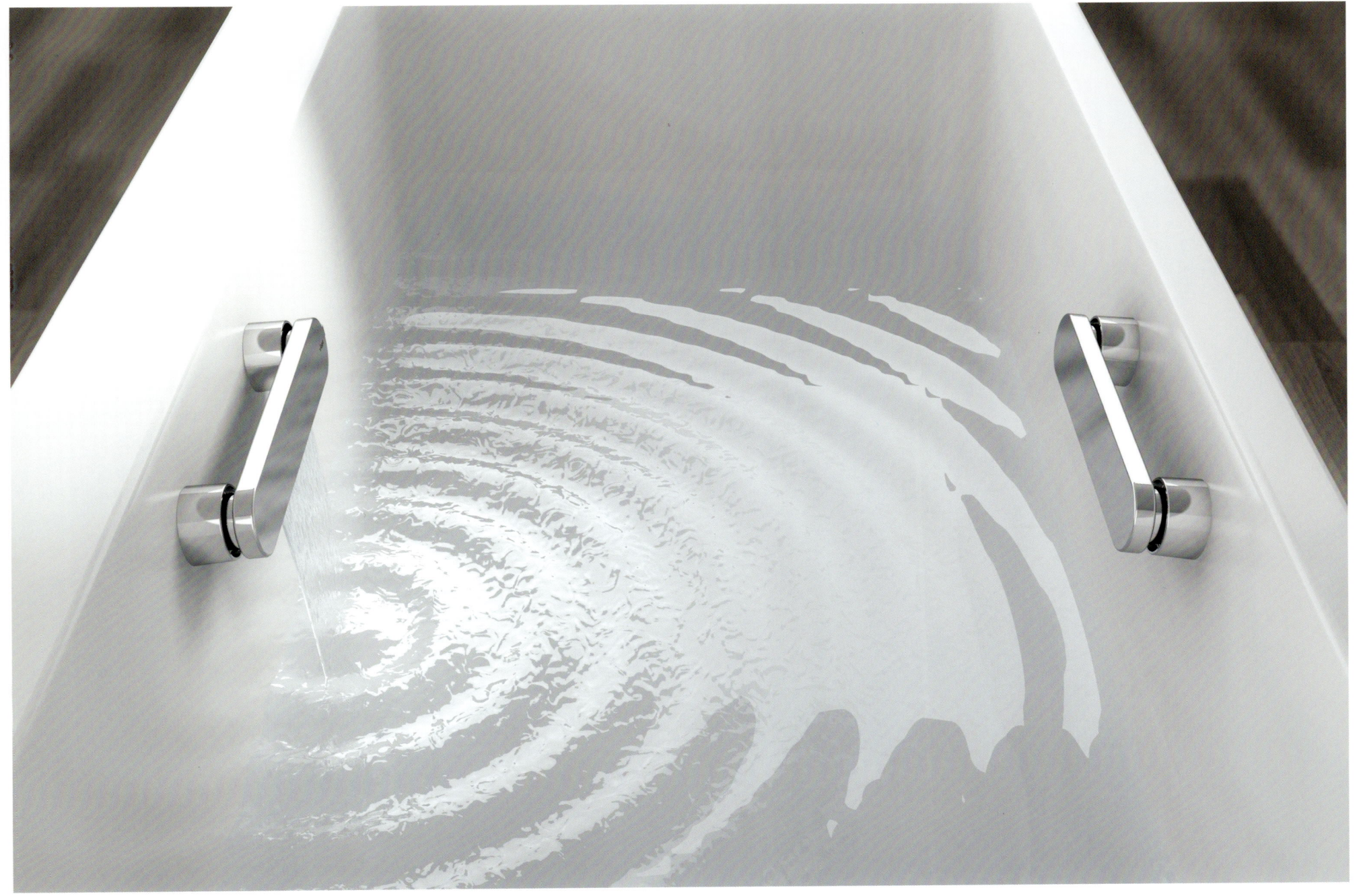

Sanitary installations

Relexa Deluxe
Shower Collection
Brause-Kollektion

Manufacturer
Grohe AG,
Düsseldorf, Germany
In-house design
Web
www.grohe.com

The Relexa Deluxe shower head was devised to use an innovative delivery of water to give the ultimate sensory shower experience. Its appearance speaks of power and performance. The design is based on concentric circles in order to create jets of water of different strengths and an intuitive link between the control and spray face. A cylindrical knob, positioned at the side makes for an easy switch between the four spray types: Rain, Normal, Champagne and Champagne Deluxe. A multidirectional swivel head ensures that the jet of water can be precisely and easily pointed in any direction.

Die Kopfbrause Relexa Deluxe wurde entworfen, um durch eine innovative Strahl-Technologie ein ultimatives sensorisches Erlebnis zu bieten. Ihre Ästhetik vermittelt Kraft und Leistung. Grundlage der Gestaltung sind konzentrische Kreise, um eine Abstufung des Wasserstrahls und eine intuitive Verbindung zwischen der Bedien- und der Strahlseite zu schaffen. Ein seitlich positionierter zylindrischer Knopf ermöglicht ein müheloses Umstellen zwischen den vier Strahlarten Rain, Normal, Champagne und Champagne Deluxe. Die Ausstattung mit einem multidirektionalen Kugelgelenk erlaubt es, den Wasserstrahl für den maximalen Komfort einfach und genau auszurichten.

Statement by the jury
There is more than a hint of luxury to the Relexa Deluxe shower head – its aesthetics and functionality will satisfy even the most demanding user.

Begründung der Jury
Mehr als einen Hauch Luxus verbreitet die Kopfbrause Relexa Deluxe – in Ästhetik wie Funktionalität bleiben keine Wünsche offen.

Rainshower F-Series Multispray 15"
Shower Collection
Brause-Kollektion

Manufacturer
Grohe AG,
Düsseldorf, Germany
In-house design
Web
www.grohe.com

The F-Series Multispray 15" is the latest addition to the Grohe Spa collection. It combines three different shower experiences, a 300 mm wide rain spray, two wide waterfall sprays and four innovative Bokoma Sprays, placed symmetrically for visual balance and enhanced water distribution. People come in different shapes and sizes, so the Bokoma Sprays can be adjusted to the optimum position. The system is available in both a wall-mounted and a super-flat concealed variant for installation in the ceiling. Its robust metal construction ensures quality and longevity and its unique spray combination delivers an unparalleled water experience.

Als jüngste Ergänzung der Grohe Spa-Kollektion kombiniert die F-Series Multispray 15" drei unterschiedliche Duscherlebnisse: einen Regenstrahl von 300 mm Durchmesser, zwei breite Wasserfälle und vier innovative Bokoma Sprays – im Sinne optischer Ausgewogenheit und optimierter Wasserverteilung perfekt symmetrisch angeordnet. Dabei lassen sich die Bokoma Sprays auf die für die jeweilige Körpergröße optimale Position einstellen. Das System ist wahlweise für die Wandmontage und als flache Einbauvariante für die Decke erhältlich. Die robuste Metallkonstruktion gewährleistet Qualität und Langlebigkeit, während die einzigartige Strahlkombination ein unvergleichliches Wassererlebnis verspricht.

Sanitary installations

F-Digital Deluxe
Shower Collection
Brause-Kollektion

Manufacturer
Grohe AG,
Düsseldorf, Germany
In-house design
Web
www.grohe.com

F-Digital Deluxe is an extremely slim, intuitive control by Grohe Spa that offers a unique shower experience to stimulate the senses. Using the external control, it is possible to choose one's own, customised wellness programme consisting of light (chromotherapy), sound (audiotherapy) and steam (aquatherapy). Thus Grohe brings to life the ambitious vision of transforming the bathroom from a purely functional room for cleaning and personal care into an inspiring and emotionally appealing private spa. This digital innovation allows every user to create a truly personalised shower experience.

F-Digital Deluxe ist die extrem schlanke, intuitive Steuerung von Grohe Spa für ein einzigartiges, alle Sinne stimulierendes Duscherlebnis. Über den extern platzierten Controller stellt man sein individuelles Wellnessprogramm aus Licht (Farbtherapie), Sound (Klangtherapie) und Dampf (Aquatherapie) zusammen. Damit wird die ambitionierte Vision realisiert, das Bad von einem funktionalen Raum der Reinigung und Pflege in ein inspirierendes und emotional ansprechendes privates Spa zu verwandeln. Mit dieser digitalen Innovation kann jeder Benutzer sein individuelles Duschvergnügen im persönlichen Wohlfühlambiente gestalten und komfortabel steuern.

Statement by the jury
The F-Digital Deluxe by Grohe Spa turns bath- and shower rooms into spas that significantly increase the physical, emotional and spiritual well-being of the user.

Begründung der Jury
Mit F-Digital Deluxe von Grohe Spa werden Bad- und Duschraum zum Wellnessbereich, der das physische, emotionale und mentale Wohlbefinden deutlich erhöht.

Extra Flat Shower Head
Superflache Kopfbrause

Manufacturer
HSK Duschkabinenbau KG,
Olsberg, Germany
In-house design
Web
www.hsk.de

The elegant look of this new, particularly flat shower head measuring only 2 mm in height is combined with a wide choice of settings. With regards to the increasing wish to individualise, it can be combined at will with the HSK shower sets and shower panels in each way required. Despite its extremely slim design, this extraordinary shower head is equipped with easy to maintain anti-scale nozzles.

Mit einer Höhe von nur 2 mm überzeugt diese neue, besonders flache Kopfbrause vor allem durch ihren edlen Look sowie eine große Kombinationsfreiheit. Im Hinblick auf den zunehmenden Wunsch nach Individualisierung lässt sie sich wahlweise mit den HSK-Shower-Sets und Duschpaneelen frei kombinieren. Trotz der flachen Bauweise besitzt diese außergewöhnliche Kopfbrause pflegeerleichternde Wasserdüsen mit Anti-Kalk-Funktion.

Sanitary installations

Rock Lake
Wash Basin
Waschbecken

Manufacturer
ZEVA CORP.,
Changhua, Taiwan
In-house design
Yung-Wen Chung
Web
www.zevalife.com

The design of this wash basin in two step-like levels was inspired by the surface erosion caused by flowing water. The lower level quickly fills to a level which is sufficient for most washing purposes. This ensures both comfortable use and a highly efficient consumption of water.

Statement by the jury
The resourceful idea of creating a cascade-shaped form for the Rock Lake wash basin is entirely based on the concept of user friendliness and efficiency.

Die Gestaltung des Waschbeckens Rock Lake in zwei abgestuften Bereichen ist inspiriert von der durch fließendes Wasser verursachten Oberflächenerosion. Der untere Teil des Beckens füllt sich schnell bis zu einer Höhe mit Wasser, die für die meisten Waschzwecke geeignet ist. Dies gewährleistet sowohl eine komfortable Nutzung als auch einen höchst effizienten Wasserverbrauch.

Begründung der Jury
Die findige Idee einer kaskadenförmigen Gestaltung beim Waschbecken Rock Lake ist ganz dem Gedanken der Nutzerfreundlichkeit und Effizienz verschrieben.

Inspire Collection
Wash Basin
Waschbecken

Manufacturer
AM.PM,
Berlin, Germany
Design
Design 3
(Bjoern Vibrans, Wolfgang Wagner),
Hamburg, Germany
Web
www.ampm-world.com
www.design3.de

The wash basin of the Inspire collection plays on the contrast of organic flow and geometric precision thereby achieving a combination of simplicity and emotion. Its clear design and outstanding ergonomic comfort result in an elegant, but distinctive appearance.

Statement by the jury
The wash basin from the AM.PM Inspire collection is so captivating mainly because of its clean form that focuses on essentials – without compromise, but nonetheless appealing.

Das Waschbecken der AM.PM Inspire-Kollektion spielt mit dem Kontrast von organischer Linienführung und geometrischer Strenge und erzeugt so eine Kombination von Schlichtheit und Emotion. Das reduzierte Design in Verbindung mit optimalem ergonomischem Komfort erzeugt ein elegantes und eigenständiges Erscheinungsbild.

Begründung der Jury
Das Waschbecken der AM.PM Inspire-Kollektion überzeugt vor allem durch seine klare, auf das Wesentliche konzentrierte Form – kompromisslos und dennoch ansprechend.

Art
Bathroom Furniture Collection
Badmöbel-Kollektion

Manufacturer
Vedum Kök & Bad AB,
Vedum, Sweden

Design
Jesper Design
(Jesper Ståhl),
Jönköping, Sweden

Web
www.vedum.se/art
www.jesperdesign.se

The Art bathroom furniture collection offers the complete range of bathroom fittings: a wash basin in two sizes, an open and a closed shelving unit, mirrors, lighting and a unique washstand. The high-quality washstand is the centrepiece of the collection. Its distinctive design was inspired by the movement of water and is reminiscent of the swirl shapes created by suction when water goes down the drain. All components exhibit the same high level of quality. Take, for example, the washstand with its picture-frame appearance and characteristic doors in natural ash or single colours with three-dimensional embossed fronts.

Die Badmöbel-Kollektion Art bietet die komplette Ausstattung für ein Badezimmer: ein Waschbecken in zwei Größen, ein offenes und ein geschlossenes Regal, Spiegel, Beleuchtung und einen außergewöhnlichen Waschtisch-Unterschrank. Der hochwertige Waschtisch ist das Kernstück der Kollektion. Sein markantes Design ist von der Bewegung des Wassers inspiriert und erinnert an den trichterförmigen Sog des abfließenden Wassers. Der hohe Qualitätsanspruch zieht sich durch alle Elemente. So besticht der Unterschrank mit seiner Bilderrahmenoptik, den charakteristischen Türen aus naturbelassener Esche oder einfarbig mit dreidimensional geprägten Fronten.

Sanitary installations, bathroom furnishings

Washlet D Shape
Shower Toilet Seat
Dusch-Toilettensitz

Manufacturer
Toto Ltd.,
Tokyo, Japan
In-house design
Minoru Tani,
Hiroyuki Takeuchi
Web
www.toto.co.jp/en

Washlet D Shape is a newly developed
toilet seat that is available separately.
In no time at all it can be fitted to
any toilet, thereby providing it with
a pleasant, hygienic and comfortable
spray cleaning function. Although the
attractive unit is narrow and flat it
offers all the features of conventional
models as well as a range of additional
ones. All functional components and the
seat are covered by a seamlessly closing
lid. Washlet D Shape integrates warm-
water cleaning, a heated seat, warm
air-drying and odour control.

Statement by the jury
This toilet seat with integrated spray
cleaning function ensures utmost
cleanliness and is usable on all existing
toilets thanks to its innovative
technology and compact shape.

Washlet D Shape ist ein neu entwickelter,
separat erhältlicher Toilettensitz, der sich
im Handumdrehen an jede Toilette anpassen lässt und diese mit einer hygienischen,
angenehmen und komfortablen Duschreinigungsfunktion ausstattet. Obwohl die
attraktiv gestaltete Einheit schmal und
flach ist, weist sie trotzdem alle Funktionen
konventioneller Modelle sowie eine Reihe
von Zusatzmerkmalen auf. Darüber hinaus
liegen die Funktionsbauteile und der Sitz
unter einem nahtlos schließenden Deckel.
Washlet D Shape umfasst Warmwasser-
reinigung, einen beheizten Sitz, Warm-
lufttrocknung und Geruchsbekämpfung.

Begründung der Jury
Größtmögliche Sauberkeit bietet dieser
Toilettensitz mit Duschreinigungsfunktion,
der dank seiner neuartigen Technik und
kompakten Gestaltung auch bei bereits
vorhandenen Toiletten einsetzbar ist.

Serel Amphora
Toilet
Toilette

Manufacturer
Matel Hammadde San. ve Tic. A.S.,
Serel Sanitary Factory,
Manisa, Turkey
In-house design
Zafer Dogan, Aldonat Sunar,
Metin Murat Elbeyli, Ali Yildiz,
Esin Cirali
Web
www.serelseramik.com.tr

The design of the Serel Amphora collection is characterised by soft flowing lines with particular emphasis being placed on ergonomic and functional aspects. Take for example the toilet, which only uses 4.5 litres of water – a reduction of 25 per cent. The Easy Release and Silent Close functions of the toilet seat and lid offer a high level of user comfort. All the products are manufactured with the Clean+ and Hygiene+ surface glazing methods which keep bacteria at bay and facilitate cleaning.

Statement by the jury
The suggestion of the form of ancient amphorae lends Serel Amphora an appealing, exotic touch though cutting edge technology and a distinctive functionality are not forgotten.

Die Gestaltung der Kollektion Serel Amphora zeichnet sich durch weiche, geschwungene Linien aus. Besonderer Wert wurde zudem auf Ergonomie und Funktionalität gelegt. So verbraucht das WC bei einer Komplettspülung mit nur 4,5 Liter 25 Prozent weniger Wasser. Die Easy Release- und Silent Close-Funktion von WC-Sitz und -Deckel bieten maximalen Benutzerkomfort. Alle Produkte werden mit den Oberflächenglasurmethoden Clean+ und Hygiene+ hergestellt, wodurch Bakterien ferngehalten werden und die Reinigung leichter ist.

Begründung der Jury
Die Anlehnung an die Form antiker Amphoren verleiht Serel Amphora einen reizvollen, exotischen Touch. Der Einsatz modernster Technologie und eine ausgeprägte Funktionalität kommen dabei aber nicht zu kurz.

Joyce WC with SlimSeat

Toilet
Toilette

Manufacturer
Villeroy & Boch AG,
Mettlach, Germany
Design
.molldesign
(Reiner Moll),
Schwäbisch Gmünd, Germany
Web
www.villeroy-boch.com
www.molldesign.de

The Joyce wall-mounted toilet displays a light and graceful form. It is equipped with a special design siphon and features both sustainable and innovative technology. Thanks to the water-saving AquaReduct flush, the toilet offers a powerful flushing performance with only a small amount of water. The patented SupraFix 2.0 attachment system makes it possible to install the toilet easily and quickly without any visible installation holes. The innovative SlimSeat perfectly complements the Joyce toilet. It has a particularly slender appearance, yet still offers the full range of comfort functions. Fitted with Quick Release, the seat is easy to remove and clean, while the Soft Closing feature ensures the lid is always lowered gently and silently.

Das Wand-WC Joyce zeichnet sich durch eine filigrane und leichte Formensprache aus. Es ist mit einem neuartigen Designsiphon sowie mit nachhaltiger, innovativer Technik ausgestattet. Dank der wassersparenden AquaReduct-Spülung bietet das WC optimale Spülleistung bei geringem Wasserverbrauch. Das patentierte Befestigungssystem SupraFix 2.0 ermöglicht eine einfache, schnelle Montage ohne sichtbare Befestigungslöcher. Perfekt ergänzt wird das WC durch den innovativen SlimSeat. Der WC-Sitz verfügt über ein besonders schlankes Design und ist trotzdem mit Komfortfunktionen ausgestattet. Dank Quick Release lässt er sich leicht abnehmen und reinigen. Soft Closing sorgt für ein sanftes Absenken des Deckels.

Statement by the jury
The slim appearance of Joyce ensures that it blends into the bathroom atmosphere. Well-engineered technology and ease of use are a given.

Begründung der Jury
Dank einer flach wirkenden Bauweise fügt sich Joyce unaufdringlich ins Badezimmerambiente ein. Eine ausgereifte Technik und höchster Komfort sind dabei selbstverständlich.

Bathrooms, spas and air conditioning

Inspire Collection

Bathtub
Badewanne

Manufacturer
AM.PM,
Berlin, Germany
Design
Design 3
(Bjoern Vibrans, Wolfgang Wagner,
Till Kobes),
Hamburg, Germany
Web
www.ampm-world.com
www.design3.de

The bathtub of the Inspire collection plays on the contrast of organic flow and geometric precision thereby achieving a combination of simplicity and emotion. Its clean and flowing lines, together with its outstanding ergonomic properties create an overall impression of comfort, rest and relaxation.

Die Badewannenserie Inspire spielt mit dem Kontrast von organischer Linienführung und geometrischer Strenge und erzeugt so eine Kombination von Schlichtheit und Emotion. Die fließende, klare Formensprache in Verbindung mit optimalen ergonomischen Eigenschaften erzeugt ein Gefühl von Komfort, Ruhe und Entspannung.

Statement by the jury
The high-quality design of this bathtub from the AM.PM Inspire collection is particularly noticeable in its elegant shape and impressive functionality.

Begründung der Jury
Die hochwertige Gestaltung dieser Badewanne der AM.PM Inspire-Kollektion zeigt sich besonders in der formalen Qualität und überzeugenden Funktionalität.

DuraStyle
Bathroom Series
Badserie

Manufacturer
Duravit AG,
Hornberg, Germany
Design
Matteo Thun & Partners
(Matteo Thun),
Milan, Italy
Web
www.duravit.com
www.matteothun.com

Individuality is important, but does not mean to stand out by any means. The design of DuraStyle shows deliberate restraint. Unmistakable in its formal simplicity, it brings a feeling of clarity and tranquillity into the bathroom. The combination of light and dark décor and wooden tones makes for an exciting contrast. A striking hallmark of the bathtub is an upstand on the side adjoining the wall. It creates order and makes getting in and out of the bath comfortable for all generations.

Individualität ist wichtig, bedeutet aber nicht, mit allen Mitteln aufzufallen. Das Design von DuraStyle zeigt sich bewusst zurückhaltend. In seiner formalen Schlichtheit unverwechselbar, sorgt es für Klarheit und Ruhe im Bad. Dabei schafft die Kombination von hellen sowie dunklen Dekors und Holztönen zusätzliche Spannung. Markantes Markenzeichen der Wanne ist eine Aufkantung am rückseitigen Rand, die Ordnung schafft und gleichzeitig generationenfreundlich und komfortabel das Ein- und Aussteigen unterstützt.

Statement by the jury
DuraStyle is notable for its expressive design details, but it still fits easily into different environments and can be used both in private spaces as well as for architectural projects.

Begründung der Jury
DuraStyle fällt auf durch ausdrucksstarke gestalterische Details, fügt sich aber dennoch bestens in das jeweilige architektonische Umfeld ein und kann zudem sowohl im Projekt- als auch im Privatbereich verwendet werden.

Happy D.2
Bathroom Series
Badserie

Manufacturer
Duravit AG,
Hornberg, Germany
Design
sieger design GmbH & Co. KG
(Christian Sieger, Michael Sieger),
Sassenberg, Germany
Web
www.duravit.com
www.sieger-design.com

The consistent geometric shape as well as the concise, minimised rim are the unifying design features of the Happy D.2 bathroom range. Its basic shape is symmetrical. All pieces offer spacious inner volumes framed by a fine, circumferential rim. The ceramic elements take up the principle of the compact exterior geometry while the bathtub's gentle transition from the rim to the inside and an optimal incline ensure users can lie in a comfortable position and enjoy a maximum degree of well-being.

Verbindendes Designmerkmal der Badserie Happy D.2 ist die durchgängige Geometrie sowie der prägnante, minimierte Rand. In der Grundform symmetrisch bietet sich so ein großzügiges Innenvolumen, das von einem feinen, umlaufenden Rand eingefasst ist. Die Keramiken greifen das Prinzip der kompakten Außengeometrie auf. Bei den Wannen sorgen der sanfte Übergang vom Wannenrand nach innen und die bequeme Liegeposition durch die optimale Rückenschräge für maximalen Wohlfühlkomfort.

Statement by the jury
A gentle shape with characteristic formal details give Happy D.2 a clear, restrained, but nonetheless striking appearance.

Begründung der Jury
Eine weiche Formgebung mit charakteristischen formalen Details sorgt bei Happy D.2 für eine klare, zurückhaltende und gleichermaßen markante Anmutung.

Bathroom furnishings

Dragon Series
Bathroom Accessories
Badezimmeraccessoires

Manufacturer
Shengtai Brassware Co., Ltd.,
Changhua, Taiwan
In-house design
JUSTIME Design Team
Web
www.justime.com

The appearance of the Dragon Series bathroom accessories is one of clean lines and a distinctive form that is strictly determined by function. This gives bathrooms an atmosphere of elegance and sophistication. The accessories are manufactured by aluminium extrusion, which not only increases their precision and stability during use, but, thanks to the seamless shape, also makes them easy to clean.

Statement by the jury
Elements of this luxuriously appointed series such as the hand towel or toilet paper holder are an asset and an attractive eye-catcher in any bathroom.

Die Gestaltung der Badezimmeraccessoires der Dragon-Serie ist von klaren Linien und einer markanten Form geprägt, die strikt ihrer Funktion folgt. Dadurch wird Badräumen eine Atmosphäre von Eleganz und Hochwertigkeit verliehen. Die Accessoires wurden im Aluminium-Strangpressverfahren hergestellt, was nicht nur die Präzision und Stabilität der Produkte im Gebrauch erhöht, sondern dank einer nahtlosen Formgebung sind sie auch leicht zu reinigen.

Begründung der Jury
Die Elemente dieser luxuriös anmutenden Serie, wie Handtuchhalter oder Toilettenpapierhalter, sind eine Bereicherung und attraktiver Blickfang für jedes Badezimmer.

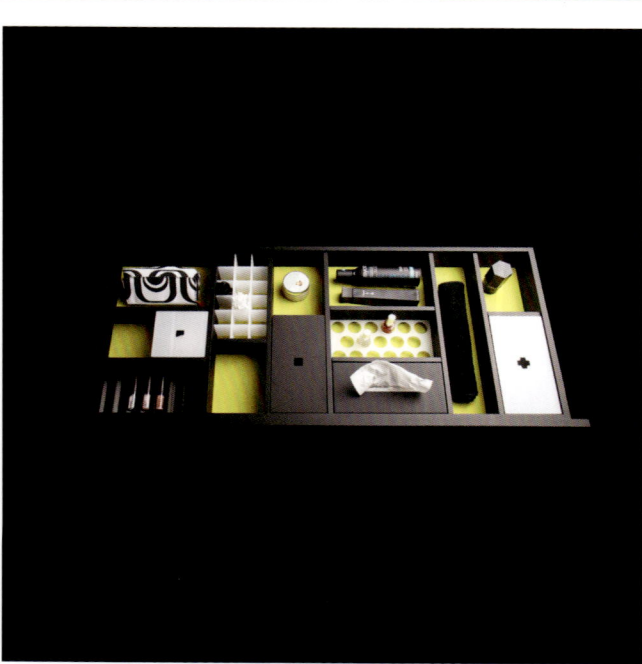

iBOX
Drawer Interior
for Bathroom Furniture
Schubladensystem
für Badmöbel

Manufacturer
cap. GmbH,
Hüllhorst, Germany
In-house design
Freimut Stehling
Web
www.cap-direct.de

The interior of bathroom furniture drawers is often subject to a rigid system. iBOX, on the other hand, leaves room for variety. The principle is simple: a steel plate with a textile cover is fitted to the base of the drawer. The drawer is sub-divided with wooden transverse and longitudinal dividers that are equipped with magnets. This achieves a sturdy yet changeable connection. Users insert the dividers according to their own requirements.

Statement by the jury
Thanks to the variable division of the space and the generous selection of materials, iBOX is a storage system for bathroom drawers that unites clarity and versatility.

Das Innenleben von Badmöbelschubladen ist meist einem starren Schema unterworfen. iBOX hingegen lässt Vielfalt zu. Das Prinzip ist einfach: Im Boden der Schublade befindet sich unter der Textilabdeckung eine Stahlplatte. Die Aufteilung der Lade erfolgt mit Quer- und Längsteilern aus Holz, welche mit Magneten ausgestattet sind. So entsteht eine feste und dennoch variable Verbindung. Der Nutzer setzt die Teiler seinem Gebrauch entsprechend ein.

Begründung der Jury
Dank einer variablen Unterteilung und einer großzügigen Materialauswahl ist iBOX ein Aufbewahrungssystem für Badmöbelschubladen, das Klarheit und Vielfältigkeit verbindet.

Kollengass Anno 1740
Washing Board
Waschbrett

Manufacturer
Schreinerei Tempel,
Wiesemscheid, Germany
Design
Jan Keller,
Werkstätten für Wohnraumgestaltung,
Kempenich, Germany
Web
www.schreinerei-tempel.com
www.jankeller.info
Honourable Mention

The washing board Kollengass Anno 1740 is as "durable as an ancient oak". The heartwood is obtained from the dismantling of old timbered houses. This is what gives each washing table its unique structure and colour shade. The timbers are hand-brushed with great craftsmanship and their natural structure is brought to the fore with a special sealing finish. The water supply and drains are covered and, in combination with its wall mounting, make the washing table appear to float.

Statement by the jury
This washing table has an air of timelessness. Each one is unique thanks to the materials used and the advanced manufacturing techniques.

„Beständig wie eine alte Eiche" ist das Waschbrett Kollengass Anno 1740. Aus dem Rückbau alter Fachwerkhäuser wird das Kernholz gewonnen, das jedem Waschtisch seine eigene Struktur und Farbnuance verleiht. Mit hoher handwerklicher Kunst werden die Holzbalken gebürstet und durch eine spezielle Versiegelung wird ihre natürliche Struktur hervorgehoben. Die verdeckten Zu- und Abläufe sowie die Wandmontage lassen den Waschtisch förmlich schweben.

Begründung der Jury
Einen Hauch von Zeitlosigkeit verbreitet dieser Waschtisch. Dank des verwendeten Materials und des ausgefeilten Herstellungsverfahrens ist jedes Exemplar ein Unikat.

Allure Aquastripe
Bath Collection
Badkollektion

Manufacturer
Grohe AG,
Düsseldorf, Germany
In-house design
Web
www.grohe.com

Aquastripe is an extension of the Allure collection that provides a practical and attractive storage solution in a harmonious form and function. At the origin of this idea was the need for more space to store cosmetics and bathroom products close at hand while finding a solution that would also provide a temporary resting place for watches and jewellery. The simple striped form incorporates all the Allure elements while the classic metal appearance enhances the whole wash basin area. The variable lengths and invisible wall mounting allow individual solutions for every bathroom.

Als Erweiterung der Allure-Kollektion entstand mit Aquastripe eine praktische und attraktive Ablagelösung, die Form und Funktion harmonisch verbindet. Ausgangspunkt war der Wunsch der Nutzer nach mehr Platz für die griffbereite Aufbewahrung von Kosmetik- und Badprodukten genauso wie für die zeitweilige Ablage von Uhren und Schmuck. Die schlichte Streifenform bindet alle Allure-Elemente ein und wertet mit ihrer edlen Metalloptik den gesamten Waschtischbereich auf. Dabei gewährleisten die variablen Längen und die unsichtbare Wandbefestigung individuelle Lösungen für jede Badsituation.

Statement by the jury
Allure Aquastripe adds a touch of elegance, unparalleled order and neatness to every bathroom.

Begründung der Jury
Allure Aquastripe bringt Eleganz ins Bad und sorgt für eine unübertroffene Ordnung und Übersichtlichkeit.

Acrobat Junior
Toothbrush
Zahnbürste

Manufacturer
Banat Firca ve Plastik San. A.S.,
Istanbul, Turkey
Design
Kilit Tasi Tasarim Mimarlik Ltd Sti
(Kunter Sekercioglu, Ozum Ozkan),
Istanbul, Turkey
Web
www.banat.com.tr
www.kilittasi.com

Acrobat Junior is a new generation
of toothbrushes for paediatric dental
hygiene. Its innovative split-body design
means it can be positioned neatly and
tidily on the rim of the toothbrush
mug. This not only keeps the wash basin
area tidy, but also promotes hygiene.
Acrobat Junior's lightweight split body
looks like a standing clown in order to
make toothbrushing more appealing to
children.

Acrobat Junior ist eine neue Generation
von Zahnbürsten für die pädiatrische
Zahnhygiene. Dank des innovativen Split-
Body-Designs kann die Bürste ordentlich
und sauber auf dem Rand des Zahnputz-
bechers aufgesteckt werden. Dies sorgt
nicht nur für Übersicht auf dem Waschbecken, sondern dient auch der Hygiene.
Acrobat Junior's leichtgewichtiger, geteilter
Split-Body-Körper hat das Aussehen eines
stehenden Clowns, um das Zähneputzen
für Kinder attraktiver zu machen.

Statement by the jury
The unmistakable shape and functional
qualities of Acrobat Junior make it an
ideal toothbrush for children.

Begründung der Jury
Unverwechselbar in der Form und funktional im Gebrauch ist Acrobat Junior ein
idealer Hygieneartikel für Kinder.

Travel Box for Denture Brushes
Reisebox für Prothesenbürsten

Manufacturer
PS Product Services GmbH,
Sankt Augustin, Germany
Design
PS-Team
Web
www.product-services.de

The high functionality and purist modern design of this travel box for denture brushes set it apart. A key design element is the subtle transition from the smoothly polished, translucent polypropylene surface to the roughened sides, which make it easy to grip the box even with damp hands. Integrated ventilation holes allow any remaining moisture to escape. Three cleverly placed bridges inside the box keep the brush firmly in place.

Die Reisebox für Prothesenbürsten zeichnet sich durch hohe Funktionalität gepaart mit puristisch-moderner Gestaltung aus. Ein wesentliches Design-Element ist der dezente Übergang von der glatt polierten transluzenten Polypropylenoberfläche zu den erosiv rauen Seiten, durch welche die Box auch mit feuchten Händen gut zu greifen ist. Die integrierten Belüftungslöcher dienen dem Entweichen der Restfeuchte. Durch drei geschickt platzierte Stege im Inneren liegt die Bürste fest in der Box.

Statement by the jury
This sturdy, functionally well thought-out travel box is an extremely practical accessory for the hygienic storage of denture brushes.

Begründung der Jury
Diese stabile, funktional durchdachte Box ist ein äußerst praktisches Accessoire für die hygienische Aufbewahrung von Prothesenbürsten.

ReAura SC5000
Laser Treatment Appliance
Laserbehandlungsgerät

Manufacturer
Royal Philips Electronics,
Eindhoven, Netherlands
In-house design
Philips Design Consumer Lifestyle Team
Web
www.philips.com

Philips ReAura is an innovative laser treatment appliance with anti-aging technology for use at home. Incorporating the same Fraxel laser technology used by professionals, it stimulates the natural cell-renewal process of skin. Fine lines are reduced, skin tones are evened out and tissues appear smoother. Its compact, ergonomic shape and simple user interface with light and sound feedback give the appliance a smooth and reassuring appearance.

Philips ReAura ist ein innovatives Gerät zur Laserbehandlung zu Hause mit einzigartiger Anti-Aging-Technologie. Es arbeitet mit der gleichen Fraxel-Lasertechnologie, die bei professionellen Behandlungen zum Einsatz kommt, und stimuliert den natürlichen Zellerneuerungsprozess der Haut. Feine Linien werden reduziert, Hauttöne ausgeglichen und Gewebe geglättet. Durch die kompakte, ergonomische Form und die einfache Benutzeroberfläche mit Licht- und Sound-Feedback wirkt das Gerät sanft und beruhigend.

Statement by the jury
An innovative design has succeeded in making professional technology available for everyday, private use.

Begründung der Jury
Durch eine innovative Gestaltung gelingt es hier, eine professionelle Technik im privaten Alltag verfügbar zu machen.

ELLE by Beurer HLE 30
Lady Shaver
Damenrasierer

Manufacturer
Beurer GmbH,
Ulm, Germany
Design
uli schade industriedesign
(Matthias Kolb),
Neu-Ulm, Germany
Web
www.beurer.de
www.schadedesign.de

This lady shaver can be used for dry as well as wet shaving in the shower. Its flexible razor head follows body contours, while the extra bright LED light helps to ensure thorough hair removal. An illuminated on/off switch indicates the operating status of the device. Hair can also be cut to a predetermined length using the integrated trimmer and two additional comb attachments.

Dieser Damenrasierer kann sowohl für die Trocken- als auch für die Nassrasur unter der Dusche verwendet werden. Dank dem flexiblen Scherkopf passt sich das Gerät der individuellen Körperkontur an. Das extra-helle LED-Licht unterstützt die sorgfältige Haarentfernung. Zusätzlich zeigt der beleuchtete An-/Aus-Schalter den Betriebsstatus an. Mittels des integrierten Trimmers und den zwei Kammaufsätzen lassen sich darüber hinaus auch Haare auf eine gezielte Länge kürzen.

Statement by the jury
The ELLE by Beurer HLE 30 lady shaver is an extremely handy appliance for guaranteed, perfect hair removal.

Begründung der Jury
Der Damenrasierer HLE 30 von ELLE by Beurer ist ein ausgesprochen handliches Gerät, das eine perfekte Haarentfernung gewährleistet.

CoolTec
Electric Shaver
Elektrorasierer

Manufacturer
Braun GmbH,
Kronberg im Taunus, Germany
In-house design
Braun Design Team
Web
www.braun.com

A switch with a snowflake? A simple, graphic symbol embodies the technical innovation: CoolTec is the shaver that cools the skin during a dry shave. As soon as the cooling function is activated the integrated Peltier element lowers the temperature of the aluminium strip in the shaver head to around five degrees centigrade, pleasantly cooling the skin during shaving and reducing skin irritation.

Ein Schalter mit einem Eiskristall? Ein einfaches grafisches Symbol visualisiert die technische Innovation: CoolTec ist der Rasierer, der während der Trockenrasur kühlt. Aktiviert man die Kühlfunktion, wird die Temperatur der Aluminiumleiste im Rasiererkopf durch das integrierte Peltier-Element auf etwa fünf Grad Celsius reduziert. Dies erfrischt die Haut während der Rasur und verringert Hautirritationen.

Statement by the jury
CoolTec is notable for its innovative technology, which is visually underlined by the metallic ice-blue of the appliance and the snowflake on the additional switch.

Begründung der Jury
CoolTec überzeugt durch seine innovative Technik, die durch das metallische Eisblau des Gerätes und das Eiskristall auf dem zusätzlichen Schalter auch visuell akzentuiert wird.

Bathroom accessories

Satin Hair 7
Hair Straightener
Haarglätter

Manufacturer
Braun GmbH,
Kronberg im Taunus, Germany
In-house design
Braun Design Team
Web
www.braun.com
Honourable Mention

Thanks to its automatic heat control, this intelligent hair straightener styles hair perfectly while providing optimal heat protection. Two sensors react twenty times a second, analysing the hair's moisture content and actively adjusting the temperature accordingly. This hair straightener is very easy to use. Once personal information has been stored, it is no longer necessary to regulate the temperature manually when styling. This innovative technology is embodied in the integrated, functional design and the user interface that is reduced to one central element.

Dieser intelligente Haarglätter sorgt durch automatische Temperaturanpassung für perfektes Styling bei optimalem Hitze-schutz. Zwei Sensoren reagieren 20-mal pro Sekunde, um den Feuchtigkeitsgehalt im Haar zu analysieren und so die aktive Temperaturanpassung zu ermöglichen. Der Haarglätter ist dadurch außergewöhnlich leicht zu benutzen. Einmal personalisiert, entfällt das manuelle Regulieren der Temperatur während des Stylens. Erlebbar wird die innovative Technologie durch das integrierte, funktionale Design und das auf ein zentrales Element reduzierte Bedien-konzept.

Statement by the jury
Innovative technology comes into its own through incredibly simple, intuitive handling.

Begründung der Jury
Die innovative Technologie kommt hier in einer ausgesprochen einfachen, intuitiven Handhabung zur Geltung.

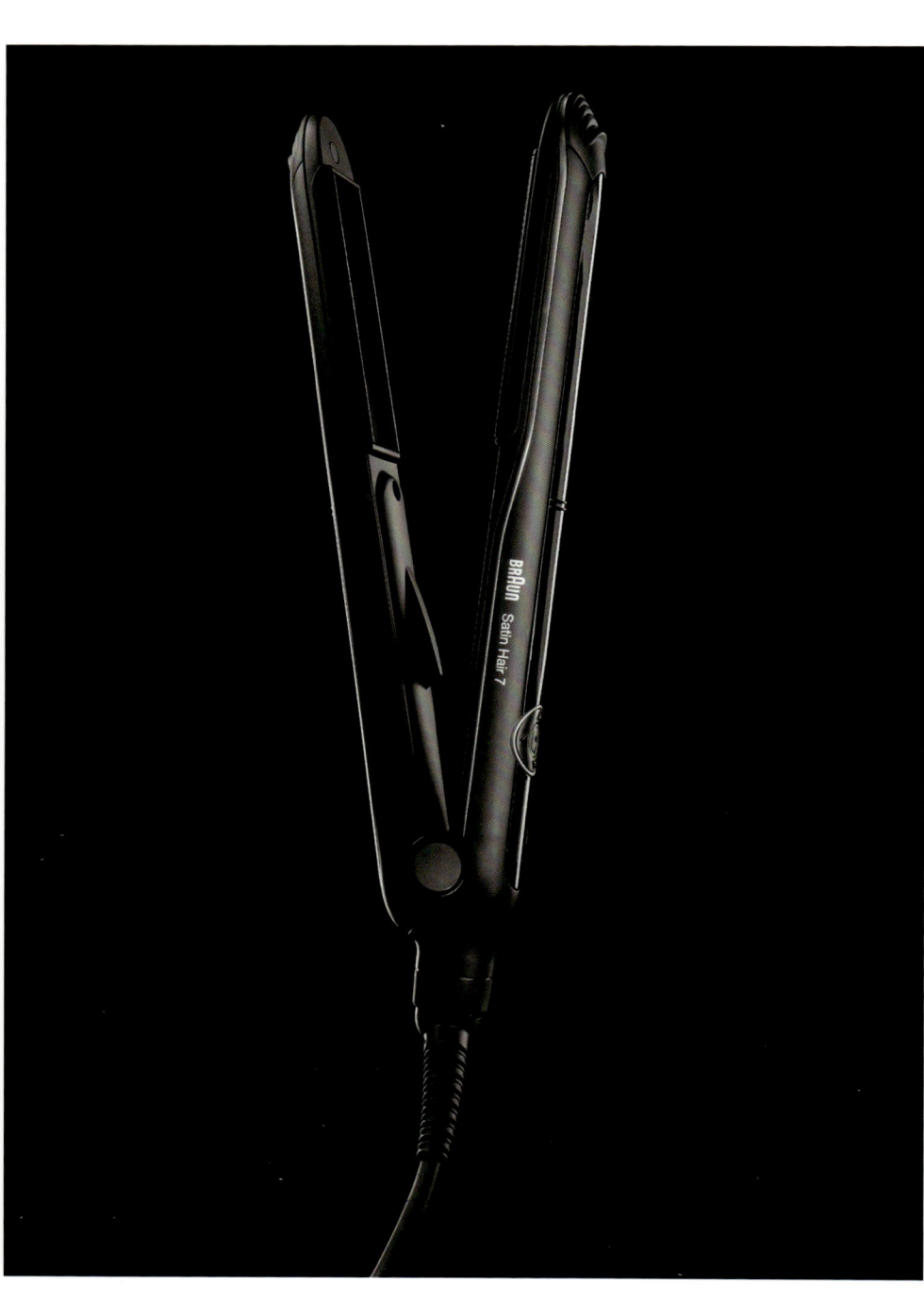

BrilliantCare Quattro-Ion
Hair Care Appliances
Haarpflege-Geräte

Manufacturer
Robert Bosch Hausgeräte GmbH,
Munich, Germany
In-house design
Yvonne Weisbarth,
Helmut Kaiser
Web
www.bosch-hausgeraete.de

The hair care appliances of the BrilliantCare Quattro-Ion range combine innovative technology and perfect ergonomics. Quattro-Ion technology's four separate ion outlets produce a very wide stream of ions that surrounds the hair from all sides and reduces static. A red LED light strip indicates whether ionisation is in progress and also accentuates the design of the device. Particular care was taken in regard to the design of the handle to ensure that all controls can be managed equally well by left- and right-handed users. Non-slip surfaces and an even weight distribution ensure comfortable use even over longer periods of time.

Die Haarpflege-Geräte der BrilliantCare Quattro-Ion-Linie überzeugen durch innovative Technik und perfekte Ergonomie. Die Quattro-Ion-Technologie schafft durch vier getrennte Ionen-Auslässe einen extra breiten Ionenstrom, der das Haar von allen Seiten umhüllt und statische Aufladung reduziert. Eine rote LED-Lichtleiste an den Geräten visualisiert, ob die Ionisation aktiv ist und akzentuiert das Gerätedesign. Dabei wurde der Gestaltung der Griffbereiche besondere Aufmerksamkeit geschenkt. Alle Bedienelemente sind sowohl für Links- als auch für Rechtshänder optimal zu erreichen. Antirutsch-Oberflächen und eine ausgewogene Gewichtsverteilung erlauben eine angenehme Nutzung auch über längere Zeiträume.

Statement by the jury
This range of hair care tools is impressive, above all, for its stringent focus on functionality and ergonomics.

Begründung der Jury
Diese Serie von Haarpflege-Geräten beeindruckt vor allem durch ihre stringente Ausrichtung an Funktionalität und Ergonomie.

Varioline (Special Edition)
Sauna Cabin
Saunakabine

Manufacturer
Saunalux GmbH
Products & Co. KG,
Grebenhain, Germany

Design
bittermann industriedesign
(Jochen Bittermann),
Gelnhausen, Germany

Web
www.saunalux.de
www.bittermann-design.de

reddot design award
best of the best 2013

Pure joy

"Room made of wood" is the literal translation of the Finnish word for "sauna", a word that in itself refers to the living tradition of sweating in a simple wooden shack. Taking a sauna is good for the health and reconnects human beings with the basic and natural elements of water and heat. The design of the Varioline sauna cabin represents a convincing expression of the maxim of relaxation and closeness to nature. The cabin's clear lines are defined by a combination of high-quality materials, including Rohol genuine-veneer nut-tree panels, and are complemented by a generously dimensioned whole glass front that extends around the front edges, forming part of the left and right side walls and lending the sauna cabin a light and spacious appearance. A floor covered with Mosa stone-tiles in black and indirect lightning in the ceiling create a luxurious and warm ambience. Functionally sophisticated details such as a comfortably adjustable middle-bank, a wheeled box for wood as well as the wooden-heated sauna stove, which can be rotated through 360 degrees, convey to sauna enthusiasts the sensations of peace and inner balance. A sauna cabin thus transforms into a lifestyle space that is inspired consistently in form and function by the origins of the traditional sauna experience.

Pures Vergnügen

„Raum aus Holz" lautet die Übersetzung des finnischen Wortes „Sauna". Diese Bedeutung verweist auf die lebendige Tradition des Schwitzens in einer einfachen hölzernen Hütte. Saunieren ist gesundheitsfördernd und führt den Menschen auf einfache und natürliche Dinge wie Wasser und Wärme zurück. Die Gestaltung der Saunakabine Varioline ist ein überzeugend zeitgemäßer Ausdruck dieser Maximen von Ruhe und Naturbezogenheit. In klaren Linien verbinden sich hochwertige Materialien wie Rohol-Nussbaum-Echtholzfurnier mit einer großzügig dimensionierten Ganzglasfront. Diese Glasfront erstreckt sich weit über die beiden Seitenwände der Kabine hinaus und lässt den Saunaraum luftig und großzügig erscheinen. Im Inneren der Kabine schaffen eine Ausstattung aus schwarzen Mosa-Steinfliesen und eine indirekte Beleuchtung des Daches ein luxuriöses und zugleich warm anmutendes Ambiente. Funktional ausgefeilte Details wie eine komfortabel verschiebbare Mittelbank, ein fahrbarer Holzbehälter sowie ein um 360 Grad drehbarer, holzbeheizter Saunaofen vermitteln dem Saunagänger die Gefühle von Ausgeglichenheit und Ruhe. Eine Saunakabine wird hier zu einem Ort des Lifestyles, der formal wie funktional stimmig an die Ursprünge des natürlichen Saunierens anknüpft.

Statement by the jury

The Varioline sauna cabin fascinates with its clear lines. Well-crafted in every detail, the sauna combines high-quality wood with generous glass surfaces. The highly functional interior places the stove in the middle of the space, defining this sauna cabin as a place for social gathering. It invites users to relax in peace while enjoying the sauna's formal beauty.

Begründung der Jury

Die Saunakabine Varioline begeistert durch klare Linien. Ihre bis ins Detail ausgearbeitete Gestaltung vereint hochwertige Hölzer mit luxuriösen Glasflächen. Sehr funktional ist im Interieur die Platzierung der Feuerstelle in der Mitte, was diese Saunakabine als Ort des sozialen Miteinanders definiert. Der Nutzer kann sich entspannen und die Schönheit der Formen genießen.

Saunas

Infrared Thermal Cabin
Infrarotwärmekabine

Manufacturer
Saunalux GmbH Products & Co. KG,
Grebenhain, Germany
In-house design
Jochen Bittermann
Web
www.saunalux.de

Selected noble woods characterise the modern design of the novus infrared cabin. The clear glass front gives the cabin its airy appearance, suffused with light. The harmonious interior offers perfect comfort while the cutting-edge control system can be managed both from in- and outside. An integrated LED panel produces balanced white light. Atmospheric LED colour lighting is available for a surcharge.

Edle und ausgesuchte Hölzer bestimmen das moderne Design der Infrarotkabine novus. Die Vorderfront aus Klarglas gibt der Kabine ihre leichte, lichtdurchflutete Optik. Die harmonische Inneneinrichtung überzeugt durch ihren perfekten Komfort. Die hochmoderne Regelung kann sowohl von innen als auch von außen betätigt werden. Die integrierte LED-Leiste sorgt für ein ausgewogenes Weißlicht, optional ist ein stimmungsvolles LED-Farblicht integrierbar.

Statement by the jury
novus makes you feel good. Its elegant appearance and range of features are enough to satisfy even the most demanding customer.

Begründung der Jury
Hier fühlt man sich wohl! novus begeistert durch das elegante Erscheinungsbild und die Ausstattung, die kaum Wünsche offenlässt.

Saunas

Concept R
Sauna Heater
Saunaofen

Manufacturer
sentiotec GmbH,
Regau, Austria
In-house design
Markus Puchegger
Design
dbgp design büro groiss peter
(Peter Groiss),
Laakirchen, Austria
Web
www.sentiotec.com
www.dbgp.at

The sauna heater is at the heart of any sauna system. This is why Concept R – "R" stands for rounded edges – can be viewed from four sides, so that the sauna heater can be placed anywhere in the room. Its inner workings are also unusual. The three-casing technology used and the optional wooden railing offer maximum protection against accidental contact and burns. A removable junction box and electronic cover protection to avoid sauna fires complete the technology package.

Statement by the jury
Its innovative, practical technology and high-quality craftsmanship make Concept R the sauna heater for those with particularly high standards.

Ein Saunaofen ist das Herzstück einer Saunaanlage, weshalb Concept R – „R" steht für runde Ecken – vier Sichtseiten besitzt, welche es ermöglichen, den Saunaofen frei im Raum zu platzieren. Auch das Innenleben ist außergewöhnlich. Die angewendete 3-Mantel-Technik und die optionale Holzreling bieten maximalen Berührungs- und Verbrennungsschutz. Ein herausnehmbarer Anschlusskasten und ein elektronischer Abdeckschutz, um Saunabränden vorzubeugen, komplettieren die Technik.

Begründung der Jury
Die innovative, praktikable Technik und hochwertige Verarbeitung machen Concept R zu einem Saunaofen für besondere Ansprüche.

Aerogor
Heat Pump
Wärmepumpe

Manufacturer
Gorenje d.d.,
Velenje, Slovenia
In-house design
Gorenje Design Studio d.o.o.
(Anton Holobar, Blaž Prestor)
Web
www.gorenje.com
www.gorenjedesignstudio.com

The Aerogor heat pump uses ambient air to provide environmentally friendly, energy- and cost-efficient heating. It consists of both an interior and exterior unit. The exterior unit is placed outdoors to take in ambient air and extract its energy using an evaporator. This energy can be used by the interior unit for heating in winter and cooling in summer. Installation of the exterior unit is quick and easy. Thanks to the well thought-out structure of the exterior unit and the ability to customise the side panels of the heating unit, Aerogor easily fits into any environment.

Statement by the jury
Shape, choice of materials and technical competence come together to create a successful product that stands for energy efficiency and sustainability.

Die Wärmepumpe Aerogor nutzt Umgebungsluft für umweltverträgliches, energiesparendes und kostengünstiges Heizen. Sie besteht aus einer Außen- und einer Inneneinheit. Die Außeneinheit wird im Freien platziert, wo sie die Außenluft aufnimmt und ihr mit einem Verdampfer Energie entzieht, welche die Inneneinheit im Winter zum Heizen und im Sommer zum Kühlen verwendet. Die Außeneinheit wird einfach und schnell aufgestellt. Durch die durchdachte Struktur der Außeneinheit und die Anpassungsmöglichkeit der Seitenwände der Heizeinheit fügt sich Aerogor gut in das jeweilige Umfeld ein.

Begründung der Jury
Formgebung, Materialeinsatz und technische Kompetenz verbinden sich hier zu einem gelungenen Produkt, das für Energieeffizienz und Nachhaltigkeit steht.

Anna by Stadler Form
Anna von Stadler Form

Fan Heater
Heizlüfter

Manufacturer
Stadler Form Aktiengesellschaft,
Zug, Switzerland
In-house design
Matti Walker
Web
www.stadlerform.ch

With its refined zinc base, this slim
fan heater shows a discreet appearance.
Its finely structured grid conceals
the underlying technology. Thus,
Anna harmoniously fits in any home
environment. The desired temperature
can be infinitely adjusted thanks to
an integrated thermostat. The quiet,
energy-efficient fan heater switches
off as soon as the desired temperature
is reached; it automatically switches
on when the temperature is dropping.

Statement by the jury
The high functionality of this fan heater
unites with an unobtrusive design that
focuses on clear lines and material
effects.

Der schlanke Heizlüfter vermittelt mit
seinem edlen Zinkfuß ein dezentes
Erscheinungsbild. Sein fein strukturiertes Gitter macht die Technik unsichtbar,
wodurch sich Anna harmonisch in jede
Wohnumgebung einfügt. Die gewünschte
Raumtemperatur ist mittels integriertem
Thermostat stufenlos einstellbar. Der leise
und energiesparsame Heizlüfter schaltet
sich aus, sobald die gewünschte Temperatur erreicht ist und bei Temperaturabfall
automatisch wieder ein.

Begründung der Jury
Die hohe Funktionalität des Heizlüfters
verbindet sich mit einer unaufdringlichen
Formensprache, die auf klare Linien und
Materialeffekte setzt.

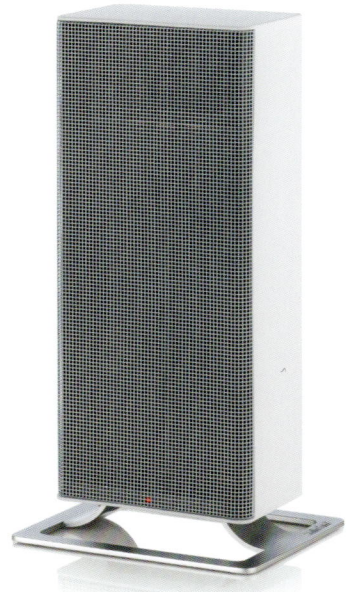

L-Style
Air Conditioner
Klimaanlage

Manufacturer
LG Electronics Inc.,
Seoul, South Korea
In-house design
In-Hyeuk Choi, Myung-Sik Kim,
Hee-Jae Kwon, Sang-Moon Jeong
Web
www.lg.com

Interior design today places great
emphasis on installing heating and air
conditioning equipment as discreetly as
possible, if not trying to hide them. This
also applies to commercial spaces. The
shape of this air conditioner meets these
requirements perfectly. The air inlet and
outlet grilles are arranged in a straight
line, thereby creating a clear, modern
design that also enhances performance.
The air conditioner is eminently suited to
cafes and restaurants, helping them to
achieve an elegant atmosphere.

Statement by the jury
This professional air conditioner
distinguishes itself thanks to its
distinctive, stylish appearance and
excellent performance.

Bei der Innenausstattung kommt es heute
auch im gewerblichen Bereich mehr denn
je darauf an, Heizungs- und Klimageräte
möglichst unauffällig und versteckt zu installieren. Die Formgebung dieser Klimaanlage erfüllt solche Anforderungen vorzüglich. Luftauslass und Lufteinlass wurden
in einer geraden Linie angeordnet, sodass
ein klares, modernes Design entsteht, das
zudem die Performance unterstützt. Das
Gerät fügt sich perfekt in die Einrichtung
von Cafés und Restaurants ein und verbreitet eine elegante Atmosphäre.

Begründung der Jury
Dieses professionelle Klimagerät zeichnet sich durch sein charakteristisches,
stilsicheres Erscheinungsbild und seine
exzellente Leistung aus.

Scape DBE
Low-Temperature Radiator
Niedrigtemperatur-Heizkörper

Manufacturer
Jaga nv,
Diepenbeek, Belgium
In-house design
Wim Grommen, Ivo Nysten
Web
www.theradiatorfactory.com

This low-temperature radiator is based on a modular system in "monobloc" design. Despite the use of only one aluminium extrusion profile, every radiator has a very individual appearance. The profile is different on the front and back and can be used horizontally or vertically. The connection between the profiles is seamless and invisible while the thermostat and DBE controls are hidden behind the removable side panel.

Statement by the jury
Scape DBE's refined method of construction is convincing. What is more, its innovative technology provides exceptional heat output.

Dieser Niedrigtemperatur-Heizkörper beruht auf einem modularen System im „Monoblock"-Design. Trotz des Einsatzes von nur einem Aluminium-Strangpressprofil erhält so jeder Heizkörper ein individuelles Aussehen. Das Profil mit seiner unterschiedlichen Vorder- und Rückseite kann horizontal oder vertikal verwendet werden. Die Verbindung zwischen den einzelnen Profilen erfolgt nahtlos und unsichtbar. Thermostat und DBE-Bedienelement befinden sich hinter dem abnehmbaren Seitenteil.

Begründung der Jury
Scape DBE überzeugt durch seine raffinierte Konstruktionsweise. Die innovative Technik sorgt zudem für eine außergewöhnliche Wärmeleistung.

ULOW E2
Low-Temperature Radiator with E2 Technology
Tieftemperatur-Heizkörper mit E2-Technologie

Manufacturer
Rettig Austria GmbH,
VOGEL&NOOT,
Wartberg, Austria
Design
LM-Design GmbH
(Manfred Lechner),
Mürzzuschlag, Austria
Web
www.vogelundnoot.com
www.lm-design.at

This radiator with E2 technology uses a unique concept to put into practice efficient, low-temperature heat emission. What is special is the use of ventilators to enhance natural convection in conjunction with an intelligent control system that switches between static or dynamic operation, either fully automatically or according to the user's requirements. All functions can be managed using the clear touchpad control panel.

Statement by the jury
A stylish design with soft, rounded forms and advanced technology that guarantees outstanding performance and energy efficiency.

Dieser Heizkörper mit E2-Technologie verwirklicht ein einzigartiges Konzept, das Tieftemperatur-Wärmeabgabe effizient ermöglicht. Das Besondere liegt in der Ausstattung mit Ventilatoren zur Unterstützung der natürlichen Konvektion in Verbindung mit einer intelligenten Regelung, die vollautomatisch oder nach Benutzerwünschen zwischen statischem und dynamischem Betrieb wechselt. Alle Funktionen werden über das übersichtliche Touchpad-Bedienfeld abgerufen.

Begründung der Jury
Eine stilvolle Gestaltung mit weichen, runden Formen und fortschrittlichster Technologie gewährleistet hier eine hervorragende Performance und Energieeffizienz.

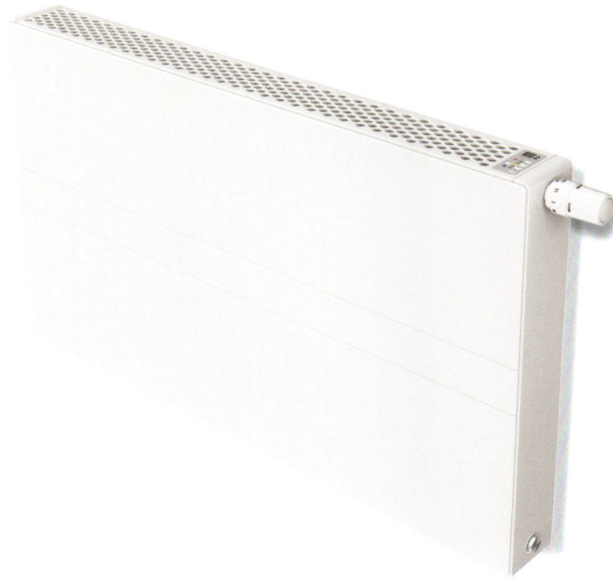

Bi2+
Fan Coil
Ventilatorspirale

Manufacturer
Olimpia Splendid,
Gualtieri (Reggio Emilia), Italy
Design
Beta Engineering
(Dario Tanfoglio),
Roncadelle (Brescia), Italy
Web
www.olimpiasplendid.com
www.betacode.it
Honourable Mention

The idea behind this product was to design a fan coil for residential buildings that was powered by water. Bi2+ offers the advantages of under floor heating, the flexibility of a fan coil and the design of a radiator. With a thickness of only 12.9 cm, Bi2+ provides cooling, dehumidifying, heating and air cleaning. An internationally patented technology allows Bi2+ to combine normal ventilated heating with radiation heating.

Statement by the jury
This inverter fan coil with radiator cover is a multifunctional, cleverly designed appliance with a high degree of efficiency.

Die diesem Produkt zugrunde liegende Idee war, eine durch Wasser gespeiste Ventilatorspirale für Wohngebäude zu entwerfen. Bi2+ bietet die Komfortvorteile einer Fußbodenheizung, die Flexibilität einer Ventilatorspirale und das Design eines Heizkörpers. Bi2+ liefert bei nur 12,9 cm Tiefe Kühlung, Entfeuchtung, Heizung und Luftreinigung. Dank einer international patentierten Technologie kann Bi2+ die normale Belüftungsheizung mit der Strahlungsheizung kombinieren.

Begründung der Jury
Die Inverter-Ventilatorspirale mit Strahlblende präsentiert sich als multifunktionales, klug konzipiertes Gerät mit hohem Wirkungsgrad.

Jaga Freedom
Hybrid Radiator
Hybrid-Heizkörper

Manufacturer
Jaga nv,
Diepenbeek, Belgium
In-house design
James Davis
Web
www.theradiatorfactory.com

The hybrid radiator Jaga Freedom harmoniously combines technology and design. The modular casing is given a slight curve, based on a double-walled profile and made from extruded aluminium. This is what makes the radiator so sturdy and gives it its unique design. Freedom is suitable for heating, cooling and ventilating thanks to a dynamic system of ultra-quiet, energy-efficient micro ventilators.

Statement by the jury
Jaga Freedom's compact, elegant shape is just as impressive as its special technology, which promises the highest level of efficiency and sustainability.

Technologie und Design sind beim Hybrid-Heizkörper Jaga Freedom harmonisch vereint. Das modulartige Gehäuse basiert auf einem leicht wellenförmigen, doppelwandigen Profil aus stranggepresstem Aluminium, welches einen extrem stabilen Heizkörper mit einzigartigem Design bildet. Freedom ist geeignet zum Heizen, Kühlen und Belüften. Dies ist möglich durch ein dynamisches System mit ultraleisen, energieeffizienten Microventilatoren.

Begründung der Jury
Jaga Freedom begeistert durch seine kompakte, elegante Form und seine spezielle Technik, die für höchste Effizienz und Nachhaltigkeit steht.

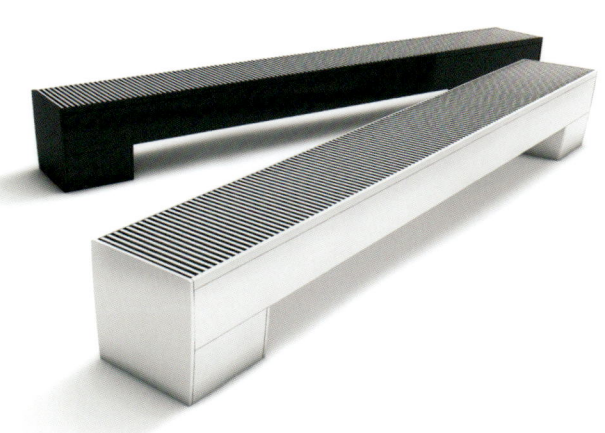

Blueair Sense
Air Purifier
Luftreiniger

Manufacturer
Blueair,
Stockholm, Sweden

Design
Claesson Koivisto Rune,
Stockholm, Sweden

Web
www.blueair.com
www.ckr.se

reddot design award
best of the best 2013

For all the senses

The air that we breathe is filled with microscopic particles and gaseous compounds. Air purifiers are ideal for cleaning the indoor air effectively and quickly of harmful pollutants and allergens for enhanced health and wellbeing. The Blueair Sense air purifier features the patented HEPASilent technology that is both whisper-quiet and low in energy consumption. This technologically sophisticated air purifier possesses a surprisingly sleek appearance that also fascinates beholders with its proportions. Its design presents itself as a harmoniously balanced combination of glass and stainless steel. Thanks to this new language of form and the option of choosing between six different colours, the Blueair Sense air purifier fits well into almost any interior. The sensitive nature of the device's user interface is also innovative: the unique motion-sensitive top allows users to change speeds intuitively with simple hand swipes above the glass surface. The Blueair Sense air purifier thus embodies a symbiotic merger of a new, elegant form vocabulary with a user interface that provides emotional user experiences.

Mit allen Sinnen

Die Luft, die wir atmen, ist angefüllt mit mikroskopisch kleinen Teilchen und Gasstoffen. Luftreiniger sind ideal, um die Innenluft von Räumen effizient und schnell von Schadstoffen und Allergenen zu reinigen und so die Gesundheit und das Wohlergehen zu fördern. Der Luftreiniger Blueair Sense arbeitet mit der patentierten HEPASilent-Technologie, welche die Atemluft sehr leise und auch energiesparend reinigt. Dieser technologisch ausgereifte Luftreiniger hat eine überraschend schlanke Anmutung, die den Betrachter auch durch die Proportionen begeistert. Seine Gestaltung kombiniert die Materialien Glas und Stahl auf eine sehr harmonische Weise. Dank dieser neuen Formensprache und der Möglichkeit, zwischen sechs Farbvarianten wählen zu können, fügt sich der Luftreiniger Blueair Sense gut in jedes Interieur ein. Innovativ ist auch die sensitive Art seiner Bedienung: Indem der Nutzer sachte über eine bewegungsempfindliche Oberfläche streicht, kann er intuitiv die Geschwindigkeit dieses Gerätes einstellen. Die neue, elegante Formensprache des Luftreinigers Blueair Sense verbindet sich so auf symbiotische Weise mit einer den Nutzer emotionalisierenden Bedienoberfläche.

Statement by the jury

The Blueair Sense air purifier fascinates with its sleek appearance and well-balanced radii. Thanks to a variety of different colours, it fits easily into almost any interior. The innovative user interface is pleasing to the touch and makes for a unique experience. The design of device enhances this product genre with an entirely novel quality.

Begründung der Jury

Der Luftreiniger Blueair Sense begeistert durch seine schlanke Gestaltung und seine ausgewogenen Radien. Er passt auch dank vieler Farbvarianten mit Leichtigkeit in jedes Interieur. Die innovative, haptisch sehr angenehme Bedienoberfläche dieses Gerätes ist ein echtes Erlebnis. Design verleiht hier einer Produktgattung völlig neue Qualitäten.

Air-conditioning technology

OXY
Oxygen Generator/ Humidifier
Sauerstoffgenerator/ Luftbefeuchter

Manufacturer
Coway,
Seoul, South Korea
In-house design
Hun-Jung Choi,
Jee-Youn Lee,
Young-Jo Kim
Web
www.coway.com

OXY is both oxygen generator and humidifier in one. The simultaneous supply of moisture and oxygen is particularly beneficial to health. At the same time, OXY is fitted with mood lighting and a wake-up light to rouse the user at a predetermined time. The oxygen generator can either be docked on the main body or can be disconnected and used as a separate unit.

OXY ist sowohl Sauerstoffgenerator als auch Luftbefeuchter. Die kombinierte Abgabe von Feuchtigkeit und Sauerstoff ist besonders gesundheitsfördernd. Zudem ist OXY mit einem Stimmungslicht und Alarmleuchten ausgestattet und kann so programmiert werden, dass man zu einer vorgegebenen Zeit geweckt wird. Der Sauerstoffgenerator kann entweder an das Hauptgehäuse angedockt oder abgenommen und als separate Einheit verwendet werden.

Statement by the jury
OXY is innovative in offering a dual function as oxygen and humidity supply which is beneficial to health and does so as a simple, decorative appliance that will look good in any environment.

Begründung der Jury
Innovativ in seiner Doppelfunktion der Sauerstoff- und Feuchtigkeitsabgabe dient OXY dem allgemeinen Wohlbefinden – und das obendrein als einfaches, dekoratives Gerät für jede Umgebung.

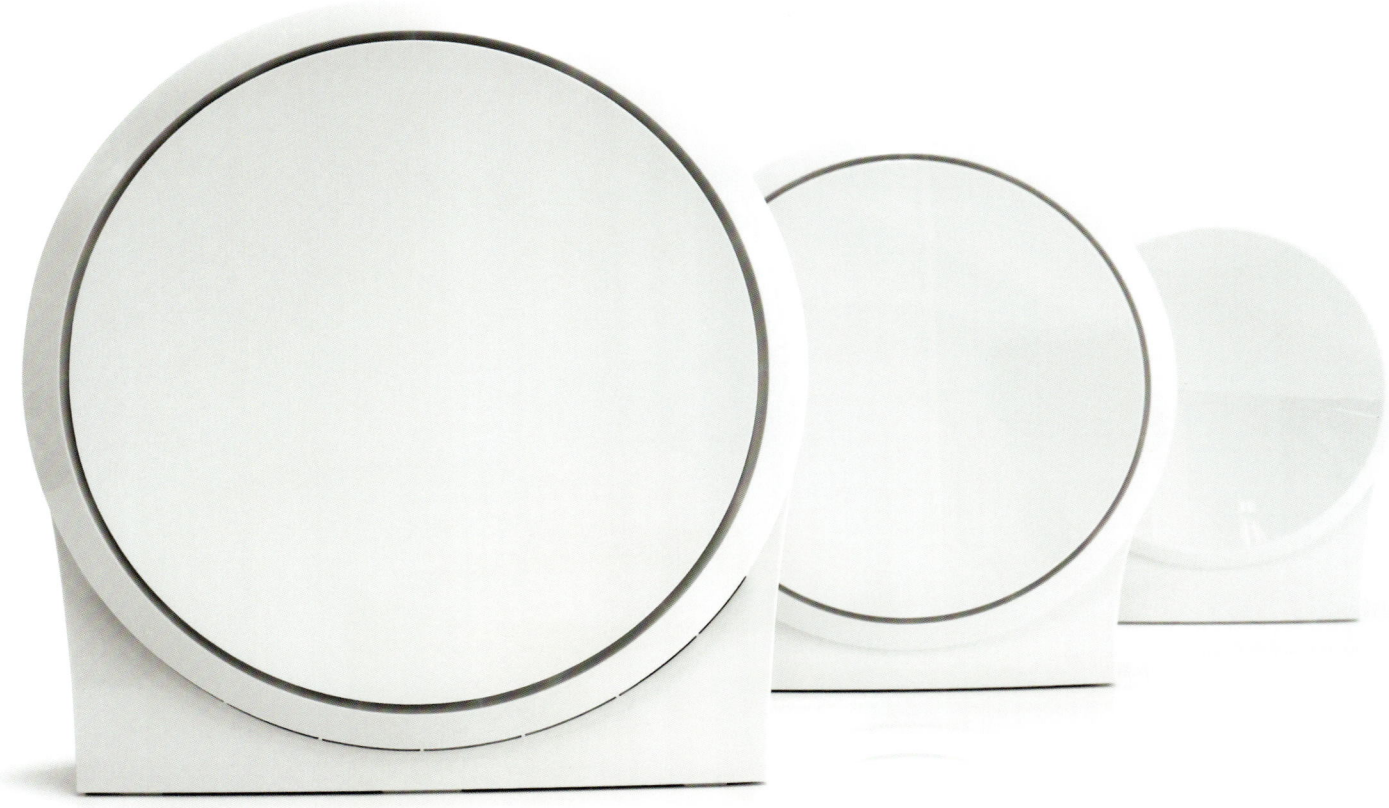

Toshiba CAF-P35/
CAF-KP40X/CAF-KP50X,
KA-P30X/KA-P50X/
KA-P70X
Air Purifier, Humidifier
Luftreiniger, Luftbefeuchter

Manufacturer
Toshiba Home Appliances Corporation,
Tokyo, Japan
In-house design
Takashi Gumisawa,
Motoyuki Suzuki,
Masaaki Sakai
Web
www.toshiba.co.jp
Honourable Mention

This range has been fitted with newly
developed filters in a donut shape.
The main components are all arranged
around a cylindrical core in order to
achieve greater efficiency and greater
compactness. The key aim of the design
was to ensure harmonious integration
into practically any type of interior,
so that the appliances could be placed
anywhere in the room. Their simple,
elegant circular design is supported
by high performance and a minimalist
appearance.

Diese Baureihe ist mit neu entwickelten
Filtern in Donut-Form ausgestattet. Die
wichtigsten Bauteile sind alle um einen
zylindrischen Kern angeordnet, um eine
höhere Effizienz und kompaktere Abmessungen zu erzielen. Bei der Gestaltung lag
der Hauptakzent auf der harmonischen
Anpassung an nahezu jede Art von Interieur, sodass die Geräte überall im Raum
platziert werden können. Das einfache,
elegante Design in Kreisform zeichnet sich
durch hohe Leistung und ein minimalistisches Erscheinungsbild aus.

Statement by the jury
The clean design without any
superfluous components is eye-
catching without being obtrusive.

Begründung der Jury
Die klare, auf überflüssige Elemente ver-
zichtende Gestaltung fällt ins Auge, ohne
aufdringlich zu sein.

Cado AP-C100
Air Purifier
Luftreiniger

Manufacturer
Eclair,
Tokyo, Japan
Design
Cado Inc.
(Ken Suzuki),
Tokyo, Japan
Web
www.product.cado.ne.jp
www.cado.ne.jp

This cylindrical air purifier was developed for the global market. With its discreet colours, it harmoniously blends in with different interiors. Even the air of large rooms can be cleaned efficiently at low-noise despite the compact size of the device's body. Seamlessly processed aluminium underscores the high quality of an air purifier that eliminates harmful substances such as bacteria and mould thanks to the photocatalytic technology.

Der zylinderförmige Luftreiniger wurde für den globalen Markt entwickelt und fügt sich mit seinen dezenten Farben harmonisch in unterschiedliche Interieurs ein. Selbst das Luftvolumen größerer Räume lässt sich trotz der kompakten Korpusgröße effizient und geräuscharm reinigen. Nahtlos verarbeitetes Aluminium unterstreicht die Hochwertigkeit eines Luftreinigers, der mittels photokatalytischer Technologie Schadstoffe wie Bakterien und Schimmel eliminiert.

Statement by the jury
In this air purifier, a corpus of simple elegance hides an innovative product solution that combines functionality with aesthetics.

Begründung der Jury
Ein Korpus von schlichter Eleganz verbirgt bei diesem Luftreiniger eine innovative Produktlösung, die Funktionalität mit Ästhetik verbindet.

Air-conditioning technology

Albert by Stadler Form
Albert von Stadler Form
Dehumidifier
Luftentfeuchter

Manufacturer
Stadler Form Aktiengesellschaft,
Zug, Switzerland
In-house design
Matti Walker
Web
www.stadlerform.ch

This puristic-elegant design concept originates from the idea to create a visually appealing, powerful and user-friendly dehumidifier. The pivotal function of the air outlet provides good air distribution. Thus, it especially facilitates the dehumidification of large rooms. With up to 20 litres per day, Albert quickly and efficiently reaches the desired relative humidity, which can be set by a hygrostat.

Statement by the jury
Rich in contrast, the ergonomically well-devised black operating panel is silhouetted against the plain white corpus of this dehumidifier.

Dieses puristisch-elegante Gestaltungskonzept entstand aus der Idee, einen visuell ansprechenden, leistungsstarken und benutzerfreundlichen Luftentfeuchter zu entwickeln. Die Schwenkfunktion des Luftauslasses sorgt für eine gute Luftverteilung und unterstützt so speziell die Entfeuchtung großer Räume. Mit bis zu 20 Liter Wasser pro Tag erreicht Albert schnell und effizient die gewünschte relative Luftfeuchtigkeit, welche per Hygrostat einstellbar ist.

Begründung der Jury
Kontrastreich hebt sich die ergonomisch durchdachte Bedienblende in Schwarz vom schlichten, weißen Korpus des Luftentfeuchters ab.

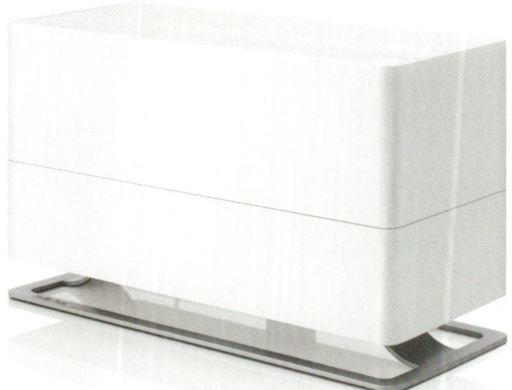

Oskar Big by Stadler Form
Oskar Big von Stadler Form
Humidifier
Luftbefeuchter

Manufacturer
Stadler Form Aktiengesellschaft,
Zug, Switzerland
In-house design
Matti Walker
Web
www.stadlerform.ch

A timeless, elegant appearance with harmonious lines characterises this powerful and quiet humidifier. Oskar Big is an economic evaporator that permits precise humidification by an integrated hygrostat. Thanks to its V4 filter technology, it distributes a lot of moisture and is recommended for rooms up to 65 sqm. Furthermore, its automatic shut-off, which is activated when the reservoir is empty, and the reminder function for changing the filter are innovative.

Statement by the jury
With plain elegance, this humidifier appealingly blends in with its surroundings. Ease of use and functionality complete the concept.

Ein zeitlos elegantes Erscheinungsbild mit harmonischer Linienführung prägt den leistungsstarken und leisen Luftbefeuchter. Oskar Big ist ein ökonomischer Verdunster, der durch den integrierten Hygrostat eine präzise Befeuchtung zulässt. Dank seiner V4-Filter-Technologie verteilt er viel Feuchtigkeit und empfiehlt sich für Räume von bis zu 65 qm. Innovativ sind zudem seine Abschalt-Automatik bei leerem Tank sowie die Erinnerungsfunktion für den Filterwechsel.

Begründung der Jury
Mit schlichter Eleganz fügt sich der Luftbefeuchter ansprechend in seine Umgebung ein. Bedienkomfort und Funktionalität runden das Konzept ab.

U200
Humidifier
Luftbefeuchter

Manufacturer
Plaston AG,
Widnau, Switzerland
In-house design
Manfred Fitsch
Web
www.plaston.com

The U200 humidifier allows simultaneously humidifying and scenting the ambient air. By means of an ultrasonic system, water is transformed into microfine mist. The fragrance container at the back of the unit easily takes up flavour oils. The puristic appearance of the device underlines its simplicity of operation. An illuminated transparent blue line sets off the horizontal separation of the upper and lower part.

Statement by the jury
The minimalist front of this humidifier visualises hygienic freshness. In addition, the ease of use and the fragrance experience are impressive.

Der Luftbefeuchter U200 verbindet die Befeuchtung mit einer gleichzeitigen Beduftung der Raumluft. Mittels Ultraschall-System wird Wasser in einen mikrofeinen Nebel umgewandelt. Über das Aromafach auf der Rückseite des Gerätes lassen sich bequem Duftöle einfüllen. Die puristische Gestaltung des Geräts unterstreicht die Einfachheit der Bedienung. Eine beleuchtete, blau-transparente Linie betont die horizontale Trennung von Ober- und Unterteil.

Begründung der Jury
Hygienische Frische visualisiert die puristisch gestaltete Gerätefront dieses Luftbefeuchters. Zudem überzeugen Bedienkomfort und Dufterlebnis.

JetClean
Air Purifier
Luftreiniger

Manufacturer
BALMUDA Inc.,
Tokyo, Japan
In-house design
Gen Terao
Web
www.balmuda.com

The JetClean air purifier features two fans, which suck in and emit the air respectively. Thus, it produces a strong airflow that reliably takes up heavy and widely spread particles such as airborne pollen. The innovative 360-degree filter catches the air particles from all directions. It filters significantly more pollen from the ambient air than conventional air purifiers.

Der Luftreiniger JetClean verfügt über zwei Gebläse, welche die Luft jeweils ansaugen und ausstoßen. Somit erzeugt er einen starken Luftstrom, der schwere und weit im Raum verteilte Partikel, wie die in der Luft befindlichen Pollen, zuverlässig aufnimmt. Der innovative 360-Grad-Filter erfasst dabei die Luftpartikel aus allen Richtungen und filtert deutlich mehr Pollen aus der Raumluft als herkömmliche Luftreiniger.

Statement by the jury
Contrasting black vents in the white corpus express the high functionality of this air purifier.

Begründung der Jury
Als Ausdruck einer hohen Funktionalität fallen bei diesem Luftreiniger die schwarz abgesetzten Lüftungsöffnungen im weißen Korpus auf.

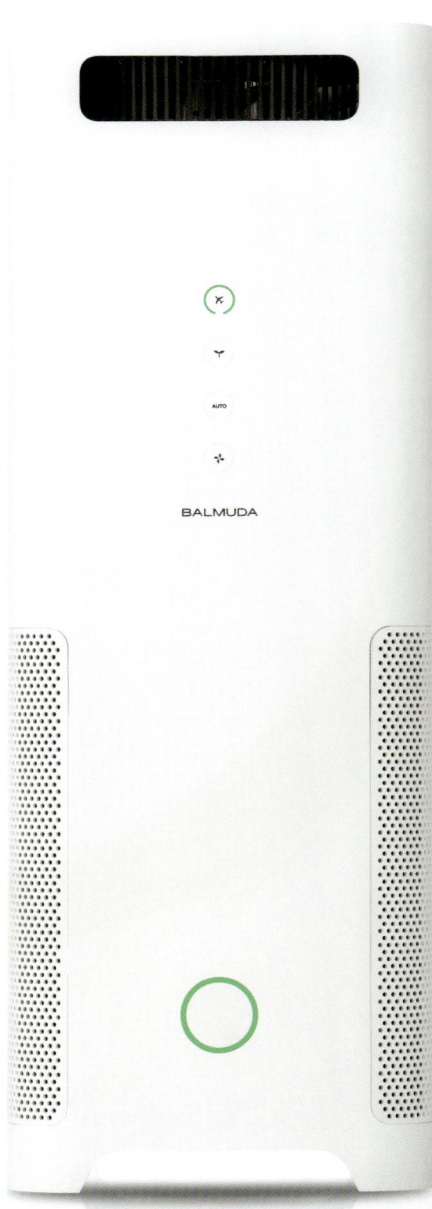

Ururu Sarara
Air Conditioner
Klimaanlage

Manufacturer
Daikin Industries Ltd.,
Kusatsu City, Shiga Prefecture, Japan
In-house design
Kouichiro Seki
Web
www.daikin.eu

The design of this wall-mounted air conditioner took as its inspiration the Japanese folding fan "Ogi". The aerodynamic flap design modifies the air stream to create a pleasant indoor environment. Air is drawn in at ground level and then fed up towards the ceiling, thereby reaching the furthest corners of the room. In contrast to conventional air conditioners, there is no noticeable draft. The use of a new refrigerant reduces environmental impact and cuts energy consumption.

Das Design dieser wandmontierten Klimaanlage ist von dem japanischen Faltfächer „Ogi" inspiriert. Durch das aerodynamische Klappendesign wird der Luftstrom so verändert, dass eine angenehme Raumatmosphäre entsteht. Die Luft wird in Bodennähe eingesaugt und dann in Richtung Decke geleitet, wodurch der Luftstrom auch die entferntesten Ecken des Raumes erreichen kann. Im Vergleich zu konventionellen Klimaanlagen ergibt sich so eine Raumerfahrung ohne fühlbaren Luftstrom. Durch ein neues Kühlmittel wird zudem die Umwelt weniger belastet und der Energieverbrauch wurde deutlich gesenkt.

Suave
Air Conditioner
Klimaanlage

Manufacturer
Vestel Beyaz Esya San. ve Tic. A.S.,
Manisa, Turkey
In-house design
Vestel White Industrial Design Group
(Burak Erbab)
Web
www.vestel.com.tr

Suave is the most recent, technically advanced air conditioning system by Vestel. When the unit is not in use, continuous clean lines give it a sleek appearance. When it is activated, the front panels slide upwards and the flaps open to allow the alternating air currents to flow. Ion technology combats dust and bacteria. Barely visible LED lights are fitted under the front panel to indicate operation status.

Statement by the jury
This air conditioning unit owes its clean look to the sliding front. At the same time, it captivates with its functionality and advanced technology.

Suave ist die neueste, technisch avancierte Klimaanlage von Vestel. Wenn das Gerät nicht benutzt wird, sorgen die durchgehenden klaren Linien für ein elegantes Erscheinungsbild. Bei Aktivierung gleitet die Frontplatte nach oben und die Klappe öffnet sich für den alternierenden Luftstrom. Dank Ionen-Technologie werden Staub und Bakterien bekämpft. Unter der Frontplatte befinden sich kaum sichtbar LED-Leuchten, die über den Betriebszustand informieren.

Begründung der Jury
Durch die verschiebbare Vorderseite gewinnt diese Klimaanlage ihr schnörkelloses Aussehen. Zugleich besticht sie durch ihre Technik und Funktionalität.

N-Style Cassette
Air Conditioner
Klimaanlage

Manufacturer
LG Electronics Inc.,
Seoul, South Korea
In-house design
Sang-Moon Jeong,
Myung-Sik Kim,
Hee-Jae Kwon,
Yong Kim
Web
www.lg.com

The four-way cassette design of this ceiling mounted air conditioner differs from the functional form of conventional air conditioners in that it can be adapted to the character of any interior. The user just chooses the most suitable front grille, which has no front suction inlet and therefore offers a sleek appearance. The rounded corners of the air inlet area ensure easy cleaning. To make installation easy, every corner is accessible separately.

Statement by the jury
The sophisticated design concept, which pays attention to the smallest detail, ensures the high quality of this air conditioner.

Das 4-Wege-Kassettendesign der deckenmontierten Klimaanlage unterscheidet sich von der funktionellen Form üblicher Klimaanlagen dadurch, dass es sich dem Charakter der Innenausstattung anpassen lässt. Der Nutzer wählt einfach die geeignete Frontplatte aus, die ohne Ansaugstutzen ein sauberes Erscheinungsbild bietet. Die abgerundeten Ecken des Lufteinlassbereichs erlauben eine einfache Reinigung, jede Ecke ist zur einfachen Installation separat zugänglich.

Begründung der Jury
Ein auch im Detail ausgefeiltes Gestaltungskonzept sorgt für die hohe Qualität dieser Klimaanlage.

Nea
Room Thermostat
Raumregler

Manufacturer
Rehau AG + Co,
Erlangen, Germany
Design
ARTEFAKT industriekultur,
Darmstadt, Germany
Web
www.rehau.com
www.artefakt.de

The design of Nea focuses on the essentials. The interactive display and the main plus/minus buttons are arranged in a horizontal line. All secondary functions are controlled by a button on the side, which is intentionally less noticeable. The sides of the casing have open grilles to ensure optimal temperature measurement. The thickness of the thermostat body is optically reduced through its cone-like shape and the intended colour contrast.

Das Design von Nea konzentriert sich auf das Wesentliche. Das interaktive Anzeigedisplay und die primär genutzten Plus- und Minustasten sind in einem horizontalen Band gefasst. Alle Sekundärfunktionen werden über einen seitlichen Taster gesteuert, welcher bewusst zurückgenommen ist. Die Gehäuseseiten weisen ein – für die Temperaturmessung optimiertes – offenes Raster auf. Die Gehäusetiefe wird durch die Konizität und den bewussten Farbkontrast optisch reduziert.

Statement by the jury
It is the clear, uncluttered appearance and thought-through functionality of the Nea room thermostat which make it win over.

Begründung der Jury
Der Raumregler Nea besticht durch sein klares, übersichtliches Erscheinungsbild und seine durchdachte Funktionalität.

Nest
Learning Thermostat
Lernender Thermostat

Manufacturer
Nest Labs, Inc.,
Palo Alto, USA
In-house design
Tony Fadell, Ben Filson
Design
bould design
(Fred Bould, Kristen Beck),
Mountain View, USA
Web
www.nest.com
www.bould.com

The second generation of the Nest learning thermostat represents significant progress. It has all the well thought-out features of the first generation product pooled into a significantly sleeker, more elegant form. A new, custom-made sensor screen results in a continuous, clean front that catches the attention. The solid stainless steel ring, for the temperature and user interface controls, is particularly striking.

Die zweite Generation des lernenden Thermostats Nest ist eine signifikante Weiterentwicklung. Er hat all die durchdachten Features der ersten Generation – konzentriert in einer deutlich dünneren und eleganteren Form. Ein neues, speziell angefertigtes Sensordisplay sorgt für eine gleichmäßige, klare Vorderseite, die den Blick fokussiert. Besonders markant ist der solide Edelstahlring für die Regelung der Temperatur und UI-Einstellungen.

Statement by the jury
The new version of this innovative thermostat that automatically regulates room temperatures has been optimised in form and design and is set to do its job in a sovereign way, just like its predecessor.

Begründung der Jury
Auch die neue, in Form und Konzept optimierte Version dieses innovativen Thermostats zur automatischen Regulierung der Raumtemperatur wird ihrer Aufgabe souverän gerecht.

MONDO Avert
Avert Heatstroke (Desk)
Hitzewarngerät (Tischmodell)

Manufacturer
Moto Design Co., Ltd.,
Tokyo, Japan
Design
Miyake Design
(Kazushige Miyake),
Tokyo, Japan
Web
www.motodesign.co.jp
www.mondo-web.com

The MONDO Avert Heatstroke displays not only time but temperature and humidity as well. It is available in different trendy colours and features a design that is reduced to the essentials. Besides the digitally displayed numbers, a vivid graphic illustrates the temperature and immediately attracts attention when it gets too hot in the room. In addition, an integrated warning signal sounds an alarm and thus protects against the risk of suffering heatstroke.

MONDO Avert Heatstroke zeigt die Temperatur und Feuchtigkeit im Raum sowie die Uhrzeit an. Das Gerät ist in verschiedenen aktuellen Farben erhältlich und besitzt eine auf das Wesentliche reduzierte Gestaltung. Neben den digital dargestellten Zahlen ergänzt eine anschauliche Grafik die Temperaturanzeige visuell und macht damit sofort auf Überwärmung aufmerksam. Zusätzlich schlägt ein eingebautes Warnsignal Alarm, sobald das Risiko eines Hitzschlags besteht.

MONDO Thermo
Thermo-Hygrometer Clock
Thermo-Hygrometer-Uhr

Manufacturer
Moto Design Co., Ltd.,
Tokyo, Japan
Design
Miyake Design
(Kazushige Miyake),
Tokyo, Japan
Web
www.motodesign.co.jp
www.mondo-web.com

The friendly and fresh appearance of this thermo-hygrometer clock catches the eye. Light pressure on the underside is all that it takes to indicate current ambient temperature, as well as previously stored information on maximum and minimum temperature and humidity values. The clock comes in various colours.

Statement by the jury
The easy, comprehensible operation as well as colourful and pleasing design of this thermo-hygrometer clock make it particularly impressive.

Diese Thermo-Hygrometer-Uhr fällt durch ihre freundliche, frische Ästhetik ins Auge. Bei leichtem Druck auf die untere Seite werden die gegenwärtig herrschenden sowie frühere abgespeicherte, maximale und minimale Temperatur- und Luftfeuchtigkeitswerte angezeigt. Die Uhr ist in vier verschiedenen Farben verfügbar.

Begründung der Jury
Ein einfaches und verständliches Bedienkonzept sowie eine farbig akzentuierte, gefällige Gestaltung beeindrucken bei dieser Thermo-Hygrometer-Uhr besonders.

MONDO Calendar + Digital
Perpetual Calendar Clock
Uhr mit ewigem Kalender

Manufacturer
Moto Design Co., Ltd.,
Tokyo, Japan
Design
Miyake Design
(Kazushige Miyake),
Tokyo, Japan
Web
www.motodesign.co.jp
www.mondo-web.com

This digital calendar, which includes a clock function, is part of the brand's product range of time and temperature devices. Its simple and functional design is intended to perfectly complement the entire range. Its discreet appearance makes the calendar – whether on a desk or shelf – a timeless accessory. This reliable and sturdy product thus integrates harmoniously into a wide variety of different environments.

Statement by the jury
This calendar clock features a functional and illustrative design and, thanks to its practical size and unobtrusive appearance, it can be used universally.

Dieser digitale Kalender samt Uhrfunktion ist Bestandteil der schlicht und funktional gestalteten Produktreihe von Zeit- und Temperaturgeräten der Marke und lässt sich daher gut mit ihnen kombinieren. Seine unauffällige Erscheinung macht den Kalender – ob auf dem Schreibtisch oder im Regal – zum zeitlosen Accessoire. Das zuverlässige und robuste Produkt fügt sich so harmonisch in unterschiedlichste Umgebungen ein.

Begründung der Jury
Diese Kalenderuhr ist funktional und anschaulich gestaltet und lässt sich dank ihrer handlichen Größe und zurückhaltenden Anmutung universell einsetzen.

Lighting and lamps
Licht und Leuchten

**Indoor and outdoor lighting, lighting systems and installations,
lighting engineering and work lighting, table / wall / stand / ceiling luminaire**
Innen- und Außenbeleuchtung, Leuchtsysteme und -installationen,
Lichttechnik und Arbeitsleuchten, Tisch-, Wand-, Stand- und Deckenbeleuchtung

6

IN-EI ISSEY MIYAKE
Lighting Collection
Leuchtenkollektion

Manufacturer
Artemide S.p.A.,
Pregnana Milanese, Italy

Design
Issey Miyake + Reality Lab.,
Tokyo, Japan

Web
www.artemide.com
www.isseymiyake.com

reddot design award
best of the best 2013

Master of transformation

The creations of Japanese designer Issey Miyake are captivating. This is due to the sensuality of the materials, the perfect design as well as the creative freedom, which the folding technique, so typical for this designer, gives the user. Again and again Issey Miyake's designs are surprising in the way in which they combine technical innovation with new shapes. The concept for the IN-EI lighting collection is based on a fabric made entirely of recycled materials, created by processing PET bottles using innovative technology. This new fabric has impressive properties and diffuses light in an interesting way. In this lighting collection, Issey Miyake combines an artistic vision of Japanese light traditions with his unique ability to transform the traditional into the modern. Every lampshade is created using mathematical 2D or 3D principles, which engender a harmonious interplay of light and shade. The structure of the recycled fabric undergoes an additional surface treatment, which allows the lights to keep their shape without using an additional frame. The IN-EI collection consists of floor, table and pendant lamps and is equipped with well-engineered LED technology. The concept achieves a successful symbiosis of efficient light technology coupled with an innovative approach to materials and design. Issey Miyake's unique folding technique creates shapes with a completely new expression.

Meister der Verwandlung

Die Kreationen des japanischen Designers Issey Miyake faszinieren durch die Sinnlichkeit der Materialien, das perfekte Design sowie die kreative Freiheit, die die für den Designer typischen Falttechniken dem Nutzer lassen. Immer wieder überraschen die Entwürfe von Issey Miyake auch durch die Art und Weise, wie sie technische Innovation mit neuen Formen vereinen. Die Gestaltung der Leuchtenkollektion IN-EI basiert auf einem vollständig aus recycelten Materialien hergestellten Gewebe, bei dem PET-Flaschen mittels einer innovativen Technik verarbeitet werden. Dieses neue Gewebe zeigt beeindruckende Eigenschaften und streut das Licht auf eine interessante Weise. Der Designer Issey Miyake verbindet für diese Leuchtenkollektion die künstlerische Vision japanischer Lichttradition mit seiner einzigartigen Fähigkeit, Tradition in Moderne zu verwandeln. Jeder Leuchtenschirm entsteht mithilfe mathematischer 2D- oder 3D-Grundsätze, die eine harmonische Wechselwirkung von Licht und Schatten hervorrufen. Die Struktur des recycelten Gewebes erhält eine zusätzliche Oberflächenbehandlung – es ist dadurch auch ohne einen zusätzlichen Rahmen formstabil. Die Kollektion IN-EI umfasst Steh-, Tisch- und Pendelleuchten und ist mit einer ausgereiften LED-Technologie ausgestattet. Ihrer Gestaltung gelingt eine Symbiose aus lichttechnischer Kompetenz und innovativer Herangehensweise an Material und Design. Die besondere Falttechnik von Issey Miyake kreiert dabei Formen mit einer völlig neuen Aussage.

Statement by the jury

This lighting collection manages to combine the unique design philosophy of Issey Miyake, which is based on Japanese traditions, with cutting edge LED technology in a fascinating way. The manner in which IN-EI was created unites deliberate, sustainable manufacture with the maxim of individual creativity. These lights are like delicate sculptures in the room. They stimulate the senses and challenge us to pose the challenge of creating ever new constellations.

Begründung der Jury

Auf eine faszinierende Art und Weise verbindet sich bei dieser Leuchtenkollektion die einzigartige, an japanischen Traditionen orientierte Designphilosophie von Issey Miyake mit modernster LED-Technologie. Die Art der Entstehung der IN-EI Leuchtenfamilie verbindet bewusstes, nachhaltiges Handeln mit der Maxime individueller Kreativität. Diese Leuchten sind filigran anmutende Skulpturen im Raum, sie beflügeln die Sinne und fordern zu immer neuen Konstellationen heraus.

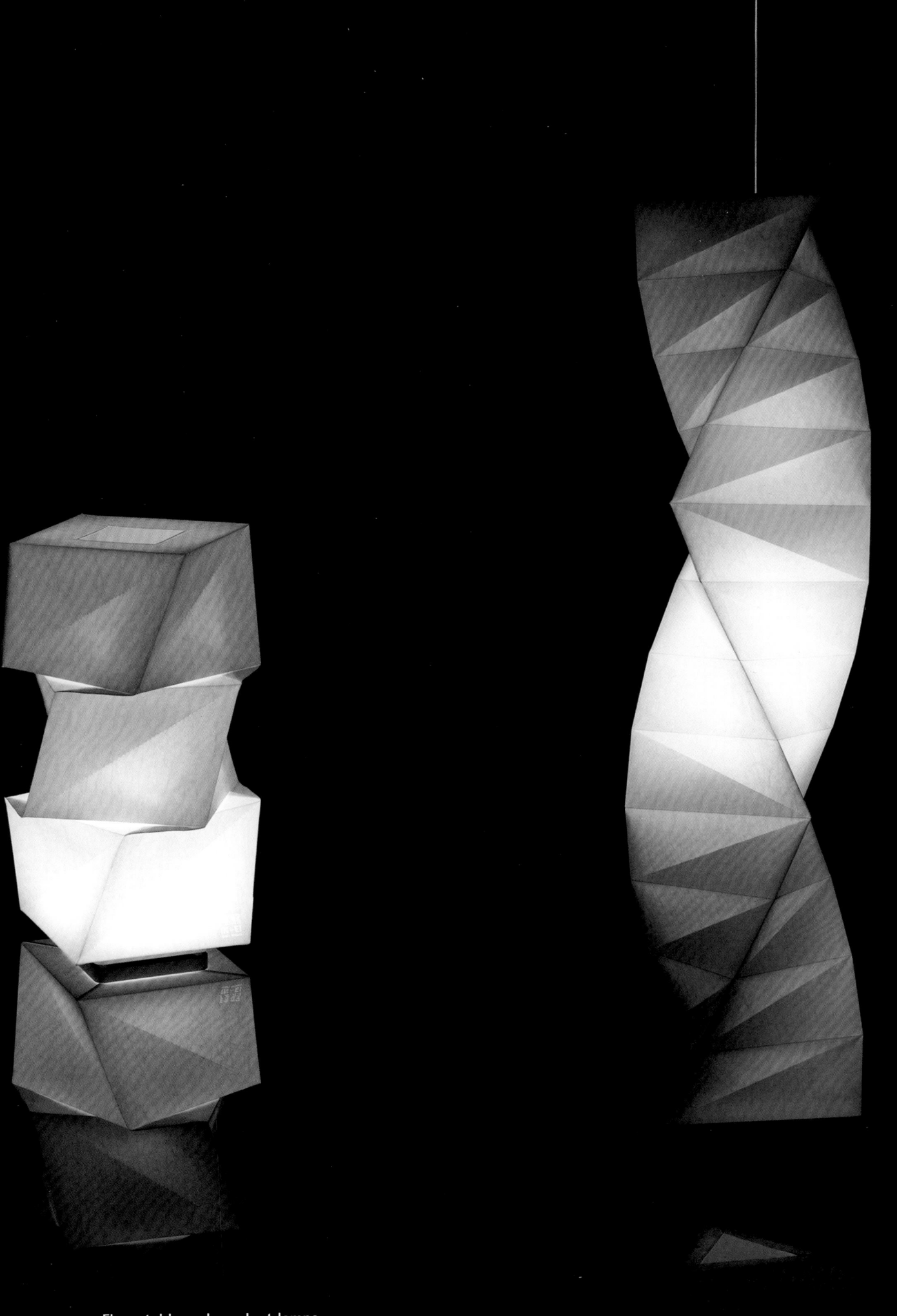

Floor, table and pendant lamps

Scopas
Pendant Luminaire
Pendelleuchte

Manufacturer
Artemide S.p.A.,
Pregnana Milanese, Italy
Design
Neil Poulton,
Paris, France
Web
www.artemide.com
www.neilpoulton.com

In Scopas, round LED modules are put together in such a way, that a sphere with incomplete structure is formed. The luminaire thereby appears different from each viewing angle, generating a particular suspense and breaking with conventional forms. The suspense is further heightened by the contrast between the black fixture of the luminary and the white, diffused light. The apparent incompleteness of the lamp contrasts with its technical efficiency.

Runde LED-Module sind bei Scopas so aneinandergesetzt, dass sie eine Kugel mit unvollständiger Struktur ergeben. Dadurch wirkt die Leuchte aus jedem Blickwinkel anders, erzeugt eine besondere Spannung und bricht mit gelernten Formen. Die Spannung wird durch den Kontrast zwischen der schwarzen Fassung der Leuchtkörper und dem weißen diffusen Licht noch verstärkt. Der scheinbaren Unvollständigkeit dieser Leuchte steht ihre technische Effizienz gegenüber.

Statement by the jury
Scopas fascinates with its unusual form which suggests perfection, yet remains incomplete. Scopas is both luminaire and light sculpture simultaneously.

Begründung der Jury
Scopas fasziniert mit einer ungewöhnlichen Form, die die perfekte Gestalt einer Kugel andeutet, jedoch unvollendet bleibt. Dadurch ist Scopas gleichzeitig Leuchte und Lichtskulptur.

Pendant lamps

Super Flat
LED Pendant Luminaire
LED-Pendelleuchte

Manufacturer
FLOS Architectural,
Antares Iluminación S.A.,
Ribarroja del Turia, Spain
In-house design
FLOS Architectural Design Team
Web
www.flos.com

The Super Flat Pendant Luminaire lies elegantly in the air suspended on strong steel hangers. The light head measuring 12.8 mm is extremely flat. The light is directed via specially developed guides, whereby the LED light sources provide optimal light emission. The Super Flat is available in various sizes, square or rectangular. It can be installed suspended on adjustable, eight metre long steel cables or directly on the ceiling.

Von kräftigen Stahlaufhängungen gehalten, liegt die Super Flat elegant in der Luft. Der Leuchtenkopf ist mit 12,8 mm extrem flach. Das Licht wird durch speziell entwickelte Führungen geleitet, wodurch die Leuchte eine optimale Lichtausgabe bietet. Die Super Flat ist in verschiedenen Größen, quadratisch oder rechteckig lieferbar. Sie kann an verstellbaren Stahlkabeln von acht Metern Länge hängend oder an der Decke installiert werden.

Statement by the jury
Super Flat is an iconic pendant luminaire which is trend-setting, thanks to its latest LED technology and its outstanding, plain and flat design.

Begründung der Jury
Super Flat ist eine ikonische Pendelleuchte, die dank neuester LED-Technologie und einer herausragend schlichten und flachen Gestaltung zukunftsweisend ist.

Shift
Interior Lighting System
Innenbeleuchtung

Manufacturer
Luxuni GmbH,
Leer, Germany
Design
Phenix Lighting (Xiamen) Co., Ltd.
(Jean Chen),
Xiamen, China
Web
www.luxuni.com
www.phenixlighting.com

Shift has an elegant and reduced form with minimised dimensions (40 x 60 mm). Its aluminium housing with matt, anodised surface makes this lamp an eye-catcher. The optical PMMA diffuser with micro-prismatic structure creates prominent, glare-free lighting. Shift opens a variety of combination options: for instance several lamps can be arranged adjacent to or above one another to form squares or hexagons.

Statement by the jury
Characteristic for these lamps are their formal-aesthetic strictness, the high grade of workmanship and the many combination options.

Shift hat eine elegante und reduzierte Form bei minimierter Größe (40 x 60 mm). Ihr Aluminium-Gehäuse mit matt eloxierter Oberfläche macht diese Leuchte zum Blickfang. Der optische PMMA-Diffuser mit Micro-Prismatik-Struktur ergibt eine auffällige, blendfreie Beleuchtung. Shift eröffnet vielfältige Kombinationsmöglichkeiten: Mehrere Leuchten lassen sich beispielsweise neben- oder übereinander, zu Quadraten oder Sechsecken arrangieren.

Begründung der Jury
Charakteristisch für diese Leuchte sind ihre formal-ästhetische Strenge, die hochwertige Verarbeitung und die vielen Kombinationsmöglichkeiten.

Friends
Pendant Luminaire
Pendelleuchte

Manufacturer
Royal Philips Electronics,
Eindhoven, Netherlands
In-house design
Philips Design Lighting Team
Web
www.philips.com

Strong as a group and iconic as single unit, Friends combines energy-saving lighting with a distinctive design. The organic silhouette puts one in mind of a drop coming from the cable on which the lamp hangs. Friends is made of a combination of plastic and metal and manages to succeed without visible connectors or constructions. The pendant luminaires are available in various sizes and in four colours.

Statement by the jury
With its organic design, the Friends collection is likeable at first glance. Furthermore, it convinces due to its high quality workmanship.

Stark als Gruppe und ikonisch als Einzelstück, verbindet Friends energiesparende Beleuchtung mit einer markanten Gestaltung. Die organische Silhouette erinnert an einen Tropfen, der aus dem Kabel, an dem die Leuchte hängt, entsteht. Friends ist aus einer Kombination aus Plastik und Metall gefertigt und kommt ohne sichtbare Verbindungen oder Konstruktionen aus. Die Pendelleuchten gibt es in verschiedenen Größen und vier Farben.

Begründung der Jury
Mit ihrer organischen Gestaltung wirkt die Friends Kollektion auf Anhieb sympathisch. Darüber hinaus überzeugt sie durch ihre hochwertige Verarbeitung.

Hangover
Pendant Luminaire
Pendelleuchte

Manufacturer
PROLICHT GmbH,
Neu-Götzens, Austria
In-house design
Web
www.prolicht.at

Hangover has the form of a very puristic, cylindrical pendant luminaire. The cylinder, however, is available in 25 different colours, the conductive hanger cables in a further four colours (white, black, red and orange), so that there is a choice of 100 different colour combinations. The product is individually assembled for the customer within 5 days.

Statement by the jury
Due to its plain, geometric form in combination with the many colour variants, the Hangover pendant luminaire matches every interior setting.

Hangover ist der Form nach eine sehr puristische, zylindrische Pendelleuchte. Der Zylinder ist jedoch in 25 verschiedenen Farben verfügbar, die stromführenden Seilabhängungen in weiteren vier Farben (Weiß, Schwarz, Rot und Orange), so dass zwischen 100 verschiedenen Farbzusammenstellungen gewählt werden kann. Das Produkt wird innerhalb von fünf Tagen individuell für den Kunden gefertigt.

Begründung der Jury
Durch ihre schlicht geometrische Form in Verbindung mit den vielen Farbvarianten passt sich die Pendelleuchte Hangover jedem Interieur an.

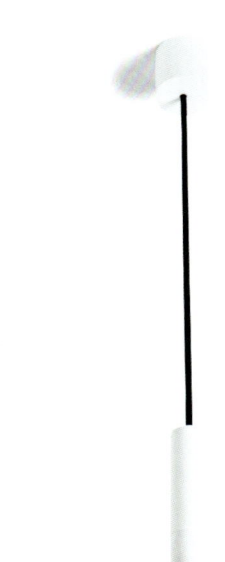

Appareo
LED Pendant Luminaire
LED-Pendelleuchte

Manufacturer
AB Fagerhult,
Habo, Sweden
Design
Howl
(Gustav Müller Nord, Jens O Johansson),
Stockholm, Sweden
Web
www.fagerhult.com
www.howlstudio.se

Appareo combines a distinctive, slim-line design with a pleasing, glare-free lighting system. This is made possible by use of acryl plastic which is fitted as disc located in the outer, narrow aluminium edge. The LEDs are arranged around this diffuser which fulfils the double function of reflector and anti-glare shield. When the light is on, the diffuser generates a clear, white glow; when switched off it is transparent.

Appareo vereint eine markante, schlanke Gestaltung mit einer angenehmen, blend-freien Beleuchtung. Ermöglicht wird dies durch die Verwendung von Acrylkunststoff, der als Scheibe in die äußere, schmale Alu-miniumkante eingesetzt ist. Die LEDs sind um diesen Diffuser angeordnet, der eine Doppelrolle als Reflektor und Blendschutz erfüllt. Ist die Leuchte eingeschaltet, erzeugt der Diffuser einen klaren weißen Schein, ausgeschaltet ist er transparent.

Statement by the jury
Its innovative use of materials makes it possible for Appareo to unite an elegant form language with pleasing LED light-ing in perfect harmony.

Begründung der Jury
Ihr innovativer Materialeinsatz ermöglicht es Appareo, eine elegante Formensprache mit einer angenehmen LED-Beleuchtung in perfekten Einklang zu bringen.

senses TOUCH
LED Pendant Luminaire
LED-Pendelleuchte

Manufacturer
senses, Steinel GmbH,
Herzebrock-Clarholz, Germany
In-house design
Thomas Möller
Design
Eckstein Design
(Stefan Eckstein, Susanne Scharf),
Munich, Germany
Web
www.senses-lights.ch
www.eckstein-design.com

In senses touch a simple, elegant form combines with an intelligent operating concept to provide an innovative pendant luminaire. By means of the LED it creates any desired light mood – from bright, cool working light to a warm atmosphere of well-being. The uplight/downlight setting facilitates in addition the change from direct to indirect lighting. A touchpad with memory function provides control.

Bei senses touch verbinden sich eine schlichte, elegante Formgebung mit einem intelligenten Bedienkonzept zu einer innovativen Pendelleuchte. Mithilfe hochwertiger LEDs schafft sie jede gewünschte Lichtstimmung – von hellem, kühlen Arbeitslicht bis hin zur warmen Wohlfühlatmosphäre. Die Up-/Downlight-Einstellung ermöglicht zusätzlich den Wechsel von direkter zu indirekter Beleuchtung. Die Steuerung erfolgt über ein Touchpanel mit Memofunktion.

Statement by the jury
With its reduced form language, this lamp remains restrained and leaves the big scenario to the light it produces.

Begründung der Jury
Mit ihrer reduzierten Formensprache nimmt sich diese Leuchte zurück und überlässt dem großen Auftritt dem Licht, das sie verbreitet.

SML LED Wall
Wall Lamp
Wandleuchte

Manufacturer
serien.lighting,
Rodgau, Germany
Design
Jean-Marc da Costa
Web
www.serien.com

The concept behind the SML LED Wall is to provide lighting in modular form. The components which comprise the system have a unified, clear form language and are minimally dimensioned. They differentiate only in their sizes (S, M and L) and can be combined with various glass covers according to which light is required. SML LED Wall is thus a very flexible lighting solution.

Das Konzept hinter der SML LED Wall ist, Beleuchtung in Form eines Baukasten-systems anzubieten. Die Elemente, aus denen sich das System zusammensetzt, haben eine einheitlich klare Formensprache und sind minimal in ihren Abmessungen. Sie unterscheiden sich allein in ihren Größen (S, M und L) und können je nach gewünschtem Licht mit verschiedenen Glasabdeckungen kombiniert werden. Damit ist SML LED Wall eine sehr flexible Beleuchtungslösung.

Statement by the jury
The SML LED Wall system provides flexible lighting solutions with a stringent, highly reduced form language.

Begründung der Jury
Das SML LED Wall System bietet flexible Beleuchtungslösungen mit einer stringen-ten, sehr reduzierten Formensprache.

Swarosphere
LED Recessed Luminaire Series
LED-Einbauleuchtenserie

Manufacturer
Swareflex GmbH,
Vomp, Austria
In-house design
Walter Ebner
Design
Bartenbach LichtLabor GmbH
(Christian Reisecker),
Aldrans, Austria
Web
www.swareflex.com
www.bartenbach.com

A bionically inspired high-grade lens of Swarovski crystal glass characterises the Swarosphere series. The light-guiding crystal glass lens generates high brilliance with soft shadow lines and homogenous light distribution. With a filigree design height of only 38 mm the facetted structure creates absolutely no glare. The crystal glass lens also serves as robust function cover and thereby enhances the considerable impression displayed by the product.

Statement by the jury
Swarosphere is at the same time representative and highly functional, providing a pleasant, glare-free light.

Eine bionisch inspirierte hochwertige Linse aus Swarovski Kristallglas prägt die Swarosphere-Serie. Die lichtlenkende Kristallglaslinse erzeugt eine hohe Licht-brillanz mit weichen Schattenverläufen und homogener Lichtverteilung. Bei einer filigranen Bauhöhe von nur 38 mm schafft die präzise Facettenstruktur absolute Blendungsfreiheit. Die Kristallglaslinse dient zudem als widerstandsfähige Funk-tionshülle und verstärkt dabei die hohe Produktanmutung.

Begründung der Jury
Zugleich repräsentativ und höchst funk-tionell, bietet Swarosphere ein angenehm blendfreies Licht.

Solar LED
Recessed Luminaire
Einbauleuchte

Manufacturer
Artemide Megalit SAS,
Saint Florent sur Cher, France
Design
Eric Solé,
Bagnères de Bigorre, France
Web
www.artemide.com

The special feature of the Solar LED is the combination of reflecting body and an innovative light pipe optics system: The light pipe captures the light beam and transmits it to a reflecting surface. This reflects the light onto the concave body which is coated with a special layer and thus scatters the light. In this way, a pleasing white light is created with exceptional light quality and a high degree of energy efficiency.

Statement by the jury
The innovative technology of the Solar LED and its distinctive concave form are mutually dependent. The result of this interplay is a high quality of light.

Die Besonderheit der Solar LED besteht in ihrer Kombination aus reflektierendem Körper und einem innovativen Lichtleiter-Optiksystem: Der Lichtleiter fängt den Lichtstrahl ein und überträgt ihn auf eine spiegelnde Oberfläche. Diese leitet das Licht zurück auf den gewölbten Körper, der mit einer speziellen, das Licht streuenden Beschichtung versehen ist. So entsteht bei hoher Energieeffizienz ein angenehm weiches Licht mit hervorragender Licht-qualität.

Begründung der Jury
Die innovative Technik der Solar LED und ihre markant konkave Form bedingen sich gegenseitig. Das Resultat aus diesem Zusammenspiel ist eine hohe Lichtqualität.

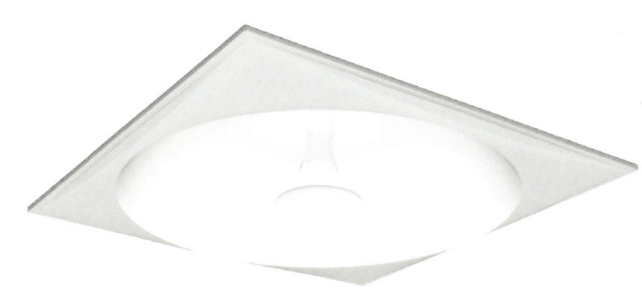

Findme
LED Spotlight Series
LED-Strahlerserie

Manufacturer
FLOS Architectural,
Antares Iluminación S.A.,
Ribarroja del Turia, Spain
Design
Jorge Herrera Studio
(Jorge Herrera Morán),
Massamagrell, Spain
Web
www.flos.com
www.jorgeherrera.es

Findme is a cylindrically designed LED spotlight series of die-cast aluminium. The special feature of the series is the fact that Findme can be inserted vertically in the ceiling structure so that only a small ring indicates the position of the light fixture. When pulled out, Findme can be positioned flexibly for accent lighting. Findme is available in three versions and colours. High grade LEDs with lenses assure optimal light control.

Statement by the jury
Findme enthralls due to its charming hiding game when recessed and its flexible accent lighting when pulled out.

Findme ist eine zylindrisch gestaltete LED-Strahlerserie aus druckgegossenem Aluminium. Die Besonderheit der Serie liegt darin, dass Findme vertikal so im Deckenaufbau versenkt werden kann, dass nur ein kleiner Ring die Position der Leuchte verrät. Herausgezogen kann Findme zur Akzentbeleuchtung flexibel ausgerichtet werden. Findme gibt es in drei Versionen und Farben. Hochleistungs-LEDs mit Objektiven gewährleisten eine optimale Lichtkontrolle.

Begründung der Jury
Findme begeistert durch ihr charmantes Versteckspiel im versenkten, und eine flexible Akzentbeleuchtung im herausgezogenen Zustand.

GO-IN
Guide Lighting Fixture
Licht-Leitsystem

Manufacturer
FLOS Architectural,
Antares Iluminación S.A.,
Ribarroja del Turia, Spain
Design
Jorge Herrera Studio
(Jorge Herrera Morán),
Massamagrell, Spain
Web
www.flos.com
www.jorgeherrera.es

The discreet, ring-shaped LED lighting signal fixtures of the Go-In system are built into plasterboard walls as orientation aids and guide the way through a building. The light's frames are produced by soft architecture technology, so that they can be fitted into the wall and form with it a homogenous surface. The body of the lamp is held magnetically for easy maintenance.

Statement by the jury
Go-In is a sophisticated guide system which, with its light circles integrated almost invisibly in the wall, is an efficient orientation aide.

Die dezenten, ringförmigen LED-Lichtzeichen des Go-In Systems werden als Orientierungshilfen in Gipskartonwände eingebaut und übernehmen so die Führung durch Gebäude. Die Rahmen der Leuchten sind mithilfe von Soft Architecture Technologie so produziert, dass sie perfekt in die Wand eingepasst werden können und eine homogene Fläche mit ihr bilden. Der Lampenkörper wird für eine einfache Wartung von Magneten gehalten.

Begründung der Jury
Go-In ist ein raffiniertes Leitsystem, das mit seinen nahezu unsichtbar in die Wand integrierten Lichtkreisen eine wirkungsvolle Orientierungshilfe ist.

Circle of Light
Ceiling Luminaire
Deckenleuchte

Manufacturer
FLOS Architectural,
Antares Iluminación S.A.,
Ribarroja del Turia, Spain
In-house design
FLOS Architectural Design Team
Web
www.flos.com

Circle of Light is a fascinating lighting solution consisting of several highly efficient LED spotlights. By means of soft architecture technology it can be perfectly integrated in the ceiling by means of a 35 mm wide, round butt joint. By this means, Circle of Light creates volume and its own carpet of light which covers the room in almost glare-free light. Circle of Light is available with a diameter of 300 mm, 600 mm and 900 mm.

Statement by the jury
Circle of Light is a poetic luminaire which fits into every architectural scheme harmoniously and smoothly, without losing its individuality.

Circle of Light ist eine faszinierende, aus mehreren hocheffizienten LED-Strahlern bestehende Beleuchtungslösung. Mittels Soft Architecture Technologie lässt sie sich über eine 35 mm breite, runde Stoßfuge perfekt in die Decke integrieren. Auf diese Weise schafft der Leuchtkreis Volumen und einen Lichtteppich, der den Raum in nahezu blendfreies Licht taucht. Circle of Light ist mit einem Durchmesser von 300 mm, 600 mm und 900 mm erhältlich.

Begründung der Jury
Circle of Light ist eine poetische Leuchte, die sich harmonisch und nahtlos in jede Architektur einfügt, ohne dabei ihre Eigenständigkeit zu verlieren.

SOLID PURE
LED Spot
LED-Strahler

Manufacturer
FLOS Architectural,
Antares Iluminación S.A.,
Ribarroja del Turia, Spain
In-house design
FLOS Architectural Design Team
Design
Knud Holscher Design,
Copenhagen, Denmark
Web
www.flos.com
www.holscherdesign.com

Solid Pure is an extremely powerful LED spotlight of die-cast aluminium alloy. Inside are high-powered LEDs with two supply options, variable light transmission and an active cooling system. Thereby the spotlight uses the full power of LED light. The light flux can be adjusted for every room – the high-powered LED is available in various light intensities and colour temperatures.

Solid Pure ist ein extrem leistungsfähiger LED-Strahler aus einer druckgegossenen Aluminiumlegierung. In ihm stecken Hochleistungs-LEDs mit zwei Versorgungsoptionen, variablem Lichtfluss und einem aktiven Kühlsystem. Damit nutzt der Strahler die volle Leistung des LED-Lichts. Der Lichtstrom kann jedem Raum angepasst werden – die Hochleistungs-LEDs sind in verschiedenen Lichtintensitäten und Farbtemperaturen erhältlich.

Statement by the jury
The clear, solid design of the Solid Pure spot is an expression of its high efficiency and gives an impression of ultimate functionality.

Begründung der Jury
Die klare, solide Gestaltung des Strahlers Solid Pure ist Ausdruck seiner hohen Effizienz und vermittelt den Eindruck höchster Funktionalität.

Ceiling lights, spotlights

Auro Drop
Recessed Spotlight
Einbauleuchte

Manufacturer
XAL GmbH,
Graz, Austria
Design
Reflexion AG
(Thomas Mika),
Zurich, Switzerland
Web
www.xal.com
www.reflexion.ch

Auro Drop is a light system of reduced design based on LED. The convex-concave form language and the shallow mounting, flush with the ceiling, make it universally adaptable. High grade LEDs combined with a freely swivelling glass lens allow optimal light beam control. The lens is slightly matted and provides a soft light with a pleasant ratio of targeted and diffused proportions.

Statement by the jury
Auro Drop is a convincingly functional lighting solution which fascinates with its convex-concave design and integrates in a great variety of contexts.

Auro Drop ist eine reduziert gestaltete Leuchte auf LED-Basis. Die konvex-konkave Formensprache und ein deckenbündiger Einbau bei geringer Einbautiefe machen sie universell einsetzbar. Hochwertige LEDs kombiniert mit einer frei schwenkbaren Glaslinse erlauben eine optimale Lichtlenkung. Die Linse ist leicht mattiert und sorgt für ein weiches Licht mit einem angenehmen Verhältnis von gerichtetem und diffusem Anteil.

Begründung der Jury
Auro Drop überzeugt als funktionelle Lichtlösung, die mit ihrer konvex-konkaven Gestaltung fasziniert und sich in unterschiedlichste Kontexte integriert.

PUNTO
Surface-Mounted Luminaire
Aufbauleuchte

Manufacturer
RIBAG Licht AG,
Safenwil, Switzerland
In-house design
Daniel Kübler
Web
www.ribag.com

The Punto luminaire combines LED technology with a high degree of aesthetics in its flat, round luminaries. The surface-mounted luminaire is available in three sizes and power ratings and can be used as complete light system or as light source with external converter. Whether mounted on the wall, the ceiling or in a protected outside area, Punto fits into every room structure. Its sturdy and heat optimised construction provides a high degree of reliability.

Statement by the jury
Punto spreads not only a pleasant light, it emanates with its classical form and precise workmanship also high quality.

Die Leuchte Punto verbindet in ihren flachen runden Lichtkörpern LED-Technologie und hochwertige Ästhetik. Die Aufbauleuchte ist in drei Größen und Leistungsstufen erhältlich und kann als Komplettleuchte oder als Lichtpunkt mit externem Konverter eingesetzt werden. An Wand, Decke oder im geschützten Außenbereich montiert, fügt sich Punto in jede Raumstruktur ein. Ihre robuste und wärmeoptimierte Bauweise sorgt für hohe Zuverlässigkeit.

Begründung der Jury
Punto verbreitet nicht nur angenehmes Licht, sondern strahlt mit ihrer klassischen Form und präzisen Verarbeitung auch eine hohe Wertigkeit aus.

Ciro ceiling
Surface Mounted Luminaire
Aufbauleuchte

Manufacturer
XAL GmbH,
Graz, Austria
Design
Kai Stania Product Design
(Kai Stania),
Vienna, Austria
Web
www.xal.com
www.kaistania.com

Ciro is part of a new LED lighting generation which combines pioneering light technology and successful form lines. The luminaire, optionally with indirect light component appears, with its minimalist form, like a hovering ring in the room. The seamlessly welded aluminium ring is available with black, grey or white texture paint and completes the clear line of the design. With its plain design, Ciro fits into every environment.

Statement by the jury
Ciro convinces due to its well-considered design with puristic, elegant form language and contemporary lighting technology.

Ciro ist Teil einer neuen LED-Leuchten-Generation, die zukunftsweisende Lichttechnologie und gelungene Formgebung vereint. Optional mit indirektem Lichtanteil wirkt die Leuchte mit ihrer minimalistischen Form wie ein schwebender Ring im Raum. Der nahtlos verschweißte Aluminiumring ist mit schwarzem, grauem oder weißem Strukturlack verfügbar und rundet die klare Linie des Designs ab. Mit ihrer schlichten Gestaltung passt sich Ciro jeder Umgebung an.

Begründung der Jury
Ciro überzeugt durch eine durchdachte Gestaltung mit puristischer, eleganter Formensprache und zeitgemäßer Beleuchtungstechnik.

Boxter
Interior Lighting
Innenbeleuchtung

Manufacturer
Delta Light nv.,
Wevelgem, Belgium
In-house design
Web
www.deltalight.com

Characteristic for the Boxter lighting
is its asymmetric design. In terms of
functionality this facilitates locating
the electronic control gear next to the
lamps instead of above them, making
the Boxter a lower and more compact
ceiling mounted lamp. The asymmetry
furthermore makes series installation
possible, giving the rooms direction and
elegance. Boxter is available with one
lamp as well as with two light sources.

Statement by the jury
Boxter interior lighting convinces with
its asymmetric design which not only
characterises the functionality but is
also aesthetically attractive.

Charakteristisch für die Boxter-Leuchten
ist ihre asymmetrische Gestaltung. Funktional gesehen ermöglicht das die Aufnah-
me des Vorschaltgeräts neben den Lampen
statt über ihnen, was die Boxter zu einer
niedrigen und kompakten Deckenaufbauleuchte macht. Ihre Asymmetrie ermöglicht darüber hinaus eine lineare Installation, die Räumen Richtung und Eleganz
verleiht. Boxter gibt es sowohl mit einer
Lampe, als auch mit zwei Leuchtmitteln.

Begründung der Jury
Boxter überzeugt mit ihrer asymmetrischen Gestaltung, die nicht nur die Funktionalität prägt, sondern auch ästhetisch
reizvoll ist.

Pixel Pro
Recessed Luminaire
Einbauleuchte

Manufacturer
iGuzzini illuminazione,
Recanati, Italy
Design
Iosa Ghini Associati
(Massimo Iosa Ghini),
Milan, Italy
Web
www.iguzzini.com
www.iosaghini.it

Pixel Pro is a recessed lamp with flowing
form, designed for the retail trade.
Its carefully considered aesthetics are
expressed particularly in the precisely
designed details: Its functional heat
conductor with its shell-shaped form
becomes an eye-catching design
feature. The extensible body can be
rotated and swivelled. Furthermore
the lamp has an enhanced colour
effect which illuminates the goods
advantageously.

Statement by the jury
This recessed lighting series impresses
from a formal viewpoint with its
exciting contrast between organic
lines and technical impression.

Pixel Pro ist eine für den Einzelhandel
konzipierte Einbauleuchte mit fließender
Form. Ihre sorgfältig durchdachte Ästhetik
kommt besonders in den präzise gestalteten Details zum Ausdruck: Ihr funktioneller
Wärmeableiter etwa wird durch seine
muschelförmige Gestaltung zum auffälligen Designelement. Der herausziehbare
Korpus ist dreh- und schwenkbar. Zudem
hat die Leuchte eine verbesserte Farbwiedergabe, die die Waren ins rechte Licht
rückt.

Begründung der Jury
Diese Einbaustrahler-Serie besticht in
formaler Hinsicht mit ihrem spannenden
Kontrast zwischen organischen Linien
und technischer Anmutung.

Tweeter
Interior Lighting
Innenbeleuchtung

Manufacturer
Delta Light nv.,
Wevelgem, Belgium
In-house design
Web
www.deltalight.com

The prominent characteristics of
Tweeter are its extreme rotation and
tilt properties which are achieved by a
special technique using asymmetrical
hinge mounting. In the case of the
recessed models the spots fit flush
with the ceiling in the base position.
The rotation mechanism is so designed
that the light beam is not interrupted
for maximal light efficiency. The ceiling
mounted light is available with one or
two spots.

Statement by the jury
Tweeter sets new standards with regard
to mobility. In the case of the recessed
lights, light and architecture also merge
into one harmonious ensemble.

Hervorstechendes Merkmal der Tweeter ist
ihre extreme Rotations- und Kippfähigkeit,
die durch eine spezielle Technik mit asym-
metrischer Scharnieraufhängung erreicht
wird. Bei den Einbaumodellen fügen sich
die Spots in der Basisposition nahtlos in
die Decke ein. Der Rotationsmechanismus
ist so konzipiert, dass der Lichtstrahl für
eine maximale Lichtwirkung nicht unter-
brochen wird. Die Deckenaufbauleuchte
gibt es mit einem oder zwei Spots.

Begründung der Jury
Tweeter setzt Maßstäbe in Sachen Beweglichkeit. Bei der Einbauleuchte verschmelzen darüber hinaus Licht und Architektur
zu einem harmonischen Ganzen.

Bullet
Track Light
Stromschienenstrahler

Manufacturer
XAL GmbH,
Graz, Austria
In-house design
Xlab
Web
www.xal.com

Bullet is so designed that it places the illuminated object in the best light. Behind the distinctive projectile form of aluminium a converter and integrated conductive track adapter are concealed. A well-considered click system allows an uncomplicated and precisely accurate alignment of the spotlight for optimal display of goods. A sophisticated aluminium die cast manufacturing technique makes the unusual form of the spotlight possible.

Statement by the jury
The distinctive Bullet can be precisely aligned to target an object with a light beam so that it is impressively illuminated.

Bullet ist so gestaltet, dass er die zu beleuchtenden Objekte ins beste Licht rückt. Hinter der markanten Projektil-Form aus Aluminium verbergen sich Konverter und integrierter Stromschienenadapter. Ein durchdachtes Klick-System erlaubt eine unkomplizierte und punktgenaue Ausrichtung des Strahlers für eine optimale Wareninszenierung. Ein aufwändiges Aluminium-Druckgussfertigungsverfahren ermöglicht die außergewöhnliche Form des Strahlers.

Begründung der Jury
Der markante Strahler Bullet lässt sich punktgenau ausrichten, um ein Objekt mit seinem Lichtstrahl genau zu treffen und es so eindrucksvoll zu illuminieren.

Supernova XS Pivot
Interior Lighting
Innenbeleuchtung

Manufacturer
Delta Light nv.,
Wevelgem, Belgium
In-house design
Web
www.deltalight.com

In this lighting unit a narrow aluminium ring holds a Plexiglas disc with 76 per cent transparency which hides a plate with modern power LEDs. A special LED arrangement guarantees a uniform and perfectly balanced light output – for an especially pleasing lighting effect. The Supernova has a flexible ceiling mounting which makes a slope of the disc of 45 and a rotation of 360 degrees possible.

Statement by the jury
The Supernova XS Pivot is timelessly beautiful and with its LED technology guarantees a particularly pleasant lighting effect.

Bei dieser Leuchte hält ein schmaler Aluminiumring eine Plexiglasscheibe mit einer 76-prozentigen Transparenz, die eine Platte mit modernen Power-LEDs verbirgt. Eine spezielle LED-Anordnung garantiert einen einheitlichen und perfekt ausgewogenen Lichtausgang – für eine besonders angenehme Beleuchtung. Die Supernova hat eine flexible Deckenbefestigung, die eine Neigung der Scheibe von bis zu 45 und eine Rotation von 360 Grad ermöglicht.

Begründung der Jury
Die Supernova XS Pivot ist zeitlos schön und garantiert mit ihrer LED-Technik eine besonders angenehme Beleuchtung.

Skyline
LED Spot
LED-Strahler

Manufacturer
Dark at night NV,
Maldegem, Belgium
Design
Lieven Musschoot & Mathias Hennebel,
Knokke, Belgium
Web
www.dark.be
www.lmmh.be

This minimalist wall and ceiling lamp consists of two rectangular block shapes of the same dimensions, one of which serves as wall mounting. The other holds the light element and cooling unit and is mounted on the central unit, so that it can be rotated 360 degrees. Skyline is also available with two light fixtures that are each available in black or white. For the panel interiors ten different colours can be selected.

Diese minimalistische Wand- und Deckenleuchte besteht aus zwei gleich großen Quadern, von denen einer als Wandhalterung dient. Der andere fasst Leuchtmittel und Kühleinheit und ist so an dem zentralen Quader befestigt, dass er sich um 360 Grad drehen lässt. Skyline ist auch mit zwei Leuchtkörpern und jeweils in schwarz oder weiß erhältlich, bei der Innenseite kann zwischen zehn verschiedenen Farbtönen gewählt werden.

Statement by the jury
Skyline impresses with its clear, geometric form language which, because of the possibility of colour accentuation, can provide an attractive contrast at the interior panels.

Begründung der Jury
Skyline beeindruckt mit seiner klaren geometrischen Formensprache, die durch die Möglichkeit der farblichen Akzentuierung an der Innenseite reizvoll kontrastiert werden kann.

Counterbalance
Wall Lamp
Wandleuchte

Manufacturer
Luceplan SpA,
Milan, Italy
Design
Studio Daniel Rybakken,
Göteborg, Sweden
Web
www.luceplan.com
www.danielrybakken.com

Counterbalance is an LED wall lamp with an almost two metre long steel arm whereby its weight is compensated by means of gearwheel and a counterweight. The counterbalance system allows a flowing alignment of the light transmitting arm along its movement axis and thus location of the lamps in unlimited positions. The arm with the rotary lamp head stands thereby perfectly balanced in the room.

Counterbalance ist eine LED-Wandleuchte mit einem fast zwei Meter langen Arm aus Stahl, dessen Gewicht mit Hilfe von Zahnrädern und einem Gegengewicht ausbalanciert wird. Das Ausgleichssystem erlaubt eine fließende Ausrichtung des lichtführenden Arms entlang seiner Bewegungsachse und damit die Positionierung der Leuchte in unendlich vielen Stellungen. Dabei steht der Arm mit dem drehbaren Leuchtenkopf jederzeit perfekt ausbalanciert im Raum.

Statement by the jury
Counterbalance fascinates due to the ease with which it seems to defy the laws of physics, even though a sophisticated technology lies behind it.

Begründung der Jury
Counterbalance fasziniert durch die Leichtigkeit, mit der sie die Gesetze der Physik außer Kraft zu setzen scheint, auch wenn dahinter eine ausgeklügelte Technik steckt.

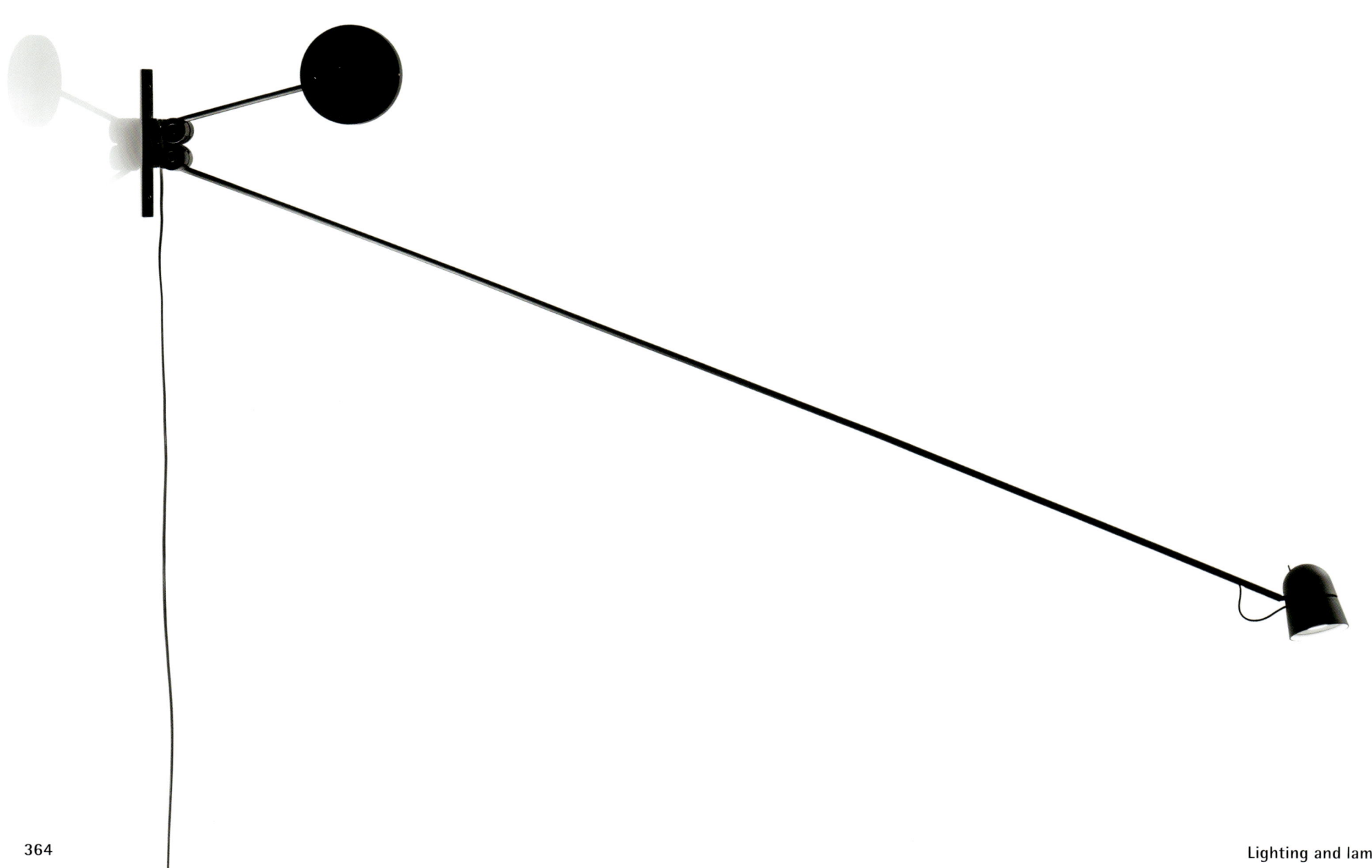

John
Desk Lamp
Schreibtischleuchte

Manufacturer
Tobias Grau GmbH,
Rellingen, Germany
Design
Tobias Grau
Web
www.tobias-grau.com

The John desk lamp is an easily movable, jointed-arm lamp. In the flat head a brilliantly shining, high-powered LED is integrated which is glare-suppressed by means of an optical lens. Two dimmers are located opposite each other in the lamp head. John is available in two versions: polished aluminium with high-gloss, white or black plastic components as well as in light colours at 2700 Kelvin (warm white) and 3500 Kelvin (white).

Die Schreibtischleuchte John ist eine leicht bewegliche Gelenkarmleuchte. In den flachen Kopf ist eine brillant leuchtende, leistungsstarke LEDs integriert, die mit einer optischen Linse entblendet wird. Im Leuchtenkopf befinden sich zwei gegen-überliegende Dimmtaster. John gibt es in zwei Ausführungen: Aluminium poliert mit hochglänzenden weißen bzw. schwar-zen Kunststoffteilen sowie in den Licht-farben 2700 Kelvin (warm weiß) und 3500 Kelvin (weiß).

SFERA
Free-Standing
LED Luminaire
LED-Stehleuchte

Manufacturer
Zumtobel Lighting GmbH,
Dornbirn, Austria
In-house design
Web
www.zumtobel.com/sfera
Honourable Mention

In every situation the appropriate lighting – this is what the Sfera free-standing LED luminaire provides. This is facilitated by a special technology which connects all LED luminaires in the room and allows them to communicate. They thus develop a kind of collective intelligence which, for example, allows a corridor lighting to function in a way that the brightness proactively increases when someone approaches in order to light the way to the workplace.

Statement by the jury
Sfera combines advanced technology with a contemporary, high-grade design.

In jeder Situation die passende Beleuchtung – das verspricht die LED-Stehleuchte Sfera. Ermöglicht wird dies durch eine spezielle Technologie, die alle LED-Stehleuchten im Raum miteinander verbindet und kommunizieren lässt. So entwickeln sie eine Art Schwarmintelligenz, die es ihnen beispielsweise mit einer Korridorfunktion erlaubt, vorausschauend hochzudimmen, wenn jemand kommt, um den Weg zum Arbeitsplatz zu weisen.

Begründung der Jury
Sfera verbindet fortschrittliche Technologie mit einer zeitgemäßen, hochwertigen Gestaltung.

XT-A FLOOR LED OSA /
XT-A LONG LED OSA
LED Floor Lamps
LED-Stehleuchten

Manufacturer
Tobias Grau GmbH,
Rellingen, Germany
Design
Tobias Grau
Web
www.tobias-grau.com

This LED floor lamp program for the office provides a considerably better light quality and energy efficiency than fluorescent lamps. Both models in the program illuminate the workplace free of glare by means of the LED OSA raster and without generating multi-shadows with white light, guaranteeing a brilliant colour emission. An integrated sensor control facilitates additional energy saving as well as various dimming and switching options.

Statement by the jury
Both lamps of this series convince with advanced LED technology, for producing exceptional working light and for their clear, high-grade design.

Dieses LED-Stehleuchten-Programm fürs Büro bietet eine deutlich bessere Lichtqualität und Energieeffizienz als Leuchtstofflampen. Beide Modelle des Programms beleuchten den Arbeitsplatz durch das LED OSA-Raster blendfrei und ohne Erzeugung von Mehrfachschatten mit weißem Licht und garantieren eine brillante Farbwiedergabe. Eine eingebaute Sensorsteuerung ermöglicht zusätzliche Energieeinsparung sowie verschiedene Dimm- und Schaltmöglichkeiten.

Begründung der Jury
Beide Leuchten dieser Serie überzeugen mit fortschrittlicher LED-Technik, durch ihr hervorragendes Arbeitslicht und ihre klare, hochwertige Gestaltung.

Lirio by Philips – Nick-Knack
LED Floor Lamps
LED-Stehleuchten

Manufacturer
Royal Philips Electronics,
Eindhoven, Netherlands
In-house design
Philips Design Lighting Team
Web
www.philips.com

Inspired by the comic figure La Linea of the Italian Osvaldo Cavandoli, Nick-Knack is a playful, versatile floor lamp which can be made into 16 different forms, according to mood. By means of two angled hinges the lamp can be bent by hand – for direct or indirect light. Six dimmable, powerful LEDs spread a warm-white light. The lamp is available in various colours and a soft-touch version.

Inspiriert von der Comic-Figur La Linea des Italieners Osvaldo Cavandoli ist Nick-Knack eine verspielte, vielseitige Stehleuchte, die je nach Stimmung in 16 verschiedene Formen gebracht werden kann. Durch zwei Winkelscharniere lässt sich die Leuchte von Hand verbiegen – für direktes oder indirektes Licht. Sechs dimmbare, leistungsstarke LEDs verbreiten ein warm-weißes Licht. Die Leuchte ist in verschiedenen Farben und einer Soft-Touch-Ausführung erhältlich.

Statement by the jury
This lamp, in its base position extremely linear, amazes with its flexible bending properties, which makes it not only very functional but also leads to ever new sculptures.

Begründung der Jury
In ihrer Basisstellung extrem geradlinig, verblüfft diese Leuchte mit ihrer flexiblen Knickbarkeit, die nicht nur sehr funktionell ist, sondern auch zu immer neuen Skulpturen führt.

Floor lamps

HF3550
Wake-up Light
Lichtwecker

Manufacturer
Royal Philips Electronics,
Eindhoven, Netherlands

In-house design
Philips Design Consumer
Lifestyle Team

Web
www.philips.com

reddot design award
best of the best 2013

Sensitive light object

Scientific observations of very simple organisms give
rise to the assumption that they began to adapt to
light and temperature at an early stage of evolution
in order to improve regulation of their metabolic
processes. The design of the HF3550 Wake-up Light
is based on a similarly natural concept: sleeping and
waking. This light alarm simulates the slow rising
of the sun. A coloured LED light slowly changes from
red to orange and then to a light sunny yellow. The
light shines gently through its translucent, organically
shaped casing and turns it into an object that
enriches any interior. The user concept of this Wake-
up Light is innovative. The neatly structured user
interface can be controlled with a free app on the
iPhone and be adapted to individual sleep patterns
so that users can select different alarm sounds or
a favourite song. Docking the iPhone to charge it
overnight is another very contemporary feature. The
organic design language and sensitive alarm function
of HF3550 Wake-up Light directly appeal to users'
emotions. The traditional shape of the alarm clock
has been completely re-defined.

Sensibles Lichtobjekt

Wissenschaftliche Beobachtungen an wenig kompli-
zierten Organismen lassen vermuten, dass diese schon
früh in der Evolution begonnen haben, sich an die
Licht- und Temperaturverhältnisse anzupassen, um auf
diese Weise ihre Stoffwechselvorgänge besser zu regeln.
Die Gestaltung des HF3550 Wake-up Light basiert auf
einem ähnlich natürlichen Konzept des Schlafens und
Aufwachens. Dieser Lichtwecker simuliert das langsame
Aufgehen der Sonne, indem ein farbiges LED-Licht sich
langsam von der Farbe Rot über Orange bis hin zu einem
hellen Sonnengelb verändert. Durch das transluzente,
organisch gestaltete Gehäuse schimmert sanft das
Licht hindurch und definiert es damit zu einem Objekt,
welches das Interieur bereichert. Eine Innovation stellt
auch das Nutzerkonzept dieses Lichtweckers dar. Sein
übersichtlich strukturiertes User Interface kann mittels
einer Free App über das iPhone gesteuert und so dem
individuellen Schlafrhythmus angepasst werden. Möglich
ist auch das Einstellen unterschiedlicher Weckgeräusche
oder die Auswahl des persönlichen Lieblingssongs. Sehr
zeitgemäß ist es, dass das iPhone auch an das HF3550
Wake-up Light angeschlossen werden kann, damit es
am nächsten Morgen geladen ist. Mit seiner organisch
anmutenden Formensprache und seinen sensitiven
Weckfunktionen spricht das HF3550 Wake-up Light
direkt die Emotionen des Nutzers an. Die bekannte Form
eines Weckers erfährt hier eine völlig neue Definition.

Statement by the jury

HF3550 Wake-up Light's design redefines a ritual.
Instead of being woken by the usual loud noises,
waking to this Wake-up Light's gentle light signals
is a much more natural experience. This concept
changes one's perception of a daily routine. The alarm
clock is no longer a merely functional tool, but turns
into a desirable design object.

Begründung der Jury

Die Gestaltung des HF3550 Wake-up Light definiert
ein Ritual auf neue Weise. Statt, wie gewohnt, mit
lärmenden Geräuschen aufgeweckt zu werden, impliziert das Aufwachen durch die sanften Lichtsignale des
Lichtweckers etwas sehr Natürliches. Dieses Konzept
verändert die Wahrnehmung im Alltag. Der Wecker
wird von einem rein funktionalen Gerät zu einem begehrten Designobjekt.

Wake-up light

X-Blaze
Headlight
Stirnlampe

Manufacturer
Favour Light Enterprises Limited,
Hong Kong
In-house design
Camellia Shiu
Web
www.favourlight.com

This battery-operated headlamp for professional use is extremely light and thanks to superior circuitry, provides a light intensity of 550 lumens. Four degrees of light intensity and a blink mode can be set via one switch. The inclining lamp head allows the setting of various beam angles. Its milled aluminium body gives the lamp not only its lightness but also makes it exceptionally sturdy.

Diese batteriebetriebene Stirnlampe für den professionellen Einsatz ist extrem leicht und bietet dank einer überlegenen Schalttechnik eine Leuchtkraft von 550 Lumen. Vier Helligkeitsstufen und ein Blinkmodus lassen sich über einen Schalter regeln. Der neigbare Leuchtkopf erlaubt die Einstellung verschiedener Strahlwinkel. Ihr gefräster Aluminiumkörper macht die Leuchte nicht nur sehr leicht, sondern auch ausgesprochen widerstandsfähig.

Statement by the jury
This headlamp is light, sturdy, technically sophisticated and well considered to the detail, so that it can provide good service even in extreme situations.

Begründung der Jury
Diese Stirnlampe ist leicht, robust, technisch ausgereift und bis ins Detail durchdacht, um selbst in Extremsituationen gute Dienste leisten zu können.

Headlight

N8LED
360-Degree LED Large Area Lighting
360-Grad-LED-Großflächenbeleuchtung

Manufacturer
ELSPRO Elektrotechnik
GmbH & Co. KG,
Hilden, Germany

In-house design
Thomas Cramer,
Hans-Werner Ribjitzki

Web
www.elspro.de

reddot design award
best of the best 2013

Perfect composition

There are many situations which require the surroundings to be lit as effectively as possible. In the case of police searches, for example, night has got to be as light as day so that they do not miss the smallest detail in their search for clues. N8LED is a well thought-out lighting concept designed for use in a number of similar situations offering 360-degree flood-lighting. The light intensity provided by cutting-edge LED technology is combined with an innovative, plate-shaped design. This plate shape makes it possible to unite several light sources to form one ball of light, which is what gives this flood-lighting its powerful radiance. The N8LED nonetheless exhibits an impressive formal coherence, by harmoniously linking the black light elements that are reminiscent of a timber-framed construction. The power of N8LED is combined with a functionality that can be developed depending on the situation. This flood-lighting can be assembled and taken apart intuitively without any tools and transported easily in an ergonomically designed bag, which is quick and simple to use. This is an innovative design concept for the effective use of LED technology in large spaces that has resulted in a product with a completely new design language. N8LED will quickly gain converts thanks to its easy handling and functionality.

Perfekte Anordnung

Es gibt viele Situationen, in denen es wichtig ist, dass die Umgebung möglichst effektiv ausgeleuchtet ist. So muss es etwa bei groß angelegten Sucheinsätzen der Polizei auch nachts taghell sein, damit dieser kein Detail bei der Spurensuche entgeht. Die N8LED ist ein sehr durchdacht gestaltetes Beleuchtungskonzept, welches für eine Vielzahl ähnlicher Ereignisse eine 360-Grad-Großflächenbeleuchtung ermöglicht. Die Lichtstärke modernster LED-Technologie verbindet sich dabei mit einer innovativen, tellerartigen Gestaltung. Diese Tellerform ermöglicht es, dass sich mehrere Lichtquellen zu einer Lichtkugel vereinen, mit der diese Großflächenbeleuchtung eine sehr helle Strahlkraft erreicht. Die N8LED zeigt dabei eine beeindruckende formale Geschlossenheit, die die fachwerkartig angeordneten schwarzen Lichtmodule harmonisch miteinander vereint. Ihre Leistungsfähigkeit verbindet sich bei der N8LED zudem mit einer nah an der Situation entwickelten Funktionalität. Diese Großflächenbeleuchtung kann intuitiv ohne Werkzeuge montiert und auch wieder demontiert werden. Transportiert wird sie unkompliziert in einer ergonomisch gestalteten Tasche, die sich dem Nutzer in ihrer Handhabung rasch und selbsterklärend erschließt. Ein innovatives Gestaltungskonzept für den effektiven Einsatz der LED-Technologie für Großflächen führte hier zu einem Produkt mit einer völlig neuen Formensprache. Die N8LED begeistert dabei durch ihre unkomplizierte Handhabung sowie ihre Funktionalität.

Statement by the jury

The N8LED significantly widens the application areas for LED technology. In fact, it is an archetype. The innovative use of the plate shape shows a fascinatingly logical approach, which combines individual light elements to form one perfect whole. This energy efficient 360-degree LED large area lighting is simple to use, thought out right down to the smallest details and is easy to transport.

Begründung der Jury

Die N8LED erweitert die Einsatzmöglichkeiten der LED-Technologie erheblich – sie ist ein neuer Archetypus. Die innovative Form eines Tellers zeigt eine faszinierende Logik, bei der sich einzelne Lichtmodule zu einem perfekten Ganzen vereinen. Diese energieeffiziente 360-Grad-LED-Großflächenbeleuchtung ist leicht zu handeln, durchdacht bis in jedes Detail und sie lässt sich gut transportieren.

LED lamps

abet
LED Light Series
LED-Leuchtenserie

Manufacturer
WILA Lichttechnik,
Iserlohn, Germany
In-house design
Andreas Henrich, Ward Murray
Web
www.wila.com

Centrepiece of the lights is their variable focussing unit: An infinitely variable fine adjustment allows various beam angles to be set. The proprietarily developed cooling device is material reduced and assures heat extraction as well as providing the lights with a high degree of recognition. The program includes round and square spotlights, wall washers and downlights. All components of the series are separable and recyclable.

Herzstück der Leuchten ist ihre variable Fokussiereinheit: Über eine stufenlose Feinjustierung lassen sich unterschiedliche Ausstrahlungswinkel realisieren. Der eigens entwickelte Kühlkörper stellt materialreduziert die Wärmeabführung sicher und verleiht den Leuchten einen hohen Wiedererkennungswert. Das Programm umfasst runde und quadratische Strahler, Wandfluter und Downlights. Alle Komponenten der Serie sind trenn- und recycelbar.

Spot 4
LED Spot
LED-Strahler

Manufacturer
Corvi,
Mumbai, India
In-house design
Vimal Soni
Web
www.corvi.com

Spot 4 is a highly efficient LED light which provides up to 600 lumens with 5 watts. The driver and a thermal management system are integrated already in the spotlight, facilitating a compact and reduced design of the lamp. The Spot 4 assures safety in case of power fluctuation as it works from 85 V to 285 V. The snap fastener of the spotlights makes installation easy; the dimming function allows flexible lighting power.

Statement by the jury
The LED lamp Spot 4 is minimalist in design, at the same time, however, highly efficient and very functional.

Spot 4 ist eine hocheffiziente LED-Leuchte, die bei 5 Watt bis zu 600 Lumen leistet. Der Treiber und ein Thermal Management System sind bereits in dem Strahler integriert, was eine kompakte und reduzierte Gestaltung der Leuchte ermöglicht. Der Spot 4 bietet Sicherheit bei Stromschwankungen, da er von 85 V bis 285 V arbeitet. Der Schnappverschluss des Spots erleichtert die Installation, die Dimmfunktion erlaubt eine flexible Beleuchtung.

Begründung der Jury
Der LED-Strahler Spot 4 ist minimalistisch gestaltet, gleichzeitig jedoch hocheffizient und sehr funktional.

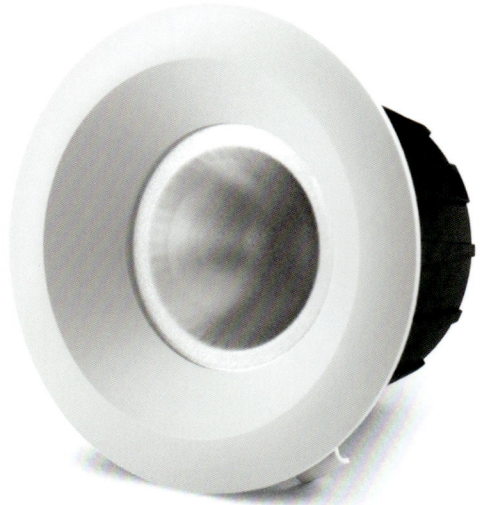

Spot 4S
LED Spot
LED-Strahler

Manufacturer
Corvi,
Mumbai, India
In-house design
Vimal Soni
Web
www.corvi.com

The exceptional property of this dimmable LED Spot 4S is its sophisticated swivel feature which makes it possible to set the lamp at various angles. Furthermore the spotlight contains innovative elements such as an integrated driver and a concealed thermal management system. The 4S can be simply installed via a snap fastener and has 35 years of life expectancy.

Statement by the jury
With the aid of an innovative swivel feature this compact LED recessed spotlight can be easily positioned for optimal illumination.

Hervorstechendes Merkmal des dimmbaren LED-Strahlers 4S ist sein ausgefeilter Schwenk-Mechanismus, der es ermöglicht, die Leuchte in unterschiedlichen Winkeln zu neigen. Darüber hinaus hat der Strahler innovative Elemente wie einen eingebauten Treiber und ein unsichtbares Thermal Management System. Der 4S lässt sich einfach mit einem Schnappverschluss installieren und hat eine Lebenserwartung von 35 Jahren.

Begründung der Jury
Mit Hilfe eines innovativen Schwenk-Mechanismus lässt sich dieser kompakte LED-Einbaustrahler für eine optimale Beleuchtung einfach ausrichten.

Downlight
LED Downlight

Manufacturer
Corvi,
Mumbai, India
In-house design
Vimal Soni
Web
www.corvi.com

This dimmable LED Downlight has a particularly purist lamp lead and thus can integrate discreetly in the ceiling structure. It is easily installed by means of a screwless snap fastener. The lamp has a concealed thermal management system which, together with the integrated driver, provides an improved, three-dimensional functionality. The highly efficient Downlight emits a light intensity of 1500 lumens at 15 watts.

Statement by the jury
With its plain appearance and simple installation method, this Downlight is suitable for almost every room.

Dieses dimmbare LED-Downlight hat einen besonders puristischen Leuchtenkopf und integriert sich so dezent in den Deckenaufbau. Mit Hilfe eines schraubenlosen Schnappverschlusses lässt es sich leicht installieren. Die Leuchte hat ein unsichtbares Thermal Management System, das zusammen mit dem eingebauten Treiber eine verbesserte dreidimensionale Funktionalität bietet. Das hocheffiziente Downlight hat einen Lichtstrom von bis zu 1500 Lumen bei 15 Watt.

Begründung der Jury
Mit seinem schlichten Erscheinungsbild und der einfachen Art der Installation eignet sich dieses Downlight für nahezu jeden Raum.

SCOTIX-1 LED
LED Spotlight
LED-Strahler

Manufacturer
PROLICHT GmbH,
Neu-Götzens, Austria
In-house design
Web
www.prolicht.at

The Scotix-1 LED spot light with its freely selectable colour temperature and a colour scheme range of 25 colours facilitates individual matching of the lamps according to each particular room situation. The easily positioned spotlight is suitable for highlighting and can be directed exactly at the target object along a 90 degree and 355 degree axis. Thanks to its compact design, the system takes up little space.

Statement by the jury
The Scotix-1 LED spotlight throws a good light on the objects in the room due to its flexible directional possibilities and its reduced form language.

Der Scotix-1 LED-Strahler ermöglicht mit seiner frei wählbaren Farbtemperatur und einer Farbgebungspalette, die 25 Farben umfasst, eine individuelle Anpassung der Leuchte auf die jeweilige Raumsituation. Der leicht positionierbare Strahler eignet sich zur Akzentuierung und lässt sich entlang einer 90- und einer 355 Grad-Achse exakt auf das Zielobjekt einrichten. Dank seiner kompakten Gestaltung nimmt das System nur wenig Platz in Anspruch.

Begründung der Jury
Der Scotix-1 LED-Strahler wirft dank seiner flexiblen Einstellungsmöglichkeiten und seiner reduzierten Formensprache ein gutes Licht auf Objekte im Raum.

i-POINT-X LED
LED Spotlight
LED-Strahler

Manufacturer
PROLICHT GmbH,
Neu-Götzens, Austria
In-house design
Web
www.prolicht.at

This plain, functional LED spotlight is designed to be flexibly usable. The versatile LED spotlight head can be set along a 105 degree and a 350 degree axis and is thus suitable for optimal highlighting. The spotlight design is reduced and space-saving; the combination options of the black elements with 25 available body colours open up possibilities for individual configurations.

Statement by the jury
This LED spotlight distinguishes itself by its high degree of functionality and contemporary design which is emphasised even more due to the black-colour contrasts.

Dieser schlichte, funktionale LED-Strahler ist so konzipiert, dass er flexibel einsetzbar ist. Der wendige LED-Strahlerkopf kann entlang einer 105- und einer 350 Grad-Achse ausgerichtet werden und eignet sich damit optimal zur Akzentuierung. Die Gestaltung des Spotlights ist reduziert und raumsparend, die Kombinationsmöglichkeiten der schwarzen Elemente mit 25 verfügbaren Korpus-Farben eröffnen individuellen Gestaltungsspielraum.

Begründung der Jury
Dieser LED-Strahler zeichnet sich durch seine hohe Funktionalität und zeitgemäße Gestaltung aus, die mit Schwarz-Farb-Kontrasten noch unterstrichen wird.

Pipes
LED Track Spotlight
LED-Stromschienenstrahler

Manufacturer
Intra Lighting,
Šempeter pri Gorici, Slovenia
Design
Serge Cornelissen,
Roeselare, Belgium
Web
www.intra-lighting.com
www.sergecornelissen.com

The Pipes LED spotlight impresses by its high quality of light with a colour rendering index of over 95. Thereby it gives the illuminated objects a particular depth, structure and lively colours and is suitable for use in museums, galleries or in the retail trade. The compact, cylindrical spotlight with its puristic aluminium housing provides various spot settings and fulfils all demands for accent lighting.

Statement by the jury
The puristic aluminium body conceals all technical components of this accurately accenting spotlight and imparts Pipes with unobtrusive, modern aesthetics.

Der LED-Strahler Pipes beeindruckt durch seine hohe Lichtqualität mit einem Farbwiedergabeindex von über 95. Damit verleiht er den angestrahlten Objekten eine besondere Tiefe, Struktur und lebendige Farben und eignet sich gut für den Einsatz in Museen, Galerien oder im Handel. Der kompakte zylindrische Strahler mit seinem puristischen Aluminiumgehäuse bietet verschiedene Strahleinstellungen und erfüllt alle Ansprüche präziser Akzentbeleuchtung.

Begründung der Jury
Der puristische Aluminiumkörper verbirgt alle technischen Bauteile dieses präzisen Akzentstrahlers und verleiht Pipes eine unaufdringlich moderne Ästhetik.

DISCUS Evolution
LED Spotlight
LED-Strahler

Manufacturer
Zumtobel Lighting GmbH,
Dornbirn, Austria
Design
EOOS Design GmbH,
Vienna, Austria
Web
www.zumtobel.com/discus
www.eoos.com

The Discus Evolution minimalist LED spotlight system was designed for accent lighting. An integral component is the innovative heat management with passive cooling by means of radial plate fins. The cooling also plays an important part in the sustainability of the spotlight, since it increases efficiency and longevity. The spot is so designed that various lens optics can be changed without the use of tools.

Das minimalistische LED-Strahlersystem Discus Evolution wurde für die Akzentbeleuchtung konzipiert. Integraler Bestandteil der Gestaltung ist das innovative Wärmemanagement mit passiver Kühlung durch strahlenförmige Lamellen. Die Kühlung spielt auch für die Nachhaltigkeit der Leuchte eine wichtige Rolle, denn sie erhöht ihre Effizienz und Lebensdauer. Der Strahler ist so gestaltet, dass sich verschiedene Linsenoptiken werkzeuglos tauschen lassen.

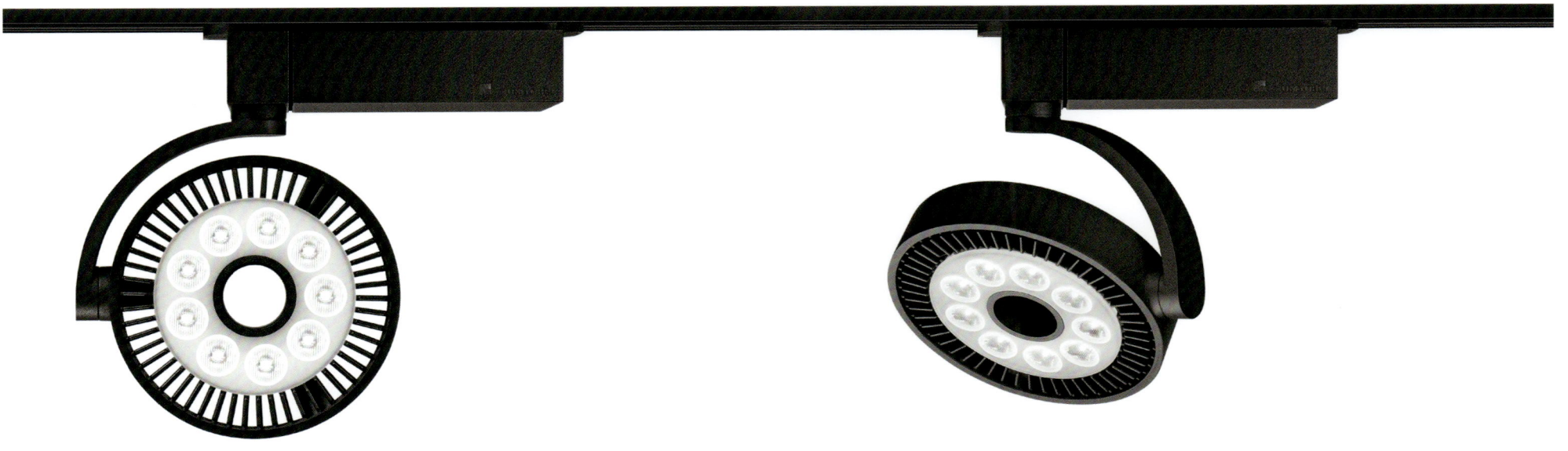

Lucid
LED Downlight

Manufacturer
ELR Australia,
North Hobart, Tasmania, Australia
In-house design
Stanley Ong, Wade Fromberg
Web
www.elr-group.com

Lucid is a premium downlight series which was specially developed for demanding commercial applications. The design of the light is classic and elegant. Its round border is extremely filigree with a thickness of under 0.9 mm and slightly bevelled towards the edge – thus Lucid fits perfectly into the ceiling structure. Lucid is available with more accessories for floodlight effects or indirect lighting.

Statement by the jury
The Lucid LED downlight integrates elegantly into every ceiling, thanks to its minimised dimensions and discreet design.

Lucid ist eine Premium Downlight-Serie, die speziell für anspruchsvolle kommerzielle Anwendungen konzipiert wurde. Die Gestaltung der Leuchte ist klassisch-elegant. Ihr kreisrunder Rand ist mit einer Stärke von weniger als 0,9 mm ausgesprochen filigran und zum Rand hin leicht abgeschrägt – dadurch fügt sich Lucid perfekt in den Deckenaufbau ein. Lucid ist mit weiterem Zubehör für Wandfluter-Effekte oder indirekte Beleuchtung erhältlich.

Begründung der Jury
Das LED-Downlight Lucid integriert sich dank seiner minimierten Abmessungen und der dezenten Gestaltung elegant in jede Decke.

Piazzo RC
LED Downlight

Manufacturer
ELR Australia,
North Hobart, Tasmania, Australia
In-house design
Stanley Ong, Wade Fromberg
Web
www.elr-group.com

Behind the puristic surface of Piazzo RC an innovative heat management is concealed which solves the problem of the heavy weight in case of high-power LED usage: extremely thin, aluminium thermal ribs form heat flow channels. Thanks to their positioning and design, these facilitate maximal airstream and simultaneously reduce the overall weight by 70 per cent. Piazzo RC is easy to install and suitable for most ceiling structures.

Statement by the jury
Piazzo RC provides an intelligent design solution for efficient output from high power LEDs while at the same time reducing the weight.

Hinter der puristischen Oberfläche von Piazzo RC verbirgt sich ein innovatives Wärmemanagement, welches das Problem des großen Gewichts bei High Power LED-Anwendungen löst: Extrem dünne thermische Rippen aus Aluminium bilden Wärmestromkanäle. Dank ihrer Anordnung und Gestaltung ermöglichen sie einen maximalen Luftstrom und reduzieren zugleich das Gesamtgewicht um 70 Prozent. Piazzo RC ist einfach zu installieren und für die meisten Deckenaufbauten geeignet.

Begründung der Jury
Piazzo RC sorgt mit einer intelligenten Gestaltungslösung für eine effizientere Leistung von High Power-LED bei gleichzeitiger Reduzierung des Gewichts.

Invader-2 LED
LED Downlight

Manufacturer
PROLICHT GmbH,
Neu-Götzens, Austria
In-house design
Web
www.prolicht.at

This recessed downlight serves to highlight points of the presentation in the room, whereby the light itself remains reservedly in the background. The compact light with a diameter of 80 mm requires little depth for mounting. With three reflector angles of 24, 32 and 50 degrees, the spotlight allows setting of the light beam direction. The light is available in 25 colours and is produced individually for the customer.

Statement by the jury
With respect to form, Invader-2 emphasises the main points in the room due to its directional beam adjustment and the colours in which it is available.

Dieser Einbaustrahler dient der punktuellen Inszenierung im Raum, wobei sich die Leuchte selbst dezent im Hintergrund hält. Die kompakte Leuchte mit einem Durchmesser von 80 mm nimmt bei der Montage nur eine mäßige Tiefe in Anspruch. Mit drei Reflektorwinkeln von 24, 32 und 50 Grad erlaubt der Strahler eine Steuerung des Lichtkegels. Die Leuchte ist in 25 Farben lieferbar und wird individuell für den Kunden produziert.

Begründung der Jury
Der Form nach ein klassischer Strahler, setzt Invader-2 durch seinen steuerbaren Lichtkegel und die Farben, in denen er erhältlich ist, Akzente im Raum.

Laser Blade
Recessed LED Downlight
LED-Einbauleuchte

Manufacturer
iGuzzini illuminazione,
Recanati, Italy
In-house design
Massimo Gattari
Web
www.iguzzini.com

This extremely minimalist LED recessed lighting for the retail trade has a particular light distribution which is characterised by an even, circular light emission. The narrow, uniform light beam allows the light to be concentrated on horizontal surfaces in order to highlight individual objects. With various spot optics, the lamps can be used not only for accent lighting but also for overall lighting.

Diese extrem minimalistische LED-Einbauleuchte für den Einzelhandel hat eine besondere Lichtverteilung, die sich durch eine gleichmäßige, kreisförmige Licht-emission auszeichnet. Der enge Lichtkegel ermöglicht es, das Licht auf horizontalen Oberflächen zu konzentrieren, um einzelne Objekte hervorzuheben. Mit verschiedenen Spotoptiken können die Leuchten sowohl für die Akzent- als auch für die Allgemein-beleuchtung eingesetzt werden.

Statement by the jury
With its linear, minimalist form language, Laser Blade generates graphic light compositions on the ceiling.

Begründung der Jury
Mit ihrer geradlinigen, minimalistischen Formensprache erzeugt Laser Blade grafische Leucht-Kompositionen an der Decke.

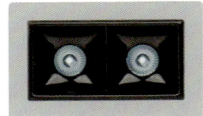

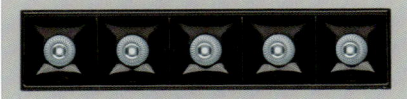

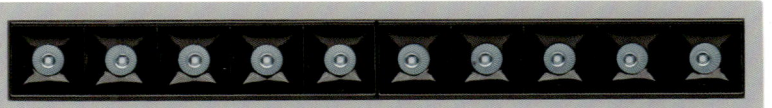

K-Design
LED Light Series
LED-Leuchtenserie

Manufacturer
Kiteo GmbH & Co. KG,
Munich, Germany
Design
ARTEFAKT industriekultur,
Darmstadt, Germany
Web
www.kiteo.de
www.artefakt.de
Honourable Mention

The K-Design program is based on three clear basic forms, which generates suspense due to the light asymmetry. Technologically it provides a colour spectrum almost identical to that of the sun and thus creates a pleasant atmosphere in the room. The lights can be controlled via iPhone or iPad to regulate the colour temperature or intensity. The series offers great freedom of planning due to the various sizes, designs and mounting possibilities.

Das K-Design-Programm baut auf drei klaren Grundformen auf, deren leichte Asymmetrie Spannung erzeugt. Technologisch bietet sie ein dem Sonnenlicht nahezu identisches Farbspektrum und schafft so eine angenehme Raumatmosphäre. Die Leuchten lassen sich über das iPhone oder iPad ansteuern, um Farbtemperatur und Intensität zu regeln. Mit verschiedenen Größen, Ausführungen und Befestigungsmöglichkeiten bietet die Serie große Planungsfreiheit.

Statement by the jury
With its reduced aesthetic and the individual control options, these lamps meet all demands of a modern lighting system.

Begründung der Jury
Mit ihrer reduzierten Ästhetik und den individuellen Steuerungsmöglichkeiten erfüllen diese Leuchten alle Ansprüche an eine moderne Beleuchtung.

PadLED
LED Surface-Mounted
Lighting System
LED-Aufbauleuchtensystem

Manufacturer
Paulmann Licht GmbH,
Springe-Völksen, Germany
In-house design
Web
www.paulmann.com
Honourable Mention

PadLED is a minimalist designed LED surface-mounted lighting system. The ceiling-mounted base elements act as power feeds, which are interconnected via a flat, self-adhesive tape with integrated conductivity. Square pads are attached to the base elements by means of magnets. The pads are of aluminium and dissipate the heat from the LEDs perfectly. Various decors can be imposed on the pads.

PadLED ist ein minimalistisch gestaltetes LED-Aufbauleuchtensystem. An die Decke montierte Basiselemente dienen als Stromeinspeiser, die über ein flaches selbstklebendes Band mit integrierter Stromführung miteinander verbunden werden. Mithilfe von Magneten lassen sich quadratische Pads auf den Basiselementen befestigen. Die Pads sind aus Aluminium und leiten die Wärme der LEDs perfekt ab. Auf die Pads können verschiedene Dekore gesetzt werden.

Statement by the jury
This surface-mounted lighting system provides a solution which is as simple as it is convincing for mounting LEDs on the ceiling without much preparation or installation work.

Begründung der Jury
Dieses Aufbauleuchtensystem bietet eine ebenso einfache wie überzeugende Lösung, LED-Leuchten ohne größere Auf- oder Einbauarbeiten direkt an der Decke anzubringen.

LED lamps

Crystal LED Candle
LED Lamp
LED-Lampe

Manufacturer
Luxram Lighting Beijing Ltd,
Beijing, China
In-house design
Shou Xun Wang, Xiao Bo Yan
Web
www.luxramlighting.com

For this lamp traditional crystal glass has been combined with the latest LED technology and a special production technique. The lamp design was inspired by diamond cutting: 132 facets have been cut in the glass, maximising the light reflection and giving the lamp great illumination power. Thanks to its LED technology, the lamp is 20 percent shorter than other candle-shaped light sources and saves 90 percent energy.

Für diese Lampe wurde traditionelles Kristallglas mit neuester LED-Technologie und einer speziellen Produktionstechnik kombiniert. Das Design der Lampe ist vom Diamantschliff inspiriert: 132 Flächen wurden aus dem Glas herausgearbeitet, was die Lichtreflexion maximiert und der Lampe große Leuchtkraft verleiht. Dank ihrer LED-Technologie ist die Lampe 20 Prozent kürzer als andere kerzen-förmigen Glühlampen und spart bis zu 90 Prozent ihrer Energie ein.

LED Premium Bulb
LED Lamp
LED-Lampe

Manufacturer
Royal Philips Electronics,
Eindhoven, Netherlands
In-house design
Philips Design Lighting Team
Web
www.philips.com

Behind this white LED lamp, with its plain and elegant form language, the latest LED technology is concealed. The classical design of the LED lamp makes it easier for consumers to convert from light bulbs to modern LED lighting. When switched off the lamps have a smooth, white surface. Their classical silhouette is the result of the absence of cooling fins and air channels. The lamp is also available as Philips Hue Connected Bulb.

Statement by the jury
The LED Premium Bulb is a reminder of classical light bulbs but has, however, a considerably more updated form language which does justice to its efficient LED technology.

Diese weiße LED-Lampe mit ihrer schlicht-eleganten Formensprache birgt neueste LED-Technologie. Die klassische Gestaltung der LED-Lampe erleichtert Konsumenten das Umrüsten von Glühbirnen auf zeitgemäße LED-Beleuchtung. Im ausgeschalteten Zustand haben die Lampen eine glatte weiße Oberfläche, ihre klassische Silhouette entsteht durch das Fehlen von Kühlrippen und Luftkanälen. Die Lampe ist auch als Philips Hue Connected Bulb erhältlich.

Begründung der Jury
Die LED Premium Bulb erinnert an klassische Glühbirnen, hat jedoch eine deutlich modernere Formensprache, die ihrer effizienten LED-Technologie gerecht wird.

LDAHV6L27CG
Modern Classic
LED Lamp
LED-Lampe

Manufacturer
Panasonic,
Wiesbaden, Germany
In-house design
Nobuyuki Mase
Web
www.panasonic.eu/led

This LED lamp is not only in its form a memento of the classical 40 Watt light bulb, it provides also the same clear and warm light. This lamp thereby conceals all advantages of the latest LED technology without the disadvantages of classical light bulbs; it consumes about 84 per cent less energy and with a life of up to 40,000 hours, lasts forty times as long. When switched on it provides a natural light immediately.

Statement by the jury
This LED lamp combines in a convincing manner the form language of the classical light bulb with the advantages of the latest LED technology.

Diese LED-Lampe ist nicht nur der Form nach eine Reminiszenz an die klassische 40 Watt-Glühbirne, sie liefert auch das gleiche klare und warme Licht. Damit birgt dieses Leuchtmittel alle Vorteile neuester LED-Technologie ohne die Nachteile klassischer Glühlampen: Sie verbraucht rund 84 Prozent weniger Energie und hält mit einer Lebensdauer von bis zu 40.000 Stunden vierzigmal so lange. Eingeschaltet sorgt sie augenblicklich für ein natürliches Licht.

Begründung der Jury
Diese LED-Lampe verbindet auf überzeugende Weise die Formensprache der klassischen Glühbirne mit den Vorteilen neuester LED-Technologie.

HeadLED
LED Lamp
LED-Lampe

Manufacturer
Santa & Cole,
La Roca (Barcelona), Spain
In-house design
Web
www.santacole.com

HeadLED is a sophisticated capsule which is light source and fitting in one. It thus contrasts with the traditional suspended lamps, whose fittings are installed independently from the light source. Thanks to this design, the HeadLED can be flexibly combined with a wide variety of different lampshades. The lamp consists of an aluminium cooling unit, a plate with four LEDs and a diffuser with high transparency and light dispersion.

Statement by the jury
The HeadLED convinces with its well-considered, innovative design which unites the LED light source with the fitting.

HeadLED ist eine raffinierte Kapsel, die Lichtquelle und Fassung in einem ist. Dadurch hebt sie sich von traditionellen Hängeleuchten ab, deren Fassung unabhängig vom Leuchtmittel angebracht wird. Dank dieser Gestaltung lässt sich die HeadLED flexibel mit den unterschiedlichsten Lampenschirmen kombinieren. Die Lampe besteht aus einem Aluminium-Kühlkörper, einer Platte mit vier LEDs und einem Diffusor mit hoher Transparenz und Lichtstreuung.

Begründung der Jury
Die HeadLED überzeugt mit ihrer durchdachten, innovativen Gestaltung, die LED-Lichtquelle und Fassung vereint.

ONYX Copilot
**LED Reading Light
for Vehicle Interior
Applications**
LED-Leseleuchte für
den Fahrzeuginnenraum

Manufacturer
OSRAM GmbH,
Munich, Germany
Design
Nerd Communications
(Daniel von Waldthausen,
Benjamin Beck),
Berlin, Germany
Web
www.osram.com
www.nerdcommunications.com

The Onyx Copilot is an elegant LED reading light powered by a car's cigarette lighter receptacle. The matte black silicon surface gives Copilot a pleasant outer texture, while there the bendable yet firm neck can be adjusted as needed. Its warm white LED-lighting provides the ideal reading atmosphere without blinding the driver. The concave on- and off-switch, integrated into the lamp's head, makes it easily findable and intuitively usable.

Statement by the jury
Onyx Copilot is a convincing reading light which combines high flexibility and the latest LED technology.

Onyx Copilot ist eine elegante LED-Leseleuchte für das Fahrzeug, die über den Zigarettenanzünder mit Energie versorgt wird. Ihre mattschwarze Silikon-Oberfläche hat eine angenehme Haptik. Der geschmeidig biegsame Hals kann je nach Bedarf ausgerichtet werden. Warmes LED-Licht schafft eine angenehme Leseatmosphäre, ohne den Fahrer dabei zu blenden. Durch seine konkave Form lässt sich der in die Oberfläche integrierte Schalter intuitiv finden und bedienen.

Begründung der Jury
Onyx Copilot überzeugt als funktionelle Leseleuchte, die dynamisches Design, hohe Biegsamkeit und aktuelle LED-Technologie in sich vereint.

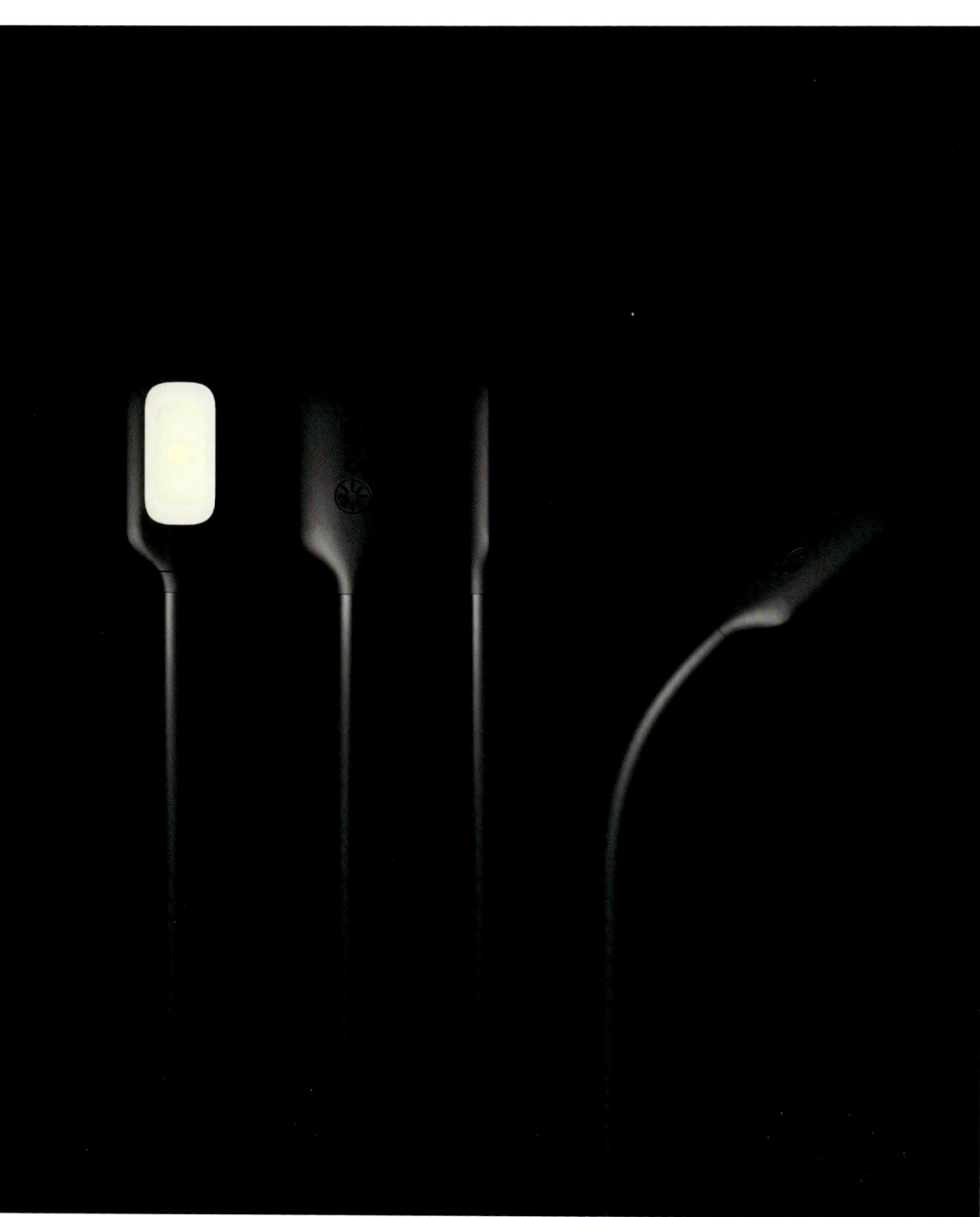

LED LENSER F1
LED Torch
LED-Taschenlampe

Manufacturer
Zweibrüder Optoelectronics
GmbH & Co.KG,
Solingen, Germany
In-house design
Andre Kunzendorf, Tobias Schleder
Web
www.zweibrueder.com

The LED LENSER F1 surprisingly provides a lighting power of 400 lumens from its minimal dimensions and one CR123 battery as energy source. At the same time, the torch combines aesthetics and practicality: Front and back caps, with their soft, flowing forms provide an overall harmonious appearance. Nevertheless, the torch provides typical elements of tactile lamps such as squared edges to prevent rolling or an exchangeable tactical ring.

Statement by the jury
This torch accomplishes well the balance between a compact and at the same time harmonious form and exceptional lighting power.

Die LED LENSER F1 überrascht bei minimalen Abmessungen und einer CR123-Batterie als Energiequelle mit einer Leuchtkraft von 400 Lumen. Gleichzeitig vereint die Taschenlampe Ästhetik und Praxistauglichkeit: Kopf- und Endkappe sorgen mit ihren weichen, fließenden Formen für ein insgesamt harmonisches Erscheinungsbild. Trotzdem bietet die Lampe typische Elemente taktiler Lampen wie einen kantigen Wegrollschutz oder einen austauschbaren taktischen Ring.

Begründung der Jury
Diese Taschenlampe bewerkstelligt souverän den Spagat zwischen einer kompakten und gleichzeitig harmonischen Form und einer herausragenden Leuchtkraft.

LED LENSER M7RX/M14X
LED Torch
LED-Taschenlampe

Manufacturer
Zweibrüder Optoelectronics
GmbH & Co.KG,
Solingen, Germany
In-house design
Andre Kunzendorf, Rainer Opolka
Web
www.zweibrueder.com

The prominent feature of the M7RX 1 and M14X torches is their powerful light of about 600 lumens. This light intensity is due to a powerful LED chip which also changes the beam: The focussed spotlight is almost three times bigger than its previous model. A new light distribution provides a great deal of light, also outside the area in focus. A titanium coloured ring at the torch head denotes this development with regard to the design.

Statement by the jury
Both these torches are sophisticated technically as well as in design and impress due to their high lighting power.

Hervorstechendes Merkmal der Taschenlampen M7RX und M14X ist ihre Lichtleistung von rund 600 Lumen. Diese Strahlkraft verdanken sie einem leistungsstarken LED-Chip, der auch den Lichtkegel verändert: Der fokussierte Spot ist fast dreimal größer als bei Vorgängermodellen, eine neue Lichtverteilung sorgt auch jenseits des fokussierten Bereichs für viel Licht. Ein titanfarbener Ring am Lampenkopf kennzeichnet diese Entwicklung in gestalterischer Hinsicht.

Begründung der Jury
Diese beiden in technischer wie gestalterischer Hinsicht ausgereiften Taschenlampen beeindrucken durch ihre hohe Lichtleistung.

Shroom
Outdoor Light Fixtures and Seats
Außenleuchten und Sitzmöbel

Manufacturer
SAINTLUC,
Saint Berthevin, France
Design
Ralston & Bau
(Birgitta Ralston, Alexandre Bau),
Dale i Sunnfjord, Norway
Web
www.saintluc.fr
www.ralstonbau.com

The Shroom series of light fixtures and seats blend into the landscape with their natural shapes. They have a unique detection system: the lights dim automatically to ten percent of their intensity if nobody is near. When a person approaches, they light up illuminating the path. This saves energy and avoids unnecessary light pollution. The organically formed lampshades are manufactured using an eco-friendly linen composite.

Die Außenleuchten und Sitzmöbel der Shroom Serie fügen sich mit ihrer natürlichen Form harmonisch in die Landschaft ein. Sie haben ein einzigartiges Detektionssystem: Das Licht dimmt automatisch auf zehn Prozent Lichtstärke herunter, wenn niemand in der Nähe ist. Sobald sich eine Person nähert, leuchten sie auf und erhellen den Weg. Das spart Energie und vermeidet unnötige Lichtverschmutzung. Die organisch geformten Lampenschirme sind aus einem umweltfreundlichen Leinen-Verbundwerkstoff hergestellt.

Statement by the jury
The organic lines of these charming lights are an expression of environmental friendliness, which is also reflected in the choice of material and in their functionality.

Begründung der Jury
Die organische Formgebung dieser charmanten Leuchten ist Ausdruck ihrer Umweltfreundlichkeit, die sich auch in Materialwahl und Funktionsweise zeigt.

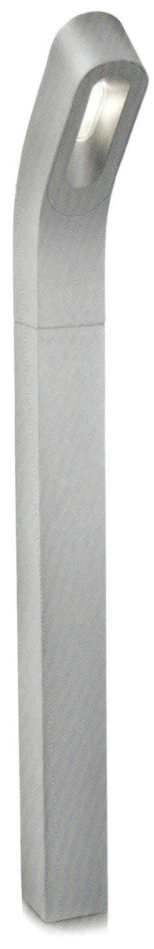

Ledino Outdoor Range Dunetop
Outdoor Luminaire Range
Außenleuchten-Serie

Manufacturer
Royal Philips Electronics,
Eindhoven, Netherlands
In-house design
Philips Design Lighting Team
Web
www.philips.com

The luminaire units of the Ledino Outdoor Dunetop range are so designed that they seem to be bowing to those passing by while they illuminate the way. The plain, aluminium lamps emit a diffused light by means of an integrated lean, white LED module. They are also energy-saving. The collection consists of a floor standing lamp in grey or anthracite and a wall lamp which is available in light grey and light anthracite.

Die Leuchten der Ledino Outdoor Dunetop-Serie sind so gestaltet, dass sie sich vor den Passanten zu verneigen scheinen, während sie dezent den Weg beleuchten. Die schlichten Aluminium-Leuchten spenden mit Hilfe eines integrierten, schlanken weißen LED-Moduls ein diffuses Licht und sind energiesparend. Die Kollektion besteht aus einer Stehleuchte in grau oder anthrazit und einer Wandleuchte, die in Hellgrau und Hell-anthrazit verfügbar ist.

Statement by the jury
These outdoor luminaire units impress with their plain elegance and seem to fulfil their task of lighting the way as pleasantly as possible with humility.

Begründung der Jury
Diese Außenleuchten bestechen mit ihrer schlichten Eleganz und scheinen sich demutsvoll ihrer Aufgabe hinzugeben, den Weg so gut und angenehm wie möglich auszuleuchten.

UrbanSky
Street Luminaire
Straßenleuchte

Manufacturer
Philips GmbH,
Unternehmensbereich Lighting,
Hamburg, Germany
Design
podpod design
(Michael Podgorschek, Iris Podgorschek),
Vienna, Austria
Web
www.philips.com
www.podpoddesign.com

UrbanSky is a modern, energy-efficient cable suspension lamp, whose design and functionally outstanding feature is a plastic bath which houses an LED module with 64 high-power LEDs and protects them optimally. Their special form with outer edges curved slightly upwards directs the light onto the road, so that safety and comfort are optimised. At the same time the adjacent house facades are discreetly illuminated.

UrbanSky ist eine moderne, energieeffizi- ente Seilleuchte, deren gestalterisch wie funktionell hervorstechendes Merkmal eine Kunststoffwanne ist, die ein LEDgine-Mo- dul mit 64 Hochleistungs-LEDs aufnimmt und optimal schützt. Ihre spezielle Form mit leicht nach oben gewölbten Außen- kanten führt das Licht so auf die Straße, dass Sicherheit und Komfort optimiert werden. Gleichzeitig werden dadurch auch die angrenzenden Häuserfassaden dezent aufgehellt.

Statement by the jury
UrbanSky is a compact streetlight with the latest LED technology which convinces due to its very complex and simultaneously timeless design.

Begründung der Jury
UrbanSky ist eine kompakte Straßen- leuchte mit neuester LED-Technologie, die mit ihrer sehr komplexen und gleichzeitig zeitlosen Gestaltung überzeugt.

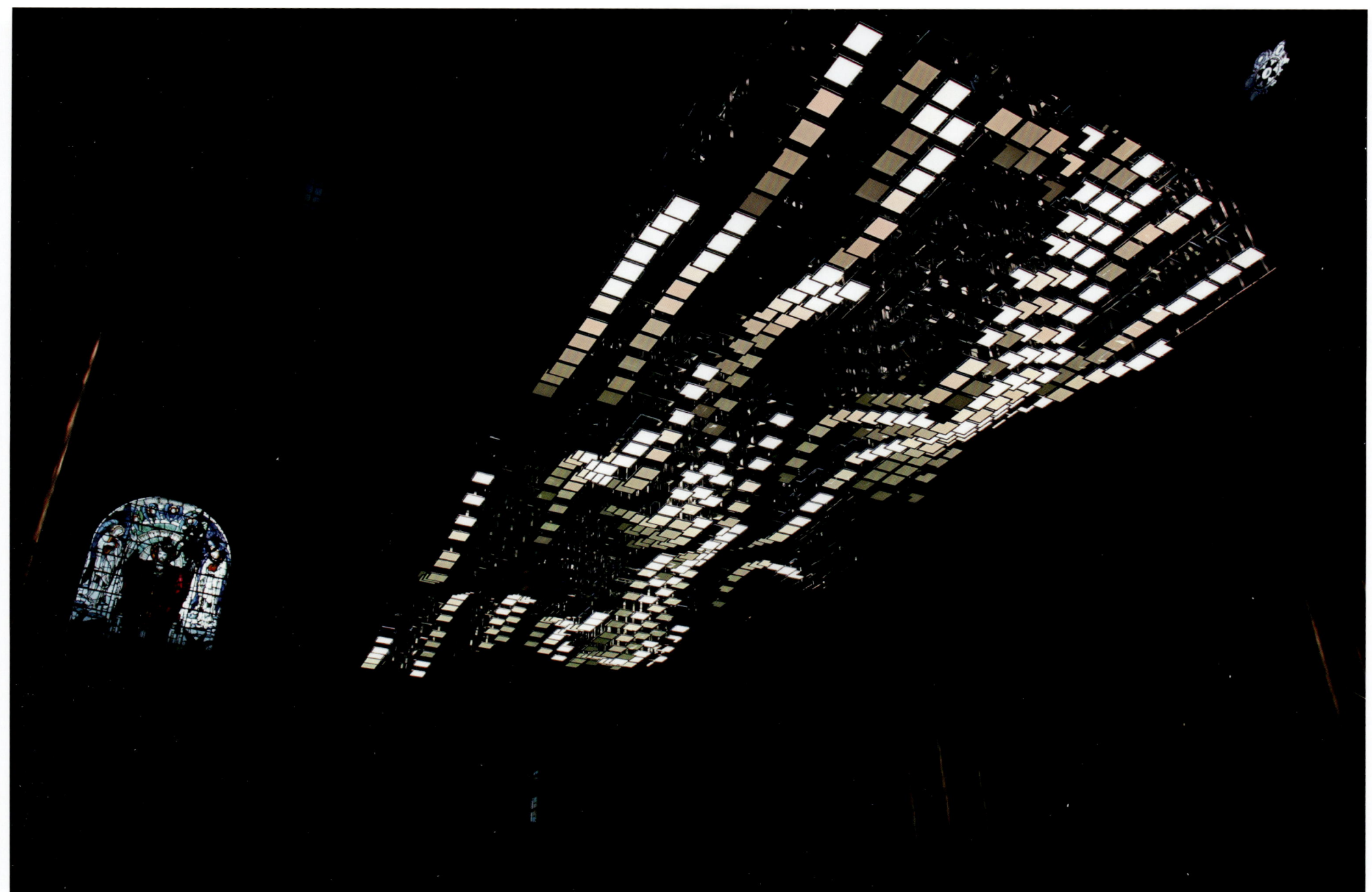

LivingSculpture
3D Module System
Modular Light Fixture
Modulares Beleuchtungssystem

Manufacturer
Philips Technologie GmbH,
Aachen, Germany
Design
WHITEvoid interactive art & design
(Christopher Bauder),
Berlin, Germany
Web
www.lighting.philips.com
www.whitevoid.com
Honourable Mention

Sheer endlessly many design possibilities for ceiling and wall lighting are provided by the LivingSculpture 3D Module System: square base plates with organic light diodes can quite easily be freely arranged on connecting rods of various lengths. This results in three-dimensional illuminated areas which, by using iPad based control software, can be individually modulated.

Schier unendlich viele Gestaltungsmöglichkeiten für die Decken- und Wandbeleuchtung stecken im LivingSculpture 3D Module System: Quadratische Basisplatten mit organischen Leuchtdioden lassen sich auf Verbindungsstäben unterschiedlicher Länge ganz einfach frei arrangieren. Das Ergebnis sind dreidimensionale Leuchtflächen, die sich mithilfe einer iPad-basierten Steuerungssoftware individuell bespielen lassen.

Statement by the jury
This modular lighting system is so amazingly simple in its concept that in principle it enables everybody to create exciting 3D light sculptures.

Begründung der Jury
Dieses modulare Lichtsystem ist so erstaunlich einfach konzipiert, dass es im Prinzip jeden in die Lage versetzt, spannende 3D-Lichtskulpturen zu kreieren.

Interior design
Interior Design

Room and building equipment, interior furnishing, micro architecture, lounges, shop furnishing and equipment, shop systems, patterns, sales displays, orientation systems and signages, object furniture, exhibition design and stands, shop fitting, flooring, wall covering, tiles, floor covering, windows, doors
Raum- und Gebäudeausstattung, Inneneinrichtung, Mikroarchitektur, Lounges, Shop-Einrichtung und -Ausstattung, Shop-Systeme, Dekors, Verkaufsdisplays, Leit- und Orientierungssysteme, Objektmöbel, Messebau und -stände, Ladenbau, Fußböden, Wandverkleidung, Fliesen, Bodenbeläge, Fenster, Türen

7

Invisible Table
Table
Tisch

Manufacturer
Kartell,
Milan, Italy

Design
Tokujin Yoshioka Inc.
(Tokujin Yoshioka),
Tokyo, Japan

Web
www.kartell.it
www.tokujin.com

reddot design award
best of the best 2013

All of a piece

The shape of a table can dominate a room; it is therefore important to adapt it to its environment. The Invisible Table is an innovative piece of furniture that will suit and enhance every interior. At a first glance it may appear rather nondescript, because it is transparent and its unobtrusive shape maintains a low profile in the room. However, closer inspection will reveal the perfection of its design and its harmonious lines. The table and its square table top measuring 100 x 100 cm are cast in an innovative, elaborate process. The starting point for the manufacture of every table is a 20 kg block of plastic. The result is a table that is as good to look at as it is to touch. At the same time, it is very versatile and combines its simultaneously graceful yet powerful appearance with a high degree of functionality. Based on an innovative production process, the Invisible Table has very individual charm. Its sophisticated design turns it into a timeless, integral part of any interior.

Wie aus einem Guss

Da die Form eines Tisches einen Raum dominieren kann, ist es wichtig, ihn gut seiner Umgebung anzupassen. Der Invisible Table ist ein innovativer Tisch, der sich in jedes Interieur einfügen kann und es stets bereichert. Auf den ersten Blick wirkt er eher unscheinbar, denn er ist durchsichtig und nimmt sich im Raum auch durch seine elegante Formensprache dezent zurück. Bei näherem Hinsehen wird dann die Perfektion seiner Gestaltung und die Harmonie seiner Linienführung deutlich. Dieser Tisch mit einer quadratischen Tischplatte in der Größe von 100 x 100 cm wird in einem innovativen und aufwendigen Gussverfahren gefertigt. Die Grundlage für die Herstellung nur eines Tisches bildet dabei ein 20 kg schwerer Kunststoffblock. Das Ergebnis ist ein Tisch, der durch seine Formen sowie seine Haptik fasziniert. Er ist dabei sehr vielseitig und vereint seine Anmutung von Leichtigkeit und Kraft mit einem hohen Maß an Funktionalität. Auf der Grundlage eines innovativen Produktionsverfahrens entstand mit dem Invisible Table ein Tisch von besonderer Anmut. Seine feinsinnige Gestaltung definiert ihn als ein integratives und zeitloses Element des Interieurs.

Statement by the jury

The Invisible Table represents a highly modern approach to materials and the use of technology. It also addresses the question of future production methods. Initially, it may appear minimalist and plain in a room, however its formal perfection and verve make it that much more impressive. This table has style.

Begründung der Jury

Der Invisible Table repräsentiert ein modernes Denken über Material, den Einsatz von Technologie und die Frage, wie man in der Zukunft etwas produzieren wird. Er wirkt auf den ersten Blick im Raum minimalistisch und klar. Umso beeindruckender ist seine formale Perfektion und seine Ausdruckskraft. Dieser Tisch hat Stil.

Interior furnishing

H2
Tables
Tische

Manufacturer
Balma SA Furniture Factory,
Tarnowo Podgórne, Poland
Design
Piotr Kuchciński,
Tarnowo Podgórne, Poland
Web
www.balma.com.pl
www.piotrkuchcinski.pl

H2 tables break the convention, because of their unusual shape. They are noticeable for the delicate, graphic form of the table base, which provides the necessary stability, even for larger table tops. The H2 collection includes conference and coffee tables, as well as one tall bar table. The colour of the metal frame as well as the shape and colour of the table top can be selected from a wide range of options.

Statement by the jury
Their minimalist, unusual design and the number of different colour and shape options make the H2 tables fit into many different aesthetic and functional environments.

Die Tische H2 brechen wegen ihrer ungewöhnlichen Form mit üblichen Schemata. Sie fallen durch die filigrane, grafische Form der Tischbasis auf, die dennoch die nötige Stabilität bietet, auch bei großen Tischplatten. Die Tischfamilie H2 umfasst Konferenztische, Kaffeetische und einen hohen Bartisch. Die Farbe des Metallgestells sowie Form und Farbe der Tischplatte können aus einer breiten Auswahl individuell bestimmt werden.

Begründung der Jury
Mit ihrer minimalistischen, ungewöhnlichen Gestaltung und den Variationsmöglichkeiten in Farbe und Form passen sich die Tische H2 problemlos unterschiedlichen ästhetischen und funktionalen Gegebenheiten an.

Smallroom
Sofa

Manufacturer
OFFECCT AB,
Tibro, Sweden
Design
Ineke Hans
Web
www.offecct.se
Honourable Mention

Smallroom consists of just a few elements, but offers many possibilities for variation and can be used in different combinations or as a single module. The "box" on the side is characteristic of the sofa. It can provide a place for plants, electric sockets or serve as a storage area. The back of the sofa can be perceived as a protective screen. Smallroom can be modified with backs and sides of varying heights, which thereby make it possible to create different environments.

Statement by the jury
Smallroom's modular nature offers many interesting options for creating interior environments in modern office settings to address individual work and meeting needs.

Smallroom besteht aus nur wenigen Elementen, erlaubt aber viele Variationsmöglichkeiten und kann kombiniert in verschiedenen Modulen oder als einzelnes Modul verwendet werden. Charakteristisch ist dabei eine seitliche „Box", die für Pflanzen, Steckdosen oder als Abstellfläche dient. Die Rückseite des Sofas kann mit einem Wandschirm verglichen werden, der Schutz bietet. Smallroom gibt es mit verschiedenen Höhen der Rücken- und Seitenteile, wodurch sich unterschiedliche Ambiente kreieren lassen.

Begründung der Jury
Smallroom bietet aufgrund seines modularen Charakters interessante Möglichkeiten der Raumgestaltung in modernen Büroumgebungen, um individuellen Arbeits- und Gesprächssituationen gerecht zu werden.

Rada
Shoe Rack
Schuhregal

Manufacturer
Frost A/S, Hadsten,
Denmark
Design
busk+hertzog
(Flemming Busk, Stephan Hertzog),
London, GB
Web
www.frostdesign.dk
www.busk-hertzog.com

Rada is a shoe rack of minimalist design in chromed steel and coated with a special paint. Its unusual shape makes it possible to store shoes in two different ways, rendering it suitable for both ladies shoes with high heels as well as trainers and boots. The mounting plate with concealed connectors also helps to protect the wall from dirt. Rada is available in two sizes: 60 or 100 cm in length.

Statement by the jury
Thanks to its clear, beautiful design, which uses a minimum of materials, the Rada shoe rack is durable and will suit almost any interior.

Rada ist ein Schuhregal mit einem minimalistischen Design aus verchromtem Stahl und spezieller Lackierung, dessen besondere Form es ermöglicht, die Schuhe auf zwei verschiedene Weisen zu platzieren, wodurch es sowohl für Damenschuhe mit hohen Absätzen als auch für Sportschuhe und Stiefel geeignet ist. Die Montageplatte mit verdeckter Befestigung dient auch als Schmutzschutz für die Wand. Rada ist lieferbar in den zwei Breiten 60 oder 100 cm.

Begründung der Jury
Durch seine klare, formschöne Gestaltung mit minimalem Materialeinsatz ist das Schuhregal Rada langlebig und für nahezu jede Einrichtung geeignet.

TwinLine
Horizontal Blind
Horizontal-Jalousie

Manufacturer
MHZ Hachtel GmbH & Co. KG,
Leinfelden-Echterdingen, Germany
In-house design
Jochen Hachtel
Web
www.mhz.de

The use of TwinLine makes it possible to move a blind up and down freely and hold it in place wherever you wish in the window. The angle of the slats can be adjusted precisely using the rotary wheel built into the handle, thus making it possible to adapt light conditions even further to individual requirements. This handle is also available in aluminium and its purist appearance particularly suits the character of a horizontal blind. TwinLine makes all light and privacy settings possible according to mood or time of day.

Statement by the jury
TwinLine offers all the many options of a horizontal blind while satisfying the most demanding expectations of form and function.

Bei TwinLine lässt sich der Behang frei verschieben und an jeder gewünschten Stelle im Fenster positionieren. Um mit Licht noch individueller zu spielen, kann an dem im Bediengriff integrierten Drehrad die Lamellenwinkeleinstellung genau justiert werden. Optional ist diese Bedieneinheit auch in Aluminium erhältlich und wird durch ihr puristisches Erscheinungsbild dem Charakter einer Horizontal-Jalousie besonders gerecht. Mit TwinLine hat man alle Möglichkeiten, Lichteinfall und Sichtschutz nach Lust, Laune und Tageszeit zu dosieren und zu modulieren.

Begründung der Jury
TwinLine bietet die vielfältigen Möglichkeiten einer Horizontal-Jalousie und wird dabei in Form und Funktion höchsten Ansprüchen gerecht.

Curv
Bench
Bank

Manufacturer
Conenna Concrete Design
(Dominique Conenna),
Dorlisheim, France
Design
Tamim Daoudi,
Grégoire Ruault,
Strasbourg, France
Honourable Mention

Curv is a bench made of high-performance concrete. Designed to have the shape of a folded surface, this bench plays on the contrast between its light, floating character and the heavy, robust nature of concrete. The intention was to increase the appeal of benches as urban furniture by re-interpreting concrete and highlighting the use of this material in a spectacular design.

Curv ist eine Bank aus Hochleistungsbeton. In ihrer Gestaltung mit der Form einer gefalteten Fläche spielt diese Bank mit dem Gegensatz zwischen ihrem leichten, schwebenden Charakter und der schweren, robusten Natur des Betons. Die Intention war, die Attraktivität des Stadtmöbels Sitzbank durch eine Neuinterpretation des Werkstoffs Beton und dessen konkrete Verwendung für eine spektakuläre Formensprache zu erhöhen.

Statement by the jury
This bench highlights the possibilities concrete as a material has to offer. Transparency and lightness are paired with expression and solidity.

Begründung der Jury
Die Möglichkeiten des Werkstoffs Beton werden bei dieser Bank eindrucksvoll gezeigt. Transparenz und Leichtigkeit gehen einher mit Ausdruckskraft und Solidität.

Beatnik
Sound Station Chair
Sessel mit Soundstation

Manufacturer
Donar d.o.o.,
Ljubljana, Slovenia
Design
Gigodesign d.o.o.
(Luka Stepan, Domen Gazvoda),
Ljubljana, Slovenia
Web
www.donar.si
www.gigodesign.com
Honourable Mention

Beatnik is an armchair with an integrated sound station for users who want to make phone calls or listen to music in comfort and peace at home, in the office or in public places. Built-in Apple AirPlay technology and Bluetooth connectivity make it possible to hook up to virtually any device that provides music and audiobooks. The position of the built-in BOSE 2.1 sound system with integrated amplifier under the seat guarantees perfect sound, while the construction and shape of the seat ensures privacy and protection from surrounding noise. A strong steel frame and sides made of MDF upholstered with polyurethane foam create a both ergonomic and comfortable chair.

Beatnik ist ein Sessel mit Soundstation, der dem Benutzer bequemes und ungestörtes Telefonieren oder Musikhören zu Hause, im Büro oder an öffentlichen Plätzen ermöglicht. Die integrierte Apple AirPlay-Technologie und Bluetooth-Konnektivität erlauben eine Verbindung mit nahezu jedem Gerät, das Musik und Audiobücher zur Verfügung stellt. Die Position des eingebauten BOSE 2.1-Soundsystems mit integriertem Verstärker unter dem Sitz gewährleistet ein hervorragendes Klangerlebnis, während die Konstruktion und Form des Sitzes für Privatsphäre und Schutz vor Umgebungsgeräuschen sorgt. Ein starker Stahlrahmen und Seiten aus mit Polyurethanschaum gepolstertem Sperrholz bilden einen ergonomischen und komfortablen Sessel.

Statement by the jury
Beatnik is an oasis of peace and sound in the midst of the daily hustle and bustle. The chair with an integrated sound system is ideal for lounging and listening to music.

Begründung der Jury
Beatnik ist eine Insel der Ruhe und des Klangs inmitten des Alltags. Der Sessel mit integriertem Soundsystem ist ideal zum Loungen und Musikhören.

Origami
Drapery
Dekorationsstoff

Manufacturer
Gebrüder Munzert
GmbH & Co. KG,
Naila-Marlesreuth, Germany

In-house design
Tobias Batrla

Web
www.munzert.de

reddot design award
best of the best 2013

New facets

There is a long tradition of folding and draping costly fabrics. Particularly Asian textile arts exhibit an enormous variety. The Origami soft furnishing fabric is an innovative, three dimensional material whose design was inspired by Japanese origami techniques. Robust single surfaces are bound together during the production process to form a three-dimensional whole with astonishing 3D effects. An innovative production process makes it possible to create special folding patterns that are pre-defined in the raw material through jacquard techniques. This results in accurate folds, as well as rapid, continuous production without complex folding and pressing. The appearance of Origami is determined by its changing patterns of light and shade. The lines that define its shape are highlighted by colour accents and therefore appear to be three-dimensional. This soft furnishing fabric is very versatile in architectural use and offers good sound-proofing. The regular folds reflect sound into different directions, which make it eminently suitable for offices and public buildings. For just such applications it is also available in flame retardant "Trevira CS" materials. Origami's design re-defines soft furnishing fabrics in an entrancing way. Its three-dimensional surfaces have innumerable expressive facets.

Neue Facetten

Das Falten und Drapieren kostbarer Stoffe hat eine lange Tradition, insbesondere die asiatische Textilkunst bot dafür eine enorme Vielfalt. Der Dekorationsstoff Origami ist ein innovatives, dreidimensionales Gewebe, dessen Gestaltung von der japanischen Origami-Technik inspiriert wurde. Bei seiner Herstellung fügen sich stabile Einzelflächen zu einem plastischen Ganzen, und es entstehen verblüffende 3D-Effekte. Möglich wird dies durch ein innovatives Herstellungsverfahren, das spezielle Faltungsmuster entstehen lässt, die bereits im Rohgewebe durch die Jacquard-Technik vordefiniert werden. Dies bedingt präzise Faltungen sowie eine schnelle, kontinuierliche Produktion ohne aufwendiges Faltenlegen und Pressen. Das Erscheinungsbild des Origami ist von seinem changierenden Schattenwurf geprägt. Die formgebenden Linien werden durch farbige Akzente betont und wirken damit sehr plastisch. Dieser Dekorationsstoff kann flexibel in der Architektur eingesetzt werden und bietet gute Schallschutzqualitäten. Seine regelmäßigen Faltungen streuen den Schall in unterschiedliche Richtungen, weshalb er der Lärmregulierung in Büros und öffentlichen Gebäuden dient. Für diese Anforderungen ist er in flammhemmenden „Trevira CS"-Materialien erhältlich. Die Gestaltung des Origami definiert einen Dekorationsstoff auf eine faszinierende Weise – seine dreidimensionalen Flächen zeigen unzählige Facetten des Ausdrucks.

Statement by the jury

The Origami soft furnishing fabric creates unusual 3D effects. Its breathtaking characteristics appear afresh from different viewing angles. This fabric has fashion-like features which make it very versatile in use. Its quality will inspire the world of interior design.

Begründung der Jury

Der Dekorationsstoff Origami erzeugt außergewöhnliche 3D-Effekte. Er entfaltet seine atemberaubende Wirkung dabei aus unterschiedlichen Blickwinkeln immer wieder neu. Dieser Dekorationsstoff besitzt die Eigenschaften von Mode und bietet dadurch vielfältige Möglichkeiten seines Einsatzes. Er hat eine Qualität, die die Welt des Interior Designs inspirieren wird.

Drapery

Viavai
Decoration Fabric
Dekorationsstoff

Manufacturer
Nya Nordiska Textiles GmbH,
Dannenberg, Germany
In-house design
Nya Nordiska Design Team
Web
www.nya.com

Viavai is a semi-transparent, soft rayon burnout fabric with a louvre effect. The slightly irregular horizontal stripes with their fringed edges are created in a sophisticated burnout process. Viavai is a purist and very sensual decorative fabric with a slightly shimmering appearance.

Statement by the jury
Viavai is a light fabric that offers interesting decorating options thanks to its semi-transparent, gently shimmering nature.

Viavai ist ein halbtransparenter, softer Viskoseausbrenner mit Jalousie-Effekt. Hinter den leicht unregelmäßigen Querstreifen mit ihren Ausfransungen steht ein raffiniert umgesetzter Ausbrenner. Viavai ist ein puristischer und sehr sinnlicher Dekorationsstoff mit leicht schimmernder Optik.

Begründung der Jury
Viavai ist ein leichter Stoff, der durch seine halbtransparente, sanft glänzende Beschaffenheit interessante Dekorationsmöglichkeiten bietet.

Benu FLOW
Sheer Curtain
Vorhang

Manufacturer
Christian Fischbacher Co. AG,
St.Gallen, Switzerland
In-house design
Web
www.fischbacher.com

Benu FLOW is Christian Fischbacher's new addition to the trademarked Benu PET collection. Now, for the first time ever it is possible to produce a flame retardant fabric whose yarn is made of recycled PET bottles. The bottles are collected, cleaned and pressed in Northern Italy. They are then shredded into flakes, mixed with flame retardant and spun into polyester yarn. This process gives the yarn its inherent flame resistance.

Statement by the jury
The softly flowing voile Benu FLOW uses an innovative process to combine aesthetics and sustainability. Its properties make it particularly suitable for modern environments.

Mit Benu FLOW ergänzt Christian Fischbacher die Kollektion Benu PET um eine attraktive Neuheit. Erstmals ist es gelungen, einen flammhemmenden Stoff herzustellen, dessen Garn aus recycelten PET-Flaschen gewonnen wird. Diese Flaschen werden in Norditalien gesammelt, gereinigt und gepresst. Anschließend werden sie zu Flocken geschreddert und mit einem flammhemmenden Zusatz zu Polyestergarn versponnen. Durch diesen Prozess besitzt das Garn eine natürliche Flammfestigkeit.

Begründung der Jury
Der weich fließende Voile Benu FLOW verbindet auf innovative Weise Ästhetik und Nachhaltigkeit. Dabei ist er aufgrund seiner Eigenschaften besonders für den modernen Objektbereich geeignet.

Weave
Rug
Teppich

Manufacturer
JAB Teppiche Heinz Anstoetz KG,
Herford, Germany
Design
Carsten Gollnick,
Berlin, Germany
Web
www.jab.de
www.gollnick-design.de

The artistic intention behind this design was to establish a link to wickerwork craftsmanship. The rug hints at a ribbon or braided relief embedded into the textile surface. The complex relief structure, which follows a geometrical principle, creates light and shade modulations. In combination with high-quality, natural yarn the result is a carpet sculpture that appears three-dimensional.

Statement by the jury
The high quality and attractive appearance of this rug, which is based on the old handicraft of wickerwork, are what make it so appealing.

Die gestalterische Intention zu diesem Entwurf war es, Bezüge zu dem kunsthandwerklichen Thema des Flechtens herzustellen. Der Teppich spielt mit der reliefhaften Andeutung einer Band-Flechtstruktur, die in einer textilen Fläche eingebunden ist. Durch die komplexe, gleichzeitig einem geometrischen Prinzip folgende Reliefstruktur entstehen Licht- und Schatten-Modulationen. In Kombination mit dem hochwertigen Naturgarn ergibt sich eine dreidimensional wirkende Teppich-Skulptur.

Begründung der Jury
Angelehnt an die alte Handwerkskunst des Flechtens, besticht dieser Teppich durch hohe Qualität und sein reizvolles Erscheinungsbild.

Pixa
Woven Carpet
Gewebter Teppichboden

Manufacturer
ANKER Teppichboden
Gebr. Schoeller GmbH & Co. KG,
Düren, Germany
In-house design
Ines Binder
Web
www.anker.eu

Pixa is a carpet with a unique flat-weave appearance that has a novel, purist, but also very colourful look. The design is based on traditional principles of size, proportion and harmony. Alongside the basic black and grey, additional colours are integrated into the base fabric to produce a sophisticated combination and achieve surprising effects. The fine pile yarn used in the flat-woven fabric creates a texture whose subtle purism creates the appropriate impression of resilience and durability.

Statement by the jury
Innovative technical processes have been used to great effect to make Pixa an effective, very versatile and hard-wearing woven carpet.

Pixa ist ein Teppichboden im eigenständigen Flachgewebe-Look mit einer neuartigen, puristischen, zugleich aber auch farbigen Optik. Das Design nutzt dabei alte Maß-, Proportions- und Harmoniegesetze. Die Farbe wird neben den Grundfarben Schwarz und Grau in einem raffinierten Verhältnis konstruktiv vom Grund eingebracht und erzeugt so verblüffende Effekte. Feines Polgarn im Flachgewebe schafft eine Textur, deren subtiler Purismus für eine angemessene Assoziation von Härte und Langlebigkeit sorgt.

Begründung der Jury
Dank innovativer technischer Verfahren ist Pixa ein effektvoller, vielseitig einsetzbarer und widerstandsfähiger gewebter Teppichboden.

Perlon Rips LCS
Woven Carpet
Gewebter Teppichboden

Manufacturer
ANKER Teppichboden
Gebr. Schoeller GmbH & Co. KG,
Düren, Germany
In-house design
Ines Binder
Design
Le Corbusier
Web
www.anker.eu

Just like the second part of Le Corbusier's colour keyboard, the brand classic Perlon Rips was originally developed in 1959. The woven carpet is characterised by its calm, timeless design and exceptional technical construction. Perlon Rips is very tightly woven and therefore achieves an unrivalled compact structure with particularly straight and very precise loops. The result is undisturbed homogeneity on the floor.

Statement by the jury
Inspired by Le Corbusier's colour keyboard, the high quality of production and timeless elegance of the woven Perlon Rips carpet are a winning combination.

Der Markenklassiker Perlon Rips wurde ebenso wie der zweite Teil von Le Corbusiers Farbklaviatur ursprünglich im Jahr 1959 entwickelt. Der gewebte Teppichboden zeichnet sich durch ein ruhiges, zeitloses Design und eine herausragende technische Konstruktion aus. Perlon Rips wird sehr dicht gewebt und hat deshalb eine unerreicht kompakte Struktur mit besonders gerade und sehr präzise stehenden Noppen. Das Resultat ist eine störungsfreie Homogenität des Bodens.

Begründung der Jury
Inspiriert durch die Farbklaviatur von Le Corbusier, überzeugt der gewebte Teppichboden Perlon Rips durch seine hohe Produktqualität und zeitlose Eleganz.

Drapery, floor covering

Quasar
Mineral Construction Material
Mineralischer Werkstoff

Manufacturer
Ecotura GmbH,
Overath, Germany
In-house design
Web
www.ecotura.de

Quasar is a novel product consisting of purely mineral raw materials. Its very high strength as well as its resistance to acids and alkali set new standards compared to stone. The extremely dense and compact structure of Quasar makes it scratch-resistant. It also does not absorb water, so that impurities cannot penetrate. In contrast to traditional quartz stone, Quasar is also UV- and heat-resistant thanks to its mineral base. Possible application areas include wall cladding, floor slabs, office and kitchen countertops in private, commercial and clinical environments. Furthermore, its elegant white also creates interesting architectural highlights.

Quasar ist ein neuartiger Werkstoff aus rein mineralischen Rohstoffen. Die sehr hohe Festigkeit sowie die Säure- und Alkalibeständigkeit setzen im Vergleich zu Stein neue Maßstäbe. Durch seine äußerst dichte und feste Struktur ist Quasar kratzfest und nimmt kein Wasser auf, sodass Verschmutzungen nicht eindringen können. Im Gegensatz zu herkömmlichem Quarzwerkstein ist Quasar aufgrund seiner mineralischen Basis auch UV- und hitzebeständig. Mögliche Anwendungsbereiche sind Wandverkleidungen, Bodenplatten, Arbeits- und Küchenplatten im privaten, gewerblichen und klinischen Bereich. Das elegante Weiß setzt zudem spannende architektonische Akzente.

Corten Steel
Cortenstahl
Surface Design
Oberflächendesign

Manufacturer
Wallenstein-Manufaktur GmbH & Co.KG,
Heilbad Heiligenstadt, Germany
In-house design
Kerstin Dorenwendt-Zarski
Web
www.wallenstein-manufaktur.de
Honourable Mention

This surface design replicates aged metal surfaces in a way that makes them look convincingly real and gives viewers a new experience of a room. Its sumptuous appearance and grace will charm anyone who sees it. Aesthetics and design here go hand in hand with architecture and space. The iridescence of the metal and its antique patina in soft gold and bronze tones are mesmerising. The materials are available on different substrates such as 19 mm MDF or 0.8 mm HPL. The coating is approx. 0.6-0.8 mm thick and is applied by hand. These surfaces are suitable for fitting out hotels and restaurants, shops, trade fairs and yachts and can be used for furniture manufacture as well. The materials can be worked using standard carpentry tools and machinery.

Mit diesem Oberflächendesign werden gealterte Metalloberflächen nachgebildet, die bestechend echt aussehen und ein neues Raumerlebnis schaffen. Mit dem Charme von Opulenz und Anmut beeindruckt es seine Betrachter. Ästhetik und Design paaren sich hier mit Architektur und Raum. Das Changieren des Metalls und der antiken Patina in sanften Gold- und Brauntönen verzaubert. Die Materialien sind auf unterschiedlichen Trägern erhältlich: MDF 19 mm sowie HPL 0,8 mm. Die Beschichtungsstärke beträgt ca. 0,6-0,8 mm und wird in Handarbeit gefertigt. Die Oberflächen sind geeignet zum Ausbau im Hotel- und Gastronomiebereich, Laden- und Messebau, Yachtausbau sowie im Möbelbau. Die Materialien lassen sich mit allen herkömmlichen Tischlerwerkzeugen und -maschinen bearbeiten.

Wall and surface covering

Plex
High Pressure Laminate
Hochdrucklaminat

Manufacturer
Formica Group,
Newcastle upon Tyne, GB
In-house design
Web
www.formica.com

Plex extends the DecoMetal laminate range by Formica Group with a new avant-garde texture that exudes the beauty and charisma of metals, giving a touch of luxury, glamour and authenticity to surfaces. Created as a texture on top of real metal foils, Plex is a versatile finish that impresses with its textile feel, yet crisp touch and rather low gloss sheen. It combines the texture, colour and appearance of metals with the practical, hardwearing, lightweight and flexible properties of a laminate. Plex is available in the colours of gold, aluminium, copper, bronze and graphite. The result is a highly attractive laminate surface that exudes quality and achieves a fresh, timeless look.

Mit Plex wird die DecoMetal-Laminatserie von Formica Group um eine neue, avantgardistische Textur erweitert, die die Schönheit und Ausstrahlung von Metall besitzt und Oberflächen Luxus, Glamour und Authentizität verleiht. Geschaffen als Oberflächentextur auf echter Metallfolie, ist Plex ein vielseitiges Finish, das mit seiner textilen, dennoch griffigen Haptik und gedämpftem Glanz beeindruckt. Es vereint die Textur, Farbigkeit und Anmutung von Metall mit den praktischen, strapazierfähigen, leichten und flexiblen Eigenschaften von Laminat. Plex ist in den Farben Gold, Aluminium, Kupfer, Bronze und Graphit erhältlich. Das Ergebnis ist eine höchst reizvolle Laminatoberfläche, die Qualität und einen frischen, zeitlosen Look ausstrahlt.

Statement by the jury
The exclusive design of Plex combines the properties of flexibility and high-quality appeal for the enhancement of contemporary interior design schemes.

Begründung der Jury
Die exklusive Gestaltung von Plex verbindet die für die heutige Inneneinrichtung so wichtigen Eigenschaften Flexibilität und Hochwertigkeit.

Wall covering

Wavy
Glass Mosaic
Glasmosaik

Manufacturer
Imex International Co., Ltd.,
Bangkok, Thailand
In-house design
Sutthisak Klinkeawnarong,
Piyanun Suwanmora
Web
www.imexinter.com

The inspiration for the Wavy glass mosaic was the beauty of the coast and the gentle waves lapping on a beach in the evening. Glass of the highest quality is heated to the correct temperature, and then undergoes an innovative moulding process in order to imitate the gently curved shape of a wave that, together with a graphic motif, reflects the beauty of the sea.

Statement by the jury
The innovative design of the Wavy glass mosaic makes it possible to create interesting embellishments, which offer new sensory experiences.

Die Schönheit der Küste und eine sanfte Meereswelle am Abend waren die Inspiration für das Glasmosaik Wavy. Feinste Glasmaterialien werden, auf die richtige Temperatur erhitzt, einem innovativen Formverfahren unterworfen, sodass sie die sanfte Form einer Welle nachbilden und in Kombination mit einem grafischen Muster die Anmut des Meeres widerspiegeln. So entsteht eine neue Art künstlerischer Dekoration, die den Seh- und Tastsinn gleichermaßen anspricht.

Begründung der Jury
Dank seiner innovativen Gestaltung ermöglicht das Glasmosaik Wavy interessante Dekorationsmöglichkeiten mit neuen sinnlichen Erfahrungen.

louvre
Glass Mosaic
Glasmosaik

Manufacturer
Imex International Co., Ltd.,
Bangkok, Thailand
In-house design
Sutthisak Klinkeawnarong,
Piyanun Suwanmora
Web
www.imexinter.com

The architecture of the Louvre in Paris and its famous glass pyramid were the inspiration for the visionary, three-dimensional form of this arresting glass mosaic. A precise glass-cutting technology leads to the creation of a work of art, which is both three-dimensional and multi-perspective. Even before the grouting takes place, a star-shaped pattern is visible thanks to an underlying stacked grid. Afterwards, further beautiful, glittering effects become apparent.

Statement by the jury
This glass mosaic is a very special artistic showpiece, which offers the viewer a spectacular visual experience.

Die Architektur des Louvre in Paris mit der berühmten Glaspyramide war die Inspiration für die visionäre, dreidimensionale Gestaltung dieses erstaunlichen Glasmosaiks. Mithilfe einer präzisen Glasschneide-Technik entsteht ein dreidimensionales und multiperspektivisches Kunstwerk. Bereits vor der Verfugung zeigt sich so aufgrund eines Stapelrasters ein Sternmuster. Nach der Verfugung werden noch schönere glitzernde Effekte sichtbar.

Begründung der Jury
Ein künstlerisches Schaustück besonderer Art präsentiert sich mit diesem Glasmosaik, das für den Betrachter spektakuläre visuelle Eindrücke bereithält.

Mosa Murals
Ceramic Tiles
Keramikfliesen

Manufacturer
Royal Mosa BV,
Maastricht, Netherlands
In-house design
Mosa Design Team
Web
www.mosa.nl

Mosa Murals provides a novel, inspiring approach to designing walls with ceramic tiles. The collection offers a wide range of tiles in various sizes, colours, relief patterns and gloss levels that can be combined to create a unique wall design expressing individuality and creative thinking. Online tools Mosa Murals Generator and Mosa Murals Library help users explore the large range of options available to create extraordinary, attractive patterns. In this way, each Mosa Murals wall is a one-off.

Mosa Murals ist eine neue und anregende Art, Keramikfliesenwände zu gestalten. Die Mosa Murals-Kollektion bietet eine breite Auswahl an Fliesen in verschiedenen Größen, Farbtönen, Reliefformen und Glanzstufen, die kombiniert werden können, um ein einzigartiges Wandmuster zu erstellen, das für Individualität und kreatives Denken steht. Die Online-Tools Mosa Murals Generator und Mosa Murals Library helfen dabei, die große Auswahl an Möglichkeiten zu erforschen, mit denen außergewöhnliche, attraktive Muster entstehen. So wird jede Mosa Murals-Wand zum Unikat.

Statement by the jury
Mosa Murals is captivating in its great aesthetic quality and because of the countless options offered for creating individual walls.

Begründung der Jury
Mosa Murals besticht durch seine hohe ästhetische Qualität und die nahezu unbegrenzten Möglichkeiten für eine individuelle Wandgestaltung.

Wall covering

Nexus
Ceramic Tiles
Keramikfliesen

Manufacturer
NG Kutahya Seramik Porselen Turizm A.S.
Seramik Fabrikalari,
Kutahya, Turkey
Design
Yigit Ozer Design Team
(Yigit Ozer),
Istanbul, Turkey
Web
www.ngkutahya.com
www.yigitozer.com

Nexus embodies the geometric perfection of nature and is inspired by the structure of the carbon atom. The collection consists of hexagonal tiles in two relief designs called Penta and Hexa. Both styles can be laid horizontally and vertically to produce a versatile honeycomb pattern. The variety of the tiles is increased by the number of possible colour combinations, as well as glazed or matt silk surfaces. This turns the Nexus range of tiles into a strong design element for offices, hotels and restaurants, but also for living rooms or bedrooms, kitchens and bathrooms, giving each their individual interior design flair.

Nexus verkörpert die geometrische Perfektion der Natur und ist inspiriert von der Struktur des Kohlenstoffatoms. Die Kollektion besteht aus sechseckigen Fliesen in den zwei Reliefformen Penta und Hexa. Beide Typen können kombiniert in horizontaler oder vertikaler Anordnung verlegt werden, um ein variantenreiches Honigwabenmuster zu erzeugen. Die Formenvielfalt wird noch erhöht durch verschiedene Farbkombinationen und glasierte oder auch seidig matte Oberflächen. Die Fliesen der Kollektion Nexus zeigen sich so als starkes Designelement für eine individuelle Raumgestaltung, das genutzt werden kann in Büros, Hotels und Restaurants, aber auch in Wohn- und Schlafräumen, Küche oder Badezimmer.

Ultra
Porcelain Tile
Feinsteinzeug

Manufacturer
VitrA Karo San. ve Tic. A.S.
(VitrA Tiles),
Istanbul, Turkey
In-house design
Erden Gulkan,
Selma Gulkan,
Huseyin Isler
Web
www.vitra.com.tr

The popular stone texture of recent years has been developed further with the Ultra range of tiles with gloss reflections. Thanks to their shiny, silky smooth surface with metallic effect, they create a sense of freshness in every room. The range is available in anthracite, grey, mink and cream colour tones and is ideally suited to stylish offices, as well as modern living areas, airports, shopping centres and restaurants.

Statement by the jury
The Ultra range of tiles is impressive due to the robustness and decorative visual effects of the surface, which makes it very versatile in use.

Die in den letzten Jahren beliebte zementartige Steintextur wurde in der Serie Ultra mit glänzenden Reflexen weiterentwickelt. Die Fliesen bringen dank ihrer seidig glänzenden Oberfläche mit metallischem Effekt ein Gefühl von Frische in jeden Raum. Die Kollektion ist in den Farben Anthrazit, Grau, Nerz und Creme erhältlich. Sie ist ideal für stilvolle Geschäftsräume und moderne Wohnbereiche, kann aber auch in Flughäfen, Einkaufszentren oder Restaurants verwendet werden.

Begründung der Jury
Die Fliesen aus der Kollektion Ultra beeindrucken durch ihre effektvolle und widerstandsfähige Oberfläche, die sie zudem vielseitig einsetzbar macht.

Balance
Wall Tiles
Wandfliesen

Manufacturer
VitrA Karo San. ve Tic. A.S.
(VitrA Tiles),
Istanbul, Turkey
In-house design
Tuba Buyukkaraduman
Web
www.vitra.com.tr

The grandeur of the third dimension comes to the fore in the relief patterns of the Balance range. Walls gain a new elegance thanks to its ultramodern metallic-printed pattern and colour range from dark to light. Balance is available in white, black, mink, pink and cream.

Statement by the jury
Three-dimensional surface structures create a feeling of spaciousness and size. The Balance range of tiles underlines this impression by the use of classic patters and colours.

Die Serie Balance präsentiert mit ihren Reliefmustern die Erhabenheit der dritten Dimension. Anhand der ultramodernen Muster mit Metallic-Druck und den Farbtönungen von hell bis dunkel wird den Wänden eine ganz neue Art von Eleganz verliehen. Balance ist in den Farben Weiß, Schwarz, Nerz, Rosa und Creme erhältlich.

Begründung der Jury
Dreidimensionale Oberflächenstrukturen vermitteln ein Gefühl von Räumlichkeit und Größe. Die Fliesen der Serie Balance unterstreichen diesen Eindruck noch durch edle Muster und Farben.

Caldo
Ceramic Tile
for Wall Heating
Keramische Kachel
für die Wandheizung

Manufacturer
To Do Product Design,
Krakow, Poland
In-house design
Katarzyna Jakubowska,
Tomasz Orzechowski
Web
www.to-do.com.pl
Honourable Mention

Caldo is a ceramic tile for the decorative design of wall heaters, stoves and other elements of interior design. Traditional technology is here put at the service of creating contemporary forms. This timeless product, which is 100 per cent environmentally friendly, is made of mouldable, fireproof clay and radiates heat in a pleasant way. Depending on the viewing angle and the incidence of light, the three-dimensional surface reveals a multitude of graphic patterns.

Statement by the jury
Caldo cleverly and innovatively makes use of traditional craftsmanship to create an intriguing, modern design.

Caldo ist eine keramische Kachel zur dekorativen Gestaltung von Wandheizung, Öfen und anderen Elementen der Innenarchitektur. Eine traditionelle Technologie wird hier zur Schaffung zeitgemäßer Formen genutzt. Dieses zeitlose, zu 100 Prozent ökologische Produkt wird aus formbarem feuerfesten Ton hergestellt und strahlt eine angenehme Wärme aus. Die dreidimensionale Oberfläche lässt abhängig vom Blickwinkel und Einfall des Lichts den Betrachter eine Vielzahl von graphischen Mustern sehen.

Begründung der Jury
Klassisches Kunsthandwerk wird bei Caldo geschickt und innovativ eingesetzt, um ein modernes, reizvolles Design zu schaffen.

Sense 316
Door Entry Panel
Außensprechstelle

Manufacturer
Comelit Group S.p.A.,
Rovetta S. Lorenzo (Bergamo), Italy
Design
Habits Srl
(Diego Rossi, Innocenzo Rifino),
Milan, Italy
Web
www.comelitgroup.com
www.habits.it

The Sense 316 door entry panel is made entirely of AISI 316 stainless steel. In contrast to traditional products, the metal surface is free of buttons, as the surface itself is touch-sensitive. The front panel is made using a sophisticated production process to achieve the required differences in material thickness needed for the capacitive sensors to work. Sense 316 sets itself apart with a generous metal surface offering the highest level of material uniformity and through the absence of any apertures on the front panel. This simplicity of look and materials makes for a very lucid and compelling appearance.

Die Außensprechstelle Sense 316 besteht komplett aus Edelstahl AISI 316. Im Unterschied zu üblichen Produkten gibt es keine Tasten, sondern die Metalloberfläche selbst ist berührungsempfindlich. Die Konstruktion der Frontoberfläche erfolgt in einem anspruchsvollen Fertigungsverfahren, um die für die Funktion des kapazitiven Sensors erforderlichen differenzierten Materialstärken zu erzielen. Sense 316 zeichnet sich so durch eine großzügige Metalloberfläche mit ausgeprägter Materialhomogenität aus, ohne Öffnungen an der Frontseite. Diese Einfachheit in Optik und Material sorgt für ein übersichtliches und zugleich kraftvolles Erscheinungsbild.

Siedle Classic
Door Station
Türstation

Manufacturer
S. Siedle & Söhne,
Furtwangen, Germany
In-house design
Eberhard Meurer
Web
www.siedle.de

Siedle Classic is a contemporary interpretation of the classic door station. Its shape is characterised by geometric structures based on a grid layout. By focusing on a few, rigidly applied principles, the system acquires tremendous openness in its appearance. This leads to almost limitless combinations of shape, function and material. Contemporary door communication consists of more than doorbell and intercom, but also requires information, sight, surveillance, access control, switches and, of course, mail delivery.

Siedle Classic ist eine zeitgemäße Interpretation der klassischen Türstation. Die Formensprache ist geprägt von geometrischen Strukturen, denen ein Gestaltungsraster zugrunde liegt. Aus der Reduktion auf wenige, konsequent angewandte Prinzipien gewinnt das System eine enorme gestalterische Offenheit. Sie eröffnet nahezu unendliche Kombinationsmöglichkeiten von Form, Funktion und Material. Zeitgemäße Türkommunikation ist mehr als Klingeln und Sprechen: Hinzu kommen Informieren, Sehen, Überwachen, Zugangskontrolle, Schalten – und natürlich der Postempfang.

Statement by the jury
Siedle Classic consistently demonstrates a high standard of quality not only in its formal and technical properties, but also with regard to the high-quality materials and workmanship.

Begründung der Jury
Siedle Classic zeigt sich durchgehend auf ausgesprochen hohem Niveau, sowohl was die formalen und technischen Eigenschaften als auch die Material- und Verarbeitungsqualität betrifft.

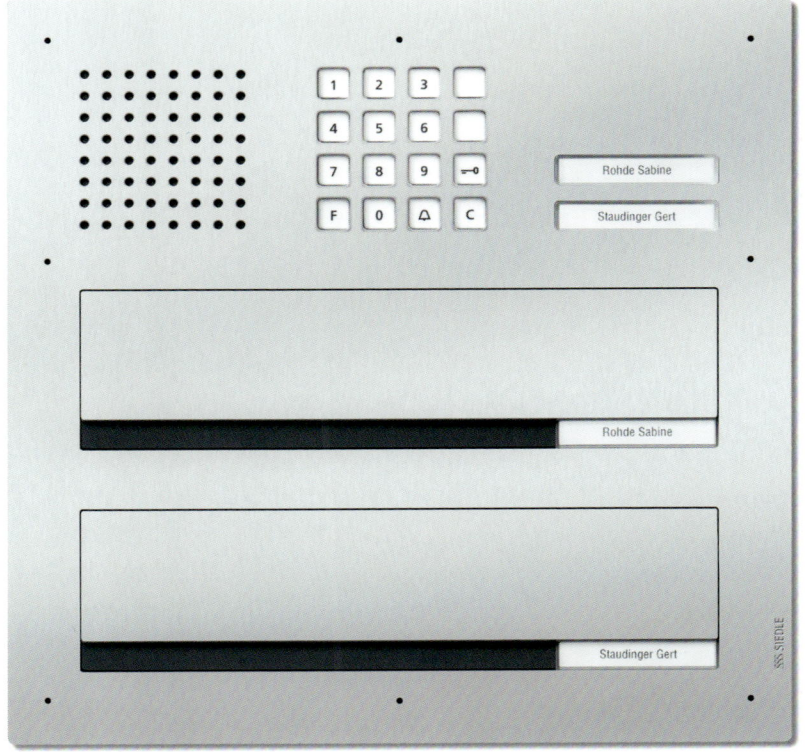

Busch-ComfortTouch 12.1
Busch-ComfortPanel 12.1
Home Automation
Hausautomation

Manufacturer
Busch-Jaeger Elektro GmbH,
Lüdenscheid, Germany
Design
PRODESIGN Brüssing GmbH & Co.KG
(Bernd Brüssing),
Neu-Ulm, Germany
Web
www.busch-jaeger.de
www.prodesign-ulm.de

Have control of the entire house at your fingertips with the Busch-ComfortTouch 12.1. Guidance through the control menu has been ergonomically improved. A simple touch of the display with the fingertips is all that is needed to control the house. Users can switch or dim lights, manage blinds, regulate room temperature, as well as store and call up all functions for complex scenarios – even remotely via smartphones and tablets. Security is also enhanced as the Busch-ComfortTouch 12.1 can simulate a presence in the house and provide alarm messages.

Statement by the jury
Thanks to its exemplary, simple method of use and elegant appearance, the Busch-ComfortTouch 12.1 is ideally suited to home automation.

Mit dem Busch-ComfortPanel 12.1 lässt sich das ganze Haus nur mit den Fingerspitzen kontrollieren. Denn die Führung durch das Menü wurde ergonomisch verbessert. Nun kann auf dem Touchdisplay mit Fingergesten gesteuert werden. Der Nutzer kann Licht schalten oder dimmen, Jalousien steuern, Raumtemperaturen regeln, sämtliche Funktionen zu komplexen Szenarien speichern und abrufen – sogar per Fernbedienung mit Smartphone und Tablet. Das Busch-ComfortPanel 12.1 bietet zudem Sicherheit durch Anwesenheitssimulation und Alarmmeldungen.

Begründung der Jury
Durch seine vorbildlich einfache Bedienung und sein elegantes Erscheinungsbild eignet sich das Busch-ComfortPanel 12.1 hervorragend für die Hausautomation.

Smart Home Manager 2
Security and Information System
Sicherheits- und Informationssystem

Manufacturer
Cham Sule Tech Co., Ltd.,
Seoul, South Korea
Design
Daewoo E&C
(Sun-Geun Kim, Jung-Min Lee),
Seoul, South Korea
Web
www.upis.co.kr
www.daewooenc.com
Honourable Mention

The Smart Home Manager 2 is an information system capable of controlling domestic installations. Upon leaving home, users can turn lights, heating and security systems on or off via a touchscreen. In addition, the device displays outdoor weather conditions such as temperature, wind speed or air humidity.

Statement by the jury
The metal frame gives the Smart Home Manager 2 a premium appearance. It is comfortably and easily operated via the touchscreen.

Der Smart Home Manager 2 ist ein Informationssystem, mit dem sich Haustechnik steuern lässt. Verlässt der Benutzer das Haus, kann er über ein Touchdisplay Beleuchtung, Heizung oder Sicherheitssysteme ein- oder ausschalten. Zusätzlich zeigt das Gerät Wetterdaten wie Temperatur, Wind oder Luftfeuchtigkeit an.

Begründung der Jury
Das Metallgehäuse verleiht dem Smart Home Manager 2 eine edle Anmutung. Über das Touchdisplay lässt er sich leicht bedienen.

eVayo IF-5735
Time and Attendance Recording Terminal
Zeiterfassungsterminal

Manufacturer
Interflex Datensysteme GmbH & Co. KG,
Stuttgart, Germany
Design
N+P Industrial Design
(Christiane Bausback),
Munich, Germany
Web
www.interflex.de
www.np-id.com

This time and attendance recording terminal can be operated intuitively via a touchscreen, which strongly simplifies user guidance. The terminal is capable of checking authorisation during identification and also saving external appointments, reasons for absence, master records and daily/weekly programmes. Moreover, it can read all current radio-frequency identification (RFID) devices. With an energy-saving mode in combination with the integrated proximity sensor, the terminal has low energy consumption, making it sustainable and guaranteeing a long service life.

Statement by the jury
The design of this time and attendance recording terminal is timeless and reserved. The selection of materials, including glass and ceramics, conveys a high degree of reliability.

Das Zeiterfassungsterminal lässt sich intuitiv über ein Touchdisplay bedienen, die Benutzerführung ist dabei sehr einfach. Das Terminal kann die Buchungsberechtigung bei einer Identifikation prüfen, Außentermine oder Fehlgründe buchen sowie Stammsätze, Tages- und Wochenprogramme speichern. Darüber hinaus verarbeitet es aktuelle RFID-Identifikationsmittel. Das Terminal verbraucht durch den Stromsparmodus in Kombination mit dem integrierten Näherungssensor wenig Energie, was nachhaltig ist und eine lange Lebensdauer gewährleistet.

Begründung der Jury
Die Gestaltung dieses Zeiterfassungsterminals ist zeitlos und schlicht. Materialien wie Glas und Keramik vermitteln darüber hinaus eine hohe Zuverlässigkeit.

Integrated Home Electronic System
Home Automation
Hausautomation

Manufacturer
POSCO E&C,
Incheon, South Korea
In-house design
Sung-Wook Hwang
Design
DESIGNK2L
(Soo-Shin Lee),
Seoul, South Korea
Web
www.poscoenc.com
www.designk2l.com

This integrated home electronic system comprises a wall-pad, light switches, a thermostat, a door station and an entry card. Equipped with touch-sensitive keys the wall-pad is intuitive to use. The functions are also easy to recognise for seniors and handicapped people. The intelligent entry card allows holders access to various areas of a building, including the parking lot, and it also calls the elevator to their floor. In addition, it also features an emergency alarm function that is activated by sliding a button.

Statement by the jury
The well thought-out design of this system excellently satisfies all requirements towards sophisticated home automation.

Dieses integrierte Hauselektronik-System umfasst eine Wand-Bedieneinheit mit Lichtschalter, Thermostat, Türstation und Zugangskarte. Der Einsatz von Sensortasten erlaubt eine intuitive Bedienung. Die Funktionen sind auch für ältere und behinderte Menschen klar erkennbar. Mit der intelligenten Zugangskarte lässt sich in Appartementhäusern das Gebäude einschließlich des Parkbereichs betreten oder der Aufzug anfordern. Zudem hat sie eine Notruf-Funktion, die aktiviert wird, wenn der Nutzer einen Schiebeknopf betätigt.

Begründung der Jury
Die durchdachte Gestaltung dieses System erfüllt die Anforderungen an eine gelungene Hausautomation vorzüglich.

BS2012
Hands-Free Audio Indoor Station
Audio-Freisprechstelle

Manufacturer
SKS – Kinkel Elektronik GmbH,
Hof, Germany
In-house design
Web
www.sks-kinkel.com

BS2012 is a hands-free indoor audio station designed to feature the core functions of an intercom station: six concave buttons simplify operation, making it suitable for people of every age and those with special needs. Mechanically moving elements were deliberately omitted in order to assure durability and easy cleaning. With a thickness of only 13 mm the station takes up minimal space.

BS2012 ist eine Audio-Freisprechstelle, die sich auf die zentralen Funktionen einer Sprechanlage konzentriert: Sechs konkav geformte Bedienflächen erleichtern die Bedienung, sodass sich die Anlage für Menschen jeder Altersklasse und mit besonderen Bedürfnissen eignet. Auf mechanisch bewegte Elemente wurde bewusst verzichtet, um eine lange Lebensdauer und einfache Reinigung zu gewährleisten. Mit nur 13 mm Bautiefe nimmt die Sprechstelle sehr wenig Platz ein.

Statement by the jury
BS2012 convinces both in its design as well as in its technical qualities with a reduction to essentials and with optimal operating ease.

Begründung der Jury
BS2012 überzeugt sowohl in gestalterischer als auch in technischer Hinsicht mit einer Reduktion auf das Wesentliche bei optimalem Bedienkomfort.

Berker R.1
Touch Sensor KNX
Room Controller
Raum-Controller

Manufacturer
Berker GmbH & Co. KG,
Schalksmühle, Germany
Design
Studio Aisslinger
(Prof. Werner Aisslinger, Nicole Losos),
Berlin, Germany
Web
www.berker.com

The soft contours, simplicity and unusual construction of the Berker R.1 Touch Sensor KNX room controller are beguiling. A gentle touch is all it takes to activate the desired function. The touch sensor consists of a base plate in black or white plastic and a glass cover in black or polar white. It controls KNX functions such as lighting, blinds, heating and air conditioning. LEDs indicate operating readiness and switch states.

Statement by the jury
This room controller is particularly appropriate for sophisticated environments thanks to its excellent design and functionality.

Das Raumbediengerät Berker R.1 Touch Sensor KNX besticht durch seine softe Kontur, seine Schlichtheit und einen ungewöhnlichen Aufbau. Eine sanfte Berührung genügt und die gewünschte Funktion wird ausgelöst. Der Tastsensor besteht aus einer Trägerplatte in Kunststoff (schwarz/weiß) und einer Glasabdeckung in Schwarz oder Polarweiß. KNX-Funktionen wie z.B. Licht, Jalousien, Heizung und Klimaanlage werden darüber gesteuert. LEDs zeigen die Betriebsbereitschaft und Schaltzustände an.

Begründung der Jury
Dieser Raum-Controller kann dank seiner ausgezeichneten Gestaltung und Funktionalität besonders in einem hochwertigen Ambiente verwendet werden.

Berker R.3
Touch Sensor KNX
Room Controller
Raum-Controller

Manufacturer
Berker GmbH & Co. KG,
Schalksmühle, Germany
Design
Studio Aisslinger
(Prof. Werner Aisslinger, Nicole Losos),
Berlin, Germany
Web
www.berker.com

The angular contours, simplicity and unusual construction of the Berker R.3 Touch Sensor KNX room controller are beguiling. A gentle touch of the immaculate surface is all it takes to activate the desired function. The touch sensor consists of a base plate in black or white plastic and a glass cover in black or polar white. It controls KNX functions while LEDs indicate operating readiness and switch states.

Statement by the jury
Its design and functionality make the Berker R.3 Touch Sensor KNX an ideal room controller for sophisticated interiors.

Das Raumbediengerät Berker R.3 Touch Sensor KNX überzeugt durch seine kantige Kontur, seine Schlichtheit und einen ungewöhnlichen Aufbau. Eine sanfte Berührung der makellosen Oberfläche genügt und die gewünschte Funktion wird ausgelöst. Der Tastsensor setzt sich zusammen aus einer Trägerplatte in Kunststoff (schwarz/weiß) und einer Glasabdeckung in Schwarz oder Polarweiß. Die KNX-Funktionen lassen sich darüber steuern, LEDs zeigen Betriebsbereitschaft und Schaltzustände an.

Begründung der Jury
In Gestaltung wie Funktionalität zeigt sich der Berker R.3 Touch Sensor KNX als vorzüglicher Raum-Controller auch für anspruchsvolle Interieurs.

Kaba star
Key
Schlüssel

Manufacturer
Kaba AG,
Wetzikon, Switzerland
Design
Process Design AG,
Lucerne, Switzerland
Web
www.kaba.ch
www.process-group.com

The innovative, mechanical Kaba star is a reinterpretation of the classic Kaba key. The round shape of the key, so typical for Kaba, has been consistently adhered to. A metal ring encloses the interior plastic clip. The front is produced using high-quality two-component injection moulding and so ensures durability. On the back, different coloured, interchangeable plastic clips act as a colour coding system that users can adapt to individual needs.

Statement by the jury
The Kaba star key is appealing thanks to its clear, consistent design and unmistakable styling, which is instantly recognisable.

Der innovative, mechanische Kaba star ist eine Neuinterpretation des klassischen Kaba Schlüssels. Die runde, für Kaba typische Schlüsselform wird konsequent weitergeführt. Ein metallischer Ring umschließt den innenliegenden Kunststoffclip. Die Vorderseite ist mit einem hochwertigen Zweikomponentenspritzguss ausgeführt und garantiert Langlebigkeit. Auf der Rückseite dienen unterschiedlich eingefärbte, austauschbare Kunststoffclips als Individualisierung und Farbleitsystem.

Begründung der Jury
Der Kaba star Schlüssel besticht durch seine klare, konsequente Gestaltung mit unverwechselbarer Formensprache und hohem Wiedererkennungswert.

Vienna
Postbox
Briefkasten

Manufacturer
Max Knobloch Nachf. GmbH,
Döbeln, Germany
Design
Beiler-Schlehaider Design
(Wolfgang Beiler-Schlehaider),
Kößlarn, Germany
Web
www.max-knobloch.com
www.beiler-schlehaider-design.com
Honourable Mention

The exterior casing of the Vienna postbox is also its door element. As it completely encloses the interior and becomes smaller towards the wall like a truncated pyramid, the casing is as watertight as possible. A light tug on the upper edge of the door releases the drop slot. A spring mechanism returns the door to its original position. This innovative concept ensures the post is secure and is the reason behind this minimalist style.

Statement by the jury
The Vienna postbox is appealing in its clean, purist design, which is also characterised by a high degree of functionality and user friendliness.

Beim Briefkasten Vienna ist das Außengehäuse zugleich das Türelement. Da es das ganze Innengehäuse umschließt und sich zur Wand hin in Form eines Pyramidenstumpfes verjüngt, wird höchste Wasserdichtigkeit erreicht. Mit einem leichten Zug an der Oberkante der Tür wird der Einwurfschlitz freigegeben, ein Federmechanismus holt die Tür zurück in ihre Ausgangsposition. Dieses innovative Konzept sorgt für die Sicherheit des Postgutes und bedingt die minimalistische Formensprache.

Begründung der Jury
Der Briefkasten Vienna überzeugt durch seine klare, puristische Gestaltung, die zudem von hoher Funktionalität und Gebrauchsfähigkeit geprägt ist.

---

d line Turtle Doorstop
Doorstop
Türstopper

Manufacturer
d line as,
Albertslund, Denmark
Design
Knud Holscher Design
(Prof. Knud Holscher),
Copenhagen, Denmark
Web
www.dline.com
www.knudholscher.dk

This is a reinterpretation of the classic turtle doorstop. The aim was to create something that is functional, robust and aesthetically appealing. This new doorstop by d line consists of a stainless steel base, covered by solid rubber and fixed to the floor. Thanks to the solid anchoring provided by the base and the quality of the rubber, this doorstop is suitable even for high traffic areas and for use with heavy doors.

Statement by the jury
This doorstop combines aesthetics and functionality. Its construction furthermore ensures that even heavy use will not cause the rubber to become detached.

Dieser Türstopper ist eine Neuinterpretation des klassischen „Schildkröten"-Türstoppers. Ziel war es, einen funktionalen, robusten und ästhetisch ansprechenden Türstopper zu kreieren. Der neue Türstopper von d line besteht aus einem im Boden verankerten Edelstahlunterteil, das mit solidem Gummi umgeben ist. Dank der festen Verankerung des Unterteils und der Qualität des Gummis eignet sich der Türstopper auch zum Einsatz in stark frequentierten Bereichen und für schwere Türen.

Begründung der Jury
Dieser Türstopper verbindet Ästhetik und Funktionalität. Seine Konstruktion sorgt zudem dafür, dass sich auch bei starker Beanspruchung kein Gummi ablöst.

---

da caster
Caster
Rolle

Manufacturer
Hammer Caster Co., Ltd.,
Osaka, Japan
Design
Hozmi Design
(Mitsunobu Hozumi, Ryo Shimizu),
Kobe City, Hyogo Prefecture, Japan
Web
www.hammer-caster.co.jp

By contrast to conventional casters with "ball bearing configurations", da caster sets itself apart through the use of a "sliding configuration" that does away with both axle and bearing. da caster consists of an aluminium casing, a roller and an inner ring made of a particular type of resin which makes it possible to create a ring-shaped wheel with a central hole. The result is a hubless caster with sufficient strength and stability that nonetheless appears to float.

Statement by the jury
The extraordinary construction of da caster ensures excellent functionality and gives the caster its distinctive appearance.

Im Gegensatz zu konventionellen Rollfüßen mit „Kugellager-Struktur" zeichnet sich da caster durch eine „Gleitlager-Struktur" aus, die weder Achse noch Lager verwendet. da caster besteht aus einer Aluminium-Hülle, einer Rolle und einem inneren Ring aus einem speziellen Harz, die ein ringförmiges Rad mit einem Loch in der Mitte ermöglichen. So entsteht ein Orbitalrollfuß, der genügend Stärke und Festigkeit hat und dennoch zu schweben scheint.

Begründung der Jury
Die besondere Konstruktion von da caster sorgt für die sehr gute Funktionalität und das charakteristische Erscheinungsbild der Rolle.

LFensterCUBEflat
Wooden-Metal Window
Holz-Metall-Fenster

Manufacturer
Lehmann Arnegg AG,
Fenster – Türen – Räume,
Arnegg, Switzerland
In-house design
Daniel Lehmann
Web
www.lehmannag.ch

The wooden-metal LFensterCUBEflat window has a very clear, reduced design that incorporates the most cutting edge technology possible. Flush mounted versions for interior and exterior use provide joint-free continuous surfaces combined with concealed fittings and a flush handle rosette to achieve the clean, angular shape of the window. By optically reducing it down to its key elements this results in a purist design that makes no compromises.

Statement by the jury
The LFensterCUBEflat is convincing both in its shape and function. Its purist, high-quality design turns it into a contemporary architectural element.

Das Holz-Metall-Fenster LFensterCUBEflat weist eine klare, reduzierte Gestaltung mit höchstmöglichen technischen Anforderungen auf. Die flächenbündige Ausführung im Innen- wie im Außenbereich sorgt durch die fugen- und phasenlose Oberfläche zusammen mit der unsichtbaren Beschlagskonstruktion und der ausgeebneten Griffrosette für die klare, winklige Form des Fensters. Die optische Reduktion auf die wesentlichen Elemente ergibt eine puristische Formensprache, ohne Einschränkungen in Kauf nehmen zu müssen.

Begründung der Jury
Das LFensterCUBEflat überzeugt in Form und Funktion gleichermaßen. Seine puristische, hochwertige Gestaltung macht es zu einem zeitgemäßen architektonischen Element.

ACTUAL ALWOOD
Window
Fenster

Manufacturer
ACTUAL Fenster Türen Sonnenschutz GmbH,
Ansfelden, Austria
In-house design
Ingo Ganzberger,
Rudolf Waldenberger
Web
www.actual.at

The window design developed by ACTUAL looks as if it was created out of a single piece. The shape of the window is cubic and angular, uncompromising in its design without slants, glazing beads or optically disruptive joins. Sash, frame and glass are flush on the outside and the sash and frame sit flush on the inside as well. The interior flush-fitting view is highlighted by the concealed fitting of invisible hinges. The minimalist sash profile allows for very narrow visible window frames.

Statement by the jury
This window system is characterised by its very clear, purist design in combination with high-quality technology and materials.

Das von ACTUAL entwickelte Fensterdesign wirkt wie aus einem Guss. Die Form des Fensters ist kubisch-kantig, kompromisslos ohne Schrägen und ohne Glasleisten mit optisch störenden Fugen. Außen sind Flügel, Rahmen und Glas flächenbündig, innen Rahmen und Flügel. Die Flächenbündigkeit innen wird durch den verdeckt liegenden Beschlag ohne sichtbare Scharniere noch betont. Das minimalistische Flügelprofil ermöglicht eine sehr schmale Fensterrahmen-Ansichtsbreite.

Begründung der Jury
Dieses Fenstersystem zeichnet sich durch eine sehr klare, puristische Formgebung in Kombination mit einer hohen Qualität in Technik und Material aus.

PLANO
Fire Rated
and Acoustic Door
Brandschutz- und Akustiktür

Manufacturer
Porseg, Sistemas de Segurança S.A.
Arcozelo (Vila Nova de Gaia), Portugal
In-house design
João Oliveira
Web
www.porseg.com

PLANO is an innovative fire rated and acoustic door, which meets current market needs with regard to design, quality and versatility. The door has a fire resistance of 60 minutes. It is notable for its minimalist design while providing maximum safety. The frame and the door leaf are on the same plane to ensure that PLANO fits perfectly into every type of environment. Locking mechanisms are hidden. PLANO is available in stainless steel, chrome-plated or painted.

PLANO ist eine innovative Brandschutz- und Akustiktür, die den aktuellen Markt-anforderungen an Design, Qualität und Vielseitigkeit gerecht wird. Die Tür weist eine Feuerbeständigkeit von 60 Minuten auf, sie zeichnet sich durch eine minima-listische Gestaltung aus – bei maximaler Sicherheit. Um sich in das jeweilige Umfeld perfekt einzufügen, befinden sich Rahmen und Flügel auf einer Ebene, die Verriegelungsmechanismen sind unsicht-bar. PLANO gibt es in Edelstahl, verchromt oder lackiert.

Doors

Minimal / Maximal
Door Handle
Türdrücker

Manufacturer
Material & Technology s.r.o.,
Nové Město nad Metují, Czech Republic
In-house design
Roman Ulich
Web
www.doorhandles-mt.com

The Minimal / Maximal door handles have a minimalist design with a covered door rosette and a handle that is pleasant to grip. The fitting is characterised by an innovative opening system, while the handle can be mounted in three different ways depending on individual requirements: pointing upwards, downwards or horizontally. This makes the handle suitable for all types of doors, even revolving and sliding ones. In each case, the same installation and construction system applies. Thanks to its progressive construction, the handle opens and closes doors quietly and precisely.

Die Türdrücker Minimal / Maximal sind minimalistisch gestaltet mit verdeckter Türrosette und einer gut in der Hand liegenden Klinke. Der Beschlag zeichnet sich durch ein innovatives Öffnungssystem aus, wobei je nach Bedarf drei Montagemöglichkeiten mit dem Türgriff nach oben, nach unten oder waagerecht zur Auswahl stehen. Daher kann das Produkt auch bei allen Türtypen, sogar bei Dreh- und Schiebetüren, verwendet werden und zwar stets mit dem gleichen Montage- und Konstruktionssystem. Dank der progressiven Konstruktion öffnet und schließt die Klinke sehr geräuscharm und präzise.

Door Handle
Türdrücker

Manufacturer
CONVEX SA,
Athens, Greece
Design
Yannis Georgaras,
Piraeus, Greece
Web
www.convex.gr

Elasticity, visual continuity and purity were the three guiding principles for the design of this door handle. It is set out to eliminate every superfluous element from its visual appearance. By creating an imaginary line from the door lock to the handle, the metal loses its rigidity and gains maximum elasticity. The design avoids all connecting elements (such as screws) and accentuates the inner structure, so that the handle appears to attach to the wooden door as if by magic and looks like an integral part of it.

Geschmeidigkeit, visuelle Kontinuität und Reinheit waren die drei Grundprinzipien bei der Gestaltung dieses Türdrückers. Jedes unnötige Element in der visuellen Erscheinung sollte eliminiert werden. Durch die Bildung einer imaginären Linie vom Türriegel zum Griff verliert das Metall seine Härte und gewinnt ein Höchstmaß an Elastizität. Die Gestaltung vermeidet alle verbindenden Elemente (Schrauben) und betont die innere Struktur, sodass sich der metallische Griff fast magisch in die hölzerne Tür einfügt und wie ein integraler Bestandteil von ihr wirkt.

Statement by the jury
The clear, purist and decidedly elegant design is proof of great aesthetic and functional quality.

Begründung der Jury
Die klare, puristische und ausgesprochen elegante Gestaltung zeugt von hoher ästhetischer und funktionaler Qualität.

Formani Fold
by Tord Boontje
Door Handle
Türdrücker

Manufacturer
Formani, Maastricht-Airport,
Netherlands
Design
Studio Tord Boontje
(Prof. Tord Boontje),
London, GB
Web
www.formani.com
www.tordboontje.com

The Fold range of door handles differs fundamentally from traditional models by combining the classic components of a door fitting – rosette, neck and handle – into one single element in an innovative way. This is achieved thanks to an astute system whose mounting is akin to a bayonet system. The result: the door handle gives the impression of floating on the door.

Statement by the jury
It is not only the technical concept of this door handle that is innovative, but also the implementation of the design down to the last ingenious detail.

Der Türdrücker aus der Serie Fold unterscheidet sich von üblichen Modellen grundlegend, da er auf äußerst innovative Weise die klassischen Komponenten eines Türgriffs – Rosette, Lochteil und Klinke – in einem Element vereint. Dafür wurde ein ausgeklügeltes System entwickelt, das sich hinsichtlich der Befestigung am besten mit einem Bajonettsystem vergleichen lässt. Das Ergebnis: Es entsteht der Eindruck, als ob der Türgriff über der Tür schwebt.

Begründung der Jury
Nicht nur das technische Konzept, sondern auch die gestalterische Umsetzung bis hin zu raffinierten Details sind ausgesprochen innovativ bei diesem Türdrücker.

Elica
Door Handle
Türdrücker

Manufacturer
pba S.p.A.,
Tezze sul Brenta (Vicenza), Italy
Design
Brunet Saunier Architecture
(Jérôme Brunet),
Paris, France
Web
www.pba.it
www.brunet-saunier.com

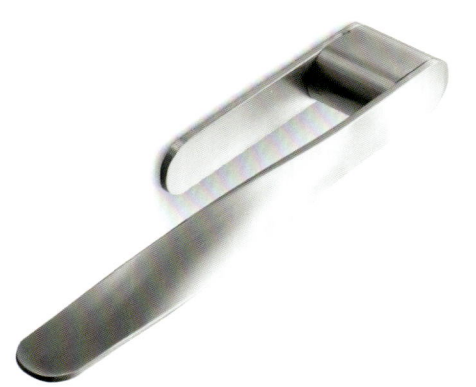

The design of the Elica handle ensures it is easy to grip and operate, particularly by people with reduced hand mobility. The flat upper part has a wide surface while the end of the handle is rounded to prevent it from getting caught on anything. Vertical handling by wheelchair-bound users is made easy, as is the installation on doors close to room corners.

Statement by the jury
Thanks to its unusual design this door handle is noteworthy for its aesthetically striking, but at the same time ergonomic styling.

Das Design des Griffs Elica sorgt für gute Griffigkeit und Handlichkeit, besonders für Menschen mit eingeschränkter Beweglichkeit der Hand. Der obere, ebene Teil bietet eine großzügige Auflagefläche, während das Ende des Griffs abgerundet ist, um ein Hängenbleiben zu vermeiden. Bei Benutzung durch Personen im Rollstuhl und bei der Anbringung an Türen in der Nähe von Wandecken erleichtert der Griff Elica die vertikale Handhabung.

Begründung der Jury
Dank seiner außergewöhnlichen Gestaltung zeichnet sich dieser Türdrücker durch eine ästhetisch auffällige und zugleich sehr ergonomische Formgebung aus.

Flat
Sliding Door Handle
Schiebetür-Griffsystem

Manufacturer
Manital Srl,
Gavardo (Brescia), Italy
Design
Studio Mazzer
(Mario Mazzer),
Conegliano (Treviso), Italy
Web
www.manital.com
www.mariomazzer.it
Honourable Mention

Flat is an innovative sliding door handle. Both the closing and opening mechanisms are integrated into a plate, which extends around three sides of the door. The opening and sliding functions are accessed by pressing a disc on the upper section of the plate. The locking mechanism is situated in the lower section and is activated by turning a knob.

Statement by the jury
A clear design, focusing on the essentials, makes this sliding door handle, with its high-quality materials and technology, very attractive.

Flat ist ein innovatives Schiebetür-Griffsystem. In einer einzigen, drei Seiten der Tür umschließenden Blende sind sowohl die Schließ- als auch die Öffnungsfunktion integriert. Die Öffnungs- und Schiebefunktionen sind über das Drücken einer Scheibe im oberen Teil des Türbeschlags zugänglich, während die mittels Drehknauf aktivierbare Schließfunktion sich im unteren Teil befindet.

Begründung der Jury
Dieses in Material und Technik hochwertig ausgeführte Schiebetür-Griffsystem gefällt durch seine klare, auf das Wesentliche konzentrierte Gestaltung.

TJSS T6
Door Closer
Türschließer

Manufacturer
TJSS Türschliesser,
Oftringen, Switzerland
In-house design
Roland Schmid
Design
synthesis design
(Michael Heimgartner),
Lenzburg, Switzerland
Web
www.tjss.ch/t6
www.synthesis-design.ch

The TJSS T6 door closer has a sliding rail and body of equal length. Combined with its high-quality finish, this creates an appearance of optical unity. Teflon coated pistons ensure there is minimal friction making the door particularly easy to open. A compact tooth-cam hybrid drive is characterised by perfect force progression and tremendous performance. Thanks to adjustable, thermally stable valves, the door closes at an even speed and with a constant force even in winter.

Statement by the jury
An ingenious technical concept makes the TJSS T6 an extremely easy-to-use door closer that fits harmoniously with every type of door.

Der Türschließer TJSS T6 erscheint durch die gleiche Länge von Schiene und Körper als optische Einheit, hochwertig gefertigt mit edlem Finish. Die teflongelagerten Kolben sorgen dabei für minimale Reibung und somit besonders leichtgängige Türen. Der kompakte Zahn-Nocken-Hybridantrieb zeichnet sich durch einen idealen Kraftverlauf und enorme Kraftentfaltung aus. Die thermostabilen Einstell-Ventile gewährleisten eine konstante Schließgeschwindigkeit und -kraft auch im Winter.

Begründung der Jury
Ein ausgeklügeltes technisches Konzept macht den TJSS T6 zu einem äußerst komfortablen Türschließer, der sich sehr harmonisch ins Türbild einfügt.

astec inline il.10
Sliding Door Fitting
Schiebetürbeschlag

Manufacturer
astec gmbh,
Albstadt, Germany
Design
id aid
(Sven von Boetticher,
Prof. Matthias Schönherr),
Stuttgart, Germany
Web
www.astec-design.de
www.idaid.com

Highly elegant and precise, the inline il.10 fitting mainly consists of aluminium, but can be customised with stainless steel accents. The larger part of the fitting is integrated into the wall, so that only the aluminium and stainless steel surfaces connected to the glass on the sliding door remain visible. il.10 is also fitted with a cushioning mechanism which makes it suitable even for heavy doors. The door's motion can be stopped gently and it can then be moved into its final position almost silently.

Statement by the jury
This sliding door fitting commands respect for its high-quality finish and the purist design that makes it very versatile in use.

Der vorwiegend aus Aluminium gefertigte Beschlag inline il.10 mit individualisierbaren Edelstahlakzenten bietet ein hohes Maß an Eleganz und Klarheit. Der Hauptteil des Beschlags wird in die Wand integriert, sodass ausschließlich Aluminium- und Edelstahloberflächen in Verbindung mit dem Glas der Schiebetür zu sehen sind. il.10 verfügt zudem über einen Dämpfmechanismus auch für große Türgewichte. Die Tür kann aus der Bewegung sanft gestoppt und nahezu lautlos in Endposition gezogen werden.

Begründung der Jury
Dieser Schiebetürbeschlag überzeugt mit hoher Fertigungsqualität und puristischer Gestaltung, die vielfältige Einsatzmöglichkeiten bietet.

Portavant 80 automatic
All-Glass Sliding Door
Ganzglasschiebetür

Manufacturer
Gebr. Willach GmbH,
Ruppichteroth, Germany
In-house design
Jens Willach
Web
www.willach.com

Portavant 80 automatic by VITRIS is an innovative, automatically operated, all-glass sliding door system for use in luxuriously appointed residential and office environments. Compared to manually operated all-glass sliding doors, Portavant 80 automatic has the advantage of offering no barriers to access and of being much easier to go through as no pushing or pulling is needed. The purist design of the sliding rail enables it to be discreetly incorporated into the system, so that it fits unobtrusively into any environment and optically harmonises with every style of interior design.

Statement by the jury
Its compact and technically well thought-out design makes Portavant 80 automatic very versatile in use while offering a high degree of comfort and safe operation.

Portavant 80 automatic von VITRIS ist ein innovatives, automatisch betriebenes Ganzglasschiebetürsystem für den Einsatz in hochwertig ausgestatteten Wohn- und Geschäftsräumen. Gegenüber manuellen Ganzglasschiebetüren hat Portavant 80 automatic den Vorteil, dass Personen barrierefrei und ohne Kraftaufwand hindurchgehen können. Durch das puristisch gehaltene Design der Laufschiene fügt sich das System unauffällig und dezent in jede Umgebung ein und passt optisch zu jedem Einrichtungsstil.

Begründung der Jury
Durch seine kompakte, technisch durchdachte Gestaltung ist Portavant 80 automatic vielseitig einsetzbar bei hohem Komfort und sicherer Bedienung.

argenta invisible neo
Concealed Design Hinge
Verdecktliegendes Design-Bandsystem

Manufacturer
Argent Alu nv,
Kruishoutem, Belgium
In-house design
Brecht Callens
Web
www.argentalu.com

argenta invisible neo is a collection of concealed design hinges for interior doors and invisible doorframes. These hinges are perfectly shaped without any visible screws and with materials made to particularly high specifications. Thanks to the built-in height adjustment system, these hinges can easily and quickly be adjusted to all needs. The patented, built-in "Easy-Hook" hook-up system ensures that the door can be hung in its frame and adjusted by just one person without the normally required wedges. The casing of the hinge can be attached in advance at the workshop. The unique, compact form of the hinge arms and the compact dimensions of the hinge itself mean the door leaf can be covered with a thicker cladding, which improves the sturdiness of the door.

argenta invisible neo ist eine Serie unsichtbarer Design-Scharniere für Innentüren und unsichtbarer Aluminium-Rahmen für Innentüren. Diese verdeckliegenden Design-Türbänder sind in einer besonders hochwertigen und formvollendeten Ausführung ohne sichtbare Schrauben gefertigt. Dank des integrierten Höhenregelungssystems kann die Feineinstellung dieser Scharniere einfach, flexibel und schnell vorgenommen werden. Mithilfe des patentierten, integrierten Einhaksystems „Easy-Hook" kann die Tür von einer einzigen Person im Rahmen montiert und eingestellt werden, ohne dabei einen Keil zu verwenden. Das Scharniergehäuse kann bereits vorab in der Werkstatt montiert werden. Durch die einzigartige, kompakte Form der Scharnierarme und die kompakten Maße des Scharniers lässt sich die Türplatte mit einer dickeren Verkleidungsschicht versehen, was der Stärke der Tür zugutekommt.

Statement by the jury
The technically well thought-out design of these hinges makes this collection very versatile in use, as they can easily be adjusted in terms of height, depth and pressure without needing to remove the door.

Begründung der Jury
Durch ihre technisch durchdachte Gestaltung sind die Scharniere dieser Serie vielseitig einsetzbar und können problemlos in Höhe, Tiefe und Anpressdruck eingestellt werden, ohne die Tür abzunehmen.

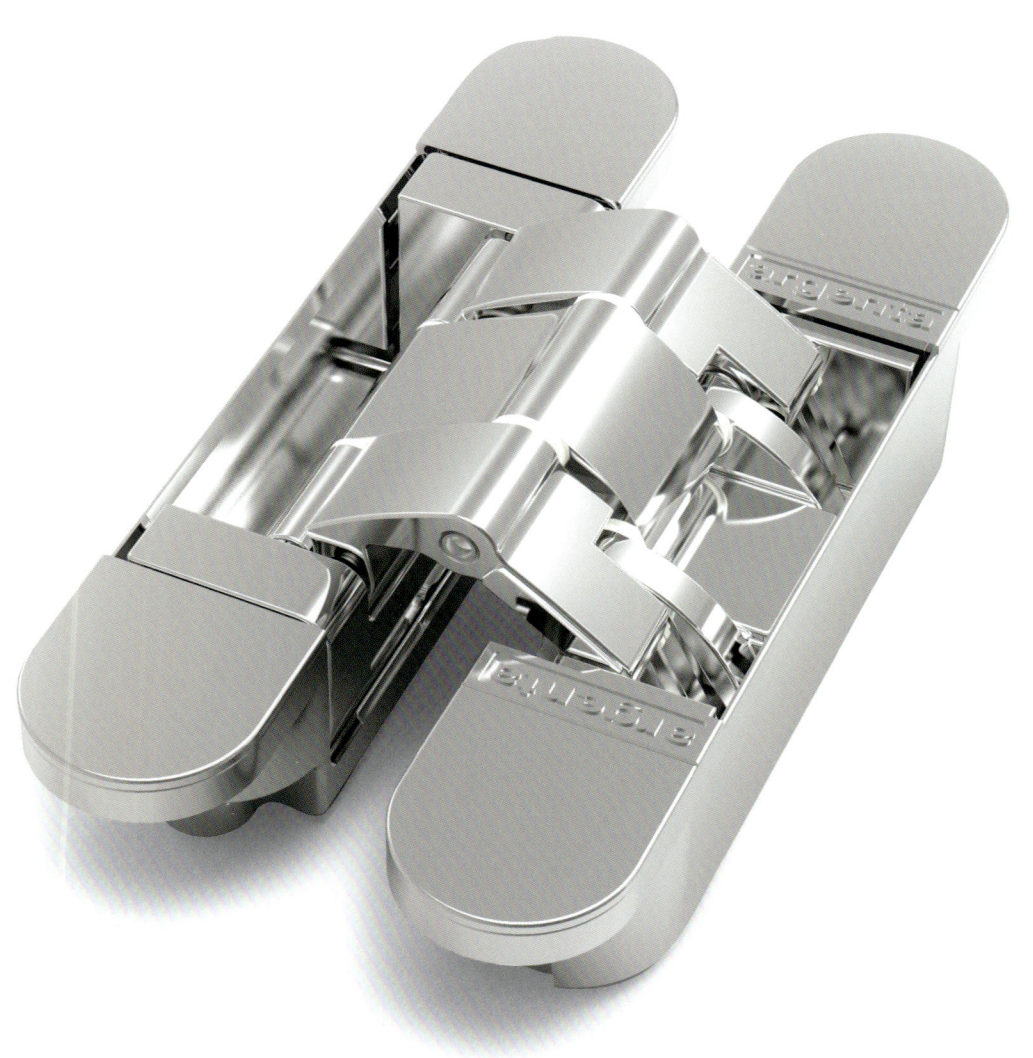

Security Door Closer
Sicherheits-Türschließer

Manufacturer
ASSA ABLOY Sicherheitstechnik GmbH,
Albstadt, Germany
In-house design
Johannes Klaszka
Design
einmaleins, Büro für Gestaltung
(Rupert Bläsi),
Burgrieden, Germany
Web
www.assaabloy.de
www.einmaleins.net
Honourable Mention

The outstanding feature of ASSA ABLOY's security door closer is the built-in escape door lock. It allows for the retrofitting of fire doors with an escape route lock. There is no need to drill, mill, grind or sand. This security door closer makes use of existing drill holes for use with DIN EN 1154 door closers by placing an extended installation panel on top. The glide rail is also extended in order to attach the escape door opener to it. The mortise latch bolt lock is mounted onto the extended installation plate – not onto the door leaf.

Das hervorstechende Merkmal des Sicherheits-Türschließers von ASSA ABLOY ist die integrierte Fluchttürverriegelung. Er ermöglicht es, Brandschutztüren nachträglich mit einer Rettungswegverriegelung auszustatten. Ohne Bohren, Fräsen, Feilen oder Schleifen nutzt der Sicherheits-Türschließer die vorhandenen Bohrlöcher für Türschließer nach DIN EN 1154 und setzt darauf eine verlängerte Montageplatte. Die Gleitschiene wird ebenfalls verlängert, um darin den Fluchttüröffner zu befestigen. Das Fallenschloss wird auf die verlängerte Montageplatte montiert – nicht auf das Türblatt.

Statement by the jury
ASSA ABLOY's security door closer is convincing thanks to its innovative, technical concept and the way in which the high-quality design has been realised.

Begründung der Jury
Der Sicherheits-Türschließer von ASSA ABLOY überzeugt durch sein innovatives technisches Konzept und dessen hochwertige gestalterische Umsetzung.

Berker R.1
Switch
Schalter

Manufacturer
Berker GmbH & Co. KG,
Schalksmühle, Germany
Design
Studio Aisslinger
(Prof. Werner Aisslinger, Nicole Losos),
Berlin, Germany
Web
www.berker.com

The R.1 range uses its design language to reinterpret the classic, circular switch. The gentle contours of the frame, combined with a round central section, are characteristic of it. The basic version of the R.1 comes in black or white plastic, but alternatives in glass, aluminium or stainless steel, mounted on a white or black plastic base plate are also very appealing. R.1 is a complete surface range with a large depth of product variety and a comfortable variety of functions.

Statement by the jury
Its classic shape and good quality make this range of switches a stylish fit for every environment.

Mit seiner klaren Formensprache interpretiert das Programm R.1 den klassischen kreisförmigen Schalter neu. Charakteristisch ist die weiche Rahmenkontur in Kombination mit dem runden Zentralstück. In der Basisvariante wird der R.1 in Kunststoff in Schwarz oder Weiß gefertigt. Auch die Varianten überzeugen: Glas, Aluminium und Edelstahl werden auf einen weißen oder schwarzen Träger aus Kunststoff aufgesetzt. R.1 ist ein vollwertiges Flächenprogramm mit großer Sortimentstiefe und komfortabler Vielfalt an Funktionen.

Begründung der Jury
Durch seine klassische Form und hochwertige Qualität fügt sich dieses Schalterprogramm stilvoll in jedes Umfeld ein.

Berker R.3
Switch
Schalter

Manufacturer
Berker GmbH & Co. KG,
Schalksmühle, Germany
Design
Studio Aisslinger
(Prof. Werner Aisslinger, Nicole Losos),
Berlin, Germany
Web
www.berker.com

The contrast between a circular central insert and angular frame is typical of the R.3 switch programme. The basic model of the R.3 is produced in black or white plastic. Alternative versions of different construction and mixed materials are equally appealing. Glass, aluminium and stainless steel are mounted on a white or black plastic base plate. Berker R.3 is a complete surface range with a large depth of product variety particularly suited for commercial properties.

Statement by the jury
This aesthetically compelling range of switches impresses above all with its clean, purist design and choice of materials.

Typisch für das Schalterprogramm R.3 ist der Gegensatz aus kreisförmigem Zentralstück und kantigem Rahmen. In der Basisvariante wird der R.3 in Kunststoff in Schwarz oder Weiß gefertigt. Durch Aufbau und Materialmix überzeugen auch die Varianten. Glas, Aluminium und Edelstahl werden auf einen weißen oder schwarzen Grundträger aus Kunststoff aufgesetzt. Der Berker R.3 ist ein vollwertiges Flächenprogramm mit großer Sortimentstiefe, das besonders für Gewerbeobjekte geeignet ist.

Begründung der Jury
Bei dieser ästhetisch überzeugend gestalteten Schalterserie beeindruckt vor allem die klare, puristische Form- und Materialgebung.

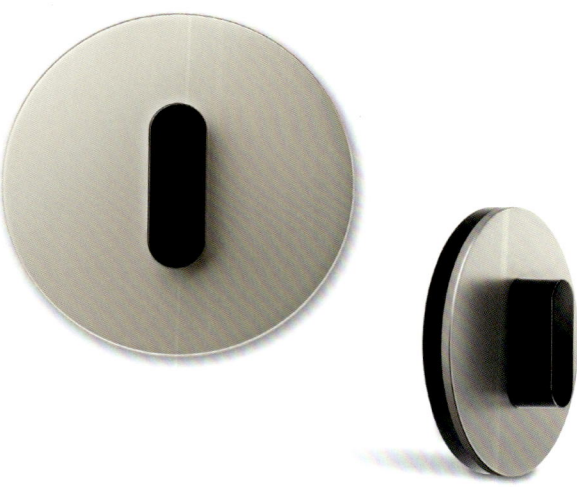

Berker Serie R.classic
Switch
Schalter

Manufacturer
Berker GmbH & Co. KG,
Schalksmühle, Germany
Design
Studio Aisslinger
(Prof. Werner Aisslinger, Nicole Losos),
Berlin, Germany
Web
www.berker.com

With its pleasant round shape and a design featuring a pure, straightforward rotary knob, the Serie R.classic harks back to old circular switches. This collection is produced in plastic (black or white) or in combinations of plastic and glass, aluminium or stainless steel by mounting a frame of the high-quality material onto a white or black plastic base plate. A wide range of functions leads to the creation of many different versions and makes the switches suitable for many different applications.

Statement by the jury
This collection re-energises the classic form of the circular switch. High-quality design makes it particularly suitable for state-of-the art architectural environments.

Mit sympathischem Radius und einer Ausführung mit pur-schlichtem Drehknebel zitiert Serie R.classic ältere runde Schalterserien. Gefertigt wird die Serie in Kunststoff (schwarz oder weiß) oder in Kombinationen aus Kunststoff und Glas, Aluminium oder Edelstahl. Dabei werden auf einen weißen oder schwarzen Kunststoffträger Echtmaterial-Platten aufgesetzt. Durch eine breite Auswahl an Funktionen lassen sich viele Anwendungen und Varianten realisieren.

Begründung der Jury
Die klassische Form des kreisförmigen Schalters wird hier neu belebt. Die hochwertige Gestaltung macht ihn besonders geeignet für architektonisch anspruchsvolle Interieurs.

5.1
Switch
Schalter

Manufacturer
Font Barcelona,
Santa Perpètua de Mogoda, Spain
Design
Guimeràicinca Studio
(Oriol Guimerà, Joan Cinca),
Barcelona, Spain
Web
www.fontbarcelona.com
www.guimeraicinca.com

The 5.1 switches of Font Barcelona have a very distinctive style and offer numerous different configuration options, making them highly adaptable to the most diverse interiors. One can choose between different covers, surfaces, frames, switch-plates, buttons, controls etc. The 5.1 collection of switches also works in conjunction with home automation systems using KNX technology.

Statement by the jury
Minimalist design and a high degree of customisation are the key characteristics of this range of switches that will also satisfy commercial requirements.

Die Serie 5.1 von Font Barcelona besteht aus Schaltern mit einer sehr klaren Gestaltung, vielen Konfigurationsmöglichkeiten und einer hohen Anpassungsfähigkeit an unterschiedlichste Interieurs. Man kann wählen zwischen verschiedenen Abdeckungen, Oberflächen, Rahmen, Schalterplatten, Tastern, Reglern etc. Die Schalter aus der Serie 5.1 sind außerdem bei der Hausautomation mit KNX-Technologie einsetzbar.

Begründung der Jury
Eine minimalistische Gestaltung und hohe Individualisierbarkeit sind die Hauptmerkmale dieser Schalterserie, die auch professionellen Ansprüchen gerecht wird.

Millenium
Room Thermostat
Raumtemperaturregler

Manufacturer
Busch-Jaeger Elektro GmbH,
Lüdenscheid, Germany
In-house design
Bernhard Heitz
Web
www.busch-jaeger.de

Finding the way around the room both by day and by night could not be easier thanks to the backlit icons on the room thermostat of the Millenium range. Using two different transparent materials, the colour of the display changes depending on the temperature. The pivot-mounted rocker provides touch feedback. Millenium is available in four frames with real metal surfaces: brushed stainless steel, matt black, matt gold and antique gold.

Statement by the jury
This KNX room thermostat is clear and purist in design. The distinctive control with built-in display is practical to use and provides a good overview.

Für eine ausgezeichnete Orientierung im Raum im Tag- und Nachtbetrieb sind die Icons bei diesem Raumtemperaturregler aus dem Schalterprogramm Millenium mit zwei unterschiedlich transparenten Materialien hinterleuchtet. Die Farbe der Anzeige ändert sich dabei entsprechend der Temperatur. Die schwimmende Wippe erzeugt ein haptisches Feedback. Millenium bietet vier Rahmen mit Echtmetall-Oberflächen: Edelstahl gebürstet, Schwarz matt, Gold matt und Gold antik.

Begründung der Jury
Dieser KNX-Raumtemperaturregler ist klar und puristisch gestaltet. Das prägnante Bedienelement mit integrierter Anzeige ist dabei praktisch und übersichtlich.

Cavius Smoke
Smoke Detector
Rauchmelder

Manufacturer
Cavius Aps,
Silkeborg, Denmark
In-house design
Glenn Højmose
Web
www.cavius.com

The smoke detector by Cavius is part of a new, high-quality collection of security products for the home. Its discreet size (a diameter of 40 mm) indicates the intention to design a product that is used for its "cool" character, as well as for its properties. "Normal" smoke detectors are large and "functional". The Cavius smoke detector is chic and well designed without compromising on quality or efficiency. In addition, it has a long battery life of ten years.

Statement by the jury
This smoke detector is impressive for its compact shape and long battery life – properties that are especially important for devices of this kind.

Der Rauchmelder von Cavius ist Teil einer neuen, hochwertigen Serie von Sicherheitsprodukten im Heimbereich. Seine diskrete Größe (40 mm Durchmesser) verweist auf die Absicht, ein Produkt zu entwerfen, das für seine „Coolness" und seine Eigenschaften benutzt wird. „Normale" Rauchmelder sind groß und „funktional". Der Rauchmelder von Cavius ist schick und gut gestaltet ohne Kompromisse bei Qualität und Effizienz. Zudem verfügt er über eine Batterielebensdauer von zehn Jahren.

Begründung der Jury
Dieser Rauchmelder beeindruckt durch seine kompakte Form und die lange Batterielaufzeit – Eigenschaften, die für ein Gerät dieser Art besonders wichtig sind.

T-Box – Multifunctional Home System
Building Block System
Baukastensystem

Design
Yang Design
(Jamy Yang, Anthony Zhang),
Shanghai, China
Web
www.yang-design.com

T-Box is a multifunctional building block system whose basic modular element is a 40 x 40 cm sized box. On the inside is a T-shaped handle, which not only facilitates transportation, but also increases stability. A single box can be used as a coffee table, stool or storage space. Several modules can be combined to create a bookshelf of any size desired, a lowboard or a semi-transparent room divider. The elements are connected with the help of X-shaped connectors that ensure the stability of the construction. The system can be extended and enlarged at will if the need arises.

T-Box ist ein multifunktionales Baukastensystem, dessen modulares Grundelement eine 40 x 40 cm große Box ist. An deren Innenseite befindet sich ein T-Stück, das die Stabilität erhöht und auch als komfortabler Tragegriff dient. Eine einzelne Box kann als Teetisch, Hocker oder Ablage genutzt werden. Mit mehreren Modulen kann man ein Bücherregal beliebiger Größe, ein Lowboard oder einen halbtransparenten Raumteiler kreieren. Die Elemente werden dabei mit Hilfe von X-förmigen Verbindungsstücken, die auch für die Stabilität der Konstruktion sorgen, zusammengefügt. Bei Bedarf kann das System beliebig erweitert und vergrößert werden.

Statement by the jury
The simplicity and versatility of T-Box are surprising. Its applications are almost limitless thanks to the modular design and simple method of use.

Begründung der Jury
T-Box zeichnet sich durch seine Einfachheit und Vielseitigkeit aus. Die Möglichkeiten der Nutzung sind dank des modularen Designs und unkomplizierten Gebrauchs nahezu unbegrenzt.

Top Time Office
Interior Design

Design
Cimax Design Engineer
(Hongkong) Limited (Bo Li),
Shenzhen, China
Web
www.libodesign.com
Honourable Mention

Located in an old plant area in the prosperous Central Business District of Beijing, Top Time Office is an office for movie and TV talents as well as creative people. The original walls and ceiling of the old plant were to be retained as much as possible. The concept utilised multiple high-quality coloured glass boxes for integrating steel plates and bars into an elaborate construction. Areas for meetings, work, make-up, fittings, discussions, reception and so on are partitioned and arranged in a tonality that is almost pure white. The specially designed working droplights and suspended ceiling lamps exude an especially ornate and dynamic appearance in this pure white world.

Das Top Time Office ist ein auf einem alten Fabrikgelände im florierenden Central Business District von Beijing gelegenes Büro für Film- und Fernseh- sowie andere Kreative. Originalwände und -decke der alten Fabrik sollten bei der Umgestaltung soweit als möglich beibehalten werden. Verschiedene hochwertige farbige Glasboxen wurden verwendet, um Stahlplatten und Stahlträger in eine ausgeklügelte Konstruktion zu integrieren. Bereiche für Meeting, Arbeit, Make-up, Anprobe, Gespräch, Empfang und so weiter sind voneinander getrennt und folgen einer Farbgebung in fast reinem Weiß. Die speziell gestalteten Arbeits-Hängeleuchten und abgehängten Deckenleuchten wirken besonders kunstvoll und dynamisch in dieser reinweißen Welt.

Statement by the jury
The clear and consistent design concept has led to the creation of a delightful, creative ambience, incorporating a suitable framework for the dynamic media of film and TV work.

Begründung der Jury
Ein klares, konsistentes Gestaltungskonzept sorgt hier für ein angenehmes, kreatives Ambiente und schafft so einen passenden Rahmen für die dynamischen Medien Film und Fernsehen.

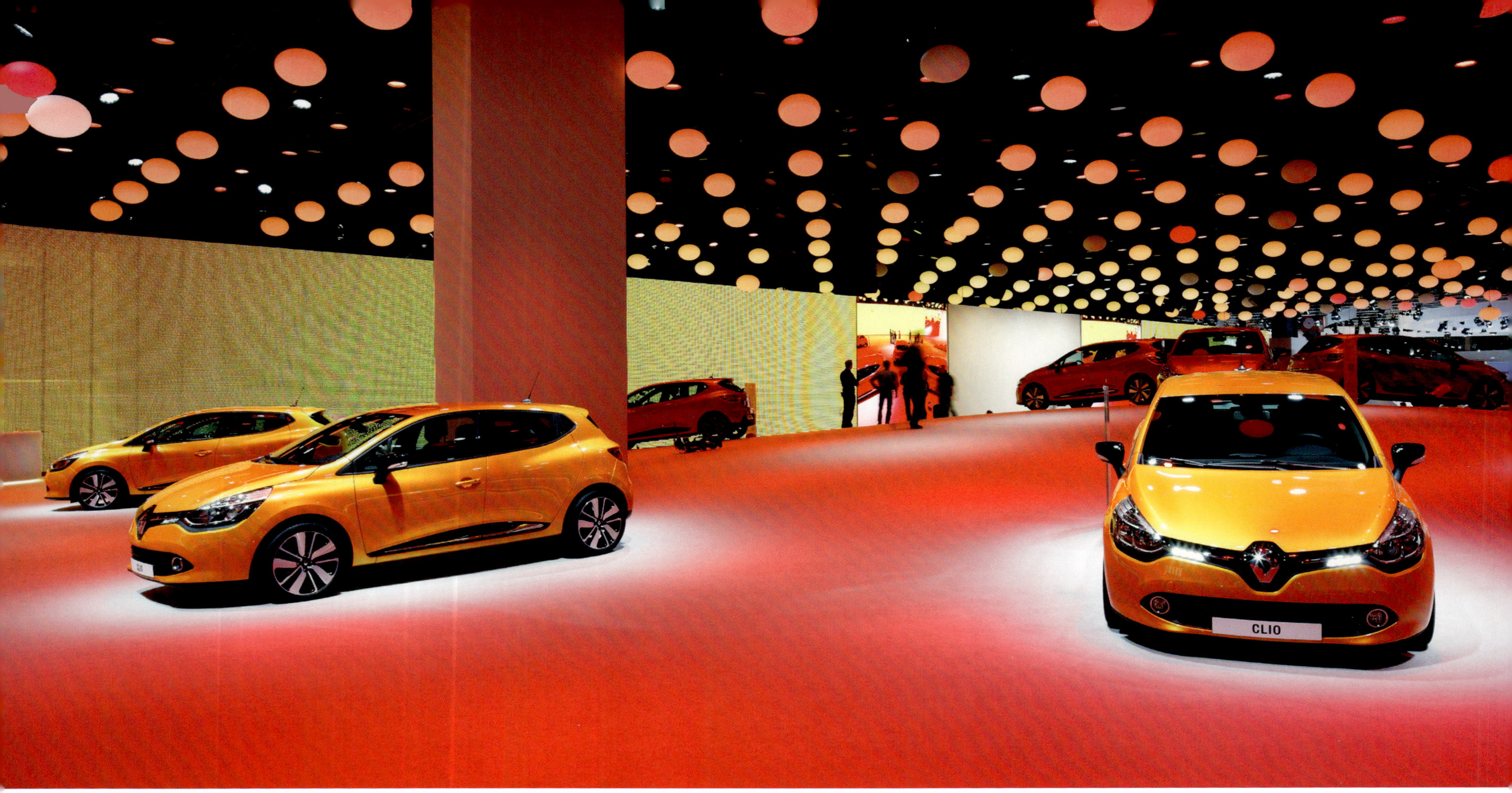
CLIO

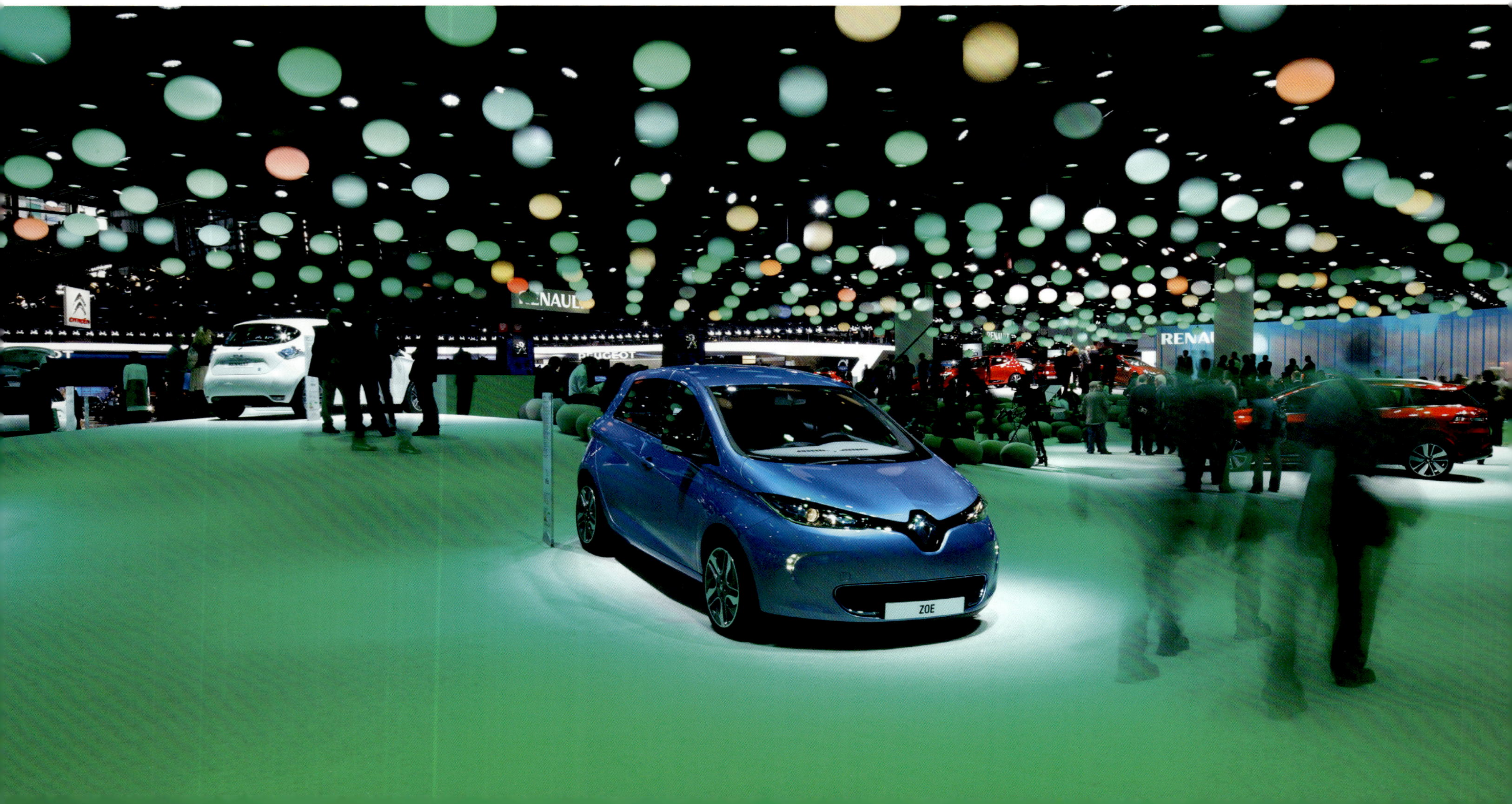
ZOE

The Bump – Renault Salon
Trade Fair Stand
Messestand

Manufacturer
Renault SAS,
Le Plessis-Robinson, France
Design
Dorell.Ghotmeh.Tane / Architects
(Dan Dorell, Lina Ghotmeh, Tsuyoshi Tane),
Paris, France
Web
www.renault.com
www.dgtarchitects.com

The new Renault stand was designed for international motor shows around the world including those in Geneva, Frankfurt, Shanghai and Buenos Aires. The design concept is inspired by a value that all cars on display on the stand have in common: motion. The idea was to translate the feeling of motion to a stand. Featuring two hills and a concentric vehicle layout, the concept cars or new vehicles spin on rotating platforms at the top. Depending on where beholders are standing, the vehicles are thus shown from different sides. The feeling of motion created by this three-dimensional layout is further enhanced by the floor and ceiling lighting. Balls of light move as one while subtly changing colour to simulate the movement of waves.

Statement by the jury
The generously spaced, animated approach to the presentation of the new Renault stand creates a vivid atmosphere that envelops beholders and adequately represents the brand values of motion and change.

Der neue Renault-Stand wurde für die internationalen Automobilausstellungen weltweit, einschließlich in Genf, Frankfurt, Shanghai und Buenos Aires, entworfen. Grundlage des Gestaltungskonzepts war dabei ein Wert, der allen ausgestellten Fahrzeugen gemeinsam ist: Bewegung. Das Gefühl von Bewegung sollte durch den Stand repräsentiert werden. So sind auf zwei Erhebungen die Konzeptfahrzeuge oder neuen Autos konzentrisch angeordnet und werden auf rotierenden Plattformen gezeigt. Dadurch werden die Fahrzeuge, je nach Standort des Betrachters, anders wahrgenommen. Die Boden- und Deckenbeleuchtung verstärkt den durch diese dreidimensionale Präsentation erweckten Eindruck von Bewegung. Lichtbälle bewegen sich im Einklang und simulieren subtil ihre Farbe verändernd Wellenbewegungen.

Begründung der Jury
Eine großzügige, animierende Rauminszenierung sorgt bei dem neuen Renault-Stand für eine lebendige, die Sinne ansprechende Atmosphäre, die die Markenwerte Bewegung und Veränderung adäquat widerspiegelt.

Stoffsüchtig Store, Hafencity Hamburg
Retail Design Concept
Retail-Designkonzept

Design
BERG – Raumkonzepte, Design, Interior
(Holger Berg),
Hamburg, Germany
Web
www.berg101.com
Honourable Mention

The concept for this store is based on an industrial atmosphere aiming to establish a link to the nearby harbour. Three-dimensional lattice structures made of untreated steel serve as hanging space. Backlit they appear to "ramble" across the walls. Plywood with a rough, textile surface was used as the base material for the furniture. The sales room is separated from the storage area by a "radiant color" cube with three fitting rooms and a space for employees. Lighting is provided by a 16 metre long light tube and two chandeliers made of fluorescent tubes.

Statement by the jury
The design concept of this store intelligently picks up on the existing industrial flair and playfully links past and future.

Das Konzept dieses Stores arbeitet mit einer industriellen Atmosphäre, um eine Bindung zum nahegelegenen Hafen zu schaffen. Dreidimensionale Gitterkonstruktionen aus unbehandeltem Stahl dienen als Hängefläche. Sie sind rückseitig beleuchtet und „wuchern" über die Wände. Als Material für die Möbel wurden Sperrholz und eine grobe, textile Oberfläche verwendet. Der Verkaufsraum wird vom Lager getrennt durch einen „Radiant Color"-Kubus mit drei Anprobekabinen und einem Mitarbeiterraum. Für das Grundlicht sorgen ein 16 Meter langes, durch den Raum laufendes Lichtrohr und zwei Kronleuchter aus Leuchtstoffröhren.

Begründung der Jury
Die Gestaltung dieses Stores greift intelligent das vorgefundene industrielle Flair auf und verbindet spielerisch Vergangenheit und Zukunft.

Google Office Düsseldorf
Interior Design

Design
Lepel & Lepel Architektur Innenarchitektur
(Monika Lepel, Angelika Van Putten),
Cologne, Germany
Web
www.lepel-lepel.de

This design concept used themed rooms to communicate company and location by association. The design followed the central idea of "Men of Steel & Girls of Pleasure". Open plan work areas were conceived as workshops and are presented as such with the help of lighting and appropriate materials. Rooms for communal use follow certain themes and use a variety of colours from glamorous to bright and trendy. Transition areas offer corners with sofas and individual workstations.

Statement by the jury
In line with the philosophy of the company, the design of its office space followed an exceptional concept that gives license to variety and creativity.

Unternehmen und Standort werden assoziativ über thematische Räume vermittelt. Der Gestaltung lag dabei die Leitidee „Men of Steel & Girls of Pleasure" zugrunde. Die Open-Space-Arbeitsbereiche werden als Werkstatt interpretiert und durch Licht und entsprechende Materialien inszeniert. Die gemeinschaftlich genutzten Räume weisen thematische Zuweisungen und Farben von glamourös bis poppig auf. In den Übergangszonen schließlich gibt es Sofaecken und einzelne Arbeitsbereiche.

Begründung der Jury
Der Philosophie des Unternehmens entsprechend wurde ein bemerkenswertes Gestaltungskonzept entwickelt, für Büroräume, die Abwechslung und Kreativität zulassen.

Transparent Sales Display
Presentation and Sales Display
Präsentations- und Verkaufsdisplay

Manufacturer
Cheil Worldwide / Samsung,
Seoul, South Korea
In-house design
Dongeon Kim, Jongheui Lee
Design
aNTS
(Daejun Kim, Kwangho Back),
Seoul, South Korea
Web
www.samsung.com
www.antscom.co.kr

The Transparent Sales Display represents a new concept in electronic merchandising displays by Samsung, aiming to draw enhanced attention and deliver information more effectively at customer touch points. It does this by playing video clips of the key attributes of new products on a transparent LCD panel placed in front of the actual products. The minimal design provides both versatility and flexibility in use. In addition, the content projections can be controlled from a remote centre.

Statement by the jury
This presentation and sales display is both an outstandingly innovative and highly practical point-of-purchase tool.

Das Transparent Sales Display stellt ein neues Konzept in der elektronischen Warenpräsentation von Samsung dar, um beim Kundenkontakt die Aufmerksamkeit zu erhöhen und effektiver Informationen bereitzustellen. Hierzu werden Videoclips über die Eigenschaften neuer Produkte auf einem transparenten, vor dem Produkt platzierten LCD-Panel abgespielt. Die minimalistische Gestaltung sorgt für Vielseitigkeit und Flexibilität. Zudem können die dargestellten Inhalte zentral ferngesteuert werden.

Begründung der Jury
Dieses Präsentations- und Verkaufsdisplay ist ein ausgesprochen innovatives und zugleich sehr praktikables Instrument der Kundenansprache.

b62™
Aluminium Frame for Stand Construction
Aluminiumrahmen für den Messebau

Manufacturer
beMatrix,
Roeselare, Belgium
In-house design
Edwin Van der Vennet
Web
www.bematrix.com

The b62 aluminium frame for constructing trade fair stands is extremely flexible to use. The built structure remains the same, but the frames and/or fillings can be changed at will to create a completely new look for the stand. b62 is suitable for both panels and textiles, which are combined by the same connectors. The construction system is lightweight and easy to handle, requiring only a limited number of connectors. Construction is quick without the use of any tools and the frame structure remains almost invisible. The frame is recyclable and of long durability.

Statement by the jury
Flexibility, speed and efficiency are particularly important when it comes to constructing exhibition stands. The b62 aluminium frame outstandingly fulfils all these criteria.

Der Aluminiumrahmen b62 für den Messebau ist extrem flexibel in der Anwendung. Die gebaute Struktur bleibt dabei stets die gleiche, aber mit verschiedenen Rahmen bzw. Füllungen kann man jeweils einen völlig neuen Look des Standes erzielen. b62 eignet sich sowohl für Platten als auch Textilien, die darüber hinaus durch die gleichen Verbinder kombiniert werden. Das Bausystem ist leicht und einfach zu handhaben. Es benötigt nur wenige Verbindungen. Der Aufbau kann sehr schnell erfolgen, ohne Werkzeug, und die Rahmenstruktur ist nahezu unsichtbar. Der Rahmen ist recycelbar und von langer Lebensdauer.

Begründung der Jury
Flexibilität, Schnelligkeit und Effizienz sind im Messebau besonders wichtig. Der Aluminiumrahmen b62 erfüllt diese Kriterien hervorragend.

Conservo Magnetic Frame
Conservo-Magnetrahmen

Manufacturer
Halbe-Rahmen GmbH,
Kirchen, Germany
In-house design
Heinrich Halbe
Web
www.halbe.de

The Conservo Magnetic Frame was developed as a picture frame for the particularly stringent requirements of restorers and museums. The frame has a hidden picture security system, height-adjustable wall spacers with enclosed felt pads to compensate for uneven walls, slanted punched holes to compensate horizontally for hanging points that are not level, a variable depth insert for artworks of different material strengths, as well as an insert frame as a spacer for the glass.

Statement by the jury
By going into great detail in its design approach and through the use of chemical-free materials, this picture frame will comply with the most stringent requirements of conservators.

Der Conservo-Magnetrahmen wurde als Bilderrahmen für die hohen Bedürfnisse von Restauratoren und Museen entwickelt. Der Rahmen hat eine unsichtbare Bildsicherung, höhenverstellbare Wandstandhalter mit eingefassten Filzpunkten zum Ausgleich bei unebenen Wänden, schräge Stanzlöcher zum horizontalen Ausgleich bei nicht waagerechten Aufhängepunkten, eine variable Einlegetiefe für Kunstwerke in unterschiedlichen Materialstärken sowie einen Einlegerahmen als Abstandhalter zum Glas.

Begründung der Jury
Durch eine im Detail durchdachte Gestaltung und den chemiefreien Materialeinsatz wird dieser Bilderrahmen höchsten konservatorischen Ansprüchen gerecht.

Display Magnetic Frame
Display-Magnetrahmen

Manufacturer
Halbe-Rahmen GmbH,
Kirchen, Germany
In-house design
Heinrich Halbe
Web
www.halbe.de

The base element of the Display Magnetic Frame (the back of the frame) is securely bolted to the wall. The actual profile frame and the plexiglass are magnetically placed onto this base element as a single unit thanks to the new Glasfix system. That makes opening the frame child's play. The second element is the specially developed Posterfix module, built into the base element that is bolted to the wall. Simply slide in the poster from below and it will automatically be held in place by the clever clamping mechanism.

Statement by the jury
The intelligent design of this frame makes it extremely simple and quick to change images.

Beim Display-Magnetrahmen wird das Grundelement (die Rückwand des Rahmens) fest an der Wand verschraubt. Der eigentliche Profilrahmen und das Plexiglas werden durch das neue Glasfix-System als Einheit magnetisch auf das Grundelement gesetzt. So lässt sich der Rahmen kinderleicht öffnen. Das zweite Element ist das speziell entwickelte Posterfix-Modul – integriert in das an der Wand verschraubte Grundelement. Das Poster wird einfach von unten eingeschoben und durch den cleveren Klemm-Mechanismus automatisch gehalten.

Begründung der Jury
Dank seiner intelligenten Gestaltung kann bei diesem Rahmen äußerst einfach und schnell das Motiv gewechselt werden.

"Italian Style Interiors" for SSJ100

Aircraft Interior Design
Flugzeug-Inneneinrichtung

Manufacturer
Alenia Aermacchi,
San Maurizio Canavese (Torino), Italy
Design
Pininfarina,
Cambiano (Torino), Italy
Web
www.superjetinternational.com
www.pininfarina.it

The aim of the interior design of this aircraft was to offer passengers on regional flights the same level of comfort as on long-haul flights. The concept includes a welcoming entrance area, a cabin with carefully designed details, as well as elegant and efficient toilets. In addition, the cabin has extremely comfortable seats, while the pleasant ambience of the space contributes to a sense of well-being. All elements were designed with a uniform, elegant design language, in order to achieve a high level of coherence throughout the interior. This has led to the correspondingly careful choice of materials, surfaces and colours to meet not only the desired level of ergonomics and cleanliness, but also to create a relaxing atmosphere.

Ziel bei dieser Flugzeug-Inneneinrichtung war es, Passagieren auf regionalen Flügen den Komfort eines Langstreckenflugzeuges zu bieten. Die Gestaltung umfasst einen einladenden Eingangsbereich, eine Kabine mit sorgfältig entworfenen Details sowie einen eleganten und effizienten Toilettenraum. Die Kabine verfügt über äußerst bequeme Sitze, während das angenehme Ambiente der Räume zusätzlich zum Komfort beiträgt. Alle Elemente sind in der gleichen eleganten Formensprache entworfen, um über das gesamte Interieur hinweg einen hohen Grad an Kohärenz zu erreichen. Materialien, Oberflächen und Farben wurden entsprechend gewählt, nicht nur um die Anforderungen an Ergonomie und Sauberkeit zu erfüllen, sondern auch um eine entspannende Atmosphäre zu kreieren.

Statement by the jury
The interior design of this regional aircraft is characterised by its elegant, harmonious forms and the fresh colours used, which are influenced by Mediterranean flair and an Italian sense of style.

Begründung der Jury
Das Interior Design für dieses Regionalflugzeug besticht durch seine eleganten, harmonischen Formen und die frische Farbgebung, die von mediterranem Flair und italienischem Stilempfinden geprägt sind.

SKYBOX
Coffin
Sarg

Manufacturer
B+B Sargmanufaktur,
Rhede, Germany
In-house design
Wolfgang Buttlar

The SKYBOX coffin has been designed with clean, purist lines leaving only the rectilinear lid, that is free of any joints, visible. All corners are mitred. The coffin is available in matt black, matt dark red or in any RAL colour. The inlaid, slightly spherical ornamental design that has been carved out of expressive hard wood which is flush with the coffin and can be omitted upon request. Six special fittings connect the lid to the coffin, which is discreetly recessed and is quite shallow.

Der Sarg SKYBOX ist in einer klaren, puristischen Formensprache gestaltet. Ausschließlich die geradlinige, fugenfreie Haube ist sichtbar. Alle Kanten sind auf Gehrung gearbeitet. Der Farbton ist wahlweise matt-schwarz, matt-dunkelrot oder nach RAL-Farbkarte. Die eingelegte, flächenbündige und leicht ballige Ornamentik aus ausdrucksstarkem Massivholz kann auf Wunsch entfallen. Die Haube wird mit sechs Spezialbeschlägen fest am Untersarg gehalten, der dezent ausgeschlagen ist und eine geringe Konstruktionshöhe hat.

Statement by the jury
The SKYBOX coffin sets itself apart with a minimalist design whose simple serenity is nonetheless extremely expressive.

Begründung der Jury
Der Sarg SKYBOX zeichnet sich durch eine minimalistische Gestaltung aus, deren schlichte Klarheit dennoch von großer Ausdrucksstärke ist.

Architecture and urban design
Architektur und Urban Design

Architecture, public design, urban planning, city and landscape planning, properties, office structures, residential buildings, garden and park architecture, hotels, restaurants, bars, clubs, shops, cultural and public amenities, building elements, constructional components, public furniture, playgrounds, museums, libraries, temporary architecture, events

Architektur, Public Design, Städteplanung, Städte- und Landschaftsbau, Immobilien, Bürobauten, Wohnhäuser, Garten- und Park-Architektur, Hotels, Restaurants, Bars, Clubs, Shops, Kulturelle & öffentliche Einrichtungen, Gebäudeelemente, Bauelemente, Stadtmobiliar, Spielplätze, Museen, Bibliotheken, Temporäre Architektur, Events

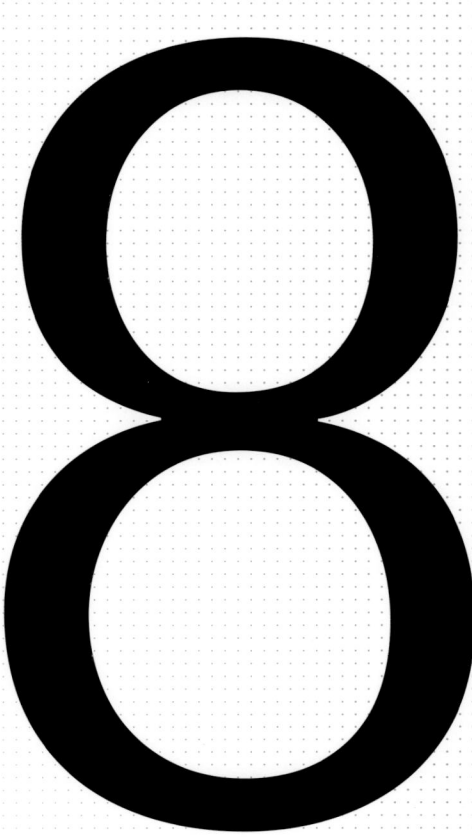

Platform for Arts and Creativity

Client
Câmara Municipal de Guimarães,
Guimarães, Portugal

Design
Pitágoras Arquitectos
(Fernando Seara de Sá,
Raul Roque,
Alexandre Coelho Lima,
Manuel Roque),
Guimarães, Portugal

Web
www.pitagoras.pt
www.cm-guimaraes.pt

A centre of life

The grounds of the historical Municipal Market in the city of Guimarães in the North of Portugal used to be a privileged and central location of public life. The urban design programme provided a comprehensive concept to restore this area by relating to its historic functions. Both the market place and the adjacent buildings were to be rejuvenated and thus reintegrated into the urban fabric. For this purpose, the functional programme for the infrastructure clearly defined three major programme areas to be implemented as an arts and culture centre. As a part of the European Capital of Culture 2012, this centre thus transformed into a multifunctional platform dedicated to various artistic, economic, cultural and social activities. The Art Centre houses a permanent exhibition area for the Collection of José de Guimarães and a temporary exhibition area, as well as a multipurpose public space for additional activities, performances and shows. The Creative Labs serve for the reception and installation of activities related to creative industries, as well as supporting and developing business projects. Finally, the Workshops to Support Emerging Creativity offer young creators in various areas the chance to develop projects on a temporary basis. In an impressive manner, this project realises the idea of a multifunctional space through urban design. In harmony with the existing architecture, this concept serves the multi-faceted purpose of supporting creative potential.

Mitten im Leben

In der Stadt Guimarães im Norden Portugals war das Gelände des historischen Marktes einst ein zentraler und privilegierter Ort des öffentlichen Lebens. Im Mittelpunkt des Urban Designs stand deshalb die Zielsetzung, durch ein weitreichendes Konzept an diese ursprüngliche Funktion anzuknüpfen. Der Marktplatz sowie die ihn umgebende Architektur sollte dabei integrativ eingebunden und neu belebt werden. Durch klar definierte Ziele für die Infrastruktur sowie ein festgelegtes Programm entstand in der Umsetzung ein Kunst- und Kulturzentrum mit drei wesentlichen Kernbereichen. Im Rahmen der Ernennung der Stadt Guimarães zur Europäischen Kulturhauptstadt 2012 ermöglichte dieses Zentrum vielseitige künstlerische, wirtschaftliche, kulturelle und auch soziale Aktivitäten. Die Einrichtung eines Art Centers bietet, neben der Dauerausstellung der Sammlung José de Guimarães, einen Wechselausstellungsbereich sowie einen vielfältig für die Öffentlichkeit nutzbaren Mehrzweckraum. Creative Labs dienen dem Aufbau und der Betreuung kreativitätsbezogener Aktivitäten sowie der Entwicklung und Wiederbelebung von Geschäftsaktivitäten. In weiteren Räumen fördern Workshops die Kreativität der Künstler und bieten ihnen zahlreiche Möglichkeiten, ihre Kunst zu entwickeln. Auf beeindruckende Weise wird hier durch das Urban Design die Idee eines multifunktionalen Raumes verwirklicht. In Harmonie mit der bestehenden Architektur dient dieses Konzept in vielerlei Hinsicht der Förderung kreativen Potenzials.

Statement by the jury

The urban design for the city of Guimarães both maintains the historically grown formal relations and blends them consistently into a contemporary architectural concept. The openness of the architecture is friendly and inviting, and thus comes close to the function of an arts and culture centre. Also fascinating is the way the Platform for Arts and Creativity factors in the future development of the city.

Begründung der Jury

Das Urban Design für die Stadt Guimarães vereint die historisch gewachsenen formalen Bezüge sehr überzeugend mit zeitgenössischen Entwürfen. Die Offenheit der Architektur wirkt einladend auf den Betrachter und kommt damit der Funktion eines Kunst- und Kulturzentrums entgegen. Die Platform for Arts and Creativity begeistert auch durch die Art und Weise, wie hier die künftige Entwicklung der Stadt mit einbezogen wird.

Architecture

Museum of the Moving Image

Client
Museum of the Moving Image,
New York, USA
Design
Leeser Architecture
(Thomas Leeser, Joseph Haberl),
New York, USA
Web
www.movingimage.us
www.leeser.com

The extensive collection of the Museum of the Moving Image in New York, which re-opened in 2011, is an exhibition of the film, television and digital media art forms and their history and technology. The concept for the renovation and extension of this unique museum is based on the interplay of the long history of moving images with innovative technologies and contemporary design. Visitors enter the building through a portal of semi-transparent mirrored glass decorated with the museum logo. The lobby has been designed with recesses and corners to provide wall space for image projections. The external façade continues this theme geometrically with a pattern of triangular metal plates.

Das 2011 wiedereröffnete Museum of the Moving Image in New York stellt mit seiner umfassenden Sammlung Kunstform, Geschichte und Technik von Film, Fernsehen und digitalen Medien vor. Die Konzeption für die Renovierung und Erweiterung dieses einzigartigen Museums basiert auf einem Wechselspiel der langen Geschichte der bewegten Bilder mit innovativen Technologien und zeitgenössischem Design. Der Besucher betritt das Gebäude durch ein Portal aus halbtransparentem Spiegelglas, welches das Museumslogo zeigt. Die Lobby hat eine Formgebung mit Winkeln und Falten, um Wandflächen für Bildprojektionen zu bieten. Die Außenfassade greift dies geometrisch auf mit einem Muster aus dreieckigen Metallplatten.

Statement by the jury
Film and architecture share common ground. The extension of the Museum of the Moving Image reflects this with its sequence of rooms, transitions, transparency and complexity.

Begründung der Jury
Film und Architektur haben manches gemeinsam. Der Anbau des Museum of the Moving Image spiegelt dies wider. Es geht um Raumfolgen und Übergänge, Transparenz und Komplexität.

Giraffe

Childcare Centre
Kinderbetreuungseinrichtung

Client
SAEM Val de Seine Aménagement,
Boulogne-Billancourt, France
Design
Hondelatte Laporte Architectes
(Raphaëlle Hondelatte,
Mathieu Laporte, Virginie Davo),
Paris, France
Web
www.ileseguin-rivesdeseine.fr
www.hondelatte-laporte.com

The Giraffe childcare centre in Boulogne-Billancourt on the outskirts of Paris is in a densely built-up environment. The aim of the project was to liven up the urban landscape through the medium of childish imagination. The building has three floors with a terrace on each floor. The façade is made of white corrugated metal and creates a neutral background for the playful sculptures of wild animals, which take over the space and bring a little poetry into everyday urban life. The building has been awarded the "Effinergie" energy-efficiency label.

Die in Boulogne-Billancourt in der Nähe von Paris gelegene Kinderbetreuungseinrichtung Giraffe befindet sich in einem dicht bebauten Umfeld. Ziel des Projektes war es, die städtische Landschaft mit den Mitteln kindlicher Phantasie zu beleben. Das Gebäude ist terrassenförmig angelegt mit drei Ebenen. Die Fassade aus weißem Wellblech stellt den neutralen Hintergrund für die spielerischen Skulpturen wilder Tiere dar, die sich den Raum aneignen und ein wenig Poesie in das Alltagsleben der Stadt bringen. Das Gebäude wurde mit dem Nullenergie-Label „Effinergie" ausgezeichnet.

Statement by the jury
This building shows how to counteract a typical, inhospitable urban silhouette and, at the same time, uses its appearance to hint at its function. The giraffe, visible from afar, sums up childish imagination and nature.

Begründung der Jury
Wie man einer typisch unwirtlichen städtischen Silhouette entgegenwirkt, zeigt dieses Gebäude, dessen Erscheinung zudem seine Funktion andeutet. Die weithin sichtbare Giraffe steht für kindliche Phantasie und Natur.

Kirche Herz-Jesu
Conversion of a Church
Umnutzung einer Kirche

Design
Schleiff Denkmalentwicklung GmbH & Co. KG,
B15 Architekten
(Christoph Spiegelhauer),
Erkelenz, Germany
Web
www.denkmalentwicklung.de
Honourable Mention

The work carried out to achieve the change in use of the Herz-Jesu church in Mönchengladbach focused on the complete preservation of the building which is classified as a historical monument. The result was the creation of 23 publicly funded apartments. The conversion used timber-frame construction according to the building-within-a-building principle. The plasterboard-covered timber-frame was erected to stand free in front of the walls and pillars of the church, thereby preserving the building's external appearance. Upon entering it, the first thing one sees is still the exposed cross-ribbed vault above the central nave.

Ziel der Umnutzung der Kirche Herz-Jesu in Mönchengladbach war der komplette Erhalt des denkmalgeschützten Gebäudes. So entstanden 23 öffentlich geförderte Wohnungen. Der Umbau wurde als Haus-im-Haus-Konzept in Holzskelettbauweise verwirklicht. Die mit Gipsplatten verdeckte Fachwerkkonstruktion wurde freistehend vor den Wänden und Säulen der Kirche montiert. Die äußere Erscheinungsform des Gebäudes blieb erhalten. Zudem fällt der Blick beim Betreten weiterhin auf das freiliegende Kreuzrippengewölbe über dem Mittelschiff.

Spijkenisse Book Mountain
Public Library
Öffentliche Bibliothek

Client
Gemeente Spijkenisse, Netherlands
Design
MVRDV,
Rotterdam, Netherlands
Web
www.deboekenberg.nl
www.mvrdv.nl

The new public library in the Dutch city of Spijkenisse lies in the centre of town. Its form and the materials used are reminiscent of a classic Dutch farmhouse and hark back to the town's agricultural past. Aside from the actual library, the building contains other rooms, that create the base upon which the platforms supporting the bookshelves sit. The platforms form a pyramid, which is covered by a glass and timber-frame construction.

Die neue öffentliche Bibliothek von Spijkenisse liegt im Zentrum der Stadt. In Form und Materialität an ein klassisches niederländisches Bauernhaus angelehnt, erinnert sie an die landwirtschaftliche Vergangenheit der Stadt. Außer der eigentlichen Bibliothek beherbergt das Gebäude verschiedene andere Räumlichkeiten, welche die Basis sind für Plattformen mit Bücherregalen. Die Plattformen bilden eine Pyramide, die von einer Konstruktion aus Glas und Holzträgern umhüllt ist.

House on the Cliff

Design
Fran Silvestre Arquitectos,
Valencia, Spain
Web
www.fransilvestrearquitectos.com

The steep gradient of the terrain and the desire to arrange all the rooms on one level meant that this house made use of a three-dimensional structure consisting of reinforced concrete elements in order to adapt to the local topography. The swimming pool is located on a lower level where the site is almost flat. The concrete structure has an outer insulation layer and is rendered with flexible, smooth white stucco, a colour that was also used for all other materials. They follow and highlight local traditional architecture, while at the same emphasising the uniform appearance of the house.

Wegen der Steilheit des Geländes und dem Wunsch, die Räumlichkeiten in einer Ebene anzulegen, kam bei diesem Haus eine dreidimensionale Struktur aus verstärkten Betonelementen zum Einsatz, die sich der Topographie der Landschaft anpasst. Der Swimming-Pool hat seinen Platz in einer tieferen Ebene, wo das Gelände schon fast flach ist. Die Betonstruktur wurde außen isoliert und dann mit einem flexiblen und glatten Weißkalkstuck versehen. Die anderen verwendeten Materialien sind alle in der gleichen Farbgebung gehalten. Sie orientieren sich an der traditionellen Architektur der Gegend und akzentuieren diese, während sie gleichzeitig das einheitliche Erscheinungsbild des Hauses betonen.

Statement by the jury
The harsh landscape and the monolithic, apparently floating concrete building appear in contrast and yet related. The building expresses the peace and serenity of the region.

Begründung der Jury
Gegensätzlich und doch zusammengehörig wirken die schroffe Landschaft und die monolithische, scheinbar schwebende Betonkonstruktion, welche die Klarheit und Ruhe der Gegend zum Ausdruck bringt.

Architecture

Heye
Room Concept
Raumkonzept

Client
Heye,
Munich, Germany
Design
tools off.architecture
(Prof. Andreas Notter, Eva Durant),
Munich, Germany
Web
www.heyegroup.de
www.tools-off.com

The Heye advertising agency has been using offices in Munich's Blumenstraße since July 2012. The building is part of a complex that was built between 1924 and 1926 in the style of the Neue Sachlichkeit (New Objectivity) movement. To make a clean break with the past, all steps of the renovation process were carried out in accordance with a consistent concept governing form, materials and colour. The spatial focus point is a glass-roofed atrium, which is the agency's central meeting area. This internal courtyard is dominated by a square steel block, which turns the abstract, minimalistic room into a place where people meet.

Seit Juli 2012 nutzt die Werbeagentur Heye die Räumlichkeiten in der Münchner Blumenstraße. Das Gebäude ist Teil eines Ensembles, das zwischen 1924 und 1926 im Stil der Neuen Sachlichkeit errichtet wurde. Um eine klare Abgrenzung gegenüber der Vergangenheit zu erreichen, wurden sämtliche Umbaumaßnahmen in einem durchgängigen Form-, Material- und Farbkonzept ausgeführt. Den räumlichen Mittelpunkt bildet ein glasgedecktes Atrium, das der zentrale Kommunikationsort für Heye ist. Dieser Innenhof wird bestimmt von einem quadratischen Block aus Stahl, der den abstrakten, minimalistischen Raum in einen Ort der Begegnung verwandelt.

Statement by the jury
The transformed internal courtyard is a successful symbiosis of old and new. Its most striking feature is a sculpture-like cube, which opens outwards to create a central communication and meeting point.

Begründung der Jury
Der umgestaltete Innenhof stellt eine gelungene Symbiose aus Alt und Neu dar. Bemerkenswert ist der wie eine Skulptur wirkende Kubus, der sich zur Nutzung auseinanderschiebt und so zum kommunikativen Treffpunkt wird.

Atrium room design and furniture

Superkilen
Urban Park
Öffentlicher Park

Client
Københavns Kommune
& Realdania,
Copenhagen, Denmark

Design
BIG Bjarke Ingels Group
(Bjarke Ingels,
Nanna Gyldholm Møller,
Mikkel Marcker Stubgaard),
Copenhagen, Denmark

Topotek 1
(Martin Rein-Cano, Lorenz Dexler),
Berlin, Germany
Superflex
(Jakob Fenger, Rasmus Nielsen, Bjørnstjerne Christiansen),
Copenhagen, Denmark

Web
www.kk.dk
www.big.dk
www.topotek1.de
www.superflex.net
www.realdania.dk

reddot design award
best of the best 2013

Global community

The district of Nørrebro in the centre of Denmark's capital Copenhagen is an ethnically highly diverse neighbourhood with people from 62 countries. Taking into account this multicultural backdrop, the urban design of Superkilen interprets a public park as a space of "urban narratives" – a place that aims to promote social integration with a lively approach. A central aspect in the implementation of this concept is to present it as an exhibition of unusual objects. Instead of using standard street furniture for the park, people from the area were asked to name specific objects such as benches, bins, trees, playgrounds, manhole covers and signage from other countries to be included in the scheme. The infrastructure of Superkilen makes up a modern park with all the typical elements including paths for pedestrians and cyclists as well as a marketplace. In addition, it also offers local inhabitants many spaces for recreation and other activities. The conceptual point of departure is the division of Superkilen into three main zones: the Red Square, the Green Park and the Black Market. The Red Square serves as an area for sports activities, the Green Park as a grassy children's playground, and the Black Market as a communal and picnic area. Due to the implementation of all represented interests, the urban design of the public Superkilen park is as diverse as the possibilities for integration. The sophisticated implementation paves the way for uniting everybody in one lively global neighbourhood.

Globale Gemeinschaft

Der Stadtteil Nørrebro im Zentrum der dänischen Hauptstadt Kopenhagen ist ethnisch sehr vielfältig: 62 Nationen sind hier vereint. Diesen multikulturellen Hintergrund verinnerlichend, interpretiert das Urban Design von Superkilen einen öffentlichen Park als einen „urbanen Erzählraum" – einen Ort, der auf eine lebendige Weise Integration ermöglichen soll. Ein zentraler Aspekt der Verwirklichung dieses Konzepts ist der einer sehr ungewöhnlichen Ausstellung. Anstatt für die Ausstattung des Parks gängiges Stadtmobiliar einzusetzen, wurden planerisch spezifische Objekte wie Bänke, Mülleimer, Bäume, Spielplätze, Gullydeckel und Beschilderung aus anderen Ländern integriert. Diese waren von den Bewohnern vorher benannt worden. Die Infrastruktur von Superkilen entspricht der eines modernen Parks mit typischen Elementen wie Fußgänger- und Fahrradwegen sowie einem Marktplatz. Er bietet den Bewohnern zudem vielfältige Aktivitäten der Betätigung und Erholung. Der konzeptionelle Ausgangspunkt ist hier die Einteilung in die Hauptzonen Roter Platz, Grüner Park und Schwarzer Markt. Der Rote Platz dient als Bereich für sportliche Aktivitäten, der Grüne Park als begraster Kinderspielplatz und der Schwarze Markt als Aufenthalts- und Picknickbereich. Das Urban Design des öffentlichen Parks Superkilen bietet durch eine planerische Einbeziehung aller vertretenen Interessen vielfältige Möglichkeiten der Integration. Die feinsinnige Umsetzung ebnet Wege hin zu einer lebendigen globalen Gemeinschaft.

Statement by the jury

Superkilen demonstrates how urban design can contribute to societal development. This park presents itself as a multicultural meeting place that provides many incentives for local inhabitants to engage in actively. The periphery of the park was integrated harmoniously into the design. It represents a concept that reveals new ways for community life in future.

Begründung der Jury

Superkilen zeigt, was Urban Design für die gesellschaftliche Entwicklung leisten kann. Mit diesem Park entstand ein multikultureller Treffpunkt, welcher der Bevölkerung vielfache Anreize bietet, sich individuell einzubringen. Die Peripherie des Parks wurde stimmig in die Gestaltung mit eingebunden. Es ist ein Konzept, welches neue Wege für das Zusammenleben in der Zukunft aufzeigt.

Urban park

ICON
Bench
Bank

Manufacturer
Vestre,
Oslo, Norway
Design
Eker Design
(Bård Eker, Katinka von der Lippe),
Gamle Fredrikstad, Norway
Web
www.vestre.com
www.ekerdesign.com

ICON is a bench with an exciting and innovative appearance whose sculptural shape and distinctive character challenge the image of traditional street furniture. It is available in fibreglass or carbon composite. The supporting frame, which makes it suitable for free standing or fixed positioning, the optional LED lighting, arm rests and the variety of colour options make a number of flexible combinations possible. The bench's characteristic design and quality of finish are underlined by the polished aluminium end covers and the acid-resistant or stainless steel supporting frame. ICON displays a high level of functionality, a stable construction and surfaces that are easy to maintain.

ICON ist eine Bank mit einer aufregenden und innovativen Gestaltung, die mit ihrer skulpturalen Form und markanten Eigenart traditionelle Stadtmöbel herausfordert. Die Bank wird in Glasfaser oder Kohlefaserverbundstoff geliefert. Das Untergestell zur freistehenden oder festen Montage, eine optionale LED-Beleuchtung, Armlehnen und viele Farboptionen bieten flexible Kombinationsmöglichkeiten. Das charakteristische Design der Bank und ihre Qualität werden von Endmuffen aus poliertem Aluminium und dem Untergestell aus säurebeständigem oder rostfreiem Stahl unterstrichen. ICON weist eine hohe Funktionalität auf, eine stabile Konstruktion und Oberflächen, die einfach zu pflegen sind.

Urban furniture

Lost in Street
Sign
Schild

Manufacturer
Ambienti D'Interni,
Proença-a-Nova, Portugal
In-house design
Carlos Silva
Web
www.wall-shape.com

Toponymy, in other words the knowledge of place names and their significance, is vital to find one's way around a town, both, in terms of space and culture. This is why the materials used on street signs as well as their size and shape are so important. "Lost in Street" is manufactured using a phenol plastic with a white finish and CNC engraving. Additional inscription with a QR code has the advantage of making supplementary and explanatory information easy to access on demand.

Statement by the jury
"Lost in Street" fulfils all the criteria of a place sign. It is robust, attractive in shape, versatile in use and informative.

Die Toponymie, also die Kenntnis der Ortsnamen und ihrer Bedeutung, ist wichtig für die räumliche und kulturelle Orientierung in einer Stadt. Die für ein Straßenschild verwendeten Materialien sowie seine Größe und Form sind deshalb von großer Bedeutung. „Lost in Street" wird aus einem Phenolkunststoff hergestellt mit weißem Finish und CNC-Gravur. Die zusätzliche Beschriftung mit einem QR-Code bietet den Vorteil, ergänzende oder erläuternde Informationen leicht abrufen zu können.

Begründung der Jury
„Lost in Street" erfüllt die für ein Ortsnamensschild wichtigen Kriterien. Es ist robust, formschön, vielseitig einsetzbar und informativ.

VILA DE MONTALEGRE

Rua Forno Velho

Signs

Jury 2013
International orientation and objectivity
Internationalität und Objektivität

The jurors of the Red Dot Award: Product Design
All members of the Red Dot Award: Product Design jury are appointed on the basis of independence and impartiality. They are independent designers, academics in design faculties, representatives of international design institutions, and design journalists.

The jury is international in its composition, which changes every year. These conditions assure a maximum of objectivity. The members of this year's jury are presented in alphabetical order on the following pages.

Die Juroren des Red Dot Award: Product Design
In die Jury des Red Dot Award: Product Design wird als Mitglied nur berufen, wer völlig unabhängig und unparteiisch ist. Dies sind selbstständig arbeitende Designer, Hochschullehrer der Designfakultäten, Repräsentanten internationaler Designinstitutionen und Designfachjournalisten.

Die Jury ist international besetzt und wechselt in jedem Jahr ihre Zusammensetzung. Unter diesen Voraussetzungen ist ein Höchstmaß an Objektivität gewährleistet. Auf den folgenden Seiten werden die Jurymitglieder des diesjährigen Wettbewerbs in alphabetischer Reihenfolge vorgestellt.

reddot design award
product design 2013

01

Prof. Masayo Ave
Japan

Jury member since 2004
Appointed six times
Jurymitglied seit 2004
Berufen sechs Mal

Professor Masayo Ave, born in 1962 in Tokyo, graduated in architecture and design from Hosei University in Tokyo. She worked with I. Ebihara Architect and Associates before moving to Milan in 1990 to study and graduate with a Master of Arts in industrial design from the Domus Academy. In 1992, she founded her own design studio under the name "Ave design corporation" with headquarters in Tokyo and Milan, received a scholarship in 1996 from the Akademie Schloss Solitude in Germany, and, in 2000, launched her own collection called "MasayoAve creation". She has received numerous international awards, including the ICFF 2000 Editors Award, as well as the A&W Mentor Award 2006, and has been working as a designer for companies such as Authentics, DuPont Corian, Yamaha, and Panasonic.

Since 2001, Masayo Ave has been conducting research into the design value of tactile sensitivity and, while a professor at the Berlin University of the Arts from 2004 to 2007, founded a design institute for haptic interface design, which she integrated into her own office in 2010 when it moved from Milan to Berlin.

Professorin Masayo Ave, 1962 in Tokio geboren, graduierte an der Hosei-Universität in Tokio in Architektur und Design. Sie arbeitete bei I. Ebihara Architect and Associates, bevor sie 1990 nach Mailand zog und einen M. A. in Industriedesign an der Domus Academy ablegte. 1992 eröffnete sie ihr eigenes Designstudio „Ave design corporation" mit Sitz in Tokio und Mailand, 1996 erhielt sie ein Stipendium der Akademie Schloss Solitude in Deutschland und im Jahr 2000 führte sie ihre eigene Kollektion „MasayoAve creation" ein. Sie erhielt zahlreiche internationale Auszeichnungen, u. a. den ICFF 2000 Editors Award sowie den A&W Mentor Award 2006, und ist als Designerin für Unternehmen wie Authentics, DuPont Corian, Yamaha und Panasonic tätig.

Seit 2001 erforscht Masayo Ave auf taktiler Sensitivität beruhende Gestaltungen und gründete während ihrer Professur an der Universität der Künste Berlin von 2004 bis 2007 ein Designinstitut für Haptic Interface Design, das sie 2010 in ihr von Mailand nach Berlin übersiedeltes Büro integrierte.

01 GENESI
Table light designed with
a cover made from a
washable open-cell polyester
and a body in chromed steel,
launched in her own collection "MasayoAve creation",
1998
Tischleuchte, die mit einem
Lampenschirm aus wasch-
barem, offenporigem Poly-
ester und einem Körper aus
verchromtem Stahl entworfen
wurde; erschienen in ihrer
eigenen Kollektion „Masayo-
Ave creation", 1998

02 "Quadrato",
"Circolo", "Triangolo"
by Bruno Munari
Book design and translation,
published by Heibonsha
Limited, Japan, 2010
Buchgestaltung und Über-
setzung, herausgegeben von
Heibonsha Limited, Japan,
2010

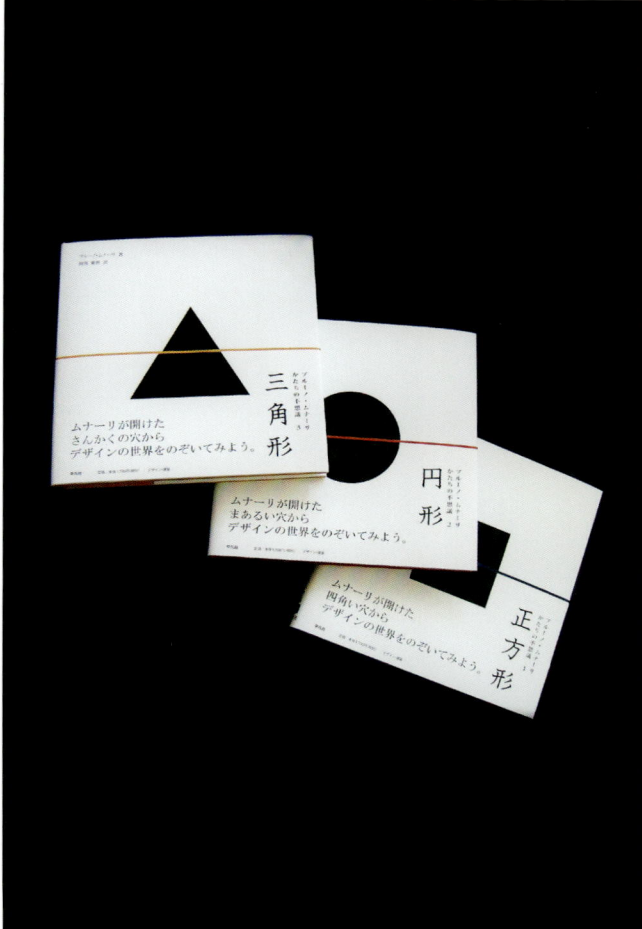

02

»I consider the sensorial value of a product as a signifier of design quality.«

»Ich erachte den sinnlichen Wert eines Produktes als Zeichen von Designqualität.«

What current trends do you see in the category "Offices"?
I have noticed that the "living office" is a new trend direction in this category. Office spaces today have to be designed not only for efficiency, but also for their living quality. I have already seen this reflected in many new products.

What are the important criteria for you as a juror in the assessment of a product?
A fine balance between advanced technology and sophisticated craftsmanship.

What challenges do you see for the future in design?
The continuous challenge that I foresee for the future of design consists in cultivating the sensorial qualities of industrial products.

Do you have a philosophy toward life?
Keeping alive my innate sense of wonder.

Welche Trends konnten Sie im Bereich „Büro" in den letzten Jahren ausmachen?
Ich sehe das „Wohnbüro" als den neuen Trend in diesem Bereich. Die Büroräume von heute müssen nicht nur der Effizienz zuliebe gestaltet werden, sondern auch Wohnqualität ausweisen, und dies schlägt sich bereits in vielen neuen Produkten nieder.

Worauf achten Sie als Jurorin, wenn Sie ein Produkt bewerten?
Eine ausgezeichnete Balance zwischen fortschrittlicher Technologie und ausgefeilter Handwerkskultur.

Welche Herausforderungen sehen Sie für die Zukunft im Design?
Die anhaltende Herausforderung, die ich für die Zukunft im Design sehe, besteht darin, die sinnliche Qualität von Industrieprodukten zu kultivieren.

Haben Sie ein Lebensmotto?
Mir meinen angeborenen Sinn des Staunens lebendig zu erhalten.

01

Marcell von Berlin
Poland/Germany

Jury member since 2013
Appointed for the first time
Jurymitglied seit 2013
Berufen zum ersten Mal

Marcell von Berlin is founder and creative director of the fashion label "Marcell von Berlin". In early 2012, the designer presented his first collection "Born for Fame" consisting of a series of high-class basics. In November 2012, he added the couture line "Atelier Marcell von Berlin". Glamorous cuts and luxurious materials – the creations are targeted at cosmopolitan customers all around Europe, including celebrities such as Judith Rakers, Anja Kling and Nazan Eckes. Before Marcell von Berlin founded his own label, he studied fashion design in New York and worked as a consultant and stylist for various fashion companies. With his own brand, he advocates the belief that collections can be successful regardless of the season, as long as they follow their own style and are further developed according to customer needs.

Marcell von Berlin ist Gründer und Creative Director des Fashion-Labels „Marcell von Berlin". Anfang 2012 präsentierte der Designer seine erste Kollektion „Born for Fame" mit einer Reihe hochwertiger Basics, im November 2012 kam die Couture-Linie „Atelier Marcell von Berlin" hinzu. Glamouröse Schnitte und luxuriöse Materialien – die Kreationen richten sich an kosmopolitische Kundinnen in ganz Europa, darunter Persönlichkeiten wie Judith Rakers, Anja Kling und Nazan Eckes. Bevor Marcell von Berlin sein eigenes Label gründete, studierte er Modedesign in New York und stand diversen Modeunternehmen beratend und als Stylist zur Seite. Mit seiner eigenen Marke vertritt er die Überzeugung, dass Kollektionen saisonunabhängig erfolgreich sein können, wenn sie einem eigenen Stil folgen und entsprechend den Kundenbedürfnissen weiterentwickelt werden.

02

»My philosophy of life is: Do what you love and love what you do.«

»Mein Lebensmotto lautet: Tue, was du liebst, und liebe, was du tust.«

What is, in your opinion, the significance of design quality in the product categories you evaluated?
The category "Fashion, lifestyle and accessories" demands products that are sold on the worldwide fashion market. It is essential that these products are targeted at a broad customer base but are unique in their designs. They should offer innovative aspects that are reflected in new, high-quality materials or cuts that are thematically linked by look and usability.

What aspects of the jury process for the Red Dot Award: Product Design 2013 have stayed in your mind in particular?
It was an incredible experience to meet, work with and exchange views with the other jurors. Not only were decisions difficult due to the high number of outstanding product submissions, but it was also challenging because every juror has a different personality, taste and ideas on design quality.

Wie schätzen Sie den Stellenwert der Designqualität in den von Ihnen beurteilten Produktkategorien ein?
Die Kategorie „Mode, Lifestyle und Accessoires" verlangt nach Produkten, die auf dem weltweiten Modemarkt vertrieben werden. Wesentlich ist, dass sie sich an eine breite Konsumentenbasis richten, in ihrer Gestaltung aber einzigartig sind. Sie sollten innovative Aspekte aufweisen, die sich in neuen, wertigen Materialien oder Schnitten widerspiegeln, in denen sich Aussehen und Gebrauchswert thematisch miteinander verbinden.

Was ist Ihnen von der Jurierung des Red Dot Award: Product Design 2013 besonders im Gedächtnis geblieben?
Es war eine unglaubliche Erfahrung, die anderen Juroren zu treffen, zusammen zu arbeiten und uns auszutauschen. Aufgrund der großen Anzahl herausragender Produkteinreichungen waren nicht nur die Entscheidungen schwierig; es war auch eine Herausforderung, da jeder Juror eine andere Persönlichkeit, Vorliebe und Vorstellungen von Designqualität hat.

01

Gordon Bruce
USA

Jury member since 2008
Appointed six times
Jurymitglied seit 2008
Berufen sechs Mal

Gordon Bruce is the managing director of Gordon Bruce Design LLC and has been a design consultant for 40 years working with many international corporations in Europe, Asia and the USA. He has worked with numerous multinational corporations on a wide range of different products – from aeroplanes to computers and medical equipment. From 1991 to 1994, Gordon Bruce was a consulting vice-president for the Art Center College of Design's Kyoto programme and, from 1995 to 1999, chairman of Product Design for the Innovative Design Lab of Samsung (IDS) in Seoul, Korea. In 2003, he played a crucial role in helping to establish Porsche Design's office in the USA. Gordon Bruce is a visiting professor at several universities in the USA and in China. For many years, he served as head design consultant for Lenovo's Innovative Design Center (IDC) in Beijing and for Changhong in China, and he is presently working with Bühler in Switzerland and Huawei Technologies, Co., LTD in China.

Gordon Bruce ist Direktor der Gordon Bruce Design LLC und seit mittlerweile 40 Jahren als Designberater für zahlreiche internationale Unternehmen in Europa, Asien und den USA tätig. Er arbeitete mit zahlreichen multinationalen Unternehmen an unterschiedlichsten Produkten in allen Größenlagen – von Flugzeugen über Computer bis hin zu medizinischen Geräten. Von 1991 bis 1994 war Gordon Bruce beratender Vorstand des Kioto-Programms am Art Center College of Design sowie von 1995 bis 1999 Vorsitzender für Produktdesign beim „Innovative Design Lab of Samsung" (IDS) in Seoul, Korea. Im Jahr 2003 war er wesentlich daran beteiligt, das Büro von Porsche Design in den USA aufzubauen. Gordon Bruce ist Gastprofessor an zahlreichen Universitäten in den USA und in China. Über viele Jahre war er leitender Designberater für Lenovos „Innovative Design Center" (IDC) in Beijing und für Changhong in China, und derzeit arbeitet er für Bühler in der Schweiz und Huawei Technologies, Co., LTD in China.

02

»Design quality is a result of experience over time with various attributes of the product and this must be considered when judging a product.«

»Designqualität zeigt sich im Erfahrungswert der verschiedenen Eigenschaften des Produkts über die Zeit hinweg, und dies muss mit in seine Beurteilung einfließen.«

What is, in your opinion, the significance of design quality in the product categories you evaluated?
From my point of view, design is all that matters in all the product categories. I think of design as a verb, not a noun. As a verb, design has multi-dimensional qualities over time. Empiric design performance takes place at every stage of interaction.

What current trends do you see in the category "Computers and information technology"?
In the laptop sector, the trend seems to be towards simplicity, refined materials and finishes, while a few unique hinge details as well as some clever transformations from laptop to tablet configurations have evolved. In desktop computers, the "all in one" classification is becoming simpler, more sophisticated and more prevalent. Thanks to novel curved-display technology, new directions have opened up in design.

Wie schätzen Sie den Stellenwert der Designqualität in den von Ihnen beurteilten Produktkategorien ein?
Meiner Ansicht nach spielt das Design des Produkts die einzige Rolle in allen Kategorien. Ich betrachte Design als ein Verb, nicht als ein Nomen. Als Verb verweist „Gestalten" auf multidimensionale Qualitäten mit zeitlichem Ablauf. In jedem Moment der Interaktion vollzieht sich eine empirische Gestaltungsleistung.

Welche Trends konnten Sie im Bereich „Computer und Informationstechnik" in den letzten Jahren ausmachen?
In der Kategorie „Laptops" hat es den Anschein, dass Schlichtheit und edle Materialien sowie Finishes immer noch im Trend liegen, während sich ein paar einzigartige Scharnierdetails sowie clevere Umwandlungen vom Laptop zur Tablet-PC-Konfiguration herausbilden. Bei Desktop-Computern wird die „All-in-one"-Klassifizierung zusehends einfacher, ausgeklügelter und verbreiteter. Mit dank neuer Technologien gewölbten Displays haben sich neue Wege in der Gestaltung eröffnet.

Gordon Bruce

01

Tony K. M. Chang
Taiwan

Jury member since 2007
Appointed seven times
Jurymitglied seit 2007
Berufen sieben Mal

Tony K. M. Chang, born in 1946, studied architecture at Chung Yuan Christian University in Chung Li, Taiwan. Since 2004 he has been chief executive officer of the Taiwan Design Center as well as editor-in-chief of DESIGN magazine. Chang has made tremendous contributions to industrial design, both in his home country and across the entire Asia-Pacific region. As an expert in design management and design promotion, he has served as a consultant for governments and the corporate sector for decades. From 2005 to 2007 and from 2009 to 2011 he was an executive board member of the Icsid and masterminded the 2011 IDA Congress in Taipei. In 2008, he was elected founding chairman of the Taiwan Design Alliance, a consortium of government-supported and private design entities aimed at promoting Taiwanese design. Chang has lectured in Europe, the United States and Asia, and he frequently serves as a juror in prestigious international design competitions.

Tony K. M. Chang, 1946 geboren, studierte Architektur an der Chung Yuan Christian University in Chung Li, Taiwan. Seit 2004 ist er Chief Executive Officer des Taiwan Design Centers und zudem Chefredakteur des Magazins DESIGN. Chang hat im Bereich Industriedesign Erhebliches geleistet, sowohl in seinem Heimatland als auch im gesamten Asien-Pazifik-Raum. Als Experte in Designmanagement und Designförderung ist er seit Jahrzehnten als Berater in Regierungs- und Unternehmenskreisen tätig. Von 2005 bis 2007 sowie 2009 bis 2011 war er Vorstandsmitglied des Icsid und federführend in der Planung des IDA Congress 2011 in Taipeh. Im Jahr 2008 wurde er zum Founding Chairman der Taiwan Design Alliance gewählt, einem Konsortium staatlich geförderter und privater Designorgane mit dem Ziel der Förderung taiwanesischen Designs. Chang hält Vorträge in Europa, den USA und Asien und fungiert häufig als Juror hochrangiger internationaler Designwettbewerbe.

02

03 / 04

»The challenges for the future of design lie in creating maximised values through minimised designs.«

»Die Herausforderung für die Zukunft des Designs besteht im Schaffen maximaler Wertigkeit durch minimale Gestaltung.«

What is, in your opinion, the significance of design quality in the product categories you evaluated?
Using the right materials and attaching importance to detailed design.

What trends have you noticed in the field of "Tableware and decoration" in recent years?
Increasing numbers of designers integrate cultural elements into their creations in order to enrich their design concepts. Silicone has been widely applied in various fields.

Do you see a correlation between the design quality of a company's products and the economic success of this company?
Undoubtedly, for a design company, design quality is a basic prerequisite in this industry. However, when it comes to the assessment of success, it is not easy to come up with a universal rule since the key factors vary depending on the situation.

Wie schätzen Sie den Stellenwert der Designqualität in den von Ihnen beurteilten Produktkategorien ein?
Sie liegt im Einsatz der richtigen Materialien und der Konzentration auf eine detaillierte Gestaltung.

Welche Trends konnten Sie im Bereich „Tableware und Dekoration" in den letzten Jahren ausmachen?
Immer mehr Gestalter integrieren kulturelle Elemente in ihre Entwürfe, um ihre Gestaltungskonzepte zu bereichern. Silikon kam in verschiedenen Bereichen ausgiebig zum Einsatz.

Sehen Sie einen Zusammenhang zwischen der Designqualität, die sich in den Produkten eines Unternehmens äußert, und dem wirtschaftlichen Erfolg dieses Unternehmens?
Zweifelsfrei ist Designqualität für ein Designunternehmen eine Grundvoraussetzung in dieser Branche. Wenn es aber um die Beurteilung von Erfolg geht, gibt es keine schnell heranziehbare universelle Regel, da die Hauptfaktoren gemäß den jeweiligen Umständen variieren.

Tony K. M. Chang

01

02

Vivian Wai-kwan Cheng
Hong Kong

Jury member since 2006
Appointed eight times
Jurymitglied seit 2006
Berufen acht Mal

Vivian Wai-kwan Cheng, born in 1962 in Hong Kong, studied industrial design at the Swire School of Design, Hong Kong Polytechnic University. In 1987, she graduated with a Bachelor of Arts degree and, in the same year, was awarded a special prize by the Federation of Hong Kong Industries in the "Young Designers of the Year" competition. She began her career as a watch designer and later continued as an industrial designer of fashion accessories. She went on to join Lambda Industrial Limited where she won the "Governor's Award for Industry: Consumer Product Design" in 1989. Vivian Wai-kwan Cheng has had a major impact on the Hong Kong design scene; she has been a member of numerous important design boards and is a senior lecturer in product design at the Hong Kong Design Institute (HKDI), where she is also in charge of international networking and collaboration.

Vivian Wai-kwan Cheng, 1962 in Hongkong geboren, studierte Industriedesign an der Swire School of Design, Hong Kong Polytechnic University. Sie schloss ihr Studium 1987 mit dem Bachelor of Arts ab und erhielt im gleichen Jahr von der Federation of Hong Kong Industries einen Sonderpreis im Wettbewerb „Young Designers of the Year". Ihre Karriere begann sie als Gestalterin für Uhren. Sie entwarf als Industriedesignerin Modeaccessoires und ging später zu Lambda Industrial Limited. Für ihre Arbeit dort gewann sie 1989 den „Governor's Award for Industry: Consumer Product Design". Vivian Wai-kwan Cheng hat in der Designszene Hongkongs viel in Bewegung gesetzt; so gehörte und gehört sie zahlreichen wichtigen Designgremien an und unterrichtet als Dozentin für Produktdesign am Hong Kong Design Institute (HKDI), wo sie zudem die Verantwortliche für internationale Zusammenarbeit und Networking ist.

03

»Everything I do today is a little better than what I did yesterday – this has been my philosophy of life since the age of 35.«

»Alles, was ich heute mache, ist etwas besser als das, was ich gestern gemacht habe – das ist meine Lebensphilosophie, seitdem ich 35 bin.«

What current trends have you noticed in the category "Fashion, lifestyle and accessories" in recent years?
This category is very much dominated by the way we live and the clothes we wear. Mobile phones are no longer just communication tools, but are also equipped with state-of-the-art technology. As such, they have also become a means for people to express their personal style and taste. There are therefore many products that have been designed to meet this rapidly growing demand.

What current trends do you see in the category "Watches and jewellery"?
We were surprised to find products that are made of recycled or environmentally friendly materials and that are produced with social responsibility in mind.

Welche Trends konnten Sie im Bereich „Mode, Lifestyle und Accessoires" in den letzten Jahren ausmachen?
Diese Kategorie wird stark von unserer Lebensart und der Kleidung, die wir tragen, dominiert. Mobiltelefone sind nicht mehr lediglich Kommunikationsinstrumente, sondern verfügen über modernste Technologie und sind zugleich Mittel, mit denen Menschen ihren persönlichen Stil und Geschmack ausdrücken. Daher gibt es eine große Anzahl an Produkten, die gestaltet worden sind, um diese schnell wachsende Nachfrage zu befriedigen.

Welche aktuellen Trends sehen Sie im Bereich „Uhren und Schmuck"?
Wir waren überrascht, Produkte vorzufinden, die aus recycelten oder umweltfreundlichen Materialien hergestellt sind und deren Herstellung soziale Verantwortlichkeit berücksichtigt.

Vivian Wai-kwan Cheng

467

01

02

Dato' Prof.
Jimmy Choo OBE
Great Britain/
Malaysia

Jury member since 2013
Appointed for the first time
Jurymitglied seit 2013
Berufen zum ersten Mal

Dato' Professor Jimmy Choo Yeang Keat OBE is descended from a family of Malaysian shoemakers and studied at Cordwainers College, which is today part of the London College of Fashion. After graduating in 1983, he founded his own couture label and opened a show store in London's East End in the late 1980s. Choo's regular customers included Diana, the Princess of Wales. In 1996, building upon his growing international reputation, Choo launched his ready-to-wear line with Tom Yeardye. He sold his share of the ready-to-wear business in 2001 to Equinox Luxury Holdings Ltd., while continuing to run his own couture line. Choo now spends his time as ambassador for footwear education at the London College of Fashion and as spokesperson for the British Council in their promotion of British education to foreign students. In 2003, Jimmy Choo was honoured for his contribution to fashion by Queen Elizabeth II, who appointed him "Officer of the Order of the British Empire".

Dato' Professor Jimmy Choo Yeang Keat OBE entstammt einer malaysischen Schuhmacher-Familie und studierte am Cordwainers College, heute Teil des London College of Fashion. Nach seinem Abschluss 1983 gründete er Ende der 1980er Jahre sein eigenes Couture-Label und eröffnete ein Schuhgeschäft im Londoner East End. Zu seiner Stammkundschaft gehörte auch Lady Diana, Prinzessin von Wales. Aufbauend auf seiner wachsenden internationalen Reputation führte er 1996 gemeinsam mit Tom Yeardye seine Konfektionslinie ein. 2001 verkaufte Jimmy Choo seine Anteile an dem Unternehmen für Konfektionskleidung an die Equinox Luxury Holdings Ltd. und kümmerte sich weiter um seine eigene Couture-Linie. Heute engagiert sich Dato' Professor Jimmy Choo als Botschafter für Footwear Education am London College of Fashion sowie als Sprecher des British Council für die Förderung der Ausbildung ausländischer Studenten in Großbritannien. Für seine Verdienste für die Mode wurde er 2003 von Königin Elisabeth II. mit dem Titel „Officer of the Order of the British Empire" geehrt.

03

»The design quality at the Red Dot Design Award 2013 was outstanding.«

»Die Gestaltungsqualität im Red Dot Design Award 2013 war herausragend.«

What trends have you noticed in the field of "Fashion, lifestyle and accessories" in recent years?
Since the recession started in 2008, there have been a few interesting trend developments in consumer behaviour. Some consumers have chosen to focus on spending more on one special piece. Others have chosen to make do and mend, which has meant an increase in crafts, as well as an interest in products that are made with traditional skills.

Do you see a correlation between the design quality of a company's products and the economic success of this company?
If the design is of a good quality and you have the right marketing for the product it will sell well. The marketing that the Red Dot Design Award offers winners is invaluable.

Do you have a philosophy toward life?
Always move forward. Work hard. Believe in yourself.

Welche Trends konnten Sie im Bereich „Mode, Lifestyle und Accessoires" in den letzten Jahren ausmachen?
Mit der Rezession seit 2008 haben sich ein paar interessante Trends im Käuferverhalten herausgebildet. Manche Verbraucher geben für ein besonderes Stück bewusst mehr aus. Andere wollen mit wenig auskommen und reparieren lieber, was zu einem Anstieg im Handwerk und einem Interesse an traditionell gefertigten Produkten geführt hat.

Sehen Sie einen Zusammenhang zwischen der Designqualität, die sich in den Produkten eines Unternehmens äußert, und dem wirtschaftlichen Erfolg dieses Unternehmens?
Wenn die Gestaltung von guter Qualität ist und man das richtige Marketing für das Produkt hat, wird es sich gut verkaufen. Das Marketing, das der Red Dot Design Award den Gewinnern bietet, ist unschätzbar.

Haben Sie ein Lebensmotto?
Immer nach vorne gehen. Hart arbeiten. An sich selber glauben.

Dato' Prof. Jimmy Choo OBE

01

Mårten Claesson
Sweden

Jury member since 2004
Appointed eight times
Jurymitglied seit 2004
Berufen acht Mal

Mårten Claesson was born in 1970 in Lidingö, Sweden. After studying at the Vasa Technical College in Stockholm in the department of Construction Engineering and at the Parsons School of Design in New York in the departments of Architecture and Product Design, he graduated in 1994 with an MFA degree from Konstfack, the University College of Arts, Crafts and Design in Stockholm. He is co-founder of the Swedish design partnership "Claesson Koivisto Rune", which is multidisciplinary in the classic Scandinavian way and pursues the practice of both architecture and design. Mårten Claesson is also a writer and lecturer in the field of architecture and design.

Mårten Claesson wurde 1970 in Lidingö, Schweden, geboren. Nach einem Studium am Vasa Technical College in Stockholm im Bereich „Construction Engineering" und an der Parsons School of Design in New York in den Bereichen „Architecture" und „Product Design" schloss er 1994 seine Ausbildung an der Konstfack, dem University College of Arts, Crafts and Design, in Stockholm ab. Er ist Mitbegründer der Design-Partnerschaft „Claesson Koivisto Rune", die sich nach klassischer skandinavischer Art multidisziplinär sowohl mit Architektur als auch mit Design beschäftigt. Mårten Claesson ist darüber hinaus als Autor und Dozent im Bereich „Architektur und Design" tätig.

02

**»A company can survive
for a while without design,
but not in the long run.«**

»Ein Unternehmen kann ohne
Design kurzfristig überleben,
aber nicht auf Dauer.«

**What is, in your opinion, the significance of design
quality in the product categories you evaluated?**
The difference between "home" and "contract"
furniture is blurred today. This means that you may
well choose to furnish your living room or office
with the same type of products. From the contract
side comes the tradition of quality in manufacturing
and professional design development and from the
home side the demand for aesthetic, poetic and
elegant design solutions.

**What current trends do you see
in the category "Offices"?**
The trend in offices is a kind of resurrection of the
cubicle office of the 1960s. Although it is described
as room-within-room furniture, it still creates
privacy.

**What are the important criteria for you
as a juror in the assessment of a product?**
Good design is like natural beauty. Not-so-good
design is like make-up or plastic surgery: it always
reveals itself. I prefer the real thing.

**Wie schätzen Sie den Stellenwert der Designqualität
in den von Ihnen beurteilten Produktkategorien ein?**
Die Unterscheidung zwischen ausgesprochenen Wohn-
und Büromöbeln verwischt zusehends. Das bedeutet,
dass man sich eben entscheiden kann, das Wohnzimmer
oder das Büro mit den gleichen Produkttypen auszustatten. Aus dem Bürosegment stammt die Tradition
der Qualität in professioneller Designentwicklung und
Herstellung. Und aus dem Wohnsegment die Forderung
nach eleganten, poetischen und ästhetischen Gestal-
tungslösungen.

**Welche Trends konnten Sie im Bereich
„Büro" in den letzten Jahren ausmachen?**
Der Trend in Büros ist eine Art Wiederauferstehung
des Zellenbüros aus den 1960ern. Obwohl als Raum-
im-Raum-Mobiliar beschrieben, entsteht so doch eine
Abgrenzung.

**Worauf achten Sie als Juror,
wenn Sie ein Produkt bewerten?**
Gute Gestaltung ist wie natürliche Schönheit. Nicht so
gute Gestaltung ist wie Makeup oder plastische Chirurgie,
sie verrät sich stets. Ich mag das Natürliche.

01

Guto Indio
da Costa
Brazil

Jury member since 2011
Appointed three times
Jurymitglied seit 2011
Berufen drei Mal

Guto Indio da Costa, born in 1969 in Rio de Janeiro, studied product design and graduated from the Art Center College of Design in Switzerland in 1993. He is design director of Indio da Costa A.U.D.T., a consultancy based in Rio de Janeiro, which develops architectural, urban planning, design and transportation projects. It works with a multidisciplinary strategic-creative group of designers, architects and urban planners, supported by a variety of other specialists.

Guto Indio da Costa is a member of the Design Council of the State of Rio de Janeiro, former Vice President of the Brazilian Design Association (Abedesign) and founder of CBDI (Brazilian Industrial Design Council). He is an active speaker for and contributor to the "ArcDesign" magazine in São Paulo and has been a jury member of many design competitions in Brazil and abroad.

Guto Indio da Costa, geboren 1969 in Rio de Janeiro, studierte Produktdesign und machte 1993 seinen Abschluss am Art Center College of Design in der Schweiz. Er ist Gestaltungsdirektor von Indio da Costa A.U.D.T., einem in Rio de Janeiro ansässigen Beratungsunternehmen, das Projekte in Architektur, Stadtplanung, Design- und Transportwesen entwickelt und mit einem multidisziplinären, strategisch-kreativen Team aus Designern, Architekten und Stadtplanern sowie mit der Unterstützung weiterer Spezialisten operiert.

Guto Indio da Costa ist Mitglied des Design Councils des Bundesstaates Rio de Janeiro, ehemaliger Vize-Präsident der brasilianischen Designvereinigung (Abedesign) und Gründer des CBDI (Industrial Design Council Brasilien). Er ist aktiver Sprecher und Mitarbeiter der Zeitschrift „ArcDesign" in São Paulo und ist als Jurymitglied in vielen Designwettbewerben in Brasilien und im Ausland tätig.

02

»Design quality has become an extremely important factor for economic success – not only for companies but also for the countries they represent.«

»Designqualität ist für den wirtschaftlichen Erfolg mittlerweile von enormer Bedeutung – nicht nur für Unternehmen, sondern auch für die Länder, die sie repräsentieren.«

What is, in your opinion, the significance of design quality in the product categories you evaluated?
As long as high quality is universal and technology is used by different manufacturers in the same way, design is the only way to differentiate products and experiences. By that I mean design in the broader sense; not only form and aesthetics, but also the way in which a product functions, the way it is manufactured, distributed and used by people. This is why design has become highly significant in every field and category.

What challenges do you see for the future in design?
I believe the world population will have to change how it lives, manufactures, uses and consumes products. To promote the correct balance between economy, energy and the environment will be the greatest challenge design has to face in the near future.

Wie schätzen Sie den Stellenwert der Designqualität in den von Ihnen beurteilten Produktkategorien ein?
Solange hohe Qualität ein allgemeines Gut ist und Technologie von verschiedenen Herstellern gleichermaßen benutzt wird, ist Design der einzige Weg, um Produkte und Erfahrungen voneinander abzuheben. Design im weiteren Sinne: nicht nur die Form und die Ästhetik, sondern auch die Art, wie ein Produkt funktioniert, die Art, wie es hergestellt, vertrieben und von den Menschen benutzt wird. Deshalb hat Design in allen Kategorien und Bereichen einen sehr hohen Stellenwert erreicht.

Welche Herausforderungen sehen Sie für die Zukunft im Design?
Ich glaube, die Weltbevölkerung wird die Art, wie sie lebt, produziert und Dinge benutzt und konsumiert, verändern müssen. In der nahen Zukunft besteht die größte Herausforderung für das Design darin, die richtige Balance zwischen Wirtschaft, Energie und Umwelt voranzubringen.

01

Vincent Créance
France

Jury member since 2008
Appointed three times
Jurymitglied seit 2008
Berufen drei Mal

Vincent Créance, born in 1961, graduated from the Ecole Supérieure de Design Industriel. He began his career in 1985 at the Plan Créatif Agency, where he became design director in 1990. He joined Alcatel in 1996 as design director for all telephone activities and became vice-president Brand for Alcatel Mobile Phone, in his role as design/UI and communication director, in 1999. In 2006, Vincent Créance was appointed president of MBD Design, one of the principal design agencies in France, providing design solutions in transportation and product design. MBD Design is also a globally leading agency for railway transportation design. He is a member of APCI (Agency for the Promotion of Industrial Creation) and the ENSCI (National College of Industrial Design) board of directors, as well as a member of the scientific advisory board of Strate College.

Vincent Créance, 1961 geboren, machte seinen Abschluss an der Ecole Supérieure de Design Industriel. Seine berufliche Laufbahn begann er 1985 bei Plan Créatif Agency, wo er 1990 zum Design Director aufstieg. 1996 ging er als Design Director für sämtliche Telefonaktivitäten zu Alcatel und wurde in seiner Funktion als Design/UI und Communication Director 1999 zum Vice-President Brand für Alcatel Mobile Phone ernannt. Vincent Créance wurde 2006 President von MBD Design, einer der wichtigsten Designagenturen in Frankreich, und entwickelte Designlösungen für Verkehrs- und Produktdesign. MBD Design ist zudem eine weltweit führende Agentur für schienengebundenes Verkehrsdesign. Er ist Mitglied von APCI (Agency for the Promotion of Industrial Creation), Vorstand von ENSCI (National College of Industrial Design) und Mitglied des wissenschaftlichen Beirats des Strate College.

02

»Above all, design must arouse emotions and desire and then link them intimately to the brand.«

»Gestaltung muss vor allem Emotion und Verlangen hervorrufen, und diese dann aufs Engste mit der Marke verknüpfen.«

What are the important criteria for you as a juror in the assessment of a product?
As always: simplicity, immediate understandability, finishing and detailing. However, I would also add beauty. It is a pity that many designers don't dare to use this word more frequently.

Do you see a correlation between the design quality of a company's products and the economic success of this company?
Yes, obviously. Good design is much more powerful than technical or marketing efficiency, because design talks primarily to the heart. It plays with desire instead of rationality, and desire always wins out over reason... If there is passion, the price is no longer so important!

Do you have a philosophy toward life?
Don't play safe! Seek out intense moments! Accept that taking risks is necessary, and be brave. In other words, conduct your own life like a design project!

Worauf achten Sie als Juror, wenn Sie ein Produkt bewerten?
Wie immer: Einfachheit, unmittelbare Verständlichkeit, Finishing und Details. Allerdings würde ich außerdem noch Schönheit hinzufügen. Es ist schade, dass sich viele Designer nicht trauen, dieses Wort öfter zu gebrauchen.

Sehen Sie einen Zusammenhang zwischen der Designqualität, die sich in den Produkten eines Unternehmens äußert, und dem wirtschaftlichen Erfolg dieses Unternehmens?
Ja, ganz offensichtlich. Gute Gestaltung ist sehr viel wirkungsmächtiger als Technik- oder Vermarktungseffizienz, denn Gestaltung richtet sich zunächst ans Herz. Es spielt mit dem Verlangen anstelle der Rationalität, und Verlangen gewinnt immer gegen Vernunft ... Wenn das Verlangen da ist, ist der Preis nicht mehr so wichtig!

Haben Sie ein Lebensmotto?
Gehe nicht auf Nummer sicher! Suche intensive Momente! Akzeptiere, dass es nötig ist, Risiken einzugehen, und sei tapfer. Anders gesagt, führe dein eigenes Leben wie ein Gestaltungsprojekt!

01

Martin Darbyshire
Great Britain

Jury member since 2008
Appointed six times
Jurymitglied seit 2008
Berufen sechs Mal

Martin Darbyshire is founder and managing director of the design studio "tangerine" in London and Seoul and has nearly 30 years of experience in the design sector. Before founding "tangerine" in 1989, he joined Moggridge Associates and worked in San Francisco at ID TWO (now IDEO). Most notably, Darbyshire led the multidisciplinary team that created both generations of the "Club World" business-class aircraft seating for British Airways – the world's first fully flat bed in the business class which, since its launch in 2000, has remained the profit engine of the airline. Martin Darbyshire also worked as visiting professor at the University of the Arts, Central Saint Martins; he is an industry spokesperson on design and innovation and was board member of the Icsid from 2007 to 2012.

Martin Darbyshire ist Gründer sowie Geschäftsführer des Designbüros „tangerine" mit Standorten in London und Seoul und kann mittlerweile auf eine fast dreißig-jährige Erfahrung in der Designbranche zurückblicken. Bevor er „tangerine" 1989 gründete, arbeitete er bei Moggridge Associates sowie bei ID TWO (heute IDEO) in San Francisco. Darbyshire leitete das multidisziplinä-re Team, das beide Generationen der „Club World", der so bezeichneten Business-Class-Flugzeugsitze für Bri-tish Airways, entwickelte. Das weltweit erste komplett flache Bett in einer Business Class hat der Airline seit seiner Markteinführung im Jahr 2000 enorme Umsatz-zahlen beschert. Martin Darbyshire arbeitete darüber hinaus als Gastprofessor an der University of the Arts, Central Saint Martins; er ist Wortführer für Design und Innovation und war von 2007 bis 2012 Vorstandsmit-glied des Icsid.

02

»Money can't buy you happiness but good design can!«

»Geld kann nicht glücklich machen, gutes Design dagegen schon!«

What trends have you noticed in the field of "Automotive and transportation" in recent years?
In automotive design, there is a continuing trend to concentrate design energy and investment on vehicle exteriors rather than what is inside and particularly on the user-interface. In transportation, notably in contract vehicles, there is some interesting use of materials with clever functionality for the user, producing "more for less". That is what clever design is all about and is one of the reasons I love judging Red Dot.

How do you assess the significance of design quality for the success of a company?
The basis of good design has to be that the product must deliver groundbreaking innovation and be commercially viable. As a jury, we always weigh up the commercial potential of a design as well as considering how it enhances and underpins the brand's reputation in the market it has been designed for.

Welche Trends konnten Sie im Bereich „Automotive und Transport" in den letzten Jahren ausmachen?
Im Fahrzeugdesign besteht ein anhaltender Trend, Investition und gestalterische Energie auf die Außen-gestaltung zu konzentrieren anstatt auf das, was im Inneren passiert, und vor allem auf die Bedienoberflä-che. Im Bereich „Transport", insbesondere bei Vertrags-fahrzeugen, zeigt sich ein interessanter Einsatz von Materialien mit ausgeklügelter Funktionalität für den Nutzer, wodurch „mehr für weniger" entsteht. Das ist, worum es bei intelligentem Design geht, und einer der Gründe, warum ich gerne Juror bei Red Dot bin.

Wie schätzen Sie den Stellenwert der Designqualität in den von Ihnen beurteilten Produktkategorien ein?
Die Grundlage guten Designs muss sein, dass das Pro-dukt bahnbrechende Innovation aufweist und finanziell realisierbar ist. Als Jury wägen wir immer auch das kom-merzielle Potenzial einer Gestaltung ab sowie die Frage, wie es die Markenreputation in dem Markt, für den es entworfen wurde, stärken und untermauern kann.

Martin Darbyshire

01

Prof. Stefan Diez
Germany

Jury member since 2011
Appointed three times
Jurymitglied seit 2011
Berufen drei Mal

Professor Stefan Diez, born 1971 in Freising, Germany, studied industrial design at the Stuttgart State Academy of Art and Design. In 2003 he opened his own studio in Munich and became professor at the Karlsruhe University of Applied Sciences in 2010. Together with two partners, he took over the art direction of Authentics from 2008 to 2009.

Stefan Diez specialises in product and exhibition design, working for Bree, e15, Established & Sons, Merten, Moroso, Rosenthal, Thonet, Wilkhahn and others; his designs have garnered many awards and are on display in various exhibitions. He is considered to be one of the most innovative and promising designers.

Professor Stefan Diez, 1971 in Freising geboren, studierte Industriedesign an der Staatlichen Akademie der Bildenden Künste Stuttgart. 2003 eröffnete er sein eigenes Studio in München und seit 2010 ist er Professor an der Staatlichen Hochschule für Gestaltung Karlsruhe. Zusammen mit zwei Partnern übernahm er von 2008 bis 2009 die Art Direction der Firma Authentics.

Stefan Diez ist im Produkt- und Ausstellungsdesign u. a. für Bree, e15, Established & Sons, Merten, Moroso, Rosenthal, Thonet und Wilkhahn tätig; seine Arbeiten wurden vielfach ausgezeichnet und in zahlreichen Ausstellungen präsentiert. Er gilt als einer der innovativsten und vielversprechendsten Designer.

01 **THIS THAT OTHER**
Seating series for e15 with
side chair, lounge chair and
barstool, made of moulded
oak-veneered plywood,
lacquered
Sitzserie für e15 mit Beistell-
stuhl, Sessel und Barhocker
aus geformten, eichenfurnierten
Schichtholzplatten, lackiert

02 **TROPEZ**
Collection of outdoor
furniture for Saskia Diez,
made of thermo-lacquered
aluminium profiles and
water-repellent fabric
Kollektion von Outdoor-
Möbeln für Saskia Diez,
gefertigt aus thermolackier-
ten Aluminiumprofilen und
wasserabweisendem Stoff

02

»Over the years the Red Dot jury has almost become a kind of circle of friends, even though there are new jurors every year and others take a break.«

»Die Red Dot-Jury ist über die Jahre fast eine Art Freundeskreis geworden, obwohl jedes Jahr neue Juroren hinzukommen und andere Pause machen.«

What is, in your opinion, the significance of design quality in the product categories you evaluated?
Besides fashion, design is currently paying most attention to furniture and lamps. Thus the jury's expectations were high. What inspired me was also the large number of innovative projects, above all in the area of architectural lighting.

What are the important criteria for you as a juror in the assessment of a product?
This always concerns the question of necessity, the logical consistency and the distinctiveness of a design. And it of course also concerns first impressions. It goes without saying that products are complex and multi-faceted, but they have to function at all levels and they have to fascinate. On top of that, I believe that the relationship between price and effort must be balanced.

Wie schätzen Sie den Stellenwert der Designqualität in den von Ihnen beurteilten Produktkategorien ein?
Neben der Mode bekommen Möbel und Leuchten gerade die meiste Aufmerksamkeit im Design. Von daher waren die Erwartungen der Jury entsprechend hoch. Was mich begeistert hat, war aber auch der hohe Anteil an innovativen Projekten, vor allem im Bereich des Architectural Lighting.

Worauf achten Sie als Juror, wenn Sie ein Produkt bewerten?
Es geht immer um die Frage nach der Notwendigkeit, um die Schlüssigkeit und um die Prägnanz eines Ent-wurfs. Und natürlich um den ersten Eindruck. Natürlich sind Produkte komplex und haben viele Schichten, aber sie müssen auf allen Ebenen funktionieren und einen fesseln. Ich finde, dass auch Preis und Aufwand in einem guten Verhältnis stehen müssen.

Prof. Stefan Diez

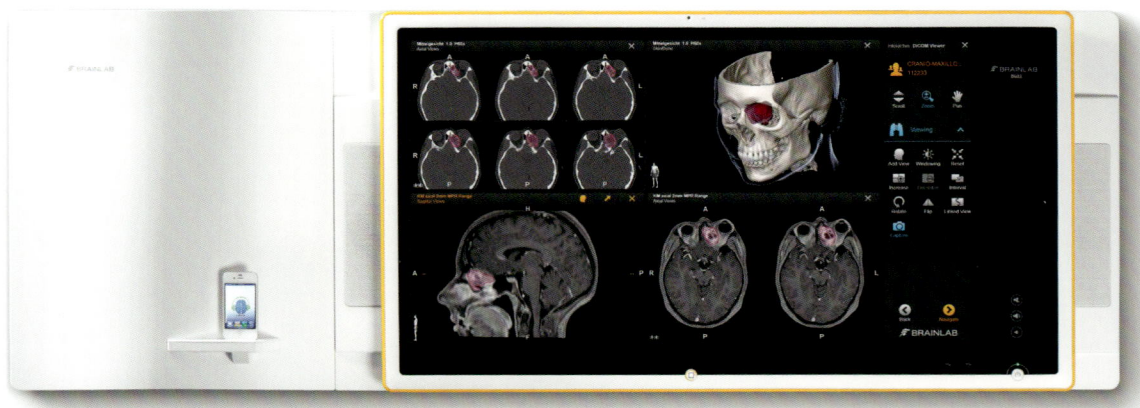

01

Stefan Eckstein
Germany

Jury member since 2013
Appointed for the first time
Jurymitglied seit 2013
Berufen zum ersten Mal

Stefan Eckstein, born 1961 in Stuttgart, studied industrial design at the Muthesius Academy of Fine Arts and Design in Kiel and attended courses at the Anthropological Institute of the Christian Albrecht University of Kiel. After holding a position as an assistant in Hamburg, he founded his own design studio in 1989 in Munich.

Since 2012, Stefan Eckstein has been the president of the Association of German Industrial Designers (VDID), giving highest priority to authenticity, responsibility and ethics. As project leader, he and his team developed the VDID Codex, which lays out the ethical values of the profession of industrial designers. His studio has received many design awards in national and international award competitions. Today, Stefan Eckstein is recognised as a renowned designer in industrial design, in particular in the fields of medical technology, as well as production and consumer goods.

Stefan Eckstein,1961 in Stuttgart geboren, studierte an der Muthesius-Hochschule in Kiel Industriedesign und besuchte Seminare am Anthropologischen Institut der Christian-Albrechts-Universität zu Kiel. Nach einer Assistenz in Hamburg gründete er 1989 sein eigenes Designstudio in München.

Seit 2012 ist Stefan Eckstein Präsident des Verbandes Deutscher Industrie Designer (VDID) und gibt Authentizität, Verantwortung und Ethik oberste Priorität. Als Projektleiter entwickelte er mit einem Team den VDID Codex, der die ethischen Werte des Berufsstandes der Industriedesigner beschreibt. Sein Büro erhielt zahlreiche Auszeichnungen in nationalen wie internationalen Wettbewerben. Stefan Eckstein zählt heute zu den renommierten Designern für Industriedesign in der Medizintechnik sowie Investitions- und Konsumgütergestaltung.

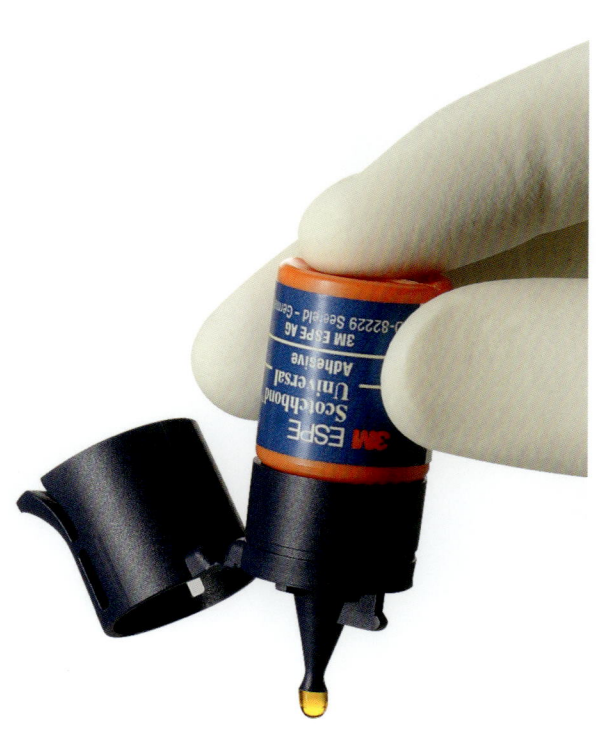

02

»In future, industrial designers will have to prove themselves with new role models and fascinating product strategies.«

»Industriedesigner müssen in Zukunft mit neuen Leitbildern und faszinierenden Produkt-strategien überzeugen.«

What trends have you noticed in the field of "Bathrooms, spas and air conditioning" in recent years?
High-quality real materials will continue to be a trend. Alongside the traditional reduced language of form, which has visibly come to the fore over the years, the bionic language of form will in future also increasingly establish itself.

How do you assess the significance of design quality for the success of a company?
The responsibility that is placed on industrial design and individual designers today is enormous. The success of all people involved in the development, production and marketing of a product, as well as the product support over its entire lifecycle, is often heightened disproportionally by the achievements of the industrial designers. Industrial design is therefore essential for companies and is clearly a critical success factor.

Welche Trends konnten Sie im Bereich „Bad, Wellness und Klima" in den letzten Jahren ausmachen?
Ein Trend werden weiter hochwertige Echt-Materialien sein. Neben der schon tradierten reduzierten Formsprache, die sich hier über Jahre sichtbar in den Vordergrund gespielt hat, wird sich in Zukunft auch die bionische Formsprache mehr und mehr etablieren.

Wie schätzen Sie den Stellenwert des Designs für den Erfolg eines Unternehmens ein?
Die Verantwortung, die Industriedesign bzw. Designer für Unternehmen heute tragen, ist enorm. Der Erfolg aller, die an der Entwicklung, Herstellung und Vermarktung eines Produkts und seiner Pflege über den gesamten Lebenszyklus mitwirken, wird häufig überproportional durch die Leistungen der Industriedesigner gesteigert. Hieraus ergibt sich, dass das Industriedesign elementar für die Zukunft von Unternehmen steht und ihren Erfolg sichtbar kennzeichnet.

Stefan Eckstein

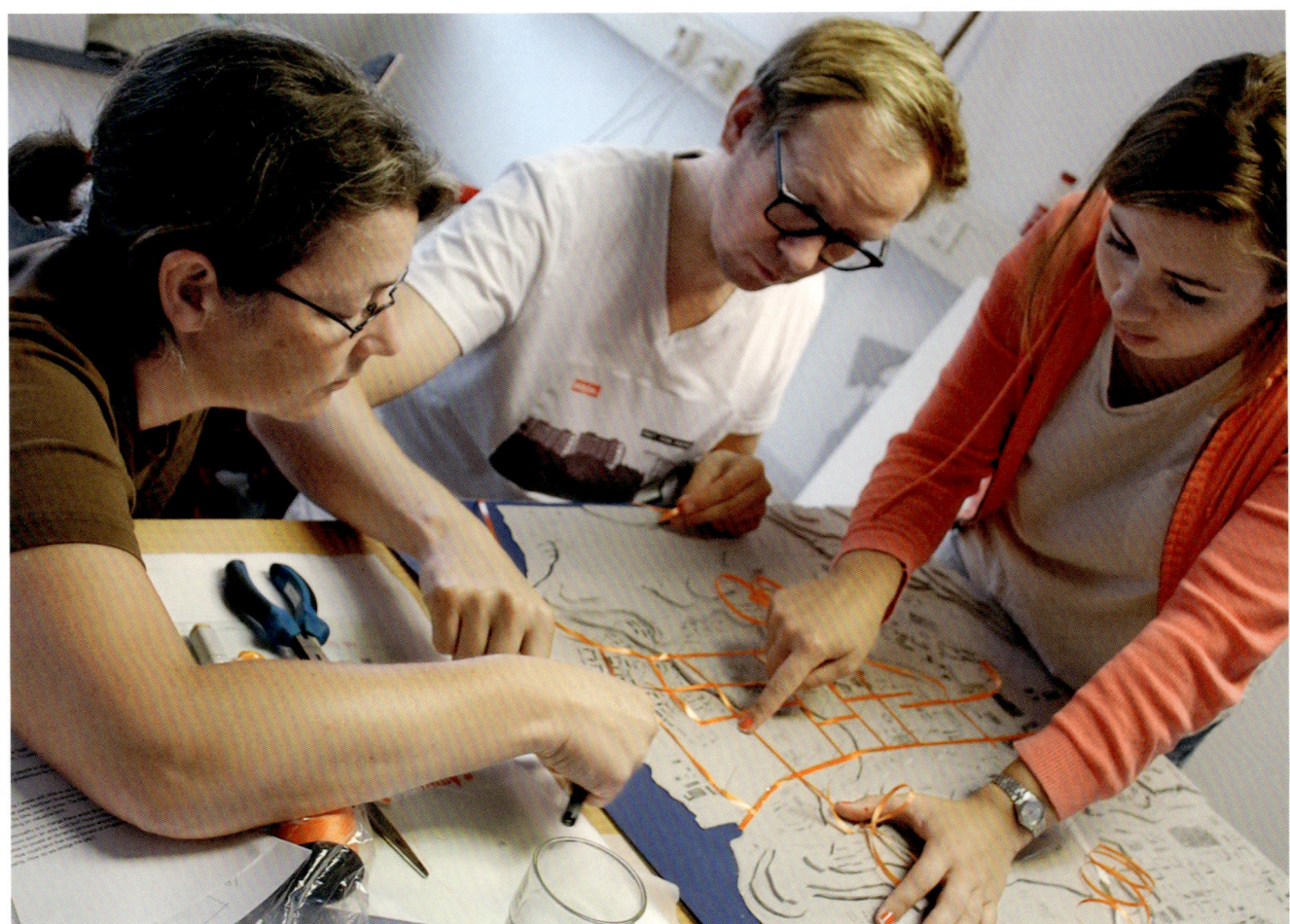

01

Robin Edman
Sweden

Jury member since 2007
Appointed six times
Jurymitglied seit 2007
Berufen sechs Mal

Robin Edman, born in 1956 and raised in Sweden, studied industrial design at the Rhode Island School of Design in Providence, USA. After graduating in 1981, he started as an industrial designer and later advanced to assistant director of Industrial Design at AB Electrolux in Stockholm. In 1989, he moved to Columbus, USA, as vice president of Industrial Design for the Frigidaire Company, where he also initiated and ran the Electrolux Global Concept Design Team for future forecasting of user needs.

In 1997, Edman moved back to Stockholm as vice president of Electrolux Global Design and was appointed chief executive of the Swedish Industrial Design Foundation (SVID) in 2001. From 2003 to 2007, Robin Edman was a board member of the International Council of Societies of Industrial Design, and from 2005 to 2007, he served as its treasurer. Since 2012 he has been a board member of the BEDA, the Bureau of European Design Associations.

Robin Edman, geboren 1956 und aufgewachsen in Schweden, studierte Industriedesign an der School of Design in Providence, Rhode Island, USA. Nach seinem Abschluss 1981 arbeitete er zunächst als Industriedesigner, später als Assistant Director für Industriedesign bei AB Electrolux in Stockholm. 1989 zog er nach Columbus, USA, um bei der Frigidaire Company die Position des Vizepräsidenten für Industriedesign zu übernehmen sowie das Electrolux Global Concept Design Team zur Vorhersage der Verbraucherbedürfnisse ins Leben zu rufen und zu leiten.

1997 kehrte Edman als stellvertretender Geschäftsführer bei Electrolux Global Design nach Stockholm zurück und wurde 2001 zum Geschäftsführer der Stiftung Schwedisches Industriedesign (SVID) ernannt. Von 2003 bis 2007 war Robin Edman Mitglied im Vorstand des International Council of Societies of Industrial Design, wobei er zwischen 2005 und 2007 das Amt des Schatzmeisters innehatte. Seit 2012 ist er Vorstandsmitglied des BEDA, Bureau of European Design Associations.

01 The Swedish Industrial Design Foundation's destination programme focuses on how the design process can develop attractive regions, locations, environments or events
Das Zielprogramm der Stiftung Schwedisches Industriedesign fokussiert sich darauf, wie der Design-prozess attraktive Regionen, Orte, Umgebungen oder Veranstaltungen entwickeln kann

02 Swedish Design Research Journal
The publication of the Swedish Industrial Design Foundation publishes research-based articles that explore how design can contribute to the sustainable development of industry, public sector and society
Die Publikation der Stiftung Schwedisches Industriedesign veröffentlicht forschungsba-sierte Artikel, die darstellen, was Design zu einer nachhal-tigen Entwicklung in Industrie, dem öffentlichen Sektor und der Gesellschaft beitragen kann

02

»I would like to see design become one of the obvious drivers of sustainable develop-ment and have it included in all innovation and change processes.«

»Ich würde Design gerne als eine der klaren Antriebskräfte für nachhaltige Entwicklung in allen Innovations- und Wandlungs-prozessen einbezogen sehen.«

What trends have you noticed in the field of "Gardens" in recent years?
Across the board there is a noticeable improvement in quality levels, a better use of materials and a "make my life easy" approach by manufacturers.

What current trends do you see in the category "Outdoor, leisure and sports"?
Multi-functionality and combinations instead of a new product for every use. Take for example clothing, strollers and toys. The improved use of new materials and clever solutions opens up new opportunities and result in better products for end-users.

What aspects of the jury process for the Red Dot Award: Product Design 2013 have stayed in your mind in particular?
Well-organised, tight schedules and 100 per cent support by the Red Dot team. A friendly and lively atmosphere and, of course, the networking and presence of so many great minds from around the world.

Welche Trends konnten Sie im Bereich „Garten" in den letzten Jahren ausmachen?
Auf ganzer Linie lässt sich ein höherer Qualitätsstan-dard, ein verbesserter Einsatz von Materialien und ein „Mach mein Leben leicht"-Ansatz durch die Hersteller beobachten.

Welche Trends konnten Sie im Bereich „Outdoor, Freizeit und Sport" in den letzten Jahren ausmachen?
Multifunktionalität und Kombinationen anstelle eines neuen Produkts für jeden Gebrauch. Beispielhaft ist dies bei Kleidung, Kinderwagen und Spielzeugen zu beobachten. Der verbesserte Einsatz neuer Materialien und intelligenter Lösungen schafft neue Möglichkeiten und bessere Produkte für die Nutzer.

Was ist Ihnen von der Jurierung des Red Dot Award: Product Design 2013 besonders im Gedächtnis geblieben?
Gut durchorganisierte, straffe Zeitpläne und 100-pro-zentige Unterstützung durch das Red Dot-Team. Eine freundliche und animierte Atmosphäre und selbstver-ständlich das Netzwerk und die Präsenz so vieler kluger Köpfe aus aller Welt.

Robin Edman

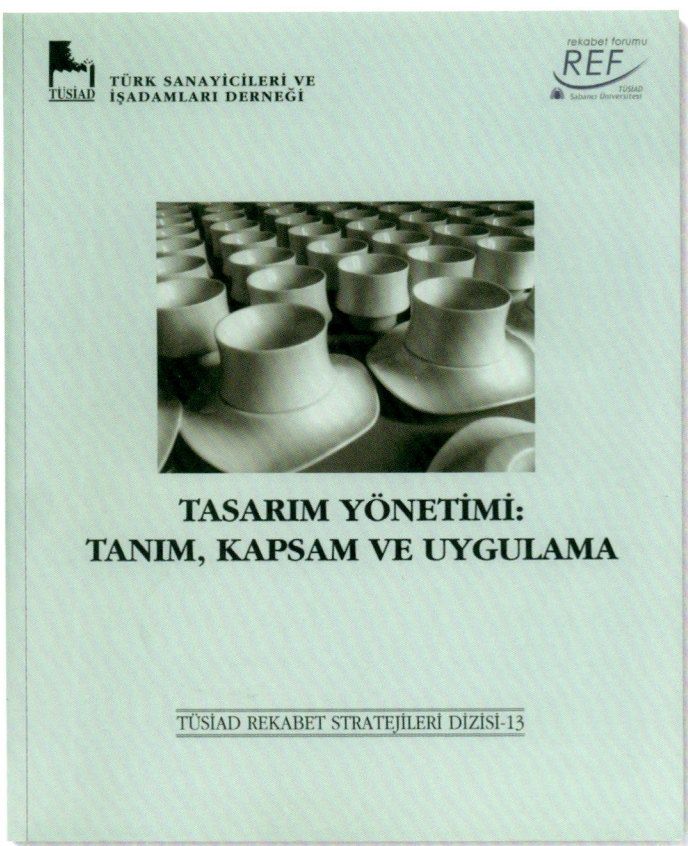

01

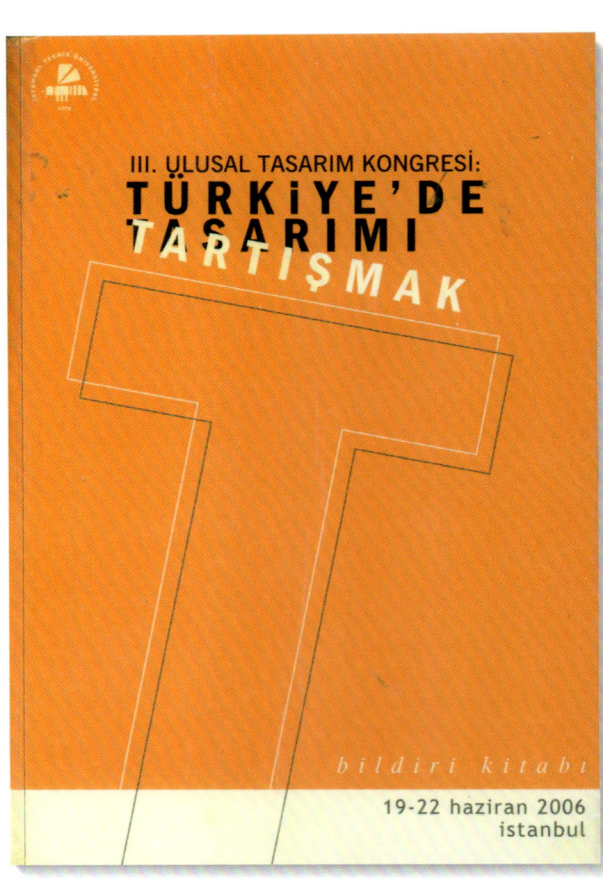

02

Prof. Dr. Alpay Er
Turkey

Jury member since 2012
Appointed twice
Jurymitglied seit 2012
Berufen zwei Mal

Professor Dr. Alpay Er studied industrial design at the Middle East Technical University (METU) in Ankara, Turkey, and completed his Ph.D. at Manchester Metropolitan University in the UK in 1994. He joined the Department of Industrial Product Design at Istanbul Teknik Universitesi (ITU) in 1997, where he served as chairperson from 2006 to 2013. Currently, he is founding chair of the Industrial Design Department at Ozyegin University in Istanbul. Alpay Er is also active in the Industrial Designers' Society of Turkey (ETMK), serving as an executive committee member as well as chairman of the ETMK Istanbul Branch. In cooperation with ITU and the Istanbul Chamber of Industry (ISO) he initiated the Industrial Design for SMEs project, the first programme for the education and promotion of design aimed at small and medium-sized enterprises (SMEs) in Turkey. In addition, he works as a consultant for various institutions and companies, is a member of the Executive Hosting Committee for the 2013 International Design Alliance (IDA) Congress hosted in Istanbul, and is a member of the Design Research Society (DRS). Alpay Er is also a member of the Icsid Executive Board (2011–2013).

Professor Dr. Alpay Er studierte Industriedesign an der Middle East Technical University (METU) in Ankara, Türkei, und promovierte 1994 in England an der Manchester Metropolitan University. 1997 trat er der Fakultät für Industriedesign an der Istanbul Teknik Universitesi (ITU) bei, wo er von 2006 bis 2013 als Vorsitzender tätig war. Derzeit ist er mitbegründender Vorsitzender der Fakultät für Industriedesign an der Universität Ozegin in Istanbul. Alpay Er engagiert sich auch in der Türkischen Gesellschaft für Industriedesigner (ETMK), sowohl als Vorstandsmitglied als auch als Vorsitzender der Abteilung ETMK Istanbul. In Kooperation mit der ITU und der Industriekammer Istanbuls (ISO) initiierte Alpay Er das Projekt „Industriedesign für KMUs", das erste, an kleine und mittelständische Unternehmen (KMUs) gerichtete Lehr- und Förderprogramm für Design in der Türkei. Zudem ist er als Berater für zahlreiche Unternehmen und Institutionen tätig und ist Mitglied des Gastgebervorstands für den 2013 in Istanbul stattfindenden Kongress der International Design Alliance (IDA) sowie Mitglied der Design Research Society (DRS). Darüber hinaus ist Alpay Er Vorstandsmitglied des Icsid (2011–2013).

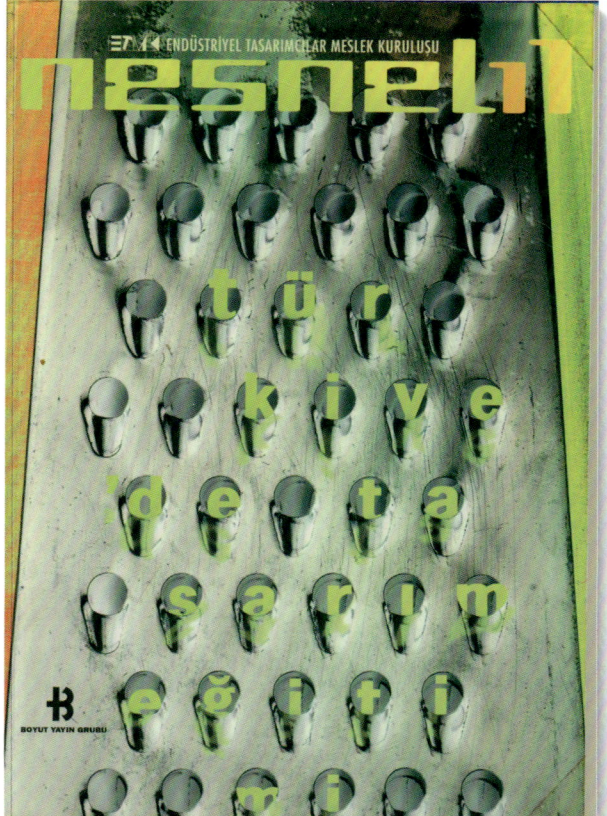

03

»Design is an indispensable part of innovation, making it more human and meaningful.«

»Design ist für Innovation unverzichtbar und macht sie menschlicher und bedeutsamer.«

What current trends do you see in the category "Life science and medicine"?
Miniaturisation continues where the function of the product allows it. Digital technologies are overtaking analogue ones. The ever increasing diversification of user needs and expectations both at global and local levels were also well represented.

What challenges do you see for the future in design?
The main challenge for design is to be able to function as one of the main drivers of innovation in competitive economic settings, while at the same time providing a meaningful contribution to significantly improving human life in a sustainable way.

Welche Trends konnten Sie im Bereich „Life Science und Medizin" in den letzten Jahren ausmachen?
Miniaturisierung setzt sich dort fort, wo es die Funktion der Produkte erlaubt, und digitale Technologien überholen die analogen. Die sich immer weiter auffächernden Bedürfnisse und Erwartungen der Anwender auf sowohl globaler wie auch lokaler Ebene wurden ebenfalls gut reflektiert.

Welche Herausforderungen sehen Sie für die Zukunft im Design?
Die größte Herausforderung für das Design besteht darin, in wirtschaftlichen Wettbewerbssituationen als ein Hauptantrieb für Innovation dienen zu können und das Leben der Menschen gleichzeitig durch bedeutende Beiträge entscheidend zu verbessern, und zwar auf nachhaltige Weise.

Prof. Dr. Alpay Er

01

Joachim H. Faust
Germany

Jury member since 2005
Appointed five times
Jurymitglied seit 2005
Berufen fünf Mal

Joachim H. Faust, born in 1954, studied architecture at the Technical University of Berlin, the Technical University of Aachen, as well as at Texas A&M University (with Prof. E. J. Romieniec), where he received his Master of Architecture in 1981. He worked as a concept designer in the design department of Skidmore, Owings & Merrill in Houston, Texas and as a project manager in the architectural firm Faust Consult GmbH in Mainz. From 1984 to 1986, he worked for KPF Kohn, Pedersen, Fox/Eggers Group in New York and as a project manager at the New York office of Skidmore, Owings & Merrill.

In 1987, Joachim H. Faust took over the management of the HPP office in Frankfurt am Main. Since 1997, he has been managing partner of the HPP Hentrich-Petschnigg & Partner GmbH + Co. KG in Düsseldorf. He also writes articles and gives lectures on architecture and interior design.

Joachim H. Faust, 1954 geboren, studierte Architektur an der TU Berlin und der RWTH Aachen sowie – bei Prof. E. J. Romieniec – an der Texas A&M University, wo er sein Studium 1981 mit dem Master of Architecture abschloss. Faust war Entwurfsarchitekt im Design Department des Büros Skidmore, Owings & Merrill, Houston, Texas, sowie Projektleiter im Architekturbüro der Faust Consult GmbH in Mainz. Anschließend arbeitete er im Büro KPF Kohn, Pedersen, Fox/Eggers Group in New York und war Projektleiter im Büro Skidmore, Owings & Merrill in New York.

1987 übernahm Joachim H. Faust die Leitung des HPP-Büros in Frankfurt am Main und ist seit 1997 geschäftsführender Gesellschafter der HPP Hentrich-Petschnigg & Partner GmbH + Co. KG in Düsseldorf. Er ist zudem als Autor tätig und hält Vorträge zu Fachthemen der Architektur und Innenarchitektur.

02

»All those award submissions were successful which expressed a clear design idea relating to the design task.«

»All jene Einreichungen waren erfolgreich, die eine klare Designidee in Bezug zur Aufgabenstellung ausdrücken konnten.«

What trends have you noticed in the field of "Architecture and urban design" in recent years?
In some architectural solutions, the consistency in the use of materials was highly convincing. They stood out in particular for their uniformity, the absence of high contrasts and a tendency towards the use of natural materials.

What are the important criteria for you as a juror in the assessment of a product?
The idea has to be clear and convincing. It then is up to the skill of the designer to translate this idea of space and material into architecture.

How do you assess the significance of design quality for the success of a company?
Today, every company acknowledges that a product is marketable only if it is well designed. Good design translates the inherent value of a product or building into an intuitively perceivable spatial quality or use.

Welche Trends konnten Sie im Bereich „Architektur und Urban Design" in den letzten Jahren ausmachen?
Bei einigen Architekturlösungen konnte die Stringenz der Verwendung von Materialien überzeugen. Einheitlichkeit, ohne große Materialwechsel, und die Tendenz zu natürlichen Materialien sind besonders aufgefallen.

Worauf achten Sie als Juror, wenn Sie ein Produkt bewerten?
Die Klarheit der Idee muss eindeutig erkennbar sein. Es ist dann die Kunst des Designers, diese Idee von Raum und Material inhaltlich in Architektur zu übersetzen.

Wie schätzen Sie den Stellenwert des Designs für den Erfolg eines Unternehmens ein?
Heute hat jedes Unternehmen erkannt, dass nur durch gutes Design ein Produkt auch marktfähig ist. Gutes Design übersetzt den inhaltlichen Wert eines Produktes oder eines Gebäudes in intuitiv erkennbare Raumqualität bzw. Bedienbarkeit eines Produktes.

Joachim H. Faust

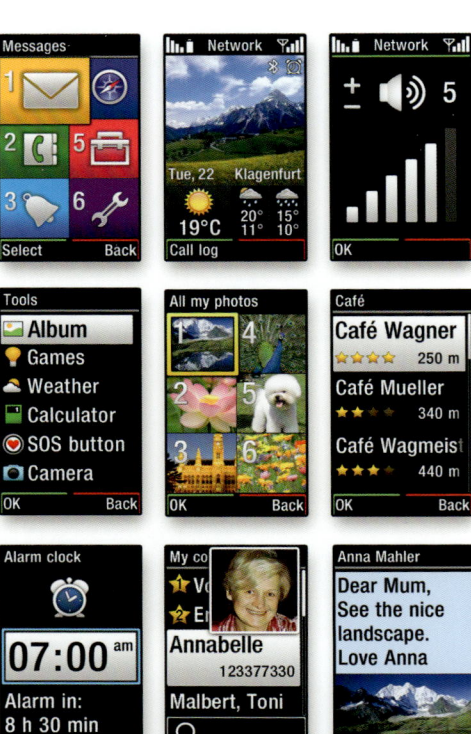

01

Andrea Finke-Anlauff
Germany

Jury member since 2004
Appointed four times
Jurymitglied seit 2004
Berufen vier Mal

Andrea Finke-Anlauff was born in Braunschweig, Germany. She studied industrial design at the Braunschweig University of Arts, during which time she spent a year in Barcelona (Facultat de Belles Arts) and also gained an MA in Design Leadership from an international degree course at the University of Industrial Arts in Helsinki, Finland. During her studies, she worked for various departments of Nokia in Great Britain, Japan and Finland. She graduated with a diploma in design and signed a consultancy agreement with Nokia.

Andrea Finke-Anlauff founded "mangodesign" in 1994. The agency's focus, aside from product design, is on interface design e. g. for agricultural vehicles and products from the mobile, entertainment and car industry. She went on to co-found the design manufactory "mangoobjects" in 2003. Her expertise has enabled Andrea Finke-Anlauff to teach interface design at art schools. She provides in-house trainings for customers and holds lectures at design events.

Andrea Finke-Anlauff wurde in Braunschweig geboren. Sie studierte Industrial Design an der Hochschule für Bildende Künste in Braunschweig, war währenddessen ein Jahr in Barcelona (Facultat de Belles Arts) und nahm an einem internationalen Studiengang MA in Design Leadership an der University of Industrial Arts in Helsinki teil. Bereits während des Studiums, das sie als Diplom-Industriedesignerin abschloss, arbeitete sie in verschiedenen Abteilungen von Nokia in Großbritannien, Japan und Finnland und erhielt im selben Jahr einen Beratervertrag bei Nokia.

1994 gründete Andrea Finke-Anlauff die Firma „mangodesign", deren Schwerpunkte – neben Produktdesign – auf Interfacedesign für landwirtschaftliche Nutzfahrzeuge sowie Produkte aus der Mobilfunk-, Unterhaltungs- und Autoindustrie liegen. Zudem war sie 2003 Mitbegründerin der Designmanufaktur „mangoobjects". Als Expertin unterrichtete Andrea Finke-Anlauff an Kunsthochschulen Interfacedesign. Sie führt betriebsinterne Schulungen für Kunden durch und hält Vorträge auf Designveranstaltungen.

01 **Emporia Connect**
   User interface, graphic
   and product design for
   a telephone for the elderly
   with Internet access:
   high-contrast displays and
   large lettering ensure
   good readability – the call
   is taken by opening the
   phone, closing it automatically ends the call
   User Interface, Grafik-
   und Produktdesign für ein
   Seniorentelefon mit Inter-
   netzugang: Hohe Kontraste
   und große Schriften sorgen
   für gute Lesbarkeit – Öffnen
   nimmt eingehende Anrufe
   an, Zusammenklappen
   beendet Telefonate automatisch

02 **TouchME**
   User interface and graphics
   for an ISOBUS terminal
   by Müller-Elektronik GmbH:
   the 12,1" touch display for
   monitoring and operating
   agricultural machinery
   can be installed vertically
   or horizontally
   User Interface und Grafik
   für ein ISOBUS-Terminal
   der Müller-Elektronik GmbH:
   12,1"-Touchdisplay zur
   Steuerung und Kontrolle
   von Landmaschinen,
   montierbar im Hoch- und
   im Querformat

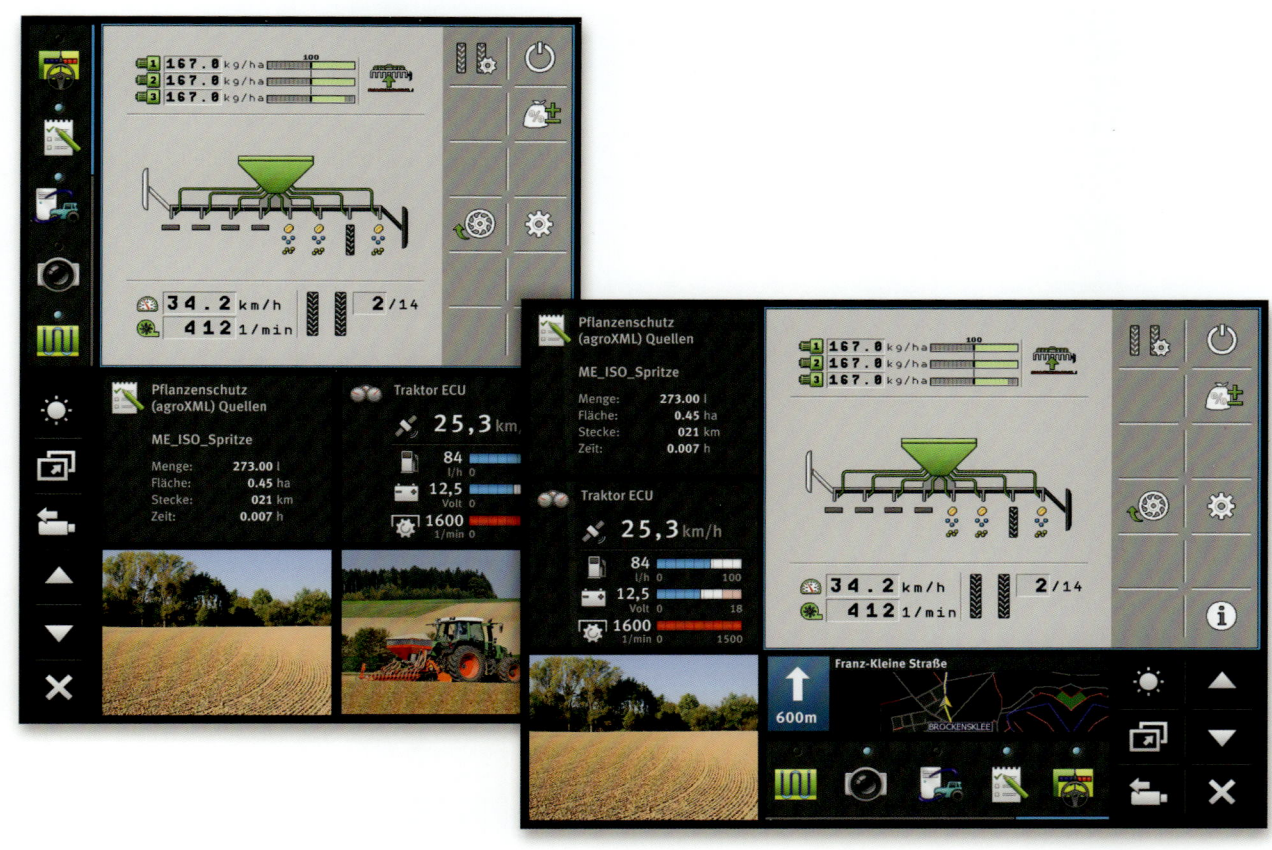

02

»Design does not only improve the visual appearance of a product, but also how it is used.«

»Design verbessert nicht nur die visuelle Anmutung, sondern auch den Umgang mit einem Produkt.«

What trends have you noticed in the field of "Computers and information technology" in recent years?
New product categories and technologies such as tablets and mobile telephones with touch screens have made computer applications much easier to use and more mobile. Many areas are marked by a merging of product types as manufacturers try out various product combinations such as cameras with a telephone function and mobile phones that could easily pass for tablets.

What aspects of the jury process for the Red Dot Award: Product Design 2013 have stayed in your mind in particular?
I was overwhelmed by the sheer number of submis-sions. The design quality of the products from Asian countries has significantly improved and the high number of submissions from the Far East is proof of a heightened awareness of design.

Welche Trends konnten Sie im Bereich „Computer und Informationstechnik" in den letzten Jahren ausmachen?
Neue Produktkategorien und Technologien wie Tablets und Mobiltelefone mit Touchbedienung haben den Umgang mit Computern erheblich erleichtert und noch mobiler gemacht. In vielen Bereichen findet eine Ver-schmelzung statt: Die Hersteller testen verschiedenste Produktkombinationen, z. B. Kamera mit Telefonfunktion oder Mobiltelefone, die als Tablets gelten können.

Was ist Ihnen von der Jurierung des Red Dot Award: Product Design 2013 besonders im Gedächtnis geblieben?
Ich war überwältigt von der Menge der eingereichten Arbeiten. Die Designqualität der Produkte aus asiati-schen Ländern ist deutlich gestiegen und die hohe Zahl der Anmeldungen aus Fernost beweist ein gesteigertes Bewusstsein für gute Gestaltung.

Andrea Finke-Anlauff

01

Prof. Lutz Fügener
Germany

Jury member since 2008
Appointed six times
Jurymitglied seit 2008
Berufen sechs Mal

Professor Lutz Fügener began his studies at the Technical University Dresden, where he completed a foundation course in mechanical engineering. He then transferred to the Burg Giebichenstein University of Art and Design in Halle/Saale, Germany, where he obtained a degree in industrial design in 1995. In the same year, he became junior partner of Fisch & Vogel Design in Berlin. Since then, the firm (today called "studioFT") has increasingly specialised in transportation design. Two years after joining the firm, Lutz Fügener became senior partner and co-owner. Since 2000, he has been chair of the BA degree course in transportation design and is a member of the board of governors of Pforzheim University.

Professor Lutz Fügener absolvierte ein Grundstudium in Maschinenbau an der Technischen Universität Dresden und nahm daraufhin ein Studium für Industrial Design an der Hochschule für Kunst und Design, Burg Giebichenstein, in Halle an der Saale auf. Sein Diplom machte er im Jahr 1995. Im selben Jahr wurde er Juniorpartner des Büros Fisch & Vogel Design in Berlin. Seit dieser Zeit spezialisierte sich das Büro (heute „studioFT") mehr und mehr auf den Bereich „Transportation Design". Zwei Jahre nach seinem Einstieg wurde Lutz Fügener Seniorpartner und gleichberechtigter Mitinhaber des Büros. Seit 2000 ist er Verantwortlicher des BA-Studiengangs „Transportation Design" und Mitglied des Hochschulrates der Hochschule Pforzheim.

»The automobile is one of those products whose design performance is explicitly perceived, judged and discussed even by customers.«

»Das Automobil ist eines der Produkte, bei dem die Designleistung auch vom Kunden explizit wahrgenommen, bewertet und diskutiert wird.«

What challenges do you see for the future in design?
Today's challenge consists of the profound integration of design into the development process of the vehicle, a process that ideally occurs not only simultaneously with the development, but which from early on represents a truly institutionalised cooperation between design and engineering.

What are the important criteria for you as a juror in the assessment of a product?
When assessing a product, for me it is important to what extent the creative work of the designers has influenced and ideally shaped the concept, development and realisation of a vehicle; that is, whether it has contributed to giving it a character easily recognisable by its users. Complementing this effect with high quality design craftsmanship in realisation yields the highest quality products.

Welche Herausforderungen sehen Sie für die Zukunft im Design?
Die heutige Herausforderung besteht in der tiefen Einbindung des Designs in den Entwicklungsprozess des Fahrzeugs, der im Idealfall nicht nur in einer Gleichzeitigkeit der Entwicklung, sondern einer wirklichen, frühzeitig institutionalisierten Kooperation von Design und Engineering besteht.

Worauf achten Sie als Juror, wenn Sie ein Produkt bewerten?
Für mich ist es bei der Bewertung wichtig, inwieweit die gestalterische Arbeit der Designer bei der Konzeption und Umsetzung eines Fahrzeugs Einfluss auf das Konzept erlangt hat und es im Idealfall prägt, also zu seinem für den Nutzer wahrnehmbaren Charakter verholfen hat. Wenn dieser Effekt mit einer hohen designhandwerklichen Qualität in der Umsetzung einhergeht, entstehen die hochwertigsten Produkte.

Prof. Lutz Fügener

01

Hideshi
Hamaguchi
Japan

Jury member since 2012
Appointed twice
Jurymitglied seit 2012
Berufen zwei Mal

Hideshi Hamaguchi graduated with a Bachelor of Science in chemical engineering from Kyoto University. Starting his business career with Panasonic in Japan, Hamaguchi later became director of the New Business Planning Group at Panasonic Electric Works, Ltd. and then executive vice president of Panasonic Electric Works Laboratory of America, Inc. In 1994, he developed Japan's first corporate Intranet and also led the concept development for the first USB flash drive. Hideshi Hamaguchi has over 15 years of experience in defining strategies and decision-making, as well as in concept development for various industries and businesses. As director of strategy at Ziba Design, he is today considered a leading mind in creative concept and strategy development on both sides of the Pacific and is involved in almost every project this renowned business consultancy takes on. For clients such as FedEx, Polycom and M-System he has led the development of several award-winning products.

Hideshi Hamaguchi graduierte als Bachelor of Science in Chemical Engineering an der Kyoto University. Seine Karriere begann er bei Panasonic in Japan, wo er später zum Direktor der New Business Planning Group von Panasonic Electric Works, Ltd. und zum Executive Vice President von Panasonic Electric Works Laboratory of America, Inc. aufstieg. 1994 entwickelte er Japans erstes Firmen-Intranet und übernahm zudem die Leitung der Konzeptentwicklung des ersten USB-Laufwerks. Hideshi Hamaguchi besitzt mehr als 15 Jahre Erfahrung in der Konzeptentwicklung sowie Strategie- und Entscheidungsfindung in unterschiedlichen Industrien und Unternehmen. Als Director of Strategy bei Ziba Design wird er heute als führender Kopf in der kreativen Konzept- und Strategieentwicklung auf beiden Seiten des Pazifiks angesehen und ist in nahezu jedes Projekt der renommierten Unternehmensberatung involviert. Für Kunden wie FedEx, Polycom und M-System leitete er einige ausgezeichnete Projekte.

02 / 03

»My philosophy of life is: All I need is less.«

»Meine Lebensphilosophie lautet: Was ich brauche, ist weniger.«

What is, in your opinion, the significance of design quality in the product categories you evaluated?
Design is significant in these categories because it forms emotional and cognitive connections. Technology is so ingrained in our lives today that it is no longer enough to be beautiful and functional – the product must also have a story and personal resonance. Design is the means to create that.

Do you see a correlation between the economic success of a company and the design quality of its products?
Definitely. If a company has the right design for all the phases of consumer interaction – attraction, engagement and ensuing actions – it should directly affect its success.

What challenges do you see for the future in design?
The challenge is finding the sweet spot between what resonates with the consumer and what is true to the brand.

Wie schätzen Sie den Stellenwert der Designqualität in den von Ihnen beurteilten Produktkategorien ein?
In diesen Kategorien ist Design wesentlich, da es emotionale und kognitive Verbindungen bildet. Technologie ist in unserem Leben heute derart tief verwurzelt, dass es nicht mehr genügt, schön oder funktional zu sein – das Produkt muss eine Geschichte und persönliche Resonanz besitzen. Design ist das Mittel, um das zu erreichen.

Sehen Sie einen Zusammenhang zwischen dem wirtschaftlichen Erfolg eines Unternehmens und der Designqualität seiner Produkte?
Auf jeden Fall. Wenn ein Unternehmen in allen Stadien der Interaktion mit dem Verbraucher – Anziehungskraft, Einbindung, Folgehandlung – über das richtige Design verfügt, sollte das seinen Erfolg direkt beeinflussen.

Welche Herausforderungen sehen Sie für die Zukunft im Design?
Die Herausforderung ist, den Punkt zwischen dem, was beim Konsumenten auf Resonanz stößt, und dem, was die Marke ausmacht, zu treffen.

Hideshi Hamaguchi

01

Prof. Renke He
China

Jury member since 2008
Appointed six times
Jurymitglied seit 2008
Berufen sechs Mal

Professor Renke He, born in 1958, studied civil engineering and architecture at Hunan University. From 1987 to 1988, he was a visiting scholar at the Industrial Design Department of the Royal Danish Academy of Fine Arts in Copenhagen and, from 1998 to 1999, at North Carolina State University's School of Design. Renke He is dean and professor of the School of Design at Hunan University in China and is also director of the Chinese Industrial Design Education Committee. Currently, he holds the position of vice-chair of the China Industrial Design Association.

Professor Renke He wurde 1958 geboren und studierte an der Hunan University Bauingenieurwesen und Architektur. Von 1987 bis 1988 war er als Gastprofessor für Industrial Design an der Royal Danish Academy of Fine Arts in Kopenhagen tätig, und von 1998 bis 1999 hatte er eine Gastprofessur an der School of Design der North Carolina State University inne. Renke He ist Dekan und Professor an der Hunan University China, School of Design, sowie Direktor des Chinese Industrial Design Education Committee. Er ist zudem stellvertretender Vorsitzender der China Industrial Design Association.

02

»Good design means good business. Nowadays, you cannot talk about companies without talking about their design.«

»Gute Gestaltung impliziert gute Geschäfte. Heutzutage kann man nicht über Unternehmen sprechen, ohne über ihre Gestaltung zu sprechen.«

What trends have you noticed in the field of "Households" in recent years?
In many countries of the world, both air and water pollution have today become serious problems that people have to deal with. This year, I have seen many air and water purifier designs that have introduced new and unique design languages to express functions and identities.

What trends have you noticed in the field of "Kitchens" in recent years?
As more and more high-tech electrical household appliances are used, kitchens have become more complicated. In order to turn kitchens back into more pleasant places, built-in design has become a trend. "Less is more" is still an important design principle.

Which product would you like to realise one day?
A mobile phone-based remote medical system for people who live far away from big cities.

Welche Trends konnten Sie im Bereich „Haushalt" in den letzten Jahren ausmachen?
In vielen Ländern der Welt sind heute Luft- und Wasserverschmutzung zu ernsten Problemen geworden, die die Menschen angehen müssen. In diesem Jahr gab es viele Gestaltungen zur Luft- und Wasserreinigung, die sich im Ausdruck ihrer Funktion und Identität neuer und einzigartiger Gestaltungssprachen bedienen.

Welche Trends konnten Sie im Bereich „Küche" in den letzten Jahren ausmachen?
Da immer mehr elektronische Hightech-Haushaltsgeräte zum Einsatz kommen, ist die Küche viel komplizierter geworden. Um sie als Ort wieder freundlicher zu machen, entwickelte sich der Trend zu Einbauentwürfen. „Weniger ist mehr" ist nach wie vor ein wichtiges Gestaltungsprinzip.

Welches Produkt würden Sie gerne einmal realisieren?
Ein per Mobiltelefon fernbedienbares medizinisches System für Menschen, die weit ab von großen Städten leben.

Prof. Renke He

01

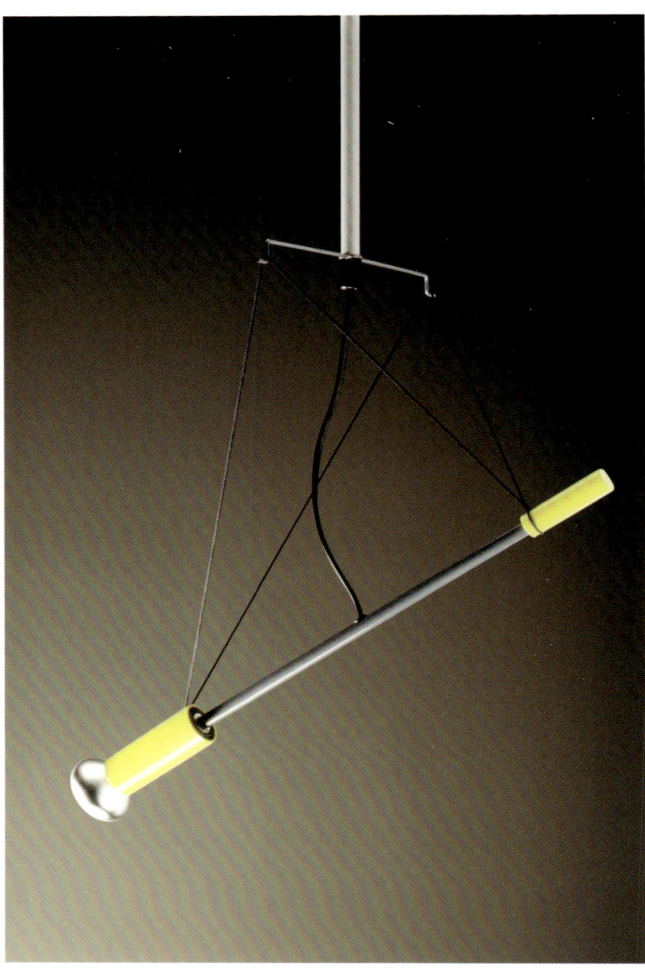

02

Prof. Herman Hermsen
Netherlands

Jury member since 1999
Appointed ten times
Jurymitglied seit 1999
Berufen zehn Mal

Professor Herman Hermsen, born in 1953 in Nijmegen, Netherlands, studied at the ArtEZ Institute of the Arts in Arnhem from 1974 to 1979. Following an assistant professorship, he began his career in teaching in 1985. Until 1990, he taught product design at the Utrecht School of the Arts (HKU), after which time he returned to Arnhem as lecturer at the Academy. Hermsen has been professor of product and jewellery design at the University of Applied Sciences in Düsseldorf since 1992. He gives guest lectures at universities and colleges throughout Europe, the United States, and Japan, and began regularly organising specialist symposia in 1998. He has also served as juror for various competitions. Herman Hermsen has received numerous international awards for his work in product and jewellery design, which is shown worldwide in solo and group exhibitions and held in the collections of renowned museums, such as the Cooper-Hewitt Museum, New York; the Pinakothek der Moderne, Munich; and the Museum of Arts and Crafts, Kyoto.

Professor Herman Hermsen, 1953 in Nijmegen in den Niederlanden geboren, studierte von 1974 bis 1979 am ArtEZ Institute of the Arts in Arnheim und ging nach einer Assistenzzeit ab 1985 in die Lehre. Bis 1990 unterrichtete er Produktdesign an der Utrecht School of the Arts (HKU) und kehrte anschließend nach Arnheim zurück, um an der dortigen Hochschule als Dozent zu arbeiten. Seit 1992 ist Hermsen Professor für Produkt- und Schmuckdesign an der Fachhochschule Düsseldorf; er hält Gastvorlesungen an Hochschulen in ganz Europa, den USA und Japan, organisiert seit 1988 regelmäßig Fachsymposien und ist Juror in verschiedenen Wettbewerbsgremien. Für seine Arbeiten im Produkt- und Schmuckdesign, die weltweit in Einzel- und Gruppenausstellungen präsentiert werden und sich in den Sammlungen großer renommierter Museen befinden, z. B. Cooper-Hewitt Museum, New York, Pinakothek der Moderne, München, und Museum of Arts and Crafts, Kyoto, erhielt Herman Hermsen zahlreiche internationale Auszeichnungen.

03

»As a juror, I essentially search for innovative aspects in form and technology.«

»Als Juror suche ich in erster Linie nach innovativen Aspekten in Form und Technik.«

What is, in your opinion, the significance of design quality in the product categories you evaluated?
The significance of design quality is very high, because these products are worn on the body. Wearers identify with them and use them to present themselves.

What current trends do you see in the category "Watches and jewellery"?
Some products were very interesting because they integrate technical innovations, for example a digital wristwatch with GPS function and a wristwatch made from recycled tin cans. Different stylistic features, which are shaped by local markets around the world, come together in this category.

What challenges do you see for the future in design?
Many issues that have been relevant for some time: environmental protection, sustainability, quality over quantity and innovation without neglecting traditional values.

Wie schätzen Sie den Stellenwert der Designqualität in den von Ihnen beurteilten Produktkategorien ein?
Der Stellenwert der Designqualität ist sehr hoch, denn diese Produkte werden am Körper getragen – und damit identifiziert und präsentiert sich der Träger.

Welche Trends konnten Sie im Bereich „Uhren und Schmuck" ausmachen?
Einige Produkte waren sehr interessant, weil sie technische Innovationen integrierten, z. B. die GPS-Funktion in einer digitalen Armbanduhr, und eine Armbanduhr etwa aus recycelten Blechdosen gefertigt war. In dieser Kategorie kommen unterschiedliche Stilmerkmale aus aller Welt zusammen, die durch die Märkte vor Ort geprägt werden.

Welche Herausforderungen sehen Sie für die Zukunft im Design?
Einige schon längst offene Türen: Umweltschutz, Nachhaltigkeit, Qualität über Quantität und Innovation, ohne die tradierten Werte zu vernachlässigen.

Prof. Herman Hermsen

01

Prof. Carlos Hinrichsen
Chile

Jury member since 2006
Appointed seven times
Jurymitglied seit 2006
Berufen sieben Mal

Professor Carlos Hinrichsen, born in 1957, graduated as an industrial designer in Chile in 1982 and went to Japan to add a Master's degree in engineering in 1991. From 2007 to 2009, he was president of the Icsid and has since served as its senator. Since then he has been heading research projects focused on innovation, design and education and, in 2010, was honoured with the distinction of "Commander of the Order of the Lion of Finland" in recognition of his valuable contribution to the development of design education, design innovation and their promotion in Chile and Finland. From 1992 to 2010, he was director of the School of Design Duoc UC, Chile. He has been a design process consultant for over two decades, and is currently design director for the Latin American Region of Design Innovation, a European design company with clients and activities across the world. Since 2002, Carlos Hinrichsen has been an honorary member of the Chilean Association of Design. He has been the keynote speaker at different conferences and seminars worldwide. He is also director of Duoc UC International Affairs.

Professor Carlos Hinrichsen, geboren 1957, schloss 1982 sein Studium als Industriedesigner in Chile ab und erwarb 1991 zusätzlich einen Ingenieurs-Masterabschluss in Japan. Von 2007 bis 2009 war er Präsident des Icsid und fungiert dort seither als Senator. Seitdem leitet er Forschungsprojekte mit Schwerpunkt auf Innovation, Gestaltung und Ausbildung und wurde 2010 in Anerkennung seiner Verdienste in Sachen Förderung der Designausbildung und -innovation sowie deren Vermittlung in Chile und Finnland mit dem „Commander of the Order of the Lion of Finland" ausgezeichnet. Von 1992 bis 2010 war er Direktor der Designschule „Instituto Profesional Duoc UC". Seit mehr als zwei Jahrzehnten ist er als Berater im Bereich Design Process tätig und derzeit der Design Director der Latin American Region of Design Innovation, einer europäischen Designfirma mit Kunden und Beschäftigungsfeldern in aller Welt. Seit 2002 ist Carlos Hinrichsen Ehrenmitglied der chilenischen Vereinigung der Designfirmen (QVID). Zudem war er Hauptredner verschiedener Konferenzen und Seminare weltweit. Darüber hinaus ist Carlos Hinrichsen Direktor der Duoc UC International Affairs.

01 **ZERO/ONE**
The initiative explores
new scenarios of mobility
for Milan, Italy, based on
different time horizons
(2010 to 2025) and propos-
als for sustainable innovation with regard to transport, logistics and usability
Die Initiative erforscht neue
Szenarien der Mobilität für
Mailand, Italien, aufbauend
auf verschiedenen Zeithori-
zonten (2010 bis 2025)
sowie Vorschläge für nachhaltige Innovation in Bezug
auf Transport, Logistik und
Anwendbarkeit

02 **Foguita**
Kerosene heater, designed
for Compañia Tecno Indus-
trial CTI in 1993: It is still in
production in Chile and sold
in local and regional markets
– currently the company is
part of Electrolux Chile
Ölheizgerät, entworfen 1993
für Compañia Tecno Industrial
CTI: Das Gerät wird immer
noch in Chile hergestellt und
lokal und regional vertrieben
– derzeit gehört die Firma zu
Electrolux Chile

02

**»Every year, this award high-
lights the latest developments
in design and altogether opens
up an unprecedented field of
knowledge and expectations.«**

»Jedes Jahr zeigt dieser
Wettbewerb die neuesten
Errungenschaften im Design
und eröffnet insgesamt
einen beispiellosen Wissens-
und Erwartungshorizont.«

**What is, in your opinion, the significance of design
quality in the product categories you evaluated?**
This year, products presented themselves as realistic
images of the desires and dreams of users, designers
and producers brought to life. In the categories I
evaluated, design quality and innovation play a key
role in turning technological innovations into business success. Product quality and performance have
also been improved from a consumer standpoint in
a wide variety of applications.

**What are the important criteria for you
as a juror in the assessment of a product?**
My criteria of assessment are as follows. I look at
the unique ways of integrating or embedding innovation into products or services, and how designers
and companies use design appropriately to imple-
ment both innovations coming from the R&D sphere
as well as innovations associated with social and
market changes in order to respond successfully to
people's new needs and requirements.

**Wie schätzen Sie den Stellenwert der Designqualität
in den von Ihnen beurteilten Produktkategorien ein?**
Dieses Jahr habe ich beobachtet, wie sich Produkte als
realistische, lebendig gewordene Träume und Wünsche
sowohl der Nutzer als auch der Gestalter und Produ-
zenten darbieten. Designqualität und Innovation spielen
eine zentrale Rolle beim Ummünzen technologischer
Neuerungen in den Geschäftserfolg. Es zeigt sich eine
große Bandbreite an Anwendungen, bei denen sich
die Produktqualität und Leistung auch aus Sicht der
Konsumenten verbessert haben.

**Worauf achten Sie als Juror,
wenn Sie ein Produkt bewerten?**
Meine Beurteilungskriterien sind wie folgt: Ich achte
auf die besondere Einbindung von Innovation in die
Produkte oder Leistungen und darauf, wie Designer
und Firmen Gestaltung angemessen nutzen, um sowohl
die Innovation aus dem F&E-Bereich umzusetzen als
auch jene Innovationen, die auf gesellschaftlichen und
marktwirtschaftlichen Veränderungen basieren – mit
dem Ziel, erfolgreich auf die neuen Bedürfnisse und
Anforderungen der Menschen zu antworten.

Prof. Carlos Hinrichsen

01

Stephan Hürlemann
Switzerland

Jury member since 2013
Appointed for the first time
Jurymitglied seit 2013
Berufen zum ersten Mal

Stephan Hürlemann, born in 1972, studied architecture at the ETH Zurich (Swiss Federal Institute of Technology). He then worked for some years as a musician and music manager, but was also active in the areas of Internet design and architectural visualisation.

In 2002, the designer joined the Hannes Wettstein's agency as CEO. He was made a partner in 2006. After Wettstein's death, Stephan Hürlemann converted the company to its new format. Today, he is one of Studio Hannes Wettstein's two creative directors, as well as partner and member of the three-person executive board.

Stephan Hürlemann, 1972 geboren, studierte Architektur an der ETH Zürich. Danach war er einige Jahre als Musiker und Musikmanager sowie in den Bereichen Internet-Konzeption und Architektur-Visualisierungen tätig.

2002 kam der Gestalter als CEO in das Büro von Hannes Wettstein, der ihn 2006 zu seinem Partner machte. Nach dessen Tod führte Stephan Hürlemann das Büro in seine neue Form über und ist heute einer der beiden Creative Directors des Studio Hannes Wettstein sowie Teilhaber und Mitglied der dreiköpfigen Geschäftsleitung.

01 **Broadcasting Studio:**
SRF Sport
Sendestudio: SRF Sport
for SRF Schweizer Radio
und Fernsehen (Swiss Radio
and Television), 2007
für SRF Schweizer Radio und
Fernsehen, 2007

02 **BN0106**
for Braun, 2011
für Braun, 2011

C3 **icon**
for horgenglarus, 2012
für horgenglarus, 2012

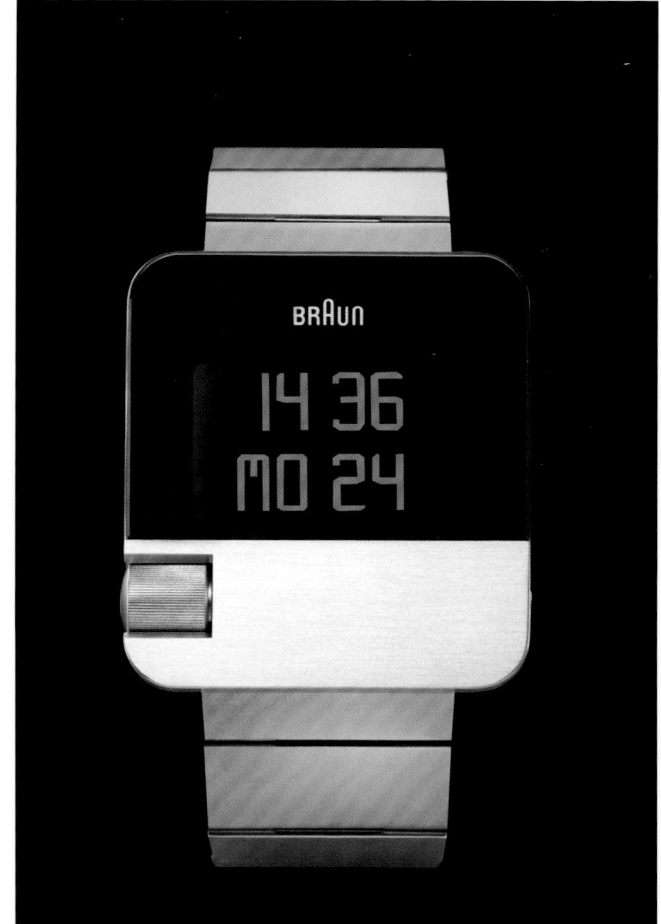

02

03

»Thanks to the standardisation of light sources and their dematerialisation design comes to the fore.«

»Durch die Vereinheitlichung der Leuchtmittel und ihre Entmaterialisierung rückt das Design in den Vordergrund.«

What aspects of the jury process for the Red Dot Award: Product Design 2013 have stayed in your mind in particular?
I was very impressed with the composition of the jury and the discussions that were held in the adjudication process. I can say with a clear conscience that the jury genuinely tried to make a contribution to the promotion of good design.

What challenges do you see for the future in design?
When design is abused in order to diversify in a saturated market, that often leads to empty products which are crowned only with short term success. I'm convinced that good design requires constant challenging and optimisation using constructive dialogue. And this can only be achieved when designers and business people work together well.

Was ist Ihnen von der Jurierung des Red Dot Award: Product Design 2013 besonders im Gedächtnis geblieben?
Ich war sehr angetan von der Zusammensetzung der Jury und von den Diskussionen, die im Jurierungsprozess geführt wurden. Ich kann mit gutem Gewissen behaupten, dass die Jury aufrichtig versucht hat, einen Beitrag zur Förderung von guter Gestaltung zu leisten.

Welche Herausforderungen sehen Sie für die Zukunft im Design?
Wenn Design missbraucht wird, um sich in einem gesättigten Markt zu diversifizieren, dann entstehen oft leere Produkte, die nur von kurzem Erfolg gekrönt sind. Ich bin überzeugt, dass gutes Design das konstante Hinterfragen und Optimieren in einem konstruktiven Dialog bedingt. Und genau dies kann nur dann entstehen, wenn das Zusammenspiel zwischen Gestalter und Unternehmer funktioniert.

Stephan Hürlemann

01

Prof. Dr. Florian Hufnagl
Germany

Jury member since 2003
Appointed ten times
Jurymitglied seit 2003
Berufen zehn Mal

Professor Dr. Florian Hufnagl, born 1948, has been director of Die Neue Sammlung – The International Design Museum, Munich, since 1990. He studied art history, classical archaeology and modern history in Munich, earning his doctorate in 1976. Thereafter, he worked for the Bavarian State Department of Monuments and Sites and, in 1980, became chief curator of Die Neue Sammlung. During this time, Hufnagl was also associate lecturer for 19th- and 20th-century art at the Institute of Art History at Ludwig-Maximilians-Universität in Munich. In 1997, he became honorary professor at the Academy of Fine Arts in Munich and, in 1998, chairman of the directors' conference of Bavaria's state museums and collections. Florian Hufnagl has written on 20th- and 21st-century architecture, painting and design in numerous publications, catalogues and essays.

Professor Dr. Florian Hufnagl, geboren 1948, ist seit 1990 leitender Sammlungsdirektor der Neuen Sammlung – The International Design Museum Munich. Er promovierte 1976 nach einem Studium der Kunstwissenschaft, Klassischen Archäologie und Neueren Geschichte in München. Anschließend arbeitete er beim Bayerischen Landesamt für Denkmalpflege und seit 1980 als Museumskurator in der Neuen Sammlung. Zugleich unterrichtete Hufnagl als Lehrbeauftragter für die Kunst des 19. und 20. Jahrhunderts am Institut für Kunstgeschichte der Ludwig-Maximilians-Universität München. Seit 1997 ist er Honorarprofessor an der Akademie der Bildenden Künste in München. 1998 wurde er Vorsitzender der Direktorenkonferenz der Staatlichen Museen und Sammlungen in Bayern. In zahlreichen Publikationen, Katalogen und Aufsätzen setzt sich Florian Hufnagl mit der Architektur, der Malerei und dem Design des 20. und 21. Jahrhunderts auseinander.

01 **Alessandro Mendini – Curiosities and Design**
2011 exhibition of Die Neue Sammlung in its branch Neues Museum in Nuremberg
Alessandro Mendini – Wunderkammer Design Ausstellung 2011 der Neuen Sammlung im Neuen Museum in Nürnberg

02 Stairway to the permanent exhibition of Die Neue Sammlung at the Pinakothek der Moderne, Munich, with objects by Zaha Hadid and Luigi Colani
Eingangstreppe zur Dauerausstellung der Neuen Sammlung in der Pinakothek der Moderne, München, mit Arbeiten von Zaha Hadid und Luigi Colani

02

»The market has become global, which also means that design must more than ever account for and factor in different cultural conditions.«

»Der Markt ist global geworden, das bedeutet auch, dass Design stärker als bisher die unterschiedlichen kulturellen Voraussetzungen berücksichtigen muss.«

What trends have you noticed in the field of "Watches and jewellery" in recent years? Are there developments that have especially attracted your attention?
Watches have followed three trends for years. Role models are the high-priced, hand-made products created by Swiss manufacturers, classic sports chronometers and the kind of minimalism that one today also finds in German and Danish products.

What trends have you noticed in the field of "Tableware and decoration" in recent years?
There have been many changes in tableware in recent years. Classical sets defined only through their form have been left behind to make way for elements that can be combined freely in terms of form, colour and pattern or used individually, and which create a highly colourful and emotional impression. New and different materials are being selected. Today's consumers prefer espresso machines to coffeepots.

Do you have a philosophy toward life?
Do it better!

Welche Trends konnten Sie im Bereich „Uhren und Schmuck" in den letzten Jahren ausmachen? Gibt es Entwicklungen, die Ihnen besonders aufgefallen sind?
Bei den Uhren gibt es seit Jahren drei Richtungen. Vorbilder sind die hochpreisigen handgefertigten Produkte aus den Schweizer Manufakturen, die klassischen Sport-Chronometer und der Minimalismus, den man inzwischen auch bei deutschen und dänischen Produkten wiederfindet.

Welche Trends konnten Sie im Bereich „Tableware und Dekoration" in den letzten Jahren ausmachen?
Bei Tableware hat sich in den letzten Jahren viel verändert, weg vom klassischen, nur durch seine Form sprechenden Service hin zu in Form, Farbe und Dekor beliebig kombinierbaren und einzeln benutzbaren Elementen, die ein sehr farbenfrohes, emotionales Bild abgeben. Es gibt neue, andere Materialien, und der Konsument bevorzugt statt der Kaffeekanne die Espressomaschine.

Haben Sie ein Lebensmotto?
Do it better!

Prof. Dr. Florian Hufnagl

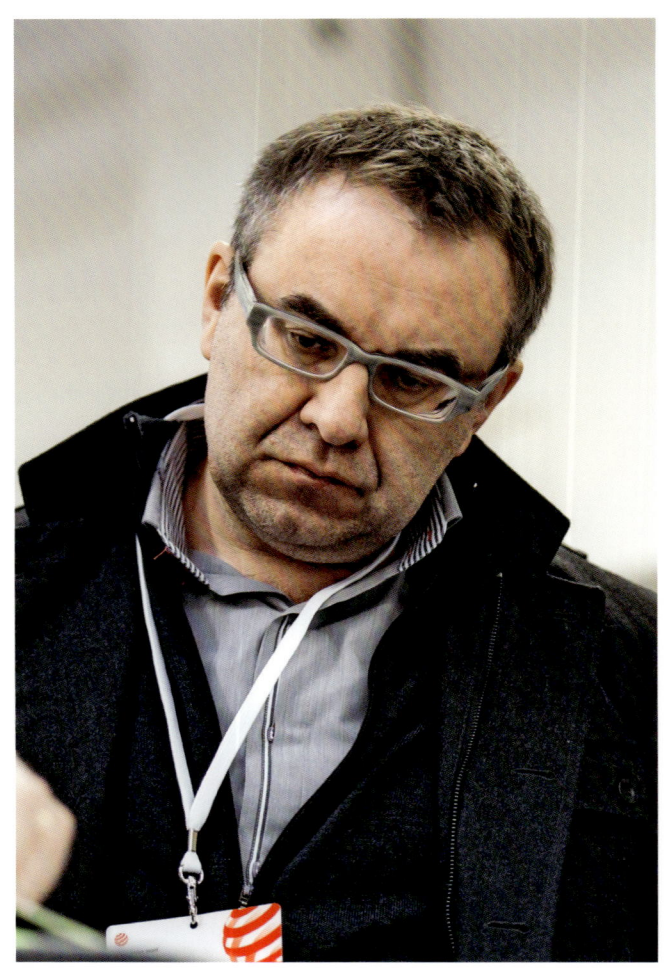

01

Gerald Kiska
Austria

Jury member since 2011
Appointed twice
Jurymitglied seit 2011
Berufen zwei Mal

Gerald Kiska studied at the University of Arts and Industrial Design in Linz, Austria. He subsequently worked for several design studios both in Austria and abroad. They included Interform Design in Wolfsburg, Germany from 1984 to 1985; Form Orange in Hard from 1985 to 1986; Agentur Idea in Stuttgart in 1986; and later Porsche Design in Zell am See. In 1991, Gerald Kiska founded his own design studio in Anif, Salzburg, which in terms of floor space (5,000 sqm) and staff (more than 110 employees from 20 nations) is one of the biggest owner-operated studios in Europe today. From 1994 to 1995, he was a visiting professor at the Offenbach Academy of Art and Design (HfG), Germany. From 1995 to 2002, he was a founding member of and lecturer at the University of Applied Sciences in Graz, Austria. Gerald Kiska became known through his work for the motorcycle manufacturer KTM. Today, he works in a wide variety of sectors, including the automotive industry, consumer goods, food and beverages, investment goods and professional tools, with a focus on the challenges posed by the development and strengthening of brands.

Gerald Kiska absolvierte die Hochschule für Gestaltung in Linz und arbeitete anschließend in verschiedenen Designbüros im In- und Ausland, darunter 1984/85 bei Interform Design in Wolfsburg, 1985/86 bei Form Orange in Hard, 1986 in der Agentur Idea, Stuttgart, und anschließend bei Porsche Design in Zell am See. 1991 gründete er sein eigenes Designunternehmen in Anif/Salzburg, das heute bezüglich seiner Fläche (5.000 qm) und Mitarbeiterzahl (über 110 Mitarbeiter aus 20 Nationen) eines der größten eigentümergeführten Studios Europas ist. Von 1994 bis 1995 lehrte er im Rahmen einer Gastprofessur an der Hochschule für Gestaltung Offenbach am Main, von 1995 bis 2002 engagierte er sich als Gründer und Dozent an der Fachhochschule für Industrial Design Graz. Bekannt wurde Gerald Kiska durch seine Arbeiten für den Motorradhersteller KTM. Heute arbeitet er für ein breites Spektrum an Branchen, darunter Fahrzeugindustrie, Konsumgüter, Nahrungsmittel & Getränke, Investitionsgüter und professionelle Werkzeuge. Der Schwerpunkt liegt auf Herausforderungen rund um die Entwicklung oder Stärkung von Marken.

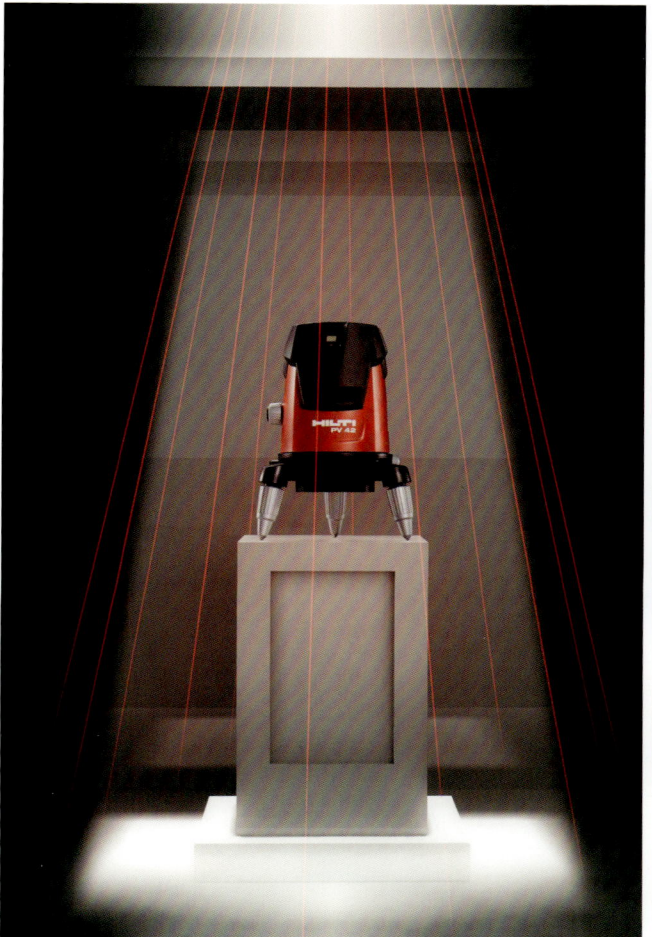

02

»Design is an important component of branding and thus indispensable for a company's success.«

»Design ist ein wichtiger Bestandteil der Markenbildung und daher für den Erfolg von Unternehmen unabdingbar.«

What trends have you noticed in the field of "Gardens" in recent years?
I have noticed that the established brands in this field, which have been using good design for a long time, have managed to greatly expand their market share, to the point where it is very difficult for almost any competitor to launch an attack.

What are the important criteria for you as a juror in the assessment of a product?
I pay attention to the usual design criteria such as aesthetics, ergonomics and surface feel, but particularly take into account branding effects: Are the manufacturer's values embodied in the product? Does the product stand out from the competition?

How do you assess the significance of design quality for the success of a company?
The strength of a brand is one of the most important parameters for a company's economic success. Products are a brand's most important messengers. Therefore, design is the most important component of branding.

Welche Trends konnten Sie im Bereich „Garten" in den letzten Jahren ausmachen?
In diesem Bereich ist mir aufgefallen, dass jene etablierten Marken, die schon seit Langem auf Design gesetzt haben, einen großen Vorsprung zum Durchschnitt aufgebaut haben, sodass es für jeden Konkurrenten sehr schwierig ist, sie anzugreifen.

Worauf achten Sie als Juror, wenn Sie ein Produkt bewerten?
Ich achte auf die üblichen Designkriterien wie Ästhetik, Ergonomie und Haptik, aber auch stark auf Branding-Effekte: Sind die Markenwerte des Herstellers ablesbar? Findet eine Differenzierung vom Wettbewerb statt?

Wie schätzen Sie den Stellenwert des Designs für den Erfolg eines Unternehmens ein?
Die Stärke einer Marke ist einer der wichtigsten Parameter für den wirtschaftlichen Erfolg des Unternehmens. Produkte sind die wichtigsten Botschafter einer Marke. Daher ist Design der wichtigste Bestandteil der Markenbildung.

Gerald Kiska

01

Wolfgang K. Meyer-Hayoz
Switzerland

Jury member since 2003
Appointed seven times
Jurymitglied seit 2003
Berufen sieben Mal

Wolfgang K. Meyer-Hayoz, born in 1947, studied mechanical engineering, visual communication and industrial design, graduating from the Stuttgart State Academy of Art and Design. In 1985, he founded the Meyer-Hayoz Design Engineering Group with offices in Switzerland (Winterthur) and Germany (Konstanz). The company offers consultancy services for business start-ups, small- and medium-sized enterprises, as well as world market leaders in design strategy, industrial design, user interface design, temporary architecture and communication design. It has received numerous international awards.

From 1987 to 1993, Meyer-Hayoz was president of the Swiss Design Association (SDA). He is a member of various other associations as well, including the Association of German Industrial Designers (VDID) and the Schweizerische Management Gesellschaft (SMG). Aside from his work as a designer and a consultant, Wolfgang K. Meyer-Hayoz is also a guest lecturer at the University of St. Gallen and serves as juror on international design panels.

Wolfgang K. Meyer-Hayoz, geboren 1947, absolvierte Studien in den Fachbereichen Maschinenbau, Visuelle Kommunikation sowie Industrial Design mit Abschluss an der Staatlichen Akademie der Bildenden Künste in Stuttgart. 1985 gründete er die Meyer-Hayoz Design Engineering Group mit Büros in der Schweiz (Winterthur) und Deutschland (Konstanz). Das Unternehmen berät Start-ups, kleine und mittelständische Unternehmen sowie Weltmarktführer in Design Strategy, Industrial Design, User Interface Design, Temporary Architecture und Communication Design und wurde bereits vielfach international ausgezeichnet.

Von 1987 bis 1993 war Meyer-Hayoz Präsident der Swiss Design Association (SDA); er ist u. a. Mitglied im Verband Deutscher Industrie Designer (VDID) und der Schweizerischen Management Gesellschaft (SMG). Neben seiner Tätigkeit als Designer und Consultant ist Wolfgang K. Meyer-Hayoz u. a. Gastdozent an der Universität St. Gallen sowie Juror internationaler Designgremien.

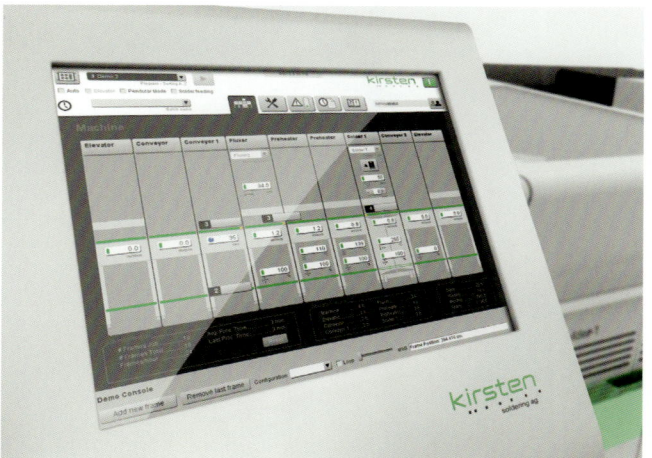
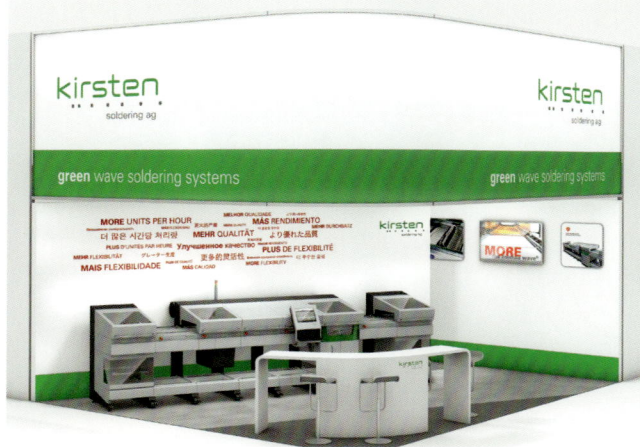

02 – 05

»My philosophy of life is to stimulate fascination for good and sustainable design.«

»Mein Lebensmotto ist, Menschen für gutes und nachhaltiges Design zu begeistern.«

What trends have you noticed in the field of "Life science and medicine" in recent years?
The obviously fast absorption of the latest research findings into new product applications (e.g., for laboratory analysis systems), but also new life-saving systems to prevent smoke poisoning. In general, a reduced language of form is coming back to the fore. This enables system solutions that provide a wide range of options in terms of application and save resources at the same time.

Do you see a correlation between the design quality of a company's products and the economic success of this company?
With the experience gathered over many industrial projects, I can say that this causality definitely exists. However, it requires a comprehensive understanding of design that includes innovation capacity, technology leadership as well as a conscious corporate management culture.

Welche Trends konnten Sie im Bereich „Life Science und Medizin" in den letzten Jahren ausmachen?
Die offensichtlich rasche Übernahme von Erkenntnissen der Forschung in neue Produktanwendungen, z. B. für Labor-Analysesysteme, aber auch neue lebenssichernde Systeme als Schutz gegen Rauchvergiftungen. Allgemein erkennt man wieder stärker eine reduzierte Formensprache. Sie erlaubt Systemdesignlösungen, welche eine große Variantenvielfalt für die Anwendung zur Verfügung stellt und gleichzeitig ressourcenschonend ist.

Sehen Sie einen Zusammenhang zwischen der Designqualität, die sich in den Produkten eines Unternehmens äußert, und dessen wirtschaftlichem Erfolg?
Aufgrund meiner in vielen Industrieprojekten gewonnenen Erfahrungen kann ich sagen, dass diese Kausalität absolut besteht. Es bedingt jedoch ein umfassendes Designverständnis, welches Innovationskraft, Technologieführerschaft sowie eine bewusste Führungskultur im Unternehmen beinhaltet.

Wolfgang K. Meyer-Hayoz

01

Jure Miklavc
Slovenia

Jury member since 2013
Appointed for the first time
Jurymitglied seit 2013
Berufen zum ersten Mal

Jure Miklavc was born in Kranj, Slovenia, in 1970. He is a graduate in industrial design from the Academy of Fine Arts in Ljubljana, Slovenia, and has nearly 20 years of experience in the field of design. Miklavc started his career working as a freelance designer with graphic designer Barbara Šušterič, before founding his own design consultancy Studio Miklavc. Studio Miklavc works in the field of product design, visual communications, brand development and consultancy for a variety of clients mainly from the areas of business and economy, but also from government and culture.

Designs by Studio Miklavc have received many prestigious awards and have been displayed in numerous exhibitions. Miklavc is also active in promoting design and its role in Slovenian society. Since 2005, he has been involved in design education as a permanent lecturer at the Academy of Fine Arts and Design.

Jure Miklavc wurde 1970 in Kranj, Slowenien, geboren und machte seinen Abschluss in Industrial Design an der Academy of Fine Arts in Ljubljana, Slowenien. Er verfügt über beinahe 20 Jahre Erfahrung im Designbereich. Zunächst arbeitete er als freiberuflicher Designer zusammen mit der Grafikerin Barbara Šušterič und gründete anschließend sein eigenes Design-Beratungsunternehmen Studio Miklavc. Studio Miklavc ist im Bereich Produktdesign, visuelle Kommunikation, Markenentwicklung und Beratung für eine Vielzahl von Kunden vor allem aus dem Unternehmens- und Wirtschaftssektor, aber auch aus Regierungskreisen und Kultur tätig.

Viele Gestaltungen aus dem Hause Studio Miklavc erhielten angesehene Auszeichnungen und wurden in zahlreichen Ausstellungen gezeigt. Jure Miklavc ist im Bereich der Designförderung und gesellschaftlichen Relevanz von Gestaltung in Slowenien aktiv und seit 2005 als Dozent an der Academy of Fine Arts and Design tätig.

01 **Intra Lighting – Etea**
Highly affordable general-purpose basic luminaire with several intelligent solutions and inner modularity for different lighting possibilities within a single casing
Äußerst preisbewusste schlichte Allzweckleuchte mit mehreren intelligenten Lösungen und innerer Modularität für verschiedene Beleuchtungsszenarien in einem Gehäuse

02 **Alpina ESK Pro**
Cross-country ski boots with a third of the world's market share; racing boots are worn by top athletes on countless podia in the highest categories of racing
Langlaufskischuhe mit einem Drittel des Weltmarktanteils; Rennschuhe werden von Topathleten auf unzähligen Podien in den höchsten Rennkategorien getragen

02

»Regardless of rational criteria, I'm open to the emotional charm of products.«

»Unabhängig von rationalen Kriterien bin ich offen für den emotionalen Charme von Produkten.«

What trends have you noticed in the field of "Industry and crafts" in recent years?
Tools are one of the most used products in our daily lives. They define who we are and the quality of our working environment. They are becoming more and more sophisticated and therefore more intuitive and ergonomic. As a result, we can carry out more precise operations with less effort and risk to our health. Thanks to well-designed products, working has become more focused and enjoyable.

What trends have you noticed in the field of "Automotive and transportation" in recent years?
I have noticed good design attempts in products and sectors that are not known for sophisticated solutions such as professional equipment for special vehicles. A greater level of intelligence is also noticeable in the development of the infrastructure for rechargeable electric cars.

Welche Trends konnten Sie im Bereich „Industrie und Handwerk" in den letzten Jahren ausmachen?
Werkzeuge gehören zu den meistgebrauchten Produkten unseres täglichen Lebens; sie bestimmen, wer wir sind und welchen Qualitätsgrad unsere Arbeitsumgebung hat. Sie werden immer durchdachter und dadurch intuitiver und ergonomischer. Wir sind daher in der Lage, immer präzisere Vorgänge mit weniger Anstrengung und Gefahr für unsere Gesundheit auszuführen. Dank gut gestalteter Produkte ist das Arbeiten konzentrierter und angenehmer geworden.

Welche Trends konnten Sie im Bereich „Automotive und Transport" in den letzten Jahren ausmachen?
Mir sind gute Gestaltungsbestrebungen bei Produkten und in Bereichen aufgefallen, die nicht für ausgeklügelte Lösungen bekannt sind, wie etwa in der professionellen Ausstattung für Spezialfahrzeuge. Mehr Intelligenz zeigt sich auch in der Entwicklung der Infrastruktur für aufladbare Elektrofahrzeuge.

Jure Miklavc

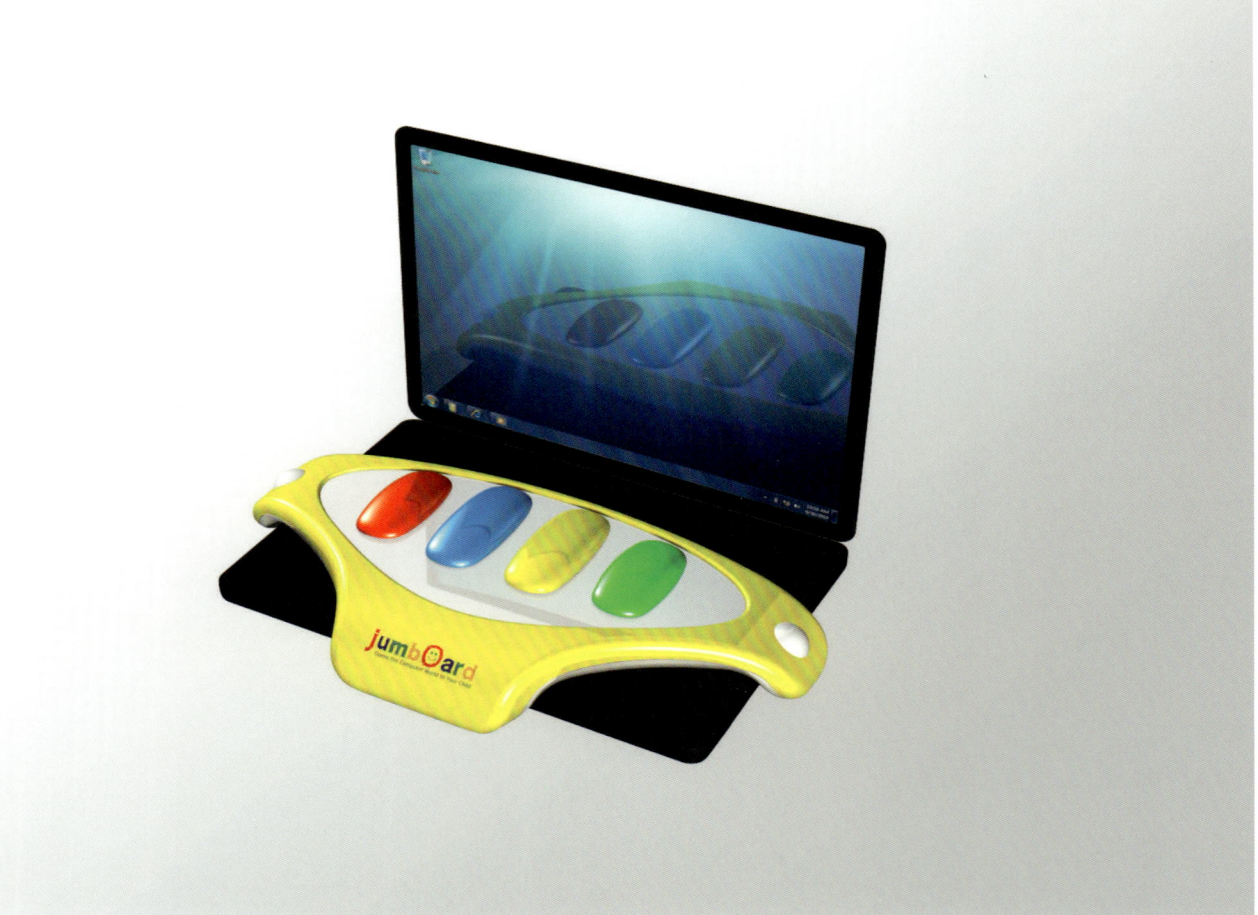

01

Prof. Ron A. Nabarro
Israel

Jury member since 2005
Appointed five times
Jurymitglied seit 2005
Berufen fünf Mal

Professor Ron A. Nabarro is an industrial designer, entrepreneur, researcher and educator. Since 1970, he has designed more than 700 products, mainly in the field of advanced technologies, and in 2009, he received the World Technology Network Award in the field of design. From 1992 to 2009, he was a professor of industrial design at the Technion Israel Institute of Technology where he founded and led the Graduate Program in Advanced Design Studies and Design Management. Currently, Ron A. Nabarro teaches at Beijing DeTao Masters Academy, China. After having been an executive board member of the Icsid from 1999 to 2003, he now acts as an Icsid regional advisor. He has lectured in over 20 countries, has acted as a consultant for a wide variety of organisations and is a frequent keynote speaker at conferences. Ron A. Nabarro is co-founder and partner of the four start-up companies Scentcom Ltd., Cellomate Ltd., MedImprove and Balance, and is also co-founder and CEO of Senior-Touch Ltd., an age-friendly R&D company and design consultancy. Its areas of research and interest are age-friendly design, design management and design education.

Professor Ron A. Nabarro ist Industriedesigner, Unternehmer, Forscher und Lehrender. Seit 1970 gestaltete er mehr als 700 Produkte, hauptsächlich im Bereich der modernen Technologien, und erhielt 2009 den World Technology Network Award im Bereich Design. Von 1992 bis 2009 war er Professor für Industriedesign am Technion Israel Institute of Technology, wo er das Graduate Program in Advanced Design Studies and Design Management begründete und leitete. Derzeit lehrt Ron A. Nabarro an der Beijing DeTao Masters Academy in China. Nachdem er von 1999 bis 2003 als Vorstandsmitglied des Icsid diente, ist er aktuell als regionaler Berater von Icsid tätig. Er hat in mehr als 20 Ländern Vorträge gehalten, ist als Berater für eine Vielzahl an Organisationen tätig und ist oft Hauptredner auf Konferenzen. Ron A. Nabarro ist Mitbegründer und Partner der vier Start-up-Unternehmen Scentcom Ltd., Cellomate Ltd., MedImprove und Balance und ebenso Mitbegründer und CEO von Senior-Touch Ltd., einem Beratungsunternehmen für altersfreundliche F&E sowie Gestaltung. Dessen Forschungs- und Interessensbereiche liegen in altersfreundlichem Design, Designmanagement und Designerziehung.

02

»My abiding impression from this jury session as well as others over the years is the respectful and conscientious attitude of all jury members throughout the adjudication process.«

»Mein bleibender Eindruck dieser Jurysitzung und anderer über die Jahre hinweg ist die respektvolle und gewissenhafte Haltung aller Juroren im Jurierungsprozess.«

What trends have you noticed in the field of "Bathrooms, spas and air conditioning" in recent years?
A dramatic change is taking place in this field. The old approach of trying to find a "practical" solution is giving way to an understanding that time spent in the bathroom and spa is supposed to be quality time for body and soul. The new designs reflect this trend, allowing the user to experience comfort and relaxation in this environment.

What current trends have you noticed in the category "Gardens"?
In the "Gardens" category, a determined effort to align design with the needs of the gardening community is becoming apparent. There are no compromises; the solutions encompass all aspects.

What challenges do you see for the future in design?
The ageing population is increasingly becoming one of the most significant social, economic and demographic phenomena of our times. I see this as one of the most important challenges for design.

Welche Trends konnten Sie im Bereich „Bad, Wellness und Klima" in den letzten Jahren ausmachen?
In diesem Bereich findet eine dramatische Veränderung statt. Der alte Ansatz, eine „praktische" Lösung zu finden, weicht dem Verständnis, dass die Zeit im Badezimmer oder Wellnessbereich eine wertvolle Zeit für Körper und Seele ist. Die neuen Gestaltungen spiegeln diesen Trend wider und ermöglichen es dem Nutzer, in dieser Umgebung Entspannung und Komfort zu erfahren.

Welche Trends konnten Sie im Bereich „Garten" ausmachen?
In der Kategorie „Garten" fällt das starke Bestreben auf, Design auf die Bedürfnisse der Gärtner abzustimmen. Es gibt keine Kompromisse, die Lösungen umfassen alle Aspekte.

Welche Herausforderungen sehen Sie für die Zukunft im Design?
Altern wird zunehmend zu einem der wichtigsten sozialen, wirtschaftlichen und demografischen Phänomene unserer Zeit. Ich halte es für eine der wichtigsten Herausforderungen im Design.

Prof. Ron A. Nabarro

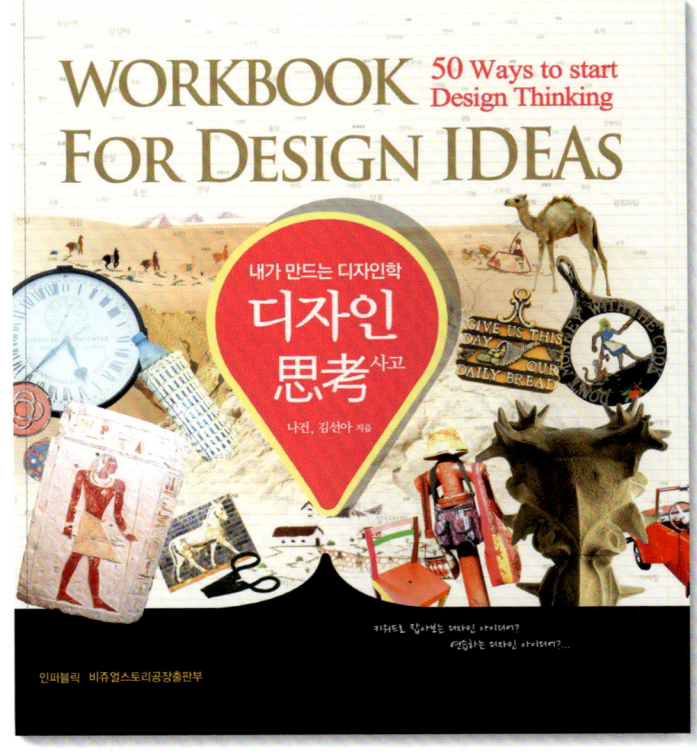

01

02

Prof. Dr. Ken Nah
Korea

Jury member since 2012
Appointed twice
Jurymitglied seit 2012
Berufen zwei Mal

In 1983, Professor Dr. Ken Nah received his B.A. from Hanyang University, South Korea, majoring in Industrial Engineering. His interest in human factors/ergonomics led him to pursue a Master's Degree from Korea Advanced Institute for Science and Technology (KAIST) in 1985. He gained his Ph.D. in 1996 in Engineering Design from Tufts University. Ken Nah is also a USA certified professional ergonomist (CPE). From 2002 to 2006, he was the dean of the International Design School for Advanced Studies (IDAS).

Currently, he is professor of Design Management and also the director of the Human and Experience Research (HER) Lab at IDAS. He has also held the post of director at the International Design Trend Center (IDTC) since 2002 and was the director general of "World Design Capital Seoul 2010". Alongside his teaching career, Ken Nah is also the vice president of the Korea Association of Industrial Designers (KAID), the Ergonomics Society of Korea (ESK), the Korea Institute of Design Management (MIDM), as well as the chairman of the Design and Brand Committee of the Korea Consulting Association (KCA).

Professor Dr. Ken Nah, der im Hauptfach Industrial Engineering studierte, graduierte 1983 an der Hanyang University in Südkorea als Bachelor of the Arts. Sein Interesse an Human Factors/Ergonomie vertiefte er 1985 mit einem Master-Abschluss am Korea Advanced Institute for Science and Technology (KAIST) und promovierte 1996 an der Tufts University. Darüber hinaus ist Ken Nah ein in den USA zertifizierter Ergonom (CPE). Von 2003 bis 2006 war er Dekan der International Design School for Advanced Studies (IDAS).

Aktuell ist er als Professor für Design Management tätig und zudem Direktor des „Human and Experience Research (HER)"-Labors an der IDAS. Von 2002 an war er Leiter des International Design Trend Center (IDTC). Ken Nah war Generaldirektor der „World Design Capital Seoul 2010". Neben seiner Lehrtätigkeit ist er Vice President der Korea Association of Industrial Designers (KAID), der Ergonomics Society of Korea (ESK), des Korea Institute of Design Management (MIDM) sowie Vorsitzender des „Design and Brand"-Komitees der Korea Consulting Association (KCA).

»I was very impressed by the diversity of products and excellent design quality of the entries this year.«

»Die Produktvielfalt und herausragende Gestaltungsqualität der diesjährigen Einreichungen hat mich sehr beeindruckt.«

What current trends do you see in the category "Computers and information technology"?
The form factors "simple" and "attractive". It was clear to me how difficult it must have been for designers to compete in this award category with innovative design products.

Do you see a correlation between the design quality of a company's products and the economic success of this company?
Definitely. Nowadays, design, especially at the sensual level, is the single most important criterion for the consumers' choice of products. It easily captivates the consumers' attention and makes them love the company's products.

What challenges do you see for the future in design?
I am a strong believer in design, since design is the most effective tool for innovation and a significant value creator. Therefore, design will continue to be increasingly important strategically and will become more inclusive in the future.

Welche Trends konnten Sie im Bereich „Computer und Informationstechnik" in den letzten Jahren ausmachen?
Die Formfaktoren „schlicht" und „schön". Daher kann ich nachempfinden, wie schwierig es für die Gestalter gewesen sein muss, in dieser Wettbewerbskategorie mit innovativen Designresultaten anzutreten.

Sehen Sie einen Zusammenhang zwischen der Designqualität, die sich in den Produkten eines Unternehmens äußert, und dem wirtschaftlichen Erfolg dieses Unternehmens?
Definitiv. Heutzutage ist Gestaltung das wichtigste Kriterium für die Produktwahl der Konsumenten, insbesondere auf der sinnlichen Ebene. Sie zieht die Aufmerksamkeit unmittelbar auf sich und bewirkt, dass die Konsumenten die Produkte des Unternehmens lieben.

Welche Herausforderungen sehen Sie für die Zukunft im Design?
Ich bin ein großer Designverfechter, da es das effektivste Instrument zur Innovation und ein wesentlicher Wertschöpfer ist. Daher wird Design weiterhin strategisch immer wichtiger und in Zukunft integrativer werden.

Prof. Dr. Ken Nah

01

Ken Okuyama
Japan

Jury member since 2010
Appointed four times
Jurymitglied seit 2010
Berufen vier Mal

Ken Kiyoyuki Okuyama, industrial designer and CEO of KEN OKUYAMA DESIGN, was born in Yamagata, Japan, 1959. He has worked as Chief Designer for General Motors, as Senior Designer for Porsche AG, and as Design Director for Pininfarina S.p.A., being responsible for Ferrari Enzo, Maserati Quattroporte and many other cars. He is also known for many different product designs such as motorcycles, furniture, robots and architecture.

KEN OKUYAMA DESIGN was founded in 2007 and provides business consultancy services to numerous corporations. Ken Okuyama also produces cars, eyewear and interior products under his original brand. He is currently a visiting professor at several universities and also frequently publishes books.

Ken Kiyoyuki Okuyama, Industriedesigner und CEO von KEN OKUYAMA DESIGN, wurde 1959 in Yamagata, Japan, geboren. Er war als Chief Designer bei General Motors, als Senior Designer bei der Porsche AG und als Design Director bei Pininfarina S.p.A. tätig und zeichnete verantwortlich für den Ferrari Enzo, den Maserati Quattroporte und viele weitere Automobile. Zudem ist er für viele unterschiedliche Produktgestaltungen wie Motorräder, Möbel, Roboter und Architektur bekannt.

KEN OKUYAMA DESIGN wurde 2007 als Beratungsunternehmen gegründet und arbeitet für zahlreiche Unternehmen. Ken Okuyama produziert unter seiner originären Marke auch Autos, Brillen und Inneneinrichtungsgegenstände. Derzeit lehrt er als Gastprofessor an verschiedenen Universitäten und publiziert zudem Bücher.

02

»My abiding impression of this year's jury session is the increased demand for more prominent corporate identity.«

»Mein bleibender Eindruck aus der diesjährigen Jurysitzung ist das Bedürfnis nach mehr hervorstechender Unternehmens- identität als zuvor.«

What trends have you noticed in the field of "Automotive and transportation" in recent years?
Driving performance is no longer a sales point. Transport design should propose not only mobility but also a new lifestyle. A car's design reflects its owner's character and lifestyle more than ever.

Do you see a correlation between the design quality of a company's products and the economic success of this company?
The correlation is the result of a clear vision and the teamwork that made it happen, plus the personalities of individual team members.

What are the important criteria for you as a juror in the assessment of a product?
A juror has to determine a product's value to society and the market. Therefore, an objective view and wide ranging knowledge of technology, materials, manufacturing, etc. are necessary.

Welche Trends konnten Sie im Bereich „Automotive und Transport" in den letzten Jahren ausmachen?
Fahr-Performance ist kein Verkaufsargument mehr. Im Segment „Transport" sollte Gestaltung nicht nur auf Mobilität abzielen, sondern auch auf einen neuen Lebensstil. Das Design eines Autos spiegelt mehr denn je den Charakter und Lebensstil seines Besitzers wider.

Sehen Sie einen Zusammenhang zwischen der Designqualität, die sich in den Produkten eines Unternehmens äußert, und dem wirtschaftlichen Erfolg dieses Unternehmens?
Diese Wechselwirkung ist das Ergebnis einer klaren Vision und der ihr zugrunde liegenden Teamarbeit – plus der Persönlichkeiten der einzelnen Teammitglieder.

Worauf achten Sie als Juror, wenn Sie ein Produkt bewerten?
Ein Juror muss den Wert bestimmen, den ein Produkt für die Gesellschaft und den Markt hat. Daher sind eine objektive Sichtweise und eine große Bandbreite an Wissen über Technik, Werkstoffe, Herstellung etc. notwendig.

01

Simon Ong
Singapore

Jury member since 2006
Appointed six times
Jurymitglied seit 2006
Berufen sechs Mal

Simon Ong, born in Singapore in 1953, holds a Master's degree in design (MDes) from the University of New South Wales and an MBA from the University of South Australia. He is the group managing director and co-founder of Kingsmen Creatives Ltd., a leading communications design and production group in the Asia-Pacific region and in the Middle East. His work has been distinguished by several awards, such as the Eddie Award, the VM&SD/ISP Design Award and the A.R.E. Design Award, the Singapore Promising Brand Award, the SRA Best Retail Concept Award, and the Annual Outdoor Advertising Award.

From 1995 to 1997, Simon Ong held the position of president of the Interior Designers Association of Singapore and from 1998 to 2007 he was a member of the advisory committee of the School of Design of the Temasek Polytechnic, Singapore. Currently he is an IDP member of the Design Singapore Council and, among others, chairman of the Design Cluster of the Singapore Workforce Development Agency.

Simon Ong, geboren 1953 in Singapur, absolvierte sein Designstudium an der University of New South Wales, Australien, mit der Promotion und erwarb einen MBA an der University of South Australia. Er ist Geschäftsführer und Mitbegründer von Kingsmen Creatives Ltd., einer führenden Gruppe von Unternehmen für Kommunikationsdesign und Fertigung im Asien-Pazifik-Raum und im Nahen Osten. Für seine Arbeiten wurde er mehrfach ausgezeichnet, darunter mit dem Eddie Award, VM&SD/ISP Design Award und A.R.E. Design Award, Singapore Promising Brand Award, SRA Best Retail Concept Award und Annual Outdoor Advertising Award.

Von 1995 bis 1997 war Simon Ong Präsident der Interior Designers Association of Singapore und gehörte von 1998 bis 2007 dem Beraterausschuss der Temasek Polytechnic, School of Design, Singapur, an. Derzeit ist er IDP-Mitglied des Design Singapore Council und u. a. Vorsitzender des Design-Clusters der Singapore Workforce Development Agency.

02

»Design quality is one of the most important tools to differentiate products from their competitors in a global marketplace.«

»Designqualität wird in einem globalisierten Markt als eines der wichtigsten Instrumente zur Unterscheidung der eigenen Produkte von denen der Konkurrenz eingesetzt.«

What is, in your opinion, the significance of design quality in the product categories you evaluated?
New technologies have not only transformed the way we lead our lives, but have opened up new opportunities for creativity. This is evident in the entries submitted by designers this year.

What are the important criteria for you as a juror in the assessment of a product?
The first impression of a product is very important. It must impress the jury enough to warrant a second look. It has to be appealing and, naturally it must possess ergonomic, innovative and functional qualities. Most of all, it must be pleasant to use.

Do you have a philosophy toward life?
Be sensitive to people and the world around us. But most of all, be happy!

Wie schätzen Sie den Stellenwert der Designqualität in den von Ihnen beurteilten Produktkategorien ein?
Die neuen Technologien haben nicht nur unsere Lebensweise verändert, sondern auch die Möglichkeit zu neuen Entwürfen eröffnet. Dies zeigt sich in den Antworten der Designer bei den diesjährigen Einreichungen.

Worauf achten Sie als Juror, wenn Sie ein Produkt bewerten?
Sehr wichtig ist der erste Eindruck, den das Produkt hinterlässt. Es muss die Jury so weit beeindrucken, dass es einen zweiten Blick rechtfertigt. Es muss seine weitere Betrachtung empfehlen und selbstverständlich ergonomische, innovative und funktionale Qualitäten besitzen. Vor allem aber muss es eine positive Nutzerfahrung bieten.

Haben Sie ein Lebensmotto?
Sei den Menschen und unserer Umwelt gegenüber aufgeschlossen. Und allem voran: Sei glücklich!

Simon Ong

01

Max Ottenwälder
Germany

Jury member since 1999
Appointed five times
Jurymitglied seit 1999
Berufen fünf Mal

Max Ottenwälder, born in 1954, graduated with a diploma in industrial design from the Schwäbisch Gmünd University of Applied Sciences (Design) in 1979. Since 1980 he has been working as a self-employed designer and, in 1990, founded the design agency Ottenwälder und Ottenwälder together with Petra Kurz-Ottenwälder. His successful work as a designer and design consultant for renowned companies in different industries and product fields has won him several international design and innovation prizes. Max Ottenwälder writes articles on design philosophy and product semantics for books and specialist magazines and gives lectures and seminars at universities, trade fairs and private institutions. As a guest lecturer for product semantics and design language he has developed a theory for the assessment of the emotional value proposition of objects. He has been a member of the jury of the Red Dot Design Award several times. In his artistic work Max Ottenwälder has initiated performances and exhibitions with "linomorph" iron wire sculptures since 1990.

Max Ottenwälder, geboren 1954, erhielt sein Diplom als Industrial Designer 1979 an der Hochschule für Gestaltung in Schwäbisch Gmünd. Seit 1980 ist er selbstständig als Designer tätig und gründete 1990 gemeinsam mit Petra Kurz-Ottenwälder das Designbüro Ottenwälder und Ottenwälder. Die erfolgreiche Tätigkeit als Gestalter und Designberater für renommierte Unternehmen in unterschiedlichsten Branchen und Produktbereichen wurde vielfach mit internationalen Design- und Innovationspreisen ausgezeichnet. Max Ottenwälder verfasst Aufsätze zu Designphilosophie und Produktsemantik in Büchern und Fachzeitschriften und hält Vorträge und Seminare an Hochschulen, auf Messen sowie an privaten Institutionen. Als Gastdozent für Produktsemantik und Formensprache entwickelte er eine Lehre zur Beurteilung des emotionalen Werteversprechens von Objekten. Er war mehrfach Jurymitglied im Red Dot Design Award. In seiner künstlerischen Tätigkeit initiiert Max Ottenwälder seit 1990 Performances und Ausstellungen mit linomorphen Eisendrahtskulpturen.

02

»The responsibility for future products includes an awareness of high-quality design and the aspects ecology and humane production.«

»Die Verantwortung für die Produkte der Zukunft umfasst eine Bewusstseinsbildung für hochwertiges Design sowie die Aspekte Ökologie und menschenwürdige Produktion.«

What trends have you noticed in the field of "Kitchens" in recent years?
What stands out in this field is that the leading manufacturers are increasingly adjusting their product design to their target markets. They achieve this through a targeted use of materials and surfaces as well as the growing use of decorative components.

What are the important criteria for you as a juror in the assessment of a product?
I approach a product from the consumer's perspective first and then from that of the manufacturer or the brand respectively. Then I assess to what extent the design fulfils its value proposition. Good function, a significant use of form and high quality materials in an adequate value-for-money ratio are the basic prerequisites for a good product.

How do you assess the significance of design quality for the success of a company?
High quality product design directly benefits a company's economic success. The significance of design is becoming increasingly important for global competition.

Welche Trends konnten Sie im Bereich „Küche" in den letzten Jahren ausmachen?
In diesem Bereich ist auffällig, dass die führenden Hersteller das Design ihrer Produkte immer mehr ihren Zielmärkten anpassen. Dies geschieht mithilfe gezielter Material- und Oberflächenauswahl sowie mit zunehmend dekorativen Komponenten.

Worauf achten Sie als Juror, wenn Sie ein Produkt bewerten?
Ich nähere mich dem Produkt zuerst aus der Perspektive des Verbrauchers und dann aus der des Herstellers bzw. der Marke. Dann beurteile ich, inwiefern das Design sein Gebrauchswertversprechen erfüllt. Gute Funktion, signifikante Formensprache und hohe Materialqualität in einem angemessenen Preis-Leistungs-Verhältnis sind die Grundvoraussetzungen für ein gutes Produkt.

Wie schätzen Sie den Stellenwert des Designs für den Erfolg eines Unternehmens ein?
Hohe Designqualität der Produkte fördert direkt den wirtschaftlichen Erfolg von Unternehmen. Der Stellenwert des Designs wird zunehmend wichtiger im globalen Wettbewerb.

Max Ottenwälder

01

Oana Radeş
Netherlands

Jury member since 2013
Appointed for the first time
Jurymitglied seit 2013
Berufen zum ersten Mal

Oana Radeş studied architecture in Bucharest, Romania, and graduated with honours in 2005 from the Technical University in Eindhoven, Netherlands. Between 2006 and 2010, she worked at MVRDV as a project leader for several large-scale public buildings and urban planning in Switzerland, Japan, India, Singapore, Germany and the Netherlands.

Since January 2011, she has been a partner of Shift architecture urbanism, together with Thijs van Bijsterveldt and Harm Timmermans. Shift operates both beyond the traditional boundaries of architecture – through self-initiated studies on current societal issues with spatial implications – and within the very core of architecture, through the continuous pursuit of craftsmanship and performance in each building project. Since 2009, Oana Radeş has taught at various architecture and design academies in the Netherlands.

Oana Radeş studierte Architektur in Bukarest, Rumänien, und schloss ihre Ausbildung 2005 an der Technischen Universität in Eindhoven, Niederlande, ab. Von 2006 bis 2010 arbeitete sie bei MVRDV als Projektleiterin für verschiedene, groß angelegte öffentliche Gebäude und Städteplanungen in der Schweiz, Japan, Indien, Singapur, Deutschland und den Niederlanden.

Seit Januar 2011 ist sie zusammen mit Thijs van Bijsterveldt und Harm Timmermans Partner von Shift architecture urbanism. Shift operiert sowohl über die traditionellen Grenzen von Architektur hinaus – mit selbst initiierten Studien zu derzeitigen gesellschaftlichen Problemen mit räumlichen Implikationen – als auch mit dem zentralen Kern von Architektur, indem sie bei jedem Bauprojekt kontinuierlich Handwerkskunst und Performance weiterverfolgen. Seit 2009 lehrt Oana Radeş an verschiedenen Architektur- und Design-Akademien in den Niederlanden.

02

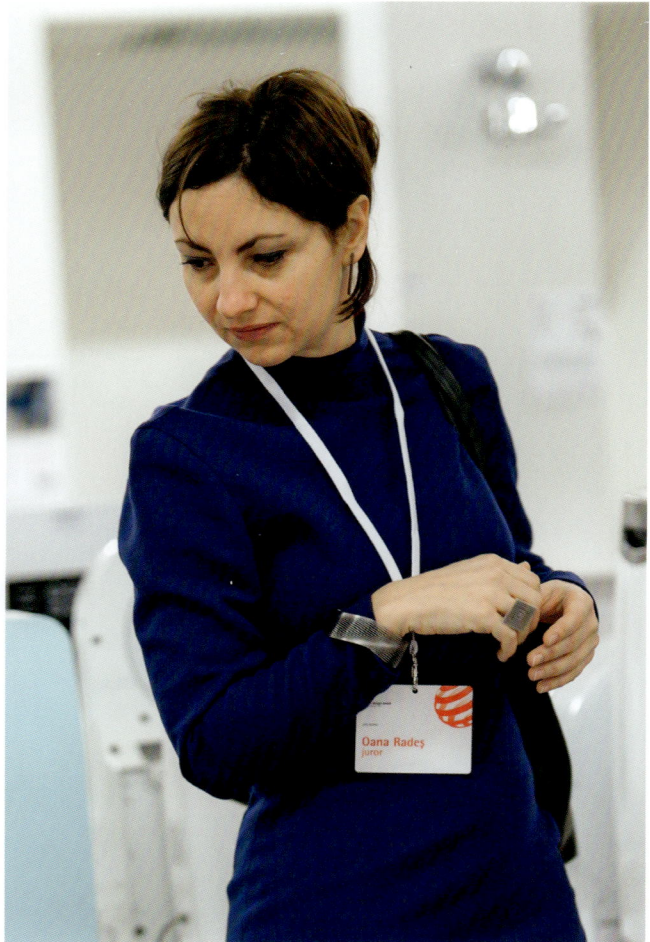

»I was impressed by the earnestness with which design was discussed and evaluated.«

»Ich war von der Ernsthaftigkeit beeindruckt, mit der Gestaltungen diskutiert und bewertet wurden.«

What is, in your opinion, the significance of design quality in the product categories you evaluated?
Well-designed spaces are crucial for our well-being, not only in terms of physical comfort, but especially in regard to mental and social aspects. At the community level, high-quality urban spaces are meaningful spaces, which can facilitate encounters, stimulate interaction and trigger a sense of belonging.

What trends have you noticed in the field of "Architecture and urban design" in recent years?
There is an increasing engagement in the architectural discourse with the social, cultural and economic needs of society. There seems to be less of a focus on iconic, spectacular forms, and more of a preoccupation with formulating creative and relevant responses to various urgent local and global issues.

Wie schätzen Sie den Stellenwert der Designqualität in den von Ihnen beurteilten Produktkategorien ein?
Gut gestaltete Plätze sind entscheidend für unser Wohlbefinden, nicht nur im Sinne körperlicher Annehmlichkeit, sondern insbesondere im Hinblick auf soziale und seelische Aspekte. Auf der Ebene von Gemeinschaft sind qualitativ hochwertige urbane Plätze bedeutsame Orte für die Begegnung, die Stimulation von Interaktion und das Ermöglichen eines Zugehörigkeitsgefühls.

Welche Trends konnten Sie im Bereich „Architektur und Urban Design" in den letzten Jahren ausmachen?
Im Architekturdiskurs herrscht ein verstärkter Dialog mit den sozialen, kulturellen und ökonomischen Bedürfnissen der Gesellschaft. Der Fokus scheint dabei weniger auf ikonischen, spektakulären Formen zu liegen als vielmehr auf der Verpflichtung, relevante und kreative Antworten auf dringliche globale und lokale Probleme zu entwerfen.

Oana Radeş

01

Dirk Schumann
Germany

Jury member since 2006
Appointed five times
Jurymitglied seit 2006
Berufen fünf Mal

Dirk Schumann, born in 1960 in Soest, studied product design at Münster University of Applied Sciences. After graduating in 1987, he joined oco-design as an industrial designer, moved to siegerdesign in 1989, and was a lecturer in product design at Münster University of Applied Sciences until 1991. In 1992, he founded his own design studio Schumanndesign in Münster, developing design concepts for companies in Germany, Italy, India, Thailand and China. For several years now, he has focused on conceptual architecture, created visionary living spaces and held lectures at international conferences. Dirk Schumann has taken part in exhibitions both in Germany and abroad with works that have garnered several awards, including the Gold Prize (Minister of Economy, Trade and Industry Prize) in the International Design Competition, Osaka; the Comfort & Design Award, Milan; the iF product design award, Hanover; the Red Dot, Essen; the Focus in Gold, Stuttgart; as well as the Good Design Award, Chicago and Tokyo.

Dirk Schumann, 1960 in Soest geboren, studierte Produktdesign an der Fachhochschule Münster. Nach seinem Abschluss 1987 arbeitete er als Industriedesigner für oco-design, wechselte 1989 zu siegerdesign und war bis 1991 an der Fachhochschule Münster als Lehrbeauftragter für Produktdesign tätig. 1992 eröffnete er sein eigenes Designstudio Schumanndesign in Münster und entwickelt Designkonzepte für Unternehmen in Deutschland, Italien, Indien, Thailand und China. Seit einigen Jahren beschäftigt er sich mit konzeptioneller Architektur, entwirft visionäre Lebensräume und hält Vorträge auf internationalen Kongressen. Dirk Schumann nimmt an Ausstellungen im In- und Ausland teil und wurde für seine Arbeiten mehrfach ausgezeichnet, u. a. mit dem Gold Prize (Minister of Economy, Trade and Industry Prize) des International Design Competition, Osaka, dem Comfort & Design Award, Mailand, dem iF product design award, Hannover, dem Red Dot, Essen, dem Focus in Gold, Stuttgart, sowie dem Good Design Award, Chicago und Tokio.

02

»Design is a versatile market-ing tool that has a significant influence on the economic success and perception of a company on the market.«

»Design ist ein vielschichtiges Marketinginstrument, das den wirtschaftlichen Erfolg und die Wahrnehmung eines Unter-nehmens am Markt signifikant beeinflusst.«

What trends have you noticed in the field of "Industry and crafts" in recent years?
There are developments that improve on the function, usability and safety of products. Especially in the professional realm, this creates high added-value for products and a positive perception of the manufacturing company, which thus documents a user-oriented focus.

What are the important criteria for you as a juror in the assessment of a product?
Individual impressions of course take over at first contact with a new product. They are followed by more in-depth considerations of aspects such as functional and formal innovation and originality, utility value and user orientation, functional intelligibility, ecological criteria and how the product relates to the manufacturer.

Which project would you like to realise one day?
Projects that are located at the interface of design, technology and architecture.

Welche Trends konnten Sie im Bereich „Industrie und Handwerk" in den letzten Jahren ausmachen?
Hier gibt es Entwicklungen, die die Funktionen, die Handhabung und die Sicherheit der Produkte ver-bessern. Speziell im professionellen Bereich verleiht dies den Produkten einen hohen Mehrwert und eine positive Wahrnehmung der Herstellerunternehmen, die dadurch eine auf den Nutzer bezogene Fokussierung dokumentieren.

Worauf achten Sie als Juror, wenn Sie ein Produkt bewerten?
Beim ersten Kontakt mit dem Produkt steht natürlich das eigene Empfinden im Vordergrund. Dann folgen vertiefende Betrachtungen von Aspekten wie funktio-nale und formale Innovation und Eigenständigkeit, Gebrauchswert und Nutzerbezogenheit, die Funktions-verständlichkeit, ökologische Kriterien und der Bezug des Produktes zum Herstellerunternehmen.

Welches Projekt würden Sie gerne einmal realisieren?
Projekte an der Schnittstelle von Design, Technologie und Architektur.

Dirk Schumann

01

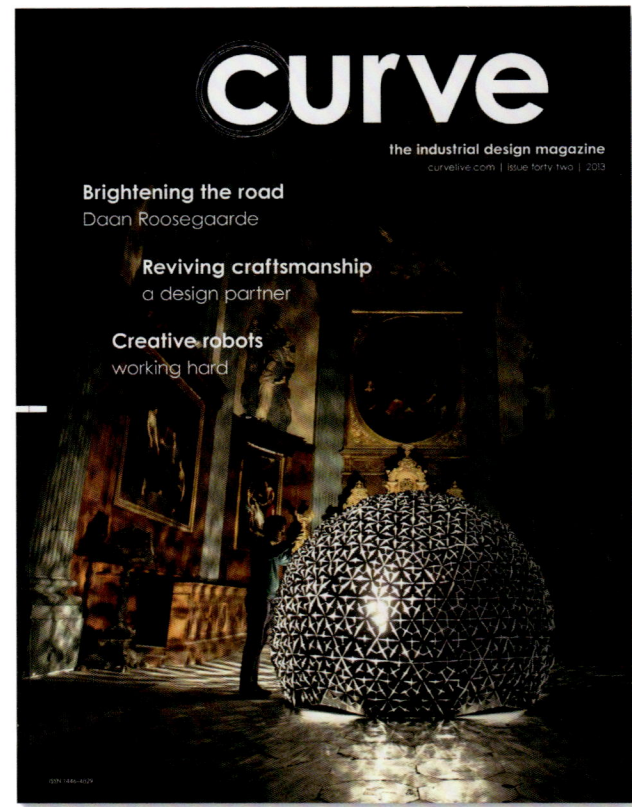

02

Belinda Stening
Australia

Jury member since 2013
Appointed for the first time
Jurymitglied seit 2013
Berufen zum ersten Mal

Belinda Stening is the founder and publisher of the industrial design magazine Curve, as well as its online counterpart "curvelive.com", which features the world's best in industrial design and product development. Since 2001 Curve aims to promote the industrial design profession, as well as manufacturing businesses developing and producing innovative products. As an internationally recognised publication, Curve is a member of the International Design Media Network, an initiative of the International Design Alliance (IDA). Belinda Stening holds a Bachelor Degree in Industrial Design and a Master of Fine Art – Sculpture from the Royal Melbourne Institute of Technology, Australia. As a professional industrial designer, she has many years of experience in design consulting, including consumer appliance design, biomedical product design, as well as packaging and furniture design. She has been a juror for design awards programs in the USA and Australia, and has worked extensively in the design education sector.

Belinda Stening ist die Gründerin und Herausgeberin des Industriedesign-Magazins „Curve" sowie seines Online-Pendants „curvelive.com", das die weltweit Besten im Bereich Industriedesign und Produktentwicklung vorstellt. Seit 2001 ist es das Ziel von Curve, den Beruf des Industriedesigners sowie die Industrieunternehmen zu fördern, die innovative Produkte entwickeln und produzieren. Als international anerkannte Publikation ist Curve Mitglied des International Design Media Network, einer Initiative der International Design Alliance (IDA). Belinda Stening hat einen Bachelor-Abschluss in Industrial Design und einen „Master of Fine Art – Sculpture" vom Royal Melbourne Institute of Technology, Australien. Als professionelle Industriedesignerin verfügt sie über langjährige Erfahrung im Design Consulting, einschließlich Consumer Appliance Design, im biomedizinischen Produktdesign sowie im Verpackungs- und Möbeldesign. Sie war als Jurorin verschiedener Designwettbewerbe in den USA und Australien sowie in der Designausbildung tätig.

03

»As a designer I'd like to think that I could develop a product that innovates the way we communicate design to the world.«

»Als Designerin gefällt mir die Vorstellung, mal ein Produkt zu entwickeln, das für die Kommunikation von Design in der Welt eine Neuerung darstellt.«

What trends have you noticed in the field of "Households" in recent years?
There are many products for compact spaces. In small homes, kitchen and laundry spaces are often integrated into living and entertainment areas. That is why household products for the laundry and kitchen are becoming more flexible and modular.

What trends have you noticed in the field of "Kitchens" in recent years?
There is a marked reduction in the use of superfluous embellishments. More "humble", simpler materials such as wood, glass and stainless steel are giving kitchen products a warmer and nostalgic style. The most appealing products are pared back and forms are plain but friendly.

What challenges do you see for the future in design?
I think it is very important for designers to remember who they are designing for. It is the designer's responsibility to be the advocate for the ultimate end-user of a product.

Welche Trends konnten Sie im Bereich „Haushalt" in den letzten Jahren ausmachen?
Es gibt viele Produkte für kompakte Räume. In kleinen Wohnungen sind Küche und Waschbereich oft in den Wohn- und Aufenthaltsraum integriert, weshalb Haushaltsgeräte für diese Anwendungen immer flexibler und modularer werden.

Welche Trends konnten Sie im Bereich „Küche" in den letzten Jahren ausmachen?
Es zeigt sich eine deutliche Reduktion im Einsatz überflüssiger Verzierungen. Einfachere und „zurückhaltendere" Materialien wie Holz, Glas und Edelstahl verleihen den Küchenprodukten ein wärmeres und nostalgisches Aussehen. Die ansprechendsten Produkte sind auf freundliche und einfache Formen zurechtgestutzt.

Welche Herausforderungen sehen Sie für die Zukunft im Design?
Ich denke, als Designer ist es sehr wichtig, sich stets zu vergegenwärtigen, für wen man eigentlich gestaltet. Die Verantwortung der Designer besteht in ihrer Rolle als Anwälte für die letztlichen Endverbraucher der Produkte.

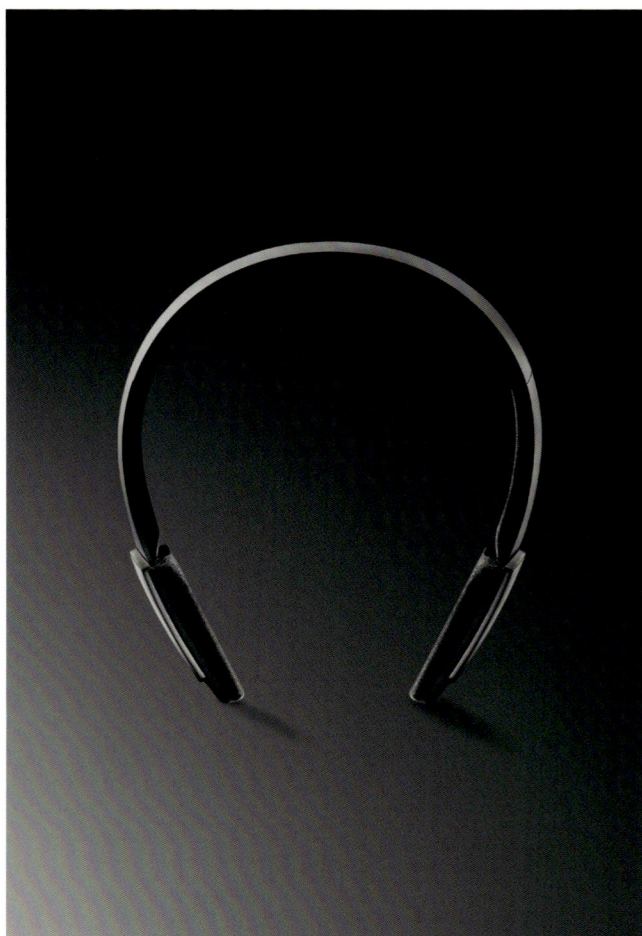

01

02

Nils Toft
Denmark

Jury member since 2006
Appointed seven times
Jurymitglied seit 2006
Berufen sieben Mal

Nils Toft, born in Copenhagen in 1957, graduated as an architect and designer from the Royal Danish Academy of Fine Arts in Copenhagen in 1985. He also holds a Master's degree in Industrial Design and Business Development. Starting his career as an industrial designer, Nils Toft joined the former Christian Bjørn Design in 1987, an internationally active design studio in Copenhagen with branches in Beijing and Ho Chi Minh City. Within a few years, he became a partner of CBD and, as managing director, ran the business. Today, Nils Toft is the founder and managing director of Designidea. With offices in Copenhagen and Beijing, Designidea works in the following key fields: communication, consumer electronics, computing, agriculture, medicine, and graphic arts, as well as projects in design-strategy, graphic and exhibition design.

Nils Toft, geboren 1957 in Kopenhagen, machte seinen Abschluss als Architekt und Designer 1985 an der Royal Danish Academy of Fine Arts in Kopenhagen. Er verfügt zudem über einen Master im Bereich Industrial Design und Business Development. Zu Beginn seiner Karriere als Industriedesigner trat Nils Toft 1987 bei dem damaligen Christian Bjørn Design ein, einem international operierenden Designstudio in Kopenhagen, das mit Niederlassungen in Beijing und Ho-Chi-Minh-Stadt vertreten ist. Innerhalb weniger Jahre wurde er Partner bei CBD und leitete das Unternehmen als Managing Director. Heute ist Nils Toft Gründer und Managing Director von Designidea. Mit Büros in Kopenhagen und Beijing operiert Designidea in verschiedenen Hauptbereichen: Kommunikation, Unterhaltungselektronik, Computer, Landwirtschaft, Medizin und Grafikdesign sowie Projekte im Bereich Designstrategie, Grafik- und Ausstellungsdesign.

01 **Jabra HALO2**
The Jabra HALO2 headset
with advanced Bluetooth®
technology ensures improved connectivity; thanks to
Multiuse™ it connects more
than one device at a time
Das mit erweiterter
Bluetooth®-Technologie
ausgestattete Headset Jabra
HALO2 ermöglicht eine op-
timierte Connectivität; dank
Multiuse™ ist der Anschluss
von mehr als einem Gerät
gleichzeitig möglich

02 **GD1000**
Professional vacuum cleaner
for institutional use as part
of a large series of machines
for professional cleaning,
designed for Nilfisk-Advance
Profistaubsauger für den
institutionellen Einsatz als Teil
einer großen Serie professioneller Reinigungsmaschinen,
gestaltet für Nilfisk-Advance

03 **Wittenborg 7100**
Espresso and fresh brew
coffee machine for
professional office use
Espresso- und Brühkaffee-
maschine für den professionellen Einsatz in Büros

03

»The great satisfaction of working as an industrial designer lies in the constant challenge presented by new industries and new products.«

»Die große Genugtuung in der Arbeit als Industriedesigner liegt in der ständigen Herausforderung durch neue Branchen und neue Produkte.«

What trends have you noticed in the field of "Bathrooms, spas and air conditioning" in recent years?
This category is focused on high-level design and consumers characterised by growing consumer expectations for design innovation. It has left its design infancy behind and entered a stage where design innovation and differentiation is important in order to maintain a competitive edge. Design just for the sake of being different is not enough; consumers are too smart and have much higher expectations.

What aspects of the jury process for the Red Dot Award: Product Design 2013 have stayed in your mind in particular?
A jury session becomes memorable when you overcome the prejudices and preconceptions that are based on a first quick glance of a product. In one jury session, I was blessed with a jury team that kept an open mind and discovered that scepticism can turn into excitement if one takes the time to understand a design.

Welche Trends konnten Sie im Bereich „Bad, Wellness und Klima" in den letzten Jahren ausmachen?
Diese Kategorie stellt eine auf hochwertige Gestaltung und auf Verbraucher fokussierte Kategorie mit wachsenden Erwartungen der Konsumenten an Designinnovation dar. Sie hat ihre gestalterische Kindheit hinter sich gelassen und eine Ebene erreicht, auf der Designinnovation und Differenzierung für die Wettbewerbsfähigkeit zentral sind. Gestaltung nur um des Andersseins willen reicht nicht aus; die Konsumenten sind dafür zu erfahren und haben höhere Erwartungen.

Was ist Ihnen von der Jurierung des Red Dot Award: Product Design 2013 besonders im Gedächtnis geblieben?
Eine Jurysitzung wird dann zum unvergesslichen Moment, wenn man seine Voreingenommenheit überwindet, die nach einem ersten kurzen Blick auf ein Produkt entstehen kann. Ich hatte das Glück, mit einem Jurorenteam zusammenzuarbeiten, das aufgeschlossen war und ebenfalls entdeckte, dass sich Skeptizismus in Begeisterung wandelt, wenn man sich für sein Verständnis eines Designs Zeit gibt.

Nils Toft

01

Prof. Danny Venlet
Belgium

Jury member since 2005
Appointed eight times
Jurymitglied seit 2005
Berufen acht Mal

Professor Danny Venlet was born in 1958 in Victoria, Australia and studied interior design at Sint-Lukas, the Institute for Architecture and Arts in Brussels. Back in Australia in 1991, Venlet joined up with Marc Newson and Tina Engelen to form "Daffodil design". Venlet then started to attract international attention with large-scale interior design projects such as the Burdekin Hotel in Sydney and Q Bar, an Australian chain of nightclubs. His design projects range from private mansions, lofts, bars and restaurants all the way to showrooms and offices of large companies. Danny Venlet has taught at several schools and universities in Australia, as well as in Belgium. Today, he is professor at the Royal College of the Arts in Ghent and at the independent College of Advertising and Design in Brussels where he also is the Artistic Director from MAD Brussels (Mode And Design Center).

Professor Danny Venlet wurde 1958 in Victoria, Australien, geboren und studierte Interior Design am Sint-Lukas, dem Institut für Architektur und Kunst in Brüssel. 1991 kehrte er nach Australien zurück und gründete zusammen mit Marc Newson und Tina Engelen „Daffodil design". Erste internationale Aufmerksamkeit erlangte er durch die Innenausstattung großer Projekte wie dem Burdekin Hotel in Sydney sowie der Q Bar, einer australischen Nachtclub-Kette. Seine Design-Projekte reichen von privaten Wohnhäusern über Lofts, Bars und Restaurants bis zu Ausstellungsräumen und Büros großer Unternehmen. Danny Venlet lehrte an zahlreichen Schulen und Universitäten sowohl in Australien als auch in Belgien. Heute ist er Professor am Royal College of the Arts in Gent und am privaten College of Advertising and Design in Brüssel, wo er zudem Artistic Director des MAD Brussels (Mode And Design Center) ist.

02

»In order to be a success for the company a product needs to have many qualities such as uniqueness, financial viability, emotional value, and transportability.«

»Um einem Unternehmen Erfolg zu bringen, muss ein Produkt viele Qualitäten haben, z. B. Einzigartigkeit, finanzielle Realisierbarkeit, emotionalen Wert und Transportierbarkeit.«

What are the important criteria for you as a juror in the assessment of a product?
If I had to narrow it down to three criteria they would be: the product's level of innovation or uniqueness, its emotional value, and the quality of its execution.

What aspects of the jury process for the Red Dot Award: Product Design 2013 have stayed in your mind in particular?
As always, it has been a very professional event. Despite being in a recession, companies see the value of winning a Red Dot more than ever.

What challenges do you see for the future in design?
The challenge we face as designers is to make sure that design will still make sense in the future. Everything is design today and we need to make sure that we don't lose the real significance of design.

Worauf achten Sie als Juror, wenn Sie ein Produkt bewerten?
Wenn ich es auf drei Kriterien beschränken müsste, wären es folgende: der Grad der Innovation oder Einzigartigkeit des Produkts, sein emotionaler Wert und die Qualität der Ausführung.

Was ist Ihnen von der Jurierung des Red Dot Award: Product Design 2013 besonders im Gedächtnis geblieben?
Wie immer war es eine sehr professionelle Veranstaltung. Und obwohl wir uns in einer Rezession befinden, erkennen Unternehmen den Wert, den der Gewinn eines Red Dot mit sich bringt, mehr als je zuvor.

Welche Herausforderungen sehen Sie für die Zukunft im Design?
Die Herausforderungen, vor denen wir als Designer stehen, bestehen darin zu gewährleisten, dass Gestaltung auch in Zukunft noch sinnvoll ist. Heutzutage ist alles Design, und wir müssen sichergehen, dass wir seine wahre Bedeutung nicht verlieren.

Prof. Danny Venlet

01

Cheng Chung Yao
Taiwan

Jury member since 2012
Appointed twice
Jurymitglied seit 2012
Berufen zwei Mal

Cheng Chung Yao studied at the Pratt Institute New York and graduated with a Master's degree in architecture. In 1991, he founded the Department of Interior Space Design at Shih Chien University and has worked as a lecturer at the Graduate School of Architecture at Tam Kang University as well as at the Graduate School of Architecture at Chiao Tung University. In 1999, he founded "t1 design" where he heads a team of architects and interior designers as well as exhibition and graphic designers.

The company's best-known products currently include the City Plaza of Taiwan Pavilion of the 2010 Shanghai Expo, the Taiwan Design Museum and the Taiwan Design Centre. Furthermore, Cheng Chung Yao curated and designed the International Interior Design Exhibition for the Expo, was president of the Chinese Society of Interior Designers, chief executive of the Asia Pacific Space Designers Association, board member of the International Federation of Interior Architects/Designers and founder of the Taiwan Interior Design Award.

Cheng Chung Yao studierte Architektur am Pratt Institute New York und schloss sein Studium mit dem Master ab. 1991 gründete er die Fakultät für Interior Space Design an der Shih Chien University und war als Dozent an der Graduate School of Architecture der Tam Kang University sowie an der Graduate School of Architecture der Chiao Tung University tätig. 1999 gründete er „t1 design" und leitet dort ein Team aus Architekten, Innenarchitekten sowie Ausstellungs- und Grafikdesignern.

Zu den aktuell bekanntesten Projekten des Büros zählen der City Plaza of Taiwan Pavilion der Expo 2010 in Shanghai, das Taiwan Design Museum und das Taiwan Design Center. Zudem kuratierte und gestaltete Cheng Chung Yao die International Interior Design Exhibition für die Expo, war u. a. Präsident der Chinese Society of Interior Designers, Hauptgeschäftsführer der Asia Pacific Space Designers Association und Vorstandsmitglied der International Federation of Interior Architects/Designers und gründete den Taiwan Interior Design Award.

02

»The selection process of the Red Dot Design Award is a great testimony of contemporary design history, aesthetics and philosophy.«

»Der Auswahlprozess im Red Dot Design Award ist eine großartige Bekundung zeitgenössischer Designgeschichte, Ästhetik und Philosophie.«

What is, in your opinion, the significance of design quality in the product categories you evaluated?
The substance of design is not just to address the specific requirements of the time; it also promotes the vision that everyone has the ability to shape their own life in a distinctive way.

What trends have you noticed in the field of "Interior design" in recent years?
Today's interior design reflects the development of lifestyle, the pursuit of innovation in our way of life, as well as the penetration of society and the quest for consolidation with contemporary technology.

What challenges do you see for the future in design?
The divergence and the convergence of the design profession, as the future of design is crossing interdisciplinary boundaries. In addition, the influence and confluence of different cultures, as the future of design is crossing intercultural boundaries.

Wie schätzen Sie den Stellenwert der Designqualität in den von Ihnen beurteilten Produktkategorien ein?
Das Wesen des Designs ist nicht nur, Antworten auf die spezifischen Anforderungen seiner Zeit zu geben; es fördert zudem die Vision, dass jeder damit sein Leben auf unverwechselbare Weise formen kann.

Welche Trends konnten Sie im Bereich „Interior Design" in den letzten Jahren ausmachen?
Das Interior Design von heute reflektiert die Entwicklung des Lifestyles, das Bestreben, das Leben innovativer zu machen, ebenso wie die Durchdringung der Gesellschaft und die Suche nach einer Verschmelzung mit zeitgenössischer Technologie.

Welche Herausforderungen sehen Sie für die Zukunft im Design?
Die Divergenz und Konvergenz der Designprofession, da die Zukunft des Designs interdisziplinäre Grenzen überschreitet; außerdem die Beeinflussung und das Zusammenfließen verschiedener Kulturen, da die Zukunft des Designs interkulturelle Grenzen überschreitet.

Cheng Chung Yao

Alphabetical index manufacturers and distributors
Alphabetisches Hersteller- und Vertriebs-Register

Alphabetical index designers
Alphabetisches Designer-Register

Alphabetical index designers
Alphabetisches Designer-Register

Imprint
Impressum

Editor | Herausgeber:
Peter Zec

Project management | Projektleitung:
Sabine Wöll

Project assistance | Projektassistenz:
Jennifer Bürling
Theresa Falkenberg
Sora Lina Loesch
Anna Kraatz
Stefanie Riechert
Anne Kämmerling
Anamaria Sumic
Lars Hofmann

Editorial work | Redaktion:
Bettina Derksen, Simmern, Germany
Kirsten Müller, Essen, Germany
Mareike Ahlborn, Essen, Germany
Klaus Dimmler, Essen, Germany
Burkhard Jacob
(Red Dot: Design Team of the Year),
Krefeld, Germany
Karin Kirch, Essen, Germany
Karoline Laarmann, Dortmund, Germany
Bettina Laustroer, Rosenheim, Germany
Astrid Ruta, Essen, Germany
Martina Stein, Otterberg, Germany

Proofreading | Lektorat:
Klaus Dimmler, Essen, Germany
Mareike Ahlborn, Essen, Germany
Jörg Arnke, Essen, Germany
Sabine Beeres, Leverkusen, Germany
Dawn Michelle d'Atri, Kirchhundem, Germany
Die Schreibweisen, Castrop-Rauxel, Germany
Annette Gillich-Beltz, Essen, Germany
Karin Kirch, Essen, Germany
Regina Schier, Essen, Germany

Translations | Übersetzung:
Heike Bors, Tokyo, Japan
Patrick Conroy, Larnaka, Cyprus
Stanislav Eberlein, Tokyo, Japan
Bill Kings, Wuppertal, Germany
Cathleen Poehler, Montreal, Canada
Jan Stachel-Williamson,
Christchurch, New Zealand
Bruce Stout, Grafenau, Germany
Philippa Watts, Exeter, Great Britain
Andreas Zantop, Berlin, Germany
Christiane Zschunke,
Frankfurt/Main, Germany

Layout | Gestaltung:
Gruschka Kramer
Visuelle Kommunikation,
Wuppertal, Germany
Lena Gruschka, Johannes Kramer

Photographs | Fotos:
Markus Benz, Walter Knoll
(portrait Foster + Partners)
Gandia Blasco/Odosdesign
(product photo juror Stefan Diez)
Gordon Bruce (product photos juror Gordon Bruce),
Gordon Bruce Design LLC, USA
Thomas De Boever (portrait Alain Gilles), Gent, Belgium
Ingmar Kurth (product photo juror Stefan Diez),
Frankfurt/Main, Germany
Flo Maeght (portrait Philippe Starck), Paris, France
Melkus Sportwagen GmbH
(product photo juror Lutz Fügener), Dresden, Germany
Ralph Richter (product photos juror Joachim H. Faust),
Düsseldorf, Germany
Rainer Viertlböck (product photos juror Florian Hufnagl),
Gauting, Germany

In-company photos | Werksfotos der Firmen

Jury photographs | Jurorenfotos:
Simon Bierwald, Dortmund, Germany

**Production and lithography |
Produktion und Lithografie:**
tarcom GmbH, Gelsenkirchen, Germany
Bernd Reinkens, Gregor Baals,
Jonas Mühlenweg, Gundula Seraphin

Printing | Druck:
Dr. Cantz'sche Druckerei Medien GmbH,
Ostfildern, Germany

Bookbindery | Buchbindung:
BELTZ Bad Langensalza GmbH,
Bad Langensalza, Germany

**Publisher + worldwide distribution |
Verlag + Vertrieb weltweit:**
Red Dot Edition | Fachverlag für Design
Contact | Kontakt:
Sabine Wöll
Gelsenkirchener Str. 181, 45309 Essen
Germany
Phone +49 201 8141-822
Fax +49 201 8141-810
E-mail edition@red-dot.de
www.red-dot.de
www.red-dot-store.de
Verkehrsnummer: 13674

Red Dot Design Yearbook 2013/2014

Softcover
Living (978-3-89939-145-9)
Doing (978-3-89939-146-6)
Working (978-3-89939-151-0)
Set = Living & Doing & Working (978-3-89939-144-2)

Hardcover
Living (978-3-89939-148-0)
Doing (978-3-89939-149-7)
Working (978-3-89939-152-7)
Set = Living & Doing & Working (978-3-89939-147-3)

**Bibliographic information published
by the Deutsche Nationalbibliothek:**
The Deutsche Nationalbibliothek
lists this publication in the Deutsche
Nationalbibliografie; detailed bibliographic
data are available on the Internet at
http://dnb.ddb.de
**Bibliografische Information
der Deutschen Nationalbibliothek:**
Die Deutsche Nationalbibliothek verzeichnet
diese Publikation in der Deutschen
Nationalbibliografie; detaillierte
bibliografische Daten sind im Internet über
http://dnb.ddb.de abrufbar.

The Red Dot Award: Product Design
competition is the continuation of the
Design Innovations competition.
Der Wettbewerb „Red Dot Award: Product Design"
gilt als Fortsetzung des Wettbewerbs
„Design Innovationen".